**Omega Squared**

$$\omega^2 = \frac{t^2 - 1}{t^2 + n_1 + n_2 - 1}$$

**Effect Size**

$$d_2 = \frac{|\mu_1 - \mu_2|}{\sigma}, \ \sigma = \frac{\hat{s}_1 + \hat{s}_2}{2} \text{ when } n_1 = n_2.$$

## STUDENT'S $t$-RATIO: INDEPENDENT GROUPS $\sigma_1 \neq \sigma_2$

$$\hat{t} = \frac{\overline{X}_1 - \overline{X}_2}{\sqrt{\left[\frac{1}{n_1}\left(\frac{SS_1}{n_1 - 1}\right)\right] + \left[\frac{1}{n_2}\left(\frac{SS_2}{n_2 - 1}\right)\right]}}$$

$$df' = \frac{\left[\frac{1}{n_1}\left(\frac{SS_1}{n_1 - 1}\right) + \frac{1}{n_2}\left(\frac{SS_2}{n_2 - 1}\right)\right]^2}{\frac{\frac{1}{n_1}\left(\frac{SS_1}{n_1 - 1}\right)^2}{n_1 - 1} + \frac{\frac{1}{n_2}\left(\frac{SS_2}{n_2 - 1}\right)^2}{n_2 - 1}}$$

## STUDENT'S $t$-RATIO: CORRELATED GROUPS

$$t = \frac{\overline{D}}{\sqrt{\frac{\Sigma D^2 - \frac{(\Sigma D)^2}{n}}{n(n - 1)}}}, \ df = n - 1$$

## PEARSON PRODUCT MOMENT CORRELATION COEFFICIENT

$$r = \frac{\Sigma XY - \frac{(\Sigma X)(\Sigma Y)}{N}}{\sqrt{\left(\Sigma X^2 - \frac{(\Sigma X)^2}{N}\right)\left(\Sigma Y^2 - \frac{(\Sigma Y)^2}{N}\right)}}$$

**Student's t-ratio for correlation**

$$t = \frac{r\sqrt{N - 2}}{\sqrt{1 - r^2}}, \ df = N - 2$$

**Fisher's z-score for correlation**

$$z = \frac{z_r - Z_r}{\sqrt{\frac{1}{(N - 3)}}}$$

## SPEARMAN RANK ORDER CORRELATION

$$r_S = 1 - \frac{6\Sigma D^2}{N(N^2 - 1)}$$

## REGRESSION ANALYSIS

**Slope**

$$b_Y = r\left(\frac{s_Y}{s_X}\right)$$

**Intercept**

$$a_Y = \overline{Y} - b_Y(\overline{X})$$

**Regression Equation**

$$Y' = a_Y + b_Y(X)$$

**Standard Error of Estimate**

$$s_{\text{est}Y} = s_Y\sqrt{\frac{N(1 - r^2)}{N - 2}}$$

# FUNDAMENTALS
# of Behavioral Statistics
### *Ninth Edition*

Richard P. Runyon

Kay A. Coleman
**Boston University**

David J. Pittenger
**Marietta College**

Boston   Burr Ridge, IL   Dubuque, IA   Madison, WI   New York   San Francisco   St. Louis
Bangkok   Bogotá   Caracas   Lisbon   London   Madrid
Mexico City   Milan   New Delhi   Seoul   Singapore   Sydney   Taipei   Toronto

# McGraw-Hill Higher Education

*A Division of The McGraw-Hill Companies*

FUNDAMENTALS OF BEHAVIORAL STATISTICS, NINTH EDITION

This book is printed on acid-free paper.

7 8 9 0 QWD/QWD 0 9 8 7 6 5

ISBN  0–07–228641–5

Editorial director: *Jane E. Vaicunas*
Executive editor: *Joseph Terry*
Editorial assistant: *Fred Speers*
Editorial coordinator: *Lai Moy*
Developmental editor: *Susan Kunchandy*
Senior marketing manager: *James Rozsa*
Project manager: *Mary Lee Harms*
Production supervisor: *Laura Fuller*
Coordinator of freelance design: *Rick Noel*
Supplement coordinator: *Brenda A. Ernzen*
Compositor: *York Graphic Services, Inc.*
Typeface: *10/12 New Aster*
Printer: *Quebecor World Dubuque, IA*

Cover/interior designer: *Sheilah Barrett*
Cover image: *©SuperStock, Inc. Image: Clouds*

The credits section for this book begins on page 579 and is considered an extension of the copyright page.

**Library of Congress Cataloging-in-Publication Data**

Runyon, Richard P.
    Fundamentals of behavioral statistics / Richard P. Runyon, Kay A.
Coleman, David J. Pittenger.—9th ed.
      p.  cm.
    Includes index.
    ISBN 0–07–228641–5
    1.  Social sciences—Statistical methods.  2.  Statistics.
I.  Coleman, Kay A.  II.  Pittenger, David J.  III.  Title.
HA29.R85      2000
519.5—dc21                         99-14482
                                          CIP

www.mhhe.com

# About the Authors

**Richard P. Runyon** lived a full and rewarding life. He received his B.A. from Drew University and his Ph.D. from Yale University, and was a fellow in the Sheffield Scientific School. At the peak of his career, he served as chair of the Department of Psychology and as Dean of the Science Faculty at C.W. Post College in Brookville, New York. He published a number of articles in psychology journals and authored or coauthored many books in statistics and psychology, including this text; *Fundamentals of Behavioral Statistics: The Core; Fundamentals of Psychology; General Statistics; Fundamentals of Statistics in Biological, Medical, and Health Sciences; Business Statistics; Psychology of Adjustment; Winning with Statistics;* and *How Numbers Lie.*

**Kay A. Coleman** is an Associate Professor of Psychology in the College of Liberal Arts at Boston University. She received her Ph.D. from Boston College and a Master's of Public Health from Harvard University. At Boston University she is Director of Undergraduate Studies for the Psychology Department, where she teaches courses in experimental design, statistics, and memory at the graduate and undergraduate levels. Her research focuses on studies of remote autobiographical memory, particularly the accuracy of memories from childhood and health-related memories. In addition to co-authoring this textbook, she is also co-author with Richard Runyon of another textbook, *Behavioral Statistics: The Core.* She is a past President of the New England Educational Research Organization and was elected to membership in the Society for Multivariate Experimental Psychology. She is an honorary member of the Golden Key National Honor Society, a member of Psi Chi and the American Psychological Society, and a Fellow in the American Psychological Association.

**David J. Pittenger** is an Associate Professor and the chair of the Department of Psychology at Marietta College in Marietta, Ohio. He received his B.A. in psychology from the College of Wooster, his Master's of Science from Texas A & M University, and his Ph.D. from the University of Georgia. In addition to teaching courses in statistics and research design, David teaches courses in physiological psychology, psychometrics, learning and behavior, and cognitive psychology. David has many interests in psychology and has written articles on the partial reinforcement extinction effect, the ethical responsibilities of psychologists, the validity of personality inventories, and the teaching of psychology. In 1987 he received the Early Career Award for teaching from Division 2 of the American Psychological Association. In 1997, David received the McCoy Teaching Fellowship from Marietta College, the college's award for excellence in teaching. He is a Fellow of the American Psychological Association, and a member of the American Psychological Society, and the American Statistical Association.

*In Memory of Richard P. Runyon*

**Friend and Scholar**

# Contents in Brief

# Contents

**CHAPTER**
**5**

Measures of Dispersion    95

**CHAPTER**
**6**

The Standard Normal Distribution    115

**CHAPTER**
**7**

**Graphs and Tables   135**

**CHAPTER**
**8**

**Correlation   161**

CHAPTER
11

Introduction to Statistical Inference 261

**CHAPTER**
**16**

## Analysis of Variance With Correlated Samples    437

**CHAPTER**
**17**

## Analysis of Categorical Data: $\chi^2$ and Binomial Tests    457

# Preface

*"Chance favors the prepared mind."*

—Louis Pasteur

Statistical reasoning is an essential component of our everyday lives. We think in terms of probability and constantly make inferences about future events. Whether we acknowledge the role of this type of reasoning on a conscious level is not important. The fact remains that we constantly predict the future and constantly use statistical reasoning to accomplish this. Given the crucial nature of this type of reasoning, it follows that these skills would be an essential component of any person's education. Thus, the underlying philosophy of this text, *Fundamentals of Behavioral Statistics*, is that statistical reasoning is a crucial element in education. In this same spirit, this ninth edition extends the book's long tradition of presenting statistical reasoning skills in a clear and meaningful way so that readers may understand and learn to appreciate the ubiquitous nature of quantitative thinking.

Today, as we usher in a new millennium, the perceived value of statistical analysis in our lives is more acute than when the first edition of this text was written. Newspapers, national news magazines, and trade journals chronicle the impact of statistics. The federal judicial system now requires judges to be conversant in basic statistical principles; these skills are needed to determine the merit of testimony offered by expert witnesses. Lawmakers use the results of statistical analysis to create policy initiatives that may have a lasting impact on the lives of their constituents. Market researchers test the reactions of the public to political events and retail products using focus groups, surveys, and statistical analysis. In brief, statistics are everywhere.

## THE NEW WORLD OF STATISTICS

As the role of statistics has become increasingly important in our lives so too has the nature of these analyses evolved. Typical undergraduate courses now cover many more types of statistical tests than they did a generation ago. The nature of the material itself has become more sophisticated. A greater emphasis is now placed on exploration of the data prior to conducting statistical tests. We now have computers that easily explore the data and perform analyses that would otherwise take hours to accomplish manually. Greater thought is now given to the importance of issues such as effect size and power analysis prior to conducting an experiment. Undergraduates now read journal articles that discuss the power of the experiment and use tests that were unknown 30 years ago. Much has changed, yet much remains the same. The change is clear. Statistical analyses have become increasingly sophisticated. What has remained constant is that we still optimistically expect our students to develop their critical thinking skills and use these skills in their coursework and later in their professional lives.

## OUR PHILOSOPHY IN WRITING

Our comprehensive review of statistical procedures strives for simplicity. While we use crucial examples from psychology to guide the reader, this text is not cluttered with distractions or superfluous information. We have maintained the book's signature of simplicity even as we have updated the pages with the most significant recent trends and advances in statistical reasoning.

### Balanced Reasoning

We believe that our book strikes a balance between teaching the conceptual foundations of statistics while providing the computational foundations of statistics. When Richard Runyon and Audrey Haber wrote the first edition of this book more than 30 years ago, they carefully balanced two extremes in teaching statistics: at one extreme, the "cookbook" approach presents formulas and leads students through them step-by-step; at the other extreme, statistics is treated as a branch of applied mathematics. It is our belief that neither extreme is useful for undergraduates in the behavioral sciences, so we continue the critical compromise created in the first edition by carefully integrating the two approaches within this latest revision.

### Critical Thinking Skills

Much has been written about the value of critical thinking skills, how to foster their development, and how to ensure that students apply the principles in their lives. From research on this topic it is clear—critical thinking does not develop in a vacuum. Memorized formulas and definitions are of little value. Blind applications of formulas and hours of mind-numbing calculations do nothing to develop critical thinking. Instead, students must expose themselves repeatedly to situations in which they practice the application of critical thinking skills. We have endeavored to structure the presentation of the material in a manner that allows students to develop their skills based on quantitative data and well-rehearsed applications of heuristics. For each test and descriptive statistic we provide the rules and procedures, illustrate their application to relevant examples, and then discuss the generalizations that can legitimately be drawn from the analysis.

### Useful Pedagogy

Students who read our textbook will learn about the theory and rationale of the various statistical tests used by behavioral scientists. When a statistical concept is introduced in the text, we may illustrate it in a number of ways. We provide both conceptual formulas and computational formulas. At the same time, we use words to explain the rationale of the statistic. Finally, we use visual illustration to help convert abstract concepts into images to help the reader understand important principles.

We recognize that once you have learned the material you will obviously need to review the material either for an exam or for an assignment in another course. Whether you use the book as a reference or for review we provide the following:

- **Basic Math Review**: *Appendix A* gives you a quick refresher on basic math.
- **Statistical Symbols Glossary**: *Appendix B* references all the major symbols you need in a clear and straight-forward manner.
- **Statistical Formula Guide**: *Appendix C* provides a step-by-step synopsis of formulas with useful examples worked out.
- **Statistical Tables**: *Appendix D* provides important tables for statistical tests.
- **Summary of Equations**: These are found on the front and back inside covers of the book and can be used as a quick reference for studying.
- **Running Glossary**: Important terms are defined as they are discussed in the text.

## A NOTE TO THE STUDENT

We understand you probably did not sign up voluntarily to study statistics. Many of you are taking this course because it is required as part of your major or minor concentration. Others of you are taking it because your parents and career counselors have suggested a course in statistics to give you a competitive edge in a difficult job market. Many of you expect to go to graduate school and are aware of the central importance of analysis of empirical data in that milieu. Just as the reasons for taking this course will vary, so too your backgrounds and prior mathematical experience will vary.

We know this because we have taught statistics to hundreds of students over many, many years. And we have learned some valuable and surprising things from our students during that time. For example, we have learned that some students grasp the most complex statistical concepts immediately while others have to struggle to master each and every one. And we have been struck by the variety of techniques students find useful and important to them in mastering the material. Their reports vary tremendously. One person will swear by a technique and five others will find it useless.

Our conclusion has been that no one teaching technique is successful for all students. Some students have the ability to read an equation and immediately understand its workings. Others have better success when they see an illustration of the concept. Some students need verbal descriptions and others find the worked-out problems, marginal definitions, and end-of-chapter exercises to be the most useful. It is remarkable, the very same formula or illustration that provides instant insight for one individual can be of little or no value to others.

What have these observations meant, in practical terms, for us as authors? We have concluded that it is not enough to provide one explanation, one study technique. We have worked hard to provide you with a range of instructional devices that students have told us over the years have worked for them. We have included techniques useful for learning the material, for reviewing it at exam time and for mastering the calculations required by the exercises. For example, we have included marginal definitions to highlight important concepts as they are presented and listings of important terms at the end of each chapter. These may be used to guide your learning and to highlight important concepts when you review for exams. The end-of-chapter exercises provide practice in how to perform the calculations as well as some questions that will force you to think about how a statistical test works, why it works that way, and some of the precautions to take when using the test.

By the way, the answers to the odd numbered exercises are presented at the back of the book. These answers won't tell you exactly how to do the calculations but they will serve as a warning if the answer you come up with differs from the one in the text.

The understanding you develop from your reading and the exercises is reinforced in summary tables in the body of the text. We have introduced these summary tables as a way for you to make your study time more efficient. In one table you can view an outline of the major concepts, their characteristics, when they are used, and cautions in their use. We have provided frequently used formulas and notation in the end pages. We have included, as well, a statistical formula guide to give you clear and easy access to review commonly used statistical procedures. This section will be of particular value to you when you study for exams and when you finish this course and are called upon in subsequent courses to review a particular statistical technique.

## A NOTE TO THE INSTRUCTOR

We don't need to tell you that quantitative analysis is an integral part of psychology. Aside from the introductory psychology course, behavioral statistics is one of the few common courses for all psychology majors. You undoubtedly studied statistics as an undergraduate and certainly were required to take some statistics courses in graduate school. In fact you may have used the Runyon and Haber text in some of your courses. If you did, then you already know of the long tradition of this text. We have attempted to maintain that tradition and at the same time we have attempted to present new material, reflective of important evolution of thought within the field and have deleted material that has outgrown its usefulness.

Two monumental developments within the world of statistics have been evolving. The first of these has been the increased recognition of the importance of power in the design and conduct of experiments. The second important development has been the questioning of the value of statistical hypothesis testing. In terms of the latter, we recognize that hypothesis testing has its limitations, yet we believe that it still can serve a useful function. Rather than discard hypothesis testing, we show students how to analyze the data from a number of perspectives in addition to using traditional hypothesis testing. In terms of power we present the concepts of power and effect size and factors such as sample size and alpha that affect the power of a test. Indeed, each chapter related to inferential statistics has a section that reviews issues related to the power of the statistic.

Another addition to the text is the inclusion of clear examples of how to present the results of research in a research paper. Several of the chapters now include short examples illustrating the editorial style of the American Psychological Association. Learning to write clearly about empirical matters is an important skill that will serve your students well. With respect to maintaining the currency of the text, we have removed some material from previous editions and added new material. We decided to finally retire the material on grouped frequency distributions. Grouped data was once a necessary computational approach. The advent of computers and other technological advances has eliminated the need for its inclusion. Instead, we focus more on how students can use exploratory data analysis and graphing techniques to augment their analysis of data.

Tradition, our own biases in the teaching of statistics, and reviewers' comments have all influenced the sequence of chapters in the text. We recognize that some may not agree with our arrangement. Thus, we intentionally wrote the chapters to be relatively free standing. In some cases, this is an impossible task. Testing hypotheses in the chapter on analysis of variance cannot be understood without a solid foundation on hypothesis testing in general. We tried to write a text that lends itself to differing orders of presentation. We hope that you find this as well as other aspects of the text accommodating.

## ACKNOWLEDGEMENTS

We would be remiss if we did not publicly acclaim the valued contributions of the many, many individuals who collaborated in the development and production of this text. At each step, from the initial proposal stages to the final production details we were blessed with input from individuals who generously provided their time and their talents.

We must especially mention our Expert Reviewers, **Dennis Cogan** of Texas Tech University and **Michael Masson** of the University of Victoria, Canada.

We would also like to extend our thanks to the following reviewers:

**Ken Hobby**, Harding University;
**Chuck Brainard**, University of Arizona;
**Fran Conner**, University of Alabama;
**Lisa Isenberg**, University of Wisconsin;
**Stuart Bernstein**, Wayne State University;
**Thomas Billimeck**, San Antonio College;
**Hilda Williams**, Drake Williams College;
**James Green**, University of Connecticut;
**Danuta Bukatko**, College of Holy Cross;
**Philip Tolin**, Central Washington University;
**Rick Jenison**, University of Wisconsin-Madison;
**Elizabeth Kudadjie-Gyamfi**, Long Island University-Brooklyn;
**Stephen Chew**, Samford University;
**Pamela Hunt**, College of William and Mary;
**Siamak Movahedi**, University of Massachusetts-Boston;
**Elizabeth Krupinski**, University of Arizona.

We gratefully acknowledge our exceptionally hard working and talented collaborators at McGraw-Hill. Executive Editor Joe Terry skillfully nurtured and coordinated the planning of this revision, along with Susan Kunchandy, the Developmental Editor, and Lai Moy, the Editorial Coordinator. Finally, Fred Speers, our Editorial Assistant, must be acknowledged for providing just the right proportion of demanding deadlines mixed with words of encouragement that kept our project on schedule.

We admire and appreciate the efforts of all those named above.

## CONCLUSION

Where do you go from here? We have outlined for you the multi-faceted approach we have taken to provide the techniques and the tools to master this material. What does this approach mean, in practical terms, for you? It means that this text is designed to allow *you* to decide how you should master this material. We have described the various instructional devices and learning aids. Try using these aids. Find the ones you feel are helpful. Use them, and keep in mind: the successful students invariably try **many** approaches and study strategies before deciding on the most useful ones. These students actively interact with the study materials and use them as tools to develop their own understanding. Trying to memorize someone else's understanding is of little value. You must be the active learner and critically examine this book and its contents. We give you all you need to become a dynamic student in this course. With some exploration and a bit of effort you have all that you need to acquire a solid, successful education in the fundamentals of behavioral statistics.

Kay A. Coleman
*Boston University*

David J. Pittenger
*Marietta College*

# 1

## Statistics: The Arithmetic of Uncertainty

## 1.1
## What Is Statistics?

Think for a moment of the thousands of complex tasks you perform each and every day and stand in awe at the marvel you represent. You are absolutely unique. No one else possesses your physical features, your intellectual makeup, your personality, or your values. Yet, you share with others the ability to survey your environment, anticipate danger, and take corrective action that may allow you to "dodge the bullet." In an instant, you can receive, integrate, and process a continuous bombardment of sensory information. What is perhaps even more impressive is that your ensuing actions reveal a wisdom that is statistically correct on most occasions. In short, you are a finely tuned and enormously sophisticated decision-making statistical instrument.

Let's look at a common example. Suppose you are driving a car in heavy traffic while engaged in conversation with a friend, a task that is, in itself, incredibly complex. In spite of this distraction, you manage to evaluate road and traffic conditions. Obviously, your sensory mechanism cannot take in everything that is going on. Rather, your observations are somewhat like a public-opinion survey: From a limited sample of sensory input you make broad judgments about your immediate environment. How good are these judgments?

Suppose that, without warning, the car in front of you stops. In an instant, you must act on the sample of information you have gathered and assess the alternative courses of action. Should you jam on the brakes? Should you turn right onto the shoulder, turn left into the oncoming lane, or pray? If you brake, what is the likelihood that you will stop in time? If this alternative appears safe, you must also judge whether the car behind you is sufficiently distant to avoid a punishing rear-end collision. Do you have a better chance of preventing an accident by turning into the oncoming left lane or onto the right shoulder? You note that there is a car in the oncoming lane but is it a safe distance ahead?

In a fraction of a second, you judge that your best chance is to turn immediately onto the right shoulder and then hit the brakes. By taking this action, you avoid a potentially devastating accident. This outcome is not surprising. Most of the time, your sensory survey is accurate and you plot a course of action that has a high probability of success. Moreover, you conduct sampling assessments and make decisions many thousands of times each and every day of your life. It is for this reason that we may consider you a sublime mechanism for generating a wealth of sophisticated statistical decisions. In other words, you are, in many ways, already a statistician.

In daily living, our statistical functioning is usually informal and loosely structured. We behave statistically, even though we may be only vaguely aware of the formal laws of probability. In this book, we will introduce you to the logic of statistics by building upon what you already know implicitly through daily experiences. Throughout this book we will provide you with the information, the techniques, and the practice to make well-reasoned decisions about numerical information. We will help you learn about collecting and analyzing data. As you will see, the data for behavioral scientists are the numbers and measurements collected as a result of making careful and systematic observations. In addition, we will help you learn how to make decisions or inferences based on careful analysis of the data.

Because you'll be building on your experience, you will often find yourself in familiar territory. Think about it a moment. You have been calculating arithmetic means almost all of your life—whenever you find the average of your test scores in a course or calculate the batting average of your favorite player on the women's or men's softball team. There is no reason to fear statistics. Much of what you will be learning you are already doing in an informal manner. Contrary to popular misconception, this course does not require sophisticated mathematics skills. The math you learned in your basic algebra course will be more than enough for this course.

## 1.2 / Why Study Statistics?

In this text we hope you will discover that statistical and empirical reasoning skills are essential for any student to develop. Perhaps the reason that some students dread taking a statistics course is that they do not understand why they have to take the course. We are all apprehensive of things we don't understand. Let's look at why you should learn more about statistics.

What was the definition of psychology you learned in your introductory psychology course? Chances are, one of the first sentences in your introductory psychology textbook read, "Psychology is the *scientific* study of behavior and mental processes." For our purposes, the key word in the definition is "scientific." All psychologists use the scientific method to understand behavior and mental processes. An essential aspect of any scientific work is collecting data and making decisions from those data. **Statistics** is the process of collecting data in a systematic way and making decisions based on these data. Therefore, statistics is a tool that helps you solve complex problems and think rationally about various problems addressed in psychology.

**Statistics:**

The process of collecting data in a systematic way and making decisions based on these data.

You may object and say that your personal experiences have allowed you to learn a lot about human behavior. If personal experiences are so valued why are they replaced with empirical methods and statistics? The truth is, personal experience has its limitations. Although such experiences may be beneficial to us in our daily lives, the process is haphazard at best. Think for a moment about the problems of basing psychology solely on personal experience. Whose personal experience should we use and trust? Are your experiences more valid than ours? Is it possible that our experiences may be biased by who we are? How do we know that our experiences are accurate for all people? Personal experience is useful, but as we shall see, the empirical method is far more satisfactory to address specific questions.

Psychologists base their knowledge of human behavior on empirical evidence. Any student who wishes to become a professional psychologist must be familiar with statistical procedures and research techniques in order to perform the job effectively. Even if you do not pursue a professional career as a psychologist, you will constantly be confronted with opportunities to make decisions based on empirical evidence. Your knowledge of statistical reasoning will help you make good decisions.

The study of statistics need not and should not become a series of progressive exercises in calculated tedium. If you approach statistics with positive expectations and attitudes, you will find the material interesting. By the end of this course you will see that statistics has applications in virtually all areas of human endeavor and is present in many fields of study. H. G. Wells, the 19th-century prophet noted, "Statistical thinking will one day be as necessary for effective citizenship as the ability to read and write." Don't forget these words. Throughout your adult life you will be asked to make many decisions, many of which will have an empirical-statistical component.

## 1.3 / Definition of Terms

Statistics is a language. Statistics provides a way of talking about research and making conclusions based on data. We use special words or terms to convey specific ideas and information to others. As you master the vocabulary of statistics and research design, you will better understand the concepts used by psychologists and other scientists as they talk about their research findings. In this section we will introduce you to some of the most commonly used statistical terms. In subsequent chapters we will introduce you to more specific terms.

In any research project, the researcher examines the relation among many different **variables.** We define a variable as a characteristic or phenomenon that takes on different values. Any measurable characteristic of a person, environment, or experimental treatment that varies from person to person, environment to environment, or situation to situation is a variable. Thus weight, intelligence, sex, and personality are variables. Subjects in a research study may have different values for each of these variables. The opposite of a variable is a **constant,** the value of which never changes. For example, $\pi = 3.1416$, the speed of light = 186,282 miles per second, and one foot = 12 inches.

We may distinguish between two classes of variables, the independent variable and the dependent variable. The **independent variable (IV)** is the variable that the experimenter manipulates in order to explain differences or changes in the dependent variable. What then is the dependent variable? The **dependent variable (DV)** is the outcome of interest that the researcher observes and measures. Consider the following example. A psychologist is interested in the effect of exercise on the mood of patients who have been hospitalized for depression. He gives a group of sedentary patients a pencil-and-paper test to assess their depression. Then he requires that they undergo six weeks of daily exercise. At the end of this period he reassesses their level of depression. In this study the independent variable is exercise. It is the variable that the researcher manipulated. The outcome of interest, change in depression test scores, is the dependent variable. The psychologist assumes that changes in the test scores *depend on* the exercise. What the researcher controls is the independent variable. What the researcher measures as the outcome is the dependent variable.

What would you say about the design of a study in which the psychologist assigned clients to different forms of treatment based on their severity of their depression—severely depressed people were assigned to Psychoanalytic Therapy and mildly depressed clients were assigned to the Placebo Condition. Bad idea! The type of treatment is no longer an independent variable. The treatment is no longer independent of the manner by which subjects are assigned treatment. The treatment a client received was dependent on another factor, the level of depression. Now if a person gets better we do not know if the improvement is due to the treatment he or she received or due to the initial level of depression. The independent variable must be independent of factors influencing the outcome of the study—thus its name.

Consider another example. A psychologist is interested in the most effective means of treating kleptomania, which is an obsessive need to

■ **Variable:**

A characteristic or phenomenon that may take on different values. Any measurable characteristic of a person, environment, or experimental treatment that varies.

■ **Constant:**

A value that does not change.

■ **Independent Variable:**

The variable that the experimenter manipulates in order to explain the differences in the dependent variable or to cause changes in the dependent variable.

■ **Dependent Variable:**

An outcome of interest that is observed and measured by the researcher in order to assess the effects of the independent variable.

steal. She compares three forms of treatment, Cognitive Behavior Modification, Psychoanalytic Treatment, and a Placebo Treatment. The psychologist monitors the patients in each treatment condition and at the end of the study she asks them if they had stolen anything in the past week. In addition she asks them to rate how strong the desire to steal has been in the past week.

What is the dependent variable in this study? Actually there are two dependent measures: the self-reports of stealing behavior and the strength of the urge to steal. What is the independent variable? The treatment condition. The researcher controls the treatment each patient receives. The treatment is presumed to affect the stealing behavior and the desire to steal. The independent variable, the treatment, is presumed to affect the behavior of the patient, the dependent variable. The measurements taken on the subjects are the dependent variables, what the researcher manipulated is the independent variable.

There are two types of independent variables, the manipulated or experimental variable and the subject variable. It is essential that you understand the difference between the two. Failure to do so will result in incorrect decisions and conclusions about the results of a research project.

A **manipulated** or **experimental variable** is a type of independent variable that the experimenter can directly control and change. In the above example of treatment of kleptomania, the researcher controlled the type of therapeutic intervention each patient received. What if the researcher had compared males and females in terms of their responsiveness to therapy designed to control kleptomania? The researcher is not changing the sex of the patients as they come into the study. She has no control over that. The patients come into the study being either male or female. Thus the sex of the subject is a subject variable. A **subject variable** is a measurable characteristic of the subject that the experimenter does not change.

A simple way to distinguish between a subject variable and a manipulated variable is to ask: "Did the condition exist for the subject prior to the experiment?" If the answer is "yes" then it is a subject variable. When you walk into an experiment, your personality, your sex, your intelligence, and many other personal characteristics are already present. By contrast, if the experimenter controls the independent variable, then it is a manipulated variable.

In all research we collect **data.** We define data as numbers or measurements that are collected as a result of observations. The important aspect of this definition is that data represent numbers. In all cases, we will base our statistical decisions and conclusions on numbers. These numbers may be frequency data, such as the number of people planning to vote for a given presidential candidate; they may be rankings, such as the order of finish of a horse race (1st, 2nd, 3rd, and so forth); or they may be measures obtained from observation or from psychological tests.

In discussions of research you will hear much about **populations** and **samples.** As with all other terms, these too have special meaning for psychologists. In psychological research we attempt to describe a wide variety of behavior. A social psychologist may study the behavior of people who are in stressful situations. A clinical psychologist may study the behavior of people diagnosed as schizophrenic. In many cases we cannot study the entire population. We cannot study *all* schizophrenics or *all* people who are under stress because these populations are potentially infinite. Researchers must use samples to represent the populations, in order to make generalizations about the population. The researcher assumes that what is true for a sample will also be true for the population.

## ■ Manipulated or Experimental Variable:

A type of independent variable that the experimenter systematically controls or manipulates and to which the subjects are assigned.

## ■ Subject Variable:

A type of independent variable that is based on a measurable characteristic of the subject that the experimenter does not change.

## ■ Data:

Numbers or measurements that are collected as a result of observations.

## ■ Population:

A complete set of individuals, objects, or measurements having some common observable characteristic.

## ■ Sample:

A subset of a population that shares the same characteristics as the population.

▦ **Statistics:**

Numbers resulting from the manipulation of sample data according to certain specified procedures; statistics for samples are variable rather than constant.

▦ **Parameters:**

Values summarizing characteristics of a population that are usually an estimate based on statistics obtained from a sample. Population parameters are constants. Parameters are represented by Greek letters.

When we think of populations we think of very large groups such as "All residents of the United States," or "All people who are schizophrenic." A population may be considerably smaller. For example, "All students enrolled in this statistics course" may be considered a population. Likewise, we could say that all college students who are members of the class of 2003 are a population. In most cases populations are too large to measure. Therefore we use a sample of individuals drawn from the population to represent the population. Our assumption is that if the sample is representative of the population, our descriptions of the sample can be applied to the population.

When we describe the characteristics of a sample we use **statistics.** When we describe the characteristics of a population we use **parameters.** Statistics are numbers based on direct observation and measurement of a sample. Parameters may be based on direct observation or measurement of a population but more often they are inferred values based on observations of samples. We use sample statistics to make inferences about population parameters. In this book, we will follow the generally accepted practice of using Greek letters to represent parameters. For example, the Greek letter $\mu$ (mu, pronounced like the cat's mew) represents the population mean whereas $\overline{X}$ (pronounced X bar) stands for the mean of a sample.

---

**Illustration of Terms Commonly Used**

A psychologist is interested in observing preschool children and the type of toys they choose to play with. He suspects that toy preference might be related to the age or sex of the child. From a list of all children enrolled in a large day care center he selects at random 20 children to observe. These children comprise the random sample. The researcher observes each child for one hour and measures with a stopwatch the time spent playing with two different toys. The toys had been previously rated as being stereotypically male (Toy A) or female (Toy B). The age and sex of each child and the time spent playing with each toy are *variables*. The age and sex of each child vary. Because age and sex of the children are not manipulated by the researcher, they are called *subject variables*. There are two *dependent variables:* Time spent playing with Toy A and with Toy B. Information recorded on the data sheet are called *data*. Data may be quantative or qualitative. Age and time are quantitative variables; sex (male or female) is a qualitative variable.

| | | | **Time in Seconds** | |
|:---:|:---:|:---:|:---:|:---:|
| **Subject ID Number** | **Age in Months** | **Sex** | **Toy A** | **Toy B** |
| 01 | 35 | F | 19 | 28 |
| 02 | 29 | M | 27 | 24 |
| 03 | 26 | M | 13 | 14 |
| 04 | 31 | F | 9 | 29 |
| 05 | 37 | M | 25 | 15 |

**DATA SHEET**

The average age in months and the average time these subjects spent playing with each toy are called *statistics* because they are based on sample data. Similarly, the percentage of males and females at the day care center are called statistics. If summaries were obtained for the entire day care center or the entire population of day care center children in the state or the country, they would be called *parameters* because they are based on population data.

Another difference between parameters and statistics is the issue of variability. We assume that parameters are constants. At a given point in time a population parameter does not change. Statistics, based on samples from the population, do vary. The reason for the variability of a statistic is simple. Consider the average height of a given population, let's say all 18-year-old women who at this moment live in Jersey City. Imagine that the average height in inches for this population is 5′5″. This summary characteristic of the population is the parameter. It is a constant. If we take a sample from this population and calculate average height, we would calculate a statistic. The statistic is variable because each sample you measure is likely to vary. Would the average of each sample be exactly the same? No. Each time we draw a sample the people we select will be of different heights—sometimes shorter, sometimes taller. Although our sample statistics will change, the parameter "average woman's height" will not.

If statistics can vary from sample to sample, how do we know that the statistics can be considered representative of the population? We can answer the question by looking at how the researcher selects members of the sample. The most frequently used collection process is **simple random sampling.** Simple random sampling is a process of selecting subjects in such a way that each member of the population has an equal likelihood of being selected. We use random sampling because it helps ensure that our sample will be representative of the population. However, it is important to realize that random sampling is a *process*. It does not ensure an outcome. Just looking at a sample does not allow us to tell if it is a random sample. It is only a random sample if the process by which it was selected allowed each member in the population an equal chance of being selected. If that process were used, then we treat the sample as representative.

For example, if we are conducting a poll of registered voters in a city, we would want to select our sample in such a way that all segments of the voting population are represented. Our goal is that the sample accurately reflect all the characteristics of the population from which it was drawn. A random sample will help ensure that. As we shall see in Chapter 10, random sampling is directly related to probability theory. We will consider random sampling in detail in that and in subsequent chapters.

Another important concept in many research designs is **random assignment.** Random assignment refers to the process by which the researcher assigns subjects to the treatment conditions. This process ensures that each individual has an equal chance of being assigned to one of the conditions. The goal of random assignment is to ensure that all groups are comparable before the experiment begins. Here is an example. Assume that a clinical psychologist wants to determine which form of psychotherapy is more effective for the treatment of depression, Psychoanalytic Therapy, Rational Emotive Therapy, or Cognitive Behavior Modification. Each client should have an equal chance of being assigned to one of the three forms of therapy. Using random assignment we attempt to avoid systematic differences among the treatment groups before the study begins. Imagine what would happen if we systematically assigned the most depressed patients to the Cognitive Behavior Modification group. It would be impossible to fairly evaluate the results of the study. As we will see shortly, random assignment is an essential component of research design.

■ **Simple Random Sampling:**

A process of selecting subjects in such a way that each member of the population has an equal likelihood of being selected.

■ **Random Assignment:**

Assigning subjects to different treatment conditions in such a way that each subject has an equal and independent opportunity to be placed in each treatment condition.

| Panel A | | | | | | | Panel B | | | | | |
|---|---|---|---|---|---|---|---|---|---|---|---|---|
| 6 | 4 | 1 | 12 | 7 | 5 | | 6 | 9 | 2 | 12 | 8 | 4 |
| 3 | 6 | 5 | 8 | 11 | 5 | | 3 | 11 | 1 | 10 | 9 | 3 |
| 2 | 9 | 7 | 9 | 4 | 10 | | 4 | 5 | 4 | 7 | 3 | 9 |
| 8 | 6 | 6 | 7 | 5 | 7 | | 5 | 8 | 10 | 2 | 9 | 3 |

**Figure** | **1.1**

Two sets of data. Look at each data set for 10 seconds and then read the instructions in the text.

## 1.4 / Descriptive Statistics

**Descriptive Statistics:**

A set of statistical procedures used to organize, summarize, and present data.

When behavioral scientists conduct research they collect a great deal of numerical information or data. In their original form, these data are usually a confusing array of scores; some might even say that the data are chaotic. To remove the confusion and to understand the data, psychologists and other behavioral scientists use **descriptive statistics** to *organize* and *summarize* the data and to *present* the data in ways that can be easily understood by others. In other words, descriptive statistics are a set of statistical tools that they use to help them understand and talk about the data. These tools include graphs as well as mathematical calculations such as means, proportions, and measures of variability.

Why must we resort to statistics in order to understand our data? Very simply, we cannot digest masses of raw data. We can comprehend only a small amount of information at a time. Take a moment and examine the numbers in Panels A and B in Figure 1.1. Study each panel for 10 seconds. Now cover the numbers. Are the two sets of numbers roughly equivalent? Are they similar? Do they differ substantially? Now turn the page and look at the distribution of scores in each panel in Figure 1.2 on page 9. You probably didn't see the differences when you were looking at the raw, unorganized data. Yet, when presented in a graph, the differences are immediately apparent. One important function of statistics, then, is to provide ways of describing and summarizing data quantitatively.

Another characteristic of descriptive statistics is that they are objective and follow a set of consistent rules. If we allow people to make general descriptions of the data based on their own impressions of the data we are likely to get many different interpretations. Statistical procedures are, however, a group of recognized and standard procedures for describing the data. Using descriptive statistics is a convention that everyone can understand and that helps remove subjective bias when interpreting the scores.

## 1.5 / Inferential Statistics

Psychologists also use statistics to make inferences from the data. There are two types of inferences we can make using statistics. The first type of inference is parameter estimation or generalization. As we noted before, we use samples to make estimates about parameters. Therefore, when we describe the results of a research study we are describing the characteristics of our sample and using those characteristics to estimate the value of population parameters. For example, a psychologist who creates an intelligence test will give the test to a large representative sample

**Figure | 1.2**

**A graphical representation of the numbers in Figure 1.1. These graphs should be easier to interpret than the raw data.**

of children between 6 and 8 years of age. In doing so, the psychologist wants to use the data from this sample to estimate how the typical 6- to 8-year-old scores. If the average score for this sample is 38, then the psychologist can estimate that the typical 6- to 8-year-old has a score of 38.

Most population parameters can never be directly known except in cases in which the population is small or if we have sufficient funds to study the population in its entirety. Election day and the census are examples of measuring the population. We could also argue that the students in your statistics class are a population. Your instructor measures the population's knowledge of statistics each time he or she administers an exam. In most cases, however, we will almost certainly never know specific population parameters such as the percentage of people afflicted with AIDS. However, sampling from populations and subsequently applying inferential statistics permits us to build a bridge between the known and the unknown.

The second type of inference allows us to make inductions about specific events. In logic, an induction is a conclusion based on our observations of various facts. For example, a clinical psychologist may note that many people who have trouble sleeping, experience constant fatigue and inability to concentrate, and who lack interest in most activities are depressed. Therefore, if the psychologist sees a client who evidences all these symptoms, the psychologist induces (concludes) that the client is probably depressed. Technically speaking, all inductions are conditional or probable. In this example, the clinical psychologist makes the diagnosis based on his or her experiences with these symptoms. There is a possibility that the person could have all these symptoms and not be depressed.

Statisticians use the same logic to make inductions or inferences about the relation between the independent and the dependent variables. Specifically, researchers attempt to infer that there is a relation between the independent variable (IV) and the dependent variable (DV) based on the observations of samples. In most psychological research we collect samples of subjects and observe their behavior. On the basis of these observations we make inferences about the populations they represent. Specifically, we conduct research under controlled settings to determine whether the dependent variable is meaningfully related to (dependent on) the independent variable. Given the research design used, we can use statistics to make inferences about a systematic relation between the IV and DV or a cause-and-effect relation between the IV and DV. We will examine the difference between a systematic and a cause-and-effect relation a little later in this chapter.

The discipline supporting **inferential statistics** is probability theory. Knowing this should alert us to the inescapable fact that inferential

■ **Inferential Statistics:**

A collection of statistical procedures that allow one to make generalizations about population parameters based on sample statistics or to assess if any systematic relation exists between the IV and the DV, and to determine if there is a cause-and-effect relation between the IV and the DV.

statistics can never *prove* anything in the ultimate sense of the word. Our conclusions are tentative. When we complete the inferential function on a set of data, our conclusions are always couched in terms of probability rather than in terms of absolute truth. Thus, we may conclude, "The probability is high that the experimental variable affected the dependent variable."

## 1.6 / Fundamentals of Research

Psychologists actively use the scientific method and make innumerable contributions to understanding the human condition by conducting scientific research. What is the scientific method and how does it relate to psychological research? Why do we conduct such research? Is psychology a scientific discipline?

Research can be conducted in any setting and can be applied to an almost endless variety of problems. It is not confined to laboratories, expensive equipment, advanced technology, and white coats. While much psychological research is conducted in laboratories, many studies are conducted in natural settings—in places where we live, work, and study. Questions of a practical nature are often asked, questions that relate to our everyday lives. For example—Has there been an increase in family violence in the past five years? Is coffee consumption related to depression? Does exercise really improve our mood? Has there really been grade inflation over the past two decades?

To understand why psychology is a scientific discipline, we need to appreciate what constitutes scientific research. All scientific research has three common features: (1) an attempt to answer empirical questions, (2) the use of publicly verifiable knowledge, and (3) the use of systematic empiricism.

**Answering Empirical Questions**   The term "research" describes a number of activities in which we ask questions about the world around and within us. We try to find the answers to these questions in a systematic manner. The first step is to describe what we are studying. This description becomes the basis for research in which we try to predict and finally gain control over a particular situation or circumstances. In order to do so, we need data—objective information required to reach a conclusion.

Take, for example, the problem of eating disorders among college students. Researchers would begin to study the problem by measuring, describing, and documenting its occurrence. Only then would they design studies in order to predict who is likely to be affected and under what circumstances. Finally, they would look for the causes of the disorder in hopes of finding ways to prevent and control it. In seeking answers to these questions, researchers rely heavily on statistics to coordinate, describe, and permit them to draw valid conclusions from the data.

Recall that statistics is a method for dealing with data. The **research design** is a systematic plan for collecting data in order to provide answers to specific questions. The questions you ask will determine the kind of design you choose which will, in turn, determine the statistics you use.

**Using Publicly Verifiable Knowledge**   One of the keys to successful research, in addition to careful planning, is the use of **operational definitions** for measuring the variables we are studying. What is an

▨ **Research Design:**

A systematic procedure for collecting data in order to provide answers to specific questions.

▨ **Operational Definition:**

The definition that a researcher uses to describe the processes by which an object, event, or a construct is measured.

operational definition? To begin with, operational definitions are different from dictionary definitions which are often descriptive and, consequently, imprecise. For example, a dictionary definition of "anxiety" may be "a state of apprehension or psychic tension." Note that apprehension and psychic tension are not directly observable. Can you see apprehension or psychic tension in another person? You cannot. Apprehension and psychic tension are conditions that an individual may experience but which cannot be directly observed by others. What you may perceive are facial expressions, oddities in behavior, a tone of voice, or a hesitance to speak, all of which you infer to mean that the person is anxious. What we need is a definition of "anxiety" that will allow other people to objectively measure the condition.

A good operational definition makes a term, such as "anxiety," observable by specifying the procedures or operations for how the construct is measured. Thus, an operational definition of anxiety could include measuring such observable variables as heart rate, sweating in the palms, dilated pupils, and a variety of other physiological changes. Operational definitions also ensure that we correctly identify the behaviors we want to observe.

Consider the concept, *spouse abuse*. The dictionary definition is "To use a spouse wrongly or improperly." This definition does not specify the measurable behaviors that operationally define spouse abuse. Defining spouse abuse by referring to physical assaults and denying financial support or social activities are measurable behaviors we can study. The definition also better defines the problem we want to examine. By operationally defining our psychological constructs, different scientists are able to communicate a common methodology with one another.

One of the most important features of a good operational definition is that it allows another scientist to replicate or repeat an experiment. As we shall see, chance factors often enter into the outcomes of research studies and our conclusions may be altered by these factors. For this reason, it is desirable that studies be repeated. If the results of an experiment are replicated, we have greater confidence that the results are real and thus greater confidence in our conclusions. There are two types of replications, direct replications and systematic replications. In a **direct replication,** the researcher repeats the study under identical conditions. The purpose of direct replication is to assess the reliability of a finding. The more often we repeat a study and obtain the same result, the greater confidence we will have in those results. **Systematic replication** refers to a general replication of an experiment but with changes to the independent variable. The purpose of systematic replication is to examine in greater detail the nature of the relation between the independent and the dependent variable and to continually explore alternative explanations.

**The Use of Systematic Empiricism** Systematic empiricism suggests that we attempt to make our observations in a controlled manner. Specifically, we attempt to account for alternative hypotheses and determine if the behavior we explore is due to the specific conditions we examine or due to other factors. For example, if it is found that individuals who exercise regularly have a lower incidence of depressive episodes, is the healthier emotional state a consequence of the exercise or do individuals with healthier emotional states exercise more frequently?

The end products of most research efforts are masses of information. As we have already noted, if this information takes numerical form,

■ **Direct Replication:**

Repeating a study under the same conditions as the earlier research. Direct replication also refers to the condition where the researcher tests the same subject several times in the same condition or the researcher may test several subjects in the same condition.

■ **Systematic Replication:**

Repeating a previous experimental preparation but with one or more changes to the independent variable.

we refer to it as data. Our task is to organize, summarize, and interpret these data so that we may obtain valid and defensible answers to the questions that prompted our research. This is where statistics come into play. Statistical analysis is concerned specifically with making sense out of data and permitting valid conclusions or inferences to be drawn from these data.

## 1.7 / Goals of Research

The types of questions for which we seek research answers are about as varied as the different settings in which the behavioral scientists and practitioners employ their skills. The goals of research can be broadly classified into four categories: gathering information, describing relationships, comparing groups, and establishing causality.

### Descriptive Research

Many research activities consist of simply gathering information about some topic of interest. For example, we may wish to learn what percent of teens know how the AIDS virus is transmitted, or the characteristics of individuals on a certain antidepressant medication, or the incidence of tobacco use among males and females in different age groups. Descriptive studies are information-gathering activities in which the major emphasis is on obtaining an accurate description of the population. Often, the results of a given study are compared to those of prior research to learn if there have been any systematic changes over time or to see if the particular group under study differs from some other group or from the larger population.

An important point to remember is that no statistic is meaningful by itself. Take, for example, the psychology professor who asked his class the following question: "Would you, for one million dollars, throw your family pet off a cliff?" He was shocked to find that 6 students out of a class of 100 said they would. Fortunately, he did not complain to the admission's office about the type of student being accepted into the college. His study provides no basis for determining whether 6% is a high, low, or typical percentage. The percentage might be even higher at other colleges.

What if the same professor asked the question, "Have you ever cheated on an exam?" Should he be shocked if 30% of the students at the school responded affirmatively to that question? Unless he had some other data against which to compare his results, he cannot evaluate his statistic. Thirty percent may be a high value or a low value relative to other schools or colleges. These single values need a context in which they can be evaluated.

A single piece of data tells us nothing about relative frequencies and absolutely nothing about causation. Take the hypothetical example of the psychologist who notices that 50% of her depressed patients test positive for a form of the herpes virus. Should she conclude that herpes causes the depression or that depression brings on herpes? Neither conclusion is warranted. Without further information, she should not conclude that there is any connection at all. The data reveal only that 50% test positive, not whether this percentage is higher or lower than any other group. Before leaping to conclusions, a prudent researcher stops, reflects, and compares the data to some meaningful comparison group. What if 75% of the general population test positive? Or 25%? Even a

**A word of caution**

Be very careful about drawing conclusions with categorical data. You absolutely cannot make causal inferences with a single piece of data. Look at the graph below. Can we conclude that the dogs in Houston are more likely to be biters than the dogs in Boston? Absolutely not. To begin with, there may be more dogs in Houston. The number of biting dogs has to be viewed in terms of total number of dogs in a given city. At the very least, a single number needs a context in order to draw conclusions.

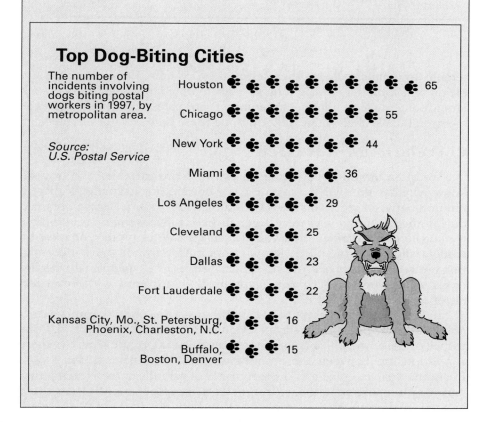

**Top Dog-Biting Cities**

The number of incidents involving dogs biting postal workers in 1997, by metropolitan area.

*Source: U.S. Postal Service*

|  |  |
|------|-----------|
| Houston | 65 |
| Chicago | 55 |
| New York | 44 |
| Miami | 36 |
| Los Angeles | 29 |
| Cleveland | 25 |
| Dallas | 23 |
| Fort Lauderdale | 22 |
| Kansas City, Mo., St. Petersburg, Phoenix, Charleston, N.C. | 16 |
| Buffalo, Boston, Denver | 15 |

large difference between the two groups would not allow you to conclude that herpes causes the depression or that depression exposes individuals to risk situations in which herpes is transmitted. We need to use other research designs before we draw causal conclusions.

Descriptive studies are frequently conducted to assist in developing public policy. For example, many adolescents—primarily females—develop serious eating disorders in which they either starve themselves (anorexia nervosa) or go on eating binges followed by purging of the food (bulimia nervosa). An ongoing series of studies by the Centers for Disease Control gathers information in regard to risk-taking behaviors among children and adolescents. Table 1.1 shows the results of one such study which is concerned with the self-perception of weight among a sample of female and male adolescents throughout the United States, including Puerto Rico and the Virgin Islands.

These data allow us to calculate such valuable statistics as: (a) the proportion (or percentage) of adolescent females and males who perceive themselves as overweight, and (b) the difference in the proportions of

**Table** | **1.1**

**A Sample of Female and Male Adolescents Perceiving Themselves as Either Overweight or Underweight.**

| | SELF-PERCEPTION | | |
|---|---|---|---|
| | **Underweight** | **Overweight** | **Row Totals** |
| Females | 419 | 1995 | 2414 |
| Males | 959 | 855 | 1814 |
| Column totals | 1378 | 2850 | 4228 |

*Source: Morbidity and Mortality Weekly Report,* 1991, 40, (43).

females and males who see themselves as overweight. Looking at the sample data in Table 1.1 we might be strongly tempted to suggest that a much larger percentage of adolescent females than males regard themselves as overweight. We shall more fully examine these data in later chapters.

## Correlational Research

We often obtain information on two or more variables and want to know whether the two "go together," or covary. For example, is there a relation between scores on the SAT and the grade point average obtained during the freshman year in college? If there is a systematic relation between the two variables then you should be able to predict how well a student should do in college knowing the SAT score. Is there a correlation between levels of testosterone and aggression? Do people with higher levels of testosterone act more aggressively than people with lower levels of testosterone?

In each of these examples, we obtain measures on two or more variables for each person, object, or event and raise the question "Do the values of these variables change together in a systematic way?" Is there a relationship between the amount of stress experienced during the freshman year in college and the number of pounds gained during that period? Do apartments near campus cost more per month than those located farther away? Is there a relation between the size of the class and the professor's course evaluation made by students at the end of the semester? Studies that ask these questions are called correlational because they attempt to describe the co-relation between two or more variables.

The diagram on page 15 describes the process of conducting a correlational study. The researcher randomly selects subjects from the population and collects information from them on two or more bits of information. The researcher then calculates a correlation coefficient, which is a statistic that describes how the two variables are related.

Note that a correlation between variables does not allow us to claim that one variable causes another variable. Let's look at a simple example. Assume that you did a survey of students in your class and found that there is a correlation between number of hours studied and overall GPA. You might be tempted to assume that studying more causes one to get higher grades. Although this sounds intuitively correct, the correlation alone *does not* allow one to infer a cause-and-effect relation. Could there be other ways to explain these results? As we will see in the following discussion, it is possible that there may be other ways of explaining

**Correlational Study**

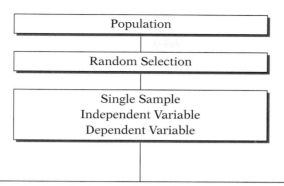

- **Statistical Analysis:** Correlation between two measures obtained from the same subject

- **Statistical Conclusion:** Relation between variables—no cause and effect conclusions

the data. Because there are these alternative explanations, we cannot directly assume cause and effect.

## Comparing Intact Groups

Sometimes we observe groups of individuals who seem to differ in terms of one or more characteristics. We might have noticed, for example, that smokers seem to be more fidgety or nervous than nonsmokers during social situations. We may notice that, on average, male students differ from female students in terms of how loud they play their stereos, or that women are less likely to talk in class than men. If you have ever pondered questions about group differences, and you undoubtedly have, you have been trying to make sense of your world in a way that would permit you to predict what your future might be like. Specifically, you are attempting to determine if there is a systematic relation between a grouping variable and some other variable. The steps of this research are shown in the flowchart on the next page.

As you can see, there is a similarity between this design and the correlational design. There are also some important differences. First, there is random selection from the population. However, when the subjects are selected they are placed into a group based on a particular subject variable. For example, we may place all women in one group and all men in the other. In another case, we may put all smokers in one group and nonsmokers in another. Similarly we could group people based on their eating habits, personality test scores, or physical characteristics. The important point to remember is that the groups represent some characteristic of the subject that existed prior to the start of the research. Once the groups are created we may use various statistical tools to compare the groups against one another.

Why is it important to distinguish between research groups that existed prior to the study and research groups in which the assignment of subjects is under the control of the experimenter? The answer is simply this: *The method of assignment of subjects affects the kinds of conclusions that can be drawn from the data*. The reason is that in the intact group design the independent variable of interest may be commingled with the presence of other variables.

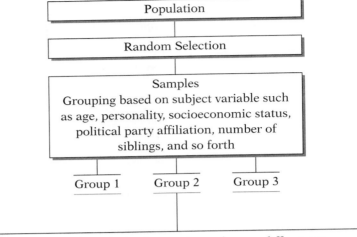

**Intact Group Comparison Study**
Group assignment is based on
subject characteristic at
the beginning of the study.

Population

Random Selection

Samples
Grouping based on subject variable such
as age, personality, socioeconomic status,
political party affiliation, number of
siblings, and so forth

Group 1    Group 2    Group 3

- **Statistical Analysis:** Comparison of group differences
- **Statistical Conclusion:** Significant difference among groups—no cause and effect conclusions

Let's look at a research question. Do pregnant women who smoke differ from those who don't smoke in terms of the weight of their babies at birth? Notice that we are not asking *why* but only *if* there is a difference in birth weight. This design does not tell us if smoking causes any difference that might exist. The reason we cannot draw *causal* inferences relates to the way in which people get into one group or another. Women who choose to smoke during pregnancy may differ from nonsmoking pregnant women in a number of different ways. They tend to be younger, to seek prenatal care later in their pregnancies, and to have different eating and drinking habits. They may also have different anxiety levels and come from a different socioeconomic class. For these reasons and others too numerous to catalogue, an intact group study does not specifically reveal whether smoking or any of these other differences affected the birth weight of the newborns.

Consider another study. A researcher compares individuals who have been in psychotherapy for 6 months with a group of individuals who have never been in therapy. Again we have an intact group comparison design. What if the researcher finds that individuals in therapy have a higher anxiety level than their counterparts who are not in therapy? Is it reasonable to conclude that psychotherapy is *causing* their anxiety level to increase? Of course not. The individuals self-selected into therapy; perhaps they are in therapy because their anxiety level is high. With this type of design, remember, we may predict differences between groups, but we cannot be sure what causes the differences.

## True Experiments

Most people use the word experiment rather loosely. If we modify some aspect of our daily lives, we dignify our new behavior with the word "experiment," such as, "I'm experimenting with getting up at 6 every morning," we proudly announce, only to experience a humiliating collapse of resolve within a few days. We even speak of people "experimenting" with drugs, thereby imparting the air of legitimacy to this activity. In this course, our use of the term "experiment" is more restrictive. The true experiment has been called the royal road to establishing cause-effect relationships. Thus it is important to distinguish the true experiment from other types of research.

Psychologists use many techniques in their attempts to establish causal relationships. Some have enthusiastic proponents as well as vocal detractors. However, few scientists question the efficacy of the experiment. In the typical experimental setting, there are three classes of variables: dependent, independent and **nuisance variables.** The latter are extraneous variables such as unplanned distractions in the experimental setting that may interfere with the assessment of the effects of the independent variable. We do all we can to keep the effects of nuisance variables to a minimum. We have already discussed the other two: The independent variable is the variable manipulated by the experimenter, such as schedule of reinforcement or length of food deprivation. The dependent variable is the measure obtained from the subjects, such as scores on a test, time required to master a task, and heart rate.

The essential elements necessary to qualify as a true experiment are the following:

**1.** The independent variable must be under the control of the experimenter.
**2.** The subjects are randomly assigned to treatment.
**3.** There must be controls for alternative hypotheses.

The question being asked with this design is, "What is the effect of the independent variable on the dependent variable?" Here is a diagram of the components of a true experiment.

The first step in an experiment is that the researcher *randomly selects* the subjects. The reasearcher then *randomly assigns* the subjects to the treatment groups. Remember, random assignment requires that each

■ **Nuisance Variables:**

Variables that may interfere with the assessment of the effects of the independent variable.

### Conducting a True Experiment

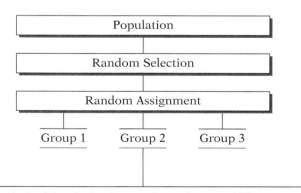

- **Statistical Analysis:** Comparison of group differences

- **Statistical Conclusion:** Significant difference among groups, significant relation between IV and DV—cause and effect conclusion

subject has an equal probability of being placed into one of the treatment conditions. Therefore, if we were to compare the treatment groups before the experiment began, we would expect no systematic difference between them. The groups should be equivalent to one another. When the subjects are assigned to a treatment condition, they are exposed to the independent variable. This variable is the experimental variable which is directly manipulated by the experimenter.

The researcher is then able to compare the differences between the groups. Remember that before the start of the experiment the groups were assumed to be equivalent. If there are differences between the groups at the end of the experiment what caused the differences? It is assumed that the differences are due to the manipulation of the independent variable. This conclusion will continue to be valid until another experiment is conducted that will support, refute, or modify the conclusion.

Here are some examples of experiments:

- What is the effect of $\frac{1}{2}$ hour of aerobic exercise on mood?
- What are the effects of attendance of the significant other at a weight loss clinic on the subsequent weight loss of the participants in the clinic?
- What effect does sleep deprivation have on performance?
- Does meditation alleviate symptoms of depression?

In each of the above examples, the experimenter controls the levels of the independent variable and the assignment of subjects to each condition. In the first example, the experimenter can randomly assign a subject to either the aerobic exercise condition or to the control condition (no exercise). In the second example, the experimenter uses random assignment to determine if the subject's significant other will or will not attend the weight loss clinic. The subjects *do not* choose which condition to join. With random assignment, each subject has an equally likely chance of being assigned to each condition. In Table 1.2 you will see that it is only the true experimental study design that provides the basis for making causal inferences.

**The Necessity of Random Selection in an Experiment**   In our discussions of experimental designs we continued to stress the importance of random selection. Although random selection is what we strive for in good research, is this goal realistic and is it practiced by all behavioral scientists? The answer escapes a simple yes or no answer. In some situations it is imperative that the researcher obtain a true random sample of the population. Political scientists who want to determine how the typical voter reacts to issues of foreign and domestic policy will want to ensure that they have a true random sample. Likewise, a psychologist studying depression among college students will want to use random sampling to achieve a sample that truly reflects the characteristics of that population. There are times, however, where random selection is neither practical nor necessary.

Consider a developmental psychologist who conducts an experiment at a local day care facility. Does the researcher really have random sampling? No, the psychologist must use the children who are available. Even if the psychologist went to several day care centers in town, true random selection may not be possible. Does this mean that the experiment is invalid? No. All it means is that the results of the experiment do need to be interpreted with caution. If the results of the experiment do apply to the population, direct and systematic replications of the experiment should yield the same results.

Simple random selection represents the ideal method for selecting subjects from a population. However, simple random selection is sometimes impractical or not essential.

**Table** 1.2

Summary of Types of Research Designs and Their Characteristics

| Design | Research Question | Process | Causal Inference |
|---|---|---|---|
| Descriptive | What are the characteristics of this group or this environment? | Each variable analyzed separately. | No |
| Correlational | What is the relation between the two variables ____ and ____ ? | At least two measures per subject are needed. | No |
| Intact group comparison | Do the two groups differ in terms of a specified variable ____? | Subjects assigned to groups based on subject variable. Subjects come into the study with that characteristic. They are not assigned that characteristic. | No |
| True experiment | What is the effect of _____ (the independent variable) on ____ (the dependent variable)? | Subjects are randomly assigned to a treatment group (the independent variable) to assess the effect of the variable on a measure of interest (the dependent variable). | Yes. Only in a true experiment is it possible to conclude that one variable *has an effect* on the dependent measure. |

**Confounding**   We spoke earlier about three types of variables in an experiment: independent, dependent, and nuisance variables. Nuisance variables are all those variables that are not considered either independent or dependent variables. There may be, for example, an unplanned distraction in the experimental setting. They may also be variables that affect the outcome of an experiment in a systematic way. When the dependent measure is affected by a variable that is linked to the independent variable, **confounding** is said to have occurred. Confounding variables are those that co-vary or are linked with the independent variable thus resulting in an experimental design that is seriously flawed. A simple example will clarify.

   Let's say a researcher is interested in the effect of experimentally manipulated stress on performance of a complex cognitive task. The study design consists of two groups. One group experiences high levels of stress and the other group experiences low stress levels. Let's further say that only males experienced the high-stress condition and females experienced the low-stress condition. If we find that the group in the high-stress condition performs poorly, can we say that it is the level of stress that caused the performance to be adversely affected? Can we say that males don't perform as well as females on this task? Obviously you can't draw either conclusion. It is impossible to disentangle the two variables—sex and level of stress. The

■ **Confounding:**

Confounding occurs when the dependent variable is affected by a variable that is related to the independent variable. Confounding is a serious flaw in an experimental design since it undermines the ability to draw causal conclusions, which is the goal of an experiment.

relative contribution of each is impossible to assess. It is possible that males are superior to females on this task and it was the stress that caused them to perform poorly. It is also possible that males don't do well on this task and the stress was a motivating factor causing them to focus their attention and improve their dismal performance. They would have done worse without the stress! Would you put money on any of these conclusions? Hopefully you wouldn't. Because of confounding it is impossible to draw any conclusions from the experiment related to the role of the independent variable as it affects the dependent variable.

You may be saying to yourself at this point that nobody would be dumb enough to design a confounded experiment. It can happen. Here's an example. Sometimes researchers, to save money and time, might run all their subjects in one experimental condition at one time, for example, in the morning. Then all the subjects in the other condition are run in the afternoon or evening. If the researcher is interested in the effect of the treatment on say, mood, there may be a confounding effect. If level of mood is related to time of day it is impossible with this design to know if it is the independent variable that is affecting their mood or if it is the time of day that accounts for their reported mood. It may be both but you won't know the relative contribution of each variable—the independent variable and the confounding variable. Here's another example. What if all the subjects during the day are college students and the evening subjects are those who are employed during the day and not able to take part in daytime experiments. If the dependent measure is a complex cognitive task then college students might have an advantage. Being in school has the effect of keeping you "up to speed" with complex verbal tasks. What if the dependent measure is affected by age of subjects? The evening group would probably be older than the daytime college students. The bottom line is, if there is a connection between your dependent measure and how you get your subjects and assign them you have confounding in your design.

**The Role of Statistics in Experiments**   So far in this chapter we have taken a look at some of the fundamental elements of research design. Our tour has been brief, but its purpose was not to cover the entire topic of research design. This is a fascinating subject in and of itself that has been covered well in a number of different volumes. Our goal was to present some basic research designs that address questions frequently asked by behavioral scientists. In subsequent chapters we will examine the various statistical techniques appropriate to those designs. But first, we formulate the questions, and then we design our investigation. Only then do we ask how statistics can help us organize, summarize, and interpret the numerical information the study yields. We cannot overemphasize the fact that the most elegant statistical techniques cannot rescue a badly designed study. The order of activities is to determine the question being asked, design a study, decide on a valid statistical analysis, conduct the study, analyze the data, and then draw conclusions.

# 1.8 / Putting It All Together: A Case of Statistical Sleuthing

A dentist practicing in Charlottesville, Virginia, made an unusual observation. Two unrelated patients, 17 and 28 years old, exhibited extensive pitting and erosion of the enamel on a number of their teeth. Such pitting is commonly found in individuals exposed to acid. An examination of their case histories revealed no medical, occupational, or dietary exposure to acid. However, the dentist noted a common factor—they were both swimmers who frequently trained at the same club.

Wisely, the dentist reported his observations to one of the finest statistical-medical-behavioral sleuthing agencies in the world: The Centers for Disease Control. In an attempt to identify additional cases, a survey questionnaire was mailed to all club members. The sample consisted of 747 replies. The population to which the investigators wished to generalize was all members of the club. The data consisted of each respondent's self-observations. In analyzing the data, members were considered to have indications of enamel erosion if they reported one or more of the symptoms "a lot" or two or more symptoms "sometimes": gritty teeth, transparent or yellow teeth, chalky white teeth, or painful teeth when chewing. Members were also considered cases if their dentists had clinically diagnosed dental enamel erosion during or after the summer months.

Note that the sample was divided into two groups: those who met the various criteria of enamel erosion and those who did not. Since the variable is a state of the individual over which the investigators had no control, the study is not an experiment but rather the comparison of two intact groups, one with dental erosion and the other without. The data subjected to statistical analyses consisted of "head counts," that is, the number of members who presented evidence of enamel erosion and those who did not. Subsequently, different groups were identified within the sample (such as frequent versus nonfrequent swimmers), appropriate sample statistics were calculated, and then inferential statistics were invoked to ascertain if there was a difference between the two groups of sufficient magnitude that it wasn't a chance or accidental occurrence.

We shall continue with this case of statistical sleuthing in Chapter 2.

## CHAPTER SUMMARY

In this chapter we saw that many people regard statistics as a mere collection of numerical facts. Scientists, however, stress the use of statistics as a method or tool concerned with collecting, organizing, summarizing, and interpreting numerical facts. We looked at the goals of research, which included gathering information, establishing relationships, comparing intact groups, and establishing causality. We noted the important role of a systematic plan—the design of the study—in accomplishing these goals.

A number of terms commonly used in statistical analysis and research design were defined and exemplified. We examined the distinction between the two functions of statistical analysis—the descriptive and the inferential. The former is concerned with the organization and presentation of the data in a convenient and communicable form. The latter addresses the problem of making broader inferences from sample data to populations.

New terms or concepts that have been introduced in the chapter are listed at the end of each chapter as well as defined, in boldface print, at the point in the chapter at which they are introduced. Some of these terms will be more precisely defined in later chapters and consequently may appear again.

_____ **TERMS TO** R EMEMBER

| | |
|---|---|
| confounding | parameters |
| constant | population |
| data | random assignment |
| dependent variable (DV) | research design |
| descriptive statistics | sample |
| direct replication | simple random sampling |
| independent variable (IV) | statistics |
| inferential statistics | subject variable |
| manipulated or experimental variable | systematic replication |
| nuisance variables | variable |
| operational definition | |

_____ E XERCISES

**1.** Indicate whether each of the following constitutes a statistic, data, or an inference from a statistic.
   **a.** A sample of 250 wage earners earn an average of $19,565.
   **b.** Based on a sample of 500 wage earners in Gotham City, it is believed that the average income of all wage earners in this city is $19,792.
   **c.** Slugs from a .22 rifle traveled 0.8, 0.96, and 1.1 miles.
   **d.** My tuition payment this year was $14,580; Sally's was $15,285.
   **e.** Based on a telephone survey, it is believed that the number of people viewing Monday night's television special was 33,520,000.

**2.** Explain the difference between a variable and a constant.

**3.** Indicate whether each of the following represents a variable or a constant.
   **a.** number of days in the month of August
   **b.** number of shares traded on the New York Stock Exchange on various days of the year
   **c.** age of freshman entering college
   **d.** time it takes to complete an assignment
   **e.** age at which an individual is first eligible to vote in a national election
   **f.** scores obtained on a 100-item multiple-choice examination
   **g.** amount of money spent on books per year by students

**4.** What is the difference between a sample and a population? Is it possible to have a population consisting of only 20 subjects?

**5.** Football commentators frequently talk about the number of first downs in a game, passes attempted, passes completed, and so on. It is not uncommon for them to say: "Here are the halftime statistics. They really tell the story of this game!" Are these numbers they report statistics? If not, what are they?

   Exercises 6 through 11 are based on the following: imagine a researcher who decides to study risk taking behavior in a randomly selected sample of male undergraduates at a large state university. He administers a standardized test designed to assess this type of behavior. Based on this study he would like to make inferences about other male undergraduates at the college.

**6.** The students selected for study constitute the
   **a.** population    **b.** statistic    **c.** parameter    **d.** sample.

**7.** In this study, risk-taking behavior measured by the test constitutes a
   **a.** statistic    **b.** variable    **c.** parameter    **d.** sample.

**8.** The scores obtained by the individuals in this study constitute the
   **a.** data   **b.** sample   **c.** statistic   **d.** population.

**9.** The average test score of the undergraduates in this sample constitutes a
   **a.** parameter   **b.** statistic   **c.** variable   **d.** data.

**10.** When we generalize our results, we make inferences to
   **a.** data   **b.** variables   **c.** statistics   **d.** populations.

**11.** The average score obtained by all undergraduates at the school would constitute a
   **a.** parameter   **b.** variable   **c.** data   **d.** population.

**12.** A researcher conducts a study in which college undergraduates are randomly assigned to one of two treatment conditions. Group 1 receives instructional materials in which line drawings are used; Group 2 receives materials in which actual photographs are used. An achievement test is given to determine the effectiveness of instruction.
   **a.** What type of design is used in this study?
   **b.** What is the independent variable?
   **c.** What is the dependent variable?
   **d.** Would it be appropriate for the researcher to assign only females to Group 1 and only males to Group 2? Explain.

**13.** Classify each of the following variables as either a manipulated variable, a subject variable, or not a variable.
   **a.** amount of drug administered in a study
   **b.** value of pi
   **c.** number of days in a week
   **d.** diagnostic categories of clients participating in a study
   **e.** gender of subjects
   **f.** amount of reinforcement
   **g.** method of instruction
   **h.** hours of food deprivation
   **i.** scores on test
   **j.** mood of experimental subjects

**14.** Tom has a problem sleeping at night. Teenagers are hanging out near his house making lots of noise. In frustration he tries an "experiment." Every night between 8:00 and 10:00 p.m. he puts stereo speakers in his window and plays classical music at maximum volume. He wants to know if the music has an effect on the teenagers, keeping them away. During a one-week period Tom counts the number of cars parked near his house when the music is playing and when it is not. At 9:00 p.m. during the week there were a total of 7 cars and at 11:00 p.m. there were a total of 61 cars.
   **a.** What is the independent variable in this experiment?
   **b.** What is the dependent variable in this experiment?
   **c.** Has Tom conducted a true experiment?
   **d.** Are you able to identify a flaw in the design of Tom's study?

**15.** What is confounding? Give an example of an experiment that is confounded and explain why confounding is a problem.

**16.** Explain the difference between an independent variable and a dependent variable.

**17.** Identify each of the following research questions as being either descriptive, correlational, intact group comparison, or experimental.

    **a.** What is the relation between number of hours spent studying and scores on a midterm exam?

    **b.** Do college students who smoke differ from those who don't smoke in terms of number of hours per week spent studying?

    **c.** What is the effect of exercise on reported mood?

    **d.** What are the characteristics of psychology majors who avoid taking the required statistics course until their senior year?

**18.** Identify the following research questions as either descriptive, correlational, intact group comparison, or experimental.

    **a.** Do coffee drinkers differ from non-coffee drinkers in terms of anxiety level?

    **b.** What is the effect of coffee consumption on mood?

    **c.** What is the relation between number of books read in the past year and score on the verbal section of the Graduate Record Exam?

    **d.** Do males differ from females in terms of the amount of time they take picking out Valentine's Day cards?

# 2

# Basic Concepts

## 2.1 / Introduction

"I'm not much good in math. How can I possibly pass statistics?" Many people feel this way when they learn that they have to take a course in statistics. And that's understandable. After all, the material may be unfamiliar and many of the formulas may appear at first to be quite imposing. It doesn't help, either, if your roommate keeps referring to the course as "sadistics."

You need not be a mathematical genius to master the statistical principles presented in this text. In years past, courses in statistics required the student to engage in tedious calculations in order to solve basic questions. Computers and calculators now free students from much of the "bookkeeping" work of statistics. Moreover, many statistical procedures contain common formulas and operations. Therefore, once you become familiar with a few basic equations, you will see them applied in slightly more complex forms. Thus, the real purpose of this course is to teach you the logic behind empirical reasoning, the use of reason underlying various statistical procedures, and how to execute problem solving techniques when interpreting the results of statistical analyses.

In this chapter we review the grammar of mathematical notation, discuss several types or classes of data, and adopt certain conventions for rounding numbers.

## 2.2 / The Grammar of Statistical Notation

Throughout this textbook, you will be learning new statistical symbols. For the most part, we define these symbols when they first appear. However there are three notations that appear throughout the text. Their introduction at this time is most helpful. They are $\Sigma$ (pronounced *sigma*), $X$, and $N$. While defining these symbols and showing their use, let's also review the grammar of mathematical notation.

Some students become lost in the forest of mathematical symbols, formulas, and operators and fail to realize that mathematics has a grammar that closely parallels spoken language. Some people would even agree that mathematics represents a special form of language. Like any sentence written in words, mathematical equations express information and have a consistent grammar and syntax. Mathematics also has its own nouns, adjectives, verbs, and adverbs.

**Mathematical Nouns** In grammar, we use nouns to represent persons, places, things, and ideas. In mathematics, our nouns are commonly quantities. The notation we use most frequently in statistics to represent quantity (or a score) is $X$, although we occasionally employ $Y$. More specifically, the letter $X$ or $Y$ represents a set of observations or data collected in a study. For example, if weight and height were two variables in a study, $X$ would represent weight and $Y$ would identify height. Another frequently used "noun" is the symbol $N$, which stands for the number of scores or quantities in the set.

**Mathematical Adjectives** In grammar we use adjectives to describe or modify nouns. When we want to modify a mathematical noun or identify

**$X$ or $Y$:**

Variables used to represent a set of observations or data.

**$N$:**

Number of scores or quantities in a set.

**$X_i$:**

Variable that represents a specific observation in the data set $X$.

it more specifically, we commonly employ subscripts. Thus, if we have a series of scores or quantities, we may represent them as $X_1, X_2, X_3, X_4$ and so on. We shall also frequently encounter $X_i$. The subscript $i$ refers to a variable, for example $X$, that may take on any value. In a study we may have 10 subjects. The subscript represents the measurement for each subject. Therefore, $X_5$ and $Y_5$ represent the $X$ and $Y$ measurements for the fifth subject.

**Mathematical Verbs**  In grammar, we use verbs to denote actions related to nouns. In mathematics, notations that direct the reader to perform something on the nouns have the same characteristics as verbs in the spoken language. One of the most important "verbs" is the symbol $\Sigma$. This notation directs us to sum all quantities or scores following the symbol. Let $X$ equal the data set with five numbers. $\Sigma X$ indicates that we should add together all the quantities from $X_1$ to $X_5$.

■ **Σ:**

The mathematical operator that indicates the summation of a set of numbers.

$$\underline{X}$$
$$X_1 = 5 \qquad \Sigma X = X_1 + X_2 + X_3 + X_4 + X_5$$
$$X_2 = 3 \qquad \Sigma X = 5 + 3 + 6 + 7 + 2$$
$$X_3 = 6 \qquad \Sigma X = 23$$
$$X_4 = 7$$
$$X_5 = 2$$

Other verbs we encounter frequently are $\sqrt{\phantom{x}}$, which directs us to find the square root, and exponents ($X^a$), which tell us to raise a quantity to the indicated power. For example, $X^2$ means the square of a number such as $3^2 = 9$. Mathematical verbs are commonly referred to as *operators*.

**Mathematical Adverbs**  In grammar, adverbs are used to describe or modify verbs. Likewise, in mathematics, adverbial notations are used to modify the verbs. We frequently find adverbial notation modifying the summation sign ($\Sigma$). Let's imagine that we want to add the following quantities:

$$X_1 + X_2 + X_3 + X_4 + X_5 + \cdots + X_N$$

Symbolically we would use the following notation:

$$\sum_{i=1}^{N} X_i$$

The notations above and below the summation sign indicate that $i$ takes on successive values from 1, 2, 3, 4, 5, up to $N$. Thus we should sum all quantities starting with $i = 1$ through $i = N$.

Sometimes this form of notation may direct us to add only selected quantities. Thus, if

$$X_1 = 7, X_2 = 5, X_3 = 9, X_4 = 8, X_5 = 11, \text{ and } X_6 = 4,$$

$$\sum_{i=2}^{6} X_i = X_2 + X_3 + X_4 + X_5 + X_6$$
$$= 5 + 9 + 8 + 11 + 4 = 37$$

At other times the notation may direct us to square each value of the variable before summing them. Thus,

$$\sum_{i=2}^{5} X_i{}^2 = 5^2 + 9^2 + 8^2 + 11^2$$
$$= 25 + 81 + 64 + 121 = 291$$

## 2.3 / Rules of Priority

**M**any statistical equations have several steps expressed in a single equation. It is vital that you remember the rules of priority for interpreting a mathematical equation. Here are the general rules that apply to all mathematical operations:

1. Work from the left to the right of the equation.
2. Perform all the operations *inside* the parentheses before performing those outside the parentheses.
3. Some mathematical operations are performed before others. The order is presented in Table 2.1.

Here are some examples of multistep problems. When you come to problems like these, make sure that you show each step. Our experience is that most students make mistakes because they try to skip steps and make an error in the process:

### Example 1

$X = 49 - (28)(5) + 23$
$X = 49 - 140 + 23$
$X = -68$

### Example 2

$X = 7^2 - (-7 + 4) + 8 - (-15)$
$X = 49 - (-3) + 8 + 15$
$X = 49 + 3 + 8 + 15$
$X = 75$

**Table** | **2.1**

**Rules of Priority for Mathematical Operations\***

| Operator | Equation Format | Example |
|---|---|---|
| 1. Exponentiation and square root | | |
|     Exponentiation | $X^2$ | $5^2 = 25$ |
|     Square root | $\sqrt{X}$ | $\sqrt{25} = 5$ |
| 2. Negation | $-X$ | $-(15) = -15$ |
| 3. Multiplication and division | | |
|     Multiplication | $X(Y)$ | $3(4) = 12$ |
| | $X \times Y$ | $3 \times 4 = 12$ |
|     Division | $X/Y$ | $12/4 = 3$ |
| 4. Addition and subtraction | | |
|     Addition | $X + Y$ | $3 + 4 = 7$ |
|     Subtraction | $X - Y$ | $12 - 4 = 8$ |

\*Rules are listed from highest to lowest priority.

Now we can apply these rules to several operations that are common to statistical analysis. For our purposes we will assume that our data sets $X$ and $Y$ each consist of the following six values:

$$X_1 = 7 \qquad Y_1 = 2$$
$$X_2 = 5 \qquad Y_2 = 7$$
$$X_3 = 9 \qquad Y_3 = 13$$
$$X_4 = 8 \qquad Y_4 = 2$$
$$X_5 = 11 \qquad Y_5 = 7$$
$$X_6 = 4 \qquad Y_6 = 8$$

***Example:*** Sum of Observations in a Set

$$\Sigma X = X_1 + X_2 + X_3 + X_4 + X_5 + X_6$$
$$\Sigma X = 7 + 5 + 9 + 8 + 11 + 4$$
$$\Sigma X = 44$$

$$\Sigma Y = Y_1 + Y_2 + Y_3 + Y_4 + Y_5 + Y_6$$
$$\Sigma Y = 2 + 7 + 13 + 2 + 7 + 8$$
$$\Sigma Y = 39$$

***Example:*** Sum of Squared Observations in a Set

$$\Sigma X^2 = X_1^2 + X_2^2 + X_3^2 + X_4^2 + X_5^2 + X_6^2$$
$$\Sigma X^2 = 7^2 + 5^2 + 9^2 + 8^2 + 11^2 + 4^2$$
$$\Sigma X^2 = 49 + 25 + 81 + 64 + 121 + 16$$
$$\Sigma X^2 = 356$$

$$\Sigma Y^2 = Y_1^2 + Y_2^2 + Y_3^2 + Y_4^2 + Y_5^2 + Y_6^2$$
$$\Sigma Y^2 = 2^2 + 7^2 + 13^2 + 2^2 + 7^2 + 8^2$$
$$\Sigma Y^2 = 4 + 49 + 169 + 4 + 49 + 64$$
$$\Sigma Y^2 = 339$$

***Example:*** Sum of Observations in a Set, Quantity Squared

$$(\Sigma X)^2 = (7 + 5 + 9 + 8 + 11 + 4)^2$$
$$(\Sigma X)^2 = 44^2$$
$$(\Sigma X)^2 = 1936$$

$$(\Sigma Y)^2 = (2 + 7 + 13 + 2 + 7 + 8)^2$$
$$(\Sigma Y)^2 = 39^2$$
$$(\Sigma Y)^2 = 1521$$

***Example:*** Sum of Cross Products

$$\Sigma XY = X_1 Y_1 + X_2 Y_2 + X_3 Y_3 + X_4 Y_4 + X_5 Y_5 + X_6 Y_6$$
$$\Sigma XY = (7 \times 2) + (5 \times 7) + (9 \times 13) + (8 \times 2) + (11 \times 7) + (4 \times 8)$$
$$\Sigma XY = 14 + 35 + 117 + 16 + 77 + 32$$
$$\Sigma XY = 291$$

***Example:*** Product of Two Sums

$$(\Sigma X)(\Sigma Y) = 44 \times 39$$
$$(\Sigma X)(\Sigma Y) = 1716$$

Note that $\Sigma X^2$ does *not* equal $(\Sigma X)^2$. Remember: Perform all operations inside the parentheses first. If you sum the scores first and then square the sum you will get a very different answer than if you first square each score and then sum them. See Table 2.2 for a review.

**Table** 2.2

**Summary of Notation for Some Frequently Used Operations**

| | $X$ | $Y$ | $X^2$ | $Y^2$ | $XY$ | $X + Y$ | $X - Y$ |
|---|---|---|---|---|---|---|---|
| | 7 | 2 | 49 | 4 | 14 | 9 | 5 |
| | 5 | 7 | 25 | 49 | 35 | 12 | −2 |
| | 9 | 13 | 81 | 169 | 117 | 22 | −4 |
| | 8 | 2 | 64 | 4 | 16 | 10 | 6 |
| | 11 | 7 | 121 | 49 | 77 | 18 | 4 |
| | 4 | 8 | 16 | 64 | 32 | 12 | −4 |
| $\Sigma$ | 44 | 39 | 356 | 339 | 291 | 83 | 5 |

$\Sigma X = 44$

$\Sigma X^2 = 356$

$(\Sigma X)^2 = (44)^2 = 1936$

$\Sigma XY = 291$

$\Sigma(X + Y) = 83$

$\Sigma X + \Sigma Y = 44 + 39 = 83$

$\Sigma Y = 39$

$\Sigma Y^2 = 339$

$(\Sigma Y)^2 = (39)^2 = 1521$

$(\Sigma X)(\Sigma Y) = (44)(39) = 1716$

$\Sigma(X - Y) = 5$

$\Sigma X - \Sigma Y = 44 - 39 = 5$

## 2.4 / Types of Data

Cultural anthropologists, psychologists, and sociologists have repeatedly called attention to the human tendency to explore the world that is remote from our experience long before we have thoroughly investigated that which is closest to us. The scientific revolution began several centuries ago and even prior to that time humans had long probed the distant stars and described with striking accuracy their apparent movements and interrelations. The science of behavior, however, was virtually ignored until the last half of the 19th century.

In many ways, a similar pattern exists in relation to children's familiarity with numbers and their thinking of the many uses of numbers. In our quantitatively oriented Western civilization, students learn to count and manipulate numbers early in their education. Nevertheless, ask a child to define a number, or to describe the ways in which numbers are used, and you are likely to be met with expressions of consternation and bewilderment, "I've never thought about it before," may be the reply. After a few moments of soul-searching and deliberation, the child may say something to the effect that numbers are symbols denoting amounts of things that can be added, subtracted, multiplied, and divided. These are all familiar arithmetic operations but do they exhaust all possible uses of numbers? At the risk of reducing our student to a state of utter confusion, you may ask, "Is the symbol 7 on a baseball player's uniform a number that readily conforms to arithmetic operations? What about your home address? Channel 2 on your television set? Does it make sense to add, subtract, multiply, or divide these numbers? Can you multiply the number on a quarterback's uniform by the number on an offensive tackle's back and obtain a meaningful value?" A careful analysis of our use of numbers in everyday life reveals an interesting fact: Most of the numbers in daily use do not have the arithmetic properties we usually ascribe to them. A few examples include the serial number of a home appliance, a postal zip code number, a telephone number, a home address, an automobile registration number, and the Dewey decimal code for books in the library.

The important point is that we use numbers in a variety of ways to achieve different goals. Much of the time, these ends do not include the representation of an amount or quantity. There are three fundamentally different ways we use numbers.

1. *Nominal scale data:* numbers used to name or identify.
2. *Ordinal scale data:* numbers used to represent position or order in a series.
3. *Interval and ratio scale data:* numbers used to represent quantity such as how many or how much.

## 2.5 / Measurement

**M**easurement is the assignment of numbers to objects or events, according to predetermined rules. Different levels of measurement represent different levels of numerical information contained in a set of observations. Some examples are: A series of house numbers, the order of finish of a horse race, a set of IQ scores, or the price per share of various companies on the stock exchange. The identification of the type of scale depends on the kinds of mathematical operations that can be legitimately performed on the numbers. The type of statistical analysis we are able to perform will depend in part on the level of measurement we use. It is important to know that some numbers do not provide the type of data that can be meaningfully analyzed. For example, the numbers on athletes' jerseys only *identify* the players. These numbers do not provide information on the importance of or on how well the athletes play the game. In sum, the level of measurement of the scale we use will affect the questions we can ask of the data, the type of analysis we are able to perform and the conclusions we can draw.

The fundamental requirements of observation and measurement are acknowledged by all the physical and social sciences. The things we observe are often referred to as variables and any particular observation is called the value of the variable. If we are studying the differences between boys and girls (the independent variable in an intact group comparison) at a day care center and the amount of time spent by each child playing with a particular toy (the dependent variable), we are using two different types of numerical scales. As we shall soon see, the independent variable (sex: male and female) represents a nominal scale and the dependent variable (time score) represents a ratio scale.

■ **Measurement:**

The assignment of numbers to objects or events according to pre-determined rules.

### Nominal Scales

When the majority of people think about measurement, they often conjure up images of scientists in white suits manipulating complex instruments in order to obtain precise measurements. Not all measurements are this precise or this quantitative. If we were to study the sex of the offspring of female rats that had been subjected to radiation during pregnancy, sex of the offspring would be the dependent variable. There are only two possible values of this variable: male or female (barring an unforeseen mutation that produced a third sex!) If we were using a computer to analyze our results, we might assign a number to each value of the variable. Thus, male might be assigned a one and female a two. The selection of the numbers to represent males and females is arbitrary, and our data would consist of the frequency of observations in each of these two classes. Note that we do not think of this variable as representing an ordered series of values, such as height, weight, or speed. An organism that is female does not have any more of the variable, sex, than one that is male.

Observations of unordered variables (such as sex, ethnic groups, or handedness) constitute a very low level of measurement and are referred to as **nominal scales** of measurement. As previously noted, we may assign numerical values to represent the various classes in a nominal scale, but these numbers have no *quantitative* properties. They serve only to identify the class. Specifically, we are characterizing some *qualitative* aspect of the condition being measured. This classification does not imply that one group is better than, larger than, or greater than another group. The purpose of the nominal scale is to indicate that one thing is different from another thing. Men are different from women with respect to sex, but our use of a nominal scale in no way indicates that one is better than the other. Likewise, when a clinical psychologist uses the current edition of the *Diagnostic and Statistical Manual* to diagnose a client, the number merely represents the clinical condition of the client. For example 300.40 represents the diagnosis *Dysthymia* (whereas 300.21 represents *Panic Disorder with Agoraphobia* (DSM-IV, 1994). The smaller number does not represent a lesser level of psychological trauma or distress.

Studies involving nominal data may be extremely useful to psychologists. Many of our studies involve counting frequencies in nominal classes in order to learn if there is a difference between, say, males and females in terms of the presence or absence of an eating disorder or marital status (married, single) and drug dependency. The data compiled with nominal scales consist of frequency counts or tabulations of the number of occurrences in each class of the variable under study. Such data are often referred to as *frequency data, nominal data,* or *categorical data,* all of which consist of the tabulations of the number of occurrences within each class of a given variable. The only mathematical relationships germane to nominal scales are those of equivalence (=) or nonequivalence (≠). Thus, a particular person or object either has the characteristic that defines the class (=) or does not have that characteristic (≠). We can say that male ≠ female but not that male > female.

How might a behavioral scientist make use of nominal scales? Recall from Chapter 1 where we examined men's and women's perception of their weight? The data are represented in Table 2.3. That study used nominal categories. In this example there are two nominal variables. The first variable is sex, males and females. The second variable divides the subjects into two mutually exclusive groups, those who see themselves as underweight and those who see themselves as overweight. Does this

**■ Nominal Scale:**

A numerical scale where the numbers represent qualitative differences among individual measurements.

**Table** 2.3

A Sample of Female and Male Adolescents Perceiving Themselves as Either Overweight or Underweight

| | SELF-PERCEPTION | | |
|---|---|---|---|
| | **Underweight** | **Overweight** | **Row Totals** |
| Females | 419 | 1995 | 2414 |
| Males | 959 | 855 | 1814 |
| Column totals | 1378 | 2850 | 4228 |

*Source: Morbidity and Mortality Weekly Report,* 1991, 40, (43).

second variable really differentiate between the weights of the subjects? No. A person could be 10 pounds overweight, normal, or severely starved and still consider themselves to be overweight. Therefore, the self-perception variable represents a qualitative construct that differentiates the subjects.

## Ordinal Scales

When we move into the next higher level of measurement, we encounter variables (such as order of finish in a race) in which the classes do represent an ordered series of relationships. An **ordinal scale** is a basic form of quantitative measurement that indicates a numerical order such as $1 < 2$, and $5 > 4$. The classes in ordinal scales are not only different from one another (the characteristic defining nominal scales) but also stand in some kind of orderly *relation* with one another. More specifically, the relationships are expressed in terms of the algebra of inequalities: $a$ is less than $b$ ($a < b$) or $a$ is greater than $b$ ($a > b$). Thus, the relationships encountered are: greater, faster, more intelligent, more mature, more prestigious, more disturbed, and so on. The numerals used in connection with ordinal scales contain more quantitative information than nominal scales but less than interval or ratio scales. They indicate position in an ordered series, not "how much" of a difference exists between successive positions on the scale. In fact, no assumptions can be made about the equality of differences between ranks.

Examples of ordinal scaling include the following: Rank ordering of soccer players according to their "value to the team," rank ordering of potential candidates for political office according to their "popularity" with voters, and rank ordering officer candidates in the military according to their "leadership" qualities. Note that the ranks are assigned according to the ordering of individuals or events within the class (see Table 2.4). Thus, the most popular candidate may receive the rank of 1, the next most popular may receive the rank of 2, and so on, down to the least popular candidate. It does not make any difference whether or not we assign the most popular candidate the highest numerical rank or the

■ **Ordinal Scale:**
A basic form of quantitative measurement that indicates a numerical order such as $1 < 2$, and $5 > 4$.

**Table** | 2.4

Ordinal Position or Rank of Response Strategies of Hairdressers and Bartenders When Clients Seek Advice and Counsel

| Strategy | Hairdresser | Bartender |
|---|---|---|
| Offer support and sympathy | 1* | 3 |
| Try to be lighthearted | 2 | 2 |
| Just listen | 3 | 1 |
| Present alternatives | 4 | 4 |
| Tell person to count blessings | 5 | 10 |
| Share personal experiences | 6 | 5 |
| Try not to get involved | 7 | 6 |
| Give advice | 8 | 7 |
| Ask questions | 9 | 9 |
| Try to get the person to talk to someone else | 10 | 11 |
| Try to change topic | 11 | 8 |

* A rank of 1 corresponds to the most frequently used strategy and 11 to the least frequently used strategy.
*Source:* Based on Emory L. Cowen (1982) "Help Is Where You Find It." *American Psychologist, 37,* 385–395.

lowest as long as we are consistent in placing each individual accurately with respect to their relative position in an ordered series. By popular usage, however, the lower numerical ranks (first, second, third) are usually assigned to those "highest" on the scale. Thus, we have valedictorians who are *first* in their class and winning candidates coming in first at the polls. The point to remember is that coming in first can mean by a landslide or by a nose.

## Interval and Ratio Scales

■ **Interval Scale:**

A measurement scale that has equal units of measurement and an arbitrary zero.

■ **Ratio Scale:**

A measurement scale that has equal units of measurement and an absolute zero.

Finally, the highest level of measurement in science is achieved with **interval** and **ratio** scales. The numerical values associated with these scales are truly *quantitative* and therefore permit the use of arithmetic operations such as adding, subtracting, multiplying, and dividing. Interval and ratio scales require a constant unit of measurement, such as inches, pounds, or seconds. Thus, equal differences between points on any part of the scale are equal. For example, the difference between 4 feet and 2 feet is the same as the difference between 9,231 and 9,229 feet. In ordinal scaling, as you will recall, we cannot claim that the difference between first and second place is the same as the difference between second and third place. With interval and ratio data, we are able to make this claim.

The interval scale differs from the ratio scale in terms of the location of the zero point. In an interval scale, the zero point is arbitrarily determined. It does not represent the complete absence of the attribute being measured. In contrast, the zero in a ratio scale does represent the complete absence of the attribute of interest. Zero length and zero weight mean the complete absence of length and weight. As a consequence of this difference in the location of the zero point, only the ratio scale permits us to make statements concerning the ratio of numbers in the scale; for example, 4 feet are to 2 feet as 2 feet are to 1 foot. The differences between these scales can be clarified by examining a well-known interval scale, for example, the Celsius scale of temperature.

The zero point on the Celsius scale does not represent the complete absence of heat. It is merely the point at which water freezes at sea level and therefore it has an arbitrary zero point. By definition, temperature is the product of the motion of atoms. When water freezes, the molecules are in solid form but the atoms are still moving. The true zero point is known as *absolute zero*, which is approximately –273° Celsius. The Kelvin temperature scale has an absolute 0° which represents the absence of atomic movement. Now, if we were to say that 40° Celsius is to 20°C as 20°C is to 10°C, it would appear that we are making a correct statement. Actually, we are completely wrong since 40°C really represents 273° + 40° = 313° of temperature; 20° represents 273° + 20° = 293° of temperature. The claim that the ratio of 313° to 293° is the same as 293° is to 283° clearly does not hold. These facts may be better appreciated graphically. Figure 2.1 shows all three temperature readings as distances from the true zero point, which is 273°C. From this graph, we see that the distance from −273°C to +40°C is not twice as long as the distance from −273°C to +20°C. Thus, 40°C is not twice as warm as 20°C, and the ratio 40°C is to 20°C as 20°C is to 10°C is clearly not correct.

Now this may not be the most exciting thing you have learned today, but it does have some implications for the conclusions you will be able to draw from the data you collect. Let's suppose you went to college in Florida and your friend decided to go to school in Minnesota. The first week of school you called your friend who told you that the

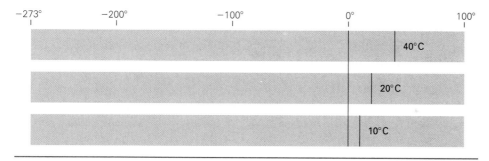

**Figure | 2.1**

| Relationships of various points on the Celsius scale to absolute zero.

temperature was 40°F. You gloat that it was 80°F where you are—twice as warm! But you have overlooked something. Because of the nature of the Fahrenheit scale (and the Celsius scale which also has an arbitrary zero point), your comment is off the mark. You would be correct only if zero degrees Fahrenheit means the absence of all warmth. But it doesn't.

Look at Figure 2.1 and see the distance from the real zero point to 40°C. Now measure twice that distance. Two times 40°C goes off the right side of the page. So you really can't say that it is twice as hot where you are. Why is this important? Because the level of measurement of a variable will affect the conclusions you can draw from the data. Many variables of interest to behavioral scientists are measured in terms of interval scales without absolute zero points. The conclusions that can be drawn from interval scales differ from those that can be drawn from ratio scales. Think, for example, of a spelling test designed for eighth graders in which one student scores 40 and another student scores 80. On that test the second student scored twice as much as the first student. But we cannot say the second student's spelling ability is twice as good as the first student. Why? Because a score of zero on the test does not mean zero spelling ability. You may draw such conclusions only if a zero score means absolutely zero amount of a trait. But spelling of words such as "if", "the", or "cat" did not appear on the test.

If a zero score means absolute absence of a characteristic, it is certainly legitimate to say that 80 pounds is twice as great as 40 pounds. It is not legitimate to say, "I've got twice as much stress as you have" if you base the statement on the fact that your score on a stress test is twice as high. If you are tempted to make such statements about test scores, ask yourself the following question: "Does a zero on this test mean an absolute absence of the trait measured by the instrument?" It probably won't!

You should note that there are other schemes for classifying numbers and identifying the way they are used. We use the nominal-ordinal-interval-ratio classification because it conveniently explains the types of data we obtain in the behavioral sciences. As you will see, we count, we place in relative position, and we obtain quantitative scores. We should note that the assignment of categories is not always clear-cut or unambiguous. In fact, sometimes it is controversial. Psychologists do not always agree as to the level of measurement represented by data. Take, for example, standardized test scores. As you will see in this text they are treated as interval level data yet some psychologists insist they provide ordinal level data. Truly interval level data should allow us to conclude that the difference between an 80 and a 100 on an IQ test is equal to the difference between 120 and 140. Most psychologists, even if they disagree on the scale of the data, are willing to treat standardized test scores as if they were interval scale data.

The implications of assigning a measurement scale to a number can extend beyond the research laboratory. Consider an example that is probably close to your heart: course grades. On the one hand they are ordinal. They represent the ranking of students on some scale of ability where the difference in grades is not always consistent. On the other hand, the dean and possibly your parents consider these grades to represent ratio scales. No credit is given for an F and it is frequently assigned a value of zero. Then D = 1, C = 2, B = 3, and A = 4. Does this mean an A is twice as good as a C, that is, $\frac{4}{2} = 2$? Well, it is certainly a better grade.

It should be clear that one of the most sought-after goals of the behavioral scientist is to achieve measurements that are at least interval in nature. Indeed, interval scaling is assumed for most of the statistical tests reported in this book. Although it is debatable whether many of our instruments achieve interval/ratio measurement, most behavioral scientists are willing to accept the assumption that they do.

One of the characteristics of higher-order scales is that they can be transformed into lower-order scales. The outcome of a race may be expressed in terms of time scores, for example, 3.56, 3.58, and 4.02 minutes. These measures represent ratio scale data since the scale has the characteristics of order, equal intervals, and a real zero point. These scores may be converted to ordinal scale (first, second, and third place) and even to nominal scale measures (winners and losers). Lower order scales may not be converted to higher order scales. Lower order scales provide less information than higher order ones. If we know only the order of finish (as in a foot race), we cannot transform the outcomes to ratio scale measures such as time scores. Although it is permissible to transform scores from higher- to lower-level scales, it is not usually recommended since precise quantitative information is lost in the transformation.

Table 2.5 summarizes the characteristics of nominal, ordinal, interval, and ratio measurement scales. Basically, when you collect data ask yourself if you want to categorize people, put them in some kind of order, or obtain a measure from them. The answer to your question will determine the type of measure you have and will affect your choice of statistical analysis.

## 2.6 / Continuous and Discontinuous Scales

In addition to the levels of measurement described above there are other ways to categorize the variables we consider in behavioral research. One of these is to assess if there is an underlying continuous scale for a variable or if there are gaps in the scale for which no intermediate values exist. Imagine that you are trying to determine the number of children per American family. Your scale of measurement would start with zero (no children) and would proceed by increments of 1 to, perhaps, 5 or 8. Note that in moving from one value on the scale to the next, we proceed by *whole numbers* rather than by *fractional* amounts. Thus, a family may have either 0, 1, 2, or more children. In spite of the statistical abstraction that the American family averages approximately 1.63 children, the

**Table** | 2.5

**Measurement Scales and Their Characteristics**

| Scale | Characteristic | Examples |
|---|---|---|
| Nominal | Unordered category | Sex of subject: male = 1, female = 2<br>DSM-IV diagnosis<br>Religion of subject<br>Political party |
| Ordinal | Order | Rank in class: 1st, 2nd, or 3rd<br>Rank on personality test: high vs. low self-esteem<br>Respect scale: 10 = high respect, 1 = little respect |
| Interval | Order, equal intervals, and arbitrary zero point | Temperature of 98.6°F<br>SAT verbal score of 540*<br>Score on an IQ test<br>Raw score on a statistics test |
| Ratio | Order, equal intervals, and real zero point | Height, weight, age, running speed<br>Number of words recalled in a memory experiment<br>Response latency<br>Grams of food consumed<br>Numbers of problems solved |

* Test scores are treated as interval scale data.

authors do not know a single couple who has achieved this interesting state of family planning. Variables such as number of children are known as **discontinuous variables.** These are variables for which the values can only be whole numbers. There are no intermediate values between each number. Discontinuous variables are sometimes called **discrete** variables and are identified by equality of *counting units.* Thus, if we are studying the number of children in a family, each child is equal with respect to providing one counting unit. Such variables permit arithmetic operations such as adding, subtracting, multiplying, and dividing. Thus, we can say that a family of four children has twice as many progeny as a family with two children. The researcher who studies the number of times a child picks up a particular toy is using a discrete variable. Similarly, the number of bar presses made by a rat in an experiment is an example of a discrete variable.

In contrast, a **continuous variable** is one that may assume any value. There are no gaps in the values of the variable; there are an unlimited number of *possible* values between any two adjacent values on the scale. Thus, if the variable consists of height measured in inches, then 4 and 5 inches would be two adjacent values of the variable.

However, there can be an infinite number of intermediate values, such as 4.5 inches or 4.7 inches. If the variable is height measured in tenths of an inch, then 4.5 inches and 4.6 inches are two adjacent values of the variable, but there can *still* be an infinite number of intermediate values, such as 4.53 inches and 4.59 inches. Similarly, with a very

■ **Discontinuous or Discrete Variables:**

Variables for which the values can only be whole numbers. There are no intermediate values between each number.

■ **Continuous Variables:**

Variables that can assume any value. There are an infinite number of values between any two numbers.

precise stopwatch a researcher could measure the number of minutes, seconds, and fractions of seconds with which a child plays with a particular toy.

It is important to note that, although our measurement of discrete variables is always exact, our measurement of continuous variables is always approximate. If we are measuring the height of American males, for example, any particular measurement is inexact because it is always possible to imagine a measuring stick that would provide greater accuracy. Thus, if we recorded the height of a person as 68 inches, we would mean 68 inches give or take one-half inch. If our scale is accurate to the nearest tenth, we can always imagine another scale with greater accuracy, say, to the nearest hundredth or thousandth of an inch. The basic characteristic of continuous variables, then, is equality of *measuring units* as opposed to equality of counting units for discontinuous or discrete variables. Thus, if we are measuring in inches, 1 inch is always the same throughout the scale. Examples of continuous variables are length, height, weight, velocity, time, and so on.

Because continuous variables are often expressed as whole numbers they may appear to be discontinuous. You may say that you are 5 feet 8 inches tall and weigh 145 pounds. However, the decision to express your height to the nearest inch and weight to the nearest pound was yours. You could have expressed height to the nearest fraction of an inch and weight to the nearest ounce. You do not have such a choice when reporting facts such as the number of children in a family or number of speeding tickets you have received. They must occur as whole numbers.

## Continuous Variables and True Limits of Numbers

We have noted that continuously distributed variables can take on an unlimited number of intermediate values. Therefore, we can never specify the exact value for any particular measure, since it is possible that a more sensitive instrument can slightly increase the accuracy of our measurements. For this reason, numerical values of continuously distributed variables are always approximate. However, it is possible to specify the limits within which the true value falls; these limits are called **true limits** or, sometimes, **real limits.** The true limits of a value of a continuous variable are equal to that number plus or minus one-half of the unit of measurement. Let's look at a few examples. You have a bathroom scale that is calibrated in pounds. When you step on the scale, the pointer will usually be a little above or below a pound marker. However, you report your weight to the nearest pound. Thus, if the pointer were approximately three-quarters of the distance between 212 and 213 pounds, you would report your weight as 213 pounds. It would be understood that the true limit of your weight, assuming an accurate scale, falls between 212.5 pounds and 213.5 pounds. At times, you may be collecting data with precision to the first decimal place, for example, 6.1, 6.2, and 6.3. In this event, you would go to the hundredths column so that 6.2, for example, would represent all values between 6.15 and 6.25. Figure 2.2 illustrates this bracketing of values of whole number scores and scores reported to the nearest tenth.

Here are some examples of true limits. The true limits of

11 are 10.5 and 11.5. Why?

11.5 are 11.45 and 11.55. Why?

112 are 111.5 and 112.5. Why?

112.2 are 112.15 and 112.25. Why?

■ **True Limits (Real Limits):**

The true limits of a value of a continuous variable are equal to that number plus or minus one-half of the unit of measurement.

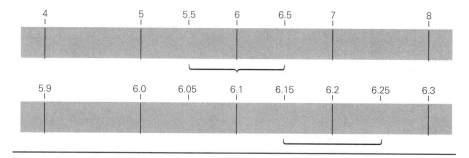

**Figure | 2.2**

Values of variables and their true limits.

## 2.7 / Rounding Numbers

**D**uring the course of the semester it is likely that you will be checking your homework calculations with a friend or with others in your class when you discover that even though you are performing the same calculations you have come up with slightly different answers. How can this be? You are both following the exact same steps. The explanation for the difference may lie in the fact that each of you is carrying out your answers to different decimal places in the intermediate steps. When you are required to express a fraction such as $\frac{1}{3}$ in decimal form, your calculator displays the following: .33333333. Since you are the compulsive one, you are carrying out your answers to eight decimal places whereas your friend carries his only to one or two places. Who is right? Actually there are a number of related questions we need to address.

1. To how many decimal places do we carry the final answer?
2. What rounding rules will we use?
3. When do you decide to round? At each intermediate step or only for the final answer?

Let us take each question in turn. First, in terms of the level of precision of our final answers, it is interesting that not all psychologists use the same convention. Many psychologists and psychological journals follow the recommendation of the *Publication Manual of the American Psychological Association* (1994) which suggests reporting summary statistics to two digits more than are in the raw data. For most examples in this text we will follow this convention. We will use whole numbers as raw data and thus will report the final results to the second decimal place. This practice will allow you to check the accuracy of your own calculations.

You should be aware that other researchers and other journals may use other conventions, most notably, they may report their summary statistics in terms of *significant digits*. Your professor may prefer to follow this convention as well. The number of significant digits typically reflects the level of accuracy of your original measurement. If you take your measures in whole numbers (e.g., numbers of seconds to complete a task) you will round your summary statistics to the real limits of the original measurement.

In terms of rounding we have some specific rules for you to follow. You are probably familiar with the concept of rounding up when your answer ends in a 5 (e.g., your grade point average of 3.25 becomes a 3.3). While this practice is widespread, it is inappropriate to use in this course because it introduces systematic bias in your analyses. Instead, when rounding, use the following steps:

1. First identify the number of decimal places to carry the final answer and mark the location with a caret. For example, to round 3.79499 to two places: $3.79_\wedge 499$.
2. Now look at the remainder to the right of the caret. If the remainder is less than 5, we drop it. Thus, $3.79_\wedge 499$ becomes 3.79.
3. If the remainder is greater than 5, we increase the last digit by 1. Thus, $3.79_\wedge 501$ becomes 3.80.
4. If the remainder is *exactly 5* we must look at the last digit. If it is an even number we drop the remainder and keep the last digit as it is. If the last digit is an odd number we round up by one. Remember this rule only applies when the remainder is exactly 5, 50, 500, and so on.

$3.78_\wedge 500$ becomes 3.78 because 8 is an even number
$3.77_\wedge 500$ becomes 3.78 because 7 is an odd number

Let's examine several illustrations. Round to the second decimal place.

| | | |
|---|---|---|
| 6.545001 | becomes 6.55 | Why? |
| 6.5450000 | becomes 6.54 | Why? |
| 1.9652 | becomes 1.97 | Why? |
| 0.02500 | becomes 0.02 | Why? |
| 0.03500 | becomes 0.04 | Why? |

Now we address the question of *when* to round. Do we round during the many intermediate steps or do we round only when we reach the final answer? This answer is straightforward. *Do not do any rounding* until after you have computed the final statistic. Otherwise, you may introduce large rounding errors. Consider the following example:

No Intermediate Rounding
$(1.7549)(3.6359)(0.8252) = 5.2653$
$= 5.27$

Much Intermediate Rounding
$(1.75)(3.64)(0.83) = 5.2871$
$= 5.29$

With more intermediate steps involved in the calculation, the rounding error can be considerably larger. Consistency in applying these rules should help you avoid large discrepancies in your answers.

On a final note, you should be aware that minor differences may occur between your calculations, the book's, or other students' in the class. These minor differences may be attributed to the fact that different calculators and computer packages will carry the intermediate steps of an analysis to a different number of decimal places. A calculator that carries the intermediate steps to four places will probably produce a slightly different final answer from one that carries all calculations to more places. Therefore, small differences that exist in the fourth or fifth decimal can be ignored (e.g., 5.5679 vs. 5.56789). Larger differences suggest a problem (e.g., 5.5679 vs. 5.1634).

## 2.8 / Ratios, Frequencies, Proportions, and Percentages

Of all the statistics in everyday use, perhaps the most misunderstood and misused involve the reporting of ratios, proportions, and percentages. An example will illustrate the differences between these terms. Imagine you are a researcher studying preschool children in a day care center. Of the 50 children at the center, 20 are girls and 30 are boys. The ratio of girls to boys is 20 to 30 or, more simply, 2 to 3.

In the total sample, the *proportion* of girls is $\dfrac{20}{50} = .40$

and the percentage equals    $(0.40)(100) = 40\%.$

In the total sample, the *proportion* of boys is $\dfrac{30}{50} = .60$

and the percentage equals    $(0.60)(100) = 60\%.$

Sometimes, when we have two numbers to compare over time, we talk of a percentage increase. For example, if the day care center expanded to enroll an additional 10 students (in addition to the original 50 students), what proportion of increase would this indicate?

$$\frac{10 \text{ new students}}{50 \text{ original students}} = \frac{10}{50} = .20$$

To convert the proportion to a percentage, we multiply by 100. The percentage increase from 50 to 60 students is $(.20)(100) = 20\%$.

If 50 students had been added to the original enrollment of 50, what would be the percentage increase?

$$\frac{50 \text{ new students}}{50 \text{ original students}} \times 100 = \frac{50}{50} \times 100 = 100\%.$$

Adding 50 new students produced a 100% increase in the total number of students. What if we asked a slightly different question: "How does total enrollment compare to previous levels?" In this case we want to compare the *current* enrollment to the enrollment *before* we added the additional children. We have:

$$\frac{50 \text{ original students} + 50 \text{ new students}}{50 \text{ original students}} \times 100$$
$$= \frac{100}{50} \times 100 = 2.00 \times 100 = 200\%.$$

That is, the addition of 50 students caused a 200% increase in enrollment. How can the answer be 100% in one case and 200% in another case when 50 children were added in both cases? The difference lies in the type of question we ask. We wanted to know the percentage *increase* in the number of students. The answer to that question is that adding 50 new students represents a 100% increase in the number of students. The second question is one of comparison between the enrollment *before* and *after* the new students were added. The answer to that question

---

The ratio of cats to rats: 3:2

The proportion of cats $= \dfrac{3}{5} = .60$

The percentage of cats $= .60 \times 100 = 60\%$

is 200%. Therefore, we must be careful to understand the comparisons that are being made.

Although the terms *percentages, proportions,* and *percent increase* are widely used, they provide fertile ground for fabricating misleading and outright fraudulent statements. Now that we have the basics down, let's see how they are applied.

## Some Examples

A topic of interest, not just to behavioral scientists but to college students as well, relates to interpersonal attraction. Under what conditions are two people attracted? How did they meet? Where is one likely to meet a mate? One way to address this issue is to ask newly married people straight out: "Where did you meet your spouse?" What worked for them might just work for others. A researcher did just that and published the results in an interesting little book entitled *Just Married* (Sinrod & Grey, 1998). The book provides a summary of a survey of 10,000 newlyweds. From this group a total of 3,876 questionnaires were returned. To calculate the response rate:

$$3,876 \div 10,000 = .3876 \times 100 = 38.76\% \text{ response rate}$$

One of the first questions put to the couples was how the two had met. Table 2.6 presents the breakdown of the responses. While the responses did vary, it looks as if friends are a good way to meet a potential mate since 25% of the respondents met the love of their lives in this way.

$$969 \div 3876 = .25 \times 100 = 25.0\%$$

The next most frequent venue for meeting a mate was school, where 15% enjoyed success. Before we draw too many conclusions beyond frequencies and percentages, keep in mind that we don't know the source of the sample or the personal characteristics of the people in it. If the sample includes many college students, of course they are likely to meet and date fellow students. We cannot draw inferences beyond our data. We can't conclude that sending an octogenarian back to college will enhance his or her dating life. In fact, if you remember what you learned in Chapter 1, you can't draw causal inferences from descriptive research studies. We *can* conclude from these data that among the individuals who responded to this survey, a quarter of them have friends to thank for introducing them to their spouse.

**Table** | **2.6**

**Summary of Responses of Newlyweds to the Question: "How Did You and Your Spouse First Meet?"**

|  | Frequency | Percentage |
|---|---|---|
| Friends | 969 | 25 |
| School | 581 | 15 |
| Bar | 388 | 10 |
| Party | 271 | 7 |
| Blind date | 233 | 6 |
| Other | 1,434 | 37 |
| Total | 3,876 | 100 |

*Source:* Based on Barry Sinrod and Marlo Grey (1998) *Just Married.* Kansas City: Andrews McMeel Publishing.

**Table 2.7**

**Summary of Frequencies of Responses of Newlyweds to the Question: "Was It Love at First Sight?"**

|  | Women | Men | Total |
|---|---|---|---|
| Frequencies |  |  |  |
| Yes | 1,017 | 1,200 | 2,217 |
| No | 1,464 | 195 | 1,659 |
| Total | 2,481 | 1,395 | 3,876 |

Source: Based on Barry Sinrod and Marlo Grey (1998) *Just Married*. Kansas City: Andrews McMeel Publishing.

## Finding Percentages in Terms of Total, Columns, and Rows

Now let us look for differences between subgroups in the sample. Let's consider differences between males and females and the reactions of each when they first met. Did any of them know at once that the person they had just met would be "the one?" Were men more likely than women to report this reaction? Table 2.7 reports the number in each group who said that it was "love at first sight." Exactly 1,200 men reported that it was love at first sight, and 1,017 of the women agreed. In terms of sheer numbers there appears to be approximately the same frequency in each group. Before jumping to the conclusion that women and men are about equally likely to feel this way, it is important to look at the overall makeup of the sample. Although the number who say yes is approximately even, there are many more women than men in the sample. Look at the bottom line of Table 2.7. There are 2,481 women versus 1,395 men. Because of the uneven size of the subgroups, the percentages are going to look very different from the raw frequencies.

When subgroups differ in size it is easier to examine responses by converting the frequencies to percentages. We can calculate percentages using the frequencies in Table 2.7. For the women in the study, 1,017 out of 2,481 or 41% said "Yes, it was love at first sight."

$$1{,}017 \div 2481 = .4099 \times 100 = 41.0\%$$

Now look at the responses of the men. There were 1,200 out of 1,395 men who agreed that it was "love at first sight" when they met their spouse-to-be.

$$1{,}200 \div 1{,}395 = .8602 \times 100 = 86.0\%$$

Eighty-six percent of the men responded yes! However, less than half of the women agreed with this sentiment. Table 2.8 presents a summary of the percentages of the subgroups. Does this mean that men have better insight, they know immediately when they meet "The One?" Not necessarily. Before we read too much into the data, remember these are reports of an event that occurred many months or even years earlier. It *is* possible that men differ from women in their reactions. It is also possible that men differ from women in their *memory* of the event. There are many possible explanations. At the very least it appears that the two sexes differ in their *reports*. Later in this text we will learn to examine group differences such as these in order to test hypotheses and to make inferences to a population.

**Table** 2.8

**Summary of Percentages of Responses of Newlyweds to the Question: "Was It Love at First Sight?"**

|  | Women | Men |
|---|---|---|
| Yes | 41 | 86 |
| No | 59 | 14 |
| Total | 100 | 100 |

*Source:* Based on Barry Sinrod and Marlo Grey (1998) *Just Married*. Kansas City: Andrews McMeel Publishing.

## 2.9
## Putting It All Together

Recall the statistical detective work introduced in Chapter 1, which might best be named "The mysterious case of dental enamel erosion among selected members of a private club." After the entire sample of 747 responses was returned, it became obvious that two groups could be separated out as the "independent" variable—frequent and infrequent swimmers. Note that the study involves intact groups so it is not a true experiment because the investigators had no control over the assignment of the subjects to the "experimental conditions."

The number of individuals in each group evidencing dental enamel erosion was tabulated. The dependent measures (Yes vs. No) represent a nominal scale of measurement. Table 2.9 presents these results in tabular form.

As we can see, the descriptive statistics show that about 10% of all respondents met the various criteria for erosion of dental enamel. However, this was not uniformly distributed among frequent and infrequent swimmers. Fully 15% of the frequent swimmers and only 3% of the infrequent swimmers met the criteria. Inferential statistics are then calculated to ascertain whether this difference in rate of erosion might reasonably be dismissed as a chance occurrence. So that your questions will not be left hanging in suspension until later in the text, let it be noted that the investigators concluded that the rate of dental erosion represented a genuine effect of some variable. Frequent swimmers were truly experiencing a higher rate of enamel erosion. We shall look later at follow-up studies that include measurements of the levels of pool acid.

Following this preliminary analysis, additional questionnaires were mailed to all 452 frequent swimmers, of whom 294 (65%) replied. Summary

**Table** 2.9

**Relative Frequency Table of Frequent and Infrequent Swimmers Evidencing and Failing to Evidence Erosion of Dental Enamel\***

| | EVIDENCE OF DENTAL ENAMEL EROSION | | |
|---|---|---|---|
| | **No** | **Yes** | **Row Totals** |
| Frequent swimmers | 383 (85) | 69 (15) | 452 (100) |
| Infrequent swimmers | 286 (97) | 9 (3) | 295 (100) |
| Column totals | 669 (90) | 78 (10) | 747 (100) |

\* Row percentages and column total percentages are shown in parentheses.

**Table** 2.10

Relative Frequency Table of Frequent Swimmers Who Swam 5 Days or More versus Those Who Swam Less Than 5 Days a Week Who Showed or Failed to Show Evidence of Dental Enamel Erosion

| | EVIDENCE OF DENTAL ENAMEL EROSION | | |
|---|---|---|---|
| | **No** | **Yes** | **Row Totals** |
| Five or more days a week | 97 (73) | 35 (27) | 132 (100) |
| Fewer than five days a week | 148 (91) | 14 (9) | 162 (100) |
| Column totals | 245 (83) | 49 (17) | 294 (100) |

data and sample statistics are shown in Table 2.10. These descriptive statistics are in line with those presented in Table 2.9 and provide further data to be subjected to inferential statistical analysis. Note that the independent measure in this study (swimmers vs. nonswimmers) consisted of nominal scales of measurement. The dependent measure achieved an ordinal scale of measurement by having experts (dental practitioners) observe the subjects' teeth and rate the degree of erosion, such as 1 for no evidence, up to 4 or 5 for an advanced degree of pitting. Such ordinal scales are commonly used in psychology, sociology, medicine, and economics. To illustrate, in a survey, the respondents rate their degree of agreement with some specific statement such as strongly agree, agree, neutral, disagree, strongly disagree. In medicine, disease processes are commonly ranked from 1 to 4 (from early to advanced stages of a disorder) and treatment outcomes are characteristically predicted on the basis of the diagnosed stage of the ailment.

In the study of enamel erosion, it would be possible to devise some physical apparatus that, by plotting the total area of pitting, would involve the use of an interval or a ratio scale of measurement. The decision of the scale to use often depends on the desired degree of precision, the availability of measuring instruments, and the funds allocated for the research. Broadly speaking, the more precise the measurements required, the more expensive and time-consuming are the research demands. Figure 2.3 shows the value of representing data analyses in graphic form.

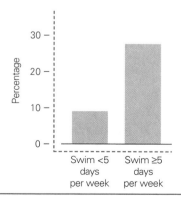

**Figure** 2.3

Percentage of frequent swimmers who swim less than 5 days or 5 or more days per week with evidence of dental erosion.

## CHAPTER SUMMARY

In this chapter, we noted that advanced knowledge in mathematics is not a prerequisite for success in this course. A sound background in high school mathematics coupled with steady application to assignments should be sufficient to permit mastery of the fundamental statistical concepts presented in this text. For the student of behavioral science, the real purpose of this course is to teach you the logic behind empirical reasoning, the use of reason underlying various statistical procedures, and the performance of problem solving techniques when interpreting the results of statistical analyses.

To assist the student who may not have had recent contact with mathematics, we have reviewed some of the basic concepts. Included in this review were the following:

1. The grammar of statistical notation
2. Summation rules, including the important rule of priority
3. Types of scales: nominal, ordinal, interval, and ratio
4. Continuous and discontinuous (discrete) scales
5. True limits of a number
6. Rounding rules
7. Counting frequencies and calculating proportions and percentages

## TERMS TO REMEMBER

continuous variable
discontinuous or discrete variables
interval scale
measurement
nominal scale
ordinal scale
ratio scale
true (or real) limits of a number
$\Sigma$
$X$ or $Y$
$N$
$X_i$

## EXERCISES

1. Apply the rules of priority to the following:
   a. $(6 + 4)^2 + (3 + 4)^2 =$
   b. $(-3 + 7)^2 =$
   c. $3(5^2 + 2^2) =$
   d. $-8(5 + 2^2) =$

2. Apply the rules of priority to the following:
   a. $(4 + 7)^2 + (^-6)^2 =$
   b. $2(-3 + 7)^2 =$
   c. $-2(5^2 + 2^2) =$
   d. $4 - (5 + 2)^2 =$

**3.** Find $Y$ when $N = 4$ and $20 + N = Y + 2$

**4.** Find $\Sigma X$ when $N = 20$ and $\overline{X} = 60$, where $\overline{X} = \dfrac{\Sigma X}{N}$

**5.** Find $N$ when $\overline{X} = 90$ and $\Sigma X = 360$, where $\overline{X} = \dfrac{\Sigma X}{N}$

**6.** Find $N$ when $\Sigma(X - \overline{X})^2 = 640$ and $s^2 = 16$ where $s^2 = \dfrac{\Sigma(X - \overline{X})^2}{N}$

**7.** Find $s^2$ when $\Sigma(X - \overline{X})^2 = 240$ and $N = 12$ where $s^2 = \dfrac{\Sigma(X - \overline{X})^2}{N}$

**8.** Determine the value of the following expressions, in which $X_1 = 2$, $X_2 = 3$, $X_3 = 5$, $X_4 = 7$, $X_5 = 9$, $X_6 = 10$, $X_7 = 13$:

   **a.** $\displaystyle\sum_{i=1}^{4} X_i =$    **b.** $\displaystyle\sum_{i=1}^{7} X_i =$    **c.** $\displaystyle\sum_{i=3}^{6} X_i =$

   **d.** $\displaystyle\sum_{i=2}^{5} X_i =$    **e.** $\displaystyle\sum_{i=1}^{N} X_i =$    **f.** $\displaystyle\sum_{i=4}^{N} X_i =$

**9.** Determine the value of the following expressions, in which $X_1 = 4$, $X_2 = 5$, $X_3 = 7$, $X_4 = 9$, $X_5 = 10$, $X_6 = 11$, $X_7 = 14$:

   **a.** $\displaystyle\sum_{i=1}^{4} X_i =$    **b.** $\displaystyle\sum_{i=1}^{7} X_i =$    **c.** $\displaystyle\sum_{i=3}^{6} X_i =$

   **d.** $\displaystyle\sum_{i=2}^{5} X_i =$    **e.** $\displaystyle\sum_{i=1}^{N} X_i =$    **f.** $\displaystyle\sum_{i=4}^{N} X_i =$

**10.** Express the following in summation notation:

   **a.** $X_1 + X_2 + X_3$        **b.** $X_1 + X_2 \ldots X_N$

   **c.** $X_3^2 + X_4^2 + X_5^2 + X_6^2$    **d.** $X_4^2 + X_5^2 \ldots X_N^2$

**11.** Using the data provided, calculate the following:

| $X$ | $Y$ |
|-----|-----|
| 4   | 9   |
| 6   | 5   |
| 1   | 6   |
| 3   | 2   |

   **a.** $\Sigma X$         **e.** $\Sigma XY$

   **b.** $\Sigma Y$         **f.** $(\Sigma X)(\Sigma Y)$

   **c.** $\Sigma X^2$        **g.** $(\Sigma X)^2$

   **d.** $\Sigma Y^2$        **h.** $(\Sigma Y)^2$

**12.** Repeat Exercises 11a. through 11h. using the following data:

| $X$ | $Y$ |
|-----|-----|
| 6   | 2   |
| 3   | 6   |
| 4   | 3   |
| 3   | 5   |

13. Using the values in Exercise 9, show that

$$\sum_{i=1}^{N} X_i^2 \neq \left( \sum_{i=1}^{N} X_i \right)^2$$

14. Name the four measurement scales described in this chapter and explain the important difference between ratio and interval scale data.

15. The answers to the following questionnaire items are based upon what scale of measurement?
    a. What is your height?
    b. What is your weight?
    c. What is your occupation?
    d. How does this course compare with others you have taken?

16. In the following examples, identify the scale of measurement of the italicized variable and determine whether it is continuous or discontinuous.
    a. *Distance* traveled from home
    b. *Time* required to complete a task
    c. Votes cast for each of *three candidates* for a political office
    d. *Number of votes* cast

17. Indicate which of the following italicized variables represent discrete or continuous scales:
    a. The *time* it takes you to complete these problems
    b. The *number of newspapers sold* in a given city on December 19, 1991
    c. The amount of *change in weight* of 5 women during a period of 4 weeks
    d. The *number of home runs* hit by each of 10 randomly selected batters during the 1991 baseball season
    e. The *number of stocks* on the New York Stock Exchange that increased in price on a given day

18. Which of the following italicized variables represent continuous scales and which represent discrete scales of measurement?
    a. The *number of light bulbs* sold each day in a hardware store
    b. The *monthly income* of graduate students
    c. The *temperatures* recorded every 2 hours in the meat department of a supermarket
    d. The *weights of pigeons* recorded every 24 hours in an experimental laboratory
    e. The *lengths of newborns* recorded at a hospital nursery
    f. The *number of textbooks* found in the college bookstore

19. State the true limits of the following numbers:
    a. 5     b. 5.0     c. 5.00     d. 0.1     e. −10     f. 0.8

20. State the true limits of the following numbers:
    a. 0     b. 0.5     c. 1.0     d. 0.49     e. −5     f. −4.5

21. Round the following numbers to the second decimal place:
    a. 0.98500     b. 0.99500     c. 9.96500     d. 0.00499
    e. 7.465     f. 1.25499     g. −9.139     h. 10.0050

22. Round the following numbers to the second decimal place:
    a. 99.99500     b. 46.40501     c. 2.96500     d. 0.00501
    e. 16.46500     f. 1.05499     g. 86.2139     h. 10.0050

**23.** Using the figures for the number of students, by sex, majoring in each of five academic areas shown in the following table, answer questions (**a.**) through (**f.**):

| Academic Area | Male | Female |
|---|---|---|
| Business administration | 400 | 300 |
| Education | 50 | 150 |
| Humanities | 150 | 200 |
| Science | 250 | 300 |
| Social science | 200 | 200 |

**a.** Of the total number of students, what percentage is female?
**b.** Considering only the males, what percentage is found in each academic area?
**c.** Considering only the females, what percentage is found in each academic area?
**d.** Of all students majoring in the five areas, what percentage is male? What percentage is female?
**e.** Among those majoring in business administration, what percentage is female?
**f.** What percentage is male among students majoring in science?

**24.** Some studies have reported high rates of childhood abuse in adults with mental illness. One study examined the self-reports of 98 hospitalized women regarding childhood physical and sexual abuse (Chu & Dill, 1990).

**Self-Reports of 98 Women with and without Histories of Physical and Sexual Abuse**

| | HISTORY OF SEXUAL ABUSE | | |
|---|---|---|---|
| History of Physical Abuse | No | Yes | Total |
| No | 36 | 12 | 48 |
| Yes | 27 | 23 | 50 |
| Total | 63 | 35 | 98 |

*Source:* Chu, J. A. & Dill, D. L. (1990). Dissociative symptoms in relation to childhood physical and sexual abuse. *American Journal of Psychiatry, 147,* 887–892.

Based on these data, answer questions (**a.**) through (**h.**).
**a.** Of the 98 women in the study, what percentage had a history of physical abuse?
**b.** What percentage of the total had a history of sexual abuse?
**c.** What percentage of the total had no history of either physical or sexual abuse?
**d.** What percentage of the total had a history of both sexual abuse *and* physical abuse?
**e.** What percentage of the total had a history of either sexual abuse *or* physical abuse or both?
**f.** Of the 35 women with a history of sexual abuse, what percentage reported also having been physically abused?
**g.** Of the 50 women with a history of physical abuse, what percentage reported also having been sexually abused?
**h.** Could you generalize these results to the general population? Could you generalize to all patients with a history of mental illness?

**25.** In a study of attractiveness and helping behavior psychologists examined whether favoritism toward the physically attractive generalizes to behavioral helping responses. (Benson, P. L., Karabenick, S. A., & Lerner, R. M. (1976), Pretty pleases: The effects of physical attractiveness, race, and sex on receiving help. *Journal of Experimental Social Psychology, 12,* 409–415.) In the study, graduate school applications, complete with mailing address, envelope, and stamps, were "inadvertently" left in a number of telephone booths at a busy metropolitan airport. Pictures of the applicants were prominently displayed, some chosen to be physically attractive and others to be unattractive. The table that follows shows the number of male subjects choosing to help attractive and unattractive female applicants. Calculate

  **a.** the percentage of males rendering help regardless of the attractiveness of the target.
  **b.** the percentage rendering help and not rendering help when the target is attractive.
  **c.** the percentage helping and not helping when the target is physically unattractive.

| | CHARACTERISTICS OF TARGET | | |
| --- | --- | --- | --- |
| | **Attractive** | **Unattractive** | **Total** |
| Helped | 17 | 13 | 30 |
| Did not help | 24 | 27 | 51 |
| Total | 41 | 40 | 81 |

**26.** Based on what you know about this study

  **a.** What is the population for this study?
  **b.** Is it likely to be representative of the general population?
  **c.** What is the independent variable in this study and what is its scale of measurement?
  **d.** What is the dependent variable and what is its scale of measurement?

# 3

# Exploratory Data Analysis, Frequency Distributions, and Percentiles

# 3.1 / Introduction

$S$uppose that your roommate walks into the room with a rather puzzled look. When you ask for an explanation, your roommate says, "I just took part in a study over in the Psychology Department. They gave a test of narcissism to the class. I got a score of 14 on the test but I haven't a clue what it means. All I know is that the higher the score, the greater is one's tendency to admire his or her own physical, sexual, or mental attributes."

Not wishing to miss an opportunity to get in a dig at your sometimes annoying roommate, you reply, "Well, knowing you as well as I do, a score of 14 must be near the top of the scale. For all we know, you may have set a new standard of narcissism." You both laugh a bit, but then have to agree that the score by itself is pretty meaningless. Scores take on meaning only when compared to some standard. The problem with a single score is that it says nothing about the relative performance of the individual. You have learned this from experience. When you take a test you most likely are interested in learning where your test score falls relative to the scores of others in your class.

Starting with this chapter, we will present techniques for examining data and evaluating individual scores relative to the rest of the data in a distribution. We will use a set of procedures known as **exploratory data analysis (EDA).** Exploratory Data Analysis, as the name implies, is a set of tools designed to help us examine data. It consists of several basic graphical and mathematical procedures for organizing and summarizing the data. In addition, EDA is an attitude about looking at numbers. Its goal is to allow researchers to learn as much as they can about the data before conducting more complex and intricate statistical procedures. As you shall see, EDA is an essential and indispensable statistical tool because it allows us to organize, summarize, and interpret the data quickly and without complicated statistical procedures.

Exploratory data analysis should *always* be the first step in the process of analyzing data from an experiment. Consider the advice of psychologist Robert Bolles (1998): "Perhaps the most basic thing I have to say is . . . *look at the data.* Always, always plot up the data to see what the numbers say. The numbers that you collect in an experiment will tell you if you have found something, even while statistical tests are fibbing, lying, and deceiving you." (p. 83)

There are two important messages in Bolles's statement. First, always look at the data to see what trends and patterns are evident. Psychologists typically have several expectations or hypotheses about the results of their experiments. Using EDA is one way that researchers can quickly confirm their expectations. In addition, EDA allows researchers to see trends or patterns in the data that they did not expect but that are important in interpreting the results of the study. EDA also helps to identify errors in the data because the procedures highlight outliers, that may be actual values or may be data entry errors.

The second important point that Bolles makes is that some statistics can be misleading. Statistical tests are misleading when researchers misapply, misuse, and incorrectly interpret them. As we will see in subsequent chapters, different statistical tests require the data to meet specific requirements. If the data are appropriate for a specific statistical test, the results of the test will provide much useful information. If the data

---

**■ Exploratory Data Analysis (EDA):**

A set of procedures for arranging and displaying numbers that allow the researcher to quickly organize, summarize, and interpret the data collected from a research project.

are not appropriate, the results of the statistical test will be meaningless. Unfortunately, many researchers rush into complex statistical analysis without carefully exploring their data. The widespread availability of the computer and software that conduct statistical tests compounds this problem. Some researchers, tempted by the speed of the computer, rush the data into a computer file and then dash off several different tests without inspecting the data. As a consequence, the interpretations may be wrong. Even worse, the impatient researcher may ignore a potentially useful insight that he or she can find by looking at the data.

Remember the old saying about computers, "Garbage in, Garbage out." This phrase means that the output of a computer is no better than the information put into it. The same is true of statistical analysis. A statistical test is just a set of mathematical operations. You can calculate a statistic on any set of numbers. If the numbers are meaningless or if the particular test is not appropriate, the results of the statistical procedure are meaningless. Therefore, Bolles's statement is not completely correct. Statistics do not fib, lie, or deceive. People do these things. In order to avoid these problems you, as a user of statistics, should know as much as possible about the data.

## 3.2 / Goals of EDA

There are several characteristics that researchers want to know about the data they collect. The first characteristic is the value or values that best represent the entire data set. Specifically, the researcher wants to determine what number best represents the entire data. We call these statistics *measures of central tendency*. The second characteristic of the data that we want to describe is amount of dispersion in the data. In other words, we want to find out if all the numbers are close to one another or extremely variable. We call these statistics *measures of dispersion*. A third characteristic of the data that we want to describe is the *shape* of the distribution. As you will see in the following chapters, it is extremely important to determine if the data are symmetrical. Finally, we want to determine if there is a *systematic relation* between two or more variables that we are examining in the research. All this information is important in understanding the data gathered from an experiment and selecting the appropriate statistical tool for more specific and detailed analysis.

**Table 3.1**

**100 Test Scores**

| 78 | 72 | 79 | 88 | 78 | 73 | 73 | 92 | 71 | 76 |
|----|----|----|----|----|----|----|----|----|----|
| 74 | 60 | 80 | 70 | 74 | 78 | 90 | 71 | 85 | 83 |
| 72 | 79 | 84 | 78 | 68 | 79 | 88 | 81 | 58 | 50 |
| 99 | 69 | 76 | 79 | 84 | 83 | 80 | 78 | 88 | 58 |
| 49 | 82 | 97 | 67 | 77 | 89 | 92 | 80 | 71 | 69 |
| 83 | 72 | 63 | 73 | 76 | 60 | 83 | 79 | 63 | 74 |
| 80 | 82 | 68 | 83 | 78 | 76 | 71 | 82 | 74 | 76 |
| 77 | 67 | 88 | 76 | 89 | 85 | 72 | 79 | 84 | 67 |
| 61 | 74 | 76 | 68 | 68 | 88 | 74 | 77 | 70 | 70 |
| 81 | 80 | 89 | 84 | 70 | 69 | 86 | 84 | 62 | 76 |

In sum, it should be clear that the time spent becoming familiar with the data using exploratory data analysis is time well invested. If done properly, EDA will allow you to better understand and interpret the results of the experiment. Thus, EDA is a guide and an aid to data analysis. As John Tukey (1977), a pioneer in the development of EDA techniques, noted "exploratory data analysis can never be the whole story, but nothing else can serve as the foundation stone—as the first step." (p. 3) In the remainder of this chapter we will investigate some of the basic EDA tools. We will review more specific and advanced EDA techniques in the following chapters.

### Organizing the Data

The first step in any data analysis is placing order onto the data. When you collect the data, they appear, for all practical purposes, to be a random jumble of numbers. Once you organize the data, you can begin to summarize and look for interesting patterns. Let's look at a simple and familiar example, grades from an exam. Table 3.1 lists grades for a class of 100 students.

## 3.3 / Stem-and-Leaf Plots

Try to answer a few simple questions based on the numbers in Table 3.1. What are the highest and lowest scores? What did most people score on the test? Are the data uniformly distributed across the range of grades? These questions are difficult to answer. You might be able to answer the first question if you are willing to hunt for the high and low scores nestled in the data set. The other questions are more difficult to answer. What we need is a quick way to organize the data that will allow us to preserve as much of the original data as possible and that will provide us with information about the shape of the data. The **stem-and-leaf plot** is a useful tool for exploring the data.

The stem-and-leaf plot is easy to construct. Figure 3.1 is a stem-and-leaf plot of the 100 test scores presented in Table 3.1. As you can see there is a large vertical line with numbers on the left and right of the line. The numbers on the left are the *stems* and represent the leftmost or leading digits of the numbers. The numbers to the right of the line are the *leaves* and represent the individual numbers. Look at the bottom stem and leaf, 9 | 02279. The stem, 9 |, represents all numbers between 90 and 99, inclusive. The leaf, 02279, represents the five numbers: 90, 92, 92, 97, and 99.

The stem-and-leaf plot is an effective means of exploring the data. You should now be able to answer the three questions asked earlier with great ease: What are the highest and lowest grades? The high score was

■ **Stem-and-Leaf Plot:**

A means of organizing data that allows for exploration of the data and its distribution while retaining the information of the original scores.

```
4 ┊ 9                                                                   1
5 ┊ 088                                                                 3
6 ┊ 0012337778888999                                                   16
7 ┊ 00001111222233334444446666666677788888889999999                  44
8 ┊ 0000011222333334444455688888999                                   31
9 ┊ 02279                                                              5
  └ ─ ─ ─ ─ ─ ─ ─ ─ ─ ─ ─ ─ ─ ─ ─ ─ ─ ─ ─ ─ ─ ─ ─ ─ ─ ─ ─ ─ ─ ─ ─
                                                                 N = 100
```

**Figure** | **3.1**

| Stem-and-leaf plot of test scores presented in Table 3.1. Note that the column to the extreme right contains the number of scores for that stem.

```
4* |                                                      0
4• | 9                                                    1
5* | 0                                                    1
5• | 88                                                   2
6* | 001233                                               6
6• | 7778888999                                          10
7* | 000011112222333444444                               21
7• | 66666666777888888999999                             23
8* | 00000112223333344444                                20
8• | 55688888999                                         11
9* | 022                                                  3
9• | 79                                                   2
   |................................................
                                          N = 100
```

**Figure** | **3.2**

**Stem-and-leaf plot of test scores presented in Table 3.1. Note that the column to the extreme right contains the number of scores for that stem.**

99; the low score was 49. What did most people score on the test? Most people scored in the 70s. Are the data uniformly distributed across the range of grades? The grades seem to fall mostly in the C–B range and there seem to be more higher grades than lower grades. By looking at the numbers arranged in the figure, you can see where the greatest concentration of scores is located (measure of central tendency), whether the data are bunched together or spread out (measure of dispersion), and the overall shape of the distribution.

The stem-and-leaf plot is also very flexible. What, for example, if we want a better way to represent the number of people who have borderline grades (e.g., 88 and 89). We could replot the scores as we did in Figure 3.2. Do you notice anything different about the data now that they have been replotted? It appears that the distribution of scores is symmetrical with the typical score in the upper 70s.

Figure 3.2 presents an alternative stem-and-leaf plot of the data from Table 3.1. In this example, we divided the leaves in half. The leaf line marked with an * presents numbers between 0 and 4 inclusive. The leaf line with the • presents the numbers between 5 and 9. Look at the numbers between 70 and 79. We grouped all numbers between 70 and 74 in the leaf line 7*. The numbers between 75 and 79 are on the leaf line, 7•.

The primary advantage of the stem-and-leaf plot is that it preserves all the information. This advantage may also be a limitation. If the amount of data will create either long leaves or many stems, the plot may become too complicated, too large, or both. There are, however, some alternatives that we can use to preserve the general quality of the stem-and-leaf plot.

Consider the 100 numbers in Table 3.2. These numbers range between 3 and 981. How would we go about constructing a stem-and-leaf plot of these data? Figure 3.3 presents the solution. As you can see, the stem numbers represent the 100s and the leaves represent the numbers in the 10s and 1s places. A comma and space separate numbers in the leaf.

Although this stem-and-leaf plot preserves the original data, the plot is growing large and cumbersome. If the data set were larger, the stem-and-leaf plot may not fit on a standard piece of paper. Therefore, we need to consider an alternative that will allow us to continue to use the logic of the stem-and-leaf plot and create a manageable representation of the data. The answer is that we will need to reach a compromise by *truncating* the numbers. Truncating means that we cut each number down to the 10s place and then use the basic stem-and-leaf format. For example, in the top line

**Table 3.2**

**100 Numbers Ranging Between 0 and 999**

| | | | | | | | | | |
|---|---|---|---|---|---|---|---|---|---|
| 765 | 648 | 196 | 93 | 801 | 304 | 455 | 20 | 53 | 35 |
| 149 | 398 | 62 | 865 | 875 | 174 | 177 | 774 | 662 | 142 |
| 684 | 269 | 851 | 111 | 165 | 264 | 952 | 678 | 973 | 732 |
| 752 | 640 | 268 | 454 | 12 | 873 | 201 | 17 | 19 | 361 |
| 452 | 419 | 963 | 719 | 981 | 775 | 809 | 520 | 312 | 876 |
| 328 | 519 | 476 | 209 | 662 | 785 | 813 | 815 | 616 | 3 |
| 346 | 248 | 232 | 383 | 640 | 366 | 355 | 686 | 905 | 358 |
| 221 | 507 | 134 | 367 | 918 | 580 | 453 | 435 | 369 | 464 |
| 446 | 702 | 329 | 128 | 402 | 519 | 593 | 546 | 168 | 689 |
| 619 | 546 | 779 | 130 | 939 | 867 | 187 | 666 | 590 | 15 |

```
100s  10s and 1s
-----------------------------------------------------------------------
  0 | 03, 12, 15, 17, 19, 20, 35, 53, 62, 93                      10
  1 | 11, 28, 30, 34, 42, 49, 65, 68, 74, 77, 87, 96              12
  2 | 01, 09, 21, 32, 48, 64, 68, 69                               8
  3 | 04, 12, 28, 29, 46, 55, 58, 61, 66, 67, 69, 83, 98          13
  4 | 02, 19, 35, 46, 52, 53, 54, 55, 64, 76                      10
  5 | 07, 19, 19, 20, 46, 46, 80, 90, 93                           9
  6 | 16, 19, 40, 40, 48, 62, 62, 66, 78, 84, 86, 89              12
  7 | 02, 19, 32, 52, 65, 74, 75, 79, 85                           9
  8 | 01, 09, 13, 15, 51, 65, 67, 73, 75, 76                      10
  9 | 05, 18, 39, 52, 63, 73, 81                                   7
                                                           N = 100
```

**Figure 3.3**

**Stem-and-leaf plot of data presented in Table 3.2. The stem represents numbers in the 100s. The leaves represent numbers in the 10s and 1s places.**

in Figure 3.3. The values may be truncated to 0, the value 12 truncated to 1, and so on. In this case the stems represent the 100s place and the leaves represent the 10s place. We drop the 0s because they are redundant. Figure 3.4 presents the revised stem-and-leaf plot.

Of course, the trade-off is that we have lost some of the original information in order to use the stem-and-leaf plot. Such a compromise is acceptable however, as our primary goal is to develop an initial impression of our data. If we wish to have more exact information about the data, we can revert to the original numbers and use other statistical techniques.

## Stem-and-Leaf Plot to Compare Two Groups

With a little creativity we can use the stem-and-leaf plot to compare two groups of data. Figure 3.5 is a stem-and-leaf plot of test grades from two classes. In this case the stem is in the middle of the leaves. The leaves on the left of the stem represent test scores in Class 1; the leaves on the right of the stem represent test scores in Class 2. You will also notice that the stems increase in units of 5. Therefore the stem |7*| includes numbers ranging between 70 and 74, inclusive. The stem |7•| includes numbers ranging between 75 and 79, inclusive.

This figure makes clear that Class 1 did not do as well as Class 2 on the test. Using this simple EDA technique we are able to determine where the majority of test scores are in each group, find the spread and shape

```
100s  10s            (i.e., 00,10,10,10,10,20,30,50,60,90)
----+-----------  ----------------------------------------------
   0 : 0111123569
   1 : 123344667789
   2 : 00234666
   3 : 0122455666689
   4 : 0134555567
   5 : 011244899
   6 : 114446667888
   7 : 013567778
   8 : 0011566777
   9 : 0135678
```

---

**Figure | 3.4**

Stem-and-leaf plot of data presented in Table 3.2. The stem represents numbers in the 100s. The leaves represent the numbers in the 10s place.

```
           Class 1              Class 2
        ----------------     ------------------
                     : 4 * :
                   9 : 4 • :
          43222111110 : 5 * :
           9988766665 : 5 • :
                 3321 : 6 * :
                 9975 : 6 • : 555666889
                   10 : 7 * : 00001122444
                    6 : 7 • : 677788
                     : 8 * : 0014
                    7 : 8 • : 55
                     : 9 * : 4
                     : 9 • : 7
```

---

**Figure | 3.5**

Stem-and-leaf plot of two groups of data.

of the scores, and make a comparison between the groups. In this example, the systematic finding appears to be that students in Class 2 did better on the test than students in Class 1.

This type of stem-and-leaf plot calls for a word of caution: The plot should be used only when the number of observations in the two groups is equal or close to equal. The plot may be misinterpreted if differences in the size of the groups are large.

# 3.4 / Frequency Distributions

Stem-and-leaf plots are very useful for presenting data. There are, however, other tools that we can use to understand data. In this section we will use frequency distributions to examine concepts such as relative proportions, percentiles, and percentile ranks.

## Qualitative Data

Where are psychologists most likely to work? Do the majority or even all psychologists work in private practice? Do many psychologists get jobs in business? These are very important questions, especially if you are thinking about a career as a psychologist. We can answer these questions by surveying psychologists and asking them to describe the type of environment in which they work.

Table | 3.3

Employment Setting for Psychologists at the Doctoral and Master's Level

| Employment Setting | Doctoral Level | Master's Level |
|---|---|---|
| University or college | 12,893 | 768 |
| Medical school | 1,558 | 114 |
| Primary school system | 789 | 1,280 |
| Independent practice | 1,635 | 225 |
| Hospital and clinics | 3,961 | 907 |
| Business or other setting | 3,547 | 903 |
| Total | 24,383 | 4,197 |

*Source:* Based on Stapp, J., Tucker, A. M., and VandenBos, G. R. (1985). Census of Psychological Personnel: 1983. *American Psychologist, 40*, 1317–1351.

The data in Table 3.3 display the survey results concerned with the employment setting of psychologists with a master's or a doctorate in psychology. The Employment-Setting Categories are *nominal* because there is no scale implied in the various work settings. No value judgment is made that one setting is better than the other or ranks higher than the other. The researchers conducting the survey simply counted the number of psychologists reporting that they worked in one of these settings.

The numbers within each category represent the frequency. For example, there were 12,893 psychologists at the doctoral level who indicated that they worked in a university or college setting. Looking at the Doctoral-Level column in Table 3.3 you can see the number of Doctoral-Level psychologists working in each of the employment settings. In essence, this column of numbers is a **frequency distribution.** It presents the number of observations that fall within each specific category or class.

In this example, the variable Employment Setting has six separate classes. A **class** represents a way of grouping together observations that are similar to one another. Consider the University or college class. This class includes all psychologists who indicated that they teach at public and private institutions, graduate schools, four-year colleges, and community colleges. The classes are *mutually exclusive* because a person could only indicate one primary type of employment setting.

Although these numbers are useful, there is room for improvement. You may want to compare the differences in employment setting between doctoral- and master's-level psychologists. We can use the frequency distributions as a general guide for interpreting the data, but the fact that there is a large difference in the number of doctoral- and master's-level psychologists makes the comparison difficult. As an example, compare the number of psychologists in independent practice. Are psychologists with Ph.D.s more likely to work in an independent practice than psychologists with MS degrees? What do these numbers mean? Who is more likely to work at a Medical School? What we need is a way to equate the numbers for easier and faster comparison. We can do this by converting the frequencies into relative percentages as shown in Table 3.4. In other words, divide the frequency in each cell by the total frequency of the column in which it appears and multiply by 100. Thus, the percentage of doctoral-level psychologists holding positions at a University or college is $12,893/24,383 \times 100 = 52.9\%$.

Is there a systematic relation between level of education and employment setting? Psychologists with doctorates appear to be more likely

■ **Frequency Distribution:**

The number of observations that fall within a specific category or class of a variable.

■ **Class:**

A mutually exclusive and nominal category that represents elements or subjects that share a common characteristic.

**Table** | **3.4**

**Employment Setting for Psychologists at the Doctoral and Master's Level**

| Employment Setting | Doctoral Level | Master's Level |
|---|---|---|
| University or college | 52.9% | 18.3% |
| Medical school | 6.4% | 2.7% |
| Primary school system | 3.2% | 30.5% |
| Independent practice | 6.7% | 5.4% |
| Hospital and clinics | 16.2% | 21.6% |
| Business or other setting | 14.5% | 21.5% |
| Total | 99.9%* | 100.0% |

*Source*: Stapp, J., Tucker, A. M. & VandenBos, G. R. (1985). Census of Psychological Personnel: 1983. *American Psychologist, 40*, 1317–1351.
*Due to rounding error column total not 100.0%

to work in higher education, whereas psychologists with a master's degree are more likely to work in the primary school system.

## Quantitative Data

Let's return to the example about your roommate's score on the narcissism test. He said he received a score of 14 on that test. To know if his score is high or low, you need to know something about the rest of the scores in the distribution.

Here are the data from the study in which your roommate participated. As you can see, the numbers are in no particular order and just looking at the numbers does not help. What we need is a way to better understand and talk about these numbers.

| | | | | | | | | | |
|---|---|---|---|---|---|---|---|---|---|
| 5 | 20 | 6 | 19 | 18 | 17 | 7 | 8 | 16 | 15 |
| 17 | 8 | 15 | 14 | 10 | 11 | 15 | 11 | 12 | 14 |
| 15 | 13 | 12 | 11 | 11 | 12 | 13 | 11 | 10 | 9 |

Let's review what we already know about the numbers. First, the number represents a *quantitative* variable that can, at the very least, be considered to be ordinal—we assume that a person with a score of 14 is more narcissistic than a person who has a score of 7. We cannot, however, determine if the data represent an interval or ratio scale. As we noted in Chapter 2, test scores are usually treated as interval scale data. Nevertheless, even though there are no fractional values in the data, we can reasonably assume that there is an underlying continuous scale of narcissism, like there is with weight and height, which would include fractional values if our measurement scale were more precise.

Figure 3.6 presents both a stem-and-leaf plot and a frequency distribution of the data. As you can see from the stem-and-leaf plot, the data from the study appear to be fairly symmetrical and the typical score is between 11 and 15. In fact, a little more than 50 percent of the scores fall between these two numbers. Specifically, there are 16 scores that fall between 11 and 15, inclusive. This block of numbers represents 53.33 percent (53.33 = 16/30 × 100) of the total scores.

The frequency distribution displays the same information but in a different format. In this plot, we count how often each value occurs. There are four columns in this display. The *X* column represents data. The letter *f* represents *frequency*, the occurrence of each value in the set. There was one individual who received a score of 20 on the test. Two

| Stem-and-Leaf | | Frequency Distribution | | | |
|---|---|---|---|---|---|
| | | X | f | Cum f | Cum % |
| | | 20 | 1 | 30 | 100.0% |
| | | 19 | 1 | 29 | 96.7% |
| | | 18 | 1 | 28 | 93.3% |
| | | 17 | 2 | 27 | 90.0% |
| | | 16 | 1 | 25 | 83.3% |
| | | 15 | 4 | 24 | 80.0% |
| * | | 14 | 2 | 20 | 66.7% |
| • | 567889 | 13 | 2 | 18 | 60.0% |
| 1* | 00111112223344 | 12 | 3 | 16 | 53.3% |
| 1• | 555567789 | 11 | 5 | 13 | 43.3% |
| 2* | 0 | 10 | 2 | 8 | 26.7% |
| 2• | | 9 | 1 | 6 | 20.0% |
| | | 8 | 2 | 5 | 16.6% |
| | | 7 | 1 | 3 | 10.0% |
| | | 6 | 1 | 2 | 6.7% |
| | | 5 | 1 | 1 | 3.3% |

**Figure | 3.6**

**Frequency distribution of 30 scores on a narcissism test.**

---

▓ **Cumulative Frequency:**

The number of scores at or below a particular value.

---

▓ **Cumulative Percentage:**

The percentage of a group that scored at or below a specific value.

---

▓ **Percentile Rank:**

The percentile rank is a value that tells us the percentage of scores that fall at or below a given point.

---

individuals received scores of 17. The Cum $f$ column represents the cumulative frequency. The **cumulative frequency** is the number of scores *at or below* the particular value. For example, 20 of the 30 students scored 14 or less. The last column is the **cumulative percentage.** The cumulative percentage tells us the percentage of a group that scored at or below a specific value. In this example, approximately 67% (66.7%) scored at or below 14. In other words, your roommate's score is at the 67th percentile.

# 3.5 / Percentiles and Percentile Ranks

A cumulative frequency and cumulative percentage distribution is useful for evaluating the relative position of a given score. With it we may examine the distribution and the scores that fall at various percentile ranks. A **percentile rank** is a value that tells us the percent of scores that fall at or below a given point. For example, a percentile rank of $P_{90}$ tells us that 90% of the scores fall at or below that point. One can calculate a percentile for any given score. The calculations are simple: Count the number of scores that are equal to and less than the specific value and divide by $N$, the sample size. For example, we determined the percentile of your roommate's score as follows. First, we determined that there were 20 scores of 14 or less. Next we divided 20 by 30 and multiplied by 100 to obtain the percentage of participants who obtained that score or a lower score ($20/30 \times 100 = 66.7\%$).

What can we conclude from this simple transformation? As you suspected, your roommate does have a higher-than-average level of narcissism. Indeed, your roommate is in the top third of the group. Don't give your roommate too much grief, however. Because of the small sample size, we cannot be sure that the data are representative of the population. Therefore, interpreting the data too broadly would be risky and unfair to your roommate.

Here is another example. Your roommate's friend received a score of 9. Six out of the 30 students taking the test received scores of 9 or below (see the Cum $f$ column). The percentile of a score of 9 is: $6/30 = .2 \times 100 = 20$.

Just as a score is meaningless in the abstract, so too a percentile has limitations in its interpretation. A percentile must always be expressed in relation to some group. Thus, if a friend claims that she scored in the 93rd percentile on a test of mathematics aptitude, you might not be very impressed if the reference group is made up of individuals who completed only the eighth grade. On the other hand, if you learned that the reference group consisted of individuals holding a doctorate in mathematics, you might be very impressed.

## Landmarks in the Data

Many researchers look for several landmarks in the data as a part of their exploratory data analysis. Specifically, they routinely calculate the 25th, 50th, and 75th percentiles because these numbers are useful in summarizing and interpreting the data. The 50th percentile is a commonly used measure of central tendency because it represents the exact middle of a distribution of scores. Another name for the 50th percentile is the median. The 25th and the 75th percentiles are the **quartiles** and are typically reported as $Q_1$ and $Q_3$. The range of scores between the 25th and 75th percentile is often used as a general measure of dispersion. These statistics are useful when comparing different groups with each other.

Let's use the Test of Narcissism as an example. First you calculate the *location* of the score by following these steps:

■ **Quartiles:**

The 25th, 50th, and 75th percentiles are the quartiles and are typically noted as $Q_1$, $Q_2$, $Q_3$. $Q_2$, the 50th percentile, is also the median.

**Step 1**   Add 1 to the sample size. In this case $N + 1 = 31$

**Step 2**   Multiply the sample size by the percentile of $X$ to determine the *location* of the desired quartile, say $Q_1$. The value 7.75 refers to the location of the score, in this case the point is somewhere after the seventh score yet not quite at the eighth score.

Location of First Quartile, $Q_1$
$$X_{.25} = (N + 1) \times .25 = 7.75$$

Location of Second Quartile, $Q_2$
$$X_{.50} = (N + 1) \times .50 = 15.5$$

Location of Third Quartile, $Q_3$
$$X_{.75} = (N + 1) \times .75 = 23.25$$

**Step 3**   If the value obtained in Step 2 is a fraction, take the average of the two adjacent $X$ values. For example, $X_{.25} = 7.75$, a decimal, indicates that the first quartile lies between the seventh and eighth scores. Take the average of $X_7$ and $X_8$, the seventh and the eighth scores. For the second quartile take the average of the 15th and the 16th scores.

Don't confuse the location of a score with the score itself. The steps we have outlined above will provide you with the *location* of the score. You must then examine the distribution to find the *score* associated with that location. Figure 3.7 illustrates the scores associated with each of the quartiles. The first quartile is located between the seventh and eighth scores. Each of these scores is 10. Thus the score at $Q_1$ is 10. The third quartile is located between the 23rd and 24th scores. These scores are both 15. Thus the score at $Q_3$ is 15.

```
 *  |
 •  | 567889
1*  | 00111112223344
1•  | 555567789
2*  | 0
2•  |
```

**Figure | 3.7**

Stem-and-leaf display with the location and the score associated with $Q_1$, $Q_2$, and $Q_3$ indicated by underlining.

## 3.6 / Box-and-Whisker Plots

The box-and-whisker plot is another useful EDA technique that incorporates many of the statistics we have already reviewed. Let's use some data to illustrate how we create and interpret a box-and-whisker graph. A psychologist wanted to evaluate the effects of different teaching strategies. She randomly assigned students to one of three conditions. Students in Group 1 represented the control group. They received a 60-item test on the history of the Korean War and had no opportunity to study for the test. Students in Group 2 listened to a 50-minute traditional lecture on the Korean War and then completed the test. Students in Group 3 attended a 50-minute class in which the instructor used multimedia tools to present the information. The data in Table 3.5 represent the scores of the three experimental groups. Notice that we have rank ordered the scores from lowest to highest and calculated the quartiles. Simply looking at the raw data tells us little.

Figure 3.8 presents the box-and-whisker plot for the data. As you can see, the rectangle extends from $Q_1$ to $Q_3$. In the middle of the rectangle is the second quartile, $Q_2$. The lines that extend from the box, called the whiskers, extend to the highest and lowest scores. The box-and-whisker

**Table | 3.5**

Scores for a Test on the History of the Korean War

| Group 1 | | | | | | | | | |
|---|---|---|---|---|---|---|---|---|---|
| 12 | 13 | 14 | 18 | 22 | 22 | 22 | 24 | 26 | 26 |
| 28 | 29 | 30 | 30 | 35 | 37 | 37 | 38 | 38 | 38 |
| | $Q_1 = 22.0$ | | | $Q_2 = 27.0$ | | | $Q_3 = 36.0$ | | |

| Group 2 | | | | | | | | | |
|---|---|---|---|---|---|---|---|---|---|
| 23 | 23 | 26 | 27 | 27 | 28 | 32 | 32 | 33 | 34 |
| 36 | 38 | 38 | 43 | 44 | 44 | 45 | 46 | 46 | 49 |
| | $Q_1 = 27.5$ | | | $Q_2 = 35.0$ | | | $Q_3 = 44.0$ | | |

| Group 3 | | | | | | | | | |
|---|---|---|---|---|---|---|---|---|---|
| 30 | 33 | 35 | 36 | 37 | 37 | 40 | 43 | 43 | 43 |
| 46 | 46 | 46 | 49 | 51 | 52 | 52 | 57 | 59 | 59 |
| | $Q_1 = 37.0$ | | | $Q_2 = 44.5$ | | | $Q_3 = 51.5$ | | |

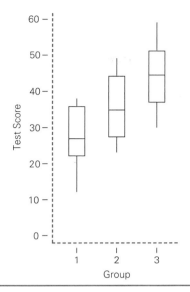

**Figure** 3.8

**Box-and-whisker plots of data presented in Table 3.5**

plot is easy to construct and offers a lot of information. Looking at the graph, you can see that the three groups differed with respect to performance on the test. The control group, Group 1, had the lowest overall performance. By contrast, the students who sat through the multimedia presentation had the greatest overall performance. The students who heard the traditional lecture, Group 2, performed better than the control group, but not as well as the multimedia group. Box-and-whisker plots do not replace statistical analysis, but they are one of the first steps in exploring research results.

## 3.7 The Shape of Distributions

When summarizing a distribution of scores, it is important to describe the shape of the distribution. The shape of the distribution is important for many reasons, many of which will be better understood as we progress through this book. For now, suffice it to say that the shape of the distribution can determine if a specific statistical procedure can be appropriately applied to the data.

To better understand the shape of a distribution, it is useful to create a graphical representation of the frequency distribution. We can create the distribution using either the stem-and-leaf plot or the **frequency histogram.** The frequency histogram is a graph that represents the frequency for each score.

Figure 3.9 is a frequency histogram of a frequency distribution of test scores. You should note that the frequency histogram is used only for interval and ratio scales. Recall that interval- and ratio-scale variables differ from ordinal-scale variables in several important ways. One of the essential differences is that interval and ratio scales have equal differences in scale values.

■ **Frequency Histogram:**

A form of graph representing a frequency distribution in which a continuous line or bars indicates the frequency of each score or group of scores.

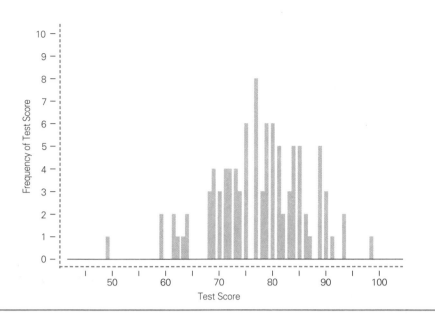

**Figure** | **3.9**

**Frequency distribution of test scores.**

## Shapes of Frequency Distributions

**Normal Distribution:**

A hypothetical frequency distribution with a characteristic bell-shaped form in which a large portion of scores is at or near the midpoint of the distribution.

**Kurtosis:**

A term that represents the degree to which scores are clustered about one common area of a distribution or distributed throughout the distribution. **Leptokurtic** refers to distributions where the scores are clustered close to a common point. **Platykurtic** refers to a distribution where the scores are spread across the distribution. **Mesokurtic** refers to a normally distributed set of data.

**Skew:**

A term that describes the relative symmetry of a distribution of scores.

Frequency histograms may take on an unlimited number of shapes. However, many of the statistical properties discussed in the text assume a particular form of distribution, namely, the "bell-shaped" or **normal distribution.** We will examine the properties of the normal distribution in Chapters 5 and 6. For now, however, let's look at several specific properties of the curve. One of the distinguishing features of the curve is its shape; many people think the curve looks like the outline of a bell. Another feature of the normal distribution is the fact that it is symmetrical about its middle. If you were to draw a line at the 50th percentile, you would see that the sides are mirror images of each other. The normal distribution is important to statisticians and psychologists because it describes many of the phenomena that we study. You will become very familiar with this curve during the remainder of this book.

One feature that we can examine in any distribution is its **kurtosis.** Kurtosis refers to the degree to which the scores are either clustered around a small portion of the scale or spread out across the entire distribution. Figure 3.10 presents several forms of bell-shaped distributions, each with different kurtosis. Although each curve is bell-shaped and symmetrical, they are not shaped the same way. We can make comparative descriptions of the three curves. Curve (a), which is characterized by the piling up of scores in the center of the distribution, is called a **leptokurtic distribution.** In contrast, we would call curve (c) a **platykurtic distribution** because all the scores are spread throughout the scale. Finally, curve (b) represents a balance between curves (a) and (c). This distribution is known as a **mesokurtic distribution.**

Another important feature to examine is the symmetry of a distribution. When we speak of a distribution's symmetry, we speak of its **skew.** Skew refers to the fact that the data are not symmetrical and that there

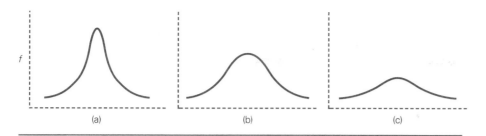

**Figure** | **3.10**

| **Three forms of bell-shaped distributions: (a) leptokurtic, (b) mesokurtic, and (c) platykurtic.**

is a tendency for the majority of scores to cluster at one end of the distribution. Figure 3.11 represents three distributions. Curve (b) represents the familiar normal curve. Because the curve is normal, we would say that the data are not skewed in either direction, they are symmetrically distributed. Curve (a) represents an obvious skew. The majority of scores are at the lower end of the distribution with a few scores trailing toward the upper end of the distribution. This curve would be said to have a **positive skew.** By contrast, Curve (c) has a **negative skew** because the majority of the scores are at the upper end of the distribution with a trailing of scores toward the lower end of the distribution. The direction of the skew, negative versus positive is always in reference to the direction of the "tail" portion of the frequency curve. If the tail of the distribution is pointed toward the upper end of the distribution, the skew is positive. If the tail of the curve is pointed toward the lower end of the distribution, the skew is negative.

■ **Positive Skew:**

Refers to a distribution where the scores are clustered at the lower end of the scale with a tail of scores at the upper end of the distribution.

■ **Negative Skew:**

Refers to a distribution where the scores are clustered at the upper end of the scale with a tail of scores at the lower end of the distribution.

## 3.8/
## Putting It All Together

When a psychologist or educator administers an achievement test, he or she will need some standardized mechanism for interpreting the person's score. In education, the use of norms is especially important because the age of a student has a considerable influence on our interpretation of the test results. Simply stated, we would expect that a fourth grader should do better on a math test than a first grader. Furthermore, it would be unfair and meaningless to judge the first grader's performance relative to older children. Therefore, psychologists create

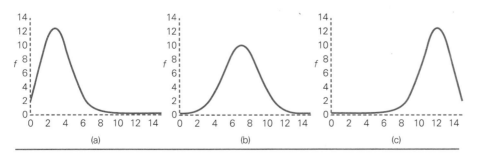

**Figure** | **3.11**

| **Three distributions with (a) positive skew, (b) no skew, and (c) negative skew.**

**Table** 3.6

**Hypothetical Scores for Students in Grades 3, 5, and 7**

| GRADE 3 | | | | | | | | | |
|---|---|---|---|---|---|---|---|---|---|
| 31 | 36 | 21 | 26 | 36 | 34 | 40 | 7 | 37 | 31 |
| 31 | 23 | 47 | 21 | 9 | 13 | 23 | 14 | 23 | 13 |
| 24 | 43 | 10 | 21 | 9 | 28 | 28 | 34 | 31 | 52 |
| 3 | 8 | 26 | 45 | 33 | 17 | 43 | 33 | 21 | 5 |
| 10 | 32 | 22 | 21 | 27 | 34 | 31 | 11 | 40 | 15 |

| GRADE 5 | | | | | | | | | |
|---|---|---|---|---|---|---|---|---|---|
| 50 | 42 | 24 | 31 | 36 | 42 | 39 | 31 | 8 | 26 |
| 34 | 20 | 41 | 31 | 29 | 41 | 42 | 46 | 40 | 36 |
| 30 | 20 | 50 | 17 | 39 | 30 | 40 | 15 | 35 | 22 |
| 13 | 44 | 43 | 35 | 37 | 67 | 42 | 44 | 29 | 6 |
| 31 | 46 | 35 | 28 | 51 | 23 | 23 | 36 | 32 | 34 |

| GRADE 7 | | | | | | | | | |
|---|---|---|---|---|---|---|---|---|---|
| 42 | 50 | 49 | 38 | 55 | 39 | 61 | 59 | 55 | 42 |
| 49 | 37 | 49 | 45 | 61 | 51 | 38 | 61 | 44 | 66 |
| 50 | 54 | 40 | 44 | 46 | 57 | 57 | 39 | 48 | 55 |
| 41 | 57 | 39 | 47 | 52 | 37 | 42 | 55 | 40 | 45 |
| 48 | 45 | 34 | 48 | 52 | 49 | 40 | 38 | 56 | 40 |

within-group norms for these achievement tests. A within-group norm is nothing more than comparison statistics for a specific population. In the case of an academic achievement test, the within-group norms would represent separate grades. Using within-group norms, we can compare an individual's score to other children in the same grade. More specifically, we can use percentile rankings to summarize a student's performance relative to other children his or her age.

```
        Grade 3                      Grade 5                      Grade 7

    * | 3                        * |                          * |
    • | 57899                    • | 68                       • |
1 * | 001334                  1 * | 3                       1 * |
1 • | 57                      1 • | 57                      1 • |
2 * | 1111123334              2 * | 002334                  2 * |
2 • | 66788                   2 • | 6899                    2 • |
3 * | 11111233444             3 * | 001111244               3 * | 4
3 • | 667                     3 • | 555666799               3 • | 77888999
4 * | 0033                    4 * | 00112222344             4 * | 0000122244
4 • | 57                      4 • | 66                      4 • | 555678889999
5 * | 2                       5 * | 001                     5 * | 001224
5 • |                         5 • |                         5 • | 555567779
6 * |                         6 * |                         6 * | 111
6 • |                         6 • | 7                       6 • | 6
```

**Figure** 3.12

**Stem-and-leaf graphs of the data presented in Table 3.6.**

**Table** 3.7

Brief Summary of Procedures to Follow When Calculating a Percentile or
Evaluating a Score in a Frequency Distribution

| If you want to | Caution |
|---|---|
| Identify a score associated with a particular percentile. <br> • Choose the percentile (e.g., the 75th percentile). <br> • Add 1 to the sample size. <br> • Determine the *location*. <br> $X_{.75} = (N + 1) \times .75$ <br> • Look in that location to identify the score. | Don't confuse the *location* with the value of the score. <br><br> When the location is a fraction, take the average of the two adjacent $X$ values. |
| Determine the percent of cases that fall at or below a given score, for example, a score of 10 in Figure 3.6. <br> • Prepare a frequency distribution with a cum $f$ column. <br> • Find the cum $f$ associated with the score (e.g., 8 out of 30 people earned a score of 10 or a lower one). <br> • Divide that cum $f$ by $N$ and multiply by 100. <br> $8 \div 30 = .267 \times 100 = 26.7$ <br> A score of 10 is approximately at the 27th percentile. | To avoid errors make sure that the top value in your cum $f$ equals $N$. <br><br> Be sure to multiply by 100. The decimal value you calculate is a proportion, not a percentage. <br><br> Be careful in your interpretation. Evaluate the percentile in terms of the reference group. |

See Section 3.5 for more complete coverage and examples.

Table 3.6 shows an example of within-group comparison for a hypothetical achievement test. For our purposes, let's assume that the test is a mathematics achievement test. The test consists of 100 multiple-choice questions designed for use with students between grades 3 through 7 inclusive. The test results for grades 3, 5, and 7 are shown in Table 3.6.

Our first step should be to examine the data more closely using a stem-and-leaf plot as we see in Figure 3.12. A visual inspection of the data reveals several interesting facts. First, as we would expect, student performance increases through the grades. We can also determine that the data are generally bell-shaped.

Finally, let's consider the third grader with a score of 52. For the third graders, a score of 52 is obviously the highest score received. What is the relative position of a score of 52 in the fifth and seventh grades? In grade 5, 49 out of 50 students had scores of 52 or less. Consequently, 98% of fifth graders (49/50 × 100 = 98%) scored at or below 52. For Grade 7, 36 students had a score of 52 or less. Therefore, for the seventh grade, 72 percent of the students scored at or below 52.

CHAPTER $S$ UMMARY

This chapter is concerned with organizing, summarizing, and interpreting raw data.

1. Exploratory data analysis (EDA) involves stem-and-leaf plots that are effective means of exploring raw data. Included were examples of plots using the original data and truncated data, and plots comparing two groups.

2. Other means of exploring raw data consist of examining frequency distributions, their graphs, and box-and-whisker plots.

3. By cumulating the frequency distributions we were able to convert scores into percentile ranks that reflect the relative positions of a score in a frequency distribution.

4. The percentile ranks that serve as landmarks in a distribution are the 25th, 50th, and 75th percentiles.

5. We discussed both the forms of frequency curves (leptokurtic, mesokurtic, platykurtic) and their skew.

6. Finally, we demonstrated the simplicity of estimating percentile ranks from stem-and-leaf plots.

TERMS TO $R$ EMEMBER

class
cumulative frequency
cumulative percentage
exploratory data analysis (EDA)
frequency distribution
frequency histogram
kurtosis
leptokurtic distribution
mesokurtic distribution

negative skew
normal distribution
percentile rank
platykurtic distribution
positive skew
quartiles
skew
stem-and-leaf plot

$E$ XERCISES

1. The accompanying table represents 40 scores for a statistics examination. The highest possible score is 100.

| 63 | 88 | 79 | 92 | 86 | 87 | 83 | 78 | 40 | 67 |
| 68 | 76 | 46 | 81 | 92 | 77 | 84 | 76 | 70 | 66 |
| 77 | 75 | 98 | 81 | 82 | 81 | 87 | 78 | 70 | 60 |
| 94 | 79 | 52 | 82 | 77 | 81 | 77 | 70 | 74 | 61 |

a. Use a stem-and-leaf plot to organize these data.
b. What were the highest and lowest scores?
c. Assuming that A = 90 or better, B = 80 to 89, down to F, how many students were in each grade category?
d. How many students were within 1 point of earning a higher grade?
e. Calculate $Q_1$, $Q_2$, $Q_3$.
f. Do the data appear skewed?

2. A statistics instructor wants to find a more efficient method of teaching statistics. She decides to do some research with two sections of a statistics course that she teaches. She teaches one class using a conventional lecture technique. We'll call this Section A. For the other class,

| 20 SCORES: SECTION A | | | | | | | | | |
|---|---|---|---|---|---|---|---|---|---|
| 73 | 84 | 76 | 70 | 69 | 76 | 46 | 81 | 92 | 66 |
| 87 | 81 | 78 | 45 | 67 | 73 | 88 | 79 | 95 | 86 |

| 20 SCORES: SECTION B | | | | | | | | | |
|---|---|---|---|---|---|---|---|---|---|
| 79 | 75 | 98 | 81 | 82 | 70 | 60 | 82 | 77 | 81 |
| 81 | 87 | 88 | 94 | 79 | 92 | 77 | 70 | 74 | 71 |

Section B, she uses much class discussion and many group exercises. At the end of the term, both sections complete the same final exam. Here are the test results for the classes.

a. Prepare a stem-and-leaf plot that compares the scores for the two sections.

b. What is $Q_2$ for each group?

c. Describe the pattern of results you observe. How does the performance in Section B compare to that in Section A?

3. The owner of a video store is interested in how many videos a customer watches during a year. She randomly selects the records of customers and counts the number of videos rented during the year. The data are presented in the accompanying table.

| | | | | | | | | |
|---|---|---|---|---|---|---|---|---|
| 67 | 63 | 64 | 57 | 56 | 55 | 53 | 53 | 54 |
| 45 | 45 | 46 | 47 | 37 | 23 | 34 | 44 | 27 |
| 45 | 34 | 34 | 15 | 23 | 43 | 16 | 44 | 36 |
| 35 | 37 | 61 | 24 | 14 | 43 | 37 | 27 | 36 |
| 25 | 36 | 26 | 5 | 44 | 13 | 33 | 33 | 17 |
| 56 | 17 | 26 | 5 | 14 | 23 | 45 | 59 | 19 |
| 37 | 42 | 32 | 29 | 90 | 44 | 46 | 45 | 66 |
| 28 | 75 | 32 | 31 | 52 | 49 | 65 | 54 | 15 |
| 59 | 61 | 40 | 41 | 43 | 49 | 38 | 31 | 19 |
| 45 | 41 | 38 | 14 | 57 | 25 | 20 | 15 | 16 |

a. Construct a frequency distribution of the data.

b. Using the frequency distribution, construct the cumulative frequency distribution and the cumulative percentage distribution.

c. Calculate $Q_1$, $Q_2$, and $Q_3$.

d. What percentage of the patrons watch 22 or fewer movies a year?

e. The store owner decides to use these data to start a new marketing campaign called the Movie of the Week Club. People who rent, on average, a movie a week will receive a 10% discount. What percentage of the clientele currently rents a movie a week (i.e., 52 or more movies a year)?

4. The head nurse of an emergency room in a small town is interested in the number of trauma cases seen each weekend (Friday at 5:00 P.M. to Sunday at 5:00 P.M.). The following are the number of cases seen each weekend for the past 52 weeks.

| | | | | | | | | | | |
|---|---|---|---|---|---|---|---|---|---|---|
| 67 | 75 | 63 | 71 | 65 | 73 | 71 | 88 | 61 | 65 | 56 |
| 62 | 58 | 72 | 66 | 76 | 77 | 75 | 61 | 70 | 64 | 71 |
| 63 | 61 | 63 | 64 | 62 | 69 | 60 | 66 | 78 | 92 | 64 |
| 64 | 69 | 64 | 65 | 75 | 72 | 67 | 88 | 74 | 65 | 73 |
| 78 | 62 | 68 | 69 | 67 | 57 | 65 | 58 | | | |

a. Construct a stem-and-leaf plot of the data and a distribution of emergency cases.

    **b.** Construct a frequency distribution of these data.

    **c.** Calculate the cumulative frequency and cumulative percentage for each number of cases.

    **d.** Assume that the nurse has been told by his supervisor that he must staff the ward as if there would be 70 cases each weekend. Assuming that next year's figures will be the same, what is the likelihood (i.e., the percentage of time) that the emergency room will be caught short of staff?

5. Draw a graph that represents each of the following types of data.
   **a.** positive skew
   **b.** negative skew
   **c.** normal distribution
   **d.** platykurtic distribution
   **e.** leptokurtic distribution

6. A teacher interested in reading ability administers tests to third graders from four elementary schools from different parts of the state. The frequency distribution for each of the four schools is presented in the accompanying table. The numbers in the first column are the raw scores for the test, and the number of students within each of these classes is indicated in the columns A through D.

| | CLASS | | | |
|---|---|---|---|---|
| Test Score | A | B | C | D |
| 20 | 1 | 0 | 6 | 5 |
| 19 | 8 | 11 | 8 | 15 |
| 18 | 12 | 28 | 16 | 15 |
| 17 | 15 | 11 | 6 | 12 |
| 16 | 11 | 0 | 9 | 3 |
| 15 | 3 | 0 | 5 | 0 |

    **a.** Relatively speaking, would it be fair to say that the pattern of results is the same for all four schools?

    **b.** Of the four schools, which shows evidence of a negative skew?

    **c.** Of the four schools, which shows evidence of a positive skew?

    **d.** Of the four schools, which distribution of scores appears to be most leptokurtic?

    **e.** What is the 50th percentile for each of the schools?

7. Describe the shape of the distributions you would expect if you were to graph each of the following.
   **a.** Annual income of U.S. families
   **b.** Heights of all women between ages 18 and 24
   **c.** Heights of all men between ages 18 and 24
   **d.** Heights of all men and women between ages 18 and 24
   **e.** IQs of children in a high school for talented and gifted students

8. The teachers of an advanced placement math class and an English class administered achievement tests to their students at the end of the term. The results of the two tests are presented in the table on page 71.
   **a.** Describe the two distributions of data.
   **b.** What are some reasonable explanations for the difference in performance between the two achievement tests?
   **c.** A local college is willing to give college credit (e.g., Math 100 or English 100) to students who score at or above the 80th percentile. What

### ACHIEVEMENT TEST SCORES

| Score | Math f | English f | Score | Math f | English f |
|-------|--------|-----------|-------|--------|-----------|
| 50 | 5 | 2 | 43 | 9 | 22 |
| 49 | 12 | 3 | 42 | 6 | 11 |
| 48 | 18 | 5 | 41 | 4 | 9 |
| 47 | 19 | 8 | 40 | 3 | 6 |
| 46 | 26 | 12 | 39 | 1 | 4 |
| 45 | 19 | 24 | 38 | 2 | 2 |
| 44 | 13 | 35 | | | |

scores are required for each test to receive credit? Approximately how many students will receive college math credit? How many will receive college English credit?

**d.** What would be the advantage, if any, of plotting these data using a stem-and-leaf plot?

**9.** A local Sunday newspaper has a large headline that reads "VIOLENT CRIME IN NORMALTOWN SKYROCKETS!!!" According to the article, the number of violent crimes this year was 566, a 15.5% increase over last year's number of 490. The editorial is an angry statement about how the police are doing a poor job of keeping the peace and ends with a demand that the chief of police resign immediately. Here are some interesting data. The accompanying table lists the population of Normaltown for the past 10 years and the violent crimes reported to the police.

| Year | Population | Violent Crimes |
|------|------------|----------------|
| 1989 | 23,450 | 294 |
| 1990 | 25,632 | 323 |
| 1991 | 25,700 | 282 |
| 1992 | 26,591 | 372 |
| 1993 | 29,781 | 387 |
| 1994 | 33,354 | 401 |
| 1995 | 37,022 | 410 |
| 1996 | 42,575 | 425 |
| 1997 | 48,961 | 490 |
| 1998 | 57,773 | 566 |

**a.** Calculate the percentage of violent crimes as a percentage of the population.

**b.** Do you believe that the newspaper is justified in its claim that crime is "skyrocketing"?

**c.** Do you think that it is more appropriate to report the crime rate as a percentage of the population? Why?

**10.** Imagine that you have a population of 12 numbers. The numbers are

1   1   2   2   3   3   4   4   5   5   6   6

As you can see, there are two of each number. Now imagine that you write each number on a slip of paper and put the slips of paper into a hat. You then draw two slips of paper from the hat and record the total for the two slips (e.g., 3 + 4 = 7).

**a.** Make a table of all possible combinations of numbers. (Hint: 3 + 4 is one combination and 4 + 3 is another combination. Therefore, there will be 36 possible combinations.)

**b.** Create a frequency distribution of the totals of the two numbers.

**c.** Based on your frequency table, what is the most frequently occurring total?

**11.** Imagine that you have a population of 14 numbers. The numbers are:

0   0   1   1   2   2   3   3   4   4   5   5   6  6

As you can see, there are two of each number. Now imagine that you write each number on a slip of paper and put the slips of paper into a hat. You then draw two slips of paper from the hat and record the total of the two slips (e.g., 3 + 4 = 7).

**a.** Make a table of all possible combinations of numbers. (Hint: 3 + 4 is one combination and 4 + 3 is another combination. Therefore, there will be 49 possible combinations.)

**b.** Create a frequency distribution of the two numbers.

**c.** Based on your frequency table, what is the most frequently occurring total?

# 4

# Measures of Central Tendency

## 4.1 / Introduction

One of the greatest sources of confusion and, perhaps, a cause for suspicion that statistics is more art than science revolves around the term "average." Television programming is said to be prepared for the average viewer; newspaper articles are written for the average fourth-grade reader; politicians express a deep concern for the welfare of the average voter; and the average family has an average of 1.8 children. Sometimes the term "average" is used as a synonym for "normal." If the temperature for a given day approaches the long-term average for the day, the TV meteorologist assures us that the day was normal even if the temperature was 95°.

In all these situations, the average represents the typical value or condition. Most people use the concept of average as a representative of some larger idea or collection of information. In a way, this is also how statisticians use the concept of average. However, because the word "average" is used in such a wide variety of contexts it no longer has a precise meaning. The word average may mean different things in different situations. Consider the case of the average wage of a worker when viewed by either the union or by management. Each side may cite statistics that are much different from the other. Management may argue that the average worker's pay is $24,000. The union negotiators, using the same data, may argue that the average worker's pay is much lower, $18,000. How can it be that both report an average, yet both cite different figures?

The problem is that there are many legitimate ways to calculate an average. Each method has its advantages and disadvantages, and its specific uses. Because of this and the lack of precision with which people use the term in everyday language, many statisticians prefer to use the phrase **measure of central tendency.** The different measures of central tendency all serve the same purpose—they are descriptive statistics that help us summarize and describe our data. In a general sense, measures of central tendency describe the typical or more commonly occurring observation in a set of data. In this chapter we will examine the more technical definition of central tendency and three of the most commonly used measures of central tendency, the mode, median, and mean.

## 4.2 / Three Common Measures of Central Tendency

There are three commonly used measures of central tendency. We will begin with a general definition of each of these measures and then continue with more specific and operational definitions. The first measure of central tendency, the **mode,** is the most frequently occurring score in the distribution. Of the three measures of central tendency, the mode is the easiest to calculate. The second measure of central tendency is the **median.** The median is the score in the middle of the distribution of scores. The third measure of central tendency is the **mean,** or what some statisticians call the **arithmetic mean.** The mean represents the sum of all the scores in a data set divided by the number of scores.

The data presented in Table 4.1 represent how the three different measures of central tendency are calculated and why each has a different value. Let's assume that these data represent the annual salaries of a corporation. In this fictitious corporation there are 15 employees. The

---

■ **Measures of Central Tendency:**

Descriptive statistics that summarize and describe data. The mode, median, and mean are measures of central tendency. They summarize data by describing the most typical or representative value in the data set.

■ **Mode:**

A measure of central tendency that represents the most frequently occurring score in a data set.

■ **Median:**

A measure of central tendency that represents the midpoint of the distribution of scores. One-half the scores fall above and one-half below this point.

■ **Mean:**

A measure of central tendency calculated by adding all the scores in a data set and dividing by the number of scores.

**Table** | **4.1**

| Annual Salaries of Management and Employees of XYZ Company

| | |
|---|---|
| $ 72,000.00 | **Mean:** Sum of scores divided by number |
| 54,000.00 | of scores. |
| 26,400.00 | Mean: $\bar{X} = \dfrac{\Sigma X}{N}$   $\dfrac{\$360,000.00}{15} = \$24,000.00$ |
| 24,000.00 ← Mean | Mean = $24,000.00 |

| | |
|---|---|
| | **Median:** Locate the score in the middle |
| 19,200.00 | of the distribution, the 50th percentile. |
| 19,200.00 | $ML = \dfrac{N + 1}{2} = 8$ |
| 19,200.00 | Count up or down to the 8th score. |
| 18,000.00 ← Median | Median = $18,000.00 |

| | |
|---|---|
| 16,800.00 | |
| 16,800.00 | |
| 16,800.00 | |
| 14,400.00 ⎫ | |
| 14,400.00 ⎪ | **Mode:** The most frequently occurring |
| 14,400.00 ⎬ ← Mode | score. |
| 14,400.00 ⎭ | Mode = $14,400.00 |

$\Sigma X = \$360,000.00$      $N = 15$

highest paid employee earns $72,000 a year, the lowest paid employee makes $14,400 a year. The table presents the location of each measure of central tendency and how it is calculated. It is easy to see how management and labor might argue about the average wage of an employee of the corporation.

Labor could use the mode, $14,400, to make its case that the typical worker is underpaid. Management, looking at the arithmetic mean ($24,000) of all the salaries, can argue that the typical employee at the corporation is well paid. A third party, such as a mediator, could concentrate on the median $18,000 as being the wage of the typical employee. Given the differences among these measures of central tendency, it is not surprising that there will be much confusion about which value best represents the wage of the typical employee. It is no wonder that Disraeli once exclaimed that "There are three kinds of lies: lies, damned lies, and statistics!" In spite of such sentiments, each measure of central tendency provides a different way of summarizing our data. To determine when it is appropriate to use each, we will need to examine them in greater detail.

# 4.3 / The Mode

Of all measures of central tendency, the mode is most easily found as it is obtained by inspection rather than by computation. The mode is simply the score that occurs with greatest frequency in a set of data. In Table 4.1, the salary with the greatest frequency is $14,400. Thus, the modal salary equals $14,400.

As it turns out, the mode is not that useful a statistic among behavioral scientists. As a descriptive statistic it is not precise, and the number is rarely used to describe the data especially when the data represent an ordinal, interval, or ratio scale. Most researchers prefer to report the mean or the median if the data are at least at the ordinal level of measurement. There are some situations in which the mode can be useful, however.

First, the mode is easily identified in exploratory data analysis. It is useful in describing the shape of a frequency distribution. In some distributions there may be two high points that produce the appearance of two humps, as on a camel's back. Such distributions are called **bimodal.** Distributions containing more than two humps are called **multimodal.** Each mode in a multimodal distribution need not have exactly equal frequencies. It is sufficient that they stand out from the remainder of the distribution.

Look at the stem-and-leaf plot in Figure 4.1 which presents the grades on an exam. As you can see, the distribution seems to be bimodal with a clustering of scores in the 60s and in the 80s. What could account for these results? Many factors could contribute to results like these. Frequently, multimodal distributions suggest that there are distinct subgroups within the sample. Perhaps the class has first-year students who did poorly on the exam and the others are seniors who did relatively well. Whatever the reason for the bimodality, we can use the concepts of mode, bimodality, and multimodal distributions to describe the data to others.

We must use the mode when the data are nominal level. Count the number of men and women in your statistics class. Are there more men or women? Your answer is the mode. Likewise, which academic program at your school has the greatest number of majors? Again, the report is the mode. When we use a nominal scale, the mode is the measure of central tendency that we can report since it does not make sense to calculate the "average sex" or the "median major."

## 4.4 / The Median

The median is defined as that score or potential score that divides the distribution in half. Half the scores are below the median and half are above the median. In other words, the median is merely a special case of a percentile rank. Indeed, the median is the score at the 50th percentile. As we saw in Table 4.1, the median salary is $18,000.

### The Median of an Array of Scores

The location of the median is easily identified with a small number of scores. Consider the following seven intelligence test scores.

| 128 | 104 | 117 | 123 | 96 | 124 | 115 |

We can use these data to examine how to calculate the median. The procedure is similar to that described in Chapter 3 for calculating $Q_2$, the 50th percentile.

**Step 1** Arrange the numbers from lowest to highest.

| 96 | 104 | 115 | 117 | 123 | 124 | 128 |

**Step 2** To locate the median, add 1 to the number of scores and divide the total by 2. In this example, the number of observations is 7. Therefore:

---

**■ Bimodal Distribution:**

A frequency distribution with two concentrations of scores.

**■ Multimodal Distributions:**

Distributions that contain more than two concentrations of scores.

```
7
6    5
5    4  6
7  4    3  2
6  3  1  2  1
7  5  0  0  0  0
5  0  0  0  0  0  0
---------------------------
4  5  6  7  8  9  10
```

**Figure 4.1**

Stem-and-leaf plot of grades on an exam.

$$\text{Median location} = \frac{N + 1}{2} = \frac{7 + 1}{2} = \frac{8}{2} = 4$$

**Step 3** Starting with the lowest score, count up to the median. In this example, count to the fourth score.

| 96 | 104 | 115 | **117** | 123 | 124 | 128 |

We find that the fourth score, the median, is 117. There are three scores below 117 and three above. The median divides the array of scores exactly in half. Be sure to note the difference between the median *location* and the value of the median.

If there is an even number of scores, the median is halfway between the two middle scores. Consider another set of test scores:

| 96 | 104 | **115** | ∧ | **117** | 123 | 124 |

$$\text{Median location} = \frac{N + 1}{2} = \frac{6 + 1}{2} = \frac{7}{2} = 3.5$$

The median is located halfway between the third and fourth scores, 115 and 117. Thus, the value of the median is $\frac{(115 + 117)}{2} = 116$.

## The Median of a Frequency Distribution

Table 4.2 shows a frequency and cumulative frequency distribution of the scores made by 30 students on a Test of Narcissism. Calculating the median from a cumulative frequency distribution requires just a few simple steps:

**Step 1** Divide $N + 1$ by 2 to find the *location* of the middle frequency. In the present example, $N + 1 = 31$. Thus, the middle frequency is $\frac{31}{2} = 15.5$—between the 15th and 16th scores.

**Step 2** This value falls between the lower and upper limits of a score of 11.5 and 12.5. You can select the midpoint of that class—a score of 12—and identify it as the median. For most purposes, this is a satisfactory estimate of the median.

**Table** 4.2

**Cumulative Frequency Distribution of Thirty Scores Obtained on a Test of Narcissism**

| | X | f | Cum f | |
|---|---|---|---|---|
| | 20 | 1 | 30 ← total number of subjects | |
| | 19 | 1 | 29 | |
| | 18 | 1 | 28 | |
| | 17 | 2 | 27 | |
| | 16 | 1 | 25 | |
| | 15 | 4 | 24 | |
| | 14 | 2 | 20 | |
| | 13 | 2 | 18 | |
| 12.5 > | **12** | **3** | **16** | <the 15.5th frequency is between the real limits of 11.5 and 12.5 |
| 11.5 > | 11 | 5 | 13 | |
| | 10 | 2 | 8 | |
| | 9 | 1 | 6 | |
| | 8 | 2 | 5 | |
| | 7 | 1 | 3 | |
| | 6 | 1 | 2 | |
| | 5 | 1 | 1 | |

■ **Arithmetic Mean ($\overline{X}$):**

The symbol is called "X bar." It is the measure of central tendency that is the sum of all the values in the data set divided by N.

$$\overline{X} = \frac{\Sigma X}{N}$$

## 4.5 / The Arithmetic Mean

When people speak of the average, they typically refer to the **arithmetic mean.** In this section, we'll show you how to calculate the mean from a set of scores and from a frequency distribution. First, let's review some symbols introduced in Chapter 2.

1. Letters of the alphabet, such as X and Y, represent variables. Subscript *numbers* identify a particular value of the variable. Thus, $X_1$ represents the first value in the data set, X. Subscript *letters* identify a specific group or condition. For example, $X_E$ may identify the Experimental group and $X_C$ the Control group.
2. The summation sign, $\Sigma$, instructs us to add the values of the variable that follows it. Thus, $\Sigma X_E$ instructs us to add together all the values of the variable X in the experimental group.
3. The letter *f* means frequency and N the number of cases. When you add together all the frequencies, $\Sigma f$, you obtain N. Thus, $\Sigma f = N$.
4. $X_N$ refers to the Nth score in the array. If you have 11 scores, $X_N$ refers to the 11th score.

### Calculating the Mean from a Set of Scores

You are probably intimately familiar with the arithmetic mean, for whenever you obtain an average grade by summing the grades (i.e., the values of the variable grades) and dividing by the number of grades (i.e., N), you are calculating the arithmetic mean. In short, the mean is the sum of the scores or values of the variable divided by their number. Stated in algebraic form:

$$\overline{X} = \frac{\Sigma X}{N} \qquad (4.1)$$

or

$$\overline{X} = \frac{X_1 + X_2 + X_3 + \dots X_N}{N}$$

where

$\overline{X}$   represents the arithmetic mean. The symbol is pronounced "X bar." Recall that we use the Roman alphabet to describe the data in a sample and Greek letters to represent population parameters. Therefore, $\overline{X}$ represents the sample mean and $\mu$ represents the population mean.

$N$   The number of scores or values of the variable.

$\Sigma X$   The symbol that directs us to sum all the measurements in the data set $X$.

Thus, the arithmetic mean of the scores 8, 12, 15, 19, 25 is:

$$\overline{X} = \frac{8 + 12 + 15 + 19 + 25}{5}$$
$$\overline{X} = \frac{79}{5}$$
$$\overline{X} = 15.8$$

## An Example

In the fall of 1997 much of the world was shocked to hear of the unexpected death of Princess Diana in an automobile accident in Paris. As part of a larger study of memory, one of the authors of this text surveyed undergraduates for their reaction to hearing the news. The students were asked to rate the intensity of their reaction on a scale of 1 to 10, with a rating of 1 being the least reaction and a rating of 10 the strongest. Table 4.3 presents the results of some selected responses of males and females.

**Table** | **4.3**

**Reported Reactions of Males and Females to News of the Death of Princess Diana**

| Male Ratings $X_M$ | Female Ratings $X_F$ |
|:---:|:---:|
| 2 | 7 |
| 6 | 3 |
| 3 | 5 |
| 5 | 8 |
| 4 | 6 |
| $\Sigma X_M = 20$ | $\Sigma X_F = 29$ |
| $N_M = 5$ | $N_F = 5$ |
| $\overline{X}_M = 4.0$ | $\overline{X}_F = 5.8$ |

The ratings are based on a scale of 1 to 10 where 1 is the least and 10 is the strongest reaction. Illustration based on selected data.

Although over 100 students participated in the study, selected responses are used to illustrate the calculations. And did the researchers find differences between the sexes in the overall study? Well, yes. The responses reported by males were, *on average,* slightly less intense than those reported by females.

### Obtaining the Mean from a Frequency Distribution

Most researchers prefer to use a computer to calculate their descriptive statistics. There are times when it is more convenient to use a calculator. Here is an example of how to calculate the mean from a distribution of scores. We can use Table 4.4 as an example. The procedure is particularly useful if the data set includes many repetitive scores. Each score, $X$, is multiplied by its frequency to obtain $fX$. These values are then summed to obtain the sum of all the scores.

## 4.6
## Some Properties of the Mean

As you will see in subsequent chapters, the mean is one of the most used statistics in the behavioral sciences. Later we will examine statistics that allow us to compare the relative differences between means and statistics that use the mean as an essential step in the computational process.

**Table 4.4**

**Calculating the Mean from a Frequency Distribution**

| Stem-and-Leaf | Frequency Distribution | | |
|---|---|---|---|
|  | $X$ | $f$ | $fX$ |
|  | 20 | 1 | 20 |
|  | 19 | 1 | 19 |
|  | 18 | 1 | 18 |
|  | 17 | 2 | 34 |
|  | 16 | 1 | 16 |
|  | 15 | 4 | 60 |
| * | 14 | 2 | 28 |
| • 567889 | 13 | 2 | 26 |
| 1* 00111112223344 | 12 | 3 | 36 |
| 1• 555567789 | 11 | 5 | 55 |
| 2* 0 | 10 | 2 | 20 |
| 2• | 9 | 1 | 9 |
|  | 8 | 2 | 16 |
|  | 7 | 1 | 7 |
|  | 6 | 1 | 6 |
|  | 5 | 1 | 5 |
|  |  | $N = 30$ | $\Sigma fx = 375$ |

$$\overline{X} = \frac{\Sigma fX}{N} = \frac{375}{30} = 12.5$$

If you are using a calculator for your computations, check your instructions to review the use of the memory function. You can save time by multiplying the frequency by the score and saving it in memory. Check to see how the function works in your calculator.

**Table 4.5**

**Two Data Sets Demonstrating That the Sum of the Differences Between the Mean and Each Score is 0**

| $X$ | $(X - \overline{X})$ | $Y$ | $(Y - \overline{Y})$ |
|---|---|---|---|
| 1 | $(1 - 3.0) = -2$ | 4 | $(4 - 6.0) = -2$ |
| 3 | $(3 - 3.0) = 0$ | 6 | $(6 - 6.0) = 0$ |
| 7 | $(7 - 3.0) = 4$ | 10 | $(10 - 6.0) = 4$ |
| 4 | $(4 - 3.0) = 1$ | 7 | $(7 - 6.0) = 1$ |
| 0 | $(0 - 3.0) = -3$ | 3 | $(3 - 6.0) = -3$ |

$\Sigma X = 15$  $\Sigma(X - \overline{X}) = 0$  $\Sigma Y = 30$  $\Sigma(Y - \overline{Y}) = 0$
$N_X = 5$  $N_Y = 5$
$\overline{X} = 3.0$  $\overline{Y} = 6.0$

Because of the importance of the mean, you should understand some of the characteristics of this important statistic.

**Summed Deviations About the Mean Equal Zero**   One of the most important properties of the mean is that it is the point in a distribution of scores or measurements about which the summed deviations or the sum of the distances from the mean are equal to zero. If we were to subtract the mean from each score and then add together the resulting deviations, the sum would equal zero. Symbolically,

$$\Sigma(X - \overline{X}) = 0$$

To illustrate, look at the data set in Table 4.5. There are two sets of data represented by variables $X$ and $Y$. The means for the two groups are 3.0 and 6.0, respectively. If we subtract the mean from a score we calculate a **deviation score.** The sum of the deviation scores is always 0 regardless of the type of numbers, the size of the mean, or other characteristics of the data.

Therefore, the mean is the score that balances the distances or deviations of all the scores on either side of it. In many ways, the mean is analogous to the balance point of a seesaw.

**Sensitivity to Extreme Scores**   When you were a child playing on a seesaw, you may have noticed that it is possible for a light person to balance a heavy person if the latter moves closer (is less deviant) to the fulcrum (the mean). This analogy leads to a second important characteristic of the mean—the mean is very sensitive to extreme measurements.

The mean is the score that balances the respective weights of numbers in a distribution. Think about two people on a seesaw, a light person and a heavy person. To balance the seesaw, the balance point must be moved toward the heavier person. The same is true with a group of numbers. Extremely large or extremely small scores will change the mean of a sample.

Consider the salary data in Table 4.1. The mean of the distribution is $24,000. The mean is pulled upward in the direction of the extreme salaries at the upper end of the scale. In contrast, the median is $18,000. The median is not sensitive to extreme scores since the location of the median depends on the *number* of scores in the distribution, not the *values* of the scores.

The sensitivity of the mean relative to the median is illustrated in Table 4.6. Note that the median of each distribution is 3 even though the

**Deviation Score:**

The difference between the score and the mean $(X - \overline{X})$. The sum of deviation scores is always 0, $\Sigma(X - \overline{X}) = 0$.

**Table** | 4.6

**Five Distributions and Their Respective Means and Medians**

|  | **A** | **B** | **C** | **D** | **E** |
|---|---|---|---|---|---|
|  | 5 | 15 | 25 | 5 | 20 |
|  | 4 | 4 | 24 | 4 | 4 |
|  | 3 | 3 | 3 | 3 | 3 |
|  | 2 | 2 | 2 | 2 | 2 |
|  | 1 | 1 | 1 | −14 | −14 |
| $\overline{X}$ | 3 | 5 | 11 | 0 | 3 |
| Median | 3 | 3 | 3 | 3 | 3 |

values differ at the extreme of each distribution. The mean of each distribution varies according to the values at either end of the distribution.

As you can see in Figure 4.2, the mean moves toward the extreme score or scores in the distribution.

**The Sum of the Squared Deviations Are Least About the Mean**   A third important characteristic of the mean involves the **sum of squares (SS),** which is the sum of the squared deviations of scores. The sum of squares about the mean is less than the sum of squares about any other score or potential score in the distribution. Table 4.7 illustrates this characteristic of the mean. It shows the squares and sum of squares when deviations are taken from the mean and various other scores in a distribution. The sum of the squares is smallest in Column 4 where deviations are taken from the mean. In other words, the mean is always the point about which the sum of the squares is minimum.

You might better understand this important property of the mean if you play tennis or racquetball. The notion is related to standing in the center of the court rather than on either side. Take a look at Figure 4.3. The mean (0) is identified by the position you have taken on the court. Your goal is to reach the ball by taking as few steps as possible. To train you to stay in center court, your tennis instructor imposes the following rules: one step will cost you $1; two steps $4 ($2^2 = $4$); three steps $9 ($3^2 = $9$); four steps $16 ($4^2 = $16$), and so on. You don't know on which side of

■ **Sum of Squares (SS):**

The sum of the squared deviation scores about the mean, $\Sigma(X - \overline{X})^2$. The sum of squares is always minimal about the mean.

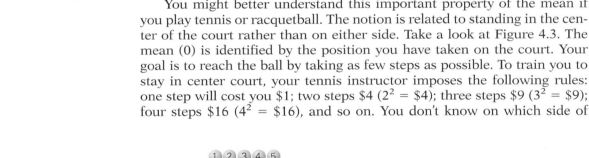
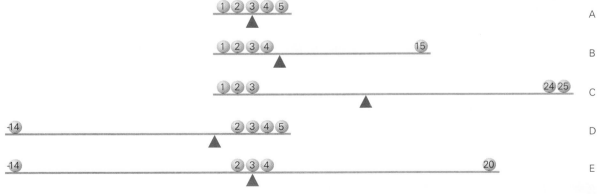

**Figure** | 4.2

Graphical representation of the five distributions presented in Table 4.6. The ▲ represents the mean of the data.

**Table 4.7**

The Squares and Sums of Squared Deviations Taken from Various Scores in a Distribution

| 1 X | 2 $(X-2)^2$ | 3 $(X-3)^2$ | 4 $(X-\overline{X})^2$ | 5 $(X-5)^2$ | 6 $(X-6)^2$ |
|---|---|---|---|---|---|
| 2 | 0 | 1 | 4 | 9 | 16 |
| 3 | 1 | 0 | 1 | 4 | 9 |
| 4 | 4 | 1 | 0 | 1 | 4 |
| 5 | 9 | 4 | 1 | 0 | 1 |
| 6 | 16 | 9 | 4 | 1 | 0 |
| $\Sigma$  20 | 30 | 15 | 10 | 15 | 30 |

$N = 5 \quad \overline{X} = \dfrac{20}{5} = 4.0$

*Mean = 4*

your court the ball will land. What you do know is that if you stand in the middle, the maximum number of steps you will have to take is three and the maximum loss is $9. If you stand on either the left side or the right side, you might have to take six steps, in which case the game could get very expensive indeed—a hefty $36. Standing in the middle would minimize your steps, your costs, and the energy you would have to expend.

Given our review of the computation and the properties of the mean, we can now provide a more detailed definition of the mean. The fact that the sum of squares about the mean is always minimized is sometimes called the concept of **least squares.** Again the value of the mean as a measure of central tendency is that it represents the smallest average difference between itself and the scores in the data. The least-squares method is a recurrent concept in statistics and one that we will encounter when we examine more advanced statistics such as regression and curve fitting.

■ **Least squares:**

The sum of squared differences between the mean and individual scores is minimal, that is, $\Sigma(X - \overline{X})^2$ is minimal.

## 4.7 The Weighted Mean

There are many times when we want to combine the results of several groups and calculate the mean of the overall group. In this situation it is appropriate to calculate a weighted mean which is a form of mean obtained from groups of data in which the different sizes of the groups are accounted for by weighting.

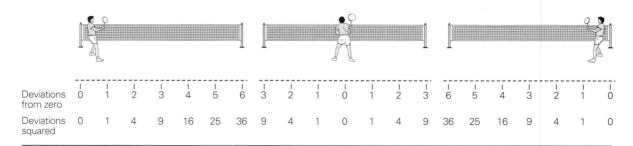

| Deviations from zero | 0 | 1 | 2 | 3 | 4 | 5 | 6 | 3 | 2 | 1 | 0 | 1 | 2 | 3 | 6 | 5 | 4 | 3 | 2 | 1 | 0 |
| Deviations squared | 0 | 1 | 4 | 9 | 16 | 25 | 36 | 9 | 4 | 1 | 0 | 1 | 4 | 9 | 36 | 25 | 16 | 9 | 4 | 1 | 0 |

**Figure 4.3**

Illustration of the squared deviations or distances from a point. When the tennis player stands in the center, the distance to reach the ball and the squared deviations are minimized.

Let's suppose that the average scores of four introductory psychology classes were: 75, 78, 72, and 80. To calculate the overall mean of the four classes, could you sum the four means together and divide by 4 (the number of means)? This could be done legitimately only if the number of students in each class is identical. What if, as a matter of fact, the mean of 75 is based on $N = 30$, the second mean is based on 40 grades, the third on $N = 25$, and the fourth on $N = 50$? When the size of the groups differ, we must calculate a **weighted mean** if we are to have an accurate measure of central tendency for the group as a whole.

To obtain the weighted mean, we need the mean and the sample size of each group. Then we apply the procedures used to calculate the mean from a frequency distribution. We regard each sample mean as if it is a score and the $N$ of each group as its frequency. The sample mean $\overline{X}$ is multiplied by $f$ to obtain $f\overline{X}$ as in Table 4.8. Note that it is not necessary to arrange these means in any particular order unless you wish to calculate the median of the sample means, which is rarely if ever done.

As you see, the weighted mean equals 77.03. Had we merely summed the sample means and divided by 4, we would have obtained an incorrect value of $\frac{305}{4} = 76.25$. Weighted means are often used when we want to do such things as obtain the average (mean) of all sections of a college course, to calculate the average amount we paid per share of stock at different prices or to calculate the lifetime batting average of a baseball player who obtained different averages per year based on different numbers of times officially at bat. The same principle applies when you calculate a grade point average (GPA). The GPA is a weighted average that takes into account each grade and the number of credits associated with each grade. As we have all learned, an A in a 2 credit course doesn't "weigh" as much as an A in a 4 credit course. Fortunately, neither does a D in a 2 credit course weigh as much as a D in a 4 credit course.

■ **Weighted Mean:**

A form of mean obtained from groups of data in which the different sizes of the groups are accounted for or weighted.

## 4.8 / Comparing the Mean, Median, and Mode

Table 4.9 summarizes the frequently used measures of central tendency. Given the choice of these measures of central tendency, which is the best one to use for a given set of data? Before considering the various facets of this

**Table 4.8**

**Obtaining the Weighted Mean by Regarding Each Sample Mean as a Score and Its Associated $N$ as a Frequency and Using Procedures for Calculating the Mean from a Frequency Distribution**

| $\overline{X}$ | $f$ | $f(\overline{X})$ | Computation |
|---|---|---|---|
| 75 | 30 | 2250 | |
| 78 | 40 | 3120 | $\overline{X}_W = \dfrac{\Sigma f(\overline{X})}{N_{total}}$ |
| 72 | 25 | 1800 | $\overline{X}_W = \dfrac{11,170}{145}$ |
| 80 | 50 | 4000 | $\overline{X}_W = 77.03$ |
| $N_{total} = 145$ | | $\Sigma f(\overline{X}) = 11,170$ | |

$\overline{X}_w$ is the Weighted Mean and $N_{total}$ is the Sum of the Frequency of Means.

**Table** 4.9

Summary of Frequently Used Measures of Central Tendency

| Measure | When used | Caution |
|---|---|---|
| Mode | Easy to obtain measure for nominal data. | Not precise. Gives very little information. Can be misleading. |
| Median | Useful when you want to know the midpoint of a distribution or if distribution is skewed. | Not sensitive to extreme scores. |
| Mean | The arithmetic average. Easily obtained, frequently used, and widely understood measure of central tendency. | Very sensitive to extreme scores. Can be misleading if outliers are present or if distribution is skewed. |
| Weighted mean | When overall mean of several groups of different sizes is needed. | Very important to use weighting, especially with much variation in size of subgroups. |

question, we will dispense with the mode as a leading candidate for use in the behavioral sciences. Because the mode is obtained by inspection rather than by computation, it is the appropriate statistic whenever a quick, rough estimate is desired or only when the most frequent value is of interest. The mode may also be useful in obtaining a quick estimate of the mean and median when the distribution of scores has one mode and is relatively symmetrical. Otherwise its use as a measure of central tendency is limited.

Apart from these considerations, we will restrict our discussion to the pros and cons of the mean and median as measures of central tendency. Specifically, we compare them in terms of ease of computation and sensitivity to skewness.

## Ease of Computation

Little justification can be made for selecting a measure of central tendency based on its ease of computation. With the increased accessibility of computers for data analysis, computational difficulty becomes, for all practical purposes, a nonissue. Once data are entered into a data file, all you need to do is type a command or choose the desired statistic from the menu. You should select the measure of central tendency most appropriate to the data and to the question being asked.

It is legitimate to consider the audience, the people who will be reading the results of your research. Most audiences will immediately understand the concept of arithmetic mean. The median is less widely understood and usually requires an explanation of its meaning. Sometimes it is appropriate to present both the mean and the median. Each provides a different measure of central tendency and, when taken together, furnish an indication of skewness in the distribution.

## Skewness

When there are extreme scores at one end of any distribution, we speak of the distribution as being **skewed.** In other words, the distribution is not symmetrical and has more scores spread out at one end of

■ **Skew:**

A descriptive term used to describe a distribution of data that is not symmetrical.

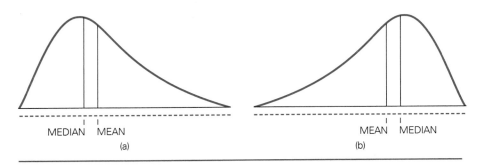

MEDIAN MEAN
(a)

MEAN MEDIAN
(b)

**Figure** | **4.4**
| **The relation between the mean and the median in (a) positively and (b) negatively skewed distributions.**

**▨ Outliers:**

An extreme score or scores at the end of the distribution.

**▨ Positive Skew:**

Refers to a skewed distribution which has a greater proportion of scores at the lower end of the scale than the upper end. The mean is greater than the median.

**▨ Negative Skew:**

Refers to a skewed distribution which has a greater proportion of scores at the upper end of the scale than the lower end. The mean is less than the median.

the distribution than the other. Scores that are a substantial distance away from the mean and the rest of the scores are sometimes called **outliers.** If there are extreme scores on the positive end of the scale (toward the right on the horizontal axis), the **skew is positive.** On the other hand, a **negatively skewed** distribution has a few scores further away from the mean at the left (negative) end of the horizontal axis. As a rule, when the mean is less than the median, the distribution is negatively skewed. When the mean is greater than the median, the data are positively skewed. Figure 4.4 illustrates both positive and negative skew. Note that the mean is pulled in the direction of the skew while the median is not. The mean is to the right of the median in a positively skewed distribution (a) and to the left of the median when there is negative skew (b).

When there is marked skewness in a distribution, the mean is an inappropriate measure of central tendency. Annual income, for example, is frequently reported in terms of median income rather than mean income. Why? Because the distribution of annual income is not symmetric. The income of a large proportion of people is at the lower end of the scale. Income does not go below zero but there is no similar restraint on the upper end of the scale where annual incomes may and do reach into the many millions of dollars. Similarly, the cost of a new home or the average length of hospital stay are both positively skewed distributions. For any such skewed distributions, the mean may be a very misleading statistic. Consider reporting both the mean and the median. Differences between the two measures indicate to the astute reader that the data are skewed and the direction of the skew.

**4.9**

**The Lake Wobegon Effect: All the Children Are Above Average**

Garrison Keillor describes what has now been known as the Lake Wobegon Effect. According to Keillor, all the children in the town of Lake Wobegon are "above average." How is it possible for all the children to be above average? The answer lies in how the children are to be compared. If the children are compared to each other, this statement cannot be true; there has to be an average and some of the children will be above or below the average. But what if a different comparison procedure is used?

All school-aged children take achievement tests during their primary school years. In many cases the state Board of Education supervises the administration of these tests. The results of the tests are then reported for the state and for each school district. It should come as no surprise that some school districts have average scores greater than or less than the state average. Because the average is assumed to be representative of all members of the group, a person could falsely assume that if the school district has a average achievement score greater than the state average, that all the children in the school district are better than average.

The Lake Wobegon Effect is really an example of the misinterpretation of the average. If we find that the average of a school district is greater than the state average, we can conclude "The average performance of students in our school district is better than the state average." It is incorrect to overgeneralize and assume that "as a consequence this proves that all our students are better than average."

## 4.10 / Putting It All Together

During the period from 1970–1971 through 1984–1985 there was a steady decline in the number of students graduating from American colleges who had majored in the natural sciences. Because we live in an increasingly technological world and because science majors provide the source from which future scientists are drawn, both the educational and the scientific community viewed this decline with concern. Many universities imposed distribution requirements; that is, they required students to take a certain number of courses outside their areas of concentration. Thus, chemistry majors find themselves enrolled in economics and poetry classes, and psychology majors find themselves in entomology and cartography courses. While this requirement may somewhat change the distribution of enrollments within departments, it is not generally believed that it alters the distribution of students majoring in certain departments.

Why is it that students decide to major in one department over another? Certainly interest in the subject matter is one factor. Future employment prospects may figure into the equation as well. However, two researchers at Williams College believe they have found evidence of a factor that has systematically and strongly influenced course enrollment over the years: *grades!*

Prompted by these concerns, Professors Richard Sabot and John Wakeman-Linn examined distributions of grades at their college and at seven other colleges and universities during the academic years 1962–1963 and 1985–1986. They found substantial inflation in the grades awarded during the latter period and, of more concern to them, the inflation was differential among departments. They present evidence of a "widening gap between low- and high-grading departments." (p.160)

Let's look at some of their findings. Table 4.10 lists the mean grades given in introductory courses taught by eight departments during two academic years. At the top of the first column, the mean grades given during 1962–1963 are presented. A 4-point scale was used, with A = 4, B = 3, and so on. A mean grade 2.62 given by the art departments is a little more than halfway between a C and a B. The average grade given in the psychology department in 1962–1963 was 2.64.

At the top of the second column you will find the percentages of grades earned that were above B+, that is, A− or A, during that period. The top of the third column shows the percentages of grades earned that were below a B−, that is C+ or lower. In the art department 9% of the grades earned were above B+ and 32% were below B−.

At the bottom portion of the first column, the grades given during the period 1985–1986 are presented. The authors divided the departments

Table | 4.10

Mean Grades and Their Distribution in Introductory Courses in Eight Departments, Williams College, 1962–1963 and 1985–1986

| Departments | Mean Grade | % above B+ | % below B− |
|---|---|---|---|
| **1962–1963** | | | |
| Art | 2.62 | 9% | 32% |
| Economics | 2.40 | 17% | 49% |
| English | 2.58 | 10% | 48% |
| Math | 2.09 | 9% | 65% |
| Music | 2.74 | 14% | 37% |
| Philosophy | 2.38 | 13% | 46% |
| Political Science | 2.43 | 8% | 55% |
| Psychology | 2.64 | 15% | 44% |
| **1985–1986** | | | |
| High-grading | | | |
| Art | 3.00 | 23% | 20% |
| English | 3.13 | 25% | 12% |
| Music | 3.26 | 28% | 17% |
| Philosophy | 2.94 | 20% | 17% |
| Political Science | 3.10 | 17% | 19% |
| Low-grading | | | |
| Economics | 2.67 | 15% | 42% |
| Math | 2.61 | 20% | 44% |
| Psychology | 2.71 | 17% | 37% |

*Source:* Richard Sabot and John Wakeman-Linn, (1991). *Journal of Economic Perspectives, 5,* No.1, Winter, 159–170.

into two groups, high-grading and low-grading departments. Examination of the mean grades given during the most recent period shows clearly that the mean grades have risen in every department. The percentages of students receiving grades higher than B+ have increased and the percentages of students receiving grades lower than B− have declined.

The authors of this study are concerned that the variation of grades among departments has increased. They do not feel, however, that it is a difference in the quality of the students that can account for the disparity in the grades awarded in the different departments. They have examined the SAT scores and grades earned in other courses by the students and have found negligible differences. Rather, they feel that it is the grading practices within departments that account for the differences. Further, they suspect that it is the grading practices that might be causing the erosion in the student enrollments in some departments. The failure of some departments to "hold the line" and stop grade inflation has led to a migration away from the departments that have the lowest amount of grade inflation. An interesting hypothesis!

Let's think about what we know concerning causal conclusions. Can we say that one factor clearly *causes* another? We could respond affirmatively to this interpretation if the results reflected the outcome of an experiment. Remember, only when a variable is manipulated under specific conditions are we able to state that one outcome is the cause of another. Since the researchers did not manipulate an independent variable but rather looked at two different time periods, they were only able to

**Table** 4.11

Percentage Increase in Mean Grades over Two Time Periods

|  | A | B | C | D |
|---|---|---|---|---|
|  | **Mean Grades 1962–1963** | **Mean Grades 1985–1986** | **Change in Grades B−A** | **% Change in Grades (C/A) × 100** |
| Art | 2.62 | 3.00 | 0.38 | 14.50* |
| Economics | 2.40 | 2.67 | 0.27 | 11.25 |
| English | 2.58 | 3.13 | 0.55 | 21.32 |
| Math | 2.09 | 2.61 | 0.52 | 24.88 |
| Music | 2.74 | 3.26 | 0.52 | 18.98 |
| Philosophy | 2.38 | 2.94 | 0.56 | 23.53 |
| Political Science | 2.43 | 3.10 | 0.67 | 27.57 |
| Psychology | 2.64 | 2.71 | 0.07 | 2.65 |

*To illustrate % change: Increase in mean art grade equals 3.00 − 2.62 = 0.38. The percentage of inflation is (0.38/2.62) × 100 = 14.50.

say that they found differences between the grades awarded 30 years ago and those given in the mid-1980s. In fact, the differences over the years may have been responsible for the migration of students from the sciences, but we cannot say with certainty.

Let's look more closely at the data and examine which grades increased the most during the time period. Table 4.11 lists the departments alphabetically. Column A shows the mean grade given during 1962–1963 by each department. Column B presents the same evidence during the 1985–1986 period. The differences between the grades awarded during these two time periods are presented in column C. As can be readily seen, the difference between the mean grade of 2.62 and 3.00 is 0.38.

Now look at column D. It contains the percentage *increase* in mean grades given by each department. In the art department, the average grade increased during the period by 14.5%. In the economics department, the grade inflation was over 11%. In contrast, there was less than a 3% increase in the psychology department. Political science and mathematics experienced the largest increases in average grades, more than 27% and almost 25% respectively.

Might we expect that there has been a disproportionate increase of students into the two departments because their average grades have increased the most? Perhaps, but we do not know. What is clear is that the examination of Table 4.11 provides us with a different picture than Table 4.10. Table 4.10 shows the mean grades by department for the two time periods. It further separates departments into two categories based on their *current* grading practices. In Table 4.11, it is not in the high-grading departments where the greatest grade inflation has occurred as measured by percentage increase in grades. In fact, it is in one of the low-grading departments, mathematics, where there has been one of the greatest increases in mean grades. Does this mean that mathematics departments are the "worst offenders" when it comes to grade inflation? Not necessarily. The lowest-grading department in 1962 was mathematics. It could evidence the largest *percentage increase* and still be among the lower-grading departments in 1985. Since it started with a lower base, the percentage increase will be larger. If there is anything that can be concluded from these data it is as follows: Be careful not to jump too quickly to conclusions. There are different ways to look at data, and it is important to examine your data from a variety of different perspectives in order for a fuller picture to emerge.

## CHAPTER SUMMARY

We began this chapter by observing that the word "average" is ambiguous and that its use often contributes to confusing issues rather than clarifying them. We then discussed, demonstrated the calculation of, and compared three indices of central tendency that are frequently used for the description of the central features of frequency distributions and arrays of scores: the mode, the median, and the mean.

We observed that the mean may be defined variously as the sum of the scores divided by their number and the point in a distribution about which the sum of the squared deviations is minimal. The median divides the distribution of score values into halves, so that the number of score values below the median equals the number of score values above the median. Finally, the mode is defined as the most frequently occurring score. We also examined the procedures for calculating the weighted mean of a set of sample means when each of the individual means is based on a different $N$ or numbers of observations.

Because it possesses special properties, the mean is the most frequently used measure of central tendency. However, the sensitivity of the mean to extreme score values that are not balanced on both sides of the distribution makes the median the measure of choice when distributions are markedly skewed.

We also demonstrated that the mean is drawn toward extreme scores in a distribution whereas the median is less affected by such scores. The difference between the mean and the median provides a way of identifying if a distribution is skewed and, if so, the direction of that skew.

## TERMS TO REMEMBER

| | |
|---|---|
| arithmetic mean | multimodal |
| bimodal | negative skew |
| deviation score | outliers |
| least squares | positive skew |
| mean | skew |
| measures of central tendency | sum of squares (SS) |
| median | weighted mean |
| mode | |

## EXERCISES

1. Find the mean, the median, and the mode for each of the following sets of measurements.
   **a.** 10, 8, 6, 0, 8, 3, 2, 5, 8, 0
   **b.** 1, 3, 3, 5, 5, 5, 7, 7, 9
   **c.** 119, 5, 4, 4, 4, 3, 1, 0

2. In which of the sets of measurements in Exercise 1 is the mean a poor measure of central tendency? Why?

3. For each of the sets of measurements in Exercise 1, show that the sum of the squares of deviations from the arithmetic mean is less than the sum of squares of deviations about any other score or potential score.

4. For each of the sets of measurements in Exercise 1, show that $\Sigma(X - \overline{X}) = 0$.

5. Tanya has calculated measures of central tendency on the weights of rats in the laboratory in terms of ounces. She decides to recompute these measures after dividing all the weights by 16 to convert them to pounds. How will this conversion affect the measures of central tendency?

6. You have calculated the maximum speed of various automobiles. You later discover that all the speedometers were set 5 miles per hour too fast. How will the measures of central tendency based on the corrected data compare with those calculated from the original data?

7. In exercise 1(c) if the score 119 were changed to a score of 19, how would the various measures of central tendency be affected?

8. On the basis of the following measures of central tendency, indicate whether or not there is evidence of skew and, if so, what its direction is.
   a. $\overline{X} = 56$, Median = 62      Mode = 68
   b. $\overline{X} = 68$, Median = 62      Mode = 56
   c. $\overline{X} = 62$, Median = 62      Mode = 62
   d. $\overline{X} = 62$, Median = 62      Mode = 30, Mode = 94

9. What is the nature of the distribution in Exercise 8(c) and (d)?

10. Calculate the mean of the following array of scores: 3, 4, 5, 5, 6, and 7.
    a. Add a constant, say, 2, to each score. Recalculate the mean.
       *Generalize:* What is the effect on the mean of adding a constant to all scores?
    b. Subtract the same constant from each score. Recalculate the mean.
       *Generalize:* What is the effect on the mean of subtracting a constant from all scores?
    c. Alternately add and subtract the same constant, say, 2, from the array of scores (that is, 3 + 2, 4 − 2, 5 + 2, etc.). Recalculate the mean,
       *Generalize:* What is the effect on the mean of adding and subtracting the same constant an equal number of times from an array of scores?
    d. Multiply each score by a constant, say, 2. Recalculate the mean.
       *Generalize:* What is the effect on the mean of multiplying each score by a constant?
    e. Divide each score by the same constant. Recalculate the mean.
       *Generalize:* What is the effect on the mean of dividing each score by a constant?

11. Sam has just finished reading in this chapter about the study of grades earned in introductory courses at Williams College. He sees that the mean grade for psychology is 2.71, whereas the mean grade in political science is 3.10. Based on this information he decides to switch his major to political science, where he feels it will be more likely he could receive an A in his courses. Do you think Sam's decision is appropriate based on these data?

12. The mean is usually more *reliable* than the median, that is, less subject to fluctuations. Suppose we conduct an experiment consisting of 30 tosses of three dice, obtaining the following results:

| | | | | | |
|---|---|---|---|---|---|
| 6,6,2 | 5,4,3 | 4,3,2 | 2,1,1 | 6,5,3 | 6,5,4 |
| 4,1,1 | 4,4,3 | 6,4,1 | 5,4,3 | 5,1,1 | 6,2,1 |
| 6,5,5 | 6,6,4 | 6,4,2 | 5,4,4 | 6,5,2 | 5,4,3 |
| 6,4,3 | 5,3,2 | 5,1,1 | 4,3,1 | 6,3,3 | 5,4,1 |
| 4,2,1 | 6,3,3 | 6,5,4 | 4,2,2 | 6,6,5 | 6,3,1 |

**a.** Calculate the 30 means.

**b.** Calculate the 30 medians.

**c.** Draw histograms for the two distributions. Do they support the contention that the mean is a more stable estimator of central tendency? Explain.

**13.** If we know that the mean and median of a set of scores are equal, what can we say about the form of the distribution?

**14.** Give examples of data in which the preferred measure of central tendency would be the
   **a.** mean.     **b.** median.     **c.** mode.

**15.** Which of the measures of central tendency is most affected by the degree of skew in the distribution? Explain.

**16.** What can we say about the relationship between the mean and the median in a negatively skewed distribution? In a positively skewed distribution?

**17.** Which measure of central tendency do you think would be most appropriate for the following data and why?
   **a.** price of new homes in a community
   **b.** yearly income
   **c.** intelligence test scores
   **d.** scores on an exam in an introductory course

**18.** What is the mean number of vacuum cleaners sold per day? Remember to weight each agent in terms of numbers of days worked.
   **a.** Amy sells a mean of 1.75 vacuum cleaners per day in 4 days.
   **b.** Bob sells a mean of 2.0 per day in 5 days.
   **c.** Carrie sells a mean of 2.4 per day in 5 days.
   **d.** Diana sells a mean of 2.5 per day in 4 days.
   **e.** Elyssa sells a mean of 2.0 per day in 3 days.
   **f.** Fred sells a mean of 1.67 per day in 3 days.

**19.** Suppose that three stores sell the following number of laptop computers from Monday through Saturday. For each store, calculate the mean, median, and the mode.
   **Store a.** 30, 30, 30, 30, 30, 30
   **Store b.** 25, 30, 35, 30, 35, 25
   **Store c.** 10, 25, 30, 36, 25, 30

**20.** Work the following problems:
   **a.** For Exercise 19 (c), show that: $\Sigma(X - \overline{X}) = 0$.
   **b.** Show that the sum of the deviations from the median and from the mode do not equal zero.
   **c.** Why do the deviations from the mean equal zero, whereas the deviations from the median and mode do not?

**21.** In a study of prior activity and its effects on the behaviors of Type A and Type B males, investigators (Ortega and Pipal, 1984) assessed the effects of different types of activity on subjects who had received extreme scores on an activity survey and were classified as either Type A or Type B. Sixty Type A subjects and 60 Type B subjects were randomly assigned to a Relaxed Condition, a Passive Condition, and an Active Condition. Thus, there were 20 Type A subjects in each of the three conditions. The Type B subjects were similarly subdivided, 20 subjects per group.

Following one of these activities, the subjects were given the opportunity to select problems from four different sets of tasks of increasing difficulty. The more difficult the problem selected was, the higher was the presumed level of challenge seeking. Note that the subjects were not required to solve these problems. Rather, they selected the level of difficulty that they were prepared to solve. The following are the scores each group received. Calculate the means for each of the six groups.

| TYPE A MALE CONDITION | | | TYPE B MALE CONDITION | | |
|---|---|---|---|---|---|
| **A** | **B** | **C** | **A** | **B** | **C** |
| 24 | 23 | 26 | 19 | 17 | 23 |
| 24 | 21 | 23 | 18 | 22 | 23 |
| 25 | 23 | 21 | 13 | 11 | 21 |
| 26 | 24 | 22 | 24 | 23 | 17 |
| 22 | 13 | 20 | 19 | 20 | 22 |
| 26 | 24 | 22 | 23 | 20 | 21 |
| 25 | 24 | 26 | 10 | 23 | 18 |
| 27 | 22 | 25 | 17 | 16 | 20 |
| 28 | 21 | 19 | 18 | 20 | 16 |
| 26 | 25 | 26 | 14 | 23 | 17 |
| 21 | 21 | 25 | 21 | 25 | 23 |
| 20 | 21 | 16 | 21 | 16 | 19 |
| 24 | 26 | 17 | 19 | 13 | 19 |
| 21 | 25 | 19 | 24 | 25 | 18 |
| 26 | 24 | 23 | 22 | 18 | 25 |
| 23 | 24 | 19 | 24 | 21 | 22 |
| 24 | 21 | 18 | 25 | 19 | 23 |
| 25 | 23 | 24 | 14 | 18 | 23 |
| 22 | 26 | 18 | 18 | 28 | 17 |
| 25 | 27 | 20 | 15 | 18 | 19 |

*Source:* Based on data from Ortega and Pipal, 1984.

22. During the summer of 1998, Survey USA, a private survey research company, interviewed 1,000 adults nationwide and asked them how much respect they have for Washington's newsmakers. The survey used a 1 to 10 scale, where 10 means the person is totally respected and 1 means the person is not respected at all. A number of prominent historical and contemporary figures are included in the ratings for context.

1. Mother Theresa — 8.9
2. Abraham Lincoln — 8.2
3. Martin Luther King — 7.4
4. Ronald Reagan — 7.0
5. Hillary Rodham Clinton — 5.5
6. President Bill Clinton — 5.2
7. Richard Nixon — 5.0
8. Larry King — 4.8
9. Matt Drudge — 4.4
10. Kenneth Starr — 4.3
11. Howard Stern — 3.2
12. Jimmy Swaggart — 2.8
13. Monica Lewinsky — 2.7
14. Linda Tripp — 2.7
15. O. J. Simpson — 2.4

Remember these ratings are a snapshot of public perception at a given point in time. Ratings can and do change daily. That is why pollsters continue to conduct their polls and their focus groups and continue to hire psychology majors to survey and analyze the data.

Based on the above data, answer the following questions.

a. Which do you think provides the best picture of the data, the rankings or the mean ratings?

b. Do you see any evidence suggesting equal intervals in the ordinal scale data?

c. Describe how one might change the names that appear on the list in a way that would affect the results of the survey.

# 5

# Measures of Dispersion

# 5.1 / Introduction

In the preceding chapters we examined different ways to describe a set of data and noted that several of the important features to describe are the central tendency, the dispersion, and the shape of the distribution. In the preceding chapter we looked at measures of central tendency of a distribution. In this chapter we will examine measures of dispersion and ways of interpreting those statistics. In addition, we will examine several methods for describing the shape of a distribution.

As is the case throughout this text, the material in this chapter will build upon what you have already learned and will prepare you for material presented in subsequent chapters. We believe that this chapter covers one of the most important concepts in statistics, **variance.** Variance is a measure of dispersion. It is a descriptive statistic researchers use to summarize and report the degree to which scores vary from one another in a data set. Variance is an essential statistical concept that is at the heart of research in the behavioral sciences. We will return to variance many times in this book.

All psychologists encounter variability in the data they collect. Consider some simple examples. An instructor gives an exam and some students do better than others. The instructor may be interested in why some students earn good grades while others struggle to pass. A researcher may want to determine if a new drug is effective for the treatment of depression. She will want to see if people treated with the drug differ from people given a placebo. The difference *between* people in the two groups is a form of variability. The differences found *within* each treatment group is also a form of variability. Therefore, measures of dispersion, like measures of central tendency, are descriptive statistics that researchers use to more fully describe their data.

Studying the variability of data is essential to the use and interpretation of many statistics. We have seen that a score by itself is meaningless and takes on meaning only when it is compared with other scores in a distribution. If we know the mean of the distribution, we can determine if a particular score is greater or less than that mean. Now comes an important question: How much? What if the mean of the distribution is 100 and an individual's score is 105? Obviously, there is a 5-point difference, and the individual's score is greater than the mean. Does this 5-point difference represent an exceptional difference or a trivial difference? We can answer the question directly by examining the distance of that score from the mean relative to the distance of the other scores from the mean.

Consider Figure 5.1, which contains two distributions of data. In both cases the mean of the distribution is 65 and the number of observations is the same. How should we interpret a score of 68 in the two distributions? In Distribution A, the data are more dispersed than the data in Distribution B. In other words, the data in Distribution A are more variable than the data in Distribution B. Look at the relative position of 68 in each of the distributions. In Distribution A, the score is relatively close to the mean. That is, the percentile ranking of the score is only slightly above the mean. In Distribution B, however, the same score appears to be exceptionally far from the mean. We would expect the percentile ranking to be high in this case. Imagine if the 68 was *your* test score on an important test. It's not enough to know that the mean was 65 and you scored above that point. Wouldn't it be important to you to know if the rest of the scores were close to the mean or very far away? Wouldn't you

**Variance:**

A descriptive statistic used to summarize and report the degree to which scores vary from one another in a data set.

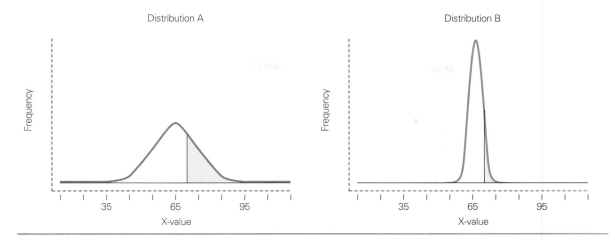

**Figure** | **5.1**

> **Two normal distributions with equal means but with different standard deviations. Vertical line represents location of a score of 68.**

want to know if you were at the top of the distribution or only slightly above average in a very dispersed distribution? Measures of dispersion will allow you to determine how much the scores are clustered around the center of the distribution or how far out the scores are dispersed.

This example illustrates our need to calculate a measure of dispersion. If we know a measure of central tendency and a measure of dispersion of a distribution, we can better interpret the meaning of individual scores in a set of data. In this chapter we will discuss four measures of dispersion or variability: the range, the semi-interquartile range, the variance, and the standard deviation. Because of their importance, we will give our greatest attention to the variance and standard deviation. These statistics serve as the foundation for other topics we will cover in this book including correlation, regression, and the analysis of variance.

## 5.2 / The Range

When you calculated measures of central tendency, you located a single value along the scale of scores and identified it as the mean, the median, or the mode. When your interest shifts to measures of dispersion, however, you must look for an index of variability that indicates the spread of scores around that central location.

One of the first measures of spread is the simplest and most straightforward measure—the **range**. Sometimes called the crude range, it is simply the distance between the largest and smallest score; that is, the range equals the highest score minus the lowest score. Thus, if the highest score is 90 and the lowest is 30, the range equals $90 - 30 = 60$. Note that the range is a single score, not two values as is commonly reported in the media. Thus the range is 60, not 30 to 90.

Although the range is meaningful, use of this simple but crude measure is limited. If there is one extreme score in a distribution, the spread of scores will appear to be large when, in fact, the distribution is quite compact except for this one outlier. Consider the example of a long distance telephone service that advertises the cost of their service. They

■ **Range:**

A measure of dispersion calculated by subtracting the value of the smallest observation from the value of the largest observation:
Range $= X_{\text{largest}} - X_{\text{smallest}}$.

claim that their calls are from 5% to 50% lower than their closest competitor's. Now do you think that *most* of the fees they charge are 50% lower or do you think that perhaps a few are 50% lower? Perhaps they are carefully wording their advertisements. It is possible that calls to only one destination are 50% lower than the competitor's. Consider another example. Imagine you are applying for a job in telemarketing. Five of the telemarketers make about $100 a week. One of them who happens to have a lot of perseverance (and relatives) makes $600 a week. It wouldn't be very fair for the company to claim that "You can earn up to $600 per week, maybe even more!" Knowing something about the variability of a distribution can be important.

There are times when knowing the range, and especially the upper values of a distribution, can be essential. Our preoccupation with averages can cause us to lose sight of the importance of the upper limits of measures. Imagine what life would be like if:

- Our highways were built to handle the average traffic load.
- Mass transit systems could accommodate only the average number of passengers per hour.
- Bridges, homes, and dams were designed to withstand the average wind velocity, the average rainfall, or the average earthquake.
- Telecommunication systems could accommodate only the average number of phone calls per hour.

Chaos is the word for it; utter chaos. Our society would crumble if everything were engineered for the average. Bridges would collapse during the first rush hour if they were designed to carry the average number of average-sized vehicles. Every aspect of our lives would be affected. We already know the discomfort of airplane seats that seem to be designed for the average jockey!

Good design decisions depend not only on measures of central tendency, but on measures of dispersion. The range and other measures of spread often provide the guidelines for important decisions. Again we see that a single statistic or number by itself is not all that useful. As W. I. E. Gates noted, "Then there was the man who drowned crossing a stream with an average depth of 6 inches." Sometimes the average can belie the depth of the data.

## 5.3 / The Semi-Interquartile Range

▨ **Semi-Interquartile Range (SIR):**

A measure of dispersion obtained by finding the difference between the 75th and 25th percentiles and dividing by 2.

$$SIR = \frac{Q_3 - Q_1}{2}$$

In order to overcome the shortcomings of the range as a measure of dispersion, we sometimes use the **semi-interquartile range (SIR).** To calculate the semi-interquartile range, subtract the score at the 25th percentile (called the first quartile or $Q_1$) from the score at the 75th percentile (the third quartile or $Q_3$). When we divide this difference by 2 (see Figure 5.2), we have a measure of the width of the semi-interquartile range on either side of the median.

If a distribution is symmetric (as in Figure 5.1), the median plus and minus the SIR cuts off the middle 50% of cases in the distribution. If, for example, a median is 70 and the SIR is 10, we can provide a useful summary statement, namely, $70 \pm 10$ (60–80) includes the middle 50% of all cases. Even with skewed distributions (see Figure 5.2), the SIR can

*page 61*

$(N+1) \times .25 = $ score at 25th percentile

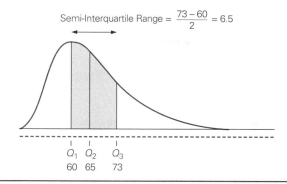

**Figure** | **5.2**

**The semi-interquartile range and a skewed distribution. Like the median ($Q_2$), the semi-interquartile range is not sensitive to extreme scores at one or the other end of the distribution.**

be useful since it focuses on the middle 50% of cases. In fact, the SIR is frequently used in conjunction with the median when extreme skew rules out the use of the mean and standard deviation as measures of central tendency and variability, respectively.

In the behavioral sciences some measures are sufficiently skewed to justify the use of the median as the measure of central tendency and the semi-interquartile range as the measure of dispersion. Some of these include physiological measures such as reaction times and heart rate as well as economic variables such as annual income, net worth, and selling price of new homes. In addition, the median and semi-interquartile range are often used to describe ordinal scale data.

Although SIR is far more meaningful than the crude range, it has two significant shortcomings: (1) like the range, it does not by itself permit the precise interpretation of a score within a distribution, and (2) like the median, it does not enter into any of the higher mathematical relationships that are basic to inferential statistics. As a consequence, we need to turn our attention to the most frequently used measures of dispersion: the variance and the standard deviation.

## 5.4 / Variance and Standard Deviation

Before we discuss these important topics we need to review some concepts from earlier chapters. Recall in Chapter 4 that we said: if the mean is subtracted from each value of a distribution, the sum of the quantities obtained is equal to zero (i.e., $\Sigma(X - \overline{X}) = 0$). When this value is divided by $N$ the quantity is said to be the **first moment about the mean.** The word "moment" is a technical term that represents the point of equilibrium between opposite forces. As you will recall from Chapter 4, the mean represents such a point of equilibrium. We said that the mean represents the balance point in the distribution. That is why the sum of the deviation scores is always 0; the mean is the point of equilibrium between high and low scores. Specifically, the first moment about the mean is calculated as:

■ **First Moment about the Mean:**

The sum of the deviation scores divided by $N$. Its value is always 0.

$$0 = \frac{\Sigma(X - \overline{X})}{N} \tag{5.1}$$

Note that the first moment about the mean will *always* equal 0 because the mean is the point in the distribution that balances the opposing forces of the larger and smaller values. Note also that we use the notation $\Sigma(X - \overline{X})$ when referring to the sum of the **deviation scores.** Other texts may also use the notation $\Sigma x$.

---

**Deviation Score (x):**

The difference between an observed score $X$ and the mean of the data set $\overline{X}$. $x = (X - \overline{X})$. The sum of the deviation scores is always zero.

---

**Sum of Squares (SS):**

The sum of the squared deviations of each observed score from the mean.

---

If we take these deviation scores and square each one, the values will become positive and larger. These squared deviations can then be summed to obtain the sum of the squared deviations or what is known as the **sum of squares.** The sum of squares is abbreviated as **SS.** The further the scores are away from the mean, the larger the sum of squares.

$$SS = \Sigma(X - \overline{X})^2 \tag{5.2}$$

It may be valuable to think of a deviation score in terms of the *distance* of that score from the mean. Now think about the impact of squaring values that are a large distance from the mean versus those that are closer to the mean. In Figure 5.3 you can see that scores farther from the mean, when squared, become larger. Small distances (deviations) when squared increase by relatively small amounts, ($2^2 = 4$, $3^2 = 9$). Numbers that are a greater distance from the mean, when squared, become much larger ($9^2 = 81$, $11^2 = 121$). This fact suggests that scores that are farther from the mean have a greater effect on the sum of squares than scores that are closer to the mean. This is an important concept to understand. Distributions that are very spread out will have much larger sums of squares than those that are less dispersed. Furthermore, the farthest scores from the mean will contribute the most to the sum of squares.

Let us consider the implications of what we have just covered. There are two factors that influence the size of the sum of squares. One, as we have just seen, is the distance of the scores from the mean of the distribution. If all the scores cluster close to the mean, the sum of squares will be small. If the scores are widely distributed, the sum of squares will be correspondingly large. The second factor that influences the sum of squares is the number of scores in the distribution. Clearly, as we add more scores to the set, the sum of squares must become larger, especially if these scores deviate from the mean. So the sum of squares becomes large when scores are spread out and when we have many scores in the data set. As a consequence, we cannot use the sum of squares as a direct measure of dispersion. We can, however, divide the sum by the total number of scores ($N$) and calculate an average of the squared

```
                              X
                        X   X   X
            X   X   X   X   X   X   X   X   X
            --------------------------------------
DISTANCE    -4  -3  -2  -1   0  +1  +2  +3  +4
(DISTANCE)² 16   9   4   1   0   1   4   9  16
```

**Figure** | **5.3**

The greater the distance of a score from the mean, the greater will be the distance squared.

deviations. Consequently, we have a statistic that represents the average squared deviation for a set of data. This average is called the **variance** and is represented by $s^2$.

Specifically, the variance of a set of data is calculated by:

$$s^2 = \frac{\Sigma(X - \overline{X})^2}{N} \tag{5.3}$$

$s^2$ may also be represented as the sum of squares (SS) divided by $N$, i.e., $\frac{SS}{N}$.

Statisticians call this equation the variance or the **second moment about the mean.** Again the concept of equilibrium between opposing forces is critical to recognize. The variance averages the effects of large and small deviations from the mean. We can use this fact to our advantage, because we can use the variance to help us characterize how much the typical score deviates from the mean.

Because we squared all the deviation scores before dividing by $N$, the variance represents the average of the sum of the squared differences between each score and the mean. If we take the square root of the variance, we will convert it into a score that is interpretable in terms of our measurement scale. The result of this transformation is called the **standard deviation,** or $s$.

$$s = \sqrt{\frac{\Sigma(X - \overline{X})^2}{N}} \tag{5.4}$$

As you can see the standard deviation is the square root of the variance, i.e., $\sqrt{s^2} = s$. Most researchers report the standard deviation when they want to describe the spread of a distribution. The variance, however, is also extremely useful. In fact, both the standard deviation and the variance are two of the most important concepts you will learn about in this course. They are the basis of many other concepts and calculations. It is important that you understand how they are derived and what they represent because you will encounter them repeatedly in subsequent chapters.

## Definitional and Computational Equations

As you progress through this text you will notice that sometimes more than one equation is presented for a given statistic. This is not done to confuse you! There can be many different algebraically equivalent formulas, each of which will give you the correct answer. We have tried to provide you with the formulae that are either easiest to use for calculations or that provide the best understanding of the underlying concepts. In the case of variance and standard deviation, the formula that is best for calculation is not the most understandable. And the most understandable formula is very inefficient for calculations. Therefore, we are going to present two equations to calculate the variance, a definitional equation and a computational equation. The definitional equation is useful for understanding what variance is all about. The computational equation, as the name implies, is useful for computing.

Equation (5.3) presented earlier is the **definitional equation** for the variance. That is, the equation defines the variance. It is useful to us in that it helps us understand what the variance represents—the average of the sum of squared deviations about the mean. Unfortunately, the equation is not very practical when we have to calculate the variance by hand. To subtract the mean from each individual score, then square each value, and sum them takes a very long time, even for a small data set,

**Variance ($s^2$):**

A measure of dispersion calculated by dividing the sum of the squared deviation scores (the sum of squares) by the number of observations. The variance is the average of the squared differences between the mean and the observed scores: $s^2 = \frac{\Sigma(X - \overline{X})^2}{N}$.

**Second Moment about the Mean:**

Another term for variance.

**Standard Deviation ($s$):**

The square root of the variance, $s = \sqrt{s^2}$.

**Definitional Equation:**

An equation that defines a measure, such as the variance.

**Computational Equation:**

An equation that simplifies the calculation of a measure, such as the variance.

and puts you at risk of the perils of rounding errors and computational errors. Fortunately there is an alternative. The **computational equation** produces the same results as the definitional equation but in a fraction of the time. Let's look at each.

Definitional equation for variance:

$$s^2 = \frac{\Sigma(X - \bar{X})^2}{N}$$

Computational equation for variance:

$$s^2 = \frac{\Sigma X^2 - \frac{(\Sigma X)^2}{N}}{N} \qquad (5.5)$$

Table 5.1 shows the procedures for calculating the variance and standard deviation from a small data set. Before looking at this table, remember that there is a difference between $(\Sigma X)^2$ and $\Sigma X^2$. In your own words, describe each of them to yourself and anticipate how they will be calculated. Now turn to Table 5.1. On the left side of the table you

$\bar{X} = 9$

**Table 5.1**

**Computational Procedures for Calculating the Variance and Standard Deviation from an Array of Scores**

| $X$ | $(X - \bar{X})$ | $(X - \bar{X})^2$ | $X^2$ |
|---|---|---|---|
| 12 | $12 - 9 = 3$ | 9 | 144 |
| 11 | $11 - 9 = 2$ | 4 | 121 |
| 10 | $10 - 9 = 1$ | 1 | 100 |
| 9 | $9 - 9 = 0$ | 0 | 81 |
| 9 | $9 - 9 = 0$ | 0 | 81 |
| 9 | $9 - 9 = 0$ | 0 | 81 |
| 8 | $8 - 9 = -1$ | 1 | 64 |
| 7 | $7 - 9 = -2$ | 4 | 49 |
| 6 | $6 - 9 = -3$ | 9 | 36 |

$\Sigma X = 81 \qquad \Sigma(X - \bar{X}) = 0 \qquad \Sigma(X - \bar{X})^2 = 28 \qquad \Sigma X^2 = 757$

$(\Sigma X)^2 = 6561$

$N = 9.0$

| Definitional Equation | Computational Equation |
|---|---|
| $s^2 = \dfrac{\Sigma(X - \bar{X})^2}{N}$ | $s^2 = \dfrac{\Sigma X^2 - \dfrac{(\Sigma X)^2}{N}}{N}$ |
| $s^2 = \dfrac{28}{9}$ | $= \dfrac{757 - \dfrac{(81)^2}{9}}{9}$ |
| $s^2 = 3.11$ | $= \dfrac{757 - 729}{9}$ |
| | $= \dfrac{28}{9}$ |
| | $s^2 = 3.11$ |
| $s = \sqrt{s^2}$ | $s = \sqrt{s^2}$ |
| $s = \sqrt{3.11}$ | $s = \sqrt{3.11}$ |
| $s = 1.76$ | $s = 1.76$ |
| Use this formula for understanding. | Use this formula for calculating. |

will find the definitional equation. Again, if you use this one, be prepared to spend much time calculating the mean, subtracting it from each value, squaring it, and summing the squared deviations. And don't be surprised if you get rounding errors in your answers. We present this equation and example to allow you to see that the variance really is based on the squared distances of the scores from the mean.

Now look at the computational equation. For it you need only $N$, the sum of the $X$ column, and the sum of the $X^2$ column. You don't need the middle two columns for this equation. The numerator, or top part of the equation is the sum of squares known as $SS$. The denominator is $N$. Sum of squares divided by $N$ equals $s^2$, the variance. The square root of the variance equals $s$, the standard deviation.

We encourage you to use a calculator or a computer to help you with the calculations. Our experience has been that many people tend to make mistakes when trying to do these calculations by hand. You should also get into the habit of preparing a neat, step-by-step account of your work. It will help you locate small, arithmetic errors. We strongly encourage you to get as much practice calculating the variance and standard deviation as possible. Once you feel confident using you calculator or computer program, the more advanced statistical procedures will be easier and less threatening.

As you can see, both the definitional and computational equations for variance and standard deviation produce the same result. Our experience is that the computational formula is easier to use if you must calculate the statistics by hand. If you plan to use a hand calculator or a computer for your computations, practice your technique on one of the odd numbered problems at the end of the chapter to assure yourself that you are using the calculator or computer package correctly.

---

**But I can't get the same answer!**

A word of warning to those of you who are discovering: "My calculator keeps giving me an answer that is different from the one in the book!!" or "My computer printout gives a different answer!" There is a good reason why this may happen. Programs and calculators may use formulas that differ slightly from the one just presented. Instead of $N$ in the denominator they may be using $N - 1$. When we get to the chapter on inference it will be clear why they are doing this. For now, the short explanation is as follows: when you are interested in using the variance to make *inferences* to a population, $N - 1$ is used. It gives a better estimate of the population value. If you are only interested in your sample and don't want to make inferences to a population then $N$ is appropriate. Either $N$ or $N - 1$ is correct, depending on what your goal is. For now let's keep it simple and use $N$.

---

## 5.5 / Computing $s^2$ and $s$ from a Large Data Set

Whenever you collect data from a large number of subjects, it is common that many of them will earn the same score. When this situation occurs, we may modify our calculations to save you time and reduce the risk of errors. In Table 5.2, you will find the Test of Narcissism data set that we presented in Chapter 3 to illustrate a frequency distribution of scores. Again we calculate $X$ and $X^2$. A score of 20 in the $X$ column becomes $20^2$ or 400 in the $X^2$ column. Because some scores are repeated, we multiply $X$

**Table 5.2**

**Test of Narcissism Scores Obtained by 30 Subjects. Computational Procedures for Calculating $s^2$ and $s$ from Larger Data Sets in Which There Are Repeated Values of the $X$-variable**

| $X$ | $X^2$ | $f$ | $fX$ | $fX^2$ |
|---|---|---|---|---|
| 20 | 400 | 1 | 20 | 400 |
| 19 | 361 | 1 | 19 | 361 |
| 18 | 324 | 1 | 18 | 324 |
| 17 | 289 | 2 | 34 | 578 |
| 16 | 256 | 1 | 16 | 256 |
| 15 | 225 | 4 | 60 | 900 |
| 14 | 196 | 2 | 28 | 392 |
| 13 | 169 | 2 | 26 | 338 |
| 12 | 144 | 3 | 36 | 432 |
| 11 | 121 | 5 | 55 | 605 |
| 10 | 100 | 2 | 20 | 200 |
| 9 | 81 | 1 | 9 | 81 |
| 8 | 64 | 2 | 16 | 128 |
| 7 | 49 | 1 | 7 | 49 |
| 6 | 36 | 1 | 6 | 36 |
| 5 | 25 | 1 | 5 | 25 |

$$N = \quad \Sigma f = \quad 30 \qquad \Sigma fX = 375 \qquad \Sigma fX^2 = 5105$$
$$\Sigma X = 375 \qquad \Sigma X^2 = 5105$$
$$(\Sigma X)^2 = 140625$$

$$s^2 = \frac{\Sigma fX^2 - \frac{(\Sigma fX)^2}{N}}{N}$$

$$s^2 = \frac{5105 - \left(\frac{140625}{30}\right)}{30}$$

$$s^2 = \frac{5105 - 4687.5}{30}$$

$$s^2 = \frac{417.5}{30} = 13.9167$$

$$s = \sqrt{13.9167}$$

$$s = 3.73$$

and $X^2$ by the frequency of the observation $f$. The frequency $f$ when multiplied by $X$ becomes $fX$. Look at the score of 17 in the $X$ column. It has a frequency of 2, which when multiplied by the score 17 is 34 in the $fX$ column. Similarly the frequency 2 is used to multiply the squared value, thus $289 \times 2 = 578$. Using these calculations we can then find the variance and the standard deviation.

# 5.6 / Errors to Avoid When Calculating $s^2$ and $s$

**M**anual Calculations   When using the computational method of calculating $s^2$ and $s$, many people commonly confuse the similar-appearing terms: $\Sigma X^2$ and $(\Sigma X)^2$ or $(\Sigma fX)^2$ and $\Sigma fX^2$. $\Sigma X^2$ represents the sum of the individually squared scores, whereas $(\Sigma X)^2$ represents all the scores that are summed first and then the sum is squared. Similarly $\Sigma f X^2$ does not equal $(\Sigma f X)^2$. Remember the rule of priority when using parentheses: Perform all operations inside the parentheses first, then square the value.

As a general rule, it is impossible to obtain a negative sum of squares (SS) or a negative standard deviation. In the event you obtain a negative sum of squares (SS), go back over your work to see if you have confused similar-appearing terms. Also, it is a good idea to write each step you take on a piece of paper and organize your answer in an easy-to-follow series of steps. If you do find that you have an error in calculation, it is easier to retrace your steps.

**Computer Computations**    Errors also crop up when you use a calculator or a computer to calculate $s^2$ and $s$. In most cases the error is due to entering the wrong data. In other words, the computer correctly calculated the standard deviation, but the answer is wrong because you entered the data incorrectly. What can you do to detect potential errors and avoid errors? The first is to be careful. Proofread your data before you ask the computer to calculate $s$. It is helpful to have someone read the numbers to you while you look at the numbers on the screen. This will help you catch typing and formatting errors. Most computer programs will print a complete frequency distribution of the data, the values of the lowest and the highest scores, and a stem-and-leaf display. Do these values make sense? Are they reasonable? Inspect your printout to ensure that the values in the data set were correctly entered. Many years ago in a large study of schoolchildren, the homeroom numbers for some children were inadvertently put in the column where their IQs were supposed to be entered. Imagine if your homeroom number was 170 versus 70! Either value should raise the suspicions of an aware researcher.

When the computer calculates the statistics, look at the mean. Does the mean correspond to your estimation based on a visual inspection of the data? For example, if the computer reports that the mean of the data is 12 and all the numbers you entered were single digit numbers, do you have a problem? Yes! It is impossible to have a double digit mean if all the numbers were single digits.

A handy rule-of-thumb for **estimating the standard deviation** is that the ratio of the range to the standard deviation is rarely smaller than 2 or greater than 6. Stated from another perspective, divide the range by 6. The answer will be a general approximation of the standard deviation. If your calculations yield a standard deviation outside this interval, you have almost certainly made an error. At a more basic level, simply look at your range. Look at its size. Do you expect your scores to vary by this much? If not, examine the distribution carefully.

■ **Estimate of the Standard Deviation:**

An approximation of the standard deviation calculated by: $s \cong \dfrac{Range}{6}$. The value should fall between 2.0 and 6.0.

# 5.7
## Interpreting the Standard Deviation

The standard deviation represents a measure of spread for a distribution. Distributions with scores that are very spread out will have a large standard deviation. If the scores cluster about the mean the distribution will have a small standard deviation. We can compare the standard deviations of different samples to determine which has the greatest amount of dispersion. Samples with relatively little dispersion are called **homogeneous** because all the scores are similar to one another. Samples with much variability are called **heterogeneous** because the scores are scattered

■ **Homogeneity:**

A term used to describe a sample of data wherein all the values are similar.

■ **Heterogeneity:**

A term used to describe a sample of data wherein all the values are dissimilar.

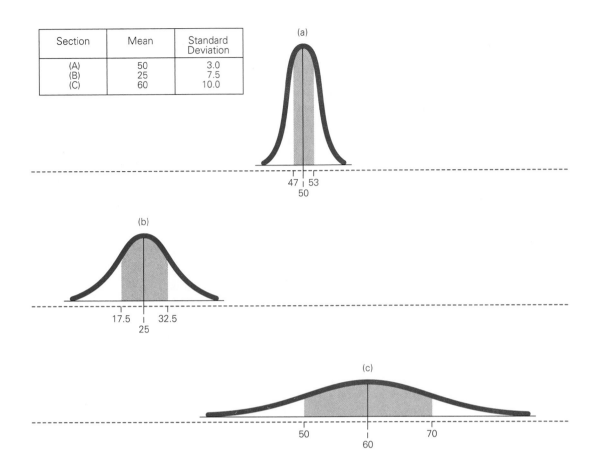

| Section | Mean | Standard Deviation |
|---------|------|--------------------|
| (A) | 50 | 3.0 |
| (B) | 25 | 7.5 |
| (C) | 60 | 10.0 |

**Figure** | **5.4**

**Distributions of test scores obtained from three sections of an introductory psychology class.**

relatively far from the mean. Take a look at Figure 5.4. Each distribution has a different mean and each differs in terms of spread. The top distribution is relatively homogeneous (least spread). The scores cluster close to the mean. The bottom distribution is heterogeneous relative to the top distribution. The bigger the standard deviation the more heterogeneous the observations. Another way of saying the same thing is: The bigger the standard deviation the more spread out are the scores in the distribution.

You will recall that we used the semi-interquartile range to assess the proportion of observations that are close to the median. Specifically, we noted that in a symmetric distribution, 50% of values are within the area of the mean plus or minus the SIR. The same logic applies to the standard deviation.

If you take the mean of a normal distribution and add and subtract the standard deviation (as shown in the shaded area), you will account for approximately 68% of the scores in the distribution. We will explain later why it is always 68%. Take, for example, the top distribution (a) in Figure 5.4. It has a mean of 50 and a standard deviation of 3.0. If we take the mean and add and subtract the standard deviation, which is 3.0, we find that 68% of the cases fall between scores of 47 and 53. The standard deviation, when added to and subtracted from the mean, provides you with a measure of spread. It tells you where slightly more than two-thirds of the scores in a distribution fall. We will have much more to say about this in the next chapter.

## 5.8 / The Shape of the Distribution: Skew and Kurtosis

We can describe the overall shape of the distribution using the two additional descriptive statistics known as **skew** and **kurtosis.** Skew refers to the symmetry of the distribution. As you may recall, we noted earlier that the direction of skew can be judged by the position of the mean relative to the median. When the mean is greater than the median, that is, when $(\overline{X} - Median)$ is a positive value, the distribution of scores is positively skewed. Conversely, when $(\overline{X} - Median)$ is negative, the scores are negatively skewed. However, these indices of *direction* of skew tell us little about the *magnitude* of skew. There are, in fact, a number of different measures of skew in use.

Technically speaking, skew is the third moment about the mean and is calculated using the equation:

$$s^3 = \frac{\dfrac{\Sigma(X - \overline{X})^3}{N}}{\left[\dfrac{\Sigma(X - \overline{X})^2}{N}\right]^{1.5}}$$ (5.6)

If the skew ($s^3$) is 0, then the distribution is said to be symmetrical, and the mean and median are the same. Numbers greater than 0 represent a positive skew, a condition that occurs when the mean is greater than the median. Numbers less than 0 represent a negative skew where the mean is less than the median.

Typically, the skew of a distribution is calculated only with a professional-quality statistics program for computers. The skew can, however, be estimated with a simple equation devised by E. S. Pearson. Pearson's coefficient for skew ($\hat{s}^3$) is:

$$\hat{s}^3 = \frac{3\,(\overline{X} - Median)}{s}$$ (5.7)

The carat (^) over the $s^3$ indicates that the statistic is an estimate of the skew rather than the actual measure of skew. Let's apply this formula to the data in Table 5.2 where $\overline{X} = 12.5$, the median is approximately 12, and $s = 3.73$. Thus, the coefficient of skew is

$$\hat{s}^3 = \frac{3(12.5 - 12)}{3.73}$$

$$\hat{s}^3 = .40$$

Remember we are only estimating $\hat{s}^3$ (for these data the real skew is .013). The positive sign indicates that the scores are positively skewed. If the distribution is symmetrical, the mean and median are the same value. The $\overline{X} - Median = 0$ and the coefficient of skew equals zero. However, it is widely accepted that data sets with indices of skew that range between $\pm 0.50$ may be considered sufficiently symmetrical for most practical applications. Because the skew of the data in Table 5.2 does not exceed the

**Skew ($s^3$):**

A statistic that describes the degree of skew of a distribution. When $s^3 = 0$, the distribution is symmetric. Positive values indicate that the data are positively skewed. When $s^3$ is negative, the data are negatively skewed.

**Kurtosis ($s^4$):**

A statistic that describes the degree to which the data are distributed closely around the mean or spread out over a wide range with many scores at either extreme.

**Table 5.3**

**Summary of Frequently Used Measures of Dispersion**

| Measure | When Used | Caution |
|---|---|---|
| Range | Easy to obtain. | Not precise. Gives very little information. Can be misleading. |
| Semi-interquartile range | Useful when you want to know roughly the middle 50% of distribution. Easy to calculate if you already have $Q_1$ and $Q_3$. | Used infrequently when reporting research. |
| Sum of squared deviations (*SS*) | The basis of many useful descriptive statistics and statistical tests. | By itself not a measure of spread. Both spread and sample size affect size of *SS*. |
| Variance | Also the basis of some very useful statistical techniques, e.g., analysis of variance. | Examine the distribution; look to see if it is symmetrical. |
| Standard deviation | Frequently used statistic for reporting where approximately two-thirds of the distribution lies. | Examine the distribution; look to see if it is symmetrical. |

absolute value of 0.50 (i.e. |0.50|), the distribution of the sample scores of the Test of Narcissism may be regarded as symmetrical*.

Statisticians also calculate what is known as the fourth moment about the mean, or the kurtosis of the distribution. The kurtosis is a descriptive statistic that tells us whether the data are bunched closely to the mean or spread out over a wide range with many scores at either extreme. The kurtosis is calculated using the equation:

$$s^4 = \frac{\dfrac{\Sigma(X - \overline{X})^4}{N}}{\left[\dfrac{\Sigma(X - \overline{X})^2}{N}\right]^2} \tag{5.8}$$

Kurtosis is sensitive to the number of observations that occur at the extremes of the distribution. As in the case of skew, kurtosis is typically calculated using a computer. We can estimate kurtosis using the equation:

$$\hat{s}^4 = 3 + \frac{Q_3 - Q_1}{2(P_{90} - P_{10})} \tag{5.9}$$

In this equation $Q_3$ and $Q_1$ represent the third and first quartiles, and $P_{90}$ and $P_{10}$ represent the 90th and 10th percentiles. As an example,

---

* Readers interested in more precise methods for determining if the skew and kurtosis are significantly large or small are encouraged to consult tables constructed by Pearson and Hartley (1970), D'Agostino and Tiejen (1973), and Gebhardt (1966).

**Table** 5.4

**Four Distributions, Each With a Different $s^2$, $s^3$, and $s^4$**

|  | DISTRIBUTION | | | |
|---|---|---|---|---|
|  | 1 | 2 | 3 | 4 |
| **X** | $f_1$ | $f_2$ | $f_3$ | $f_4$ |
| 11 | 1 | 3 | 1 | 16 |
| 10 | 1 | 2 | 0 | 0 |
| 9 | 2 | 1 | 1 | 1 |
| 8 | 2 | 1 | 0 | 0 |
| 7 | 8 | 1 | 16 | 1 |
| 6 | 2 | 1 | 0 | 0 |
| 5 | 2 | 1 | 1 | 1 |
| 4 | 1 | 2 | 0 | 0 |
| 3 | 1 | 8 | 1 | 1 |
| $\Sigma X$ | 140 | 120 | 140 | 200 |
| $N$ | 20 | 20 | 20 | 20 |
| $\overline{X} =$ | 7.0 | 6.0 | 7.0 | 10.0 |
| Median = | 7.0 | 4.5 | 7.0 | 11.0 |
| $s^2 =$ | 3.50 | 10.10 | 2.00 | 5.00 |
| $s^3 =$ | 0.00 | 0.48 | 0.00 | −2.15 |
| $s^4 =$ | 3.03 | 1.55 | 6.80 | 6.25 |

consider the data for Distribution 1 in Table 5.4. We can estimate the distribution's kurtosis as:

$$\hat{s}^4 = 3 + \frac{8 - 6}{2(9.5 - 4.5)}$$
$$\hat{s}^4 = 3.2$$

# 5.9 / Putting It All Together

To better understand the relationship among the descriptive measures we have just covered, let's examine the means, standard deviations, skew, and kurtosis of several distributions. Table 5.4 presents four distributions. Each distribution ranges between 3 and 11 and each distribution has 20 observations. The difference among the distributions is the relative frequency of each of the observations.

We can begin by examining Distribution 1 which has a mean of 7.0, a variance of 3.50, a skew of 0.0, and a kurtosis of 3.03. The top left graph in Figure 5.5 represents the frequency distribution of the data. As you can see, the majority of the scores are at or close to 7. There are very few scores at either extreme in this distribution. We can, therefore, describe several of the attributes of the data. First, the data are not skewed. As you can see, $s^3 = 0.0$, and the mean and median are both 7. Therefore, the data are symmetrical about the mean. In describing the kurtosis of the data, we would say that the data are **mesokurtic.** In general, mesokurtic distributions are "bell-shaped" or what statisticians call "normally distributed." This means that the majority of the scores are

■ **Mesokurtic:**

A descriptive term for the distribution of data when the kurtosis $s^4 = 3$. This distribution is in-between the extreme shapes represented by leptokurtic and platykurtic distributions.

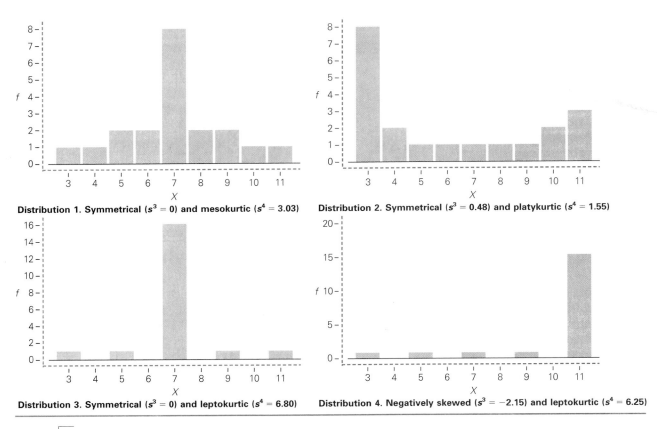

Distribution 1. Symmetrical ($s^3 = 0$) and mesokurtic ($s^4 = 3.03$)

Distribution 2. Symmetrical ($s^3 = 0.48$) and platykurtic ($s^4 = 1.55$)

Distribution 3. Symmetrical ($s^3 = 0$) and leptokurtic ($s^4 = 6.80$)

Distribution 4. Negatively skewed ($s^3 = -2.15$) and leptokurtic ($s^4 = 6.25$)

**Figure** | **5.5**

Graphical representation of four distributions from Table 5.4.

■ **Platykurtic:**

A descriptive term for the distribution of data when the kurtosis $s^4 < 3$. This distribution represents one where the distribution of data is flattened. There are many scores at either extreme of the distribution.

■ **Leptokurtic:**

A descriptive term for the distribution of data when the kurtosis $s^4 > 3$. This distribution represents one wherein the data are gathered close to the mean and there are few that are distant from the mean.

close to the center of the distribution and that there are relatively few scores at either extreme. As you can see from Table 5.4, the kurtosis is 3.03. Mesokurtic curves typically have a kurtosis that equals 3.00.

A much different pattern is evident in Distribution 2 (see Table 5.4 and Figure 5.5), where the data are much more spread out. As you can see, there are few scores in the middle of the distribution and many scores at either extreme of the distribution. The distribution is flattened out; we would call this distribution **platykurtic.** In other words, when $s^4$ is less than 3 the distribution is platykurtic. You will notice that the kurtosis of this curve is $s^4 = 1.55$, whereas the skew is still relatively small, $s^3 = 0.48$. Thus we can conclude that variance, skew, and kurtosis each provide different information about a distribution.

Distribution 3 is characterized by the fact that nearly all the observations are at the point of central tendency (see Table 5.4 and Figure 5.5). In other words, there are few if any scores at the extremes of the distribution. When the data are arranged in such a way, we say that the distribution is **leptokurtic.** As you can see, this distribution has no skew, but the kurtosis is extremely high, $s^4 = 6.80$.

In Distribution 4, we see that the data are skewed and that the data are centered around a single point at the upper end of the distribution (see Table 5.4 and Figure 5.5). Therefore, we can say that the data are negatively skewed *and* leptokurtic. These observations are confirmed by examining the third and fourth moments of the mean. The skew is large, $s^3 = -2.15$ as is the kurtosis, $s^4 = 6.25$.

## CHAPTER S UMMARY

In this chapter, we saw that to fully describe a distribution of scores we require more than measures of central tendency. We must be able to describe how scores are dispersed about the measure of central tendency. In this connection, we looked at four measures of dispersion: the range, the semi-interquartile range, the standard deviation, and the variance.

For normally distributed variables, the two measures based on the squaring of deviations about the mean, the variance, and the standard deviation are most useful. To obtain the variance and the standard deviation it is first necessary to calculate the sum of squares, SS. We examined the procedures for calculating the standard deviation using the definitional formula and also using a computational formula. While the answers obtained from each are the same, the definitional formula is valuable for understanding the nature of these measures of spread. The computational formula is the one to use when performing calculations. It is superior, both in terms of time efficiency and error reduction. Also covered was a method for calculating the standard deviation and variance for a large data set in which many subjects receive the same score.

As the mean is a measure of central tendency, the variance and standard deviations are measures of spread. Using both the mean and standard deviation it is possible to describe a distribution in terms of two important characteristics, its location (central tendency), and its spread. Based on these two statistics one is able to determine, in a normal distribution, where approximately 68% of the cases in that distribution lie. In addition, one can assess the shape of a distribution using estimates of skewness and kurtosis. Skewness refers to the symmetry of a distribution and kurtosis describes the extent to which cases cluster closely around the mean or distribute in the extremes.

## TERMS TO R EMEMBER

| | |
|---|---|
| computational equation | mesokurtic |
| definitional equation | platykurtic |
| deviation score ($x$) | range |
| estimate of the standard deviation | second moment about the mean |
| first moment about the mean | semi-interquartile range (SIR) |
| heterogeneity | skew ($s^3$) |
| homogeneity | standard deviation |
| kurtosis ($s^4$) | sum of squares (SS) |
| leptokurtic | variance ($s^2$) |

## E XERCISES

1. Calculate $s^2$ and $s$ for the following array of scores: 3, 4, 5, 5, 6, 7.
   a. Add a constant, say, 2, to each score. Recalculate $s^2$ and $s$. Would the results be any different if you had added a larger constant, say, 200? *Generalize:* What is the effect on $s$ and $s^2$ of adding a constant to an array of scores? Does the variability increase as we increase the magnitude of the scores?
   b. Subtract the same constant from each score. Recalculate $s^2$ and $s$. Would the results be any different if you had subtracted a larger constant, say, 200?

*Generalize:* What is the effect on $s$ and $s^2$ of subtracting a constant from an array of scores?

**c.** Alternately add and subtract the same constant from each score (i.e., $3 + 2$, $4 - 2$, $5 + 2$, etc.). Recalculate $s$ and $s^2$. Would the results be any different if you had added and subtracted a larger constant? *Generalize:* What is the effect on $s$ and $s^2$ of adding and subtracting a constant from an array of scores? (Note: This generalization is extremely important with relation to subsequent chapters where we discuss the effect of random errors on measures of variability.)

**d.** Multiply each score by a constant, say, 2. Recalculate $s$ and $s^2$. *Generalize:* What is the effect on $s$ and $s^2$ of multiplying each score by a constant?

**e.** Divide each score by the same constant. Recalculate $s$ and $s^2$. *Generalize:* What is the effect on $s$ and $s^2$ of dividing each score by a constant?

2. Compare your generalizations with those you made in relation to the mean (see Exercise 10, Chapter 4).

3. Due to a scoring error, 10 points were added to the test scores of everyone taking a final examination in a psychology course. What will be the effect of this error on the mean of the distribution and on the standard deviation?

4. How would $s$ be affected by the situations described in Exercises 5 and 6, Chapter 4?

5. What is the nature of the distribution if $s = 0$?

6. Calculate the standard deviations for the following sets of measurements:
   **a.** 10, 8, 6, 0, 8, 3, 2, 2, 8, 0
   **b.** 1, 3, 3, 5, 5, 5, 7, 7, 9
   **c.** 20, 1, 2, 5, 4, 4, 4, 0
   **d.** 5, 5, 5, 5, 5, 5, 5, 5, 5, 5

7. Why is the standard deviation in Exercise 6c. so large? Describe the effect of extreme deviations on $s$.

8. Determine the range for the sets of measurements in Exercise 6. For which of these is the range a misleading index of variability, and why?

9. List at least three specific instances in which a measure of variability was important in comparing a group of people.

10. A number of formulas were presented in this chapter to calculate the variance. Which formula is most appropriate to use in the following situations and why?
    **a.** You want to explain the concept of variance to your friend.
    **b.** You want to calculate the variance for a data set in which $N = 14$.
    **c.** You want to calculate the variance for a large data set.

11. A comparison shopper compares prices of plums at a number of different supermarkets. She finds the following prices per pound (in cents): 56, 65, 48, 73, 59, 72, 63, 65, 60, 63, 44, 79, 63, 61, 66, 69, 64, 71, 58, 63.
    **a.** Find the mean.
    **b.** Find the range and the semi-interquartile range.
    **c.** Find the standard deviation and variance.

**12.** Describe the advantage of using the standard deviation rather than the variance as a measure of spread. Why would you use the standard deviation instead of the sum of squares as a measure of spread?

**13.** Presented below is the monthly normal precipitation (in inches) for four urban areas.
   **a.** It is possible to calculate means and measures of variability by columns (months of the year) or by the rows by analyzing each community. Which corresponds to a within-subject measure of variability and which is a between-subject measure? Explain.
   **b.** Determine the yearly mean, range, variance, and standard deviation of precipitation for each city.
   **c.** Find the mean, range, variance, and standard deviation of the precipitation during each month.
   **d.** Which seems to yield the higher measures of variability—the within- or between-subject?
   **e.** Which cities have the most and the least consistent monthly precipitation data?

| Stations | Jan | Feb | Mar | Apr | May | June | July | Aug | Sept | Oct | Nov | Dec |
|---|---|---|---|---|---|---|---|---|---|---|---|---|
| Barrow, AK | 0.2 | 0.2 | 0.1 | 0.1 | 0.1 | 0.4 | 0.8 | 0.9 | 0.6 | 0.5 | 0.2 | 0.2 |
| Burlington, VT | 2.0 | 1.8 | 2.1 | 2.6 | 3.0 | 3.5 | 3.9 | 3.4 | 3.3 | 3.0 | 2.6 | 2.1 |
| Honolulu, HI | 3.8 | 3.3 | 2.9 | 1.3 | 1.0 | 0.3 | 0.4 | 0.9 | 1.0 | 1.8 | 2.2 | 3.0 |
| Seattle-Tacoma, WA | 5.7 | 4.2 | 3.8 | 2.4 | 1.7 | 1.6 | 0.8 | 1.0 | 2.1 | 4.0 | 5.4 | 6.3 |

*Source:* Based on data from National Climatic Center, NOAA, U.S. Department of Commerce.

**14.** A team of researchers examined the effects of intense prior emotional experiences on the subsequent emotional reactions in situations that evoke contrasting states. They sought to determine if horror is more intense when it is preceded by humor and if humor is funnier when preceded by horror. As part of that study, the rating of pleasantness of humor was obtained from male and female subjects when humorous scenes alone were shown (humor first) or when humorous scenes were preceded by five scenes of horror (1-minute excerpts from the movie *Halloween*). The following table presents the pleasantness ratings made by the four groups of subjects (the lower the score was, the greater was the pleasantness).

| HUMOR FIRST | | HUMOR PRECEDED BY HORROR | |
|---|---|---|---|
| Male | Female | Male | Female |
| 17 | 9 | 17 | 10 |
| 24 | 12 | 11 | 15 |
| 13 | 20 | 25 | 14 |
| 13 | 18 | 20 | 7 |
| 24 | 23 | 6 | 10 |
| 18 | 18 | 10 | 13 |
| 21 | 21 | 6 | 6 |
| 28 | 32 | 31 | 6 |
| 12 | 12 | 8 | 11 |
| 9 | 12 | 17 | 14 |

*Source:* Based on data from Manstead et al., 1983.

a. Calculate the mean, median, range, variance, and standard deviation for each of the four groups.
b. Combine the male and female scores in humor first and find the mean, median, range, variance, and standard deviation.
c. Combine the male and female scores in humor preceded by horror and find the mean, median, range, variance, and standard deviation. Are the means consistent with the emotional contrast hypothesis that would predict lower scores when humor is preceded by horror?

# 6

# The Standard Normal Distribution

## 6.1 / Introduction

As we have said over and over, individual scores are meaningless without a context. To take on meaning, a score needs a reference group for comparison. For example, let's say you received a score of 62 on an important exam. Is this good or bad? It may be very bad if the majority of the class earned scores of 100. On the other hand, it is possible that yours is the top score. You have no way of knowing. A score of 62 is meaningless unless you have a reference group against which to compare it. Then you can find out where you stand relative to others. Are you above or below the mean? A lot above or just a little bit? What percent of the others scored higher than you, what percent lower? As you will see in this chapter, it is an easy matter to answer these questions if you know the mean and the standard deviation. The technique we use to provide meaning to individual scores and allow for their interpretation is the **z-score.**

■ **z-score:**

A descriptive statistic that represents the distance between an observed score and the mean relative to the standard deviation.

## 6.2 / The Concept of z-Scores

A z-score takes into account the distance of an individual score above or below the mean. Thus, if a mean of a distribution is 50, and your score is 62, you are 12 points above the mean. But knowing only that you are above the mean isn't enough. Were you above most of the others or only a few? How far above the mean were you relative to everyone else? A z-score allows you to answer that question with precision. First it looks at the difference between your score and the mean. Then it evaluates that difference in terms of a standard. Before we see how a z-score works and how we calculate it, let's do a quick review.

Remember we talked in the last chapter about using the mean and the standard deviation to determine where 68% of the distribution falls? If the mean is 50 and the standard deviation equals 6, then about 68% of the scores fall between 44 and 56. We can find 68% of the distribution when the standard deviation is added to and subtracted from the mean. If the mean is 50 and the standard deviation is 10, approximately 68% of the scores fall between 40 and 60. Remember the larger the standard deviation, the more spread out the scores. Notice, however, that the percentage of the distribution is the same, 68%.

Now let's return to the z-score. We can define a z-score as:

$$z = \frac{X - \overline{X}}{s} \tag{6.1}$$

$X$ represents the score of interest, your score of 62. The mean we already know is 50. Your score is 12 points above the mean. The value for $s$ is the standard deviation of the distribution which we calculated as 6.

$$z = \frac{62 - 50}{6} = \frac{12}{6} = 2.0$$

Notice in the numerator, a score of 62 is greater than the mean of 50. The distance of your score 12 points above the mean is evaluated relative to a standard distance, the standard deviation. In this case, your distance, 12 points, when compared to a standard of 6 is 2.0 standards above the mean. Had you been 12 points below the mean, your $z$-score would be negative, $z = -2.0$. Scores that are larger than the mean will always be positive. Scores below the mean will be negative.

A $z$-score provides an answer to the question, "How many standard deviations away from the mean is a given score?" Using the $z$-score we have a way of expressing the relative distance of an observed score from the mean.

We have presented an example using data from a sample. Sometimes our data set consists of measures taken from a population. In that case we use the following formula:

$$z = \frac{X - \mu}{\sigma} \hspace{3cm} (6.2)$$

Recall that $\mu$ is the mean of a population and $\overline{X}$ is the mean of a sample, and that $\sigma$ is the standard deviation of a population and $s$ is the standard deviation of a sample. The only difference between Equations 6.1 and 6.2 is whether sample statistics or population parameters are used for the comparison.

There is nothing magical about $z$-scores. They are simply a way of looking at a score relative to other scores in a distribution. In our illustration, a score of 62 is 12 points above the mean. With a standard deviation of 6, a score of 62 is two standard deviations above the mean. Thus, your $z$-score is 2. What if you had received a score of 56?

$$(56 - 50.0)/6.0 = 1.0. \hspace{1cm} \text{The } z\text{-score is } 1.0.$$

Here are some examples of raw scores converted to $z$-scores:

*If the raw score is 53* $\hspace{1cm} z = (53 - 50)/6 = \hspace{0.5cm} 3/6 = \hspace{0.5cm} 0.5$

*If the raw score is 47* $\hspace{1cm} z = (47 - 50)/6 = -3/6 = -0.5$

*If the raw score is 41* $\hspace{1cm} z = (41 - 50)/6 = -9/6 = -1.5$

In effect, a $z$-score looks at the distance of a score from the mean relative to a "standard" distance.

$$z = \frac{\text{distance of a score above or below the mean}}{\text{standard deviation}}$$

Now, if we were to convert every score in a distribution into a $z$-score, each $z$ would represent the deviation or distance of a specific score from the mean, expressed in standard deviation units. Those above the mean will be positive. Those below the mean will be negative. Those exactly on the mean will have values equal to zero. Finally, those farther away from the mean will have larger values than those scores close to the mean.

Suppose we were to take all raw scores in a distribution, subtract the mean from each [$(X - \overline{X})$, the familiar deviation score] and then divide each deviation score by the standard deviation. Would the transformed distribution possess any characteristics that are common to all distributions transformed in this way? The answer is "Yes."

The transformation of observed scores (also known as raw scores) to $z$-scores converts a distribution with any mean and standard deviation to a distribution where the mean is 0 and the standard deviation is 1.

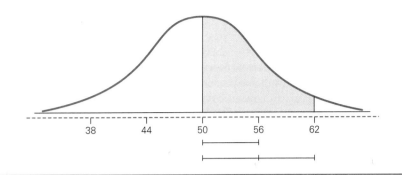

**Figure** | **6.1**

| **A distribution of scores in which the mean is 50 and the standard deviation is 6.**

Also, if all $z$ scores in a distribution are squared, their sum, $\Sigma z^2$, will be equal to $N$, the number of scores in the distribution. This fact may not seem important now but it will have important implications when we study correlation. The $z$-score transformation is often called a standardized transformation because all scales are converted to a standard scale.

$$\Sigma z = 0 \qquad \Sigma z^2 = N$$

What is the purpose of transforming to $z$-scores? The conversion to $z$-scores always yields a mean of 0 and a standard deviation of 1, but it does not "normalize" a distribution that is not normal to begin with. In fact, it doesn't change the shape of a distribution at all. If a distribution is skewed to begin with, transforming the scores to $z$-scores will not affect the skew of the distribution. However, if the population of scores on a given variable is normal, we may express any score as a percentile rank by comparing the $z$-score to the standard normal distribution. In addition, because $z$-scores represent abstract numbers, as opposed to the concrete values of the original scores (inches, pounds, IQ scores, etc.), we may compare an individual's position on one variable with his or her position on a different variable. To understand these important characteristics of $z$-scores, we must make reference to the standard normal distribution.

Before we move on to another topic, we want to close with a comment about the value of the $z$-score. There are many reasons that we want you to learn about $z$-scores. First, they are a useful descriptive statistic that you may use to better understand the data. Moreover, the $z$-score has important implications for several advanced statistics. For example, we will show you how the $z$-score can be used to calculate and understand the correlation coefficient. In addition, we will use the $z$-score to introduce you to some important aspects of probability in Chapter 10. Therefore a little practice and patience in learning about the $z$-score will be well repaid later in the book.

## 6.3 / The Standard Normal Distribution

As we have seen, many variables are distributed in such a way that the majority of the observations are concentrated near the center of the distribution. As you move from the center of the distribution, the frequencies of actual observations decrease, both above and below this central concentration of frequencies. This yields a bell-shaped distribution that is commonly referred to as the **normal distribution.** The normal distribution is a mathematical abstraction that statisticians use to describe events that happen in nature. Although the normal distribution is the invention of mathematicians, it is extremely useful in helping us describe natural events and various principles in statistics. As we will see in subsequent chapters, the normal distribution is one of the key elements in many statistical concepts.

Let's look at some of the important features of the normal distribution. One of the most important characteristics of the normal distribution is that it has a known mathematical function. Mathematical functions are important because they allow us to describe specific objects. For example, you probably recall from a math course that the formula for the area of a circle is:

$$Area = \pi(r^2)$$

Therefore, no matter how large the circle, you could calculate its area with this simple equation. The same is true for the normal distribution: we can use the same mathematical equation to describe a normal distribution regardless of the mean and standard deviation of the data. The equation for the normal distribution is:

$$f(X) = \frac{1}{\sqrt{2\pi\sigma^2}}\, e^{-(X-\mu)^2/2\sigma^2} \qquad (6.3)$$

where,

   $f(X)$ = the relative frequency of a particular score
    $X$ = the observed score
    $\mu$ = the population mean
    $\sigma^2$ = the population variance
    $\pi$ = the constant pi, $\pi \cong 3.1416$ (the symbol $\cong$ means "equals approximately"
    $e$ = the base of the natural logarithm, $e \cong 2.7183$

One of the most important aspects of defining the distribution mathematically is that we can determine the proportion of the area that is within specific parameters of the distribution. For example, in all normal distributions, approximately 34% of the distribution is between the mean and the first standard deviation. Because the distribution is symmetrical, we can say that approximately 68% of the normal distribution is ±1 standard deviations from the mean.

Examine the normal distribution presented in Figure 6.2. We can use this illustration to note several important points. First, note that the scale along the bottom of the distribution is in $z$-score units. That is, the mean of a normal distribution is 0 and the other numbers represent the standard deviation units above and below the mean. A $z$-score of $-2$ represents a score that is 2 standard deviations below the mean whereas a $z$-score of 3 represents a score that is 3 standard deviations above the mean.

A second characteristic of the distribution is its shape. It is bell-shaped and symmetric. As you can see the distribution has no skew ($s^3 = 0.0$) and is mesokurtic ($s^4 = 3.0$).

A third characteristic of the distribution relates to the proportion of the areas under different parts of the curve. This is where the value of having a constant mathematical function becomes essential. When we

■ **Normal Distribution:**

The normal distribution is a theoretical distribution used to describe various statistical concepts and empirical distributions. The shape of the distribution is defined by the equation:

$$f(X) = \frac{1}{\sqrt{2\pi\sigma^2}}\, e^{-(X-\mu)^2/2\sigma^2}.$$

The normal distribution has a $\mu = 0$ and a $\sigma = 1$. The normal distribution has no skew and is mesokurtic.

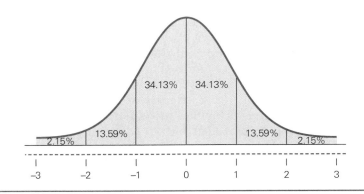

**Figure** | **6.2**

**Areas between selected points under the normal curve.**

convert a raw score into a z-score, we are able to assess the proportion of the area above and below that value and thus determine its percentile ranking. We are also able to assess the proportion of the area between two values. For normally and near-normally distributed variables, the proportion of the area between the mean and

±1 standard deviation is approximately .68, or 68%

±2 standard deviations is slightly more than .95, or 95%

±3 standard deviations is approximately .997 or 99.7%.

The value of the normal distribution lies in the fact that many real-world distributions—including values of a variable as well as values of sample statistics (e.g., means, variances, standard deviations)—approach the form of the normal distribution. This enables us to use the characteristics of the theoretical model to our advantage in real-world applications.

## 6.4 Comparing Test Scores

One of the most common uses of the z-score is comparing two different measures that have different means and standard deviations. Using the z-score transformation we can make direct comparisons among these different scales. Let us illustrate how this works. Take a situation in which we have three sets of test scores. The tests are designed to measure math, verbal, and logic aptitude. The three distributions are very different from one another in terms of central tendency and spread. The math test has the highest average test score. It also has the largest standard deviation. The logic test has the lowest average score and also the smallest standard deviation. Because of the difference in these distributions it doesn't make sense to compare a test score of 55 on the math test with a score of 14 on the test of logic. If we could convert all three test scores to a common scale we could compare the performance of an individual on the three very different measures.

As shown in Figure 6.3, we convert the observed or raw scores to z-scores to make these comparisons. Consider, for example, data from the math and the verbal test. A score of 57 is 1.0 standard deviation above the mean on the math test because $(57 - 50)/7 = 1.0$. A raw score of 4.2 is also 1 standard deviation above the mean for the verbal test because

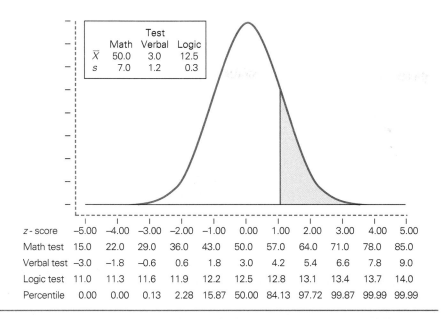

| z - score | −5.00 | −4.00 | −3.00 | −2.00 | −1.00 | 0.00 | 1.00 | 2.00 | 3.00 | 4.00 | 5.00 |
|---|---|---|---|---|---|---|---|---|---|---|---|
| Math test | 15.0 | 22.0 | 29.0 | 36.0 | 43.0 | 50.0 | 57.0 | 64.0 | 71.0 | 78.0 | 85.0 |
| Verbal test | −3.0 | −1.8 | −0.6 | 0.6 | 1.8 | 3.0 | 4.2 | 5.4 | 6.6 | 7.8 | 9.0 |
| Logic test | 11.0 | 11.3 | 11.6 | 11.9 | 12.2 | 12.5 | 12.8 | 13.1 | 13.4 | 13.7 | 14.0 |
| Percentile | 0.00 | 0.00 | 0.13 | 2.28 | 15.87 | 50.00 | 84.13 | 97.72 | 99.87 | 99.99 | 99.99 |

**Figure** | **6.3**

**Illustration of how the z-score allows different tests with different means and standard deviations to be compared to one another.**

(4.2 − 3.0)/1.2 = 1.0. Therefore, we can say that, relatively speaking, a score of 57 and 4.2 are equivalent to one another because they are the same relative distance above the mean. What would one standard deviation above the mean for the logic test be? A score of 12.8 represents a score that is one standard deviation above the mean for that distribution. As you can see in Figure 6.3, the three scores (57, 4.2, and 12.8) are each one standard deviation above the mean, and each is at the 84th percentile for the distribution.

## 6.5 / Areas Under the Curve

We confined our preceding discussion of areas under the standard normal curve to the selected points shown in Figure 6.2. As a matter of fact, it is possible to determine the percent of area between any two values in a distribution by making use of the tabled values under the normal curve (see Table A in Appendix C). To illustrate the use of this table, excerpts are presented in Table 6.1. The values in the left-most column, Column (A), represent the deviations of a score from the mean expressed in z-scores. For each z-score you can find in Column (B) the area between that score and the mean. The area is expressed in terms of a proportion and is in decimal form. That area will be larger the farther a score is from the mean. Column (C) contains the area beyond that z-score.

Take the example of Sally, who obtained a score of 25 on a normally distributed variable with $\mu = 16.0$ and $s = 5.0$. We can calculate the z-score as

$$z = \frac{(25 - 16)}{5} = \frac{9}{5} = 1.80$$

**Table** 6.1

**Excerpted Values from "Proportions of Area Under the Normal Curve"**

| (A) | (B) area between | (C) area | (A) | (B) area between | (C) area |
|-----|------------------|----------|-----|------------------|----------|
| $z$ | mean and $z$ | beyond $z$ | $z$ | mean and $z$ | beyond $z$ |
| 1.80 | .4641 | .0359 | 2.37 | .4911 | .0089 |
| 1.81 | .4649 | .0351 | 2.38 | .4913 | .0087 |
| 1.82 | .4656 | .0344 | 2.39 | .4916 | .0084 |
| 1.83 | .4664 | .0336 | 2.40 | .4918 | .0082 |
| 1.84 | .4671 | .0329 | 2.41 | .4920 | .0080 |

(From Table A in Appendix C)

Stop and think for a minute. What does 1.8 represent? It is 1.8 standard deviations away from the mean. The value is positive, so it represents the number of standard deviations above the mean. Now locate $z = 1.80$ in Column (A) of Table 6.1. Immediately to the right in Column (B) we find that .4641 is the proportion of area between that $z$-score and the mean. A proportion of .4641 may be converted to a percentage of 46.41% of the area. Because 50% of the area under the curve falls below the mean in a symmetrical distribution, we may conclude that 96.41% (50% + 46.41%) of all the area falls below Sally's score of 25. We can now say that her percentile rank is approximately 96.

Let's suppose that another individual obtained a score of 7 on the same normally distributed variable. Her $z$-score would be below the mean and would be negative:

$$z = \frac{(7 - 16)}{5} = -\frac{9}{5} = -1.80$$

Because the normal curve is symmetrical, only the areas corresponding to the positive $z$-scores are given in Table A of Appendix C and in Table 6.1. Negative $z$-scores have precisely the same proportions as their positive counterparts. Thus, the area between the mean and a $z = -1.80$ is also 46.41%. The percentile rank of any score below the mean may be obtained either by subtracting the value in the B column from .5000, or directly from Column (C), which shows proportions of areas farther from the mean. Using either approach, the percent of scores below a value of 7.0 is approximately 3.59 for a percentile rank of about 4.

Transforming the raw scores to standard scores does not in any way alter the form of the original distribution. The only change is to convert the mean of the resulting $z$-distribution to 0.0 and the standard deviation to 1.0. Thus, if the original distribution of scores is nonnormal, the distribution of $z$-scores will also be nonnormal.

## 6.6 Illustrative Examples

Let's take several examples in which we assume that $\mu = 100.0$ and $\sigma = 16.0$ on a standard IQ test. The test has been constructed so as to yield a normal distribution.

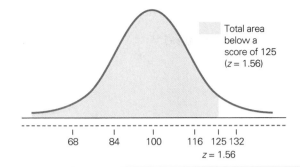

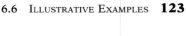

Total area
below a
score of 125
($z = 1.56$)

68    84    100    116  125 132
$z = 1.56$

**Figure** 6.4

An illustration of Example 1. The mean of the distribution is 100.0 and the standard deviation is 16.0. The observed score is 125.0. Using the calculations described in the text, a score of 125 is equal to a $z$-score of 1.56, which corresponds to the 94th percentile.

*Example 1*   Frank obtained a score of 125 on an IQ test. What percent of cases fall between his score and the mean? What is his percentile rank in the general population? Let's start by drawing a diagram of the problem as we did in Figure 6.4. We can begin by assuming that the data are normally distributed. Therefore, we can draw a normal distribution. Next, we know that a score of 125 is above the mean. Therefore, the $z$-score will be positive. To find the value of $z$ corresponding to $X = 125$, we subtract the population mean from 125 and divide by 16. Thus,

$$z = \frac{(125 - 100)}{16}$$

$$z = \frac{25}{16}$$

$$z = 1.56$$

Looking up 1.56, in Table A in Appendix C, we find from Column (B) that 44.06% of the area falls between the mean and 1.56 standard deviations above the mean. Therefore, Frank's percentile rank is 50.0 + 44.06 = 94.06. His IQ exceeds those of 94% of the general population.

*Example 2*   Corinne scores 93.0 on the IQ test. What is her percentile rank in the general population? To answer this question examine Figure 6.5. Her score is below the mean so we would expect to calculate a negative $z$-score and the percentile to be less than 50.0.

$$z = \frac{(93 - 100)}{16}$$

$$z = -\frac{7}{16}$$

$$z = -0.44$$

The minus sign indicates that the score is below the mean. Looking up a $z$-score of 0.44 in Table A in Appendix C, we find in Column (C) that 33.0% of the cases fall below her score. Thus, her percentile rank is 33. Note that we could also have taken the value in Column (B) and subtracted it from .5000.

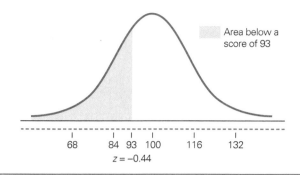

**Figure** | **6.5**

An illustration of Example 2. The mean of the distribution is 100 and the standard deviation is 16. The observed score is 93. Using the calculations described in the text, a score of 93 is equal to a *z*-score of –0.44, which corresponds to the 33rd percentile.

*one score is > mean*
*one score is < mean*

***Example 3*** What percent of cases fall between a score of 120 and a score of 88? Look at Figure 6.6. Note that to answer this question we do not subtract 88 from 120 and divide by $\sigma$. The areas under the normal curve are designated in relation to the mean as a fixed point of reference. We must therefore separately calculate the area between the mean and a score of 120 and the area between the mean and a score of 88. We then add the two areas together. The procedure is:

**Step 1** To find the $z$ corresponding to $X = 120$:
$$z = \frac{(120 - 100)}{16} = 1.25$$

**Step 2** To find the $z$ corresponding to $X = 88$:

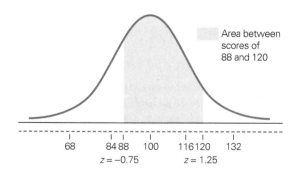

**Figure** | **6.6**

An illustration of Example 3. The mean of the distribution is 100 and the standard deviation is 16. The observed scores are 88 and 120. Using the calculations described in the text, a score of 88 is equal to a *z*-score of –0.75. The area of the normal curve between 100 and 88 represents 27.34% of the distribution. A score of 120 is equal to a *z*-score of 1.25. The area of the normal curve between 100 and 120 represents 39.44% of the distribution. Therefore, 66.78% (27.34 + 39.44 = 66.78) of the normal curve is between 88 and 120.

$$z = \frac{(88 - 100)}{16} = -0.75$$

**Step 3**  Find the required areas by referring to Column (B), Table A:
Area between the mean and $z = 1.25$ is 39.44%
Area between the mean and $z = -0.75$ is 27.34%

**Step 4**  Add the two areas together. Thus, the percent of area between IQs of 125 and 88 is 39.44% + 27.34% = 66.78%.

*Example 4*  What is the percent of area between a score of 123 and 135 (Figure 6.7)? Here again, we cannot obtain the answer directly; we must find the area between the mean and a score of 123 and subtract this from the area between the mean and a score of 135. The procedures are as follows:

*both scores are > mean*

**Step 1**  Find the $z$ corresponding to 135:
$$z = \frac{(135 - 100)}{16} = 2.19$$

**Step 2**  Find the $z$ corresponding to 123:
$$z = \frac{(123 - 100)}{16} = 1.44$$

**Step 3**  Find the required areas by referring to Column (B):
Area between the mean and $z = 2.19$ is 48.57%
Area between the mean and $z = 1.44$ is 42.51%

**Step 4**  Subtract to obtain the area between 123 and 135:
48.57% − 42.51% = 6.06%.

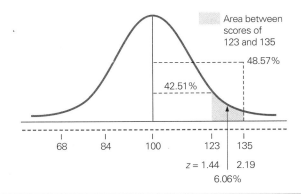

**Figure** | **6.7**

An illustration of Example 4. The mean of the distribution is 100 and the standard deviation is 16. The observed scores are 135 and 123. Using the calculations described in the text, a score of 135 is equal to a *z*-score of 2.19. The area of the normal curve between 100 and 135 represents 48.57% of the distribution. A score of 123 is equal to a *z*-score of 1.44. The area of the normal curve between 100 and 123 represents 42.51% of the distribution. Therefore, 6.06% (48.57 − 42.51 = 6.06) of the normal curve is between 123 and 135.

***Example 5***   We stated earlier that our transformation to $z$-scores permits us to compare an individual's position on one variable with her or his position on another. Let's look at this important use of $z$-scores.

On a standard aptitude test, Andrea obtained a score of 245.0 on the verbal scale and 175.0 on the mathematics scale. The means and standard deviations of each of these normally distributed variables are as follows:

Verbal Test: $\mu = 220$, $\sigma = 50$
Math Test: $\mu = 150$, $\sigma = 25$

On which test did Andrea perform better? To answer this question we must first convert each raw score to a $z$-score.

$$\text{Verbal } z = \frac{(245 - 220)}{50} = 0. \qquad \text{Math } z = \frac{(175 - 150)}{25} = 1.0$$

Her verbal score was 0.5 standard deviation above the mean and her math score was 1.0 standard deviation above the mean. We conclude that, even though her raw score was lower on the math scale, her relative performance was better on the math test than on the verbal test. Her percentile rank was 84.13 for math and 69.15 on the verbal test.

***Example 6***   In each of the preceding examples, we knew the mean, the standard deviation, and the value of the variable for which we wished to find the corresponding percentage of area. There are occasions when the percentage of area is known and we wish to find the value of the variable that yielded this percentage. To illustrate, imagine that you wish to join a highly selective intellectual society that requires that its members be in the upper 2% of the population in intelligence. The IQ test used for selection has a mean of 100 and a standard deviation of 16.

The first step is to find the value of $z$ that cuts off the upper 2% (i.e., 0.0200) of area under the standard normal curve. Referring to Column (C) in Table A of Appendix C, we find that the area beyond a $z$ of 2.05 excludes 2.02% of the area under the normal curve. This is a bit more than 2%. However, a $z$ of 2.06 excludes only 1.97% of the area under the curve. We will use a $z$ of 2.05 in our calculations. Using the formula $X = z\sigma + \mu$, we find $X = (2.05 \times 16) + 100 = 132.8$. Thus, a minimum IQ of 133 would be needed to qualify for membership in this society.

## 6.7 / Using *s* to Estimate Error and Precision

In the absence of any specific information, what is our best single basis for predicting a score that is obtained by any given individual? If the data are drawn from a normally distributed population, the mean is our best single predictor. However, the dispersion of the scores determines just how precise a predictor it is. The more compactly our scores are distributed about

**Table** 6.2

**Two Distributions with Identical Means but Widely Different Variability\***

| | PLAYER A | | PLAYER B | |
|---|---|---|---|---|
| | $X_A$ | $X_A^2$ | $X_B$ | $X_B^2$ |
| | 14 | 196 | 10 | 100 |
| | 15 | 225 | 18 | 324 |
| | 12 | 144 | 9 | 81 |
| | 15 | 225 | 19 | 361 |
| | 14 | 196 | 14 | 196 |
| | 15 | 225 | 6 | 36 |
| | 13 | 169 | 22 | 484 |
| Σ | 98 | 1380 | 98 | 1582 |

$$SS_A = 1380 - \frac{98^2}{7}$$
$$= 1380 - 1372$$
$$= 8$$
$$s_A = \sqrt{\frac{8}{7}} = 1.07$$

$$SS_B = 1582 - \frac{98^2}{7}$$
$$= 1582 - 1372$$
$$= 210$$
$$s_B = \sqrt{\frac{210}{7}} = 5.48$$

\*These data are the number of points earned by two basketball players during a seven-game period. Both players obtained precisely the same mean, but note how much variability there was in the performance of Player B.

the mean, the smaller our errors in prediction will be. Conversely, when the scores are widely spread about the mean, we will make larger errors in prediction.

Consider the data presented in Table 6.2 that consist of the number of points scored by the star forwards on two different basketball teams. Each player, A and B, scores *on average* 14 points per game. Notice how much more variable Player B's performance is. You would surely feel more confident in predicting that Player A rather than Player B would score about 14 points in a given game. Because the standard deviation reflects the dispersion of scores, it becomes, in a sense, an estimate of error. The smaller the standard deviation, the smaller the error in predicting any given score. This point is illustrated in Figure 6.8.

## 6.8 / The Transformation to *T*-Scores

Many psychological and educational tests have been purposely constructed to yield a normal distribution of z-scores. Recall that z-scores include negative values and are expressed in decimal form. Since the lay public often finds it confusing to deal with decimals and negative numbers, the z-scores of normally distributed variables are sometimes converted to *T*-scores. A *T*-score is a standard score that is always a positive value and is a whole number rather than a decimal value. We use the following transformation equation to convert z-scores to *T*-scores:

$$T = \overline{T} + s(z) \tag{6.4}$$

"I have some good news and some bad news, Captain. The bad news is that first we were 150 meters past the target; then 150 meters under; next 75 meters under and, then, 75 meters over. Not a single #*!#* shell on target. The good news is that, on the average, we were right on target!"

**Figure | 6.8**

A cartoon illustrating the need to recognize that the mean, by itself, tells only part of the story. We need to know the standard deviation in order to understand how accurately the mean represents each of the observations.

where
$T$ = transformed score
$\overline{T}$ = mean of scale as determined by researcher
$s$ = standard deviation of scale to be determined by researcher
$z$ = z-score

Here is an example of a z-score of $-1.52$ transformed to a standard T-score with a mean of 100 and a standard deviation of 10.

$$T = 100 + 10(-1.52)$$
$$= 100 - 15.2 = 84.8$$

For T-scores it is traditional to round to the nearest whole number. In this case the T-score would be 85.

We may readily convert T-scores back to units of the standard normal curve:

$$z = \frac{T - \overline{T}}{s} \tag{6.5}$$

Thus, a person obtaining a T of 84.8 (we will use the more precise decimal value) would have a corresponding z of

$$z = \frac{84.8 - 100}{10} = -1.52$$

A z-score of $-1.52$ may then be evaluated using Table A in Appendix C to determine the proportion of the area under the normal curve that is lower than this value. We find that the area below a z of $-1.52$ (see Column C) is .0643 and thus the score has a percentile rank of 6.43.

An important benefit of the T-score transformation is that it allows us to compare people from different age groups. Consider, for example, two people who take a standardized memory test—an 18-year-old and a 42-year-old. There are many reasons that we might not want to compare the younger person's performance on the test to the older person's score. As an alternative, we are interested in how the younger person scored relative to other young people. Likewise, we want to compare the older

**What score did you get on your Scholastic Aptitude Test?**

At this point you may be interested in evaluating a score you (or a friend) earned on a test of scholastic aptitude. Some of these aptitude tests have a mean of 500 and a standard deviation of 100. If you received a score of 560, what proportion of test takers scored below your score? To answer the question you must first convert your *T*-score back to a *z*-score. Thus,

$$z = \frac{560 - 500}{100} = \frac{60}{100} = 0.6$$

For a z-score of .6, the area between the mean and that score is .2257. Thus 22.57% of test takers scored between the mean and that *z*-score. We already know that 50% of the group fell below the mean. So 50% and 22.57% taken together equals 72.57%. More than 72% of those taking the test scored lower than you did.

individual to people of similar age and background. Basically, we are evaluating each individual's score relative to his/her peer group. Here is a hypothetical example of what we might find.

For the population of young people (18–19) the average raw score is 147 points with a standard deviation of 12 points. The 18-year-old receives a score of 153. For the population of older people (35–44) the average raw score is 153 points with a standard deviation of 7 points. The 42-year-old receives a score of 161 points.

**Step 1**  Convert raw scores to *z*-scores

| **18-Year-Old** | **42-Year-Old** |
|---|---|
| $\dfrac{153 - 147}{12} = 0.5$ | $\dfrac{161 - 153}{7} = 1.14$ |

**Step 2**  Convert *z*-scores to *T*-scores

$T = 100.0 + 10.0(0.5)$      $T = 100.0 + 10.0(1.14)$

                             $T = 111.4$

$T = 105.0$                  $T = 111.0$

In the last step we rounded to the nearest whole number. Using these *T*-scores, we can now directly compare the two people. In essence we can say that the score of the 42-year-old, relative to his or her peers, scored higher than the 18-year-old individual, relative to his or her peers.

# 6.9 / Putting It All Together

Table 6.3 shows the scores of Mary Cardinale on six scales of a standardized aptitude test. Also shown are the mean and standard deviation for each scale. The conversion of each of Mary's scores into *z*-scores and percentile ranks is shown in Table 6.4.

Take note of the fact that Mary's raw score on Logical Reasoning is the second to lowest of all her scores. Nevertheless, her percentile rank on this scale is her highest, exceeding 96% of the group against which this test was standardized. Conversely, her highest raw score, 105, was on the Numerical Reasoning Scale, but her percentile rank was

**Table** 6.3

**The Mean and Standard Deviation on Six Scales of a Standardized Test and the Scores Made by Mary Cardinale**

|  | Clerical Ability | Logical Reasoning | Mechanical Ability | Numerical Reasoning | Spatial Relations | Verbal Fluency |
|---|---|---|---|---|---|---|
| Score | 41 | 47 | 100 | 105 | 90 | 70 |
| Mean | 50 | 40 | 120 | 100 | 70 | 60 |
| $\sigma$ | 15 | 4 | 25 | 10 | 20 | 6 |

**Table** 6.4

**Conversion of Six Scores on a Standardized Test to Percentile Ranks**

| Scale | z-score | Percentile Rank |
|---|---|---|
| Clerical ability | $(41 - 50) / 15 = -0.60$ | 27 |
| Logical reasoning | $(47 - 40) / 4 = 1.75$ | 96 |
| Mechanical ability | $(100 - 120) / 25 = -0.80$ | 21 |
| Numerical reasoning | $(105 - 100) / 10 = 0.50$ | 69 |
| Spatial relations | $(90 - 70) / 20 = 1.00$ | 84 |
| Verbal fluency | $(70 - 60) / 6 = 1.67$ | 95 |

considerably lower than her rank on the Logical Reasoning Scale. How is it possible that a "high" raw score can be low and a "low" raw score can be high?

This example illustrates that performance is not necessarily judged on the basis of raw scores. What must be taken into account is the mean

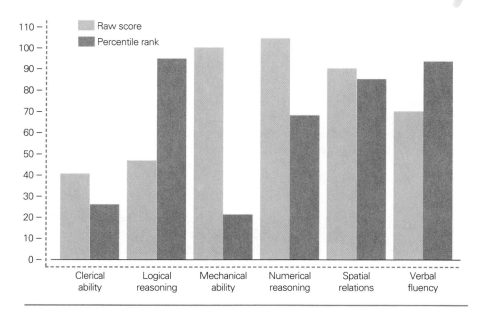

**Figure** 6.9

**Bar graph of Mary Cardinale's relative performance on six scales of an aptitude test. The blue bars show her raw scores, whereas the grey bars represent a measure based on relative performance (percentile rank).**

and the standard deviation of the comparison group on each scale of the aptitude test. Converting each score to a common scale of values (the $z$-scale) and a common reference standard (the standard normal curve) enables us to compare an individual's relative performance (percentile rank) on a diverse spectrum of abilities. Figure 6.9 shows a bar graph of Mary's raw scores and her relative performance (percentile rank) on several different measures of ability. Note again how misleading your estimates of Mary's abilities would be if you based your conclusions exclusively on her raw scores.

## CHAPTER SUMMARY

In this chapter, we saw that when distributions take the form of the symmetrical bell-shaped curve, the standard deviation is useful in interpreting the relative position of scores in that distribution. A raw score is first converted to a standard score or $z$-score, and then it is possible to evaluate that score relative to the rest of the distribution. Standard scores are also used to compare scores on two or more variables. A series of examples demonstrated how to convert raw scores into standard or $z$-scores and to assess areas under the curve. The $z$-scores were also converted to percentile ranks.

We discussed the standard deviation as an estimate of error and of precision. We demonstrated the use of the T-transformation as a means of eliminating decimals and negative values. Finally we examined the ability profile of an individual, using raw scores and standard scores. Standard scores were then converted to percentile ranks.

## TERMS TO REMEMBER

normal distribution
$z$-score

## EXERCISES

1. Given a normal distribution with a mean of 45.2 and a standard deviation of 10.4, find the standard score equivalents for the following scores:
   **a.** 55　　　　**b.** 41　　　　**c.** 45.2
   **d.** 31.5　　　**e.** 68.4　　　**f.** 18.9

2. Find the proportion of area under the normal curve between the mean and the following $z$-scores:
   **a.** −2.05　　　**b.** −1.90　　　**c.** −0.25
   **d.** +0.40　　　**e.** +1.65　　　**f.** +1.96
   **g.** +2.33　　　**h.** +2.58　　　**i.** +3.08

3. Assume a normal distribution based on 1,000 cases with a mean of 50 and a standard deviation of 10.
   **a.** Find the proportion of area and the number of cases *between* the mean and the following scores:
   　　60　　70　　45　　25
   **b.** Find the proportion of area and the number of cases *above* the following scores:
   　　60　　70　　45　　25　　50
   **c.** Find the proportion of area and the number of cases *between* the following scores:
   　　60 and 70　　25 and 60　　45 and 70　　25 and 45

4. Below are Debbie's scores, the mean, and the standard deviation on each of three normally distributed tests.

| Test | $\mu$ | $\sigma$ | Score |
|------|------|------|-------|
| Arithmetic | 47.2 | 4.8 | 53 |
| Verbal comprehension | 64.6 | 8.3 | 71 |
| Geography | 75.4 | 11.7 | 72 |

   a. Convert each of Debbie's test scores to standard scores.
   b. On which test did Debbie stand the highest? On which the lowest?
   c. Debbie's score in arithmetic was surpassed by what proportion of the population? Her score in verbal comprehension? In geography?

5. On a normally distributed mathematics aptitude test, for females,

$$\mu = 60 \qquad \sigma = 10$$

and for males,

$$\mu = 64 \qquad \sigma = 8$$

   a. Richard obtained a score of 62. What is his percentile rank on both the male and the female norms?
   b. Lois has a percentile rank of 73 on the female norms. What is her percentile rank on the male norms?

6. If frequency curves were constructed for each of the following, which would approximate a normal curve?
   a. Heights of a large representative sample of adult American males
   b. Means of a large number of samples with a fixed $N$ (say, $N = 100$) drawn from a normally distributed population of scores
   c. Weights, in ounces, of ears of corn selected randomly from a cornfield
   d. Annual income, in dollars, of a large number of American families selected at random
   e. Weight, in ounces, of fish caught in a popular fishing resort in a season

7. In a normal distribution with $\mu = 72$ and $\sigma = 12$:
   a. What is the score at the 25th percentile?
   b. What is the score at the 75th percentile?
   c. What is the score at the 90th percentile?
   d. Find the percent of cases scoring above 80.
   e. Find the percent of cases scoring below 66.
   f. Between what scores do the middle 50 percent of the cases lie?
   g. Beyond what scores do the most extreme 10 percent lie?
   h. Beyond what scores do the most extreme 1 percent lie?

8. Answer questions 7 a. through h. for:
   a. $\mu = 72$ and $\sigma = 8$
   b. $\mu = 72$ and $\sigma = 4$
   c. $\mu = 72$ and $\sigma = 2$

9. Using the following information, determine whether Larry did better on Test I or Test II. On which test did Jessica do better?

| | Test I | Test II |
|------|------|------|
| $\mu$ | 500 | 24 |
| $\sigma$ | 40 | 1.4 |
| Larry's scores | 550 | 26 |
| Jessica's scores | 600 | 25 |

**10.** Are all sets of $z$-scores normally distributed? Why?

**11.** Is there more than one normal distribution?

**12.** Transform the following $z$-scores to $T$-scores, using $T = 50 + 10(z)$. Round to the nearest whole number.
    **a.** −2.43      **b.** 1.50      **c.** −0.50      **d.** 0.00

**13.** The transformation to $T$-scores yields the following values when $T = 500 + 100(z)$. Convert back to the original $z$-scores.
    **a.** 230      **b.** 500      **c.** 780      **d.** 640      **e.** 460

**14.** Transform the raw scores presented in Exercise 13 a. through e. to $T$-scores, when $T = 100 + 15(z)$.

**15.** In what sense can the standard deviation be regarded as a measure of precision?

# 7

# Graphs and Tables

# 7.1 / Introduction

Consider this lucid passage about classical conditioning: The standard learning curve, which represents the strength of the conditioned response, is a negatively accelerating hyperbolic function with the asymptote representing a complete association between the conditioned stimulus and the unconditioned stimulus. Perfectly clear, right? If you have studied mathematics or engineering, and are familiar with "negatively accelerating hyperbolic functions" and recall all the subtleties of the meaning of "asymptote," you should have no problem understanding this description. Chances are, however, that the sentence has no meaning for you at all. We could try to rewrite it and use more words to describe the same thing, but if we did, it would be much longer and there would be a good chance that some readers might not fully understand all the details.

What if we told you that Figure 7.1 represents the results of a simple classical conditioning experiment using a dog and Pavlov's conditioning procedure? In this experiment the psychologist rang a bell (the Conditioned Stimulus) and then presented the dog with a small piece of meat (the Unconditioned Stimulus). The vertical line of the graph represents the amount of saliva produced when the bell rang. The horizontal line represents the number of trials in the experiment. As you can see, the conditioned response increased very quickly during the first several trials and eventually leveled off and remained constant.

Graphs and tables are essential parts of the data analysis and the research report. Like other statistical tools, graphs and tables help us organize, summarize, and interpret data based on research. A well-constructed graph or table will help you and others understand the data. Indeed, you may find that the data are easier to understand and explain when you use a graph or a table. Good graphs allow the reader to quickly perceive complex trends that would otherwise be difficult to describe in words. As you may have already experienced, it can take the reader several minutes to read a written description of the results but only seconds

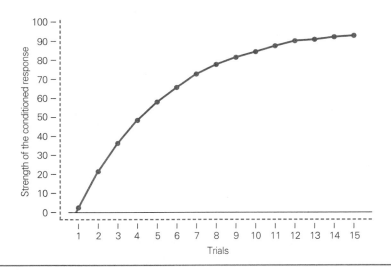

**Figure** | **7.1**

**Strength of a conditioned response (CR) as a function of the number of trials of pairings of the conditioned stimulus and unconditioned stimulus.**

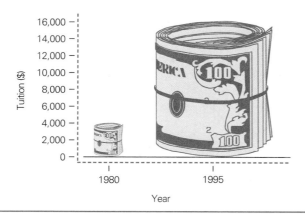

**Figure** | 7.2

A pictograph representing the increase in the average cost of tuition at a 4-year college between 1980 and 1995.

to "read" a graph. Finally, good graphs are easy to remember. People are more likely to remember a picture than a list of facts and numbers.

You have probably seen thousands of graphs in newspapers, magazines, books, and on television. This fact confirms the importance of graphs for relaying information in a quick and easy-to-understand manner. In this chapter we will examine graphing techniques that researchers use. As you will soon learn, there are important differences between graphs used in the popular press and those used by scientists.

As an example of this difference, look at Figure 7.2, which represents the increase in the cost of a college education between 1980 and 1995. Technically speaking, this graph is a pictograph because we use a picture of $100 bills to represent the data. This graph presents the simple fact that the average four-year college tuition increased between 1980 and 1995. Specifically, the tuition in 1995 was four times greater than the tuition in 1980 ($16,000/$4,000 = 4).

If you look at the tops of the bundles of $100 bills, you can see that they accurately represent the value of the average tuition as indicated on the vertical or *Y*-axis. If we concentrate our attention on the size of the bundles of $100 bills, we may falsely conclude that the tuition increase during the 10-year period was much greater than the actual increase. The problem is that the area covered by the bundles of bills for 1995 is approximately 16 times larger than the area of the 1980 bundle. Therefore, many people may be misled by this graph. This is one of the main reasons why researchers do not use pictographs. The goal of scientific graphing is to present accurate representations of the data in as simple a manner as possible.

# 7.2 / Characteristics of a Graph

Let's begin by looking at the common features of good graphs and the general form they take. Researchers follow several general guidelines when constructing graphs. By following these guidelines, a knowledgeable reader can interpret the meaning of a graph quickly and with minimal effort. Figure 7.3 represents the foundation for most of the graphs you will probably construct.

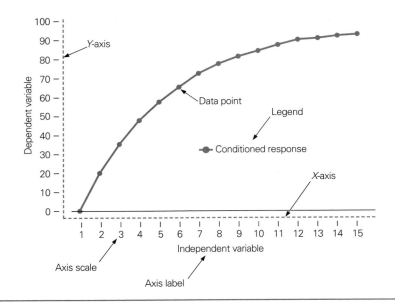

**Figure | 7.3**

**Example of a graph with the primary features noted. Note that the independent variable is always plotted along the *X*-axis, and the dependent variable is plotted along the *Y*-axis. See the text for a more detailed discussion of the common elements of a graph.**

Although each graph is unique, all graphs share several fundamental features. The following is a brief list and explanation of these features.

**Feature 1**    All graphs have two axes that are drawn at a right angle. The horizontal axis is the abscissa or *X*-axis. The vertical axis is the ordinate or the *Y*-axis. For the remainder of the book, we will call the axes the *X*-axis and *Y*-axis.

**Feature 2**    We plot the independent variable along the *X*-axis and the dependent variable along the *Y*-axis. Remember that the researcher uses the independent variable to predict, describe, or explain differences in the dependent variable. The response of the subject, the dependent variable, is the variable of interest in the research.

**Feature 3**    The length of the *X*- and *Y*-axis conforms to the golden rectangle. Many people find the golden rectangle to be aesthetically pleasing. An example of the golden rectangle is a box that is 3 inches high and 5 inches wide. In other words, the width of a graph is approximately 1.7 times its height.

**Feature 4**    There is a clear label for both the *X*-axis and the *Y*-axis. All graphs must include the measurement scale and the names of the variables presented. As you can see in Figure 7.3, each axis contains a label and scale. The tics along the axis are also important and give the reader a visual guide for the axis scale. The legend defines the lines within the body of the graph.

**Feature 5**   The *Y*-axis is a continuous scale. Do not break the *Y*-axis unless you have a compelling reason to do so.

**Feature 6**   The graph contains information related to the data. There is no need to embellish the graph with items other than those presented in Figure 7.3.

Now that we have examined some of the basic features of graphs, let's look at some of the techniques available for presenting data. The graphs that we present are the ones most often used in the behavioral sciences.

## 7.3 / The Bar Graph

A **bar graph** has several unique features. First, the *X*-axis presents nominal data or categorical information. In other words, we use the bar graph whenever the information plotted along the *X*-axis represents categories that can be arranged in different patterns. Therefore, we use bar graphs to present *qualitative* categories as opposed to *quantitative* data.

A second feature of the bar graph is that the bars do not touch. This is an important feature of the graph. Because the information along the *X*-axis is qualitative, we need to represent each bar as a different class and show that the classes do not represent a continuous variable. The gap suggests to the reader that there is no meaningful continuum along the *X*-axis.

The *Y*-axis of the bar graph may present frequencies, percentages, or descriptive statistics such as the mean. For example, you could use a bar graph to present the number of students who select the various majors across campus, the percentage of students selecting each major, or the average cumulative grade point average of students in each major.

Figures 7.4 and 7.5 are two examples of bar graphs. These data present the number of adolescents who perceive themselves to be underweight or overweight. Although both graphs present the same information, there are several important differences.

First, Figure 7.4 presents the frequencies for the four classes. There were 2,414 females and 1,814 males in the study. The fact that there are many more women in the study may cause us to misinterpret the results. A suitable alternative would be to convert the data to percentages as was done in Figure 7.5. Converting from frequencies to percentages allows us to directly compare the percentage of males and females who see themselves as overweight or underweight.

The second difference between the two graphs is how we arranged the categories along the *X*-axis. In Figure 7.4, the emphasis is to compare the underweight and overweight categories within each sex. The emphasis in Figure 7.5 is to compare males and females within each category. Which arrangement is better? The answer to that question must come from the purpose of the graph. In essence, the arrangement in Figure 7.4 is better if the goal is to look at the pattern within each sex. If the goal is to compare males and females, then Figure 7.5 may be better.

■ **Bar Graph:**

A form of graph that uses rectangles, or bars, to represent nominal categories. The bars do not touch.

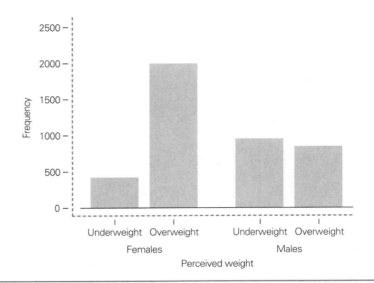

**Figure** | 7.4

**Number of female and male adolescents who perceive themselves as being either overweight or underweight.**

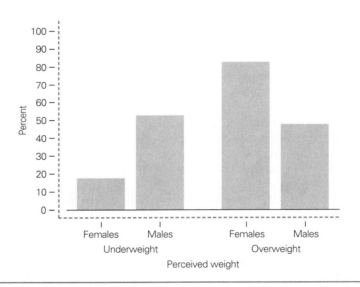

**Figure** | 7.5

**Percentages, by sex, of male and female adolescents who perceive themselves to be underweight or overweight.**

■ **Dot Chart:**

An alternative to the bar graph. Each line represents a separate category. The scale is arranged along the horizontal axis.

## 7.4 / The Dot Chart

An alternative to the bar graph is the **dot chart**. Cleveland (1984a, 1984b, 1985) invented dot charts as an improvement over bar graphs. The dot chart has several advantages over the bar graph. First, it is easier to sort the data into meaningful groups and subgroups when using a dot chart. Another advantage of the dot chart is that it is easy to create and makes better use of space. Finally,

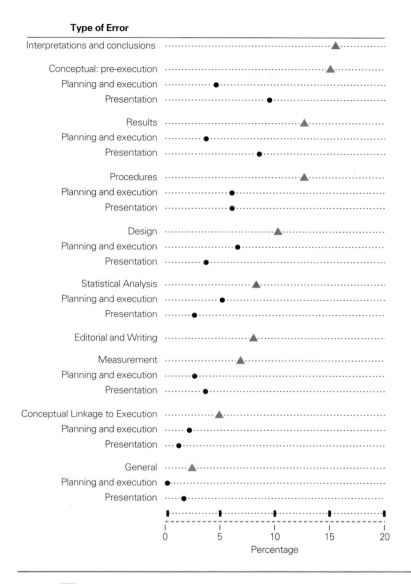

**Figure** | 7.6

An example of a dot chart. For each major category the ▲ represents the total percentage error for that category. The subdivisions, represented by the ●, indicate the degree to which the error was due to planning or executing the study, or to the presentation of information in the manuscript.

many people find dot charts easier to read than bar graphs. Figure 7.6 provides an example of a dot chart.

Fiske and Fogg (1990) reviewed the editorial decisions written in reaction to 153 manuscripts submitted for publication in journals published by the American Psychological Association. The authors then categorized the editorial reactions by different types and determined if the problem with the manuscript had to do with the planning and execution of the research or with the presentation of the material. As you can see, the types of errors are ranked from the most to the least common type. For example, it is clear that the highest percentage of errors involved interpretations and conclusions.

## 7.5 / The Histogram

The main difference between the histogram and the bar graph is the measurement scale for the *X*-axis. For the **histogram,** the scale is ordinal or higher. Therefore, the *X*-axis of the histogram presents a quantitative variable—the scale represents a continuum that ranges from low to high scores.

Histograms use bars to present the data. The bars represent a class interval. **A class interval** is a category of numbers with specified limits. Letter grades on an exam represent class intervals. The letter grades

**■ Histogram:**

A form of bar graph used to present information where the *X*-scale is ordinal or better.

**■ Class Interval:**

A group of numerical values organized according to a specified range or width.

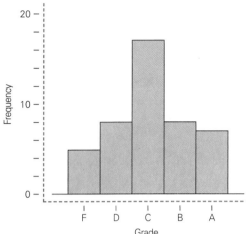

**Figure | 7.7**

Histogram of grades between F and A. Do you think that this is the best way to present grades? Note that the lower end of the *X*-axis is the F category and the upper end of the axis is the A category. We chose this scale because As are better grades than Fs. Some people may, however, find the graph unsettling because the order of letters appears to be backward.

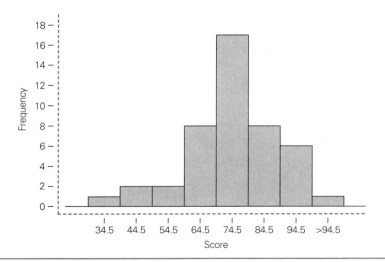

**Figure | 7.8**

Histogram of grades, showing midpoint of each class interval.

represent ranges of scores. For example, most professors assign a B to exams with a score between 80% and 89%. Similarly, an A represents a score between 90% and 100%.

Figure 7.7 is an example of a histogram. The X-axis represents the letter grades F through A. Note that the bars touch, indicating that the grades represent a meaningful continuum. Figure 7.8 presents the same information, but in a slightly different form. In this figure, the instructor reported the data using the test scores. Each number represents the midpoint of the class. For example 84.5 represents the middle of the B grade $[(80 + 89)/2 = 84.5]$.

## 7.6 / The Stem-and-Leaf Plot

We spent considerable time examining the merits of the stem-and-leaf plot in Chapter 3. As you may recall, we suggested that this plot is a useful tool for learning about your data. It can also be an effective method for presenting the data to others. Figure 7.9 presents a version of the stem-and-leaf plot that follows the format of the histogram. The data are the same exam grades presented in Figures 7.7 and 7.8. As you can see, the numbers replace the bars. Using this form of the stem-and-leaf plot, the instructor can quickly show the students the distribution of grades. The plot also retains all the original information. Therefore, it is easy for anyone to see how they did relative to others in the class.

## 7.7 / The Box-and-Whisker Plot

John Tukey (1977) devised the box-and-whisker plot as a graph to represent as much of the data as possible while keeping the graph as simple as possible. The **box-and-whisker plot** represents information about the central tendency, dispersion, and shape of the distribution all in a single form. Figure 7.10 presents four sets of data using the box-and-whisker plot.

■ **Box-and-Whisker Plot:**

A form of graph consisting of a rectangle and several lines. The rectangle represents the interquartile range $(Q_3 - Q_1)$. The vertical lines extend from the rectangle to the extreme scores. A horizontal line represents the median.

```
                        8
                        7
                        6
                        6
                        5
                        5
                        5
                        5
                        5
                9   4   8
                9   3   7
                8   3   6   9
                7   3   6   5
                7   2   5   2
                6   2   2   1
        9   9   6   1   1   1
    1   0   9   6   1   1   1   0
    ----------------------------------
    3   4   5   6   7   8   9   10
```

**Figure** | **7.9**

Stem-and-leaf plot of the data shown in Figure 7.8.

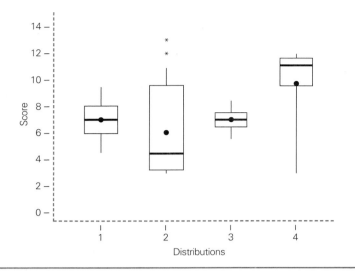

**Figure** | **7.10**

Box-and-whisker plots. This figure presents plots of four different distributions. Note that the solid circle (•) within each plot represents the arithmetic mean and that the horizontal line represents the median. The vertical lines above and below each rectangle identify the range. The two asterisks above the whisker for Distribution 2 represent two outliers.

The "box" in the box-and-whisker plot refers to the rectangular portion of the graph. The lower edge of the plot represents the 25th percentile, and the upper end represents the 75th percentile. Therefore, the box represents the interquartile range. The size of the box (height in our example) implies the variability of the data. The greater the distance on the scale between the 25th and 75th percentile, the greater the variability of the data.

The "whiskers" of the plot extend from the lower and upper edges of the box to the extreme scores in the data set. Specifically, the lower whisker extends from the lowest score to the 25th percentile. Similarly, the upper whisker extends from the 75th percentile to the highest score.

Some researchers and computer programs draw the whisker differently. For example, some researchers prefer to draw the whisker to the 10th and 90th percentiles and then mark the extreme scores with an asterisk (*). There are many versions and variations of the box-and-whisker plot. Because of this variability, it is important that you pay special attention to the caption of these graphs. Also, if you use a computer to generate these graphs, be sure you understand how the program draws the figure.

The final characteristics of the box-and-whisker plot are the figures within the box. As you can see, our plot contains both a solid circle (•) and a bold horizontal line. The circle represents the arithmetic mean and the horizontal line represents the median. You can use this information to infer the skew of the data. Skew refers to the fact that the data are not symmetrically distributed. The mean is sensitive to extreme scores in the data whereas the median is not. Consequently, when the mean is greater than the median, we say that the data are positively skewed. Distribution 2 in Figure 7.10 represents a positive skew. The skew is negative when the mean is less than the median, as is illustrated in Distribution 4 of Figure 7.10.

# 7.8 / The Line Graph

The **line graph** is a popular and effective method of presenting data. There are many advantages to this graph. One of the most important advantages of the line graph is that we can simultaneously present data from several conditions. Consider Figures 7.11 and 7.12. Both present data reported by Hare (1965). Hare compared normal people to people diagnosed as having an antisocial personality disorder. For part of his research, Hare examined how these groups of people would react to standard classical conditioning. On each trial, a subject heard a tone, and after a brief interval, received a mild shock. The dependent variable was the strength of the conditioned responses to the tone.

Figure 7.11 is a histogram presenting Hare's data. Figure 7.12 presents the same data using a line graph. Although both Figures 7.11 and 7.12 present the same data, we believe that Figure 7.12 is easier to interpret. The lines create a clear link from one data point to the next. This visual continuity gives the clear impression that the data represent a continuous set of data. In addition, because we use different lines, it is easy to compare the two groups over time. As you can see, the normal subjects quickly developed a conditioned response to the tone and that this response became quite strong.

## Treatment of the *Y*-axis

Huff (1954), in his humorous and informative book *How to Lie with Statistics*, tells the reader to beware of the graph that has no absolute 0 for the *Y*-axis. Huff's concern is that someone can be economical with the truth and present misleading information with a graph that has a

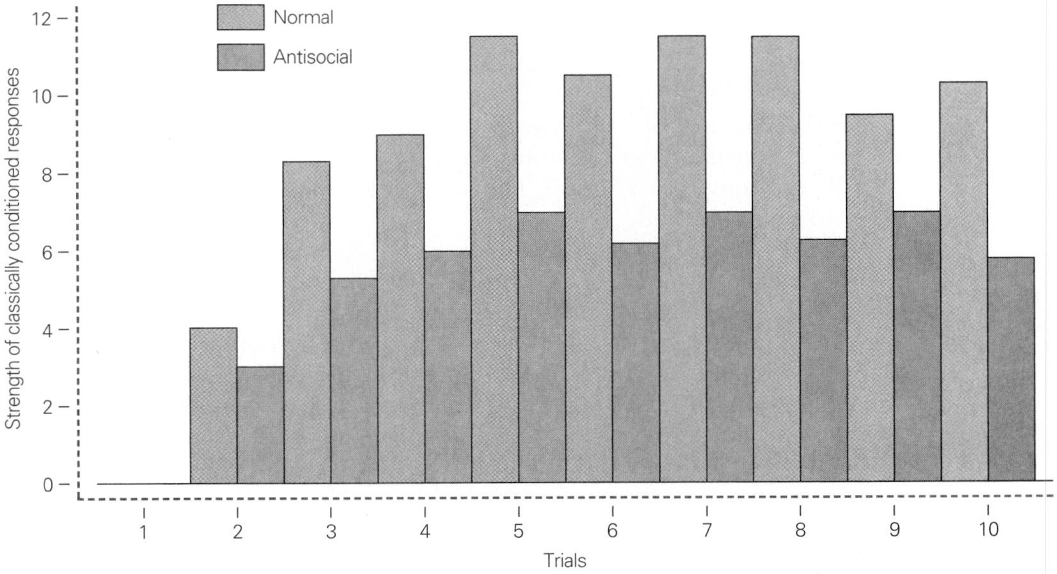

**Line Graph:**

A form of graph representing a frequency distribution in which a continuous line indicates the frequency or statistic presented along the *Y*-axis.

**Figure 7.11**

**An example of a histogram representing normal and antisocial individuals' responses to a stimulus. The data came from a study conducted by Hare (1965).**

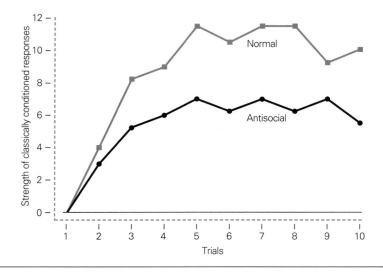

**Figure** | 7.12

Hare's (1965) results presented as a line graph. It is much easier to read than Figure 7.11.

broken $Y$-axis. Figure 7.13 helps to illustrate how to be deceptive with a graph. The data presented in Figures 7.13(a) and 7.13(b) present the tuition of a hypothetical private 4-year college.

Figure 7.13(a) presents the rise in tuition for the college between 1980 and 1990. The line appears to be almost flat. Someone who just glanced at the graph would assume that tuition barely changed over the 10-year period. The graph is deceptive because of its scale. True, there is an absolute 0, but look at the top of the graph. The range of the $Y$-axis is extremely large at $30,000. The upper end of the $Y$-axis is almost twice as great as the 1990 tuition. Therefore, the nearly four-fold increase of tuition in the decade appears small.

Figure 7.13(b) is no less deceptive. It looks as if tuition has sky-rocketed. The author of this graph achieved the graphical slight of hand by using a broken $Y$-axis. Note that there is no 0. The $Y$-axis begins at $3,500 and moves to $11,500. This technique allows any difference in tuition to be magnified.

Figure 7.13(c) is a better way to present the data. The most important component of this graph is that there are points of comparison. The four lines in the graph represent the tuition of four different colleges. The extra data allow us to compare the change in the hypothetical college's tuition. These data suggest that the change in the college's tuition matches the changes in tuition at other colleges. The graph also implies that tuition at state universities was much lower and did not increase at the same rate.

Huff's (1954) rule that all graphs must have an absolute 0 for the $Y$-axis is too rigid. Although it is a useful guideline, there are many reasonable conditions where it need not be applied. As long as the scale of the $Y$-axis is well labeled, the break clearly defined, and appropriate comparative data are included, the $Y$-axis can take any form necessary for presenting the information.

## Things to Avoid in Graphs

Tufte (1983) coined the term "chartjunk" to describe graphical embellishments that add nothing to the quality of a graph. Many graphs

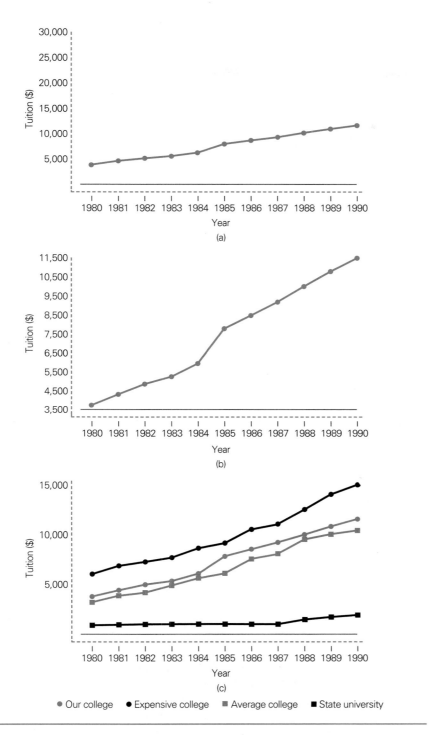

**Figure** | **7.13**

**Three examples of how the same data can be presented. See the text for more details.**

in the popular press contain lots of chartjunk. In addition, many computer programs create graphs with lots of chartjunk. Because **chartjunk** represents superfluous visual information that is distracting and obscures the important information in the graph, Tufte argued that researchers should avoid chartjunk at all costs. Most researchers

■ **Chartjunk:**

Superfluous visual information added to a graph that is distracting and makes the graph harder to interpret.

in the behavioral sciences follow Tufte's advice. Although scientific graphs look rather Spartan, the fact is that when preparing graphs, less is more.

Figure 7.14 is a graph loaded with chartjunk. The data represent the results of a cognitive dissonance experiment. During the experiment, the researcher had participants complete an extremely boring task. When the participants completed the task, the researcher asked them to tell another person that the task was interesting and informative. Some participants received $20 for their deception, others received $1, or nothing at all. In the final part of the experiment, the researcher asked the participants to rate the task on a 100-point scale (high scores mean they liked the task).

There are many things wrong with this graph. Although it does display the relevant information, it also includes many unnecessary features. Let's look at the bits of chartjunk.

1. *There is a title at the top of the graph.* Graphs in the behavioral sciences do not have titles as a part of the graph.
2. *The description of the X-axis is misplaced.* The description of the three treatment conditions ($0, $1, and $20) should be located on the *X*-axis. Labeling the three bars at the axis makes it easier for the reader to know what the bars represent.
3. *The three-dimensional effect for the graph adds no new information.* Although 3D graphs are popular, they are no better at presenting the data. Indeed, many professionals (e.g., Tufte, 1983) see the 3D as the worst case of chartjunk.
4. *There are too many divisions along the Y-axis.* There is no reason to divide the scale into so many units. An alternative would be to use 10-point increments.
5. *The grid adds nothing to the graph.* The grid on the back wall of the graph makes the whole graph look busy.
6. *The bars should not be touching.* The continuity of the bars suggests that the differences in the payoffs are equal units. The difference between $0 and $1 is much different from the difference between $1 and $20.

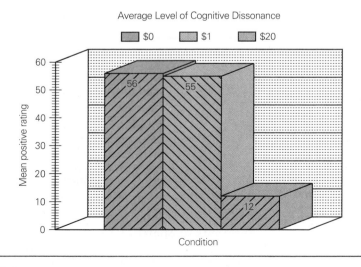

**Figure** | **7.14**

An example of a graph with much unnecessary information. See the text for a discussion of specific problems with this figure.

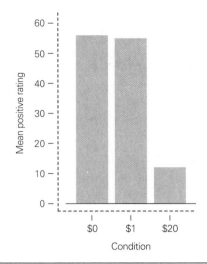

**Figure** | **7.15**

An example of a graph that is easier to read because unnecessary and superfluous information has been removed.

**7.** *The crosshatches in the bars make the graph look busy.* Tufte (1983) calls this shading *moiré* (*moiré* means a wavy pattern), and argues that it is a needless distraction. As a rule, avoid using cross-hatching in bars.

**8.** *The numbers in the bars are redundant.* If the numbers are so important, why not just include them in the text and/or in a table and drop the graph all together. The purpose of a graph is to present a quick representation of the data, not a precise recount of each detail. If you need to present precise details, use a table.

Figure 7.15 presents the same information using a simple bar graph. Although the bar graph does not have any fancy features, it is simple and easy to interpret.

During the remainder of this book we will make much use of graphs. As we introduce new statistical tools, we will show you how to use graphs to present the data. We also use graphs to help explain many important statistical concepts.

## 7.9 / Tables

Graphs present pictures. The pictures allow us to quickly interpret the results of the data. Although graphs are extremely useful as a research tool, there are many times when we need to present numbers to the reader. Constructing useful and easy-to-read tables is like constructing good graphs. There are some simple rules to follow that will help you present your data well. Ehrenberg (1977) identified six basic features for constructing good tables. Table 7.1 is an example of a single table.

**Feature 1** Round the numbers to a meaningful number. If your numbers have decimal values, you will usually round to two digits (e.g., 123.45 rather than 123.4544321). As a rule, your report of numbers should follow the precision of your measurement.

Table | 7.1

Example of Simple Table Presenting Average SAT Scores for Men and Women Living in Low and in High Social Economic Status Homes (Fictitious Data)

|         | Low SES | High SES | Average |
|---------|---------|----------|---------|
| Men     | 950     | 1100     | 1025    |
| Women   | 960     | 1150     | 1055    |
| Average | 955     | 1125     | 1040    |

**Feature 2** If possible, include row and column averages. These summary statistics help the reader discern general trends in the data and differences among groups.

**Feature 3** Orient the most important data in a column. Readers find it easier to scan a vertical column of numbers than to scan a row of numbers.

**Feature 4** If possible, rank-order the data from largest to smallest or smallest to largest. Ranking the data helps the reader find the extremes in the data.

**Feature 5** Keep row and column spacing relatively small. The distance between each line and column should clearly distinguish each number. In addition, the numbers should be close enough to allow quick comparisons.

**Feature 6** Use tables only when it is essential to present the quantitative data or when there is no alternative for presenting the data.

Table 7.2 presents the relative prevalence of schizophrenia among pairs of related individuals. These data are interesting, but we can present the data in a better format. Table 7.3 presents the same data but in a different format. Notice that in Table 7.2, the data are organized alphabetically by type of relationship. By contrast, the data in Table 7.3 are ordered in terms of relationship. This reordering of the data allows us to see that the closer the familial relationship, the greater the rate of schizophrenia.

Table | 7.2

Percentage of Schizophrenia Observed in Pairs of Individuals by Relationship (Alphabetical Ordering)

| Relationship    | N    | Pairs with Schizophrenia (%) |
|-----------------|------|------------------------------|
| Child           | 1578 | 11.3                         |
| DZ twin*        | 329  | 13.7                         |
| First cousin    | 1600 | 1.6                          |
| Grandchild      | 739  | 2.8                          |
| Half-sibling    | 499  | 3.4                          |
| MZ twin*        | 261  | 45.6                         |
| Niece or nephew | 3966 | 2.7                          |
| Sibling         | 8817 | 8.4                          |
| Spouse          | 194  | 2.1                          |

*DZ, Dizygotic or nonidentical; MZ, monozygotic or identical.

**Table** 7.3

**Percentage of Schizophrenia Observed in Pairs of Individuals by Relationship (Ordering by Percentage)**

| Relationship | *N* | Pairs with Schizophrenia (%) |
|---|---|---|
| MZ twin* | 261 | 45.6 |
| DZ twin* | 329 | 13.7 |
| Child | 1578 | 11.3 |
| Sibling | 8817 | 8.4 |
| Half-sibling | 499 | 3.4 |
| Grandchild | 739 | 2.8 |
| Niece or nephew | 3966 | 2.7 |
| Spouse | 194 | 2.1 |
| First cousin | 1600 | 1.6 |

*MZ, monozygotic; DZ, dizygotic.

# 7.10 / Putting It All Together

## Example 1

Galanter, Dermatis, Egelko, and DeLeon (1998) examined the history of 327 patients receiving treatment for crack cocaine abuse at a large metropolitan medical center. Of these patients, 315 had intact and complete medical histories. Table 7.4 presents the nonsubstance abuse psychiatric diagnoses.

Table 7.4 is an effective way to present the data. We can also use a bar graph to provide a visual presentation of the data. Figure 7.16 presents the same data using a bar graph.

## Example 2

Proactive interference occurs when previously learned information decreases your ability to learn new material. In 1972, D. D. Wickens conducted an interesting experiment that examined the effects of proactive interference. He randomly assigned subjects to either the experimental group or the control group. Wickens then had the participants perform a standard memory test. For each trial, the subjects heard three related words (e.g., rose, daisy, and tulip). After completing a distraction task that kept the subjects from practicing the words, the experimenter asked the subjects to recall the three words. During the first three trials,

**Table** 7.4

**Number and Percent of 315 Crack Cocaine Abusers Who Have Been Previously Diagnosed with a Nonsubstance Abuse Psychiatric Disorder**

| | | |
|---|---|---|
| Schizophrenia | 52 | 16% |
| Affective disorder | 59 | 19% |
| Personality disorder | 75 | 24% |
| No previous disorder | 129 | 41% |
| Total | 315 | 100% |

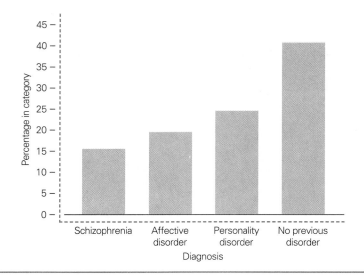

**Figure | 7.16**

**Percentage of crack cocaine abusers with previous psychiatric diagnoses. Data based on a report by Galanter, Dermatis, Egelko, and DeLeon (1998).**

subjects in both the experimental and control groups were required to recall different sets of related words (e.g., names of flowers). The fourth trial was the critical test. Subjects in the control group heard another list of flower names. By contrast, subjects in the experimental group heard a list of words from a different category (e.g., law, medicine, and psychology). Table 7.5 presents the results of the experiment.

Figure 7.17 presents the same data. The graph makes clear the dramatic effect of changing the type of words for the experimental group. As is clear in the graph, both groups show the effects of proactive interference. On each of the first three trials, the average performance of the subjects decreased. On the fourth trial, the subjects in the experimental group showed a sizable improvement due to the change in the meaning of the words to be remembered.

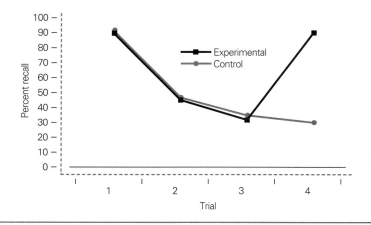

**Figure | 7.17**

**Percentage of words recalled in Wickens' (1972) experiment examining proactive interference.**

**Table | 7.5**

**Percentage of Words Recalled in Wickens' (1972) Experiment Examining Proactive Interference**

| | TRIAL | | | |
|---|---|---|---|---|
| **Condition** | **1** | **2** | **3** | **4** |
| Experimental | 90 | 45 | 32 | 90 |
| Control | 92 | 47 | 35 | 30 |

## CHAPTER SUMMARY

In this chapter we looked at fundamental aspects of data analysis and subsequent written presentations, namely, tables and graphs. When well done, research results are easier to remember and more readily understood by the reader.

Some of the graphic techniques presented in this chapter include the following.

1. The bar graph is used when the $X$-axis involves nominal numerical scales.
2. The dot chart is used as a useful alternative to the bar graph, particularly when the abscissa contains a large number of classes and subclasses.
3. The histogram is used when the abscissa involves ordinal, interval, or ratio scales. The values are arranged along the abscissa in either ascending or descending order of magnitude. When interval or ratio scales are used and the values are grouped in class intervals or class widths, the histogram displays the midpoints of each class along the $X$-axis.
4. The stem-and-leaf plot is visually almost identical to the histogram. Its main advantage over the histogram is that the original data are preserved rather than compacted into class intervals.
5. The box-and-whisker plot permits the representation of much of the data while keeping the graphical image simple and easy to interpret. It can be used to represent information about central tendency, dispersion, and the shape of the distribution in a single form.
6. The frequency curve or line graph can reduce the clutter caused by adding more variables and conditions to a study. It consists of joining the midpoints where the tops of the bars would otherwise be.
7. The various issues to consider when preparing a graph include the following.
   a. The efficiency of the various graphic techniques.
   b. Broken versus continuous scale for the $Y$-axis.
   c. Factors that should and should not be included in a graph.
   d. Representing variance in a graph.

   Finally, we examined Ehrenberg's six basic recommendations for constructing numerical tables.

**TERMS TO**R EMEMBER

bar graph                    dot chart
box-and-whisker plot         histogram
chartjunk                    line graph
class interval

E XERCISES

1. The following numbers are 36 scores on a statistics examination. The highest possible score is 100.

| 88 | 79 | 92 | 86 | 87 | 83 | 78 | 40 | 67 |
|----|----|----|----|----|----|----|----|----|
| 76 | 46 | 81 | 92 | 77 | 84 | 76 | 70 | 66 |
| 75 | 98 | 81 | 82 | 81 | 87 | 78 | 70 | 60 |
| 79 | 52 | 82 | 77 | 81 | 77 | 70 | 74 | 61 |

   a. Use a stem-and-leaf plot to organize these data.
   b. Draw a histogram of the data.
   c. Draw a box-and-whisker plot of the data.
   d. Which graph do you prefer? Which do you believe is more helpful in interpreting the data?

2. The owner of a video store is interested in how many videos a typical customer watches during a year. He randomly selects the records of 100 customers and counts the number of videos rented during the previous year. Here are the data.

| 67 | 63 | 64 | 57 | 56 | 55 | 53 | 53 | 54 | 54 |
|----|----|----|----|----|----|----|----|----|----|
| 45 | 45 | 46 | 47 | 37 | 23 | 34 | 44 | 27 | 44 |
| 45 | 34 | 34 | 15 | 23 | 43 | 16 | 44 | 36 | 36 |
| 35 | 37 | 24 | 24 | 14 | 43 | 37 | 27 | 36 | 26 |
| 25 | 36 | 26 | 5  | 44 | 13 | 33 | 33 | 17 | 33 |
| 56 | 17 | 26 | 5  | 14 | 23 | 45 | 59 | 19 | 49 |
| 37 | 42 | 32 | 29 | 90 | 44 | 46 | 45 | 66 | 28 |
| 28 | 75 | 32 | 31 | 52 | 49 | 65 | 54 | 15 | 23 |
| 59 | 61 | 40 | 41 | 43 | 49 | 38 | 31 | 19 | 24 |
| 45 | 41 | 38 | 14 | 57 | 25 | 20 | 15 | 16 | 12 |

   a. Construct a box-and-whisker plot of the data. Be sure that you mark the 25th, 50th, and 75th percentiles. Also indicate the location of the mean.
   b. How would you describe the shape of the distribution of scores? Are they normally distributed or are they skewed?

3. A teacher interested in reading ability tests third graders from four elementary schools from different parts of the state. The frequency distribution for each of the four schools is presented in the accompanying table. The Score column represents the raw scores for the test, and the $f$ column represents the number of students within each of these classes.

| SCHOOL A | | SCHOOL B | | SCHOOL C | | SCHOOL D | |
|---|---|---|---|---|---|---|---|
| Score | f | Score | f | Score | f | Score | f |
| 20 | 1 | 20 | 0 | 20 | 6 | 20 | 5 |
| 19 | 8 | 19 | 11 | 19 | 8 | 19 | 15 |
| 18 | 12 | 18 | 28 | 18 | 16 | 18 | 15 |
| 17 | 15 | 17 | 11 | 17 | 6 | 17 | 12 |
| 16 | 11 | 16 | 0 | 16 | 9 | 16 | 3 |
| 15 | 3 | 15 | 0 | 15 | 5 | 15 | 0 |

   **a.** Construct a box-and-whisker plot for each of the schools. Be sure you represent the 25th, 50th, and 75th percentiles as well as the mean.

   **b.** Using the box-and-whisker diagram, compare the performance of the students in each of the schools. Which school had the highest overall performance? Which school had the greatest variance in scores?

**4.** A local newspaper has a large headline in the Sunday newspaper that reads "VIOLENT CRIME IN NORMALTOWN SKYROCKETS!!!" According to the article, the number of violent crimes last year was 566, a 15.5% increase from the number of crimes the previous year $[(566 - 490)/490 = 76/490 = 0.155(100) = 15.5\%]$. The editorial is an angry statement about how the police are doing a poor job of keeping the peace and ends with a demand that the chief of police resign immediately. Here are some interesting data. The accompanying table lists the population of Normaltown for the past 10 years and the violent crimes reported to the police.

| Year | Population | Violent Crimes |
|---|---|---|
| 1990 | 23,450 | 294 |
| 1991 | 25,632 | 323 |
| 1992 | 25,700 | 282 |
| 1993 | 26,591 | 372 |
| 1994 | 29,781 | 387 |
| 1995 | 33,354 | 401 |
| 1996 | 37,022 | 410 |
| 1997 | 42,575 | 425 |
| 1998 | 48,961 | 490 |
| 1999 | 57,773 | 566 |

   **a.** Using the number of violent crimes, draw two line graphs. On the first graph, make it appear that the number of violent crimes has skyrocketed. On the second graph, make it appear that the number of crimes has barely changed over the 10 years.

   **b.** Draw a third line graph that presents the number of crimes as a proportion of the population.

   **c.** Which of the three graphs do you believe best represents the "crime problem" of Normaltown? Should the police chief resign?

**5.** Create a dot chart for the following data. Make sure that the chart allows you to compare the proportion of doctoral-level and master's-level psychologists who work within each employment setting.

| Employment Setting | Doctoral Level (%) | Master's Level (%) |
|---|---|---|
| University or college | 52.9 | 18.3 |
| Medical school | 6.4 | 2.7 |
| Primary school system | 3.2 | 30.5 |
| Independent practice | 6.7 | 5.4 |
| Hospital and clinics | 16.2 | 21.6 |
| Business or other setting | 14.6 | 21.5 |
| Total | 100.0 | 100.0 |

*Source:* Based on Stapp, Tucker, & VandenBos (1985). *American Psychologist, 40,* 1317–1351.

6. One of the more famous experiments in experimental psychology was one conducted by Peterson and Peterson in 1959. Their research has been used as evidence of short-term memory. In that experiment, they showed subjects a meaningless three-letter word such as "RUW" for 1 second. The word was then removed, and the subjects were engaged in a distracting task for several seconds. Between the time the three-letter word was removed and the time the subjects were asked to recall the word was called the retention interval. The subjects were then asked to recall the word they had seen. Here are the data. The numbers represent the average proportion of correct recall for each retention interval.

| | RETENTION INTERVAL (SEC) | | | | | | |
|---|---|---|---|---|---|---|---|
| | **0** | **3** | **6** | **9** | **12** | **15** | **18** |
| Correct recall (%) | 90 | 53 | 40 | 22 | 13 | 10 | 7 |

   a. Draw a line graph that presents these data.
   b. Describe the pattern of results you see.

7. Rats were trained to press a bar for a piece of food. Half the rats received food every time they pressed the bar. The experimenter called this condition the 100% group. The other rats received food, on average, 60% of the time. After some time, the experimenter stopped providing food when a rat pressed the bar and then counted the number of times the rat pressed the bar over the next 10 minutes. The data presented here are the average number of bar presses each rat in each group made during each of the 10-minute sessions.

| | MINUTE | | | | | | | | | |
|---|---|---|---|---|---|---|---|---|---|---|
| **Group** | **1** | **2** | **3** | **4** | **5** | **6** | **7** | **8** | **9** | **10** |
| 100% | 65 | 62 | 48 | 32 | 26 | 15 | 9 | 5 | 3 | 1 |
| 60% | 65 | 63 | 64 | 57 | 52 | 48 | 35 | 16 | 9 | 7 |

   a. Draw a line graph that compares the performance of the two groups of rats over time.
   b. Describe the pattern of results you see. Which group took longer to stop pressing the bar once the food was removed?

8. A group of researchers was interested in the relation between memory, the age of a person, and the amount of information to be remembered. They asked people in different age groups to memorize a list of numbers with 3, 7, or 10 digits. The data are shown in the accompanying table.

| | AGE | | | | |
|---|---|---|---|---|---|
| **Number of Digits** | **18–39** | **40–49** | **50–59** | **60–69** | **70–85** |
| 3 | 99 | 98 | 97 | 97 | 97 |
| 7 | 96 | 96 | 94 | 93 | 91 |
| 10 | 77 | 75 | 72 | 63 | 64 |

**a.** Draw a line graph of these data so that we can compare the performance of these age groups in remembering lists of numbers.

**b.** Describe the pattern of results you see. What is the relation between the number of digits to be remembered and accuracy of recall? What is the relation between the age of the person and the accuracy of recall? Are older people really all that more forgetful?

**9.** A teacher tells a class that a guest speaker is coming to give a lecture. In one section of the course the teacher tells the students that the guest is a "warm and caring" individual, and in the other section that the guest is a "cold and reserved" person. The speaker gives exactly the same lecture in both classes. The students are asked to rate the lecturer on a number of characteristics, and the data are shown in the accompanying table. *Note:* The lower the rating, the lower the characteristic being rated.

| | **Warm** | **Cold** |
|---|---|---|
| Self-centered | 6.0 | 9.5 |
| Formal | 6.3 | 9.5 |
| Unsociable | 5.2 | 11.6 |
| Unpopular | 4.0 | 7.2 |
| Humorless | 8.3 | 11.9 |

**a.** Draw a histogram to present these data.
**b.** Draw a dot chart to present these data.
**c.** Do you prefer one graph over the other? If so, why?
**d.** How would you explain these data?

**10.** Look through your local newspaper or a popular daily newspaper (such as *USA Today*) and find examples of graphs with many embellishments (e.g., pictographs). Examine each one and consider the following issues.
**a.** How easy is the graph to interpret?
**b.** Can you redraw the graph, using the principles learned in this chapter, to make it easier to understand?
**c.** Are there features of the graph that are potentially misleading?

**11.** Look through a journal published by the American Psychological Association, the American Psychological Society, or another professional society for behavioral researchers and find a few examples of graphs.
**a.** What information does the graph represent?
**b.** What are the independent and dependent variables?
**c.** What pattern of results do you see in the data?
**d.** Do you think the same data could be presented using another type of graph?

**12.** A researcher at a local mental health center has examined the types of clients served by the staff at the facility. Here are the primary diagnoses and their frequency.

| Psychoactive Substance Abuse | *f* |
|---|---|
| Alcohol abuse | 750 |
| Cannabis abuse | 53 |
| Cocaine abuse | 329 |
| Nicotine dependence | 243 |

| Schizophrenia | *f* |
|---|---|
| Catatonic | 2 |
| Disorganized | 53 |
| Paranoid | 12 |
| Undifferentiated | 70 |

| Mood Disorders | *f* |
|---|---|
| Major depressive episode | |
|    Chronic | 377 |
|    Seasonal pattern | 153 |
| Bipolar disorders | 36 |
| Depressive disorders | |
|    Major depression | 750 |
|    Dysthymia | 69 |

**a.** Prepare a table of these data that will help the reader to see the most frequently occurring disorders observed at the clinic.

**b.** Would it help to also report the percentage of the total for each number?

**c.** Do you think that the table or the dot chart is more efficient in presenting the data? What are the relative merits of each?

**13.** A researcher tested the hypothesis that people who have expertise about a topic or activity can remember more details about that topic than people who do not have that expertise. The researcher gathered three groups of students from her campus. The first group consisted of 10 football players, the second group of 8 law students, and the last group of 10 computer science majors. All subjects were shown the following: (i) a 3-minute clip of a professional football game, (ii) a simple contract for the lease of a house, and (iii) a code for a computer program that calculates polynomials. Twenty-four hours later the researcher had the subjects return and describe in as much detail as possible the three things they had seen. The scores represent overall accuracy and detail (1 = low accuracy and detail; 10 = high accuracy and detail).

| Football Players | | | | | | | | | |
|---|---|---|---|---|---|---|---|---|---|
| Memory of football clip | | | | | | | | | |
| 9 | 8 | 9 | 10 | 7 | 8 | 8 | 6 | 8 | 10 |
| Memory of contract | | | | | | | | | |
| 6 | 5 | 4 | 5 | 2 | 5 | 4 | 3 | 4 | 2 |
| Memory of computer program | | | | | | | | | |
| 9 | 8 | 6 | 7 | 10 | 2 | 4 | 3 | 5 | 6 |

## Law Students

Memory of football clip

| 6 | 7 | 5 | 8 | 7 | 9 | 6 | 5 |

Memory of contract

| 9 | 8 | 10 | 10 | 8 | 9 | 7 | 9 |

Memory of computer program

| 3 | 4 | 3 | 6 | 7 | 5 | 6 | 3 |

## Computer Science Majors

Memory of football clip

| 6 | 7 | 5 | 8 | 4 | 6 | 6 | 7 | 8 | 9 |

Memory of contract

| 4 | 5 | 3 | 6 | 3 | 7 | 2 | 2 | 5 | 6 |

Memory of computer program

| 10 | 10 | 9 | 8 | 10 | 9 | 8 | 9 | 8 | 10 |

a. Calculate the mean for each data set. Use the mean to create a bar graph of the data.
b. Describe the results of these data. Do you think the hypothesis was confirmed?

# 8

# Correlation

# 8.1 / Introduction

Up until this chapter we have examined statistical procedures that describe single variables. These descriptive statistics have allowed us to examine a distribution and interpret individual scores within that distribution. These descriptive statistics represent the foundation for all statistical procedures but they have limitations. They do not allow us to examine relationships between two or more variables. As you may recall from Chapter 1, one of the primary goals of the behavioral sciences is to look for systematic relationships. You may recall that behavioral scientists use correlational studies to see if two variables change in a systematic way, or covary. If we find a correlation between two variables, we can use this information to help us describe and possibly predict future behaviors or events. Let's look at an example.

Why is it that some people become passionately committed in a romantic relationship whereas others remain relatively uncommitted? Why do some people seem to cherish a long-term relationship and others move from one to another? Snyder and Simpson (1984) suspected that the differences in people's romantic lives may be explained by their personalities. Specifically, they predicted that the personality characteristic known as self-monitoring is related to commitment. Briefly, self-monitoring describes the degree to which behavior is controlled by the context or situation. People high on this dimension are likely to change their behavior as the situation changes. In contrast, people who are low on self-monitoring are likely to behave consistently in different situations. Snyder and Simpson hypothesized that people who score low on the self-monitoring scale would be more likely to maintain a long-term relationship than people who score high on the scale. To examine this hypothesis, they administered a questionnaire to college students asking them to complete the self-monitoring scale and to describe their dating histories. Table 8.1 presents hypothetical data based on their study.

Scores on the first variable $X$, the self-monitoring scale, can range from 0 to 25. The second variable $Y$ consists of the number of months the person has dated his or her current partner. Snyder and Simpson (1984) viewed the self-monitoring scale as the *independent variable* because they use self-monitoring to describe or explain another behavior. The *dependent variable* is the number of months in the relationship. Why? Remember that the independent variable is used to describe or explain the differences in the dependent variable. The dependent variable is an outcome of interest that is assumed to be affected by the independent variable. We will represent self-monitoring by the variable $X$, and the number of months dating by the variable $Y$. Usually, the independent variable is the $X$ variable and the dependent variable, the $Y$ variable.

As you can see, examining the raw data and the descriptive statistics for each of the variables is not very helpful. Looking at the means and standard deviations of the two variables tells us nothing about how $X$ and $Y$ are related. To examine the relationship between the two variables, we will have to see if there is any systematic pattern in the size of the values for $X$ and $Y$. If you look through the data you may be able to find an interesting trend; people with lower scores on the self-monitoring scale seem to have had longer dating relationships. Consider Subjects 2 and 4 as examples. Subject 2 has a high self-monitoring score ($X_2 = 19$) and a short dating history ($Y_2 = 4$). By contrast, Subject 4 has a lower self monitoring score ($X_4 = 9$) and many months with his or her partner ($Y_4 = 14$).

**Table** 8.1

**Hypothetical Data from a Study Examining the Relation Between Self-Monitoring and the Number of Months a Person Has Dated His or Her Current Partner**

| Subject | SELF-MONITORING SCORE | | MONTHS DATING | |
|---|---|---|---|---|
| | $X$ | $X^2$ | $Y$ | $Y^2$ |
| 1 | 14 | 196 | 8 | 64 |
| 2 | 19 | 361 | 4 | 16 |
| 3 | 12 | 144 | 4 | 16 |
| 4 | 9 | 81 | 14 | 196 |
| 5 | 15 | 225 | 8 | 64 |
| 6 | 6 | 36 | 14 | 196 |
| 7 | 21 | 441 | 10 | 100 |
| 8 | 14 | 196 | 14 | 196 |
| 9 | 12 | 144 | 14 | 196 |
| 10 | 15 | 225 | 4 | 16 |
| 11 | 14 | 196 | 10 | 100 |
| 12 | 11 | 121 | 10 | 100 |
| 13 | 7 | 49 | 16 | 256 |
| 14 | 6 | 36 | 18 | 324 |
| 15 | 15 | 225 | 6 | 36 |
| 16 | 15 | 225 | 8 | 64 |
| 17 | 10 | 100 | 10 | 100 |
| 18 | 16 | 256 | 8 | 64 |
| 19 | 16 | 256 | 14 | 196 |
| 20 | 10 | 100 | 12 | 144 |

$N = 20$    $\Sigma X = 257$    $\Sigma X^2 = 3613$    $\Sigma Y = 206$    $\Sigma Y^2 = 2444$

$\overline{X} = 12.85$    $\overline{Y} = 10.30$

$s_X = 3.94$    $s_Y = 4.01$

**STEM-AND-LEAF PLOT**

| Self-Monitoring Score | | Months Dating |
|---|---|---|
| | 0–4 | 444 |
| 9766 | 5–9 | 68888 |
| 44422100 | 10–14 | 0000244444 |
| 9665555 | 15–19 | 68 |
| 1 | 20–21 | |

What is needed is an objective method for examining the data. The stem-and-leaf plot in Table 8.1 provides a visual representation of each distribution singly. These plots are used to identify extreme scores and outliers and to examine the distributions for deviations from normality. The **scatterplot** in Figure 8.1 is used to visually examine the relationships between the two variables. In the scatterplot, as you can see, each dot represents the two scores for a subject. The data for Subject 1 has been highlighted in the figure. The point on the scattergram represents the intersection of lines $X_1 = 14$ and $Y_1 = 8$. That subject received a score

■ **Scatterplot:**

A visual representation of the relationship between two variables. Each point in a scatterplot represents the value for the $X$ and $Y$ variable for a subject.

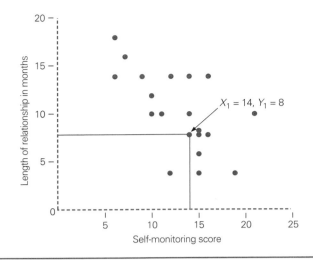

**Figure** | **8.1**

Scatterplot of the relation between self-monitoring score and length of a dating relationship, in months. These hypothetical data are based on a study conducted by Snyder and Simpson (1984).

---

■ **Negative Relationship:**

Variables are said to be negatively related when scores that are high on one variable are accompanied by scores that are low on the other variable.

---

■ **Positive Relationship:**

Variables are said to be positively related when scores that are high on one variable are accompanied by scores that are high on the other variable.

---

■ **Correlation Coefficient:**

A statistic used to express quantitatively the extent to which two variables are related and the direction of that relationship. The size of a correlation coefficient may range from −1.00 ≤ $r$ ≤ +1.00.

of 14 on the self monitoring scale and had been in a relationship for 8 months.

It is easier to see the relationship between the two variables now that we have examined the visual representation of the two variables. It appears that Snyder and Simpson's (1984) prediction was correct—people with lower self-monitoring scores are more likely to be involved in long-term dating relationships than people who score high on the self-monitoring scale. In this case, we would say that there is a **negative relationship** between self-monitoring and length of dating relationship—as the self-monitoring score goes up, the length of the relationship goes down. We can also see that the relationship between the two variables is not perfect. There are several people with approximately the same self-monitoring score who have had either shorter or longer romances with their current partner. If we had a **positive relationship** between the two variables, people who scored high on one variable would tend to also score high on the other variable.

Having examined the scatterplot, we are ready to begin calculating a descriptive statistic that allows us to assign a numerical value to the degree to which the two variables are related. This statistic is known as the **correlation coefficient,** and is the focus of this chapter.

## 8.2 / The Concept of Correlation

The correlation is a fascinating and powerful statistical tool that researchers use to examine the relationship between two or more variables. A correlation can answer many interesting questions about the nature of the relationship between two variables. In the example of the relationship between self-monitoring and dating, we saw that some of the variations in the amount of time in a committed relationship can be accounted for by the personality variable self-monitoring.

The correlation coefficient tells us first about the *direction* of the correlation. The correlation coefficient may be a positive or a negative value.

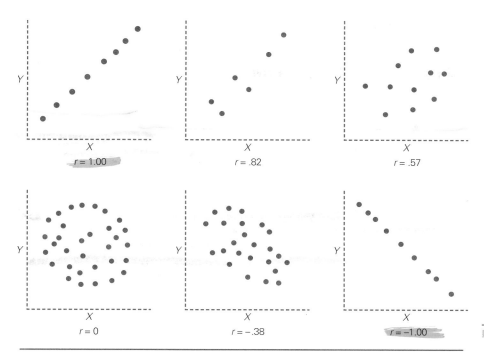

**Figure 8.2**

Scatter diagrams showing various degrees of relationship between two variables.

Positive values indicate a positive relationship between the variables; negative values of the coefficient indicate a negative relationship. A data set with a **positive correlation** is one in which high values on one variable are associated with high values on the other variable. Low values on one variable tend to be associated with low values on the other variable. A data set may have a **negative correlation,** meaning that as the values on the $X$ variable increase, the values on the $Y$ variable tend to decrease. The scatterplots in Figure 8.2 represent positive and negative correlations. The scatterplot with a correlation of $r = 1.00$ represents a perfect positive correlation; increases in the $X$ variable are perfectly matched with increases in the $Y$ variable. In contrast, the correlation of $r = -1.00$ represents a perfect negative correlation. Low $X$ scores are related to high $Y$ scores, and as $X$ increases, $Y$ decreases. Notice that the closer the correlation is to either 1.00 or $-1.00$ the more the data fall along a straight line. When we calculate a correlation coefficient we expect that a straight line can best describe the data. This straight line represents a **linear relationship.**

The correlational analysis also allows us to examine the *degree* to which two variables are interrelated. The correlation coefficient will vary in size from 0 to 1.00. A 0 indicates absolutely no relationship between the two variables; a 1.00 indicates the strongest possible relationship. The closer the values are to 1.00, the stronger the relationship. Values such as .85, .90, or .96 indicate increasingly strong relationships. The closer the values are to 0, the weaker the relationship. Values such as .26, .15, and .07 are examples of what would be called weak correlation coefficients. No matter what the strength of the relationship is, a coefficient may be positive or negative. When a correlation is $r = +.9$ we are able to conclude that there is a strong, positive relationship between the

**Positive Correlation:**

A correlation coefficient that is $0 < r \leq 1.00$. This correlation indicates that there is a direct relation between the two set of scores—a high score of $X$ is related to a high score of $Y$, a low score of $X$ is related to a low score of $Y$.

**Negative Correlation:**

A correlation coefficient that is $-1.00 \leq r < 0$. This correlation indicates that there is an inverse relation between the two sets of scores—a high score of $X$ is related to a low score of $Y$, a low score of $X$ is related to a high score of $Y$.

**Linear Relationship:**

A condition wherein the relationship between two variables can be best described by a straight line. The linear relationship may represent either a positive correlation or a negative correlation.

two variables. When $r = -.9$, we can still conclude that there is a strong relationship but that the relationship is a negative one. When $r = 0.0$ there is no systematic relationship between the two variables. Look again at the scatterplots in Figure 8.2. When $r = 1.00$ and when $r = -1.00$ the data points fall on a straight line. This means that all the differences in one variable can be described by the other variable. As $r$ gets closer to 0, there is less of a linear relation between $X$ and $Y$.

Although the correlation is a useful statistic, it does not by itself allow us to infer a cause-and-effect relation between two variables. As you may recall from Chapter 1, we cannot assume a causal relation between the two variables unless the experimenter randomly assigned subjects to the different treatment groups and manipulated the levels of the independent variable. In correlational research, the researcher has no direct control over either of the variables. Therefore, it is safe to say that a correlation coefficient allows one to describe the degree to which two variables are related. To assume that there is a cause-and-effect relation, the independent and dependent variables must be correlated *and* the data must be derived from a true experiment.

## 8.3 / Other Correlation Coefficients

There are many types of correlation coefficients. Table 8.2 shows several different types. The choice of a coefficient depends on factors such as (1) the type of scale of measurement in which each variable is expressed, (2) the nature of the underlying distribution (continuous or discrete), and (3) the characteristics of the distribution of scores (linear or nonlinear). We present two correlation coefficients in this text: the Pearson $r$ (also known as the Pearson Product Moment Correlation Coefficient) that is used with interval/ratio scaled variables; and $r_s$ or the Spearman rank-order correlation coefficient, employed with rank-ordered or ordinal data.

No matter which correlational technique you use, all have the same basic characteristics:

1. Two or more sets of measurements are obtained on the same individuals (or events), or on pairs of individuals who are matched on some basis.
2. The values of the correlation can range between $r = -1.00$ and $r = +1.00$. Both extremes represent perfect relationships between the variables, and $r = 0.00$ represents the absence of a linear relationship.
3. A high correlation does not, by itself, establish a causal link between variables.

## 8.4 / Calculating the Pearson Product Moment Correlation Coefficient

There are many formulas for the Pearson Product Moment Correlation Coefficient. Once again we will present both a definitional and a computational equation. The definitional equation is useful for understanding and explaining the foundation of the statistic;

**Table** 8.2

**Several Different Types of Correlation Coefficients and Numerical Scales with Which They Are Used**

| Scale | Symbol | Used With |
|-------|--------|-----------|
| Nominal | $r_{phi}$ (phi coefficient) | Two dichotomous variables. |
| | $r_b$ (biserial $r$) | One dichotomous variable with underlying continuity assumed; one variable that can take on more than two values. |
| | $r_t$ (tetrachoric) | Two dichotomous variables in which underlying continuity can be assumed. |
| Ordinal | $r_s$ (Spearman $r$) | Ranked data. Both measures must be at least ordinal. They must be expressed as ranks prior to calculating Spearman $r$. |
| | $\tau$ (Kendall's tau or rank order correlation) | Ranked data. |
| Interval or ratio | Pearson $r$ | Both scales interval or ratio. |
| | Multiple $R$ | Three or more interval- or ratio-scaled variables. |

the computational equation, as the name implies, is useful for computing the statistic. We will begin by examining the definitional equation for $r$ first as it will allow us to examine the underlying logic of the correlation coefficient. We will then present the step-by-step procedures for calculating this statistic.

## Pearson $r$ and $z$-scores

Before proceeding, you may wish to go back to Chapter 6 and review the section on $z$-scores. One way to understand the concept of correlation is to think of the variables in terms of $z$-scores. Recall that the $z$-score is a measure of how far above or below the mean a given score lies, relative to the standard deviation. Look at the *size* and the *sign* of the $z$-score. A large positive $z$ represents a score that is greater than the mean and a negative $z$ represents a score that is less than the mean. A positive $z$-score of 2.0 indicates that the score is 2 standard deviations above the mean, whereas a negative $z$-score of $-1.5$ indicates that a score is 1.5 standard deviations below the mean. In your review, be sure to note the following. First, the mean of a distribution of $z$-scores equals 0. Second, the standard deviation equals 1. Third, the sum of the squared z-scores equals $N$, that is, $\Sigma z^2 = N$. You should also recall that the purpose of the z-score is to create a standardized scale for the comparison of numbers drawn from different distributions with different means and standard deviations. These facts will help us understand the Pearson correlation coefficient.

A high positive Pearson $r$ indicates that each individual or event obtained approximately the same z-score on both variables. In other words, the score for each subject is located approximately in the same location in each distribution, the $X$ and the $Y$ distribution. In a perfect positive correlation ($r = 1.00$), each person obtains precisely the same z-score on both variables. Likewise, with a perfect negative $r$, each individual obtains exactly the same z-score on both variables, but opposite in sign. We may now describe the meaning of **Pearson $r$:**

---

**Pearson $r$:** The Pearson Product Moment Correlation Coefficient, $r$, represents the extent to which individuals or events occupy the same relative position in two distributions. The defining formula for $r$ is:

$$r = \frac{\Sigma z_X z_Y}{N} \tag{8.1}$$

---

In order to explore the fundamental characteristics of the Pearson $r$, let us examine a simplified example of a perfect positive correlation. The first set of calculations in Table 8.3 shows that the z-scores of each subject are identical on both variables. Hence, with the perfect alignment of z-scores, $r = 1.00$. The scatterplot of the data demonstrates that all the points are arranged in a straight line (see Figure 8.3). This scatterplot is a little different than the other graphs that you have seen because we included the original scales for $X$ and $Y$, and the z-score transformations for both scales. We did this to help remind you that the correlation coefficient is a statistic that describes the degree to which the *relative position of the two variables is the same.*

Now look at the column headed by $z_X z_Y$. To calculate each entry in that column, multiply the value in the $z_X$ column by the value in the $z_Y$ column. You can see that $z_X$ and $z_Y$ are identical when you have a perfect positive correlation. Thus, when you multiply them together, you get the same result you would get if you took each value in the $z_X$ (or $z_Y$) column and squared it.

Earlier in this section, and in Chapter 6, we noted that $\Sigma z^2 = N$. By extension, the sum of the cross products, $\Sigma z_X z_Y$, will also equal $N$ if each $z_X$ equals its corresponding $z_Y$. In addition, the sum of the products of $z_X$ and $z_Y$ will be maximum only when each $z_X$ is equal to its corresponding $z_Y$. No other combination of the sum of the products will be as large as when the two values are identical.

There is a final feature of the correlation coefficient that needs to be highlighted. Notice how the standard deviations of the two distributions are not equal. The standard deviation for $X$ is much smaller than the one for $Y$ (4.00 vs. 6.00). Remember that a consequence of converting the raw scores into z-scores is that the data are converted to a common or standard scale. In this example, the first pair of scores, 1 and 4, are equally distant from the mean of their respective distributions; they are 1.5 standard deviations below the mean. Therefore, the obvious advantage of the Pearson $r$ is that we can correlate variables that were

**Table** 8.3

**Raw Scores and Corresponding *z*-Scores Made by 7 Subjects on Two Tests, *X* and *Y***

| Subject | X | Y | $z_X$ | $z_Y$ | $z_X z_Y$ |
|---------|---|---|-------|-------|-----------|
| A | 1 | 4 | −1.5 | −1.5 | 2.25 |
| B | 3 | 7 | −1.0 | −1.0 | 1.00 |
| C | 5 | 10 | −0.5 | −0.5 | 0.25 |
| D | 7 | 13 | 0.0 | 0.0 | 0.00 |
| E | 9 | 16 | 0.5 | 0.5 | 0.25 |
| F | 11 | 19 | 1.0 | 1.0 | 1.00 |
| G | 13 | 22 | 1.5 | 1.5 | 2.25 |

$N = 7$    $\Sigma X = 49$    $\Sigma Y = 91$    $\Sigma z_X = 0.0$    $\Sigma z_Y = 0.0$    $\Sigma z_X z_Y = 7.00$

$\Sigma X^2 = 455$    $\Sigma Y^2 = 1435$

$\overline{X} = 7.0$    $\overline{Y} = 13.0$

$s_X = 4.0$    $s_Y = 6.0$

$$r = \frac{\Sigma z_X z_Y}{N} = \frac{7.00}{7} = 1.00$$

measured with scales that have different means and standard deviations because the *z*-score transformation will always convert the numbers to a scale for comparison.

Now look at the second data set in which two scores are transposed, 7 and 4 on the *Y*-variable, as was done in Table 8.4. The *z*-scores are no longer perfectly aligned. With this small change in the alignment of the data, you can see that the sum of the products of the *z*-scores is less than *N*. In fact, any rearrangement of the alignment of *z*-scores reduces the

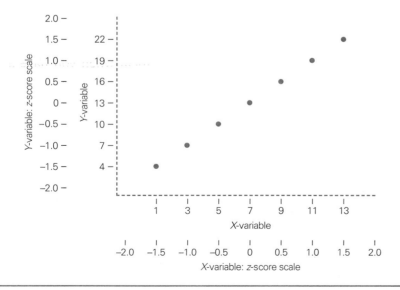

**Figure** 8.3

**Scatterplot of data presented in Table 8.3. Notice that each axis represents the original and *z*-score scales for each variable.**

**Table** 8.4

**Same Data as in Table 8.3 Except That the First Two Scores for the Y Variable (4 and 7) Are Reversed**

| Subject | X | Y | $z_X$ | $z_Y$ | $z_X z_Y$ |
|---------|---|---|-------|-------|-----------|
| A | 1 | **7** | −1.5 | −1.0 | 1.50 |
| B | 3 | **4** | −1.0 | −1.5 | 1.50 |
| C | 5 | 10 | −0.5 | −0.5 | 0.25 |
| D | 7 | 13 | 0.0 | 0.0 | 0.00 |
| E | 9 | 16 | 0.5 | 0.5 | 0.25 |
| F | 11 | 19 | 1.0 | 1.0 | 1.00 |
| G | 13 | 22 | 1.5 | 1.5 | 2.25 |
| $N = 7$ | $\Sigma X = 49$ | $\Sigma Y = 91$ | $\Sigma z_X = 0.0$ | $\Sigma z_Y = 0.0$ | $\Sigma z_X z_Y = 6.75$ |

$$r = \frac{6.75}{7} = .96$$

size of the sum of the products. See for yourself what happens when Subject A gets −1.5 on the X-variable and −1.0 on the Y-variable and Subject B obtains a z-score of −1.0 on the X-variable and −1.5 on the Y-variable. Clearly, the less the z-scores are aligned, the smaller are the sums of their products. From the scatterplot of these data (see Figure 8.4) it is evident that the relationship between X and Y is not perfect; however, there is still an obvious positive correlation between the two variables.

This point leads to another way of thinking about the z-score formula for correlation. In it, r may be viewed as a ratio of the sum of the products relative to what that sum would be if all the z-scores were all

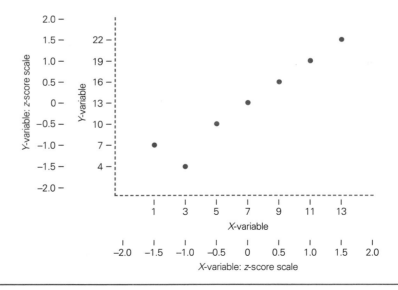

**Figure** 8.4

**Scatterplot of data presented in Table 8.4. Notice that each axis represents the original and z-score scales for each variable.**

**Table 8.5**

**Same Data As Presented in Table 8.3 Except That the Order of the *Y* Variable Has Been Randomly Arranged**

| Subject | X | Y | $z_X$ | $z_Y$ | $z_X z_Y$ |
|---------|-----|-----|-------|-------|-----------|
| A | 1 | 10 | −1.5 | −0.5 | 0.75 |
| B | 3 | 16 | −1.0 | 0.5 | −0.50 |
| C | 5 | 19 | −0.5 | 1.0 | −0.50 |
| D | 7 | 4 | 0.0 | −1.5 | 0.00 |
| E | 9 | 22 | 0.5 | 1.5 | 0.75 |
| F | 11 | 7 | 1.0 | −1.0 | −1.00 |
| G | 13 | 13 | 1.5 | 0.0 | 0.00 |

$$N = 7 \qquad \Sigma X = 49 \qquad \Sigma Y = 91 \qquad \Sigma z_X = 0.0 \qquad \Sigma z_Y = 0.0 \qquad \Sigma z_X z_Y = -0.50$$

$$r = \frac{-0.50}{7} = -.071$$

perfectly aligned with one another. With perfect alignment, that ratio yields a perfect correlation of 1.00. The term in the numerator is the largest it can be and is equal to the sum of the squared $z$-scores that, in turn, equals $N$. Since the numerator can never be larger than $N$, the correlation cannot be larger than 1.00. As the alignment of $z$-scores decreases, the value of the numerator becomes smaller, until finally it becomes zero.

Now look at Table 8.5 wherein the values of $Y$ have been randomly ordered. There appears to be little or no order in the relationship between the $X$ and $Y$ variables. As you can see in Figure 8.5, the data are scattered all over the graph. The correlation coefficient confirms this observation. Because the position of the $z$-scores for $X$ and $Y$ is not systematic, the effects of the positive and negative values of the $z$-scores are canceled out producing a small sum of cross products, $\Sigma z_X z_Y = -0.50$.

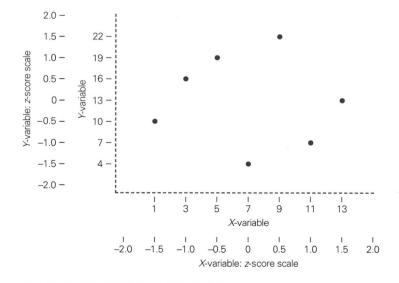

**Figure 8.5**

**Scatterplot of data presented in Table 8.5. Notice that each axis represents the original and *z*-score scales for each variable.**

**Table** | **8.6**

Same Data as Presented in Table 8.3 Except That the Order of the *Y* Variable Has Been Reversed

| Subject | X | Y | $z_X$ | $z_Y$ | $z_X z_Y$ |
|---------|---|---|-------|-------|-----------|
| A | 1 | 22 | −1.5 | 1.5 | −2.25 |
| B | 3 | 19 | −1.0 | 1.0 | −1.00 |
| C | 5 | 16 | −0.5 | 0.5 | −0.25 |
| D | 7 | 13 | 0.0 | 0.0 | 0.00 |
| E | 9 | 10 | 0.5 | −0.5 | −0.25 |
| F | 11 | 7 | 1.0 | −1.0 | −1.00 |
| G | 13 | 4 | 1.5 | −1.5 | −2.25 |

$N = 7$    $\Sigma X = 49$    $\Sigma Y = 91$    $\Sigma z_X = 0.0$    $\Sigma z_Y = 0.0$    $\Sigma z_X z_Y = -7.00$

$$r = \frac{-7.00}{7} = -1.00$$

Therefore, the correlation coefficient for these data is $r = .071$. This small correlation can be interpreted to mean that there is little or no meaningful linear relationship between the $X$ and $Y$ variables. We could also say that the two variables are independent of one another because changes in one variable are not related to changes in the other variable.

Now let us go back to our original distribution as it appears in Table 8.3. In it, the $z$-scores for the $X$ variable were perfectly aligned with those for the $Y$-variable. Compare this table with Table 8.6 in which the entire $z$-distribution for $Y$ is reversed relative to $X$. In fact, the distance from the mean of each $z$-score remains constant, but the signs of the $z$-scores are opposite. In other words, a low score for $X$ is matched with a high score for $Y$ and the $z$-scores are aligned in a reverse direction (see Figure 8.6). As you can see, the positive $z$-scores are matched with negative

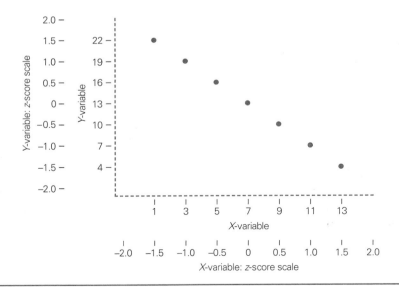

**Figure** | **8.6**

Scatterplot of data presented in Table 8.6. Notice that each axis represents the original and *z*-score scales for each variable.

*z*-scores. This arrangement will result in the sum of the cross products and the correlation to be maximum negative. In this example, the correlation is $-1.00$, a perfect negative correlation. Thus, a perfect negative correlation is one in which there is a perfect alignment of *z*-scores but one of the scales is in reversed order.

Although the *z*-score formula for *r* is a useful way to define the correlation, it is not practical to use. Imagine the Herculean task of calculating *r* when *N* equals 25 or more cases, as it often does in behavioral research! You would have to calculate the *z*-score for each number, then calculate the cross products of the *z*-scores, total the cross products, and then divide by the number of pairs. When we introduced you to the standard deviation and variance, we showed you that there are two formulas that can be used to calculate the same statistic. The computational formula is excellent for calculating a statistic but provides little basis for understanding the meaning of the statistic. The definitional formula is useful for understanding the logic of a statistic but is of limited value for practical calculations. The *z*-score formula for *r* is of the latter type, it helps us understand how to think about a correlation coefficient. Don't use it for calculating *r*, however. A useful and more time-efficient means of calculating *r* is the raw score formula which we now present.

**Raw Score Formula for Pearson *r***   In Chapter 5, we saw the important role the sum of squares (*SS*) plays in calculating the two major indices of variability, specifically the variance and the standard deviation. As we progress toward more complex statistical formulas, their complexity is simplified and clarified by the fact that *SS* is at the very core of many of these formulas. In this section, we examine how the sum of squares can be applied to the calculation of the correlation coefficient. Here is another formula which is useful for understanding the concept of correlation.

$$r_{XY} = \frac{\Sigma(X - \overline{X})(Y - \overline{Y})}{\sqrt{\Sigma(X - \overline{X})^2 \Sigma(Y - \overline{Y})^2}} \tag{8.2}$$

This equation may appear different and intimidating, but if you look carefully, you see that there are some familiar terms in the equation. To begin, look at the denominator. the two separate terms $\Sigma(X - \overline{X})^2$ and $\Sigma(Y - \overline{Y})^2$ are the sums of squares for the variables *X* and *Y*, respectively. As you remember, this form of the sum of squares is the definitional formula and can be easily replaced with the computational forms:

$$SS_X = \Sigma X^2 - \frac{(\Sigma X)^2}{N} \quad \text{and} \quad SS_Y = \Sigma Y^2 - \frac{(\Sigma Y)^2}{N}$$

Now look at the numerator of the equation. This is also a form of sum of squares. Specifically, this is the sum of squares for the covariance between the two variables *X* and *Y*. We can rewrite the numerator using the equation $\Sigma XY - \frac{(\Sigma X)(\Sigma Y)}{N}$. Therefore, the computational equation for the correlation coefficient is

$$r_{XY} = \frac{\Sigma XY - \frac{(\Sigma X)(\Sigma Y)}{N}}{\sqrt{\left[\Sigma X^2 - \frac{(\Sigma X)^2}{N}\right]\left[\Sigma Y^2 - \frac{(\Sigma Y)^2}{N}\right]}} \tag{8.3}$$

**Table** 8.7

**Calculating the Pearson Correlation Coefficient**

| Subject | $X$ | $X^2$ | $Y$ | $Y^2$ | $XY$ |
|---------|-----|-------|-----|-------|------|
| A | 1 | 1 | 4 | 16 | 4 |
| B | 3 | 9 | 7 | 49 | 21 |
| C | 5 | 25 | 13 | 169 | 65 |
| D | 7 | 49 | 16 | 256 | 112 |
| E | 9 | 81 | 10 | 100 | 90 |
| F | 11 | 121 | 22 | 484 | 242 |
| G | 13 | 169 | 19 | 361 | 247 |

$N = 7$    $\Sigma X = 49$    $\Sigma X^2 = 455$    $\Sigma Y = 91$    $\Sigma Y^2 = 1435$    $\Sigma XY = 781$
$(\Sigma X)^2 = 2401$    $(\Sigma Y)^2 = 8281$

Using computational formula as a whole

$$r_{XY} = \frac{\Sigma XY - \frac{(\Sigma X)(\Sigma Y)}{N}}{\sqrt{\left(\Sigma X^2 - \frac{(\Sigma X)^2}{N}\right)\left(\Sigma Y^2 - \frac{(\Sigma Y)^2}{N}\right)}}$$

$$r_{XY} = \frac{781 - \frac{(49)(91)}{7}}{\sqrt{\left(455 - \frac{2401}{7}\right)\left(1435 - \frac{8281}{7}\right)}}$$

$$r_{XY} = \frac{781 - 637}{\sqrt{(455 - 343)(1435 - 1183)}}$$

$$r_{XY} = \frac{144}{\sqrt{(112)(252)}} = \frac{144}{\sqrt{28224}} = \frac{144}{168}$$

$$r_{XY} = .857$$

Calculating component separately then combining

$$\Sigma XY - \frac{(\Sigma X)(\Sigma Y)}{N} =$$

$$781 - \frac{(49)(91)}{7} =$$

$$781 - 637 = 144$$

$$SS_X = 455 - 343 = 112$$

$$SS_Y = 1435 - 1183 = 252$$

$$r = \frac{144}{\sqrt{(112)(252)}} = \frac{144}{\sqrt{28224}}$$

$$r = \frac{144}{168}$$

$$r = .857$$

Before proceeding, compare Formula 8.2 with Formula 8.3. Note that they both are equations for calculating $r_{XY}$. Why do we need two? Why not just one? Simply because Formula 8.2 is useful for understanding correlation and seeing how it is related to concepts learned earlier. Formula 8.3, however, is much more efficient for *calculating r*, but don't use it to try to explain the concept of correlation to your roommate! For that, use a definitional formula. Now let's examine Formula 8.3 more carefully.

The numerator of this equation is known as the sum of squares for the covariance. **Covariance** is an index of the degree to which the two variables share common variance. As you have seen in the previous examples, the covariance will be the largest possible number for the given data when there is a perfect linear relation between $X$ and $Y$. The covariance will equal 0 when there is no relation between $X$ and $Y$ or when the relation between $X$ and $Y$ cannot be described as a straight line. By itself, the covariance has no real meaning, just as the cross products of the $z$-scores have no meaning. When we divide the numerator by the

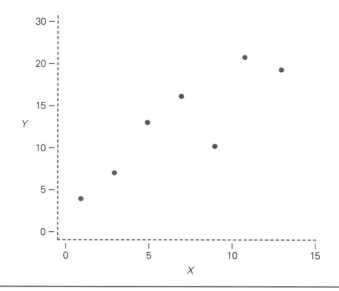

**Figure** 8.7

Scatterplot of the data presented in Table 8.7.

denominator (also represented by $\sqrt{SS_X \times SS_Y}$), which is an index of the variance for $X$ and $Y$, we convert the covariance into a descriptive statistic, the correlation coefficient, $r$.

---

**Sum of Squares for Covariance:**
   The total of the cross products of the deviation
   scores for two sets of data:

| Definitional Equation | Computational Equation |
|---|---|
| $Cov_{XY} = \Sigma(X - \overline{X})(Y - \overline{Y})$ | $Cov_{XY} = \Sigma XY - \dfrac{(\Sigma X)(\Sigma Y)}{N}$ |

---

We can apply this equation to some simple data for the sake of illustration. Consider the data in Table 8.7. The scatterplot of these data is presented in Figure 8.7.

Now that we have examined how to calculate the correlation on some simple data, let's look at the calculation of a correlation coefficient on a larger set of data. For this exercise we can use the data presented in Table 8.1. To compete our calculations, we will need to calculate the sum of the cross products, $\Sigma XY$. These calculations are presented in Table 8.8.

## 8.5 / How the Pearson Product Moment Correlation Coefficient Got Its Name

Sir Francis Galton developed the concept of correlation in the late 1800s. Galton, who was a cousin of Charles Darwin, was very interested in evolutionary theory and the degree to which physical and psychological traits are inherited from one's parents. Galton believed that families shared

**Table 8.8**

**Calculation of the Pearson Product Moment Correlation Coefficient, Based on Data Presented in Table 8.1**

| $N = 20$ Self-Monitoring | Months Dating | Cross Products |
|---|---|---|
| $\Sigma X = 257$ | $\Sigma Y = 206$ | $\Sigma XY = 2452$ |
| $\Sigma X^2 = 3613$ | $\Sigma Y^2 = 2444$ | |

$$r_{XY} = \frac{\Sigma XY - \dfrac{(\Sigma X)(\Sigma Y)}{N}}{\sqrt{\left(\Sigma X^2 - \dfrac{(\Sigma X)^2}{N}\right)\left(\Sigma Y^2 - \dfrac{(\Sigma Y)^2}{N}\right)}}$$

$$\text{Covariance} = \Sigma XY - \frac{(\Sigma X)(\Sigma Y)}{N}$$

$$= 2452 - \frac{(257)(206)}{20}$$

$$= 2452 - 2647.1 = -195.10$$

$$SS_X = 3613 - \frac{257^2}{20} = 3613 - 3302.45 = 310.55$$

$$SS_Y = 2444 - \frac{206^2}{20} = 2444 - 2121.80 = 322.20$$

$$r_{XY} = \frac{-195.10}{\sqrt{(310.55)(322.20)}}$$

$$r_{XY} = \frac{-195.10}{316.32}$$

$$r_{XY} = -.617$$

similar traits because of their biological "co-relation." Such an observation is in keeping with our understanding of genetics. Identical twins are perfectly co-related because they share the same genetic material. Because of the high co-relation, identical twins are very similar to one another. Brothers and sisters share only 50% common genetic material. Consequently, siblings are similar to one another, but there are large differences among individuals. Randomly selected people share little common ancestry and are therefore likely to be very different from one another.

Although Galton first conceived the concept of an index of "co-relation," it was the mathematician Karl Pearson who developed the mathematics of the statistic that bears his name. The other parts of the name are mathematical terms. In statistics, the deviation of scores about the mean are called *moments*. If you multiply two moments together, you get the *product* of the moments. A *coefficient* is a mathematical term for the result of a specific mathematical operation. Hence the name of this statistic is really quite meaningful.

## 8.6 Interpreting the Correlation Coefficient

Although the correlation coefficient is a statistic with a common scale (it ranges between $-1.00$ and $+1.00$), the number has little meaning by itself. Let's examine some general issues that need to be considered when we interpret the correlation coefficient. To help us interpret the correlation, we can review the questions that the correlation coefficient allows us to address.

### The Magnitude and Sign of the Correlation Coefficient

The first question we can ask is whether the two variables are correlated and the way in which the variables are correlated. As we have seen previously, the sign of the correlation is very meaningful for our interpretation. A positive correlation indicates that there is a *direct* relation between the two variables. A negative correlation indicates that there is an *inverse* relation between the two variables.

A second question we can ask about the correlation coefficient is about its magnitude. There are many ways that we can judge the size of the correlation coefficient. The first way to judge a correlation coefficient is to follow some general guidelines that many behavioral scientists follow. Cohen (1988) suggests that correlation coefficients can be characterized as "Small," "Medium," or "Large." Table 8.9 presents the ranges for these three levels of correlation.

Remember that the correlation coefficient can have positive and negative values. Indeed, the correlation coefficient is symmetrical about 0. This means that a correlation of $-.50$ represents the same strength of relationship as a correlation of .50. Many people make the mistake of assuming that a negative correlation means a small correlation. Such an interpretation is wrong. The negative sign merely means that the relation between the two variables is inverted. Therefore, the larger the absolute value of the correlation, the greater the degree of relation between the two variables.

From this table we can see that the correlation for our hypothetical data for the self-monitoring study is "Large." The observed correlation $r = -.617$ is within the range of $-1.00$ to $-.50$. Although Cohen's guide is useful, it is incomplete and not all scientists agree on the values that Cohen chose, therefore, many researchers use other techniques to judge the magnitude of the correlation coefficient.

Another technique for interpreting the correlation coefficient is to square its value. The correlation coefficient squared, $r^2$, is known as the **coefficient of determination**. The coefficient of determination tells us the percentage of variance in one variable that can be described or explained by the other variable. In our example the correlation is $r = -.617$, therefore the coefficient of determination is $r^2 = .381$. We can interpret

**Coefficient of Determination ($r^2$):**

The proportion of variance in one variable that can be described or explained by the other variable.

**Table 8.9**

**Cohen's (1988) Guidelines for Small, Medium, and Large Correlation Coefficients**

| Correlation | Negative | Positive |
|---|---|---|
| Small: | $-.29$ to $-.10$ | .10 to .29 |
| Medium: | $-.49$ to $-.30$ | .30 to .49 |
| Large: | $-1.00$ to $-.50$ | .50 to 1.00 |

the coefficient of determination to mean that 38.1% of the differences among the length of time people have been involved in a romantic relationship can be predicted by a characteristic of personality, self-monitoring.

We can also calculate the **coefficient of nondetermination** which tells us the proportion of variance in one variable that *cannot* be described or explained by the other variable. The coefficient of nondetermination is calculated as $1 − r^2$. In our example, $1 − .381 = .619$. Therefore, 61.9% of the differences in the length of a romantic relationship is due to other factors that have yet to be identified.

One way to think about the coefficient of determination is presented in Figure 8.8. These diagrams represent different correlations. Imagine that the circles represent the $X$ and $Y$ variables. When the correlation between $X$ and $Y$ is 0, there is no overlap between the two circles. As the magnitude of the correlation coefficient increases, the amount of overlap increases. The coefficient of determination between two variables is represented by the overlap of the two circles.

There are still some basic questions that have not been addressed: "What is a *good* correlation between $X$ and $Y$?" and "How do I know if I have a significant correlation?" These are two very different questions. The first question has to do with the *importance* of a correlation coefficient. When researchers talk about the importance of a correlation coefficient, they are indicating that the correlation coefficient helps them to better understand a complex phenomenon. The importance of a correlation will depend on the type of research that is being conducted. A correlation of .2 may be considered *important* by one researcher and *trivial* by another, depending on the context in which the data are to be interpreted.

It is always important to interpret statistics with respect to the context in which the data were collected and the decisions that will be based on the statistical conclusion. Would you consider $r = .10$ to be trivial? The correlation is small and $r^2 = .01$, suggesting a very slight relation between the two variables. Would you be willing to suggest that the

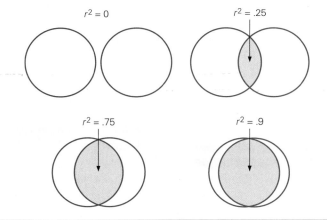

**Figure** | **8.8**

Schematic diagram of four increasingly strong correlations. Each circle represents a variable. The overlap of the two circles represents the correlation between the variables. Specifically, the overlap represents the coefficient of determination, $r^2$. The parts of the circles that are not overlapping represent the coefficient of nondetermination, $1 − r^2$.

correlation is trivial if you learned that it represents the effectiveness of a new drug and that the correlation means an improvement of 10 lives in 1,000 (Rosenthal, 1994)? Being able to improve the quality of life for 10 individuals is rarely considered to be trivial!

The concept of the *significance* of a correlation coefficient is another issue. Statistical significance is a mathematical concept that describes the probability that the results are due to chance factors. We will present the concept of statistical significance in greater detail starting with Chapter 11. For now it is enough to know that a correlation coefficient is, in and of itself, a descriptive statistic. Later in this text we will see how researchers evaluate the importance and the significance of the correlation coefficients using inferential statistics.

# 8.7
## Several Words of Caution

We must exercise some caution when interpreting a correlation coefficient. There are several important factors that can cause the correlation coefficient to be artificially high or low. These extreme correlations are sometimes known as **spurious correlations** because they do not represent the true relationship between the variables or represent the effect of some confounding factor. Sometimes the correlation will be small or close to 0. Some researchers assume that a low correlation means that there is little or no relationship between the two variables under study. There are many reasons why there may be an apparent lack of correlation between two variables. There are also conditions that will lead to an extremely high correlation that is unrelated to the true relation between the two variables. A good researcher will attempt to account for these alternative explanations before coming to any conclusion about the meaning of the correlation coefficient. The following is a list of potential reasons for spurious correlations.

**■ Spurious Correlation:**

A correlation coefficient that is artificially high or low because of the nature of the data or method for collecting the data.

**Lack of a Linear Relation Between the Variables**   One must remember that Pearson *r* reflects only the *linear relationship* between two variables. In other words, the relationship is such that a straight line would summarize any systematic correlation between the two variables. To illustrate, if we were plotting age against strength of grip, we might obtain a picture somewhat like the scatterplot or diagram shown in Figure 8.9.

It is usually possible to see if there is a substantial departure from linearity by examining a scatter diagram. If the distribution of points are scattered in what would appear to be a fairly straight line, it may safely be assumed that the relationship is linear. Any small departures from linearity will not greatly influence the size of the correlation coefficient, however, major departures from linearity will. It is inappropriate to use a Pearson product moment correlation on data that are markedly curvilinear. Therefore, it is important to remind you that you should examine your scatterplot before calculating any correlation coefficient.

When there is marked **curvilinearity**, as in Figure 8.9, Pearson *r* will be misleading and inappropriate as a measure of linear relationship. The overall correlation may be extremely low because the positive and negative components on each side of the curve are antagonistic and would tend to cancel out each other. A curvilinear coefficient of correlation would better reflect the relationship of the two variables under investigation. Although it is beyond the scope of this text to investigate nonlinear coefficients of correlation, you should be aware of this possibility.

**■ Curvilinearity:**

A condition where the relation between two variables is better described by a curved line than a straight line.

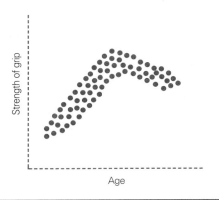

**Figure** | **8.9**

Scatter diagram of two variables that are related in a nonlinear fashion (hypothetical data). Note that there appear to be two components in the scatter diagram: a positive component from birth to the middle years and a negative component thereafter.

The assumption of linearity is a most important requirement to justify the use of Pearson $r$ as a measure of relationship between two interval- or ratio-scaled variables. It is not necessary that $r$ be calculated only between normally distributed variables. So long as the distributions are *unimodal* and relatively *symmetrical*, a Pearson $r$ may legitimately be computed.

**Truncated Range**   A spuriously low correlation coefficient may also be the product of truncated range. Truncated range refers to a condition where the range of values for one or both of the variables is restricted. For example, if we were interested in the relationship between age and height between ages of, say, 1 and 16 years of age, we would undoubtedly obtain a rather high positive correlation between these two variables. However, suppose we were to restrict the range of one of our variables. What effect would this have on the size of the coefficient? Let us look at the same relationship between age and height but only for those children between 9 and 10 years of age. We would probably wind up with a rather low Pearson $r$, as shown graphically in Figure 8.10.

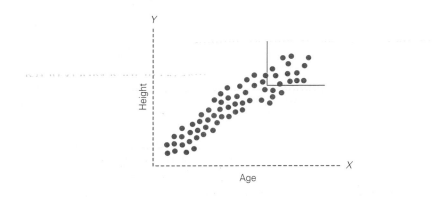

**Figure** | **8.10**

Scatter diagram illustrating a high correlation over entire range of *X*- and *Y*-values but a low correlation when the range is restricted as illustrated by the inserted graph.

The problem of truncated range is fairly common in behavioral research where subjects have been preselected for intelligence and related variables. Thus, they represent a fairly homogeneous group with respect to these variables. Consequently, when an attempt is made to demonstrate the relationship between variables such as SAT scores and college grades, the resulting coefficient may be lowered because of the truncated range. The correlation coefficients would be expected to be lower among colleges that select their students from a narrow range of SAT scores.

The primary remedy for this problem rests with the design of the study. If you are planning a correlational study, you want to be sure that, for the variables you are examining, you do *not* restrict the range. You want to maximize variability in your sample. In other types of research, particularly experimental studies, you may want to minimize variability in the sample in order to allow the effect of the independent variable to be detected. We will discuss this further when we cover inferential statistics and the design of experiments. For correlational studies, be sure that your sample is sufficiently diverse (i.e., your subjects exhibit a wide range of scores on both the independent and the dependent variables).

**Sample Size** Many times a spurious correlation occurs because the sample size is too small. In the behavioral sciences it is not uncommon for some researchers to use 50 or more subjects to find a meaningful correlation between two or more variables. How large should your sample size be? That is a good question, but one that we will defer answering for now until we have reviewed some more statistical concepts. Until that time, do not assume that a small sample will result in a small correlation coefficient or that a large sample will increase the size of your $r$. This assumption is a common misconception. As a matter of fact, sample size and strength of relationship are independent. The general rule is that your sample should be sufficiently large to be representative of the population you are attempting to describe.

**Outliers** One problem that a small sample size creates is that a single subject whose $X$ and $Y$ scores are extremely high or low can have a considerable impact on the data. The problem arises from the fact that the correlation is based on the relative position of the scores from the mean. As you may recall from our discussion of descriptive statistics, the mean is sensitive to extreme scores especially when the number of observations is small. The same is true for correlations. One pair of scores that is extremely deviant from one or both means can greatly influence the size of the correlation.

Although the effect of outliers diminishes as the sample size increases, it is important to examine the distributions and the scatterplot to identify deviant scores. Extreme scores may occur for a variety of reasons. They may be typographical errors or may represent an exceptional case. A good researcher examines extreme scores to determine if the data should be included in the analysis.

**Multiple Populations** Examine the data presented in Figure 8.11. There are two clusters of data points, one represented by 10 squares, the other by 10 circles. If we combine all 20 points and calculate the correlation coefficient, we obtain a moderate correlation, $r = .358$. The correlation coefficients calculated for each of the clusters is larger, however. The correlation for the cluster of squares is $r = .722$; the correlation for the circles is $r = .681$.

How is it that the correlation for the entire data set is smaller than the correlation for each of the individual groups? This situation can

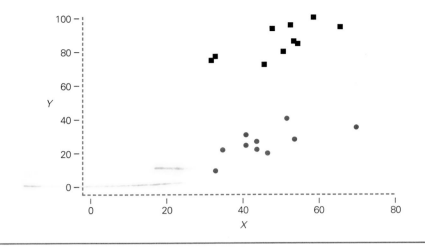

**Figure** | **8.11**

A scatterplot containing two distinct populations. The correlation for all the data is less than the correlations for each of the two subgroups.

happen when there are subgroups within the sample that behave in different ways. In the present example the difference is due to the fact that the means of the $Y$ variable for the two clusters are different. For the squares, the mean of $Y$ is 84.7; for the circles, the mean of $Y$ is 25. The squares could represent, for example, data obtained from adults whereas the circles could represent the measures obtained from children. Both the level of development of the subject and the $X$ variable influence the results.

This example illustrates the value of exploratory data analysis, indeed the necessity of exploring data, prior to performing statistical calculations. Without examining this scatterplot we might well have concluded that the relationship between the $X$ and $Y$ variables is weak. Instead we are able to determine from this visual representation that the strength of the relationship is strong *and* there appears to be two distinct subpopulations within our sample. These conclusions could not have been reached without a prior examination of the data.

**Extreme Scores** Sometimes misguided researchers select only the extreme cases in their sample and attempt to look at the relationship between two variables. Consider the example of a researcher interested in the correlation between depression and short-term memory. He administers a depression test and a test of short-term memory. He then takes subjects who scored in the top 25% and the bottom 25% of the depression test and uses only these subjects in his calculations. What's the problem?

An illustration of the problem is presented in Figure 8.12. These are 50 scores that represent a moderate correlation between $X$ and $Y$, $r = .317$. If we ignore the 30 scores in the center of the sample (those scores represented by the circles), the correlation is much higher, $r = .808$.

The problem with using the extreme scores to perform the calculation is that it provides an inflated estimate of the correlation between the two variables. Variables $X$ and $Y$ are correlated, but the degree of the relationship is better represented by the correlation based on the broader set of data.

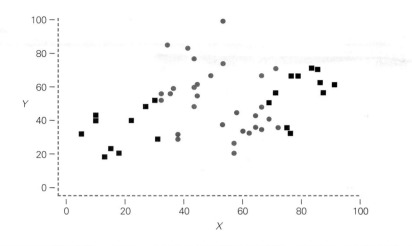

**Figure | 8.12**

An example of how a spurious correlation can be found using extreme groups.

**Causation** Just because two variables are highly correlated does not mean that one is causing the other. As noted earlier in this text, when you have two variables, *X* and *Y*, correlational studies tell you only that some kind of relationship exists. They do not tell you that *X causes Y*. There are two general problems with causation that the correlation coefficient cannot address. First, causes must precede the event. This means that the independent variable must occur in time before the dependent variable. This issue is known as *temporal directionality*. Second, there must not be other variables that can cause *X* and *Y* to change. The latter problem is sometimes known as the *third variable problem*.

Let's consider the example about personality characteristics and longevity of romantic relationships presented earlier in the chapter. Can we assume that personality *causes* the longevity of romantic relationships? Absolutely not! With respect to our requirement of temporal directionality, we do not know if it is personality that influences the dating behavior. It may be that dating experiences influence the personality of the individual. A correlational design is merely an empirical snapshot of a series of events and does not allow us to examine the sequence through which the current conditions developed. Even if we know the sequence, a correlation cannot allow us to draw causal conclusions. Consider the example of a researcher who finds a strong positive correlation between the number of books in the homes of some elementary school children and the reading achievement scores of those children. Can you conclude that the number of books in the home *causes* the children to have higher reading achievement scores? If that were the case, the school system should pack up some books and deliver boxes of them to the students' homes immediately. Imagine being able to raise test scores in such an efficient manner. In fact, there are many other variables that potentially contribute to the differences in reading performance. The children who come from homes with many books probably are from a higher socioeconomic class, and their parents probably have more years of schooling. The children with fewer books in the home are probably poorer and have parents with less schooling. The parents may not speak English and their children may have missed early exposure to the language. Many factors are possibly contributing to the lower reading test scores. A correlation coefficient will provide a quantitative measure of the relationship between variables but it will *not* provide understanding or any explanations of why the relationship exists.

---

**TWO MISGUIDED GRADUATE STUDENTS**

Two graduate students uncovered the most remarkable correlation! While working on a national survey, as part of their studies, they found there was a high positive correlation (r = .9) between the number of churches and the number of taverns in cities and towns across the country. The very religious graduate student saw this as evidence of the responsiveness of the clergy and the willingness of the clergy to move into areas with the greatest need. The other, more cynical student exclaimed, "Aha, religion is driving people to drink!" In fact, neither conclusion can be drawn. There is a simple explanation. If you need a hint, think in terms of a third variable!

Answer: There is a third factor, population. Large cities have a larger population with many churches and many taverns. Small towns have fewer of either.

---

## 8.8 / Correlation as a Measure of Reliability

**Reliability:**

The extent to which a measurement procedure produces a consistent outcome.

An important concept in psychological research is that of **reliability.** Reliability refers to the consistency with which a measurement technique produces the same outcome. A test is reliable if it produces consistent results when administered under standardized conditions. Reliability is frequently evaluated using the correlation coefficient. Let's look at an example in which Pearson $r$ can be used to measure the reliability of a psychological test.

Reliability is an essential component of any measurement, including psychological tests. Thus, psychologists routinely examine their tests for this important characteristic. The concept of reliability of a test is simple. If a test is reliable, the relative standing of subjects on the first testing should be similar to their standing on the second testing. A high correlation between scores obtained from the two test administrations indicates that the test is reliable. Scores obtained on one day will be similar to those obtained on another day. An unreliable test is one for which the correlation is low between scores obtained by the same individuals at two different times. Imagine a graduate school admission test on which you scored in the top 10% the first time you took the test and in the bottom 10% the next time you took it. Assuming the conditions were the same for the two administrations, you could rightfully complain that the test was not reliable!

Although correlation is widely used as a measure of reliability, don't be fooled into concluding that a high correlation is evidence that the scores obtained on two different time periods will remain the same or even close. A correlation indicates not that the scores must be the same or close to the same at each administration, rather, it indicates that the scores for each administration should be at or near *the same relative position* in the distribution. To illustrate, imagine a situation in which you administer a scholastic achievement test to a group. Then you provide intensive instruction about taking the test. When you readminister the test, everyone's score has increased by exactly 100 points. Interestingly, the correlation between the two test scores will be a perfect 1.00. Why?

Every member of the sample has remained in the *same relative position*, and it is relative position rather than absolute score that is assessed in correlational analyses. So when you evaluate test-retest reliability, be sure to look at before-after means to arrive at a more accurate picture of what is taking place.

A note of caution is needed here. Don't confuse the concept of reliability with that of **validity**. Validity is the extent to which a test measures what it purports to measure. If a test is supposed to measure spelling ability then it should provide a good assessment of that ability. If it is supposed to be a good measure of word problem solving, it should measure that ability and not be measuring reading ability instead. Validity, like reliability, is assessed using a correlation coefficient. Scores obtained on a test are correlated with scores obtained from a performance measure or from another test. If the correlation is high, the test is said to be valid.

There is an easy way to remember the difference between the two related concepts. Let's say you put your little brother on the bathroom scale two or three times in a row. Each time the scale says he weighs 70 pounds. You may say that the scale provides a reliable measure of his weight. If, however, you want to say that the 70 is a valid measure of his IQ you would be wrong. Your bathroom scale may be a reliable one but it is not a valid indicator of IQ.

## 8.9 / A Correlation Matrix

**Validity:**

The extent to which a test measures what it purports to measure.

Sometimes we hold beliefs that are not based on documented evidence. Take for instance the notion that an overweight child is destined to be overweight as an adult. Parents worry that their chubby little baby will morph into a chubby adolescent. Some of us chubby adolescents have worried that we had a life sentence to this condition. Is there a basis for our concerns? Folklore would say there is. But is there an empirical basis? What does the evidence say? Correlational studies often provide evidence that either substantiates or refutes common beliefs. What do you think? Is your weight during childhood a reliable indicator of your weight throughout life?

Researchers have examined this question of lifetime weight using a measure called the Body Mass Index (BMI). This index takes into account weight relative to height. For our purposes we can think of it as a measure of fatness. A group of subjects were followed over four decades and their weights were obtained at different times—childhood, early adolescence, and at 18, 30, and 40 years of age. The measures obtained at these different times were then correlated with each other.

The data are presented in Table 8.10 in the form of a correlation matrix. This type of matrix is used to present the correlation coefficients obtained from the intercorrelation of many variables. That is, the variables listed in the column on the left side are the same as the variables presented across the top of the matrix. On the top row, the correlation between measures taken during childhood and later times in life are presented. Thus the correlation between fatness in childhood and fatness during early adolescence is positive and strong, $r = .81$. The correlation between fatness in childhood and at 18 years of age is less strong, $r = .53$. The correlation between fatness during childhood and fatness at 40 years of age is almost zero, $r = -.03$. If you are curious about your relative weight at age 18 and at age 40, look down the left column to

**Table** 8.10

**Pearson Correlation of Body Mass Index\* from Childhood to 40 Years in a Longitudinal Study of Female Subjects**

|  | Childhood | Early Adolescence | 18 years | 30 years | 40 years |
|---|---|---|---|---|---|
| Childhood | 1.00 | .81 | .53 | .21 | −.03 |
| Early adolescence | — | 1.00 | .82 | .50 | .31 |
| 18 years | — | — | 1.00 | .66 | .62 |
| 30 years | — | — | — | 1.00 | .84 |
| 40 Years | — | — | — | — | 1.00 |

\*Body mass index (BMI) is a technical term that considers weight of an individual relative to his or her height.

*Source:* Adapted from V. A. Casey, J. T. Dwyer, K. A. Coleman, and I. Valadian (1992) *American Journal of Clinical Nutrition, 56,* by permission © 1992 American Society for Clinical Nutrition.

where it says 18 years and look directly to your rightmost column. Note that the longer the time period between weighing, the smaller the correlations. It is quite clear, however, that if you want to predict the relative weight of an adult female based on her weight as a child, you might just as well flip a coin and predict heads for higher weight, tails for lower weight. According to the data, the coin toss will be as accurate as any attempt to make a prediction from the data. Many of us worry about adding too many pounds as we get older, but because we were chubby as young children does not mean that we have to worry more than our skinnier siblings. They're at risk too!

## 8.10 / Ordinally Scaled Variables and $r_s$

Imagine that you are a teacher in the primary grades. After years of classroom observation, you have developed a strong suspicion that intelligence and leadership are related variables, specifically the higher the IQ of a child the stronger his or her leadership qualities. However, you are unable to find any ratio or interval scales available to measure classroom leadership. Moreover, you can think of no satisfactory way to quantify this variable. Nevertheless, based on numerous observations of the children in different leadership circumstances, you feel confident that you are able to *rank* the children who are highest to lowest in leadership qualities. The resulting measurements constitute an ordinal scale. Although we could obtain a Pearson r with ranked data, there is a variant of the product moment coefficient which is referred to as the **Spearman r, $r_s$,** or the **rank correlation coefficient.** The correlation coefficient employed with rank data reduces the computational task in obtaining the correlation coefficient. The Spearman r is appropriate when one scale constitutes ordinal measurement and the remaining scale is either ordinal or interval/ratio. The Spearman r is also a preferred measure of correlation when the data are greatly skewed.

The primary difference between the Spearman r and the Pearson r is the method of scaling the numbers. As we have reviewed previously, the Pearson r scales the observed scores by converting them to z-scores. Therefore the scale represents relative distance from the mean. By contrast, the Spearman r converts the observed scores into ranks. Therefore the transformed scale represents a ranking from lowest to highest. The assumption is that highly correlated variables will have the same or

**Spearman r, $r_s$, or the Rank Correlation Coefficient:**

Correlation coefficient used with ordered or ranked data.

**Table 8.11**

**Procedures for Calculating $r_s$ from Ranked Variables (Hypothetical Data)**

| IQ Rank | Leadership Rank | D | $D^2$ |
|---|---|---|---|
| 1 | 4 | −3 | 9 |
| 2 | 2 | 0 | 0 |
| 3 | 9 | −6 | 36 |
| 4 | 1 | 3 | 9 |
| 5 | 7 | −2 | 4 |
| 6 | 10 | −4 | 16 |
| 7 | 8 | −1 | 1 |
| 8 | 13 | −5 | 25 |
| 9 | 5 | 4 | 16 |
| 10 | 3 | 7 | 49 |
| 11 | 11 | 0 | 0 |
| 12 | 6 | 6 | 36 |
| 13 | 12 | 1 | 1 |

$$\Sigma D = 0 \qquad \Sigma D^2 = 202$$

$$r_s = 1 - \frac{6\Sigma D^2}{N(N^2 - 1)} = 1 - \frac{6 \times 202}{13 \times 168} = 1 - \frac{1212}{2184}$$

$$r_s = 1 - .555 = .445$$

similar rank order. Let's return to our example to examine the statistic in greater detail.

Realizing that your knowledge of the children's IQ scores might lead to contaminated or biased estimates of their leadership qualities, you ask a teaching associate to provide estimates of the ranking of leadership qualities on his or her students. You then obtain, independent of leadership estimates, an assessment of their IQs based on prior testing. You then rank the IQs from highest to lowest.

The rank correlation coefficient requires that you obtain the differences in the ranks, square and sum the squared differences, and substitute the resulting value into the formula

$$r_s = 1 - \frac{6\Sigma D^2}{N(N^2 - 1)} \tag{8.4}$$

where
$D^2$ = difference between ranks, squared
$N$ = number of pairs of data

The procedures for calculating the Spearman $r$ are presented in Table 8.11. The obtained $r_s$ is .445.

As a matter of course, $\Sigma D$ should be calculated even though it is not called for in the formula. It provides a useful check of the accuracy of your calculations, because $\Sigma D$ always equals zero. If you get a value other than zero, you should recheck your original ranks and subsequent subtractions.

## Tied Ranks

Occasionally, when it is necessary to convert scores to ranks, you will find two or more tied scores.* In this event, assign the mean of the tied ranks to each of the tied scores. The next score in the array receives the rank normally assigned to it. Thus, the ranks of the scores 128, 122, 115, 115, 115, 107, 103 would be 1, 2, 4, 4, 4, 6, 7, and the ranks of the scores 128, 122, 115, 115, 107, 103 would be 1, 2, 3.5, 3.5, 5, 6.

## 8.11 / Putting It All Together

H. G. Wells, the 19th-century prophet, remarked, "Statistical thinking will one day be as necessary for efficient citizenship as the ability to read and write." This was a rather profound statement because statistics now occupies a prominent place in the thinking in areas such as philosophy and all of the sciences—physics, biology, and the behavioral sciences. Along a more applied vein, statistical analysis is used by many agencies of the government and is an essential element of techniques used by Wall Street 'quants,' economists, and market researchers. Even college professors use statistical techniques.

Let us suppose you are a professor and you want to know if there is a relationship between student performance in a statistics class and overall achievement in other courses. You randomly select 10 students in your statistics class, record their grades on the final examination, and look up their grade point average at the registrar's office. The hypothetical results are shown in Table 8.12.

Figure 8.13 shows the scatter diagram of the two variables, final exam in statistics, and cumulative grade point average. As is readily seen, the

---

* When there are numerous tied ranks on either or both the $X$- and $Y$-variables, the Spearman formula tends to yield spuriously high coefficients of correlation. When there are many ties, it is preferable to apply the Pearson $r$ formula to the *ranked* data.

**Table** 8.12

**Final Examination Scores and Grade Point Averages (GPA) for 10 Randomly Selected Students**

| Student | Exam($X$) | GPA($Y$) | $X^2$ | $Y^2$ | $XY$ |
|---------|-----------|----------|-------|-------|------|
| 1 | 90 | 2.5 | 8100 | 6.25 | 225 |
| 2 | 85 | 2.0 | 7225 | 4.00 | 170 |
| 3 | 80 | 2.5 | 6400 | 6.25 | 200 |
| 4 | 75 | 2.0 | 5625 | 4.00 | 150 |
| 5 | 70 | 1.5 | 4900 | 2.25 | 105 |
| 6 | 70 | 1.0 | 4900 | 1.00 | 70 |
| 7 | 70 | 1.0 | 4900 | 1.00 | 70 |
| 8 | 60 | 0.5 | 3600 | 0.25 | 30 |
| 9 | 60 | 0.5 | 3600 | 0.25 | 30 |
| 10 | 50 | 0.5 | 2500 | 0.25 | 25 |
| | $\Sigma$ 710 | 14.0 | 51750 | 25.5 | 1075 |

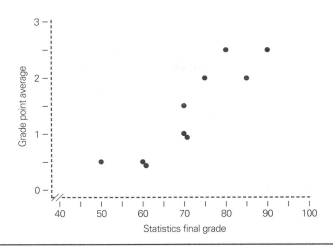

**Figure** 8.13

**Scatter diagram for two variables—final exam in statistics and grade point average.**

data points go from the lower left-hand corner to the upper right-hand corner. Therefore, there is a positive relationship. Visually there appears to be a relationship. A quantitative measure of the strength and direction of the relationship is obtained by calculating the correlation.

The steps for obtaining this correlation are shown below.

**Step 1** Square each value of $X$ and place the result in the column labeled $X^2$. See Table 8.12.

**Step 2** Sum the values of $X^2$ to obtain $\Sigma X^2 = 51750$.

**Step 3** Square each value of $Y$ and place the result in the column labeled $Y^2$.

**Step 4** Sum the values of $Y^2$ to obtain $\Sigma Y^2 = 25.5$.

**Step 5** Multiply each value of $X$ by its corresponding value of $Y$ and sum the column $XY$ to obtain $\Sigma XY = 1075$.

**Step 6** Find $\Sigma XY - \dfrac{(\Sigma X)(\Sigma Y)}{N}$

$$= 1075 - \frac{9940}{10}$$
$$= 1075 - 994$$
$$= 81.$$

**Step 7** Find $SS_X = \Sigma X^2 - \dfrac{(\Sigma X)^2}{N}$

$$= 51750 - \frac{504100}{10}$$
$$= 51750 - 50410$$
$$= 1340.$$

**Step 8**   Find $SS_Y = \Sigma Y^2 - \dfrac{(\Sigma Y)^2}{N}$

$$= 25.5 - \frac{196}{10}$$

$$= 25.5 - 19.6$$

$$= 5.9$$

**Step 9**   Find $r$ by substituting the values found in steps 6, 7, and 8 in Formula 8.3.

$$\text{Thus, } r = \frac{\Sigma XY - \dfrac{(\Sigma X)(\Sigma Y)}{N}}{\sqrt{(SS_X)(SS_Y)}} = \frac{81}{\sqrt{(1340)(5.9)}} = \frac{81}{88.916} = .91$$

As we can see, in this sample of $N = 10$, $r = 0.91$ is a high positive relationship between final grades on a statistics exam and cumulative grade point averages of these students.

## CHAPTER SUMMARY

In this chapter we investigated the concept of correlation and presented the calculation of two types of correlation coefficients (i.e., the Pearson $r$ and Spearman rank order correlation). The former, Pearson $r$, is employed with interval- or ratio-scaled data, and the latter, the Spearman correlation coefficient ($r_s$) is used with ordinally scaled measures.

We saw that the correlation coefficient assesses the extent to which the values of two variables are related and the direction of that relationship. The values of correlation coefficients vary from $-1.00$ to $+1.00$; both extremes represent perfect relationships. Two factors that are important in assessing a correlation coefficient are its sign and its size. The sign speaks to the direction of the relationship, the size relates to its strength. A correlation coefficient of 0.00 indicates the absence of a relationship. We noted that a high correlation coefficient does not, in itself, establish a causal relationship between two variables.

There are times when a number of different variables are correlated with one another. A correlation matrix is used to display the interrelationships among a number of variables. An example of a correlation matrix was presented in which relative body weight at different ages was correlated.

We reviewed a number of considerations to keep in mind when interpreting correlation coefficients. The Pearson $r$ is appropriate only for variables that are related in a linear fashion. When there is marked curvilinearity it is inappropriate to use the Pearson $r$ as a measure of relationship. The range of the values on one or both of the variables is important in the interpretation of Pearson $r$. With restricted range on one or both of the variables the resulting correlation will be lower. On the other hand, outliers or extreme scores can cause a spuriously high coefficient, especially in small samples. Subgroups within the sample may also affect the size of the obtained correlation coefficient. The question of correlation and causation was addressed. Although it may be tempting to do so, it is extremely important not to draw causal conclusions based on correlational data. One can only tell if there is a relationship. It is not possible to say which variable is causing the other to vary or if there is a third variable affecting them both.

With ranked data, the Spearman rank order coefficient is the counterpart of the Pearson $r$. The various computational formulas for Pearson $r$ may be employed in calculating $r_s$ from ranked data. A computational formula for $r_s$ was presented that considerably simplifies the calculation of this coefficient.

## TERMS TO REMEMBER

coefficient of determination ($r^2$)  
coefficient of nondetermination ($1 - r^2$)  
correlation coefficient  
covariance  
curvilinearity  
linear relationship  
negative correlation  
negative relationship  

Pearson $r$  
positive correlation  
positive relationship  
reliability  
scatterplot  
Spearman $r$ ($r_s$, or rank correlation coefficient)  
spurious correlation  
validity  

## EXERCISES

1. The data in the accompanying table show the scores obtained by a group of 20 students on a college entrance examination ($X$) and a verbal comprehension test ($Y$).

| Student | College Entrance Exam X | Verbal Comprehension Test Y |
|---------|-------------------------|------------------------------|
| A | 52 | 49 |
| B | 28 | 34 |
| C | 70 | 45 |
| D | 51 | 49 |
| E | 49 | 40 |
| F | 65 | 50 |
| G | 49 | 37 |
| H | 49 | 49 |
| I | 63 | 52 |
| J | 32 | 32 |
| K | 64 | 53 |
| L | 43 | 41 |
| M | 35 | 28 |
| N | 66 | 50 |
| O | 26 | 17 |
| P | 44 | 41 |
| Q | 49 | 29 |
| R | 28 | 17 |
| S | 30 | 15 |
| T | 60 | 55 |

a. Draw a scatterplot of these data and describe the relation between the two tests.
b. Calculate the correlation coefficient between these two variables. Does the correlation coefficient support your description of the scatterplot?
c. Using the coefficient of determination, $r^2$, describe the strength of the relation between the two tests.

**d.** Would it be fair to state that knowledge of a student's performance on the college entrance exam allows you to infer the student's performance on the verbal comprehension test?

2. A statistics professor believes that knowledge of math is essential for students to do well in a statistics course. At the start of the semester, she administers a standardized test of general math ($X$). Later she compares these scores to the final grades students receive for the course ($Y$).

| Student | Test X | Grade Y |
|---------|--------|---------|
| A | 90 | 94 |
| B | 85 | 92 |
| C | 80 | 81 |
| D | 75 | 78 |
| E | 70 | 74 |
| F | 70 | 73 |
| G | 70 | 75 |
| H | 60 | 66 |
| I | 60 | 53 |
| J | 50 | 52 |

**a.** Draw a scatterplot of these data and describe the relation between the two tests.
**b.** Calculate the correlation coefficient between these two variables. Does the correlation coefficient support your description of the scatterplot?
**c.** Using the coefficient of determination, $r^2$, describe the relation between the two tests.
**d.** Would it be fair to state that knowledge of a student's performance on the math test allows you to infer the student's performance in the statistics course?

3. The data in the accompanying table are from a group of students majoring in psychology. They include the student's overall GPA and salary for the first year after college.

| GPA | Salary ($) |
|-----|-----------|
| 2.0 | 18,000 |
| 2.1 | 22,000 |
| 2.1 | 25,000 |
| 2.1 | 26,000 |
| 2.7 | 27,000 |
| 2.0 | 28,000 |
| 2.0 | 28,000 |
| 2.9 | 30,000 |
| 2.3 | 31,000 |
| 2.6 | 31,000 |
| 2.1 | 32,000 |
| 2.2 | 35,000 |
| 3.4 | 38,000 |
| 3.1 | 36,000 |
| 3.2 | 38,000 |
| 3.4 | 39,000 |
| 3.8 | 42,000 |
| 3.2 | 45,000 |
| 3.0 | 49,000 |

**a.** Draw a scatterplot of these data and describe the relation between the two variables.

**b.** Calculate the correlation coefficient between these two variables. (Hint: Divide the salary by 1,000 first to convert to two-digit numbers.) Does the correlation coefficient support your description of the scatterplot?

**c.** Using the coefficient of determination, $r^2$, describe the strength of the relation between the two variables.

**d.** Would it be fair to state that knowledge of a student's GPA allows you to infer the student's future salary? Would these data motivate you to raise your GPA (and major in psychology)?

**4.** Roger wants to study the relation between the personality dimension locus of control and leadership ability. Assume that he uses valid and reliable measures of locus of control and leadership. Also assume that he administers the two measures to 25 college students. Roger finds no meaningful correlation between the two variables ($r$ is a very small number). Should he automatically assume that there is no relation between the two variables? What would you recommend that he do in order to determine whether the correlation between the two variables is a fair estimate of the true relation between the two variables?

**5.** Each of the following examples represents an opportunity to examine the correlation between two variables. For each example, identify and describe the potential problems with how the data are collected, the interpretation of the results, or both.

**a.** The relationship between age and reaction time for subjects from 1 year to 65 years of age.

**b.** The correlation between IQ and grades for honor students at a large university.

**c.** The correlation between vocabulary and reading speed among children in an economically disadvantaged community.

**d.** The correlation between years of education and annual income for men and women between the ages of 18 and 35.

**6.** Each of the following statements is based on a correlation between two variables. Evaluate each statement to determine whether it can be considered fair and accurate.

**a.** There is a correlation between the amount of education the subjects have obtained and the likelihood that they will seek psychological counseling. Therefore, greater education leads to greater psychological stress that requires counseling.

**b.** There is a correlation between the number of years a child has played a musical instrument and his or her grade point average. Therefore, playing a musical instrument enhances a student's academic performance.

**c.** There is a negative correlation between two variables; this means that they are unrelated.

**7.** Eva is the director of human resources management for a large corporation that owns many stores. There is a considerable need to continually hire staff to work at the cash register. Given the importance of this job, the company wants to ensure that it hires the best staff for the job. After some general research Eva finds four tests and compares the results of these tests to evaluations of employees' performance. Here is a correlation matrix for all possible correlations.

| | Job Performance | Test 1 | Test 2 | Test 3 | Test 4 |
|---|---|---|---|---|---|
| Job performance | 1.000 | .286 | .350 | −.410 | .031 |
| Test 1 | | 1.000 | .678 | −.782 | .126 |
| Test 2 | | | 1.000 | −.633 | .193 |
| Test 3 | | | | 1.000 | −.120 |
| Test 4 | | | | | 1.000 |

**a.** Of the four tests, which is best correlated with job performance?

**b.** Assume that Eva wants a test that accounts for twice as much of the variance of job performance. What would the correlation between the test and job performance have to be?

**c.** Why do you think that two tests will correlate with each other more highly than with job performance?

8. A teacher needs a test that she can use to find children who may have difficulty reading. She finds a research report that compares the scores of four tests to reading performance. According to the report, these are the correlations.

| | Reading Ability | Test 1 | Test 2 | Test 3 | Test 4 |
|---|---|---|---|---|---|
| Reading ability | 1.000 | .153 | .225 | −.126 | .633 |
| Test 1 | | 1.000 | .678 | −.452 | .326 |
| Test 2 | | | 1.000 | −.843 | .793 |
| Test 3 | | | | 1.000 | −.120 |
| Test 4 | | | | | 1.000 |

**a.** Of the four tests, which is best correlated with reading ability?

**b.** Assume that the teacher wants a test that accounts for twice as much of the variance of reading ability. What would the correlation between the test and reading ability have to be?

**c.** Why do you think that two tests will correlate with each other more highly than with reading ability?

9. How well do you remember the names of the seven dwarfs from Disney's animated classic, *Snow White and the Seven Dwarfs*? The accompanying table shows the order in which they were recalled, the percentage of subjects who recalled the names of each one, and the percentage who correctly identified the dwarf in a recognition task. [These data are based on a study reported by Meyer and Hildebrand (1984).]

| Dwarf | Order of Recall | Percentage Recalled | Percentage Recognized |
|---|---|---|---|
| Sleepy | 1 | 86 | 91 |
| Dopey | 2 | 81 | 95 |
| Grumpy | 3 | 75 | 86 |
| Sneezy | 4 | 78 | 93 |
| Doc | 5 | 58 | 80 |
| Happy | 6 | 62 | 70 |
| Bashful | 7 | 38 | 84 |

Using these data, perform the following steps.

**a.** Draw three scatterplots, the first depicting the relation between order of recall and percentage recalled, the second depicting the relation between order of recall and percentage recognized, and the third depicting the relation between percentage recalled and percentage recognized.

**b.** What type of correlation procedure is appropriate for each of these comparisons?

**c.** Calculate the appropriate correlation for each of the three comparisons. (Remember, if you calculate a Spearman $r$ you must first rank both variables.)

**d.** What generalizations can you draw from these correlations? Does it "pay" to be Bashful?

**10.** Emory Cowens (1982) wanted to demonstrate that many nonpsychologists listen to the psychological problems of their clients. For example, many people share their problems with their hairdressers and bartenders. Cowens surveyed hairdressers and bartenders and asked them to indicate how often they heard about different types of problems from their clients. The data are shown in the accompanying table. The numbers represent the rank based on the frequency of each problem identified (1—highest frequency, 10—lowest frequency).

| Problem | Hairdressers | Bartenders |
|---|---|---|
| Difficulties with children | 1 | 7 |
| Physical health | 2 | 6 |
| Marital problems | 3 | 2 |
| Depression | 4 | 5 |
| Anxiety or nervousness | 5 | 8.5 |
| Job | 6 | 1 |
| Finances | 7 | 3 |
| Sex | 8 | 4 |
| Drugs | 9 | 10 |
| Alcohol | 10 | 8.5 |

**a.** Draw a scatterplot of the data. How would you describe the relation between these two variables?

**b.** What is the appropriate correlation coefficient to use for these data?

**c.** How would you explain the magnitude of the correlation?

**11.** How do people feel when others tell them about their problems? Cowens (1982) asked hairdressers and bartenders to select one word from a list of 11 words that best described their feelings when a customer shared some problem with them. The rankings associated with the 11 terms (1—most frequently selected, 11—least frequently selected) are listed in the accompanying table.

| Feeling | Hairdressers | Bartenders |
|---|---|---|
| Gratified | 1 | 4 |
| Sympathetic | 2 | 3 |
| Encouraging | 3 | 1 |
| Supportive | 4 | 2 |
| Puzzled | 5 | 7 |
| Helpless | 6 | 5.5 |
| Uncomfortable | 7 | 9 |
| Bored | 8 | 8 |
| Trapped | 9.5 | 5.5 |
| Depressed | 9.5 | 10 |
| Angry | 11 | 11 |

**a.** Draw and describe a scatterplot of these data.

**b.** Describe the differences between this scatterplot and the scatterplot drawn for Exercise 10.

**c.** What is the appropriate correlation statistic to use for these data?

**d.** What is the correlation between the two occupations?

**e.** Explain the differences between the correlations observed for the data for this question and for Exercise 10.

**12.** Sleep studies continue to provide a wealth of surprising findings. For example, in one study (Sewich, 1984) the subjects were awakened from sleep [as defined by an electroencephalograph (EEG)] by the ringing of a telephone. The experimenter recorded the time required for the subject to make a verbal response. Each subject was asked if he or she was awake or asleep when the telephone rang. Surprisingly, a number of subjects reported having been awake when, according to the EEG record, they were asleep. The accompanying table shows the mean reaction times over a number of trials for each of 10 subjects when they perceived themselves as being awake or asleep. For purposes of this analysis, we will treat each subject's mean as a score.

| Subject | Awake | Asleep |
|---------|-------|--------|
| 1 | 5.7 | 6.2 |
| 2 | 8.6 | 4.3 |
| 3 | 1.9 | 2.2 |
| 4 | 3.7 | 5.2 |
| 5 | 2.2 | 4.7 |
| 6 | 7.8 | 12.9 |
| 7 | 3.4 | 7.3 |
| 8 | 2.2 | 4.2 |
| 9 | 4.0 | 25.1 |
| 10 | 3.4 | 4.1 |

**a.** Draw and describe a scatterplot of the relation between the awake and asleep conditions.

**b.** What is the appropriate correlation coefficient for these data?

**c.** What is the correlation between the awake and asleep conditions?

**d.** Note that the performance of Subject 9 appears to be considerably different from that of the other subjects. Such observations are known as outliers and often initiate an inquiry into the reasons for the difference. Such differences can result from errors in collecting, coding, entering the data into a computer, or some specific characteristic of the subject. What is the correlation between the two conditions when the data for Subject 9 are removed? Does this change in the data greatly change the interpretation of the data?

**13.** Research has shown that there is a moderate positive correlation between anxiety and health problems. Stuart believes that this high correlation shows that anxiety is one of the contributors to poor health. Why is it inappropriate for Stuart to assume a cause-and-effect relation between these variables?

**14.** A psychological study involved the ranking of rats along a dominance-submissiveness continuum in which a lower numerical rank means high dominance. In order to determine the reliability of the rankings, we tabulated the ranks given by two different observers. The data are presented in the accompanying table.

| | RANK BY OBSERVER | |
|---|---|---|
| Animal | A | B |
| A | 12 | 15 |
| B | 2 | 1 |
| C | 3 | 7 |
| D | 1 | 4 |
| E | 4 | 2 |
| F | 5 | 3 |
| G | 14 | 11 |
| H | 11 | 10 |
| I | 6 | 5 |
| J | 9 | 9 |
| K | 7 | 6 |
| L | 10 | 12 |
| M | 15 | 13 |
| N | 8 | 8 |
| O | 13 | 14 |
| P | 16 | 16 |

a. Draw a scatterplot of these data.
b. What is the appropriate correlation coefficient to use for these data?
c. What is the correlation between the rankings?
d. How reliable are the rankings?

15. For a group of 50 individuals, $\Sigma z_X z_X = 41.3$. What is the correlation between the two variables?

16. How does the range of scores sampled affect the size of the correlation coefficient?

**9**

# Regression and Prediction

# 9.1
## A Brief Look Ahead

When you first encountered terms like correlation and regression, you probably thought you were entering new and alien territories. Nothing could be further from the truth. You make judgments every day that implicitly involve correlation and regression analysis. You may not use these exact terms to describe what you are doing, but in many ways you are a natural statistician. We are all natural statisticians: We use past experiences to predict the future. Consider the relation between your golf score and the time you spend practicing. In general, the more time you practice, the better your performance. Similarly, you have probably seen data suggesting that people with more education (e.g., college or professional degree) have a higher annual income than people with less education. Knowing the amount of time we have spent practicing or the amount of education we have, we are able to make calculated guesses about the consequences of our behavior or about outcomes that are correlated with our behavior.

Let's look at an example. Jessica is finishing the semester. She has completed all her assignments in statistics and the only hurdle remaining is the final exam. She would like to estimate what score she will earn on the final exam. Based on discussions with her instructor, she learns that the exam is designed to yield a mean of approximately 75. If this is the only information available, her best guess is that she will score about 75 on the final. (More in this chapter about why the mean is the best guess if we have limited information.) But Jessica has more information. She knows that she earned a 74 on the midterm and that the class mean of that exam was 70. How can she use this information to make a better prediction? She might reason that a score above the mean on the midterm exam would probably be followed by a score above the mean on the final. At this point she appears to be closing in on a more accurate prediction of her expected performance. However, simply knowing that she scored above the mean on the midterm would not provide a clear understanding of her relative standing on that exam. How might she introduce more precision in specifying her performance on the midterm?

With further investigation, Jessica discovers that the standard deviation on the midterm exam was $s = 4$. Thus her $z$-score was: $(74 - 70)/4 = 1.00$. Her score was exactly one standard deviation above the mean. If the standard deviation on the final is also 4, she might predict a final exam score of $75 + (1.00)(4) = 79$.

Jessica's reasoning is impeccable up to a point. Let's look at the steps she took and the assumptions she made along the way. First, Jessica determined that her midterm score was 1.00 standard deviation above the mean. Then, she tried to figure out what one standard deviation above the mean would be on the final. She knows that the final exam will have a mean of 75 and a standard deviation of 4. She accepts this statement as being accurate since the professor made that prediction based on previous experience. Jessica is correct that a score of 79 is 1.00 standard deviation above the mean for the final exam. Will two correct steps lead to the conclusion that she will do as well on the final? What other information do we need to know?

One important bit of information is still missing. What is the relationship between scores earned on the midterm and those earned on the final exam? In other words, is there any systematic relationship between scores on the two tests? The stronger the relationship between the two exams, the better the prediction Jessica can make. In the previous chapter you learned that a positive $r$ represents the extent to which the same individuals or events occupy the same relative position on both variables. Therefore, if the correlation between the midterm and the final is perfect ($r = 1.00$) Jessica could predict without error what she would score on the final.

What could Jessica predict if there was no systematic relationship between the midterm and final grades, that is, if $r = 0$? If there is zero correlation between the two tests she cannot use the midterm to predict the final grade; she will be as likely to score above the mean as below the mean on the final. Therefore, her *best guess* would be that her grade on the final will be a 75. To illustrate this point, look at Figure 9.1

The scatterplot below presents a set of hypothetical data for a midterm and final exam. As you can see, there is no orderly relation between the midterm grades and the final. The vertical line represents Jessica's midterm score of 74. The horizontal line represents the mean of the final exam, 75. You should conclude that Jessica is not guaranteed a good grade. It is true, she *could* receive a high grade of 82 or a low grade of 66 on the final. Because there is no apparent relation between midterm and final grades, our best guess is that she will receive a score somewhere around a 75, the mean of the $Y$ distribution of scores.

What if the correlation between the grades on the two tests were $r = .86$? This should suggest to you that Jessica will probably do better than average on the final. Remember, if two tests are highly positively correlated, those scoring well on one test will probably score well on the other. This situation is illustrated in Figure 9.2

As you can see from the scatterplot, there is a strong positive relation between the two exams. Students who did well on the midterm

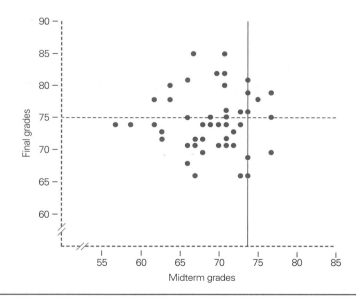

**Figure** | **9.1**

Hypothetical scatterplot of the relation between a midterm exam and a final exam. The correlation between the two tests is $r = 0$. The vertical line represents a midterm score of 74. The horizontal line represents the mean of the final exam—best estimate for performance on the test.

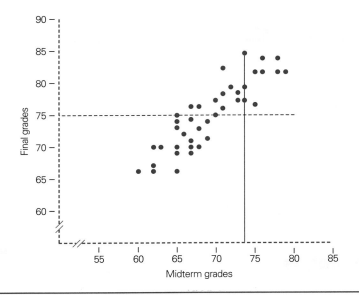

**Figure** 9.2

**Hypothetical scatterplot of the relation between a midterm exam and a final exam. The correlation between the two tests is $r = .86$. The vertical line represents a midterm score of 74. The horizontal line represents the mean of the final exam, 75.**

generally did well on the final whereas students who did poorly on the midterm performed poorly on the final exam. Based on these data, we can predict that Jessica will do well on the final. But is Jessica assured that she will receive a grade exactly 1.0 standard deviation above the mean? No. As the data suggest, there is still some variance in the score she could receive. We do predict her score will be above the mean, but it could be well above the mean (i.e., a score of 85) or only slightly above the mean (a score of 77). We could still be way off. Remember we are talking about a *predicted* score. We have to wait to see her actual score and determine just how close our prediction is.

This example illustrates the value of correlation and regression analysis. Using one bit of information we can make predictions about another event. In this example, we saw how a student could use the information about the correlation between two tests to predict her final score. Psychologists, educators, biologists, sociologists, stockbrokers, and economists constantly perform this function in their professional careers. In the remainder of this chapter we will examine the more formal and mathematical processes that researchers use to make these predictions. This procedure is known as linear regression.

## 9.2 / Linear Regression

Let us begin with an example of two variables that are perfectly or almost perfectly related: monthly salary and annual income. Table 9.1 presents the monthly incomes of eight wage earners in a small software company. A scatter diagram of these data is shown in Figure 9.3. Recall that it is customary to refer to the horizontal axis as the *X*-axis and the vertical as the *Y*-axis. If one of the variables occurs before the other in time, the

**Table** 9.1

**Monthly Salaries and Annual Income of Eight Employees**

| Employee | Monthly Salary ($) | Annual Income ($) |
|----------|--------------------|--------------------|
| A | 2,000 | 24,000 |
| B | 2,050 | 24,600 |
| C | 2,200 | 26,400 |
| D | 2,275 | 27,300 |
| E | 2,350 | 28,200 |
| F | 2,425 | 29,100 |
| G | 2,500 | 30,000 |
| H | 2,600 | 31,200 |

prior variable is plotted on the X-axis. In regression analysis we call the X-variable the independent variable because we want to use the variable to predict or estimate the dependent variable. Note that because $r = 1.00$, the paired scores fall on a straight line extending from the lower left corner of the scatter diagram to the upper right corner.

## Formula for Linear Relationships

The formula relating monthly salary ($X$) to annual income ($Y$) may be represented as

$$Y = 12(X)$$

You may substitute any value of $X$ into the equation and obtain the value of $Y$ directly. For example, if another employee were added to the payroll at $2,800 per month her annual income would be

$$Y = 12(2800) = \$33,600$$

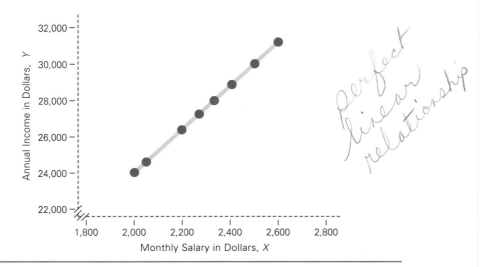

**Figure** 9.3

**Monthly salaries and annual income of eight employees.**

Let's add one more factor to this perfect linear relationship. Suppose that the firm had an exceptionally good year and the management decided to award a year-end bonus of $1,000. The equation would now read:

$$Y = 1000 + 12(X)$$

Perhaps, thinking back to your days of high school algebra, you will recognize the preceding formula as a special case of the general equation for a straight line; that is,

$$Y = a + b_Y(X) \qquad (9.1)$$

in which $X$ and $Y$ represent variables that change from individual to individual and $a$ and $b_Y$ represent constants for a particular set of data. More specifically, $b_Y$ represents the **slope** of a line relating values of $Y$ to values of $X$. This line is known as the regression of $Y$ on $X$. In the present example, the slope of the line is 12, which means that $Y$ changes by 12 for each change of one unit in $X$. The letter $a$ represents the value of $Y$ when $X = 0$ and is known as the **intercept.** The intercept is the point at which the regression crosses or intercepts the $Y$-axis. The information presented in Figure 9.4 will help you understand the meaning of the intercept and slope.

As you can see, there are three lines represented in Figure 9.4. All three lines have an intercept of 50; each line crosses the $Y$-axis at 50. Each of the lines, however, has a different slope. The slope refers to the increase or decrease in $Y$ that occurs as $X$ increases. Consider the line

**▨ Slope:**

Describes the angle of a line. The slope represents the change in $Y$ that occurs when $X$ is changed;
$$b_Y = \frac{\text{Change in } Y}{\text{Change in } X}$$

**▨ Intercept:**

The point at which the line intersects the $Y$ axis.

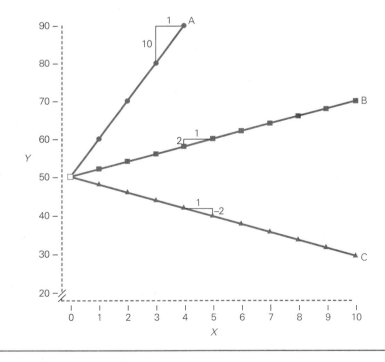

**Figure 9.4**

A graph representing lines with different slopes. The size of the slope value will determine if the line is more horizontal (small slope) or steep (large slope). The slope for Line A is 10, for Line B the slope is 2, and for Line C it is −2. The intercept for all lines is 50.

that rises the fastest, Line A. This line has a slope of 10; each single unit increase of $X$ equals a 10-unit increase in $Y$. For this line we would say that the slope is 10 to 1 or more simply 10. Another way of thinking about the slope of this line is:

$$b = \frac{\text{Change in } Y \uparrow}{\phantom{xxxxxxxxxx}}$$

In words, the slope is the ratio of the change in $Y$ for every unit of $X$. When change in $Y$ is positive, the regression line increases from left to right, as in a positive correlation. When $Y$ is negative, the line decreases from left to right, as in a negative correlation. The larger the increment, the steeper the slope.

Line C represents a line within a negative slope. Each time $X$ is increased, $Y$ gets smaller. You have already seen diagrams like this when we examined negative correlations. For this line the slope is $-2$, which means that each unit increase in $X$ corresponds to a 2-unit decrease in $Y$.

We can use Equation 9.1 to describe each of the lines in Figure 9.4:

A:     $Y = 50 + 10(X)$

B:     $Y = 50 + 2(X)$

C:     $Y = 50 + -2(X)$

*[handwritten: Value of the intercept is 50,]*

Using any value of $X$ we can estimate the corresponding value of $Y$ by multiplying the slope and adding the value of the intercept. When the correlation is 1.00 (as in the present cases) the predictions are perfect.

## Predicting $Y$ from $X$

In behavioral research, it is rare for data to fall exactly on a straight line. In the last chapter we saw scatter diagrams in which most of the data were not perfectly aligned. (That's why they call them *scatter* diagrams!) So usually we must find a line that best fits a scattering of points and use this line to make accurate predictions. This line is sometimes called a *line of best fit*. What do we mean by "best fit?" How should we go about drawing a line that best fits the data?

Before we go into detail about how to construct a line of best fit, let's examine some data. Figure 9.5 consists of the same data we presented earlier in Figure 9.2. In addition we include a line of best fit or what is also known as the **regression line.** Notice the new symbol, $Y'$. This may be read as "$Y$ prime." It is also sometimes called "$Y$ predicted," or "$Y$ estimated." The symbol, $\hat{Y}$, pronounced "$Y$ carat" or "$Y$ hat" is used interchangeably with $Y'$. The prime mark or the caret are used to indicate that the value is an estimated or predicted value.

In Figure 9.5 the line of best fit has an intercept of 11.4 and a slope of .915. Note that the intercept is the value of $Y$ when $X = 0$.* We can use the line to predict the final exam grade of any student based on his or her midterm grade. Here is an example. What if someone had a midterm grade of 72? See the $X$-axis at 72 and the vertical line that extends upward to the regression line. Now from that point on the line,

----

**Regression Line:**

A straight line which best represents the linear relationship between two variables, $X$ and $Y$. The regression line is defined by the equation $Y' = a + b_Y(X)$. The regression line is considered to be the "line of best fit" as the average squared distance between each of the actual scores ($Y$) and predicted scores ($Y'$) is minimal; $\Sigma(Y - Y')^2$ is minimal.

----

* Some graphs do not show the $Y$-intercept in order to save space. In Figure 9.5, the $Y$-intercept appears to be about 62 because neither the $X$-axis nor the $Y$-axis is brought down to 0. However, if done so, the $Y$-intercept when $X = 0$ would be 11.4.

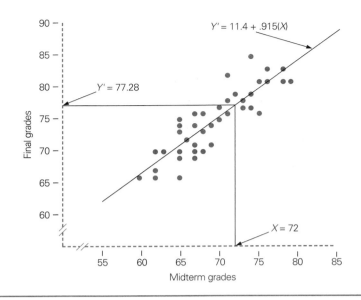

**Figure** | **9.5**

A scatterplot of the relation between midterm grades and final grades. The diagonal line represents the line of best fit or the regression line. The line is defined by the equation $Y' = 11.4 + .915(X)$.

connect to the $Y$-axis to the left. At that point on the $Y$-axis our predicted score is 77.28. We can obtain the same value using the linear equation, $Y' = 11.4 + .915(72) = 77.28$. For any value of $X$ we use the equation $Y' = 11.4 + (.915)X$ to predict a value of $Y$.

How did we determine exactly where to draw the prediction line? What would you do if you were drawing the line "by eye?" Chances are that you would try to draw the line so that it would cover as many of the points as possible. As you decide on drawing the line you probably try to imagine a line that is as close to all of the points as possible. Your line would probably be similar to the one we drew. However, we want to use a more objective technique to draw our line of best fit, therefore we will use what is called the *least squares method*.

You may recall that, when discussing the mean and standard deviation, we defined the mean as the point in a distribution that makes the sum of squared deviations minimal. We called this minimal deviation the least squares because the sum of the squared distance of each score from the mean $\Sigma(X - \overline{X})^2$ is smallest when $\overline{X} = \Sigma X/N$. In regression statistics we want to do the same thing. (Remember back in Chapter 4 our tennis player stood in the middle of the court to avoid having to run long distances to reach the ball.) If $Y$ represents the obtained score and $Y'$ represents the predicted value, we want our line to minimize the squared difference between $Y$ and $Y'$. Therefore, when applying the least squares method to correlation and regression, the best-fitting straight line is defined as the line that makes $\Sigma(Y - Y')^2$ minimal. The quantity $\Sigma(Y - Y')^2$ is a sum of squares. In this case we are summing the squared differences between actual $Y$ scores and $Y'$ scores predicted by the regression line.

## 9.3 / Determining the Regression Line

Returning to the equation for a straight line, $Y' = a + b_Y X$, we are faced with the problem of determining

> **WHY PREDICT Y WHEN WE ALREADY KNOW IT?**
>
> You may be asking a perfectly reasonable question at this point. If we already have X and we already have Y, why are we *estimating* Y'? A real score should be better than an estimated one. True. But regression analysis uses data collected previously to estimate some future outcome or future score. Colleges, for example, use the grade point average of high school students to predict their later success in college. They take data obtained from last year's class or the year before, perform a regression analysis, and calculate the regression equation. This regression equation is now used to predict the success of future high school students who are applying now for admission.

$b_Y$ and $a$ for a particular set of data. There is a raw score formula for calculating $b_Y$, one that uses terms we are already familiar with.

$$b_Y = \frac{\Sigma XY - \dfrac{(\Sigma X)(\Sigma Y)}{N}}{\Sigma X^2 - \dfrac{(\Sigma X)^2}{N}} \tag{9.2}$$

If you look carefully at the equation you will see that the denominator, the bottom quantity, is the sum of squares for $X$. (Remember, $SS_x$ is the sum of the squared deviations for the $X$ variable.) The numerator consists of the sum of squares for cross products. The slope is then the ratio of these two quantities. Fortunately, this equation can be reduced to a more manageable formula:

$$b_Y = r\left(\frac{s_Y}{s_X}\right) \tag{9.3}$$

Once you have calculated the slope, the intercept is easy to determine if you know the mean of $X$ and the mean of $Y$.

$$a_Y = \overline{Y} - b_Y\overline{X} \tag{9.4}$$

These components provide us with a useful equation for obtaining $Y'$ for individual scores. The following equation is used when you have the value $X$ for an individual and you want to make a prediction about their score on the $Y$ variable.

$$Y' = \overline{Y} + r\left(\frac{s_Y}{s_X}\right)(X - \overline{X}) \tag{9.5*}$$

Equation 9.5 will produce the same results as Equation 9.1. The main reason that we will use Equation 9.5 is that it will help us to better explain the concept of regression analysis. Let us begin to examine the regression equation in greater detail.

---

* Because $Y' = a + b_Y X$, $a = \overline{Y} - b_Y\overline{X}$, and $b_Y = r\frac{s_Y}{s_X}$, then $Y' = \overline{Y} - r\frac{s_Y}{s_X}\overline{X} + r\frac{s_Y}{s_X}X$.
Thus, $\overline{Y} + r\frac{s_Y}{s_X}(X - \overline{X})$.

**Table 9.2**

**A Series of Examples That Illustrate Three Factors That Affect the Size of the Slope: The Size and the Sign of the Correlation Coefficient and the Ratio of the Differing Spreads of the Two Variables**

| | | | | |
|---|---|---|---|---|
| $r = 1.0$ | $\frac{s_Y}{s_X} = \frac{2}{1}$ | $b_Y = 2.00$ | $\frac{s_Y}{s_X} = \frac{1}{2}$ | $b_Y = 0.50$ |
| $r = .5$ | $\frac{s_Y}{s_X} = \frac{2}{1}$ | $b_Y = 1.00$ | $\frac{s_Y}{s_X} = \frac{1}{2}$ | $b_Y = 0.25$ |
| $r = 0.0$ | $\frac{s_Y}{s_X} = \frac{2}{1}$ | $b_Y = 0.00$ | $\frac{s_Y}{s_X} = \frac{1}{2}$ | $b_Y = 0.00$ |
| $r = -0.5$ | $\frac{s_Y}{s_X} = \frac{2}{1}$ | $b_Y = -1.00$ | $\frac{s_Y}{s_X} = \frac{1}{2}$ | $b_Y = -0.25$ |
| $r = -1.0$ | $\frac{s_Y}{s_X} = \frac{2}{1}$ | $b_Y = -2.00$ | $\frac{s_Y}{s_X} = \frac{1}{2}$ | $b_Y = -0.50$ |

$$Y' = \overline{Y} + r \frac{s_Y}{s_X} (X - \overline{X})$$

| Predicted value of $Y$ | = | Mean of $Y$ | + | Correlation between $X$ and $Y$ | $\dfrac{\text{SD of } Y}{\text{SD of } X}$ | Deviation score |

A key element of this equation is the slope of the regression line, $r\left(\frac{s_Y}{s_X}\right)$. Three factors affect the slope of the regression line: (a) the *size* of the correlation, (b) the *sign* of the correlation, and (c) the *ratio* of the spread of the two distributions. The data in Table 9.2 illustrate the relation among these three factors.

The sign of the slope depends completely on the sign of the correlation. Positive correlations produce positive slopes, negative correlations produce negative slopes, correlations of 0 produce flat lines, lines with no slopes.

The magnitude of the slope depends on the size of the correlation and the size of the ratio $\frac{s_Y}{s_X}$. This ratio represents the proportional change in $Y$ that will occur when $X$ changes. As we have mentioned many times before, one of the advantages of correlation and regression statistics is that they allow us to use two scales that may have different means and standard deviations. The ratio $\frac{s_Y}{s_X}$ allows us to estimate the distance of the predicted score from the mean of $Y$, $(Y' - \overline{Y})$ given the distance of the $X$-score from the mean of $X$ $(X - \overline{X})$. It allows us to adjust our predicted score if the two measures differ in terms of variability. If both $X$ and $Y$ have the same spread $(s_X = s_Y)$, then the ratio will equal 1.0 and no adjustment is needed. There are two examples of the ratio $s_X = s_Y$ presented in Table 9.2. In one case the ratio is 2:1. As a consequence, small changes along the $X$ scale correspond with large changes along the $Y$-scale. In the other example, the ratio is 1:2. This smaller ratio means that changes along the $X$-scale correspond with relatively small changes along the $Y$-scale.

Many researchers make the mistake of assuming that the larger the slope the better. From an inspection of Table 9.2, however, you should be able to see that the size of the slope is not a measure of the magnitude of the relationship between $X$ and $Y$. Consider two examples presented in Table 9.2. When $\frac{s_Y}{s_X} = 2$ and $r = .5$ the slope of the line is 1.00. In contrast when $\frac{s_Y}{s_X} = .5$ and $r = 1$ the slope of the line is 0.5. Although it is smaller, a slope of 0.5, in this example, represents a greater degree of relatedness between the two variables. The slope is a function of both relatedness and the ratio of the spreads of the two variables. Thus, only the correlation coefficient can be used to describe the magnitude of the relation between two variables. The slope describes the amount of change in the $Y$ variable produced by changes in the $X$ variable.

Now look at the last part of the equation: $(X - \overline{X})$. This value tells us the distance of a score from the mean and if it is above or below the mean. The further the distance from the mean, the larger the deviation score. This distance above or below the mean, when multiplied by the slope, will provide the location of the predicted score $Y'$ from the mean of $Y$. If $X$, the observed score, is below the mean $\overline{X}$, then the predicted score $Y'$ will be below the mean on the $Y$ variable. The exact location of $Y'$ will be a function of both the slope and the distance of the predictor score above or below the mean of its distribution.

When there is a perfect correlation, there will be a perfect correspondence between the relative position of each score. When the correlation is 0, there is no way to accurately predict $Y$ from $X$. Thus, when $r = 0$, $Y' = \overline{Y}$. This confirms what we noted earlier: When the correlation is 0 and no other information is available, the mean is our best predictor of individual performance.

## Illustrative Examples

Let's return to our example of performance on the midterm and predicting the final exam grade. Let us consider Jessica and another student, Hugh. Jessica scored 74 on the midterm, Hugh earned a 63. The mean of that test was 70 and the standard deviation, 4.0. Remember that the professor had given these tests before, so he knew from past experience that the mean of the final exam was 75 with a standard deviation of 4.0. He knew that the correlation between the two tests was $r = .60$. With this information it is possible to predict performance on the final exam from scores earned on the earlier test as shown in Table 9.3.

Figure 9.6 presents graphs of the two regression lines. The solid line represents the regression line when $r = .6$, the dotted line represents the regression line for $r = 1.0$. The vertical lines represent the midterm scores for Jessica and Hugh. We can use this graph to make several

**Table** 9.3

Estimated Scores for Final Exam Based on Results of Midterm Exam

| Midterm Exam<br>$X$ | | Final Exam<br>$Y$ |
|---|---|---|
| $\overline{X} = 70$ | | $\overline{Y} = 75$ |
| $s_X = 4$ | $r = .60$ | $s_Y = 4$ |

Jessica made 74 on the midterm.   Hugh made 63 on the midterm.

$$Y' = \overline{Y} + r\left(\frac{s_Y}{s_X}\right)(X - \overline{X}) \qquad\qquad Y' = \overline{Y} + r\left(\frac{s_Y}{s_X}\right)(X - \overline{X})$$

$$= 75 + .6\left(\frac{4}{4}\right)(74 - 70) \qquad\qquad = 75 + .6\left(\frac{4}{4}\right)(63 - 70)$$

$$= 75 + (.6)(1)(4) = 75 + 2.4 \qquad = 75 + (.6)(1)(-7) = 75 + (-4.2)$$

$$= 77.4 \qquad\qquad\qquad\qquad\qquad = 70.8$$

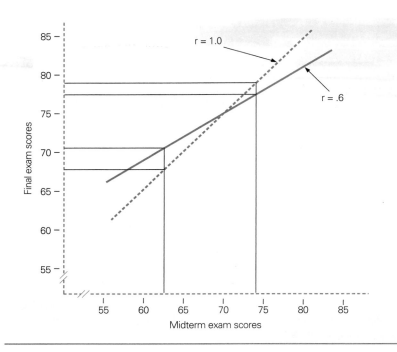

**Figure** 9.6

A regression analysis of the relationship between midterm exam scores and predicted final exam scores. The solid regression line represents the estimated final grades when the r = .6. The dotted regression line represents the estimated final grades when r = 1.0.

observations. First, Jessica will score above average and Hugh will score below average. What is interesting is that if the correlation between the midterm and final were perfect (r = 1.0) Jessica's predicted score would be higher and Hugh's predicted score would be lower than if the correlation between the midterm and final were r = .6. We can better understand what is presented in this graph as we present a more detailed account of how the estimated scores were derived.

Let's start with Jessica. Her midterm score was a 74. What prediction can we make about her final grade? First of all, her score on the first exam is above the mean, so we will predict that her score on the final will also be above the mean. According to the regression equation presented in Table 9.3, we can predict that:

$$Y' = 75 + .6\left(\frac{4}{4}\right)(74 - 70)$$

$$Y' = 75 + .6(4)$$

$$Y' = 77.4$$

Note that her hope of obtaining a grade of B (i.e., $Y \geq 80$) is diminished by the fact that the correlation was not 1.00. If the correlation had been 1.00, her predicted score would have been:

$$Y' = 75 + 1(4) = 79$$

She would almost have reached her goal of 80.

Let us look at another example. Hugh, on the same midterm test, scored 63. What is the best prediction concerning his score on the final exam? Note that he is below the mean on the first exam and since the correlation between the two tests is positive then his predicted score will be below the mean on the second exam.

$$Y' = 75 + .6\left(\frac{4}{4}\right)(63 - 70)$$
$$Y' = 75 + .6\,(-7)$$
$$Y' = 75 + -4.2$$
$$Y' = 70.8$$

According to our prediction, Hugh will be expected to just squeak by with a C. What would happen to Hugh's grade if the correlation were 1.00? According to the regression equation Hugh's grade would be much lower, 68. $Y' = 75 + 1.0\,(-7) = 68$. Hugh had better hope that he can study extra hard for the exam in the hopes of boosting his grade. Remember, we are talking about prediction. Hugh *could* score well above 70.8 or well below that value. In fact, the lower the correlation between the two variables, the less accurate we will be in our predictions. The error in our predictions, $\Sigma(Y' - Y)^2$, that is, the squared difference between what we predict ($Y'$) and what Hugh actually scores ($Y$) will be less as $r$ approaches 1.0 and greater as $r$ approaches 0.

### Predicting $z_Y$ from $z_X$

Sometimes the measures taken by researchers have been converted to standard scores. It is not necessary to convert these scores back to raw scores in order to predict future performance on a second test. There is a simple way of using the standard score of one variable to predict the standard score on another variable. The formula is:

$$z_Y = r\,(z_X) \tag{9.6}$$

In words, the predicted standard score on the $Y$ variable, $z_Y$, is simply the z-score on the $X$ variable, $z_X$, multiplied by the correlation between the two tests. With a perfect correlation, the z-score on one test will equal the z-score on the other test. (Sound familiar?) The stronger the correlation between the two tests, the further away from the mean the predicted score will be located.

Consider the student who has scored two standard deviations above the mean on a test. His predicted standard score on the second test will depend completely on the correlation between the two tests. See what happens when the correlation goes from a perfect relationship, $r = 1.0$, to increasingly weaker relationships and finally to a zero relationship, $r = 0$.

$$
\begin{aligned}
z_Y = \quad & r \quad\;\; z_X \\
= \;\; & 1.0 \;\; (2.0) = 2.0 \\
= \;\; & .9 \;\; (2.0) = 1.8 \\
= \;\; & .5 \;\; (2.0) = 1.0 \\
= \;\; & .2 \;\; (2.0) = \;\; .4 \\
= \;\; & 0.0 \;\; (2.0) = 0.0
\end{aligned}
$$

The predicted score, which is at first two standard deviations above the mean, moves toward 0 as the correlation declines between the two tests. When they are not at all related, ($r = 0$), the best prediction of performance on the second test is the mean of that distribution, that is,

$z_Y = 0$. On the other hand if the relationship between the two tests is perfect and positive, the obtained score on the first test will be equal to the predicted $z$-score on the second test. Using this formula it is clear that one has more predictive power the stronger the relationship between the two variables. Look back at the raw score formula and see the same influence of the size of the correlation coefficient on the distance of the predicted scores from the mean of the distribution.

## Why the Line of Best Fit Is Called a Regression Line

Why do we call this statistical procedure "regression?" Why is the line of best fit called a regression line? The answer to these questions goes back to Sir Francis Galton, the originator of correlation and regression statistics. Galton was interested in how family traits are inherited. As you know, we inherit many of our personal characteristics from our parents. Height, hair and eye color, skin tone, and many other features are determined, in part, by our genetics. Galton spent much time studying how different physical and psychological traits were inherited by families. In his research he noticed an extremely interesting phenomenon. He called this phenomenon *regression to the mean.* What was it that Galton saw? We can explain regression to the mean with an example.

Imagine that two extremely tall people are married and have children. We would expect their children to be tall; height is a physical trait that is influenced by genetics as well as environmental conditions such as diet. Will these children be as tall as their parents? We would predict that the children will be closer to the average height of other children in their generation. Correlation and regression examine the *relative* distance of scores from the mean. The children's predicted height will *regress toward the mean*; their height will move toward the average of the heights of their age cohort.

What Galton discovered is an extremely important phenomenon. Whenever we take a measure of one variable, there is a tendency for the scores to cluster around the mean. If two variables are independent of one another, as is the case when $r = 0$, then an extreme score on one measure is as likely to be associated with a high or a low score on the other measure. More specifically, if we obtain an extreme score on one measure, the companion score is most likely to regress toward the mean for that measure. By contrast, if two variables are perfectly related, as is the case when $r = 1$, then extreme scores for one variable will be associated with extreme scores for the other variable, and there will be no regression toward the mean.

Keep in mind that we are talking about predicted scores regressing toward the mean. Using the least squares method which penalizes us when we are far off in our predictions (as a tennis player is penalized when his or her position is far from when it should be in order to make a satisfactory return), we are "safer" standing in the center of the tennis court. But we all know that predictions are sometimes inaccurate and will become increasingly inaccurate as the correlation between the two variables moves toward 0.

Consider a student who gets an extremely low score on a test and then takes a similar test shortly thereafter. If there is no correlation between the tests, then we would predict the student's performance on the second test to be closer to the mean. If there is a high correlation between the tests, there will be less regression to the mean.

The regression toward the mean phenomenon explains Jessica's and Hugh's estimated scores. The fact that the correlation between the midterm and the final is not perfect means that both scores will tend to regress toward the mean—Jessica's score may decrease whereas Hugh's score may increase. Only when the correlation between the two tests is perfect will there be no regression toward the mean. Therefore, the closer $r$ is to 0.0 the greater is the regression toward the mean.

Many people fail to recognize the regression to the mean effect when examining the results of an experiment. For example, suppose that a researcher claims that a new reading program is useful for helping students learn how to read. To justify her claim, she administers a reading test to 100 students and then selects the 25 students with the lowest scores, the "poor readers." After a year with the reading program all 25 students are reading at average grade level. Has the researcher demonstrated the effectiveness of the reading program? No! The improvement observed in the 25 "poor readers" may have simply been a case of regression to the mean. On the day that they were first tested they received low scores for reasons that cannot be identified. According to the regression to the mean phenomenon, we should not be surprised that they had "normal" scores the second time they were tested.

## Predicting $X$ from $Y$

Thus far, we have been directing our attention to the regression of $Y$ on $X$. There are times when we wish to predict $X$ values from known values of $Y$ (such as predicting IQ from GPA). It should not surprise you that there are a series of equations relating variable $X$ to variable $Y$. These would involve the regression of $X$ on $Y$ and permit estimation of $X$-values from known $Y$-values. The slope of the regression line of $X$ on $Y$ becomes:

$$b_X = \frac{\Sigma XY - \dfrac{(\Sigma X)(\Sigma Y)}{N}}{\Sigma Y^2 - \dfrac{(\Sigma Y)^2}{N}} \tag{9.7}$$

or

$$b_X = r\frac{s_X}{s_Y} \tag{9.8}$$

Therefore, the regression equation for predicting scores on the $X$-variable from values of the $Y$-variable is

$$X' = \overline{X} + r\frac{s_X}{s_Y}(Y - \overline{Y}) \tag{9.9}$$

The main point you should take away from this section is that in correlation and regression the relation between the two variables is reciprocal—we can use the $X$-variable to predict $Y$ and the $Y$-variable to predict $X$. This fact means that the selection of the independent variable can be arbitrary. In practice, however, most behavioral scientists use only one variable as the independent variable and the other as the dependent variable. Figure 9.7 illustrates the regression of $X$ on $Y$ and of $Y$ on $X$.

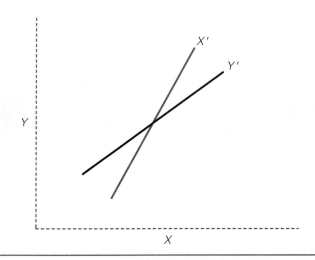

**Figure** 9.7

Illustration of two regression lines. **Y′** is the regression line for predicting values of **Y** from known values of **X**. **X′** is the regression line for predicting values of **X** from known values of **Y**.

## 9.4 / Residual Variance and Standard Error of Estimate

Figure 9.8 presents a series of scatter diagrams showing the regression of $Y$ on $X$. As you can see, not all the obtained scores fall on the regression line. However, if the correlation had been $r = +1.0$ or $r = -1.0$, all the scores would have fallen right on the regression line. The deviations between the predicted and obtained scores $(Y - Y')$ in Figure 9.8 represent our errors in prediction.

Each panel of Figure 9.8 represents a different type of variation. The left panel represents the total variation of $Y$. Specifically, the distance between the horizontal line, which represents the mean of $Y$, and each of the points is a deviation. Therefore, $\Sigma(Y - \overline{Y})^2$ represents the sum of squares for the total variability of $Y$.

The middle panel represents the differences among $Y$-scores that can be predicted or explained by $X$. In this panel we are measuring the distance between the mean of $Y$ and our predicted values of $Y$. In other words $\Sigma(Y' - \overline{Y})^2$ allows us to predict how much of the differences among $Y$-scores can be accounted for by $X$. You may recall that the coefficient of determination $(r^2)$ predicts the percentage of the variance in one variable that can be accounted for by another variable. As we will show below $\Sigma(Y' - \overline{Y})^2$ and $r^2$ are directly related.

The last panel represents the variance among $Y$-scores that cannot be predicted by $X$. This quantity can be thought of as error in our predictions. We use the equation $\Sigma(Y - Y')^2$, the sum of the squared difference between our predicted and our actual scores, to estimate the variance in $Y$ that cannot be accounted for by $X$. This equation is directly related to $1 - r^2$ the coefficient of nondetermination.

Note the similarity of $Y - Y'$ (the deviation of a score from the regression line) to $Y - \overline{Y}$ (the deviation of a score from the mean). If either of these values are summed they will always equal 0. Earlier we saw that the sum of the deviations around the mean is always 0 because the mean is the moment of the distribution that balances the effects of large

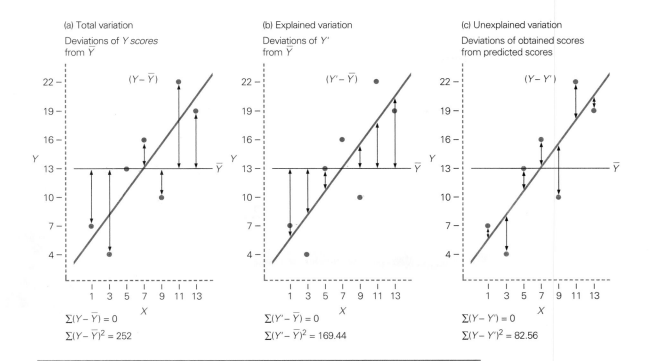

**Figure 9.8**

Scatter diagrams of paired scores on two variables, regression line for predicting *Y*-values from known values of *X*, and the mean of the distribution of *Y*-scores ($\overline{Y}$) when *r* = 0.82. (a) Deviations of scores ($Y - \overline{Y}$) from the mean of *Y*. (b) Deviations of predicted scores ($Y' - \overline{Y}$) from the mean of *Y*. (c) Deviations of scores ($Y - Y'$) from the regression line.

and small numbers. The same concept applies to the regression line. The deviations of actual scores from predicted scores, when summed, equal 0. The regression line is a sort of "floating mean." Indeed, as we discussed above, the regression line is the line that minimizes the average squared distance between the raw scores and the corresponding predicted scores.

You may recall that to calculate a variance we must square deviations from a mean, sum them, and divide by *N*. We can perform the same operations on these quantities to obtain their variance. If we now square and sum the deviations of scores from the regression line, $\Sigma(Y - Y')^2$ (the amount we were off in our predictions), we would have a basis for calculating variance. This variance around the regression line is known as the residual variance and is defined as follows:

$$s^2_{\text{est } Y} = \frac{\Sigma(Y - Y')^2}{N - 2} \tag{9.10}*$$

The difference between the predicted score, *Y'*, and the actual score, *Y*, is our error in prediction. Thus, the variance around the regression line is also called error variation.

---

* For now, don't be concerned about why the denominator is *N* − 2 rather than *N*. The explanation is concerned with making biased estimates of population parameters. We will discuss that shortly.

The standard deviation around the regression line (referred to as the standard error of estimate) is obtained from the square root of the residual variance. Thus

$$s_{\text{est } Y} = \sqrt{\frac{\Sigma(Y - Y')^2}{N - 2}} \tag{9.11}$$

You may be justifiably aghast at the amount of computation that is implied in the preceding formulas for calculating the standard error of estimate. However, as has been our practice throughout the text, we have shown the basic formulas so that you may have a conceptual grasp of the meaning of the standard error of estimate. It is, as we have seen, the standard deviation of scores around the regression line (a floating mean) rather than around the mean of the distribution.

Fortunately, as in our previous illustrations in the text, there is a simplified method for calculating $s_{\text{est } Y}$.

$$s_{\text{est } Y} = s_Y \sqrt{\frac{N(1 - r^2)}{N - 2}} \tag{9.12}$$

Note that when $r = +1.0$ or when $r = -1.0$, $s_{\text{est } Y}$ equals 0, which means that there are no deviations from the regression line and, therefore, no errors in prediction. Visualize a regression line when the correlation is perfect. All the points fall exactly on the line. There is no deviation from the line and thus there is no error and the $s_{\text{est } Y}$ will equal 0. On the other hand, when $r = 0$, the errors in prediction are maximal for that distribution and are close to $s_Y$. That is, $s_{\text{est } Y} = s_Y \sqrt{\dfrac{N}{N - 2}}$. When the sample size is large, $\sqrt{\dfrac{N}{N - 2}} \cong 1$ and $s_{\text{est } Y} \cong s_Y$.

As you have seen, $Y'$ is a *good* estimate of $Y$ when we know about the relation between two variables, but unless the correlation is perfect, $Y'$ will not be perfectly accurate. We know that there is a chance that the real value of $Y$ may be somewhat greater than or less than $Y'$. Consider the relation between two tests, a general college entrance exam and a verbal comprehension exam.

| College Entrance Exam (X-Variable) | Verbal Comprehension Exam (Y-Variable) |
|---|---|
| $N = 20$ | |
| $\overline{X} = 47.65$ | $\overline{Y} = 39.15$ |
| $s_X = 13.82$ | $s_Y = 12.35$ |
| $r = 0.8466$ | |
| $s_{\text{est } Y} = s_Y \sqrt{\dfrac{N(1 - r^2)}{N - 2}}$ | $b_Y = r\left(\dfrac{s_Y}{s_X}\right)$ |
| $_{\text{est } Y} = 12.35 \sqrt{\dfrac{20(1 - .8466^2)}{20 - 2}}$ | $b_Y = .8466(12.35/13.82)$ |
| $= 12.35(.5611)$ | $b_Y = .8466(.8936)$ |
| $= 6.93$ | $b_Y = .7565$ |
| $Y' = 39.15 + .7565(X - 47.65)$ | |

We noted earlier that the regression line is analogous to the mean and shares its properties. The sums of the deviations about the mean and about the regression lines are zero and the sums of the squared deviations about the mean and the regression line are minimal. Similarly, the standard error of estimate has properties that are similar to those of the standard deviation. Both reflect the degree of dispersion about their measures of central tendency, namely the mean and the regression line, respectively. Thus, the greater the standard error of estimate is, the greater is the dispersion of scores about the regression line.

For each value of $X$, there is a distribution of scores of the $Y$-variable. The mean of each of these distributions is $Y'$, and the standard deviation of each distribution is $s_{est\ Y}$. When the distribution of $Y$-scores for each value of $X$ has the same variability, we refer to this condition as homoscedasticity. In addition, if the distribution of $Y$-scores for each value of $X$ is normally distributed, we may state relationships between the standard error of estimate and the normal curve. We can, for example, predict a value of $Y$ from a given value of $X$ and then describe an interval within which it is likely that the true value of $Y$ will be found. For normally distributed variables, approximately 68% of the time, the true value of $Y$ ($Y_T$) will be within the following interval:

Interval including true value $Y_T$

$$Y_T = Y' \pm s_{est\ Y} \sqrt{1 + \frac{1}{N} + \frac{(X - \overline{X})^2}{\Sigma X^2 - \frac{(\Sigma X)^2}{N}}} \tag{9.13}$$

For example assume that $X = 25$. Using our regression equation we determine that $Y' = 22.02$ ($Y' = 39.15 + .7565(25 - 47.65)$). Using equation 9.13 we can estimate a range of scores in which we would expect $Y_T$ to fall.

$$\text{Interval including } Y_T = 22.02 \pm 6.93 \sqrt{1 + \frac{1}{20} + \frac{(25 - 47.65)^2}{3819.53}}$$

$$= 22.02 \pm (6.93)(1.088)$$

$$= 22.02 \pm 7.54$$

$$\text{Interval including } Y_T = 14.48 \text{ to } 29.56$$

In other words, when $X = 25$, about 68% of the time the true value of $Y$ will be found between scores of 14.48 and 29.56. How do we know this? The answer refers back to standard deviations and the normal distribution. Remember in earlier chapters you learned that 68% of the normal distribution is $\pm 1$ standard deviation about the mean. In essence we can use $s_{est\ Y}$ as a standard deviation of scores about $Y'$. For each predicted score we can add and subtract $s_{est\ Y}$, just as we add and subtract a standard deviation. We then are able to come up with a 68% interval. What would you do if you wanted to be 95% confident in the prediction you made about $Y'$. Approximately 95% of a normal distribution is represented by $\pm 1.96$ standard deviations. Therefore $1.96 \times 7.54 = 14.78$, and we can be 95% confident that $Y_T$ will be within the range of 7.24 to 36.80.

Using these data, we draw two lines, one above and one below the regression line for predicting $Y$ from $X$ as in Figure 9.9. For normally distributed variables, approximately 68% of the time the true values of $Y$ will be found between these two lines when we use Equation 9.13 to predict $Y$-values from various values of $X$. Note that these lines are more

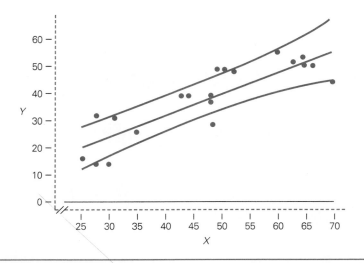

**Figure** | **9.9**

Line of regression for predicting *Y* from *X* with parallel lines one $s_{est\ Y}$ above and below the regression line. Dots indicate individual scores on *X* and *Y*.

spread out with *Y*-values from extreme values of *X*. The results are two slightly bowed lines, with minimum difference between them at the mean of the *X*-variable. (It should be noted that these relationships refer to the distributions of *both* the *X*- and *Y*-variables).

## 9.5 / Explained and Unexplained Variation

If we look again at Figure 9.8, we see that there are three separate sums of squares that can be calculated from these data. These are:

1. **The total sum of squares for *Y* ($SS_{total}$):** This sum of squares is given by $\Sigma(Y - \overline{Y})^2$ (i.e., $SS_Y$) It is basic to finding the variance and standard deviation of the distribution.

2. **The sum of squares for explained variance in *Y:*** The variation of predicted scores about the mean (Figure 9.8b). This variation is given by $\Sigma(Y' - \overline{Y})^2$ and is referred to as the **regression sum of squares ($SS_{exp}$).** The reason for this terminology should be clear from our discussion in the preceding paragraph and our prior reference to predicted deviation. Recall our observation that, the greater the correlation, the greater will be the predicted deviation from the sample mean. It follows further that the greater the predicted deviation, the greater is the explained variation. When the predicted deviations are maximum, the correlation is perfect and 100% of the variation is explained. When the predicted deviations are minimum, the correlation is 0 and there is no variation to be explained.

3. **The sum of squares for unexplained variance in *Y:*** The variation of scores around the regression line or line of predicted scores (Figure 9.8c). This variation is given by $\Sigma(Y - Y')^2$ and is referred

**■ Regression Sum of Squares:**

The variation of predicted scores about the mean of a distribution. Also called the explained variance.

to as either the unexplained sum of squares (**SS**$_{unexpl}$) or as **error sum of squares** (**SS**$_{err}$). It is based on the sum of the differences between the obtained scores and the predicted scores. The reason for this terminology should be clear. If the correlation between two variables is $\pm 1.00$, all the scores fall on the regression line. Consequently, we have explained all the variation in $Y$ in terms of variations in $X$ and, conversely, all the variation in $X$ in terms of variations in $Y$. In other words, in the event of a perfect correlation, there is no unexplained variation. However, when the correlation is less than perfect, many of the scores will not fall right on the regression line. The deviations of these scores from the regression line represents variation that is not accounted for in terms of the correlation between the two variables. Hence the term "error" is used.

**■ Error Sum of Squares:**

The variation of scores about the regression line, also called the unexplained sum of squares.

It can be shown mathematically that the total sum of squares ($SS_{total}$) consists of two components, which may be added together. These two components represent explained variation and unexplained variation, respectively. Thus

$$\Sigma\,(Y - \overline{Y})^2 \;=\; \Sigma\,(Y' - \overline{Y})^2 \;+\; \Sigma(Y - Y')^2 \qquad (9.14)$$

| Total sum of squares | = | Explained variation or regression sum of squares | + | Unexplained variation or error sum of squares |

We can use the data presented in Table 9.4 to illustrate this point.

As you can see, total variation consists of explained variation plus unexplained variation.

$$\Sigma(Y - \overline{Y})^2 \;=\; \Sigma\,(Y' - \overline{Y})^2 \;+\; \Sigma(Y - Y')^2$$

| 2011.5971 | = | 1451.7275 | + | 559.8696 |
| Total variation | = | Explained | + | Unexplained |

**Table 9.4**

**Partitioning $SS_{total}$ into Two Components: Explained Variation and Unexplained Variation**

| | $X$ | $Y$ | $Y'$ | Total $(Y - \overline{Y})^2$ | Explained $(Y' - \overline{Y})^2$ | Unexplained $(Y - Y')^2$ |
|---|---|---|---|---|---|---|
| | 139.60 | 136.10 | 131.6269 | 152.3461 | 282.7766 | 20.0087 |
| | 213.30 | 179.50 | 180.5297 | 964.5461 | 1029.5645 | 1.0602 |
| | 162.30 | 133.10 | 146.6892 | 235.4033 | 3.0752 | 184.6669 |
| | 166.90 | 150.40 | 149.7415 | 3.8304 | 1.6865 | 0.4336 |
| | 157.80 | 141.70 | 143.7033 | 45.4661 | 22.4634 | 4.0132 |
| | 165.70 | 166.60 | 148.9453 | 329.6818 | 0.2524 | 311.6902 |
| | 149.00 | 131.70 | 137.8642 | 280.3233 | 111.9089 | 37.9968 |
| Total | 1154.60 | 1039.10 | 1039.1000 | 2011.5971 | 1451.7275 | 559.8696 |
| Mean | 164.94 | 148.44 | 148.4429 | | | |
| $s$ | 21.70 | 16.95 | | | | |
| Pearson $r$ | 0.8495 | | | | | |
| slope | $0.6635 = .8495\left(\dfrac{16.95}{21.70}\right)$ | | | | | |

$Y' = 148.4429 + .6635(X - 164.9429)$

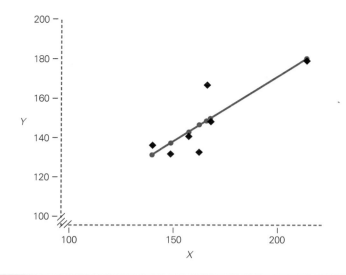

**Figure** | **9.10**

Scatterplot of the data in Table 9.4. The solid diamonds represent the actual values of *X* and *Y*, and the circles represent the predicted scores, *Y'*, given the regression equation and values of *X*.

Also, $r^2$ is equal to explained variation divided by total variation.

$$r^2 = \frac{\text{explained variation}}{\text{total variation}} = \frac{1451.7275}{2011.5971} = .7217$$

Finally, the square root of $r^2$ equals the correlation coefficient, *r*.

$$r = \sqrt{r^2} = \sqrt{.7217} = .8495$$

Figure 9.10 shows a scatter diagram based on the data in Table 9.4, showing one regression line: the line for predicting *Y* from known values of *X*. Although our present discussion is directed only to this regression line, all conclusions we draw apply equally to the line of regression of *X* on *Y* and the regression line of *Y* on *X*.

The regression line represents one way for predicting values of *Y* from values of *X*. As you can see, not all the obtained scores fall on the regression line. If they had, Pearson *r* would have been 1.0. But because the correlation is high, the scores tend to cluster about the regression line. Figure 9.8c shows the deviations of the obtained scores from the regression line. These represent our errors in prediction $(Y - Y')$. You can see that, because of the high correlation, these errors are low in magnitude. In contrast, the deviations between the predicted scores and the mean $(Y' - \overline{Y})$ in 9.8b are considerably larger. This is as it should be. Assuming, for example, that amount of musculature and strength are correlated, we would expect Arnold Swartzenegger's strength to deviate far from the population mean on this variable. Remember when actual scores deviate little from predicted scores, the correlation is strong. When the correlation is strong, the regression line will move away from the means of *Y*, thus maximizing the difference between the predicted *Y* scores and the mean of *Y*.

## 9.6 / Coefficients of Determination ($r^2$) and Nondetermination ($1 - r^2$) Revisited

In the last chapter we introduced you to the coefficient of determination, $r^2$, and the coefficient of nondetermination, $1 - r^2$. You may recall that the coefficient of determination was used to indicate the proportion of variance shared between the two variables. The coefficient of nondetermination represents the proportion of variance that is not shared by the two variables. Let us examine these concepts in more detail. The coefficient of determination is defined by the formula:

$$r^2 = \frac{\text{Regression Sum of Squares}}{\text{Total Sum of Squares}} = \frac{\Sigma(Y' - \overline{Y})^2}{\Sigma(Y - \overline{Y})^2} \qquad (9.15)$$

We can apply this formula to the data presented in Table 9.4. Specifically:

$$r^2 = \frac{\Sigma(Y' - \overline{Y})^2}{\Sigma(Y - \overline{Y})^2} = \frac{1451.7275}{2011.5971} = .7217$$

From Table 9.4 you will see that $r = .8495$. Therefore our calculations are in agreement: $\sqrt{.7217} = .8495$. To reiterate, the coefficient of determination represents the proportion of the variation in $Y$ that can be accounted for by the regression of $Y$ on $X$. Stated in other words, the coefficient of determination represents the proportion of variation that is shared between the two variables.

We can use the same logic to examine the coefficient of nondetermination. As we have seen, $\Sigma(Y - Y')^2$ is the sum of squares for the differences between the predicted and actual values of $Y$. We consider this term to be the "error term" because it represents a deviation from our prediction and we have no way to explain this difference. Therefore, it we divide this term by the total sum of squares we will have the coefficient of nondetermination:

$$1 - r^2 = \frac{\text{Error Sum of Squares}}{\text{Total Sum of Squares}} = \frac{\Sigma(Y - Y')^2}{\Sigma(Y - \overline{Y})^2} \qquad (9.16)$$

For our current example:

$$1 - r^2 = \frac{\Sigma(Y - Y')}{\Sigma(Y - \overline{\overline{Y}})} = \frac{559.8696}{2011.5971} = .2783$$

This finding confirms that $1 - r^2 = 1 - .7217 = .2783$. Thus we can see that the coefficient of nondetermination is the proportion of the total variation that is unaccounted for by the regression of $Y$ on $X$.

Figure 9.11 presents the relation between the size of $r$ and $r^2$. One important aspect of this graph to recognize is the fact that small changes in $r$ represent large changes in $r^2$. Look at the difference between $r = .4$ and $r = .2$, and $r = .8$ and $r = .6$. In both cases there is a difference in $r$ of .2. Compare the difference in $r^2$. For the first set the difference is $.16 - .04 = .12$, for the second set the difference is much larger, $.64 - .36 = .28$. The differences in these values suggest that we should use $r^2$ to compare the relative size of the correlations. Here is an example. If you found

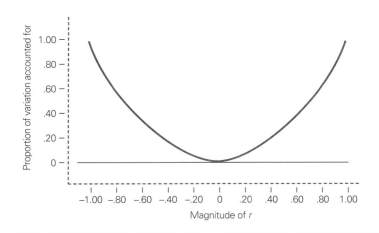

**Figure** 9.11

**The proportion of the variation of one variable accounted for in terms of variations of a correlated variable at varying values of r.**

that the correlation between two variables was $r = .20$ what correlation coefficient would represent twice as much shared variance? The answer is best understood by squaring the correlation. Thus $r^2 = .04$. Now what correlation represents $r^2 = .08$? The answer is $r = .2828$. Why would $r = .4$ be the wrong answer? Again we need to look at $r^2$. In this example $r^2 = .4^2 = .16$, which is 4 times greater than $r^2 = .2^2 = .04$.

## 9.7 / Regression and Causation

You have seen that, when two variables are related, it is possible to predict the values of one variable from values of another. This relationship between correlation and prediction often leads to a serious error in reasoning: a high relationship between two variables frequently carries with it the implication that one has caused the other. This is especially true when one variable precedes the other in time. What is often overlooked is the fact that the variables may not be causally connected in any direct way, but they may vary together by a common link to other variables. Thus, if you are a bird-watcher, you may note that the increase of bird migration to your area is followed by a greening of the grass (see Figure 9.12). However, recognizing that variables such as increasing hours of sunlight in the spring accompanied by increasing warmth of the sun are other factors influencing bird migration and the greening accompanying spring, you are not likely to conclude that the birds cause the grass to turn greener. Unfortunately, there are may occasions in the behavioral sciences when it is not easy to identify other factors.

Suppose you have demonstrated that there is a high positive correlation between the number of hours students spend studying for an exam and their subsequent grades on that exam. You may be tempted to conclude that the number of hours of study causes the grades to vary. Let's look more closely at this imputation of causality. On the assumption that a greater number of hours of study causes grades to increase, we would expect any student who has a love affair with his/her texts to achieve higher grades than one whose love has dimmed. This is not necessarily

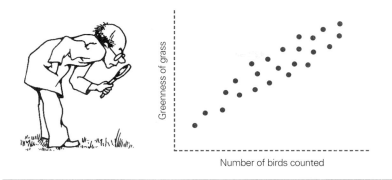

**Figure** | **9.12**

Correlation is not causation. Note that when the census count of birds is low in the northern U.S., the grass is not very green. Therefore, the number of birds will determine how green the grass will become. What is wrong with this conclusion?

the case. We have overlooked the possibility that the better student performs better by virtue of higher intelligence, stronger motivation, better study habits, supporting companions, or simply because she or he has a greater capacity to perform better. Longer hours of study and better grades may be welcome by-products of these factors.

What we are saying is that correlational studies simply do not permit inferences concerning causation. Correlation is a *necessary* but not *sufficient* condition to establish causal relationships between two variables. In short, establishing a causal relationship requires that the experimental conditions or values of the random variable are randomly assigned to the subjects. A correlational study lacks the requirement of independent random assignment.

A book by D. Huff includes an excellent chapter devoted to the confusion of correlation and causation. He refers to faulty causal inferences from correlational data as the post hoc fallacy.

> Reams of pages of figures have been collected to show the value in dollars of a college education, and stacks of pamphlets have been published to bring these figures—and conclusions more or less based on them—to the attention of potential students. I am not quarreling with the intention. I am in favor of education myself, particularly if it includes a course in elementary statistics. Now these figures have conclusively demonstrated that people who have gone to college make more money than those who have not. The exceptions are numerous, or course, but the tendency is strong and clear. The only thing wrong is that along with the figures and facts goes a totally unwarranted conclusion. This is the *post hoc* fallacy at it best. It says that these figures show that if *you* (your son, your daughter) attend college you will probably earn more money than if you decide to spend the next four years in some other manner. This unwarranted conclusion has for its basis the equally unwarranted assumption that since college-trained folks make more money, they make it because they went to college. Actually we don't know whether these are people who would have made more money even if they had *not* gone to college. There are a couple of things that indicate rather strongly that this is so. Colleges get a disproportionate number of two groups of kids—the bright and the rich. The bright might show good earning power without college knowledge. And as for the rich ones—well, money breeds money in several different ways. Few sons of rich men are found in low-income brackets whether or not they go to college. (Huff, 1954, pp. 93–94)

## 9.8 / The Marriage of Regression Analysis and Experimental Design

A distinctive characteristic of a true experiment is that the subjects are randomly assigned to the experimental conditions and the experimenter can manipulate the independent variable. In the typical experiment, the independent variable is some aspect of the subject's environment that is manipulated by the experimenter to assess its effects on one or more aspects of the subject's response system (the dependent variable(s)). Thus, if the experimenter wishes to assess the effects of a drug on the activity level of a randomly selected and randomly

**Table 9.5**

Regression Analysis of Data from an Experiment in Which the Independent Variable Is Milligrams of a Drug and the Dependent Variable Is Activity Level

| Subject Number | X-Variable (Independent) | Y-Variable (Dependent) | $X^2$ | $Y^2$ | $XY$ |
|---|---|---|---|---|---|
| 1 | 1 | 12 | 1 | 144 | 12 |
| 2 | 3 | 11 | 9 | 121 | 33 |
| 3 | 4 | 15 | 16 | 225 | 60 |
| 4 | 5 | 17 | 25 | 289 | 85 |
| 5 | 6 | 19 | 36 | 361 | 114 |
| 6 | 7 | 18 | 49 | 324 | 126 |
| 7 | 9 | 23 | 81 | 529 | 207 |
| 8 | 11 | 20 | 121 | 400 | 220 |
| 9 | 12 | 26 | 144 | 676 | 312 |
| $N = 9$ | | | | | |
| Sum | 58 | 161 | 482 | 3069 | 1169 |
| Mean | 6.44 | 17.89 | | | |

$$\Sigma(X - \overline{X})(Y - \overline{Y}) = \Sigma XY - \frac{(\Sigma X)(\Sigma Y)}{N}$$

$$= 1169 - \frac{(58)(161)}{9}$$

$$= 169 - 1037.556$$

$$= 131.444$$

$$SS_X = \Sigma X^2 - \frac{(\Sigma X)^2}{N} = 482 - \frac{58^2}{9} = 482 - 373.778 = 108.222$$

$$SS_Y = \Sigma Y^2 - \frac{(\Sigma Y)^2}{N} = 3069 - \frac{161^2}{9} = 3069 - 2880.111 = 188.889$$

$$r = \frac{\Sigma XY - \frac{(\Sigma X)(\Sigma Y)}{N}}{\sqrt{SS_X SS_Y}} = \frac{131.444}{\sqrt{(108.222)(188.889)}} = \frac{131.444}{142.975} = .919$$

$$s_X = \sqrt{\frac{SS_X}{N}} = \sqrt{\frac{108.222}{9}} = 3.47$$

$$s_Y = \sqrt{\frac{SS_Y}{N}} = \sqrt{\frac{188.889}{9}} = 4.58$$

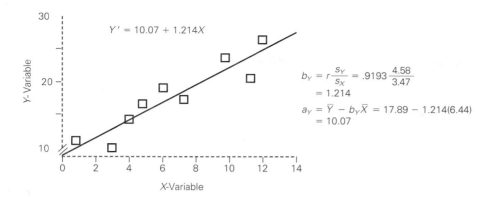

**Figure** | **9.13**

Scatter diagram, regression line, and regression equation for data presented in Table 9.5. The relationship between X and Y is linear.

assigned sample of experimental animals, there are often two experimental conditions, the control condition and the experimental condition. The subjects in the control condition do not receive the active ingredient of the compound whereas subjects in the experimental condition will receive the active ingredient for the drug. The effects of the independent variable are usually judged in terms of the difference between the means for the control and experimental groups.

Let's suppose that we design a study so that the features of regression analysis and experimental design are combined. Specifically, the subjects are randomly assigned to different dosages of the experimental variable and their corresponding dependent measures are then measured. Since there are two measures on each subject (the independent variable is the amount of the compound administered and the dependent measure involves some aspect of behavior, such as activity level), such a study combines the features of both a true experiment and a regression analysis. To illustrate, Table 9.5 shows the raw data and the regression analysis of a hypothetical study.

Figure 9.13 shows the data in the form of a scatter diagram with an accompanying line of regression of Y on X. It should be noted that the merger of the experimental design with regression analysis is plausible only when both the independent and the dependent variables are either interval or ratio scales. When this is the case, there are distinct advantages of the experimental/regression analysis over the traditional experimental design:

1. What is the relation between a dosage of a drug and its effect on behavior? In a simple two group design we might ask: What is the effect on activity of administering 2 milligrams of the drug to subjects in the 2-mg condition compared to the activity level of subjects in the 12-mg condition? In contrast, the experimental/regression design makes it possible to relate a whole spectrum of values of the independent variable to another wide spectrum of outcomes with respect to the dependent variable. To illustrate, as Figure 9.13 shows, the predicted activity level of a subject receiving 2 milligrams of the drug is approximately 12. In contrast, as the level of administration of the drug increases so also does the general activity level of subjects receiving these increased levels of the independent variable. See the much higher predicted activity level of a subject who receives 12 milligrams of a drug.

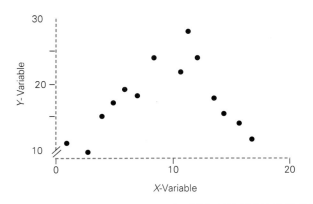

**Figure** | 9.14

Scatter diagram depicting a curvilinear relationship between the independent variable and the dependent variable. A typical two group design might lead to different conclusions depending on the level of drug administered in the experiment.

2. When the correlation between the independent and dependent variable is high, as in the present case when $r = 0.92$, the regression line can be used to predict the effect of administering different dosages of the drug on the dependent measures. Note that when using the regression equation in Figure 9.13, the predicted $Y' = 10.07 + 1.214(9) = 21$. Such prediction is not possible when using a traditional two-group experimental design.

3. The scatter diagram in Figure 9.14 depicts a curvilinear relationship between the dosage level and the activity level. As can be seen, dosages up to 12 mg increase the activity level. Beyond that dosage, the effect is inverse. Dosages beyond 12 mg lead to decreasing activity levels. A typical experimental two-group design might lead to two different conclusions if the administered dosage levels of the two experimental conditions are 12 mg as opposed to 17 mg. On the other hand, when the correlation between the independent and the dependent variable is high, as in the present example, it is possible to detect the level at which the independent variable has its greatest effect on the dependent variable.

   However, we must keep in mind that we are still dealing with descriptive statistics. The procedures for making conclusions from these data will appear in the inferential section of this text.

## CHAPTER S U M M A R Y

In this chapter we saw that it is possible to fit two straight lines to a bivariate distribution of scores, one for predicting $Y$ scores from known values of $X$ and the other for predicting $X$-values from known values of $Y$. It is the $Y$-score that is traditionally the predicted score, and the $X$-score that is predictor. We noted that when the correlation is perfect ($r = \pm 1.00$), all the scores fall on the regression line and there is no error in prediction. The lower the relationship is, the greater will be the dispersion around the regression line and the line will rotate toward the mean of the predicted variable. Our errors in prediction increase as the correlation lowers toward 0. Finally, when $r = 0$, the regression line becomes the mean of the predicted variable and the mean becomes our "best" predictor for that variable.

The regression line was shown to be analogous to the mean: The summed deviations around it are 0 and the sums of squares are minimal. The standard error of estimate was shown to be analogous to the standard deviation. This standard error is useful in determining the spread of the scores around the regression line and for calculating the interval in which the true value of $Y$ can be expected to fall.

We noted that three separate sums of squares, reflecting different sources of variability, may be calculated.

1. Variation about the mean of the distribution for each variable. This familiar variation is known as the total sum of squares.
2. Variation of each score about the regression line. This variation is called the unexplained variation.
3. Variation of each predicted score about the mean of the distribution for each variable. This is the explained variation.

We concluded that the sum of the unexplained variation and the explained variation is equal to the total variation (i.e., $SS_{total} = SS_{unexp} + SS_{exp}$).

Next, we saw that the ratio $\dfrac{SS_{exp}}{SS_{total}}$ indicates the proportion of the total variation that is explained. This proportion is known as the coefficient of determination. In addition, the converse concept of coefficient of nondetermination $\left(\dfrac{SS_{unexp}}{SS_{total}}\right)$ was discussed.

## Summary of Formulas Presented in This Chapter and When They Are Used

| When you want to | Use this formula |
| --- | --- |
| predict a raw score, $Y'$ and you have a raw score $X$ | $Y' = \overline{Y} + r\frac{s_Y}{s_X}(X - \overline{X})$ |
| predict a standard score $z_Y$ and you have a standard score $z_X$ | $z_Y = r\,(z_X)$ |
| determine the slope of the regression line and you know $r$ and the spreads of both distributions | $b_Y = r\left(\frac{s_Y}{s_X}\right)$ |
| determine the slope of the regression line from a distribution of raw scores | $b_Y = \dfrac{\Sigma XY - \dfrac{(\Sigma X)(\Sigma Y)}{N}}{\Sigma X^2 - \dfrac{(\Sigma X)^2}{N}}$ |
| understand how the standard error of the estimate is related to unexplained variation | $s_{est\ Y} = \sqrt{\dfrac{\Sigma(Y - Y')^2}{N - 2}}$ |
| obtain standard error of the estimate and you know $N$ and $r$ | $s_{est\ Y} = s_Y\sqrt{\dfrac{N(1 - r^2)}{N - 2}}$ |
| Determine the interval that will include $Y_T$ | $Y_T = Y' \pm s_{est\ Y}\sqrt{1 + \dfrac{1}{N} + \dfrac{(X - \overline{X})^2}{\Sigma X^2 - \dfrac{(\Sigma X)^2}{N}}}$ |

We noted that correlation and regression analysis do not, in general, lead to the establishment of causal relationship. However, there is a marriage of correlation and experimental design that permits us to draw causation between the X- and Y-variables. This occurs when a variety of values of the X-variable are assigned at random to a randomly selected pool of subjects and the correlation is calculated between the values of X and the values of the dependent variable.

## TERMS TO REMEMBER

coefficient of determination ($r^2$)
coefficient of nondetermination
   $(1 - r^2)$
error sum of squares
   $(\bar{z}(Y - \overline{Y}')^2)$
homoscedasticity
intercept $a_Y$
nondetermination
post hoc fallacy

regression line
regression sum of squares
   $(\bar{z}(Y' - \overline{Y})^2)$
regression to the mean
residual variance
slope by $s^2_{est\ Y}$
standard error of estimate
unexplained or unaccounted for
   variation

## EXERCISES

1. A researcher believes that the older a child is, the fewer irrelevant responses he or she will make when engaged in a problem-solving situation. The data are shown in the accompanying table.

| Age | Responses |
|-----|-----------|
| 2 | 11 |
| 4 | 10 |
| 5 | 11 |
| 6 | 10 |
| 7 | 12 |
| 9 | 7 |
| 11 | 6 |
| 12 | 5 |
| 3 | 12 |
| 4 | 14 |
| 5 | 9 |
| 7 | 7 |
| 9 | 8 |
| 10 | 3 |
| 11 | 5 |
| 12 | 3 |

Using these data,
a. Draw a scatterplot.
b. Describe the relation between the two variables in several short sentences.
c. Determine if the researcher's conclusion appears to be valid.
d. Calculate the correlation between the two variables.
e. State what proportion of the differences among numbers of irrelevant responses can be accounted for by age according to the correlation.
f. Find the equation of the regression line of Y on X for the data.
g. Determine the most probable number of irrelevant responses that the experimenter would predict for Mandy, age 8.

**2.** Pat, a librarian, wants to know if there is a relation between the number of books a person checks out of the library and grade point average. She randomly selects 100 college seniors and compares the relation between number of books read, $X$, and grade point average, $Y$. Pat obtained the information shown in the accompanying table.

$\overline{X} = 98.0 \qquad \overline{Y} = 3.30$
$s_X = 10.0 \qquad s_Y = 0.55$
$\qquad r = \quad .70$
$\qquad N = 100$

---

**a.** Find the equation of the regression line of $Y$ on $X$ for these variables.
**b.** Draw a sketch of the regression line of $Y$ on $X$ for these variables.
**c.** Sally checked out a total of 110 books; estimate her GPA.
**d.** Pat predicts that Bill will have a GPA of 2.8. Approximately how many books would you predict that Bill has read?
**e.** Determine the standard error of estimate of $Y$.

**3.** A study was undertaken to find the relationship between "emotional stability" and performance in college. The results shown in the accompanying table were obtained.

| Emotional Stability | GPA |
|---|---|
| $\overline{X} = 49.0$ | $\overline{Y} = 2.85$ |
| $s_X = 12.0$ | $s_Y = 0.50$ |
| $r =$ | .36 |
| $N = 60$ | |

**a.** Find the equation of the regression line of $Y$ on $X$ for these variables.
**b.** Draw a sketch of the regression line between these variables.
**c.** Norma obtained a score of 65 on the $X$-variable. What is your prediction for her score on the $Y$-variable?
**d.** Determine the standard error of the estimate for $Y$.
**e.** What proportion of the total variation is accounted for by explained variation (e.g., the regression model)?

**4.** Assume that $\overline{X} = 30$, $s_X = 5$ and $\overline{Y} = 45$, $s_Y = 8$. Draw a separate graph for each pair of regression lines for the following values of $r$.
**a.** $r = \quad .00$ **b.** $r = \quad .20$ **c.** $r = \quad .40$ **d.** $r = \quad .60$ **e.** $r = \quad .80$
**f.** $r = -.20$ **g.** $r = -.45$ **h.** $r = -.60$ **i.** $r = -.80$ **j.** $r = -.90$

**5.** For each of the following data sets, what is the slope of the regression line?

| **a.** $r = .3$ | **b.** $r = -.6$ | **c.** $r = .25$ | **d.** $r = -.8$ |
|---|---|---|---|
| $s_X = 3.5$ | $s_X = 8.4$ | $s_X = 2.0$ | $s_X = 12.0$ |
| $s_Y = 3.4$ | $s_Y = 9.1$ | $s_Y = 6.0$ | $s_Y = 3.0$ |

**e.** Write a short essay describing the relation among the slope of the regression line, $r$, $s_X$, and $s_Y$.
**f.** Using these data, explain why the size of the slope does not represent the strength of the relation between the two variables.

**6.** A researcher examines the correlations among three different tests and an outcome measure. The correlations are (1) $r = .45$, (2) $r = -.78$, and (3) $r = .62$. All else being equal, which of these correlations will produce the best overall prediction? Which correlations will have the greatest standard error of estimate?

7. A student takes the SAT and earns a score that is 1.5 standard deviations ($z = 1.5$) above the mean. The following are hypothetical correlations for people who take two versions of the SAT on different occasions.
   **a.** $r = 0$ **b.** $r = .40$ **c.** $r = .80$ **d.** $r = .97$ **e.** $r = .60$
   **i.** On the basis of each of these correlations, estimate the student's standard score for the second test. (Hint: Remember that the standard deviation of the $z$-scores is 1.)
   **ii.** For which of the five correlations will the regression to the mean be the greatest?
   **iii.** Describe the relation between the size of the correlation coefficient and the amount of regression to the mean.

8. A personnel manager made a study of employees involved in one aspect of a manufacturing process. She finds that after they have been on the job for a year, she is able to obtain a performance measure that accurately reflects their proficiency and obtains a correlation of $r = .65$ between the proficiency measure ($\underline{Y}$) and the selection test. The mean of the selection test, $\overline{X} = 50$, $s_X = 6$, $\overline{Y} = 100$, $s_Y = 10$, and $N = 1000$. Answer the following questions based on these facts (assume that both the selection test and the proficiency measures are normally distributed).
   **a.** Herman obtained a score of 40 on the selection test. What is his predicted proficiency score?
   **b.** How likely is it that he will score as high as 110 on the proficiency measure?
   **c.** A score of 80 on the $Y$-variable is considered satisfactory for the job; below 80 is unsatisfactory. If the $X$-test is to be used as a selection device, which score should be used as the cutoff point? (Hint: Find the value of $X$ that leads to a predicted score of 80 on $Y$. Be sure to employ the appropriate prediction formula.)
   **d.** Sonya obtained a score of 30 on $X$. How likely is it that she will receive an acceptable score on $Y$?
   **e.** Leona obtained a score of 60 on $X$. How likely is it that she will fail to achieve an acceptable score on $Y$?
   **f.** For a person to have prospects for a supervisory position, a score of 120 or greater on $Y$ is deemed essential. What value of $X$ should be employed for the selection of potential supervisory personnel?
   **g.** If 1,000 people achieve a score on $X$ that predicts a $Y = 120$, approximately how many of them will obtain scores below 120? Above 130? Below 110? Above 110?

9. An admissions counselor conducts a study of students applying to a large state college. He finds that the correlation between a college entrance exam, $X$, and the first year GPA, $Y$, is $r = .40$. The mean of the test is 500 and $s_X = 25$. The mean GPA is 2.95, $s_Y = .4$, and $N = 2500$. Answer the following questions based on these facts (assume that both the exam and the first year GPA are normally distributed).
   **a.** Robert obtained a score of 510 on the entrance exam. What is his predicted GPA?
   **b.** How likely is it that Robert will earn a GPA as high as 3.5?
   **c.** A GPA of 2.00 is essential to stay in school. What exam score predicts a GPA of 2.00?
   **d.** Nancy obtained a score of 300 on the entrance exam. How likely is it that she will have a GPA above 2.00?
   **e.** Peggy obtained a score of 550 on the entrance exam. How likely is it that she will fail (have a GPA below 2.00)?
   **f.** For a student to be in the honors program, he or she needs a GPA of 3.4. What test score could be used to identify students who will have a GPA of 3.4 or greater?

**10.** A psychologist examined the relation between hours of sleep deprivation, $X$, and performance on a cognitive task, $Y$. Results are as follows:

$$\overline{X} = 5.0 \qquad \overline{Y} = 125.0$$
$$s_X = 1.0 \qquad s_Y = 12.0$$
$$r = -.40$$
$$N = 30$$

    **a.** If someone has been kept up for 8 hours, what would you expect that his or her score on the task will be?

    **b.** The correlation between these two variables is not perfect. Can you offer an explanation for why it is not higher?

**11.** A researcher is convinced that the moon causes abnormal behavior. Indeed, the word "lunacy" comes from the Latin word for moon, *luna*. To prove this point, the researcher plots the relation between the phase of the moon and the number of calls received by a 911 line. According to the data, there is a strong positive correlation between the two events. Is the researcher justified in concluding that the moon causes increases in abnormal behavior?

**12.** A psychologist wants to study the effectiveness of a new psychological treatment for depression. He administers a standard test of depression to a large number of subjects, selects those who are the most depressed, and provides them with the new treatment. The vast majority of the subjects experience some improvement in their mood. Can the psychologist assume that the treatment has brought about a relief from the depression? What concept have you learned about in this chapter that can explain these results?

**13.** A sociologist is convinced that greater levels of education cause reduced levels of violent behavior. Based on the results of an extremely large data set, the sociologist finds that the correlation between years of education and number of criminal acts is $-.25$. On the basis of these results, the sociologist argues that everyone should be required to complete a 12th-grade education. According to the results, a person who completes 12 years of school will commit, on average, 0.80 violent crimes. Do you think that the researcher's conclusions are justified? Defend your answer.

**14.** A researcher finds that the slope of the regression equation is small ($b = 0.03$) and concludes that there is no meaningful relation between the two variables. Is this necessarily a correct conclusion?

**15.** Bob has just taken a job placement test. He is disappointed because he did very poorly. You discover that the correlation between the test scores of a person who takes the test on two occasions is .20. Would you encourage Bob to take the test again? Why? What if you discovered that the correlation between testings is .90?

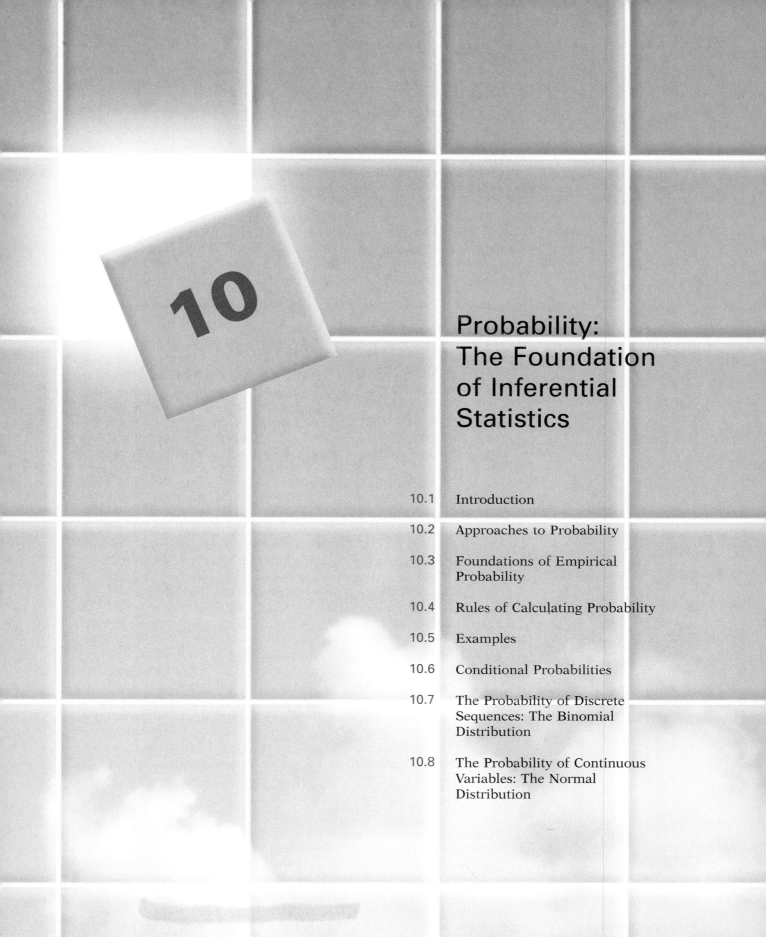

# 10

# Probability: The Foundation of Inferential Statistics

## 10.1 / Introduction

Previously, we learned how to use statistics to summarize and describe data. We are now ready to move toward a more sophisticated use of statistics, inference. As behavioral scientists, we conduct research on samples to better understand the behavior we study. In other words, we want to use the results from a sample to generalize to the population as a whole. In order to make the conceptual leap from samples to populations, we will need to examine the foundations of probability. As you will see in this and the following chapters, the mathematics of probability is the foundation of inferential statistics. This chapter provides you with a short introduction to different ways of examining issues related to probability.

## 10.2 / Approaches to Probability

The thought of probability causes many people to go into a cold sweat. For some reason, many people think probability is an abstract form of math that requires the intelligence of a rocket scientist. Trust us, probability theory is not as strange or difficult to understand as many would think. Indeed, you are constantly making decisions based on probabilities. When you hear that there is a 60% chance of thunderstorms, you may take your umbrella with you when you leave the house. You may not have to use your umbrella, but the forecaster's prediction leads you to believe that you should be prepared. You may also be deciding whether to continue reading this chapter or stop studying for the rest of the day. Your decision may be based, in part, on the probability that you will have an exam tomorrow in your statistics course. If your instructor gives unannounced quizzes, you may not want to take the risk of being unprepared. On the other hand, if the next test is two weeks from now, you may make a different decision. The decision can become even more complicated when you begin to consider the probability that there will be an exam or quiz in your other courses.

Although you may not know the formal laws of probability, you may have an intuitive knowledge of how to use probability information. Typically, your intuitive knowledge of probability is sufficient for you to make good decisions. In more complex situations, such as interpreting the results of an experiment, it is essential that you move beyond relying upon subjective reactions to probability and develop an appreciation for the rules of probability. The following are three types of probability that psychologists study. Understanding them should help you understand why you need to study the formal rules of probability.

### Subjective Probability

There are many times when we lack objective data for making good decisions. Nevertheless, we may have strong feelings that we call "a hunch," "common sense," or an "intuition." These **subjective probabilities** come from our experiences and expectations, and influence how we behave.

Although we may believe that we can trust our intuitions, there is considerable reason to be suspicious of subjective probability. Psychologists have studied human decision making for some time and have found some interesting examples of errors that we commonly make. Let's look at a few of these errors.

■ **Subjective Probability:**

An estimate of probability that is based on one's experiences, intuitions, and opinions about an event.

**The Gambler's Fallacy**   The Gambler's Fallacy refers to the fact that many people over- or underestimate the probability of a specific event. Imagine that you have tossed a quarter four times in a row and that each time it has landed "heads." What do you think will happen on the fifth toss of the coin? Many people predict that the quarter will land "tails" because it is unlikely to get a run of five "heads" in a row. Some people may even say that the coin is overdue to land "tails" because half the tosses should be "heads" and other half should be "tails." They may say something like: "The law of averages says that half the coin tosses should be 'tails.' Because all four tosses of the coin came up 'heads,' the coin is overdue for a 'tails.' Therefore the next toss should be 'tails.' "

Although these arguments sound reasonable, they are wrong. On the next toss of the quarter there is an equal probability that it will be "heads" or "tails." The problem with the belief that the coin should land "tails" is that it assumes the quarter has a memory for what happened on the last four tosses and the moral sense to correct its behavior in order to obey the laws of probability. Of course coins are not aware of what has happened to them and do not attempt to behave according to any "law of averages." If the coin is fair, there is an equal chance that the next toss will produce a "heads" or a "tails."

Let's look at another example. If you tossed a fair coin six times in a row, which of the following outcomes do you think is more likely, TTTHHH or HHTTHT? If you said that they were equally likely, you are beginning to catch on. Because each toss of the coin is independent of what happened on the previous toss, it is equally likely that either pattern would occur. If you thought the pattern HHTTHT was more likely, the problem may be that you are relying on your subjective estimate of which pattern looks more random. The pattern HHTTHT looks random whereas TTTHHH does not. Two cognitive psychologists, Amos Tversky and Daniel Kahneman (1974, 1982, 1983) found that many people solve probability problems using personal heuristics. A personal heuristic is a method for solving a problem based on one's personal experiences. Tversky and Kahneman have shown that many people make errors in judgment concerning probability because their personal heuristic contradicts the mathematics of probability. The moral of the story is that hunches and intuitions are often misleading.

**Self-Fulfilling Prophecies**   Other factors influence our intuitive assessments of probability. One of these is selective memory, or what social psychologists call the self-fulfilling prophecy (Snyder, 1984). If we believe something to be true, we are more likely to remember occurrences that confirm our beliefs and to forget conflicting information. Indeed, we may even reinterpret events to conform to our expectations. The self-fulfilling prophecy is a real problem for researchers and one of the reasons why scientists go to great pains to use research procedures and statistical techniques to remain objective concerning the data they collect.

**"Man-Who" Statistics**   Another type of error that many people make when interpreting statistical information is what Richard Nisbett and Lee Ross (1980) call "Man-Who Statistics." (p. 61) The effect refers to the fact that some people give undue consideration to anecdotal evidence or to a single exception to a generalization. Here is an example. As a generality, people who smoke are more likely to suffer health problems that arise from their habit. A friend of yours may discredit this generalization by saying, "Those data are all wrong! My uncle has been a two-pack-a-day smoker for the past 20 years and is as healthy as an ox."

**■ Statistical Generalization:**

A statement about a characteristic or feature of a population.

In this example, your friend does not appreciate the fact that a **statistical generalization** is not an absolute pronouncement. A statistical generalization represents a reliable trend that is likely to be true when we discuss the differences among populations. Therefore, it is acceptable to generalize that, all else being equal, people who smoke are more likely to suffer specific kinds of health problems than are those who do not smoke. Although there may be exceptions, we expect the statistical generalization to be true more often than not. To restate an important point, the goal of probability statistics is to estimate attributes of the population, not necessarily the individual cases.

As you can see, subjective probability often leads to wrong conclusions about important information. Consequently, psychologists use the scientific method and inferential statistics to avoid the types of mistakes associated with subjective impressions and preconceived expectations. Therefore, we need to learn and practice formal methods to make decisions concerning complex issues. Developing these skills will help you better understand and interpret the research you are conducting.

## Classical Approach to Probability

**■ Classical Definition of Probability:**

A mathematical index of the relative frequency or likelihood of the occurrence of a specific event.

The **classical approach to probability** uses mathematical rules to determine the probability of different events under known conditions. Classical probability theory evolved from mathematicians' study of games of chance. In all gambling situations, the mathematician knows the specific conditions of the game. As an example, we can determine the probability of selecting a king from a deck of cards. All standard decks have 52 cards, 4 of which are kings. If we draw one card at random, the probability of selecting a king is 4/52 or .0769.

We define probability as the likelihood that a given event will occur relative to all the other events that can occur. In the example of selecting a king from a deck of cards, the number of kings in the population is 4. We can represent this value with the variable, $f(A)$, which reads as, *"frequency of event"* A. The number of cards that are not kings is 48, which we represent as $f(\text{not } A)$. We read $f(\text{not } A)$ as, *"frequency of events that are not"* A. We use $p(A)$ to represent the probability of Event A. Formally, the mathematical definition of the probability is:

$$p(A) = \frac{Number\ of\ Outcomes\ of\ Interest}{Total\ Number\ of\ Possible\ Outcomes} \qquad (10.1)$$

or

$$p(A) = \frac{f(A)}{f(A) + f(\text{not } A)}$$

## Empirical Approach to Probability

**■ Empirical Definition of Probability:**

A mathematical estimate of the relative frequency of the occurrence of a specific event that is based on samples made from the population under identical conditions.

In the classical approach to probability, the statistician knows all the population parameters. This is not the case in most real-life research because we never know the parameters of the population. Instead, we must sample from the population to estimate the relative frequency of different events. Once we estimate the relative frequency of those events, we can then make specific predictions. Therefore, the essential difference between the classical and **empirical** **approaches to probability** is the method of assigning relative frequencies of events. In the classical approach we know the parameters, in the empirical approach we use samples to estimate the relative probabilities.

## 10.3 / Foundations of Empirical Probability

Before we move too far into our formal discussion of probability, we should review a few basic concepts. Once you have mastered these, you will be able to move on to the calculation of probability.

## Discrete vs. Continuous Variables

The first concept that we will examine is the type of variables we use, discrete variables and continuous variables. As you should recall from Chapter 2, a discrete variable is one that we represent with whole numbers. Many researchers use discrete variables. For example, an educational psychologist may want to know whether a student passed a test. Similarly, a clinical psychologist may want to know if a treatment cured an emotional problem. In both examples, there are two outcomes: *Pass vs. Fail* and *Cured vs. Not Cured*.

Continuous variables, by contrast, can take on intermediate or fractional values. Your height, the number of calories you eat each day, and your intelligence are all examples of continuous variables. We will focus on estimating the probability of discrete variables in the first part of the chapter and then move on to continuous variables.

## Sample Space

**Sample space** refers to all the possible outcomes that can occur when we collect data. Let's use a simple example to illustrate our point. Imagine that you are conducting a poll of registered voters to determine if they are willing to vote for a countywide levy to support a mental health center. As you conduct your poll, you call registered voters and ask if they: (a) will vote for the tax, (b) will not vote for the tax, or (c) are still undecided. We could also ask the voters about their political party affiliation. Consequently, the sample space consists of voters who are affiliated with (a) the Democratic Party, (b) the Republican Party, or (c) another political party, and their opinion of the tax. Table 10.1 presents the sample space for our survey.

■ **Sample Space:**

The sample space consists of all possible outcomes that can occur in an experiment.

## Random and Independent

Randomness and independence are two important concepts in probability. Random means that the outcome of an event is not known. At best, all we can do is *estimate* the probability of the event. For example, a coin toss is random because we do not know if it will land heads or tails. Our best prediction is to estimate that there is a 50% chance of the

**Table** | **10.1**
| **Sample Space for a Hypothetical Political Survey\***

| Democrat | Republican | Other |
|----------|------------|-------|
| For | For | For |
| Against | Against | Against |
| Undecided | Undecided | Undecided |

*The sample space includes the voter's political party and whether or not they intend to vote for or against an issue.

coin landing heads. If you knew how it would land, then the event would not be random because its outcome would be predetermined. A long sequence of random events will have no pattern or consistent feature.

Independent means that one event does not influence another. Consider again flipping a coin. Each time you flip the coin, the probability that it will land heads or tails is independent of all the previous tosses. If the coin tosses are not independent, then they cannot be random.

In our example of the political poll, we would want to ensure that our data represents random and independent samples from the population. By random, we mean that every registered voter in the county has an equal probability of being selected for our survey. Similarly, we want to ensure that selecting one voter does not influence our choice of other voters. If the data represent a random and independent sample, then we are justified in making predictions about the outcome of the next election.

Randomness is extremely important to researchers. Whenever we use random selection or random assignment techniques, we want to be sure that the procedures represent random events. In 1955, the Rand Corporation published an important book that contains a million random numbers. The book was very popular among researchers who wanted a guaranteed source of random numbers. Table B of Appendix D contains an example of a random number table. Today, many computer programs can generate a series of random numbers that meet your particular needs.

## Methods of Sampling

Because researchers rely on samples drawn from populations, it is essential that we ensure that the sample is representative of the population. Many programs of research fail because the sample data are not representative of the population. Consider a common example. A popular magazine conducts a mail-in poll of its readers. The magazine then reports that 70% of all married couples say that they would not marry their current spouse if given the choice. According to the article, this result is based on the 20,000 readers who mailed in the questionnaire. Should we conclude that the vast majority of married people are dissatisfied with their marriage? Absolutely not! Although the sample consists of an impressive number of responses, they can hardly be considered representative of the population. You can probably see the problems with the data collection technique. For example, only people who read the magazine had an opportunity to respond. In addition, not all the readers responded to the questionnaire. In other words, these data represent a biased sample because they do not represent a fair approximation of the population. There are several sampling techniques that we can use to ensure that the data are representative of the population.

**Simple Random Selection**   Simple random selection means that every member of the population has an equal probability of being selected. To generate a random sample, you would use a table of random numbers or a computer program that generates random numbers. For example, assume that you wanted to conduct a poll of students at your college. Also assume that there are currently 12,000 students enrolled at the school, and you decided to create a sample of 100 students. If you were using a computer, you would program it to generate 100 numbers between 1 and 12,000. Then, using an alphabetical list of the students, you would select the names corresponding to the random numbers.

**Systematic Selection**   Another form of probability sampling is systematic selection. For this procedure, you select every Xth person on a list. Using the previous example, you would take the alphabetical list of students at your college and then select every 120th student. Although the procedure is not random sampling, the procedure does provide a representative sample in most cases.

**Stratified Random Selection**   Sometimes there may be meaningful subgroups in the population. For example, you may want to ensure that the sample accurately represents the proportion of men and women in the population. Similarly, you may wish to ensure that people of different age groups, ethnic origin, or religious preference are accurately represented in the sample. The first step is to identify these important subgroups and their relative size in the population. Once you have identified the size of these subgroups, you can then customize your random selection procedure to ensure that the sample matches the population.

As an example, assume that for your survey of college students, it is important to identify the year of the student. According to the Records Office, the proportion of each class is: Freshman = .30, Sophomore = .28, Junior = .25, Senior = .17. Armed with this information, you can now use random sampling to select from each class. Specifically, you would randomly select 30 Freshmen, 28 Sophomores, 25 Juniors, and 17 Seniors.

## Mutually vs. Nonmutually Exclusive Events

The concept of mutually exclusive describes events in our sample space that cannot occur together or overlap. Technically speaking, a person cannot be a registered Republican and a registered Democrat. One's political party is a mutually exclusive condition—in the eyes of your state's Board of Elections, you belong to one, and only one, political party. Similarly, your votes are mutually exclusive events because you can only vote for or against a proposition.

Although there are many examples of mutually exclusive events, there are many situations where events are not mutually exclusive. In our example, one can be a Democrat and vote for a tax. One way to illustrate the concept of a joint probability is to use a Venn diagram. A Venn diagram is nothing more than a set of circles. Each circle represents a separate event. The degree to which the circles overlap represents the degree of **joint probability**. Figure 10.1 is an example of two Venn diagrams. Figure 10.1(a) represents a mutually exclusive condition whereas Figure 10.1(b) represents a joint probability.

____

■ **Joint Probability:**

The joint probability is the probability of selecting from the sample space an element where two conditions are present. A joint probability is represented as $p(A \text{ and } B)$.

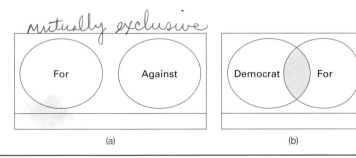

(a)        (b)

**Figure** | **10.1**

A Venn diagram of the voter example. **The entire rectangle represents the sample space. Figure (a) represents two mutually exclusive events, voters who will vote For or Against a tax. Figure (b) represents two events that intersect or overlap. The circles represent Democrats and voters who will vote For a tax. The overlap represents Democrats who will vote For the tax.**

## Expressing a Probability

There are several ways to express a probability. Many researchers find it convenient to express the probability as a percentage or as the relative frequency in 100 chances. In the example of drawing a king from a deck of cards, if we shuffled the deck and selected a card at random, the probability of selecting a king is $p = .0769$. If we repeated those same steps 100 times—shuffle, draw, reshuffle—we can predict that 7.69% of the draws will result in a king. Therefore, to convert a probability into a percentage, multiply the probability by 100.

You may have noticed that when we report probabilities we do not have a "0" before the decimal point. This practice comes from the editorial guidelines of the American Psychological Association (1994). According to their editorial rules, any number that cannot be greater than 1 need not have a "0" in front of the decimal point. Therefore, we express probabilities as $p(A) = .64$.

## 10.4 / Rules of Calculating Probability

With this brief introduction we can now consider some simple rules of probability. The two rules we will examine are the Addition Rule and the Multiplication Rule. These rules represent different ways of deriving probabilities under specific conditions. We will examine each and then see how they can be applied to specific situations.

### Addition Rule: $p(A \text{ or } B)$

We use the addition rule when we want to know the probability of selecting an element that has one or more conditions. For example, we may be interested in selecting a voter who is either in favor of a new tax or is still undecided. Similarly, we may be interested in the probability of selecting a person from a mental clinic who has been diagnosed as depressed or alcohol-dependent. We use the addition rule to determine probabilities in these situations.

> **Addition Rule:** The probability of selecting a sample that contains one or more elements is the sum of the individual probabilities for each element less the joint probability. When A and B are mutually exclusive, $p(A \text{ and } B) = 0$.
>
> $$p(A \text{ or } B) = p(A) + p(B) - p(A \text{ and } B) \qquad (10.2)$$

Here is a quick example. Based on your survey, you estimate that 40% of the voters are for the levy, 35% are against the levy, and 25% are still unsure. If you selected a registered voter at random, what would be the probability that the person would be for or undecided about the levy? According to the addition rule $p(A \text{ or } B) = .40 + .25 - 0 = .65$. Because the voting categories are mutually exclusive there can be no $p(A \text{ and } B)$, therefore its value is 0. Thus, the probability of selecting one of the two types of voters is 65%. We will show you what to do when there are non-mutually exclusive events later in the chapter.

## Multiplication Rule for Independent Events: $p(A) \times p(B)$

We apply the **multiplication rule for independent events** in situations where we want to know the probability of specific events that are mutually exclusive. Using the multiplication rule, we can determine the probability of two or more events occurring at the same time. For example, if a student completes a five-question multiple choice exam for which he or she has not studied, what is the probability that he or she will get at least three of the questions correct? Let's assume that the student has to guess randomly to get the correct answer and that each question has four alternative answers. Therefore, the probability that the student will guess the correct answer to any question is $p(Q_j) = 1/4 = .25$. According to the multiplication rule, $p(Q_1 \text{ and } Q_2 \text{ and } Q_3) = .25 \times .25 \times .25 = .0156$. Therefore, the student has a 1.56% chance in guessing three out of five correctly.

---

**Multiplication Rule for Independent Events:**
The probability of obtaining a specific sequence of independent events is the product of the probability of each event.

$$p(A \text{ and } B \text{ and } \ldots) = p(A) \times p(B) \ldots \qquad (10.3)$$

---

## 10.5 / Examples

Suppose that in an effort to obtain data on current reasons for seeking professional help, a psychologist sent a questionnaire to a random sample of mental health clinics throughout the state. One part of the questionnaire dealt with the abuse of drugs and alcohol among those receiving care at the clinics. Table 10.2 presents the results of the survey. Let's define alcohol abuse as Event A and drug abuse as Event B. We can use these data to illustrate many practical applications of the addition and multiplication rules.

### Joint and Marginal Probabilities

Let's begin with a simple form of probabilities, joint and marginal probabilities. These probabilities refer to the proportion of an event as a fraction of the total. To calculate the probability of an event, we divide the frequency of the event by the total. Table 10.3 presents these probabilities.

**Table  10.2**

Observed Frequencies of the Number of People Who Abuse Alcohol, Drugs, or Both

|  | CONDITION OF CLIENT | | |
| --- | --- | --- | --- |
|  | Alcohol Abuse (A) | No Alcohol Abuse (not A) | Row Total |
| Drug abuse (B) | 118 | 118 | 236 |
| No drug abuse (not B) | 236 | 5428 | 5664 |
| Column total | 354 | 5546 | 5900 |

**Table** | **10.3**

**Joint and Marginal Probabilities of the Number of People Who Abuse Alcohol, Drugs, or Both**

| | CONDITION OF CLIENT | | |
|---|---|---|---|
| | **Alcohol Abuse (A)** | **No Alcohol Abuse (not A)** | **Marginal Probability** |
| Drug abuse (B) | $p$(A and B) 118/5900 = **.02** | $p$(not A and B) 118/5900 = **.02** | $p$(B) 236/5900 = **.04** |
| No drug abuse (not B) | $p$(A and not B) 236/5900 = **.04** | $p$(not A and not B) 5428/5900 = **.92** | $p$(not B) 5664/5900 = **.96** |
| Marginal probability | $p$(A) 354/5900 = **.06** | $p$(not A) 5546/5900 = **.94** | 5900/5900 = **1.00** |

We use the term *joint probability* to refer to the probability estimates within the body of the table. These values represent the conjunction of two events (e.g., A and B). According to the data, the probability of selecting people who abuse alcohol but not drugs is $p$(A and not B) = .04. By contrast, we use the term **marginal probabilities** to refer to the column and row values. For example, the probability of selecting a person who does not abuse drugs is $p$(not B) = .96.

■ **Marginal Probability:**

The probability that reflects independent or unconditional events.

## Addition Rule

Using the values in Table 10.3 and the probability rules, we can find the answer to several interesting questions. For example, what is the probability that a given patient, selected at random, will be either alcohol or drug dependent? You might be tempted to add the proportion of clients abusing alcohol and the proportion abusing drugs to obtain: $p$(A or B) = $p$(A) + $p$(B) = (.06 + .04) = .10. This answer is wrong because it does not take into account the 118 people who are counted twice—once as alcohol abusers and again as drug abusers. In other words, the two categories are not mutually exclusive.

Figure 10.2 illustrates the relation between the two conditions. If you look at the definition for the addition rule, you will see that we must

Alcohol *and* drug abuse

Alcohol abuse     Drug abuse

**Figure** | **10.2**

Venn diagram of clients of a mental health clinic, some of whom are alcohol abusers, some of whom are drug abusers, some of whom are both. The overlap represents both.

**Table** 10.4

**An Example of the Addition Rule for Determining Probability***

|  | CONDITION OF CLIENT | |
|---|---|---|
|  | Alcohol Abuse (A) | No Alcohol Abuse (not A) |
| Drug abuse (B) | $p$(A or B) .06 + .04 − .02 = **.08** | $p$(not A or B) .94 + .04 − .02 = **.96** |
| No drug abuse (not B) | $p$(A or not B) .06 + .96 − .04 = **.98** | $p$(not A or not B) .94 + .96 − .92 = **.98** |

*Each probability printed in bold represents the probability of either condition.

subtract the joint probability from the sum of the combined probability. To determine the probability of Event A and Event B, we must subtract the 118 cases that overlap both categories. In the present example $p$(A or B) is:

$$p(\text{A or B}) = p(\text{A}) + p(\text{B}) - p(\text{A and B})$$

$$p(\text{A or B}) = \frac{354}{5900} + \frac{236}{5900} - \frac{118}{5900}$$

$$p(\text{A or B}) = .06 + .04 - .02$$

$$p(\text{A or B}) = .08$$

We can apply the logic of this procedure to all the cells in Table 10.4.

## 10.6 Conditional Probabilities

**N**ow that we have examined the basics of probability calculations, we are ready to examine more complex probability topics. Specifically, we will examine **conditional probabilities**. We use conditional probabilities when the categories or groups are not mutually exclusive. Consider an example. In the population there are people who suffer from depression, people who suffer from substance dependence, and people suffering from both. Because a person can be depressed and substance dependent, we would say that the categories are not mutually exclusive.

When we examine conditional probabilities we want to know the probability of a specific event given the existence of another condition. Using our example of drug and alcohol abuse, we can ask, "What is the probability that someone will abuse alcohol if they also abuse drugs?" A different question we can ask is "What is the probability that someone will abuse drugs if they abuse alcohol?" Although these questions may sound as if they ask the same thing, they are quite different. The first question could be reworded as "If a person is abusing drugs, what is the probability that he or she is abusing alcohol?" Rewording the second question would be, "If a person is abusing alcohol what is the

■ **Conditional Probability:**

The probability of an event that is dependent upon the presence of another event.

probability that they will abuse drugs?" As we will see, the answers to these questions are very different.

It is easy to convert a conditional probability question into a mathematical statement. Take the question "What is the probability that someone will abuse alcohol if they also abuse drugs?" In mathematical terms we write $p(A \mid B)$. The vertical line ($\mid$) represents the phrase "given the condition." Therefore, we can read the equation $p(A \mid B)$ as "probability of A given the condition B." The following equation represents the different conditional probability questions we can raise and their solutions.

$$p(A \mid B) = \frac{p(A \text{ and } B)}{p(B)}$$

$$p(A \mid \text{not } B) = \frac{p(A \text{ and not } B)}{p(\text{not } B)}$$

$$p(\text{not } A \mid B) = \frac{p(\text{not } A \text{ and } B)}{p(B)}$$

$$p(\text{not } A \mid \text{not } B) = \frac{p(\text{not } A \text{ and not } B)}{p(\text{not } B)}$$

(10.4)

$$p(B \mid A) = \frac{p(A \text{ and } B)}{p(A)}$$

$$p(B \mid \text{not } A) = \frac{p(\text{not } A \text{ and } B)}{p(\text{not } A)}$$

$$p(\text{not } B \mid A) = \frac{p(A \text{ and not } B)}{p(A)}$$

$$p(\text{not } B \mid \text{not } A) = \frac{p(\text{not } A \text{ and not } B)}{p(\text{not } A)}$$

Let's put the concept of conditional probabilities into action. Table 10.5 presents the conditional probabilities of the different conditions given the presence of alcohol abuse. As you can see $p(B \mid A) = .3333$. From this conditional probability we can conclude that if someone abuses alcohol, there is a 33.33% chance that they will also abuse drugs. In addition, the probability that some people will abuse drugs and not abuse alcohol is remote because $p(B \mid \text{not } A) = .0213$ or 2.13%.

**Table** | **10.5**

**An Example of Conditional Probabilities***

| | CONDITION OF CLIENT | |
|---|---|---|
| | **Alcohol Abuse (A)** | **No Alcohol Abuse (not A)** |
| Drug abuse (B) | $p(B \mid A)$ .02/.06 = **.3333** | $p(B \mid \text{not } A)$ .02/.94 = **.0213** |
| No drug abuse (not B) | $p(\text{not } B \mid A)$ .04/.06 = **.6667** | $p(\text{not } B \mid \text{not } A)$ .92/.94 = **.9787** |
| | $p(A)$ .06/.06 = **1.00** | $p(\text{not } A)$ .94/.94 = **1.00** |

*In this example, all probabilities are conditional on the presence or absence of Condition A.

**Table** 10.6

An Example of Conditional Probabilities*

| | CONDITION OF CLIENT | | |
|---|---|---|---|
| | Alcohol Abuse (A) | No Alcohol Abuse (not A) | |
| Drug abuse (B) | $p(A \mid B)$ <br> .02/.04 = **.5000** | $p(\text{not } A \mid B)$ <br> .02/.04 = **.5000** | $p(B)$ <br> .04/.04 = **1.00** |
| No drug abuse (not B) | $p(A \mid \text{not } B)$ <br> .04/.96 = **.0417** | $p(\text{not } A \mid \text{not } B)$ <br> .92/.96 = **.9583** | $p(\text{not } B)$ <br> .96/.96 = **1.00** |

*In this example, all probabilities are conditional on the presence or absence of Condition B.

Table 10.6 presents the same data, but uses the existence of drug abuse as the conditional event. As you can see, this table offers us a different perspective on the relation between alcohol and drug abuse. For example, what is the probability that there will be alcohol abuse if there is drug abuse? From the table, $p(A \mid B) = .50$. In words, this means that if someone abuses drugs, there is a 50% chance that they also abuse alcohol. The fact that $p(B \mid A) \neq p(A \mid B)$ is important. The inequality reflects the fact that conditional probabilities are not symmetrical. In our example, we might find that people who abuse drugs have a high probability of also abusing alcohol. The opposite is not true however, people who abuse alcohol are not as likely to abuse drugs.

Before we close this section of the chapter, we need to examine a special form of the multiplication rule. As you recall, when two events are mutually exclusive, we can determine the joint probability by taking the product of the two probabilities (e.g., $p(A \text{ and } B) = p(A) \times p(B)$). When the events are not mutually exclusive, we need to use the conditional probability and the probability of the event. For example, if we want to know the probability of randomly selecting a client who abuses alcohol and drugs, we use $p(A \text{ and } B) = p(A \mid B)p(A)$. In Table 10.7, we converted the conditional probabilities to joint probabilities. The obvious feature of the table is that the joint probabilities match those presented in Table 10.3.

**Table** 10.7

An Example of Determining Joint Probabilities Using Conditional and Marginal Probabilities

| | CONDITION OF CLIENT | | |
|---|---|---|---|
| | Alcohol Abuse (A) | No Alcohol Abuse (not A) | Marginal Probability |
| Drug abuse (B) | $p(A \text{ and } B)$ <br> .3333 × .06 = **.02** | $p(\text{not } A \text{ and } B)$ <br> .0213 × .94 = **.02** | $p(B) =$ **.04** |
| No drug abuse (not B) | $p(A \text{ and not } B)$ <br> .6667 × .06 = **.04** | $p(\text{not } A \text{ and not } B)$ <br> .9787 × .94 = **.92** | $p(\text{not } B) =$ **.96** |
| Marginal probability | $p(A) =$ **.06** | $p(\text{not } A) =$ **.94** | **1.00** |

---

**Multiplication Rule for Dependent Events:**
The probability of obtaining a specific sequence of dependent events is the product of the probability of the event and the conditional probability.

$$p(A \text{ and } B) = p(B \mid A) \, p(A) \tag{10.5}$$

---

## 10.7 The Probability of Discrete Sequences: The Binomial Distribution

There are many times when researchers examine the sequence of discrete outcome events. For example, in a clinical study, we may want to know the number of clients who were cured by a treatment and the number who were not cured. In the classroom, a teacher may want to know how many students correctly answered a question and how many did not. In both these examples, we see an example of a discrete variable. Moreover, this variable has just two levels (e.g., 1 = cured or correct, 0 = not cured or incorrect).

Let's take a concrete example. Imagine that you receive a quiz containing 10 true-false questions. To make things more interesting, imagine that the test asks questions about some obscure topic you have never studied. How will you do on the test? What is the probability that you will guess at least 7 of the 10 correctly? What about answering correctly 6 of the 10 questions? Do you have any chance of getting all 10 correct? The answer to these questions comes to us using an important statistical tool, the binomial distribution.

In essence, the binomial distribution describes the probability of different sequences of outcomes for a series of independent trials where each trial has two outcomes. We can use the binomial distribution to predict your performance on the test. First, your test score is a discrete variable. Your answer to each question is correct or incorrect. Consequently, your total score is also a discrete variable. Second, we can assume that your answer to each question is independent of the previous questions. This assumption is fair to make if you know nothing about the topic. Reading one question should do nothing to help you solve another question.

The formula that describes the binomial distribution is:

$$p(X) = \frac{N!}{X!(N-X)!} \, p^X q^{N-X} \tag{10.6}$$

where
    $X$ = Number of specified outcomes.
    $N$ = The number of events in the sample space.
    $!$ = Factorial symbol. The product of all integers between 0 and $X$. We set $0! = 1$. $5! = 5 \times 4 \times 3 \times 2 \times 1 = 120$.
    $p$ = Probability of a positive outcome. Typically, we use $p$ to represent the presence of the variable.
    $q$ = Probability of a negative outcome. The value of $q$ is always the complement of $p$. Specifically, $q = 1 - p$.

**Table** 10.8

**An Example of How to Calculate the Probabilities of Specific Events Described by a Binomial Distribution***

| Number Correct X | X! | X!(N − X)! | A $\dfrac{N!}{X!(N-X)!}$ | B $p^X$ | C $q^{N-X}$ | A × B × C = p(X) |
|---|---|---|---|---|---|---|
| 0 | 1 | 3628800 | 1 | 1.000000 | .000977 | .0010 |
| 1 | 1 | 362880 | 10 | .500000 | .001953 | .0098 |
| 2 | 2 | 80640 | 45 | .250000 | .003906 | .0440 |
| 3 | 6 | 30240 | 120 | .125000 | .007813 | .1172 |
| 4 | 24 | 17280 | 210 | .062500 | .015625 | .2051 |
| 5 | 120 | 14400 | 252 | .031250 | .031250 | .2461 |
| 6 | 720 | 17280 | 210 | .015625 | .062500 | .2051 |
| 7 | 5040 | 30240 | 120 | .007813 | .125000 | .1172 |
| 8 | 40320 | 80640 | 45 | .003906 | .250000 | .0440 |
| 9 | 362880 | 362880 | 10 | .001953 | .500000 | .0098 |
| 10 | 3628800 | 3628800 | 1 | .000977 | 1.000000 | .0010 |

*For this binomial distribution, $N = 10$ and $p = .5$

$7 \times 6 \times 5 \times 4 + 3 \times 2 \times 1$       $5040 \left( 1 - 10 \right)$

In our example, we assume that you guess the answer to each question. Therefore, the probability that you will give a correct answer for any question is $p = .50$. We can use this information to create the binomial distribution. Table 10.8 and Figure 10.3 represent the numerical and graphical versions of the binomial distribution. As you can see, you are most likely to score 5 out of 10 items on this exam. We can calculate the mean and standard deviation of the binomial distribution using Equations 10.7 and 10.8.

$$\mu = Np \quad \textit{Mean} \tag{10.7}$$

$$\sigma = \sqrt{Npq} \quad \textit{Sd} \tag{10.8}$$

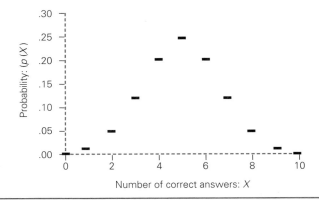

**Figure** 10.3

The frequency distribution of the data presented in Table 10.8. For this binomial distribution, $N = 10$ and $p = .5$

What is the probability that you will score a C, or 70%? According to our calculations, $p(7) = .1172$, or 11.72%. The probability that you will score *at least* a C will include the possibility of scoring even higher.

We can use the addition rule and Table 10.8 to solve a number of specific questions. What is the probability that you will score 6 or greater?

$$p(X \geq 6) = p(6) + p(7) + p(8) + p(9) + p(10)$$

$$p(X \geq 6) = 0.2051 + 0.1172 + 0.0440 + 0.0098 + 0.001$$

$$p(X \geq 6) = .3771$$

You have a 37.71% chance of earning a score of 6 or greater. What is the probability that you and your roommate will get a score of 6 or greater?

$$p(X \geq 6 \text{ and } X \geq 6) = .3771 \times .3771$$

$$p(X \geq 6 \text{ and } X \geq 6) = .1422$$

There is a 14.22% chance that you and your roommate will get a score of 6 or greater.

Now, let's make things interesting. Imagine that you now have 10 multiple-choice questions, each with five alternative answers. Again, we will assume that you know nothing about the subject matter. Therefore, we can assume that each question represents an independent trial and that the chance of guessing any one item correctly is $p = 1/5 = .20$. Table 10.9 and Figure 10.4 represent the results of this scenario.

As you can see, the value of $p$ changes the shape of the distribution of the binomial distribution. Specifically, when $p = .5$ the distribution is symmetrical. When $p < .5$ there will be a positive skew. In contrast, when $p > .5$ the distribution will have a negative skew.

## Relation Between the Binomial and Normal Distributions

As you can see in Figure 10.3, the binomial distribution appears to be relatively bell-shaped when $p = .5$. In fact, the binomial distribution is a fair approximation of the normal distribution. This approximation

**Table 10.9**

**An Example of How to Calculate the Probabilities of Specific Events Described by a Binomial Distribution***

| Number Correct X | X! | X!(N − X)! | A $\dfrac{N!}{X!(N-X)!}$ | B $p^X$ | C $q^{N-X}$ | A × B × C = p(X) |
|---|---|---|---|---|---|---|
| 0 | 1 | 3628800 | 1 | 1.000000 | .107374 | .10737 |
| 1 | 1 | 362880 | 10 | .200000 | .134218 | .26844 |
| 2 | 2 | 80640 | 45 | .040000 | .167772 | .30199 |
| 3 | 6 | 30240 | 120 | .008000 | .209715 | .20133 |
| 4 | 24 | 17280 | 210 | .001600 | .262144 | .08808 |
| 5 | 120 | 14400 | 252 | .000320 | .327680 | .02642 |
| 6 | 720 | 17280 | 210 | .000064 | .409600 | .00551 |
| 7 | 5040 | 30240 | 120 | .000013 | .512000 | .00079 |
| 8 | 40320 | 80640 | 45 | .000003 | .640000 | .00007 |
| 9 | 362880 | 362880 | 10 | .000001 | .800000 | .00000 |
| 10 | 3628800 | 3628800 | 1 | .000000 | 1.000000 | .00000 |

*For this binomial distribution, $N = 10$ and $p = .2$

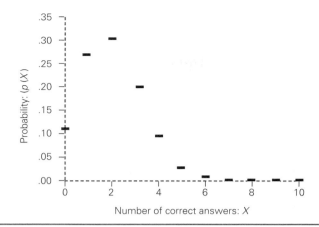

**Figure | 10.4**

The frequency distribution for the data presented in Table 10.9. For this binomial distribution, **N** = 10 and **p** = .2

becomes more accurate as sample size increases. As a generality, when $N \times p \times q \geq 9$, the binomial distribution will approximate a normal distribution.

Although these facts may not be the most exciting things you learned today, they are extremely important. Because the binomial distribution will approximate the normal distribution when $N \times p \times q \geq 9$, we can use everything we learned about the normal distribution to solve problems related to the binomial distribution. When $N \times p \times q \geq 9$, we can use Equation 10.9 to convert an observed score to a z-score.

$$z = \frac{X - Np}{\sqrt{Npq}} \qquad (10.9)$$

Recall that for the binomial distribution, $\mu = Np$ and $\sigma = \sqrt{Npq}$. Therefore, this form of the z-score is exactly like the one you learned in Chapter 6.

We can close this section with a brief example. Assume that you randomly select 100 students from your campus. Also, assume that there are equal numbers of men and women on your campus. Given these assumptions, determine the mean and standard deviation of the binomial distribution.

Given:

| Sample Size | Proportion of Men | Proportion of Women |
|---|---|---|
| N = 100 | p = .50 | q = .50 |

Then:

$\mu = Np \qquad \sigma = \sqrt{Npq}$

$\mu = 100 \times .50 \qquad \sigma = \sqrt{100 \times .50 \times .50}$

$\mu = 50.0 \qquad \sigma = 5.0$

mean        stndrd deviation

Knowing that $\mu = 50$ and that $\sigma = 5.0$, we can convert any score between 0 to 100 to a z-score. Table 10.10 presents several examples on the

**Table | 10.10**

**An Example of How to Convert X to z for a Binomial Distribution***

| X | z |
|---|---|
| 43 | $-1.4 = \dfrac{43 - 50}{5}$ |
| 50 | $0.0 = \dfrac{50 - 50}{5}$ |
| 55 | $1.0 = \dfrac{55 - 50}{5}$ |

*In this example $\mu = 50$ and $\sigma = 5$

conversion of X to z for the binomial distribution. In the next section we will show you how to convert a z-score into a probability.

## 10.8 The Probability of Continuous Variables: The Normal Distribution

Earlier in this book we introduced you to the normal distribution. In Chapter 6 we introduced you to the z-score and how you could use the z-score to determine the area under the normal distribution. As you might guess, you were learning how to use z-scores to determine probabilities. Now that you have a better understanding of the concept of probability, we can combine your knowledge of z-scores with your understanding of probability. Learning how to determine probability using the normal distribution will help you master other skills presented later in this book.

*Example 1* A student takes a standardized test with a mean of 100 and a standard deviation of 15: $\mu = 100$, $\sigma = 15$. What is the probability of randomly selecting a person with a test score of 130 or greater?

First, draw a sketch of a normal distribution and indicate the approximate location of the criterion score of 130. You can also shade in the region of the curve representing scores greater than 130 as we did in Figure 10.5.

Now we convert the criterion score (130) into a z-score:

$$z = \frac{X - \mu}{\sigma} \qquad z = \frac{130 - 100}{15} \qquad z = 2.00$$

Turn to Table A from Appendix D. Because the criterion score is above the mean and we want to calculate the probability of getting a score at or beyond 130, we will use Column C. According to the table, the probability of the proportion of the curve that is more than 2.00 standard deviations beyond the mean is .0228. Therefore, the probability of selecting an individual with a score of 130 or greater is $p = .0228$.

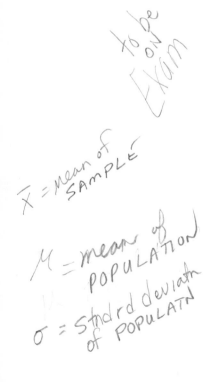
to be on Exam

$\overline{X}$ = mean of SAMPLE

$\mu$ = mean of POPULATION

$\sigma$ = Standrd deviatn of POPULATN

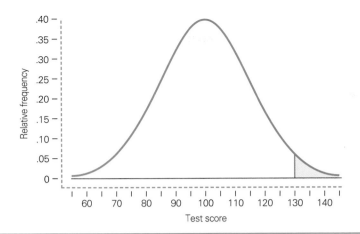

**Figure** 10.5

Illustration of Example 1. The shaded area represents the proportion of area above a score of 130 in a normal distribution with $\mu = 100$, $\sigma = 15$.

***Example 2*** A student takes a standardized test with a mean of 100 and a standard deviation of 15: $\mu = 100$, $\sigma = 15$. What is the probability of selecting at random an individual with a test score of 95 or greater? We can use the same steps to answer the question.

First, draw a graph of the conditions we have described (Figure 10.6). As you can see, a score of 95 is below the mean, therefore our $z$-score will be a negative value. Indeed,

$$z = \frac{95 - 100}{15} \qquad z = -0.33$$

Because we want to find the proportion of the normal curve at and above 95 we need to follow two steps. First, what is the proportion of the curve between a $z$-score of $-0.33$ and the mean? The answer is in Column B of the Table of Normal Distributions. The proportion of the curve

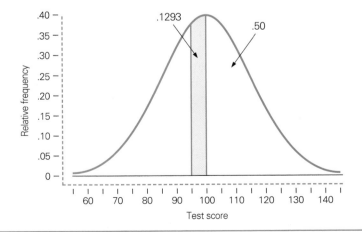

**Figure** 10.6

Illustration of Example 2. The shaded area represents the proportion of the area between $X = 95$ and the mean in a normal distribution with $\mu = 100$, $\sigma = 15$.

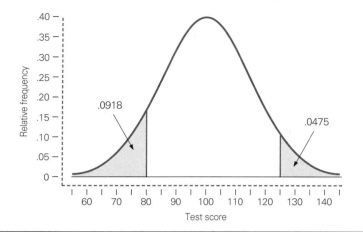

**Figure** | **10.7**

Illustration of Examples 3 and 4. The left-most shaded area represents the area of the normal distribution less than 80. The right-most shaded area represents the area of the normal distribution greater than 125. We assume that $\mu = 100$, $\sigma = 15$.

between the criterion score and the mean is .1293. What is the proportion of the normal curve that is greater than the mean? You should remember that the answer is .5 because the mean of a normal distribution is also the median of the distribution. We can now add the two proportions: .1293 + .5 = .6293. Therefore, the probability of selecting someone with a score of 95 or greater is $p = .6293$.

**Example 3**   Using the same information from Example 1, suppose we wanted to know the probability of selecting at random a person whose score is at or below 80 or a person whose score is at or above 125.

First, draw a sketch of the data as in Figure 10.7. As you can see, we have to calculate two probabilities. The first probability is associated with selecting a score less than 80, the second probability is associated with a score greater than 125. To begin, we convert each criterion score into a z-score, and the z-score into the appropriate probability:

$$z = \frac{80 - 100}{15} = -1.33 \qquad z = \frac{125 - 100}{15} = 1.67$$

$$p(X \le 80) = .0918 \qquad p(X \ge 125) = .0475$$

Using the addition rule we can solve the problem by adding the two probabilities.

$$p(X \le 80 \text{ or } X \ge 125) = p(X \le 80) + p(X \ge 125)$$

$$p(X \le 80 \text{ or } X \ge 125) = .0918 + .0475$$

$$p(X \le 80 \text{ or } X \ge 125) = .1393$$

Because the two probabilities are mutually exclusive, we do not have to determine the joint probability.

**Example 4**   For the last example we will need to use the multiplication rule. In this situation we will randomly sample, record the scores, replace the person in the population, and select another random sample. What is the probability of selecting three people with a test score of 125 or greater?

We know that the probability of selecting a score of 125 or greater is $p(X \geq 125) = .0475$. Consequently, the probability of selecting three such cases in a row is

$$p(X \geq 125) = p(X \geq 125) \times p(X \geq 125) \times p(X \geq 125)$$

$$p(X \geq 125) = (.0475) \times (.0475) \times (.0475)$$

$$p(X \geq 125) = .000107$$

In other words, the probability of selecting three such scores is approximately 1 in 9,346 (9345.7944 = 1/.000107).

## CHAPTER S UMMARY

We began the chapter describing the various approaches to probability, subjective probability, classical probability, and empirical probability. The review of subjective probability examined many of the common errors people make when thinking about statistics. The more common errors are the Gambler's Fallacy, Self-Fulfilling Prophecies, and the "Man-Who" statistic. These common errors reveal that many people's "common sense" ideas about probability are wrong. Consequently, people tend to make mistakes when they rely upon their subjective impressions of probabilities. For this reason, and many others, researchers prefer to use the formal mathematics that supports the analysis of probability.

Classical probability defines the basic rules for determining the probability of different events. We use these rules in most statistical tests and procedures. The basic rules that you need to learn for this course are the rules of addition and multiplication. These skills are useful throughout the text.

Empirical probability is an extension of classical probability. In all research, we do not know the parameters of a population. Therefore, we must use samples to estimate the population parameters. Using sampling techniques such as random sampling, systematic sampling, and stratified sampling, we can ensure that the sample is an unbiased representation of the population. Using the rules of probability derived from classical probability, we can then determine the likelihood of different events in our data.

You also learned about two important ways to determine probability. First, you learned how to use the binomial distribution. The binomial distribution is extremely useful for describing discrete variable data. We will see the use of the binomial distribution again in Chapter 17. You also learned how to use the normal distribution and the $z$-score to determine the probability of events measured with a continuous scale.

As you progress through the following chapters, you will see that probability is at the heart of statistics. Specifically, you will see how we use classical and empirical probability to make conclusions about our data. We call these conclusions inferences, and the statistics, inferential statistics.

## TERMS TO REMEMBER

addition rule

classical definition of
   probability

conditional probabilities

empirical definition of
   probability

joint probability

marginal probabilities

multiplication rule for
   independent events

multiplication rule for
   dependent events

sample space

statistical generalization

subjective probability

## EXERCISES

1. Mr. and Mrs. Smyth want a large family. So far they have five children, all boys. Mrs. Smyth is pregnant with another child. Mr. Smyth is sure that the next child will be a girl and says that the odds are in favor of a girl being born. Is Mr. Smyth correct to assume that the next child is more likely to be a girl? Defend your answer.

2. Dr. Jones gives unannounced quizzes. She tells the class that she uses a random number table to determine whether to give a quiz. For the past 3 weeks Dr. Jones has given the quiz on Monday. It is late Sunday afternoon, and Mark is about ready to study. His roommate says that there is a great movie on television. Mark decides that there is very little chance that there will be a quiz tomorrow and decides to watch the movie. Is Mark's conclusion about the quiz correct? Defend your answer.

3. Mary is taking a general biology course. In class her professor starts a lecture on environmental toxins. The professor states, "Of course, you all know that smoking is a serious health risk and leads to lung cancer." Mary objects to the professor's conclusion. She notes that her 85-year-old grandfather has been smoking two packs of cigarettes a day for the past 65 years and is still in relatively good health. Has Mary provided a good argument against her professor's claim?

4. Alexander is trying to tell his son about the importance of a college education. To persuade his son he cites the general statistic that the annual income of the average college graduate is many thousand dollars greater than that of the average high school graduate. Alex Jr. says "No way. Dave Thomas, the founder of Wendy's, doesn't have a high school education and look at where he is. In addition, Bill Gates, the cofounder of Microsoft, is the richest man in the United States and he dropped out of college. All I need is a lot of spunk and energy and I'll be real successful without a college education." Does Alex Jr. have a good point and counterargument?

5. The registrar of a large university wants to conduct a survey of transcripts. For the study the registrar needs a representative sample of the student population. The university is divided into four colleges. According to current records, the enrollment in each of the colleges is

| | |
|---|---|
| College of Arts and Sciences | 12,546 |
| College of Business | 8,534 |
| College of Education | 2,543 |
| College of Engineering | 10,343 |

*(handwritten: 12,546 ÷ 33966 = .3694 or 36.94%)*

Use this information to answer the following questions.
   **a.** What is the probability of selecting, at random, a student from each of the four colleges?
   **b.** Assume that the registrar decides to use simple random sampling. How would the students be selected? What are some advantages and disadvantages of this procedure?
   **c.** The registrar decides to select 1,000 records and tells the staff to "pull" every 333rd transcript. What is this selection procedure called? What are some of the relative advantages and disadvantages of this procedure?
   **d.** Someone suggests that the registrar use stratified random selection. How would this procedure be executed? What would be the advantage of such a method?

**6.** Which of the following selection techniques will result in a true random sample? Explain your answers. If you believe that the sampling technique is not random, what would you do as an alternative?
   **a.** *Population:* Students attending a college. *Sampling technique:* Select every fifth person enrolled in Psychology 101.
   **b.** *Population:* Viewers of a talk show. *Sampling technique:* Select at random half of the studio audience for one evening chosen at random.
   **c.** *Population:* All children in a suburban high school. *Sampling technique:* Have each homeroom teacher select one student from the class.
   **d.** *Population:* Voters in a congressional district. *Sampling technique:* Calling a randomly selected group of voters on a Saturday.

**7.** Imagine that there is a bowl filled with an equal number of three types of colored balls—red, white, and blue. Assume that Peggy selects one ball at random, records the color of the ball, returns it to the bowl, and then randomly selects another ball. Use this information to complete the following. What is the probability that Peggy will select
   **a.** two white balls?
   **b.** two balls of the same color?
   **c.** one red ball and one white ball?

**8.** Rebecca is a marketing major. She is studying the effects of advertising on buying habits. A large retail store printed an advertisement in the local newspaper announcing a large sale. Rebecca surveys 150 randomly selected customers who enter the store the day after the advertisement appears. According to the survey, 83 people entering the store said they had seen the advertisement. Her survey data also reveal that 66 people made purchases, 32 of whom had seen the advertisement. Use this information to complete the following.
   **a.** Draw a Venn diagram that illustrates the shoppers in the survey who saw the advertisement and the shoppers who made purchases.
   **b.** What percentage of the surveyed shoppers saw the advertisement?
   **c.** What percentage of the surveyed shoppers made a purchase?
   **d.** What percentage of the surveyed shoppers saw the advertisement and made a purchase?
   **e.** What percentage of the surveyed shoppers who made a purchase did not see the advertisement?

**9.** A social psychologist studied the relation between physical attractiveness and helping behavior. The person in need of help was a male whose appearance was either normal (regular clothes, clean) or unattractive (filthy clothes, unwashed hair), and the subjects were female students. The results are shown in the accompanying table.

| Response | Normal (A) | Unattractive (not A) | Row Total |
|---|---|---|---|
| Helped (B) | 19 | 13 | 32 |
| Did not help (not B) | 22 | 27 | 49 |
| Column total | 41 | 40 | 81 |

   **a.** Prepare a joint probability table of the results.
   **b.** Calculate the conditional probabilities of the B events given A.
   **c.** Calculate the conditional probabilities of the A events given B.

**10.** A psychologist conducted a longitudinal study of 272 couples who sought pre-marriage counseling. The psychologist examined whether the man was ever physically abusive toward the woman before the marriage and 30 months into the marriage.

**AGGRESSION: PRIOR TO MARRIAGE**

| Aggression: 30 Months of Marriage | Yes (A) | No (not A) | Row Total |
|---|---|---|---|
| Yes (B) | 37 | 31 | 68 |
| No (not B) | 47 | 157 | 204 |
| Column total | 84 | 188 | 272 |

   **a.** Prepare a joint probability table of the results.
   **b.** Calculate the conditional probabilities of the B events given A.
   **c.** Calculate the conditional probabilities of the A events given B.

**11.** A psychologist conducted a longitudinal study of 98 women who had experienced sexual abuse. The researcher asked whether the women had also experienced physical abuse.

**SEXUAL ABUSE**

| Physical Abuse | Yes (A) | No (not A) | Row Total |
|---|---|---|---|
| Yes (B) | 12 | 36 | 48 |
| No (not B) | 23 | 27 | 50 |
| Column total | 35 | 63 | 98 |

   **a.** Prepare a joint probability table of the results.
   **b.** Calculate the conditional probabilities of the B events given A.
   **c.** Calculate the conditional probabilities of the A events given B.

**12.** A psychologist administered a lie detector test to 306 people who applied for a job. The test identified some people as having lied about having been convicted of a crime whereas the test indicated that the others told the truth. The psychologist then examined police records for evidence of prior convictions.

**APPLICANT'S LEGAL STATUS**

| Lie Detector Test Results | No Record (A) | Conviction (not A) | Row Total |
|---|---|---|---|
| Truth teller (B) | 204 | 12 | 216 |
| Liar (not B) | 69 | 21 | 90 |
| Column total | 273 | 33 | 306 |

**a.** Prepare a joint probability table of the results.
**b.** Calculate the conditional probabilities of the B events given A.
**c.** Calculate the conditional probabilities of the A events given B.

**13.** The proportion of people with type A blood in a city is .20. What is the probability that
   **a.** a given individual, selected at random, will have type A blood?
   **b.** two out of two individuals will have type A blood?
   **c.** an individual selected at random will not have type A blood?
   **d.** two out of two individuals will not have type A blood?

**14.** A researcher has developed a new test for a chemical associated with depression. The advantage of the procedure is that it is inexpensive to administer. The regular test, which is extremely accurate, requires expensive laboratory equipment and takes much time to complete. To test the accuracy of the new test, the researcher selected 385 subjects who are depressed and administered the two tests. Here are the results.

| Sample | New Test | Regular Test |
|---|---|---|
| 385 | 154 Positive | 110 Positive |
| | | 44 Negative |
| | 231 Negative | 30 Positive |
| | | 201 Negative |

**a.** Using these data, calculate the conditional probability that the new test will correctly identify the presence of the chemical.
**b.** What is the conditional probability that the test will fail to detect the chemical?
**c.** What is the probability that the new test will provide a correct result?

**15.** Maleah wanted to conduct a study in which family size was a critical variable. As a preliminary step, she administered a questionnaire to students enrolled in the college's required English Composition course. One question asked the students to indicate the number of brothers and sisters in their family. Use these data to answer the following questions.

**NUMBER OF BROTHERS AND SISTERS**

| | 0 | 1 | 2 | 3 | 4 | 5 | 6 | 7 |
|---|---|---|---|---|---|---|---|---|
| Frequency | 98 | 258 | 57 | 43 | 21 | 18 | 3 | 2 |

.196  .516  .114  .086  .042  .036  .006  .004

$\Sigma = 500$
$\overline{X} = 62.5$

**a.** Convert the frequencies to probabilities.
**b.** If Maleah uses random sampling of students at this college, what is the probability that she will randomly select subjects with
   **i.** 2 or more brothers and sisters.

144

    **ii.** fewer than 2 brothers and sisters.

    **iii.** at least one and lower than 3 siblings.

  **c.** What is the average number of siblings according to these data?

  **d.** Are these data normally distributed or are they skewed?

16. Robert, the registrar of a large university, is interested in the number of times students change their majors. He collects a random sample of 125 students who graduated within the last year and counts the number of times they changed their major. Use these data to answer the following questions.

| | 0 | 1 | 2 | 3 | 4 | 5 | 6 | 7 |
|---|---|---|---|---|---|---|---|---|
| **NUMBER OF CHANGES IN MAJORS** | | | | | | | | |
| **Frequency** | 1 | 5 | 35 | 45 | 23 | 12 | 3 | 1 |

  **a.** Convert the frequencies to probabilities.

  **b.** What proportion of the students changed their major 3 or more times?

  **c.** What proportion of the students changed their major at least twice?

  **d.** What proportion of the students changed their major between 2 and 4 times?

  **e.** What is the average number of major changes according to these data?

  **f.** Are these data normally distributed or are they skewed?

17. Tests of deception typically work by asking a series of questions that represent honest behaviors that few people actually perform. These questions include "I always obey the speed limit when driving" or "I always tell people the truth even if it may hurt their feelings." According to a recent study, when given eight questions of this type and told to answer truthfully, the typical person will agree with two of these statements. Assuming that these data are valid, respond to the following questions.

  **a.** What is the proportion of questions that the typical person will say is true of them (e.g., $p$)?

  **b.** What is the proportion of questions that the typical person will say is not true of them (e.g., $q$)?

  **c.** Using these data, create a binomial distribution that describes potential outcomes.

  **d.** What are the mean and standard deviation of the distribution? What are the probabilities of the following outcomes?

  **e.** $X \geq 4$

  **f.** $X > 5$

  **g.** $X \leq 2$

  **h.** $X \geq 6$

  **i.** Assume that your roommate takes this test and earns a score of 7. Do you think your roommate is answering honestly?

18. In this chapter we saw that we can use the $z$-score to determine the proportion of the normal curve that is within specific ranges. Use Table A of Appendix D to find the proportion of the normal curve that is

  **a.** between a $z$-score of 1.00 and the mean.

  **b.** between a $z$-score of 1.65 and the mean.

  **c.** at or above a $z$-score of 1.65.

  **d.** at or below a $z$-score of 1.65.

  **e.** at or below a $z$-score of $-1.96$.

  **f.** at or above a $z$-score of $-1.96$.

  **g.** between the $z$-scores of $-1.00$ and 1.00.

**h.** between the $z$-scores of $-1.65$ and $1.65$.
**i.** between the $z$-scores of $-1.96$ and $1.96$.

19. Use Table A of Appendix D to find the proportion of the normal curve that is
    **a.** between a $z$-score of $0.50$ and the mean.
    **b.** between a $z$-score of $1.50$ and the mean.
    **c.** at or above a $z$-score of $1.20$.
    **d.** at or below a $z$-score of $1.20$.
    **e.** at or below a $z$-score of $-1.60$.
    **f.** at or above a $z$-score of $-1.60$.
    **g.** between the $z$-scores of $-1.00$ and $0.50$.
    **h.** between the $z$-scores of $-1.65$ and $0.50$.
    **i.** between the $z$-scores of $-1.96$ and $0.50$.

20. In this chapter we saw that we can use the $z$-score to determine the proportion of the normal curve that is within specific ranges. Use Table A of Appendix D to answer the following questions.
    **a.** What $z$-score is associated with the lowest 2.5% of the normal distribution?
    **b.** What $z$-score represents the 25th percentile of the normal distribution?
    **c.** What $z$-score represents the 80th percentile of the normal distribution?
    **d.** What $z$-score is associated with the highest 5% of the normal distribution?
    **e.** What are the upper and lower $z$-scores that represent the interquartile range (the middle 50%) for the normal distribution?
    **f.** What are the upper and lower $z$-scores that represent the middle 95% of the distribution above and below the mean?

21. Use Table A of Appendix D to answer the following questions. What is the probability of obtaining a score whose $z$-score is
    **a.** less than $-3.00$?
    **b.** greater than $-2.00$?
    **c.** less than $-1.96$?
    **d.** greater than $-1.00$?
    **e.** greater than $0.00$?
    **f.** less than $1.96$?

22. Use Table A of Appendix D to answer the following questions. What is the probability of obtaining a score whose $z$-score is
    **a.** greater than $-3.00$?
    **b.** less than $-2.00$?
    **c.** greater than $-1.96$?
    **d.** less than $-1.00$?
    **e.** less than $0.00$?
    **f.** greater than $1.96$?

23. Use Table A of Appendix D to answer the following questions.
    **a.** What $z$-score is associated with the lowest 5% of the normal distribution?
    **b.** What $z$-score represents the 20th percentile of the normal distribution?
    **c.** What $z$-score represents the 75th percentile of the normal distribution?
    **d.** What $z$-score is associated with the highest 10% of the normal distribution?
    **e.** What are the upper and lower $z$-scores that represent the middle 90% of the normal distribution?
    **f.** What are the upper and lower $z$-scores that represent the middle 25% of the distribution above and below the mean?

24. A well-known test of intelligence is constructed to have normally distributed scores with a mean of 100 and a standard deviation of 16.
    a. What is the probability that someone picked at random will have an IQ of 122 or higher?
    b. There are IQs so high that the probability is .05 that they will occur in a random sample of people. Such IQs are beyond what value?
    c. What is the probability that someone picked at random will have an IQ between 90 and 110?
    d. What is the probability of selecting two people at random
        i. with both having IQs of 122 or greater?
        ii. with both having IQs between 90 and 110?
        iii. with one having an IQ of 122 or greater and the other having an IQ between 90 and 110?
    e. An elementary school creates a special curriculum for talented and gifted students. Part of the entry requirement for the curriculum is to be in the 90th percentile for IQ. What IQ score will a child require to be considered for this curriculum?

25. A well-known college entrance test is constructed to have a normally distributed score with a mean of 500 and a standard deviation of 100.
    a. What proportion of all people who take the test will score 150 or higher?
    b. A large state university will admit any applicant who has a score of 550 or greater. What proportion of applications will the college reject because their scores are too low? (Assume that all people who take the test also apply to the university.)
    c. Another state university will admit any applicant who has a score at or above the 45th percentile. What score is required to be admitted to this university?
    d. Nancy scores 664 on the test. Convert her score to a percentile.
    e. Pat scores 405 on the test. Convert Pat's score to a percentile.
    f. What scores on the test are associated with the 25th and 75th percentiles?

26. A well-known test of artistic ability has a mean of 50 and a standard deviation of 2. Assume that the data are normally distributed.
    a. What is the probability that someone picked at random will have a score on this test of 54 or higher?

    What scores are associated with
    b. the 25th percentile?
    c. the 50th percentile?
    d. the 90th percentile?
    e. the 95th percentile?
    f. What is the probability that someone picked at random will have a score on this test between 48 and 52?

    What is the probability of selecting two people at random
    g. with two having scores of 54 or greater?
    h. with two having scores between 48 and 52?
    i. An elementary school creates a special curriculum for talented and gifted students. Part of the entry requirement for the curriculum is to be in the 85th percentile for artistic ability. What test score will a child require to be considered for this curriculum?

# 11

# Introduction to Statistical Inference

# 11.1 / Introduction

■ **Statistical Inference:**

A series of procedures in which data obtained from samples are used to make statements about some broader set of circumstances.

In earlier chapters we discussed samples and populations, sampling, and probability. We will now extend this discussion to examine how we use data obtained from samples to make inferences about populations. More specifically, we will investigate a series of procedures known as **statistical inference.** Using these procedures we draw conclusions and then make statements about the probability that the conclusions are correct.

Take a step back and consider how we make inferences. First, we use bits of information to draw a general conclusion. For example, your roommate returns home one night in a foul mood. You know that he was with his "significant other." You may also know that he has had doubts about the relationship and has talked about breaking up. Based on these "facts" you come to the conclusion that the date did not go well and the relationship has finally ended. Can you be absolutely certain that you are correct? No, you cannot. There is a chance (probability) that you are wrong.

The same lack of certainty is true of any induction or statistical inference. When we conduct research we use small samples or bits of information to make statements about some broader set of circumstances. When we do this we must recognize that there is a probability that other conclusions are correct and our induction is wrong. You are no doubt familiar with weather predictions. When a weather forecaster says that there is an 80% chance of rain, he or she makes a prediction based on a set of observations (e.g., barometric pressure and cloud formation) and his or her previous experience with weather patterns. The 80% chance represents the forecaster's recognition that he or she may have failed to recognize other important factors that contribute to a rain shower.

In all research we make inductions or inferences based on our observations. When we do this we recognize that there is some probability that we will be wrong. Let's begin by looking at some scenarios.

*Psychic abilities:* A friend of yours claims he can predict the future. He suggests that you flip a coin 10 times and he will predict the outcome of each toss. What if your friend gets 5 out of 10 correct? 7 out of 10 correct? All 10 correct? How many would he have to get correct before you infer that he has psychic powers?

*Cause of illness:* You work for your state's public health service. There is concern about the high rate of cancer in a community near a chemical plant. What if the incidence is 1% above the national average? 10% above? 20% above? At what point do you decide that these cases are probably not due to chance but rather due to something in the environment, possibly the chemical plant?

*Treatment effectiveness:* Your clinic is conducting two weight-loss workshops. One workshop uses traditional dietary counseling; the other uses behavioral modification techniques. The clients in the behavior modification group lose an average of two pounds more than the other group. Do you think this approach is superior to the traditional approach? What if the group lost an average of five pounds more? Ten pounds more? How much of a difference in outcome will you need before you decide that one technique is superior to the other?

What do each of these scenarios have in common? In essence you are asking questions about a parameter of a population to which you want to generalize but are unable to study in its entirety. Because many populations can be infinitely large, it may be impossible to study all the members of a population. In each of the scenarios presented above there is a population and a sample. Consider the friend who claims to be able to predict the outcome of a coin toss. Theoretically you could toss the coin an infinite number of times, the population of coin tosses. Your friend, however, wants his abilities examined using a sample of 10 tosses. In the example involving the diet workshops your sample consists of clients who have already received treatment at your facility. The results of your study will determine how all potential clients, the population, will be treated.

In some research settings, the population is a hypothetical entity or what researchers call a **treatment population.** In the typical experiment, the treatment population does not exist except when the experiment is conducted. The research we conduct is an attempt to find out something about the characteristics of the treatment population if it did exist. Here is a concrete example that is also illustrated in Figure 11.1.

A pharmacologist develops a new drug for the treatment of AIDS. There is a real population of people who have contracted AIDS, but there is no population of people who have AIDS *and* are taking the drug. The pharmacologist wants to know what would happen if a group of people who have AIDS receive the drug. From this group, individuals are randomly assigned to one of two groups. The first group, the control group, consists of people with AIDS who receive a placebo. Those individuals assigned to the treatment group receive the experimental drug. Results

**Treatment Population:**

A hypothetical population which exists only when an experiment is conducted. The research is conducted to find out about a characteristic of the treatment population if it did exist.

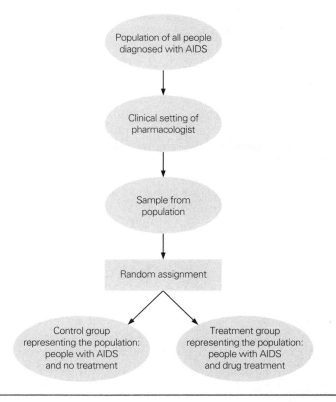

**Figure** | **11.1**

Subjects in the control group represent all people diagnosed with AIDS who receive the placebo. The subjects in the treatment group have AIDS and are treated with the new drug.

obtained from the sample are generalized to the population. This population is, of course, hypothetical because it exists only when we administer the drug. If the research is successful, the pharmacologist will find that the drug does help slow the progression of AIDS. She can conclude that people who have AIDS and take the drug (a population) will be in better health than those who have AIDS and who do not take the drug (another population).

Because populations can rarely be studied exhaustively, we must depend on samples as a basis for arriving at an inference concerning various characteristics, or parameters, of the population. Note that our interest is not in sample statistics per se but in making inferences from sample data.

The question that we need to examine is how we go from calculating basic descriptive statistics to making large and complex inferences about populations and the differences among these populations. We answer this question by examining what is known as inferential statistics. As we will show you in this and subsequent chapters, inferential statistics includes a combination of descriptive statistics, probability, logic, and common sense.

## 11.2 Inferential Procedures

Using sample data to make inferences about a population involves two very different types of procedures. The first consists of *estimating population parameters* and the second involves *hypothesis testing*. As you will see, these procedures evolve from a common set of statistical principles. Let us examine them in greater detail.

### Estimating Population Parameters

When we estimate a population parameter using a sample statistic, the estimate is known as a point estimate. A sample statistic such as a mean ($\overline{X}$) can be used to estimate the population mean which is called $\mu$. We have introduced you to many sample statistics in this text. Each of these sample statistics can be used to estimate a corresponding population parameter. This type of inference is known as **point estimation** because we use the sample statistic to infer the corresponding population parameter. Symbolically we say that $\overline{X} \cong \mu$ or $r \cong \rho$. Examples of point estimation include the following.

■ **Point Estimation:**

Using a sample statistic to estimate the value of the corresponding population parameter.

| Sample Statistic | Population Parameter That Is Estimated | |
|---|---|---|
| $\overline{X}$ | $\mu$ (mu) | Mean of the population |
| $s^2$ | $\sigma^2$ (sigma squared) | Variance of the population |
| $s$ | $\sigma$ (sigma) | Standard deviation of the population |
| $r$ | $\rho$ (rho) | Correlation between populations |
| $b_Y$ | $\beta_Y$ (beta $Y$) | Slope of the regression line |

Because we can estimate the population parameter from the sample, we must recognize that our estimate of the parameter is inexact and may include some error. Is there any way to determine the size of the error we are likely to make with a point estimate? We can't know for sure but we can estimate what our error is likely to be. It is possible to determine the range of potential scores our sample statistic can take using

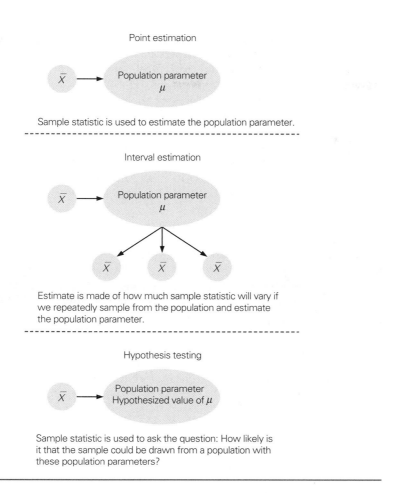

Point estimation

Sample statistic is used to estimate the population parameter.

Interval estimation

Estimate is made of how much sample statistic will vary if we repeatedly sample from the population and estimate the population parameter.

Hypothesis testing

Sample statistic is used to ask the question: How likely is it that the sample could be drawn from a population with these population parameters?

**Figure | 11.2**

**Illustration of point estimation, interval estimation, and hypothesis testing.**

**interval estimation**. Interval estimation allows us to estimate how much the sample statistic would vary if we repeatedly sample from the population. See Figure 11.2 for illustrations of point estimation and interval estimation.

> **Interval Estimation:**
>
> Estimation of the amount of variability in a sample statistic when many samples are taken repeatedly from the same population.

You are probably already familiar with point and interval estimation. During an election, newspapers and television stations conduct voter opinion polls. You may hear on the evening news that according to a national poll of potential voters, 54% are ready to vote for Jones and 46% are ready to vote for Smith. The report then goes on to say that the poll is accurate to within 3 percentage points (i.e., ±3%). The poll suggests that if the election were held immediately, 54% of the votes would be cast for Jones. Therefore, we infer that the final vote for Jones may well be between 51% and 57% (54% ±3%). Is it possible that Jones could lose to Smith? Yes, the sample could be in error and Smith could receive more votes; however, our interval estimation suggests that that outcome is of low probability.

## Hypothesis Testing

Another form of statistical inference is **hypothesis testing.** Our primary concern with hypothesis testing is the comparison of sample results

> **Hypothesis Testing:**
>
> The comparison of sample results with some known or hypothesized population parameters.

with some known or hypothesized population parameters. In some cases we use statistics to compare samples from two or more treatment populations. Consider the example presented earlier in the chapter in which two weight-loss workshops are compared. We want to determine if people who are treated with one form of therapy evidence greater improvement than people treated with another form of therapy. We use the results obtained from the samples to make inferences about the population.

Sometimes we have a single statistic and we want to test a hypothesis. Let's say we have a sample in which we have found a correlation of $r = .36$ between income and favorability rating of a political candidate. It is *possible* that in the population of voters there is no correlation between income and favorability ratings. It is also *possible* that in the population there *is* a correlation between the two variables. We can use hypothesis testing based on our sample to make inferences about the population.

In summary we use point estimation to make inferences about a population parameter. We use interval estimation to make inferences about how much the sample statistic varies. We use hypothesis testing to estimate how likely sample results vary from a known or hypothesized population parameter. In the first two cases we are describing features of the population, in the latter case we are using inferential processes to test a hypothesis. We will examine these concepts in greater detail later. At this point we need to digress in order to examine some principles essential to understanding inferential statistics.

## 11.3 / The Concept of Sampling Distributions

When we conduct research in the behavioral sciences, we use samples of known size drawn from a population of unknown size and shape. We then use descriptive statistics, which describe the characteristics of the sample, to make inferences about the population. But how confident can we be in our inferences? How can we take the results of a small group and generalize to an entire population? If we continue to draw samples of the same size from the population, we are likely to get slightly different values of sample statistics. On one occasion we might by chance select a set of observations that produces an average that is lower than the population. On another occasion we might by chance select a set of observations that produces an average that is higher. Yet another sampling may provide a mix of high and low scores with an average quite close to that of the population. How can we make any conclusions based on this variability? The answer is that we draw conclusions knowing the range of variability we can expect to occur by chance alone. In this section we will show you that we can actually predict how much change will occur in our sampling and then use that information to make point and interval estimates.

The concept that we will examine is known as a sampling distribution. A **sampling distribution** is a theoretical probability distribution of the possible values of some sample statistic that would occur if we were to collect an infinite number of same-sized samples from a population. You are already familiar with a frequency distribution for a sample. Using a frequency distribution, you can determine where the majority of the observations in the sample occur and the percentile rank of the scores. The sampling distribution serves the same function as the frequency distribution (see Figure 11.3).

■ **Sampling Distribution:**

A theoretical probability distribution of the possible values of some sample statistic that would occur if we were to draw an infinite number of same-sized samples from a population.

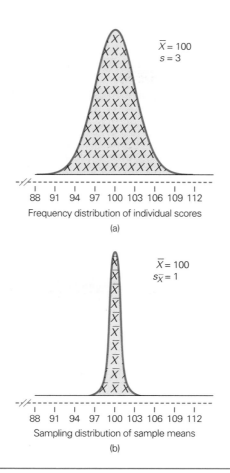

Frequency distribution of individual scores

(a)

Sampling distribution of sample means

(b)

**Figure** | **11.3**

> **Frequency distribution of observed data drawn from a population (a) and a sampling distribution of means (b). The $X$s represent individual scores. $\overline{X}$s represent the means of the samples.**

There are several important differences between frequency distributions and sampling distributions. The first difference is how the two distributions are derived. A frequency distribution is derived *empirically:* We collect real observations and plot the frequency with which each score occurs. A sampling distribution, however, represents a *theoretically* derived distribution. A second difference between the two distributions is the type of data that are plotted. In a frequency distribution, we plot the raw data or individual scores. In a sampling distribution we plot a theoretical distribution of sample statistics. For example, we can develop a sampling distribution of means. To do this we randomly select observations from the population. We then calculate the mean of the sample and then place the means in the sampling distribution. We then repeat the process until the sampling distribution of means is formed.

There is a sampling distribution for every statistic—including means, standard deviations, proportions, and correlations. Furthermore, we can describe these distributions mathematically. As you can see from the definition, a sampling distribution represents what we assume to be true if we could take an infinite number of samples from a population. Sampling distributions are one of the most important concepts in inferential statistics.

Remember when we calculated $z$-scores in order to look at the relative position of an individual score in a distribution? Sampling distributions allow us to look at the relative positions of sample statistics within a hypothetical distribution of sample statistics. Sampling distributions provide us with a benchmark for comparing statistical results. Remember that no number or statistical result can be interpreted independently; it must be placed in some broader context. Just as a single test score is meaningless until we know the mean and standard deviation of the test grades, a statistic is generally meaningless until we know the sampling distribution that represents the population from which that statistic was drawn.

## Discrete Distributions: The Binomial Distribution

We can begin our discussion of sampling distributions with a special type of sampling distribution known as the binomial distribution. The binomial distribution is a special type of distribution used to describe events that have two possible outcomes. Tossing a coin 10 times can be described by a binomial distribution. If you toss a coin 10 times in a row, what could happen? You could get anything from 10 heads in a row to 10 tails in a row. You are also likely to get some patterns of heads and tails that lie somewhere in between these extremes.

As we showed you in Chapter 10, the binomial distribution has a known mathematical formula:

$$p(X) = \frac{N!}{X!(N-X)!} \, p^X (q)^{N-X} \tag{11.1}$$

where
$\quad p(X) =$ probability of $X$
$\quad\quad N =$ number of cases in a sample
$\quad\quad N! =$ factorial for number of cases in a sample
$\quad\quad\quad$ (Note that $5! = (5)(4)(3)(2)(1) = 120$ and $0! = 1$)
$\quad\quad X =$ number of specified outcomes
$\quad\quad p =$ probability of event occurring
$\quad\quad q =$ probability of event not occurring

We can use our coin-tossing example to illustrate the use of the equation. First, we need to predict the probability of some event. For example, what is the probability that in 10 tosses of a coin we will get 5 heads? Because we are tossing the coin 10 times, $N = 10$. We want to know the probability of getting 5 heads, and therefore we let $X = 5$. We can assume that the coin is fair and is equally likely to land heads as tails; therefore, we set $p$ at .5. Using this information and the equation, we can calculate $p(X)$, the probability of getting 5 heads within 10 tosses.

$$p(X) = \frac{N!}{X! \, (N-X)!} \, p^X (q)^{N-X}$$

$$p(5) = \frac{10!}{5!(10-5)!} \, (.5^5)(.5)^{10-5}$$

$$p(5) = \frac{3{,}628{,}800}{120(120)} \, (.03125)(.03125)$$

$$p(5) = .246$$

Therefore, if we were to toss a fair coin 10 times, the probability that we would have 5 heads is $p = .246$.

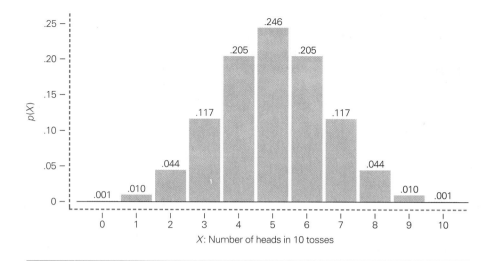

**Figure** | **11.4**

**Histogram of a binomial sampling distribution of various numbers of heads obtained by tossing an unbiased coin 10 times or by tossing 10 coins once.**

Figure 11.4 presents the theoretical sampling distribution for 10 tosses. What can we learn from looking at this graph? First, we can determine the expected probability of each type of outcome. For example, the probability of getting 5 heads in 10 tosses is 24.6%. Second, the distribution is symmetrical, which means that the probability of getting 3 heads (7 tails) is the same as getting 7 heads (3 tails), 11.7%. We can also see that as we deviate from the center of this distribution, the probability of the number of heads decreases. Finally, if you total all the proportions listed in the graph, they will equal 1.00 (within rounding error).

Assume that you decide to test your friend's psychic ability by having him guess the outcome of 10 coin tosses. You toss a coin, catch it in midair, and ask your friend to report heads or tails. If your friend is correct it is a "hit" and if not, it is a "miss." After the 10th toss you add the number of hits and find that your friend was correct 7 times. What does this number mean? We can use the information presented in Table 11.1 to help us interpret the results.

If your friend is just guessing, we would predict that there is a 50% chance ($p = .5$) that he would be correct on each toss of the coin. We know that 7 hits is above what we would expect as an average, but how extraordinary is 7 hits? Looking in Table 11.1, you will see that we have calculated the cumulative probabilities of each of the possible outcomes. The cumulative probabilities will help us interpret the meaning of 7 hits. The column labeled cum $p(10 - X)$ represents the probability of obtaining $X$ or more hits. As you can see, the probability of getting 7 or more hits is .1720 or 17.2%. This value is obtained by adding together from the second column the probabilities of obtaining no hits (.001) plus the probability of getting one hit (.010) plus the probability of two hits (.044), and so on until seven hits.

Do you find this to be impressive evidence of your friend's psychic ability? What if your friend had been correct on 8 of the 10 tosses? The probability of guessing correctly 8 or more times in a series of 10 is .055 or 5.5%. Perhaps such data would provide more convincing evidence. If you

Table | 11.1

**Sampling Distribution of Number of Possible Hits in Tossing a Single Coin 10 Times in a Row and the Cumulative Probability of These Events**

| | | PROBABILITY OF A HIT | |
|---|---|---|---|
| Hits $X$ | $p(X)$ | $X$ or Fewer cum $p(X)$ | $X$ or More cum $p(10 - X)$ |
| 10 | .001 | 1.000 | .001 |
| 9 | .010 | .999 | .011 |
| 8 | .044 | .989 | .055 |
| 7 | .117 | .945 | .172 |
| 6 | .205 | .828 | .377 |
| 5 | .246 | .623 | .623 |
| 4 | .205 | .377 | .828 |
| 3 | .117 | .172 | .945 |
| 2 | .044 | .055 | .989 |
| 1 | .010 | .011 | .999 |
| 0 | .001 | .001 | 1.000 |

were a real skeptic, you might want your friend to be perfectly correct because the probability of 100% accuracy is .001 (0.1%), 1 chance in 1,000.

## Continuous Distributions: The Central Limit Theorem

In most behavioral research we use measures that are continuous rather than discrete. Psychologists, educators, and other researchers in the behavioral sciences are interested in measuring variables that may take on different values. When we conduct research, we sample from the population and calculate a mean for the sample. How should we evaluate the mean? What sampling distribution best represents the means of samples drawn at random from a population? According to the **central limit theorem,** the normal distribution best describes the sampling distribution of means.

Using the central limit theorem, statisticians have developed a wide array of inferential statistics. We can use the central limit theorem for point and interval estimation as well as hypothesis testing. As you will see, the central limit theorem is of fundamental importance in inferential statistics. It states:

> If random samples of a fixed $N$ are drawn from any population (regardless of the shape of the population distribution), as $N$ becomes larger, the distribution of sample means approaches normality, with the overall mean approaching $\mu$, the variance of the sample means $\sigma_{\bar{X}}^2$ being equal to $\sigma^2/N$ and a standard error $\sigma_{\bar{X}}$ of $\sigma/\sqrt{N}$.

Let us examine this important theorem more carefully and the several assumptions that we must make for the theorem to be accepted. First, we will assume that the population has a mean and a standard deviation that are fixed. This means that during our sampling the mean and standard deviation of the population do not change. Second, we assume that our sampling is random, that each unit in the population has an equal probability of being selected. We do not want any *systematic*

**■ Central Limit Theorem:**

If random samples of a fixed $N$ are drawn from any population (regardless of the shape of the population distribution), as $N$ becomes larger, the distribution of sample means approaches normality, with the overall mean approaching $\mu$, the variance of the sample means $\sigma_{\bar{X}}^2$ being equal to $\sigma^2/N$ and a standard error $\sigma_{\bar{X}}$ of $\sigma/\sqrt{N}$.

*bias* in our sampling procedure that would cause the sample means to be artificially inflated or deflated. Finally, we assume that each sample will have the same number of observations. If we can accept these assumptions, we can now present three predictions or propositions derived from the central limit theorem.

---

**Proposition 1:** The mean of the sampling distribution will equal the mean of the population; $\mu_{\bar{X}} = \mu$.

---

The symbol $\mu_{\bar{X}}$ represents the mean of the sampling distribution. For example, if we were to collect 100 samples from a population and calculate the mean of each of these samples, the mean of these sample means would be the mean of the sampling distribution, $\mu_{\bar{X}}$. We can define the mean of the sampling distribution as

$$\mu_{\bar{X}} = \frac{\Sigma \bar{X}}{N_k} \tag{11.2}$$

Note that we sum the mean of each sample ($\bar{X}$) and then divide by the number of means ($N_k$).

This proposition is accurate when we draw many samples from the population, especially as $N$, the size of each sample, approaches infinity. You should be clear about the difference between the *sample size* and the *number of samples* drawn from the population. Sample size refers to the number of observations in each sample, and the number of samples refers to the number of samples drawn from the population. Notice that this proposition says nothing about sample size, mentioning only the number of samples ($N_k$) collected.

---

**Proposition 2:** The sampling distribution of means will be approximately normal, regardless of the shape of the population.

---

This is an interesting and important proposition. It states that the sampling distribution will be approximately normal regardless of the population from which the samples are drawn. The population may be normally distributed, skewed, bimodal, U-shaped, L-shaped, or any other potential configuration, and the sampling distribution will still be normally distributed when the sample size is sufficiently large.

Figure 11.5 presents three populations, a U-shaped, a uniform, and an L-shaped distribution. Below each population is the sampling distribution that will develop when the sample size (number of elements in each sample) is $N = 2$, $N = 4$, and $N = 30$. In each case the mean of the sampling distribution approximates the mean of the population. In addition, as the sample size increases, the sampling distribution of the means becomes more normal. As a generality, the sampling distribution for the means becomes normal with sample sizes of 30 observations or more.

---

**Proposition 3:** The standard deviation of the sampling distribution equals the standard deviation of the population divided by the square root of the sample size; $\sigma_{\bar{X}} = \dfrac{\sigma}{\sqrt{N}}$.

---

In essence this proposition predicts that when the sample size is large, the means will tend to cluster close to the mean of the population.

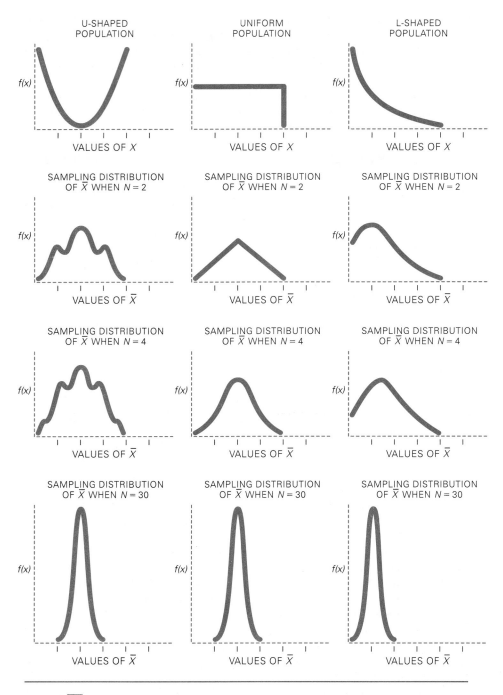

**Figure 11.5**

**Sampling distributions of means of samples $N = 2$, $N = 4$, and $N = 30$ from three different types of populations. These figures illustrate how, regardless of the shape of the parent population, the sampling distribution of means approaches normality as $N$ increases.**

This prediction makes sense. Large samples should give better estimates of the population parameter. Look at Figure 11.5. The population is represented in the top panel. If we select individuals at random, you will see that the distribution of scores equals that for the population. What happens as we begin to make our sample sizes larger, taking 2, 4, or 30 people at a time for each sample? As you can see, the means tend to cluster about the mean of the population, and the standard deviation of the sampling distribution decreases as the sample size increases. These observations suggest that our sample mean will be more representative of the population mean as we increase the sample size. In addition, you can see that the amount of spread in the population ($\sigma$) also affects the amount of spread in the sampling distribution. Clearly, as the population spread gets larger, for any fixed sample size, the standard deviation of the sampling distribution will also increase.

## 11.4 Applications of the Sampling Distribution

On the basis of the central limit theorem we can say that the normal distribution represents the sampling distribution when the sample size is greater than 30. The advantage of knowing this is that we can apply all that we know about standard deviations, $z$-scores, percentiles, and areas under the normal curve to the sampling distribution of the mean. We can begin to examine how this information is used by introducing an important statistical concept, sampling error.

### Sampling Error

Whenever we sample from a population, it is likely that our sample mean will not be *exactly* equal to the population mean. The difference between the sample mean and the population mean, represented as $\overline{X} - \mu$, is due to **sampling error**. In brief, sampling error reflects a host of possible events that can cause the sample mean to be an inexact estimate of the population mean. Almost anything can contribute to sampling error, and sampling error is present in all forms of research.

We assume that all sampling error is random. In other words, the error is as likely to artificially inflate as to decrease the mean. Because sampling error is random, we can assume that the distribution of sampling errors will be normally distributed. Indeed, as you saw in the preceding discussion, if we continually sample from a population, the means of the samples will be normally distributed. Therefore, if we take many samples from the population, we would expect that $\Sigma(\overline{X} - \mu) = 0$. This fact allows us to estimate the range of values the sample mean may take. Let's use an example to illustrate this concept.

Imagine that you drew a sample of 100 subjects from a population. The mean of the sample was 45, and the standard deviation was 3.5. If you took another sample, how much would you expect the next mean to differ from the first? Let's look at what we have learned so far. First, we know that if we were to draw another random sample, the new sample would probably have a slightly different mean. The difference between these means would be due to sampling error, assuming that there is no systematic bias in our sampling or in our measurement of the data. We also know that if we continued to sample from the population, the sampling distribution of means would be randomly distributed with a mean of $\mu_{\overline{X}}$ and a standard deviation of $\sigma_{\overline{X}} = \dfrac{\sigma}{\sqrt{N}}$. Using what we know, we can take a step forward.

You will recall that we previously defined the variance of a sample as

$$s^2 = \frac{\Sigma(X - \overline{X})^2}{N}$$

**Sampling Error:**

The difference between a sample mean and the population mean $\overline{X} - \mu$. Sampling error is assumed to be random and nonsystematic.

The standard deviation, $s$, is the square root of this value. These definitions are perfectly appropriate so long as we are interested only in *describing* the variability of a sample. However, when our interest shifts to *estimating* the population variance from a sample value, we find this definition inadequate, since $\Sigma(X - \overline{X})^2/N$ tends on the average to *underestimate* the population variance. In other words, it provides a **biased estimate** of the population variance.

We define an **unbiased estimate** as an estimate that equals, on the average, the value of the parameter. That is, when we make the statement that a statistic is an unbiased estimate of a parameter, we are saying that the mean of the distribution of an extremely large number of sample statistics, drawn from a given population, tends to center on the corresponding value of the parameter. We now employ the symbol $\hat{s}^2$ to represent a sample variance providing an *unbiased estimate of the population variance*, and $\hat{s}$ to represent a sample standard deviation based on the unbiased variance estimate. Thus

$$\text{Unbiased estimate of } \sigma^2 \cong \hat{s}^2 = \frac{\Sigma(X - \overline{X})^2}{N - 1}$$

and

$$\text{Estimated } \sigma \cong \hat{s} = \sqrt{\hat{s}^2}$$

We are now able to estimate $\sigma_{\overline{X}}^2$ and $\sigma_{\overline{X}}$ from sample data. We don't know them exactly but we have estimates for them. We shall employ the symbols $s_{\overline{X}}$ and $s_{\overline{X}}$ to refer to the estimated variance and standard error of the mean, respectively. Since we do not know $\sigma^2$, we accept the unbiased variance estimate $\hat{s}^2$ as the best estimate we have of the population variance. Thus, the formula for determining the variance of the sampling distribution of the mean from sample data is

$$\text{Estimated } \sigma_{\overline{X}}^2 \cong s_{\overline{X}}^2 = \frac{\hat{s}^2}{N}$$

**■ Biased Estimate:**

An estimate of a population parameter that tends to under- or overestimate that parameter.

**■ Unbiased Estimate:**

An estimate that equals, on average, the value of the corresponding parameter.

**Table** | 11.2

**Summary of Measures of Spread Used to Describe Samples and Populations and to Estimate Spread in Populations and Sampling Distributions**

| Goal | Symbols | How Obtained or Used |
|------|---------|----------------------|
| Describe the spread of a sample | $s, s^2$ | Values are calculated from sample data and used to describe that sample. |
| Estimate the spread of a population | $\hat{s}, \hat{s}^2$ | Values are calculated from sample data in order to estimate the population parameters. |
| Describe the spread of a population | $\sigma, \sigma^2$ | Not estimates but actual parameters of the population. Usually we don't know the population parameters and have to estimate them. |
| Estimate spread in the sampling distribution | $s_{\overline{X}}, s_{\overline{X}}^2$ | Sample variability used to estimate variability in the sampling distribution. |

We estimate the standard error of the mean by finding the square root of this value:

$$\text{Estimated } \sigma_{\overline{X}} \cong s_{\overline{X}} = \sqrt{\frac{\hat{s}^2}{N}} = \frac{\hat{s}}{\sqrt{N}}$$

If the sample variance (not the unbiased estimate) is used, we may estimate $\sigma_{\overline{X}}$ as

$$\text{Estimated } \sigma_{\overline{X}} \cong s_{\overline{X}} = \frac{s}{\sqrt{N-1}} = \sqrt{\frac{\Sigma(X-\overline{X})^2}{N(N-1)}} = \sqrt{\frac{SS}{N(N-1)}}$$

The above formula is the one most frequently employed in the behavioral sciences to estimate the standard error of the mean. We shall follow this practice.

## 11.5 Standard Error of the Mean and Confidence Intervals

We can estimate how much variability there is among potential sample means by calculating the standard error of the mean. The standard error of the mean is calculated as

$$s_{\overline{X}} = \frac{\hat{s}}{\sqrt{N}} \tag{11.3}$$

Notice we are using the <u>unbiased</u> estimate obtained from sample data. The standard error of the mean is thus the standard deviation of the sampling distribution of the means estimated by the sample statistics. In other words, we assume that $s_{\overline{X}} \cong \sigma_{\overline{X}}$. Specifically, we use $s_{\overline{X}}$ as an unbiased estimate of $\sigma_{\overline{X}}$. We can now take another step and develop a confidence interval for our mean.

If we took another sample from the population, would we be able to predict how much the next sample mean is likely to differ from the first? <u>A confidence interval is a probability statement that indicates the likely range of values sample means can take</u>.

Using the example we presented earlier, in which a sample of 100 subjects was drawn from a population and the standard deviation was found to be 3.5, we can determine that the standard error of the mean is

$$s_{\overline{X}} = \frac{s}{\sqrt{N-1}}$$
$$= \frac{3.5}{\sqrt{99}}$$
$$= \frac{3.5}{9.95}$$
$$= .35$$

Now that we have estimated the standard error of the mean, we can construct a confidence interval for the mean. Because the sampling distribution for the mean is normally distributed, and because we have a large sample size, we can use our knowledge of standard scores to create the confidence interval (i.e., $CI_{\bar{X}}$). We know that approximately 68% of a normal distribution lies 1.0 standard deviations above and below the mean. Therefore, the mean plus and minus $s_{\bar{X}}$ represents a 68% confidence interval. That is,

$$45 - .35 = 44.65$$
$$45 + .35 = 45.35$$

Thus, the 68% confidence interval for the mean is 44.65 − 45.35. We can broaden the confidence interval by multiplying by the z-score that represents the percentage of the normal distribution that we want to estimate. Two of the most common confidence intervals are the 95% and the 99% confidence intervals. As you will recall from our discussion of the normal curve, between the z-scores of ±1.96 represents 95% of the distribution about the mean; a z-score of ±2.58 represents 99% of the distribution. We can, therefore, define the confidence interval for the mean as

$$CI_{\bar{X}} = \overline{X} \pm z_{CI}\frac{\hat{s}}{\sqrt{N}} \tag{11.4}$$

It should be noted that this formula is used when we have a sample that is large, when $N$ equals or is greater than one-hundred. Later in this text we will discuss confidence intervals for smaller sample sizes.

We can now create the confidence intervals for the three ranges in probability as shown in Table 11.3. It may be useful to describe the confidence interval using a picture of a normal distribution as in Figure 11.6. Here the mean of the distribution is the mean of our sample, 45. We use the mean of the sample as the mean of the sampling distribution because it is the best estimate of the population mean. The $X$-axis of the distribution indicates the z-scores that correspond to the three confidence intervals and the values based on the sample statistics.

Some words of caution in interpreting the confidence interval. In establishing the interval within which we believe the population mean falls, we have *not* established any probability that our obtained mean is correct. In other words, we cannot claim that the chances are 95 in 100 that the population mean is 45. Our statements are valid only with respect to the interval and not with respect to any particular value of the sample mean. In addition, because the population mean is a fixed value and does not have a distribution, our probability statements never refer to $\mu$. The probability we assert is about the interval—that is, the probability that the interval contains $\mu$.

Finally, we are not saying that there is a .95 probability that the population mean "falls" in the confidence interval. The population mean is constant, it is fixed; it is the intervals that will vary from sample to sample. It should be clear that if we were to select repeated samples from a population, both the sample means and the standard deviations would differ from sample to sample. Consequently, our estimates of the confidence interval would also vary from sample to sample. When we have established the 95% confidence interval of the mean, then we are stating that if repeated samples of a given size are drawn from the population, 95% of the interval estimates will include the population mean.

**Table** | **11.3**

**Example of the 68%, 95%, and 99% Confidence Intervals for Data Where the Mean is 45, the Standard Deviation is 3.5, and the Sample Size is 100**

| | RANGE OF CONFIDENCE INTERVAL | | |
|---|---|---|---|
| | **68%**<br>$z = 1.00$ | **95%**<br>$z = 1.96$ | **99%**<br>$z = 2.58$ |
| | $45 \pm 1.00(0.35)$<br>$= 45 \pm 0.35$ | $45 \pm 1.96(0.35)$<br>$= 45 \pm 0.69$ | $45 \pm 2.58(0.35)$<br>$= 45 \pm 0.90$ |
| Upper limit of CI | 45.35 | 45.69 | 45.90 |
| Lower limit of CI | 44.65 | 44.31 | 44.10 |

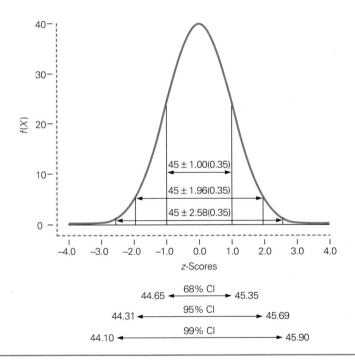

**Figure** | **11.6**

**Illustration of a normal distribution with three common confidence intervals.**

In summary, we see that we can use the concept of sampling distributions to help us make inferences about point and interval estimation. We can now turn our attention to the study of hypothesis testing. As you will see, much of what we have already learned will be applied in hypothesis testing. We will, however, have to introduce some new concepts to explain how hypothesis testing is conducted.

## 11.6
### One- and Two-Tailed Probabilities

In making estimates we frequently try to determine the probability of some event and specifically the probability an event will deviate from an expected outcome. Sometimes we are only interested in whether the outcome will deviate in one direction. We might ask, "What is the probability of getting a score greater than a certain value?" In this case we are asking about the probability of an event that is on one side of the probability distribution. This type of probability is known as a **one-tailed probability value**. "One-tailed" refers to the fact that we are looking at one extreme end of a distribution. When we calculate this probability, we call it the *one-tailed p-value*.

Our question might also be framed as, "What is the probability of getting a score that differs from a certain value?" It could be higher, it could be lower. This type of question is known as a **two-tailed probability value** because we are looking at both tails of the probability distribution—both above and below the mean.

You practiced the skills for determining one- and two-tailed probabilities when you studied the normal distribution and the z-score. We will examine a few examples to refresh your memory.

Let's begin with a one-tailed probability. What is the probability of obtaining a score of 60 or greater? To answer this question, we need to know the mean and the standard deviation of the population from which the score was drawn. In this case, let us assume that $\mu = 50$ and $\sigma = 10$. Recall that we can convert the raw score into a z-score using

$$z = \frac{X - \mu}{\sigma} = \frac{60 - 50}{10} = 1.00$$

Here we are looking at a score that is 10 points above the mean. The standard deviation equals 10. The score is exactly one standard deviation above the mean. We have transformed the observed score of 60 to a z-score of 1.00. Looking at Table A in Appendix D, we find in Column C that 15.87% of the area of the normal distribution is beyond a z-score of 1.00. Thus, the probability of obtaining a score greater than 60 is $p = .1587$ or almost 16%.

Now, let's look at a one-tailed test in another way. What if we decided our probability first and then wanted to determine what score was within that probability? What if we wanted to know the raw score associated with the top 5% of the distribution. Using Table A, we find that when the z-score is 1.64, 5% of the distribution is above that point. Look in Column C to find the area beyond z that contains the value closest to .05; its associated z-score in Column A is 1.64. We can now use the same formula, this time to solve for X rather than z,

$$1.64 = \frac{X - 50}{10}$$

to find that a raw score of 66.4 is the raw score associated with the top 5% of the distribution. In other words, the probability of obtaining a score of 66.4 or higher is $p = .05$.

What about a two-tailed probability? Let's look at the problem stated above. What is the probability of getting a score below 40 or above 60? Both scores are 1.00 standard deviation from the mean. Using Table A

**One-Tailed Probability:**

The probability that an observation will occur at one end of the sampling distribution.

**Two-Tailed Probability:**

The probability that an observation will occur at either extreme of a sampling distribution.

of Appendix D, Column C, we find that the proportion of the normal distribution beyond a $z$-score of 1.00 is .1587. Therefore, 15.87% of the distribution is less than 40 and 15.87% of the distribution is above 60. The answer to our question is that 31.74% of the distribution is beyond these two points.

We can say that the probability of a score less than 40 or greater than 60 is $p = .3174$. Of course, the probability that the score will be within that range is $1 - .3174$ or .6826.

What scores above and below the mean have a 5% probability of being selected? We can use the same procedure we used before. We are asking for the raw scores whose probability, when totaled, represents a total of 5%. To do this we need to divide the probability level in half so that 2.5% is in the top part of the distribution and 2.5% is in the lower part. Specifically, $.05/2 = .025$. We can now follow the familiar steps.

According to Table A of the Appendix, a $z$-score of 1.96 represents the value that when added to or subtracted from the mean, encompasses 95% of the distribution; 2.5% of the distribution is beyond that point on each end. Therefore,

| Lower limit | Upper limit |
|---|---|
| $-1.96 = \dfrac{(X - 50)}{10}$ | $1.96 = \dfrac{(X - 50)}{10}$ |
| $-19.6 = X - 50$ | $19.6 = X - 50$ |
| $-X = +19.6 - 50$ | $-X = -19.6 - 50$ |
| $X = 30.4$ | $X = 19.6 + 50$ |
| | $X = 69.6$ |

The probability of obtaining a score less than or equal to 30.4 is $p = .025$; the probability of obtaining a score greater than or equal to

**Table 11.4**

**Summary of Steps to Take in Calculating One- and Two-Tailed Probabilities and Their Associated z-Scores**

| To Convert | One-Tailed | Two-Tailed |
|---|---|---|
| $z$-score to $p$ | 1. Convert $X$ to a $z$-score.<br>2. Use Table A to find area beyond $z$. | 1. Convert $X$ to a $z$-score.<br>2. Use Table A to find area beyond $z$.<br>3. Multiply area by two. |
| $p$ to $z$-score | 1. Use Table A to find the $z$-score that corresponds to the probability.<br>2. Solve for $X$ using $X = z\sigma + \mu$. | 1. Divide the probability by 2.<br><br>2. Use Table A to find the $z$-score that corresponds to $p/2$.<br>3. Use that $z$-score to find the upper (ul) and lower (ll) limits of $X$:<br>$X_{ll} = -z\sigma + \mu$ and<br>$X_{ul} = z\sigma + \mu$. |

69.6 is $p = .025$. The probability of obtaining a score less than or equal to 30.4 or greater than or equal to 69.6 is $p = .05$.

## 11.7 / Hypothesis Testing

**Conceptual Hypothesis:**

A general statement about the relation between the independent and dependent variables.

**Statistical Hypothesis:**

A statement that can be shown to be supported or not supported. It is designed to make inferences about a population or populations.

Let us talk again about hypothesis testing. There are generally two types of hypotheses, conceptual hypotheses and statistical hypotheses. A **conceptual hypothesis** is a general statement about the relation between the independent and the dependent variables or about the magnitude of observation. A **statistical hypothesis** is a mathematical statement that can be shown to be supported or not supported.

To illustrate the difference between the two types of hypotheses consider an experiment designed to study the effectiveness of an antidepressant. The psychologist may state as the conceptual hypothesis that "the antidepressant decreases the severity of depressive symptoms." In this statement the independent variable (the exposure to treatment) is thought to influence the dependent variable (depressive symptoms). What would the statistical hypothesis look like? To answer this question, we need to look at the experiment.

Twenty-five depressed clients are randomly assigned to a placebo treatment group. Another 25 depressed clients are placed in a treatment group in which they receive an antidepressant.* The subjects in the placebo group represent the population of depressed people who receive no drug, and the subjects in the antidepressant group represent the population of depressed people who receive the antidepressant. Level of depression is measured by a standard psychological test. A high score represents profound depression, and a low score represents the normal mood.

Using this information, the psychologist may form the statistical hypothesis: "Subjects exposed to the antidepressant will have a lower depression score than subjects not exposed to the drug." In many ways the statistical hypothesis is similar to the conceptual hypothesis. In both, the psychologist is saying that the treatment is effective in alleviating depression. The difference is the fact that the statistical hypothesis specifies the mathematical relationship between the two groups. The statistical hypothesis can be converted from words to symbols as $\mu_t < \mu_c$. That is, the mean of subjects in the treatment condition is lower than the mean of the subjects whom we assigned to the control condition. Notice that the hypothesis is stated in terms of population means. We use the population means because we are generalizing to the broader population.

There are two types of hypotheses we can create, directional and nondirectional. In a directional hypothesis the researcher states explicitly the direction of the relation between the populations. Specifically, the researcher states that either $\mu_t < \mu_c$ or $\mu_t > \mu_c$. Directional hypotheses are always associated with one-tailed tests because we can use them to determine whether the predicted score will be above or below the criterion.

In a nondirectional hypothesis the researcher predicts that there will be a difference between the means but is unable to or does not want to predict the exact relation between the means. A nondirectional statistical hypothesis is written as $\mu_t \neq \mu_c$. In this example the researcher can predict that there will be a difference between the two groups but does not want to hypothesize the direction of the difference. As you may have

* Subjects enrolled in studies in which placebos are used must, for ethical reasons, be told beforehand that they may be assigned to a treatment in which the drug or treatment they receive has little or no known therapeutic value.

guessed, nondirectional hypotheses are associated with two-tailed tests.

## 11.8 / Indirect Proof of a Hypothesis

How do we decide when our statistical hypothesis is a correct statement? As we have already seen, we must use the mean of a sample to make inferences about the mean of the population, and sample means are by their nature subject to variability. Another problem is more philosophical—what constitutes adequate evidence to confirm that some statement is true? If your friend claims he has psychic abilities, how much evidence do you need before you decide he might be correct or before you decide his claims are not correct?

### Falsification: Null and Alternative Hypotheses

One of the basic rules of logic is that claims can often be proved false but never proved true. Consider the simple statement, "All crows are black." Can you *prove* this statement true? In fact, you cannot. The word "all" in the statement refers to crows that are currently living, crows that are dead, and crows yet to be hatched. Have you now and will you have the opportunity to observe all crows to confirm this statement to be true? The answer is no. You may be confident that the statement is true because all the crows you have seen are black and therefore make an *induction* that based on your experience the statement is true. Unfortunately, there may be a group of crows that you have never seen that are not black. Indeed, if you found one red crow, your initial statement, "All crows are black," would be proved wrong. Thus, with one disconfirming case you are able to falsify or prove wrong the statement "All crows are black." How does this problem relate to a statistical hypothesis?

The problem is that no statement can ever really be proved to be true, only false. Think about it for a minute. You could flip a coin all day long and have your friend predict if it is heads or tails. He could show himself to be a psychic fraud in the first 5 coin tosses. On the other hand, just because he is correct the first 10 times doesn't mean he will continue to be correct. It is easy to dismiss his claims, but 10 coin tosses don't prove his abilities, nor do 100 or even 1,000 tosses.

In scientific research we use a logical procedure called **modus tollens,** which is also known as the procedure of falsification. *Modus tollens* relies on the fact that a single observation can lead to the conclusion that the premise or prior statement is incorrect. To use *modus tollens* in research, statisticians create two special types of statistical hypotheses, the **null hypothesis ($H_0$)** and the **alternative hypothesis ($H_1$).** The null hypothesis is presented as the prior statement that can be shown to be false with sufficient empirical information. That is, we use the results of the experiment to demonstrate that the statement is false. In its typical form, the null hypothesis is stated to indicate that all conditions are equal. If the null hypothesis is found to be incorrect, we can reject the null hypothesis as false and tentatively accept the alternative hypothesis as being a more accurate statement.

To illustrate, let's use the example of the psychologist studying the effectiveness of an antidepressant by comparing a treatment group with a control group. The null and alternative hypotheses are

$$H_0 : \mu_t = \mu_c$$
$$H_1 : \mu_t \neq \mu_c$$

**Modus Tollens:**

A procedure of falsification that relies on the fact that a single observation can lead to the conclusion that the premise or prior statement is incorrect.

**Null Hypothesis ($H_0$):**

A statement that specifies hypothesized values for one or more of the population parameters. Commonly involves the hypothesis of "no difference."

**Alternative Hypothesis ($H_1$):**

A statement specifying that the population parameter is some value other than the one specified under the null hypothesis.

The null hypothesis states there is no difference between the two means and that the drug treatment has no effect on depression. Does this mean that the two sample means $\overline{X}_t$ and $\overline{X}_c$ will be equal? No. If the null hypothesis is true—the drug had no effect—the differences we observe between $\overline{X}_t$ and $\overline{X}_c$ will be due to sampling error.

If the null hypothesis is false—the drug is effective—the researcher should find that any difference between the two means is too large to be accounted for by chance alone. Therefore, the psychologist has reason to say that the evidence does not support the null hypothesis and that the alternative hypothesis can be accepted as a more accurate description of the two populations.

In the above example, we are interested in testing a null hypothesis ($H_0$) of no difference against the alternative hypothesis ($H_1$) of any difference, whether the treatment is more or less effective. This is a nondirectional test and is sometimes called a two-tailed test. Sometimes we are interested in whether the treatment group differs in a particular direction. Then we would use a directional test:

$$H_0 : \mu_t \geq \mu_c \qquad\qquad H_0 : \mu_t \leq \mu_c$$

$$\text{or}$$

$$H_1 : \mu_t < \mu_c \qquad\qquad H_1 : \mu_t > \mu_c$$

Table 11.5 shows examples of null and alternative hypotheses in correlational, single sample, and two sample research.

Which hypotheses should the researcher use, directional or nondirectional? The answer to this question is not always a straightforward one. In fact, researchers may not agree on the answer. In general, the selection of the hypotheses depends on the type of research being conducted and the degree to which the researcher can predict the outcome of the research. If there is strong evidence to support your belief that the results will come out in a specific way, you might want to consider using directional hypotheses. For example, if you have reason to predict that there will be a positive correlation between two tests you will select the alternative hypothesis $\rho > 0$. Similarly, if you predicted that a sample mean will be less than the population mean you would use the directional alternative hypothesis (i.e., $\mu > 5$). Keep in mind that just because you *hope* to find your treatment group superior to your control

**Table** 11.5

**Examples of Null and Alternative Hypotheses When Directional and Nondirectional Tests Are Used**

| Testing the Significance of | Nondirectional Test | Directional Test |
|---|---|---|
| Correlation: | | |
| $H_0$: | $\rho = 0$ | $\rho \geq 0$ |
| $H_1$: | $\rho \neq 0$ | $\rho < 0$ |
| Single sample mean: | | |
| $H_0$: | $\mu = 5$ | $\mu \geq 5$ or $\mu \leq 5$ |
| $H_1$: | $\mu \neq 5$ | $\mu < 5$ or $\mu > 5$ |
| Two sample means: | | |
| $H_0$: | $\mu_t = \mu_c$ | $\mu_t \geq \mu_c$ or $\mu_t \leq \mu_c$ |
| $H_1$: | $\mu_t \neq \mu_c$ | $\mu_t < \mu_c$ or $\mu_t > \mu_c$ |

group does not mean you should always use a directional hypothesis. In many cases you will not want to predict a specific outcome other than to say that the null hypothesis is not a true statement. In such cases you should use the nondirectional hypotheses.

All researchers establish their null and alternative hypotheses before the data are collected. Many researchers call such hypotheses *a priori* (the Latin phrase meaning "before the fact") tests. If hypotheses are created after the data are collected, there is the chance that their selection will be biased by the outcome of the experiment. We will examine the logic of this requirement shortly; however, it is important to note that honest and ethically responsible researchers state their primary research hypotheses *a priori*.

## 11.9 / Rejecting the Null Hypothesis

We now come to one of the most critical questions in inferential statistics: When do we have sufficient evidence to reject the null hypothesis? Let's return to the example of your friend who claims to have psychic powers. What are your hypotheses in this case? The null hypothesis should be that your friend does not have psychic abilities. We can begin with the null hypothesis as $H_0 : \mu = .5$. The null hypothesis suggests that your friend's ability to predict the outcome of a coin toss is equal to chance. What is your alternative hypothesis? We know that it should be directional because your friend claims that he can do better than chance. Both the null hypothesis and the alternative hypothesis must reflect this directionality. Therefore, $H_0 : \mu \leq .5$ and $H_1 : \mu > .5$. Now the problem. How much better than chance must your friend be for you to reject the null hypothesis in favor of the alternative?

One thing is clear. The *true proportion* of correct responses from your friend can never be known. You could start tossing coins now and have your friend guess the outcome of each toss, and you will never exhaust the population of possible outcomes because the population of coin toss predictions is unlimited.

The fact that the *true values* of the population parameters are unknown does not prevent us from trying to estimate what they are. We can rely on samples to estimate the parameters and use the outcome of our samples to make our conclusion. For example, if your friend makes 5 correct predictions out of a total of 10 predictions, do we suspect that he is psychic? Of course not, because this is exactly what we would predict would occur if he were guessing. What if he is correct 6 times? Again this is not all that unusual. In fact, we have already seen that the probability of getting 6 or more correct guesses is 37.7%.

What about 8 correct guesses or 9 correct responses? Would you be more likely to be impressed? The probability of guessing correctly 8 or more times is 5.5%, a little more than 1 chance in 18 ($1/.055 = 18.18$). The probability of guessing correctly 9 out of 10 times is 1.1%—a probability of a bit more than 1 in 100. Where do we draw the line between deciding between the null hypothesis and the alternative hypothesis?

### Alpha Level and Significance Level

The answer to this question reveals the basic nature of science. Decisions are based on <u>probabilistic rather than definitive</u> information. Therefore, we must determine a probability level where we are willing

■ **Alpha (α) Level:**

The level of significance set by the experimenter. It is the confidence with which the researcher can decide to reject the null hypothesis.

■ **Significance Level:**

The probability value used to conclude that the null hypothesis is an incorrect statement. Common significance levels are .05, .01, and .001.

to reject the null hypothesis and accept the alternative hypothesis. This point is known as the **alpha (α) level** and the cutoff point as the **significance level**.

The researcher chooses the alpha level. It establishes the confidence with which the researcher can decide to reject the null hypothesis. In essence, the researcher states, "if the null hypothesis is true, then the probability of getting results this extreme by chance or sampling error is equal to $\alpha$; this probability is sufficiently small to allow me to conclude that the null hypothesis is an incorrect statement." For the sake of example, let's assume that you agree to establish your significance level at 9 or more correct guesses. You have determined that the probability of guessing correctly 9 or 10 times in a series of 10 guesses is small. In other words, if the null hypothesis is correct (your friend has no psychic abilities), the probability of getting 9 or more correct predictions is small. If your friend does get 9 correct guesses, you must conclude that the results are too unlikely to have occurred by chance. Therefore, you will reject the null hypothesis and accept the alternative hypothesis as correct.

We should note that failure to reject the null hypothesis does not mean that the null hypothesis is correct, merely that we have not collected sufficient information to reject it as a false statement. By the same token, we have not *proved* the alternative hypothesis to be true. When we reject the null hypothesis, we *conditionally* accept the alternative hypothesis as a correct statement. We must recognize that our decision to accept the alternative is based on probability and that further research may require us to further modify our conclusion.

## Comparing $\alpha$ and $p$

The researcher sets the $\alpha$-level to determine when to reject $H_0$ and when not to reject $H_0$. Once $\alpha$ is set, the data can be collected and the probability of the outcome calculated. If $p \leq \alpha$, then reject $H_0$ in favor of the alternative hypothesis. If $p > \alpha$, then we cannot reject $H_0$. For example, if the $\alpha$-level is .05 and the probability of the sample statistic is $p = .02$, then $p < \alpha$ and we can reject the null hypothesis. If $p = .06$ then we cannot reject the null hypothesis because $p > \alpha$.

When $H_0$ is rejected, many researchers write or say that they have statistically significant results. What does the term "statistically significant" really mean? For us it means that the results are worthy of further consideration and discussion. "Statistically significant" is a way of saying, "These results are not likely to be due to chance or random events and are worthy of further analysis." Does "significant" mean "important"? Not necessarily. There are many times when the results can be statistically significant but not all that important. As we will see, many factors contribute to statistical significance including the size of the sample. Using a large sample, it is possible to obtain results that are statistically significant yet have little meaning in everyday life. For example, researchers have found that there is a significant difference between men and women on standardized math tests. Although this difference is significant, the difference between the average scores of men and women is very small relative to the variance within each group (Hyde, Fennema, & Lamon, 1990). There are other cases where statistical significance does translate into important differences. What you should learn is that rejecting $H_0$ is just one step in a long line of steps taken in any research project.

# 11.10
## Two Types of Error

**Y**ou may now ask, "But aren't we taking a chance that we are wrong in rejecting the null hypothesis? Isn't it possible that we have in fact obtained a statistically rare occurrence by chance?" The answer to these questions must be a simple yes. This is precisely what we mean when we say that science is probabilistic. If there is any absolute statement that scientists are entitled to make, it is that we can never assert with complete confidence that our findings or propositions are true. There are countless examples in science in which an apparently firmly established conclusion has had to be modified in the light of further evidence.

In the coin-tossing study, even if all the tosses had resulted in correct predictions, it would be possible that your friend was not psychic. By chance alone, once in every 1,024 tests, on average, your friend could be correct 10 out of 10 times. When we employ the .05 level of significance, approximately 5% of the time we will be wrong when we reject the null hypothesis and assert its alternative.

These are some of the basic facts of the reality of inductive reasoning to which researchers must adjust. Students of behavior who insist on absolute certainty before they speak on issues are people who have been mute throughout all their years and who will remain so the rest of their lives (probably). These same considerations have led statisticians to identify the probable errors that are made using hypothesis testing and the probabilities associated with each.

### Type I Error ($\alpha$ Error)

Back pain has become one of the most common disabling disorders of this century. In a number of cases, trauma and aging have caused the discs (shock absorbers) between the vertebrae to lose elasticity and the gap between the vertebrae to narrow. Many years ago surgeons developed the spinal fusion procedure because they believed that the treatment would allow the spine to absorb shock and thereby reduce pain. The initial results of this surgical procedure were so positive that the null hypothesis ($H_0$: Spinal fusion does not relieve pain) was rejected. More recent evidence no longer supports the view that spinal fusion is effective in relieving back pain. That is, additional research has not confirmed the original findings—these studies did not replicate the original findings. Consequently, spinal fusion is now a less frequently performed procedure. As a result of this Type I error, in which $H_0$ was falsely rejected, many people underwent expensive and temporarily incapacitating surgery without achieving any pain relief.

In a **Type I error,** we reject the null hypothesis when it is actually true. The probability of making a Type I error is $\alpha$. In plain terms, a Type I error occurs when we decide to reject the null hypothesis when we should not. We have already pointed out that if we set our rejection point at the .05 level of significance, we will mistakenly reject $H_0$ approximately 5% of the time. So the good news is that we can decide how much risk we should take regarding the null hypothesis. In order to avoid this type of error, we should set the rejection level as low as possible. For example, if we were to set $\alpha = .001$, we would risk a Type I error only about one time in every thousand ($.001 = \frac{1}{1000}$). It should be noted that the .05 level is rather routinely used in the social and behavioral sciences unless there is a particular reason to be extremely conservative about making a Type I error.

**■ Type I Error ($\alpha$ Error):**

When a researcher rejects $H_0$ when in fact it is true. The probability of a Type I error is $\alpha$.

Suppose we are comparing a totally new teaching method to the technique currently in use. Suppose also that the null hypothesis is really true; that is, there is no difference in the comparison between the two methods. If we make a Type I error (we reject the null hypothesis when we should not), the error could conceivably lead to an extremely costly and time-consuming changeover to a teaching method that is in fact no better than the one being used. Similarly, in medicine a Type I error could lead to the implementation of a procedure that is costly, involves high levels of risk, and leads to severe discomfort for the patient. In situations such as these, we might want to set a more conservative level of significance (e.g., $\alpha = .01$). To familiarize you with the use of both levels, we have arbitrarily employed the $\alpha = .01$ and $\alpha = .05$ levels in examples that are presented throughout the text. However, keep in mind that the lower we set $\alpha$ the greater the likelihood that we will make a Type II error.

## Type II Error ($\beta$ Error)

When DDT was first introduced into households and on farms as a pesticide, there was no accumulated evidence that permitted the null hypothesis ($H_0$: DDT is not harmful) to be rejected. As a result of widespread use over a period of years, evidence accumulated concerning its harmful effects on humans (cancer), domestic animals, and wildlife. Failure to reject $H_0$ had led to the false conclusion that DDT was not harmful, indeed that it was safe. The decision-making error exemplified by DDT and many later pesticides and solvents is known as a Type II error. As you can see, the consequences of such an error can be devastating.

In a **Type II error,** we fail to reject the null hypothesis when it is actually false. In other words, a Type II error occurs when we do not reject the null hypothesis when we should. Beta ($\beta$) is the probability of making a Type II error. The reason for this fact rests in the observation that the critical region of $\alpha$ is always the smallest region of the sampling distribution. This type of error is far more common than a Type I error. For example, if we employ the .01 level of significance as the basis for rejecting the null hypothesis and then conduct an experiment in which the result we obtain would have occurred by chance only 2% of the time, we cannot reject the null hypothesis. Consequently, we cannot claim an experimental effect even though there very well may be one.

When we plan to conduct research, there is a trade-off between committing a Type I and a Type II error. If we attempt to protect ourselves from Type I errors by lowering $\alpha$, we increase the risk of committing a Type II error. Likewise, if we attempt to protect against a Type II error by increasing $\alpha$, we run the risk of committing a Type I error. The only way to resolve this conflict is to give careful consideration to the consequences of committing each type of error.

Table 11.6 summarizes the types of errors made as a function of the true status of the null hypothesis and the decision we have made. We should note that Type I and Type II errors are sampling errors and refer to samples that are drawn from hypothetical populations. Let's look at a few examples in which for illustrative purposes we supply the following information about the underlying population: $H_0$, $\alpha$-level, obtained $p$, statistical decision made, and the true status of $H_0$.

1. $H_0$: $\mu_1 = \mu_2$, $\alpha = .05$, two-tailed test. Obtained $p = .03$, two-tailed value. *Statistical decision*: $H_0$ is false. Actual status of $H_0$ is true. *Consequence*: Type I error—rejecting a true $H_0$.

2. $H_0$: $\mu_1 = \mu_2$, $\alpha = .05$, two-tailed test. Obtained $p = .04$, two-tailed value. *Statistical decision*: $H_0$ is false. Actual status of $H_0$: false.

**▨ Type II Error ($\beta$ Error):**

An error that occurs when a researcher fails to reject a null hypothesis that should be rejected. The effect is ignored by the researcher. The probability of committing a Type II error is $\beta$.

Table | 11.6

Various Statistical Decisions and Their Outcomes When $H_0$ is True or False*

| Decision | TRUE STATUS OF $H_0$ | |
| --- | --- | --- |
| | $H_0$ is True | $H_0$ is False |
| Fail to reject $H_0$ | Correct $p = 1 - \alpha$ | Type II error $p = \beta$ |
| Reject $H_0$ | Type I error $p = \alpha$ | Correct $p = 1 - \beta$ |

*Each cell represents the decision made and the probability, p, that the decision is correct or in error.

> *Consequence*: No error has been made. A correct conclusion was drawn because $H_0$ is false and the statistical decision was that $H_0$ is false.
> 3. $H_0$: $\mu_1 = \mu_2$, $\alpha = .01$, two-tailed test. Obtained $p = .10$, two-tailed value. *Statistical decision*: fail to reject $H_0$. Actual status of $H_0$: false. *Consequence*: Type II error—failure to reject a false $H_0$.
> 4. $H_0$: $\mu_1 = \mu_2$, $\alpha = .01$, two-tailed test. Obtained $p = .06$, two-tailed value. *Statistical decision*: fail to reject $H_0$. Actual status of $H_0$: true. *Consequence*: No error has been made because the statistical decision has been to accept $H_0$ when $H_0$ is actually true.

You may now ask, "In actual practice, how can we tell when we are making a Type I or a Type II error?" The answer is simple, we cannot! If we examine once again the logic of statistical inference, we can see why. As already stated, with rare exceptions we cannot know the true parameters of a population. Without this knowledge, how can we know whether our sample statistics have approximated or have failed to approximate the true value? How can we know whether or not we have mistakenly rejected a null hypothesis? If we knew a population value, we could know whether or not we made an error. Under these circumstances, however, the need for sampling statistics is eliminated. We collect samples and draw inferences from them only because our population values are unknowable for one reason or another. When they become known, the need for statistical inference is lost.

Is there no way, then, to know which experiments reporting significant results are accurate and which are not? The answer is a conditional yes. If we were to repeat the experiment and obtain similar results, we would have increased confidence that we are not making a Type I error. For example, if we tossed our coin in a second series of 10 trials and our friend correctly called heads or tails each time, we would feel far more confident in rejecting the null hypothesis that he had no psychic abilities. After the fourth, fifth, or sixth series of tosses, if he continued his successful predictions our confidence would increase.

## CHAPTER S UMMARY

We have seen that one of the basic problems of inferential statistics involves estimating population parameters from sample statistics. In inferential statistics we are frequently called upon to compare our obtained values with expected values. Expected values are given by the appropriate sampling distribution, which is a theoretical probability distribution of the possible values of a sample statistic.

We have seen how to use sampling distributions to interpret sample statistics. We discussed the null hypothesis and the alternative hypothesis. The null hypothesis frequently asserts that there is no difference and the alternative hypothesis asserts the alternative conclusion that a difference exists. If the outcome of an experiment indicates that a difference exists and it is unlikely to have happened by chance, we reject the null hypothesis and assert its alternative. If the difference we find is likely to have occurred by chance, we fail to reject the null hypothesis.

Failure to reject the null hypothesis is not evidence that it is true. We use probability statements to define what we mean by "rare." Sometimes our definition of "rare" may be large ($\alpha = .1$), sometimes our definition of "rare" is moderate (e.g., $\alpha = .05$), and sometimes our definition of "rare" is extreme (e.g., $\alpha = .001$).

We can define $\alpha$ on the basis of our concern about committing one of two errors:

*Type I error*. Rejecting a null hypothesis that is correct.

*Type II error*. Failing to reject a false null hypothesis.

When a scientist wants to be conservative, he or she establishes a low level of significance (e.g., $\alpha = .01$ or $\alpha = .001$), resulting in a greater incidence of Type II errors than Type I errors. When a scientist wants to avoid Type II errors, a less stringent significance level may be chosen (e.g., $\alpha = .1$ or $\alpha = .05$).

One of the primary themes of this chapter was that all scientific knowledge is based on probabilities and inference. There are no absolute truths in science or statistics, only best guesses, estimates, and forecasts.

## TERMS TO R EMEMBER

| | |
|---|---|
| alpha ($\alpha$) level | sampling distribution |
| alternative hypothesis ($H_1$) | sampling error |
| biased estimate | significance level |
| central limit theorem | statistical hypothesis |
| conceptual hypothesis | statistical inference |
| hypothesis testing | treatment population |
| interval estimation | two-tailed probability |
| modus tollens | Type I error ($\alpha$ error) |
| null hypothesis ($H_0$) | Type II error ($\beta$ error) |
| one-tailed probability | unbiased estimate |
| point estimation | |

## E XERCISES

1. Explain in your own words how samples are used to draw inferences in behavioral sciences and why conclusions that are drawn are termed conditional.

2. For each of the following sample statistics name the associated population parameter and its symbol: $\overline{X}$, $s^2$, $s$, $r$, $b_Y$.

3. Explain the difference between a point estimate and an interval estimate.

4. Frequency distributions differ from sampling distributions in two important ways. What are they?

5. Using the data presented in Figure 11.4, determine the probability of obtaining the following outcomes when tossing a coin 10 times.
   a. exactly 5 heads
   b. exactly 3 heads
   c. 3 or fewer heads
   d. 0 heads
   e. 7 or more heads
   f. all 10 heads

6. If a coin is tossed in the air 10 times, what is the probability of obtaining as many as 8 or more heads? 2 or fewer heads?

7. What are the three propositions derived from the central limit theorem?

8. In discussing the central limit theorem, a distinction is made between the sample size and the number of samples drawn from the population. Explain.

9. Describe what happens to the distribution of sample means when you
   a. increase the size of each sample.
   b. increase the number of samples.

10. A psychologist develops a reading achievement test that is used nationally. After years of study he has found that $\mu = 50$ and $\sigma = 10$. Based on these data what proportion of those taking the test received a score
    a. between 40 and 60?
    b. between 30 and 70?
    c. 70 or higher?
    d. 65 or higher?

11. Based on the data presented in Exercise 10, if one were to select at random a single individual from among those tested, what is the probability of selecting one who received a score
    a. between 40 and 60?
    b. between 30 and 70?
    c. 70 or higher?
    d. 65 or higher?

12. Again based on the data described in Exercise 10 determine
    a. between what two scores do the middle 50% of the cases lie?
    b. between what two scores do the middle 95% of the cases lie?
    c. between what two scores do the middle 99% of the cases lie?
    d. beyond what scores do the most extreme 5% of the cases lie?
    e. beyond what scores do the most extreme 1% of the cases lie?

13. After completing a study in experimental psychology Josh concluded, "I have proved that no difference exists between the two experimental conditions." Criticize his conclusion according to the logic of drawing inferences in science.

14. Does the null hypothesis in a one-tailed test differ from the null hypothesis in a two-tailed test?

15. Does the alternative hypothesis in a one-tailed test differ from the alternative hypothesis in a two-tailed test? Give an example.

16. Identify each of the following as either $H_0$ or $H_1$:
    a. The population mean in intelligence is 100.
    b. The proportion of Democrats in Watanabe County is not equal to .50.
    c. The population mean in intelligence is not equal to 100.
    d. The proportion of Democrats in Watanabe County is equal to .50.

17. An experimental psychologist hypothesizes that drive affects running speed. Assume that she has set up a study to investigate the problem employing two different drive levels. Formulate $H_0$ and $H_1$ using a nondirectional test.

18. If the researcher described in Exercise 17 had decided to use a directional test, how would the null and alternative hypotheses be stated?

19. A researcher decides to test a hypothesis about the correlation between IQ and head circumference. Symbolically, how would one state the null and alternative hypotheses for a nondirectional test? How would one state them for a directional test?

20. An efficiency expert conducts a study in which she compares two types of visual displays, circular and rectangular dials. She determines the amount of time it takes to read each type of dial and finds a significant difference between the two types. For each of the following levels of significance, state how many times in 1,000 this difference would be expected to occur by chance.
    - **a.** .001
    - **b.** .01
    - **c.** .005
    - **d.** .36
    - **e.** .05
    - **f.** .095
    - **g.** .004
    - **h.** .10

21. If $\alpha = .05$, what is the probability of making a Type I error?

    In Exercises 22 through 26, $H_0$, obtained $p$, and true status of $H_0$ are given. State whether or not an error in statistical decision has been made. If so, state the type of error.

22. $H_0$: $\mu_1 \geq \mu_2$, $\alpha = .01$, one-tailed test. Obtained $p = .008$, one-tailed value (in predicted direction). Actual status of $H_0$: True.

23. $H_0$: $\mu_1 = \mu_2$, $\alpha = .05$, two-tailed test. Obtained $p = .08$, two-tailed value. Actual status of $H_0$: True.

24. $H_0$: $\mu_1 = \mu_2$, $\alpha = .05$, two-tailed test. Obtained $p = .06$, two-tailed value. Actual status of $H_0$: False.

25. $H_0$: $\mu_1 = \mu_2$, $\alpha = .05$, two-tailed test. Obtained $p = .03$, two-tailed value. Actual status of $H_0$: False.

26. $H_0$: $\mu_1 = \mu_2$, $\alpha = .01$, two-tailed test. Obtained $p = .005$, two-tailed value. Actual status of $H_0$: False.

27. In Exercise 13, Josh drew some erroneous conclusions about his experimental results. Josh's friend Matthew asserted: "It can be said that the purpose of any experiment is to provide the occasion for rejecting the null hypothesis." Explain what he meant by that statement.

28. Give examples of experimental studies in which a
    **a.** Type I error would be considered more serious than a Type II error.
    **b.** Type II error would be considered more serious than a Type I error.

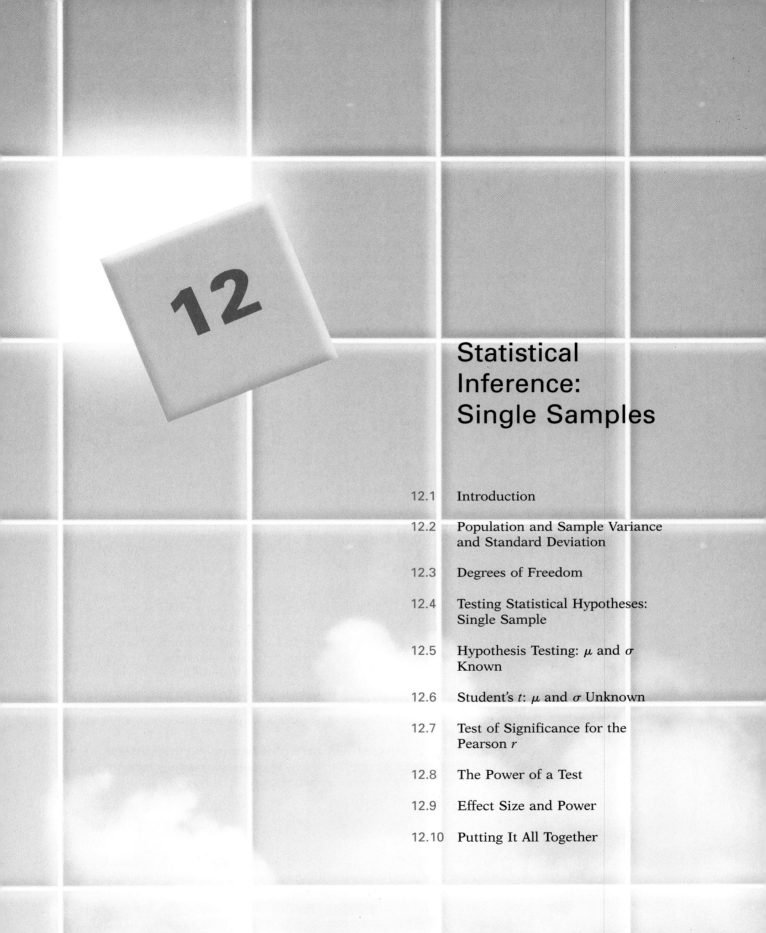

# 12

# Statistical Inference: Single Samples

## 12.1 / Introduction

In Chapter 11 we introduced you to the concept of statistical inference and hypothesis testing. In this chapter we will continue our exploration of this important topic and examine additional concepts that allow you to work toward a more comprehensive understanding of inferential statistics. As with each chapter in this book, we build upon material that you have already mastered. Specifically, we will use what you have learned about the normal distribution, descriptive statistics, sampling distributions, and probability to introduce you to inferential statistics. In addition, we will show you how to apply inferential statistics to various practical problems including testing of the significance of sample and population means and the correlation coefficient, $r$. We will also show you how the central limit theorem helps us interpret data and plan our research. Finally, we will introduce you to new concepts that serve as the foundation for material to be presented in subsequent chapters. Let's begin by revisiting a familiar topic, the variance and standard deviation.

## 12.2 / Population and Sample Variance and Standard Deviation

In Chapter 5, we defined the sample variance as

$$s^2 = \frac{\Sigma(X - \overline{X})^2}{N} \qquad (12.1)$$

and the sample standard deviation as

$$s = \sqrt{\frac{\Sigma(X - \overline{X})^2}{N}} \qquad (12.2)$$

We use these statistics to describe the variance and the standard deviation of the sample. Although they work well as descriptive statistics, we cannot use them to estimate the population parameters $\sigma^2$ and $\sigma$. As you learned in Chapter 11, $s^2$ and $s$ provide a **biased estimate** of the population parameters. To be exact, Equations 12.1 and 12.2 *underestimate* the population parameters. Therefore, you should use Equations 12.1 and 12.2 only when the data represent the population. When you wish to estimate the population variance and standard deviation, you will need to use another set of equations.

Statisticians discovered that they could estimate the magnitude of the bias and thus adjust for this bias using a correction term. Mathematically, the relation between $s^2$ and $\sigma^2$ is

$$\sigma^2 \cong \frac{N}{N-1}\, s^2 \qquad (12.3)$$

There are several implications of Equation 12.3. First, using sample data we can never predict the population parameter, $\sigma^2$, without bias. We can create only an estimate of $\sigma^2$ using the conventional definition of $s^2$. Another observation is that the bias is largest when the sample size is small and that the error decreases as sample size increases. Try a simple

■ **Biased Estimate:**

Any descriptive statistic that consistently underestimates or overestimates a population parameter.

comparison; use a sample size of 5 and another of 500 for the correction term. Compare the size of the two correction terms.

$$1.250 = \frac{5}{5 - 1} \qquad 1.002 = \frac{500}{500 - 1}$$

With the small sample size, the amount of error is great (1.250). When the sample is large, the error is small (1.002).

We can use Equation 12.3 to help us create a measure of variance and standard deviation that is a better estimate of $\sigma^2$ and $\sigma$. Specifically, if we incorporate the correction factor from Equation 12.3 with Equation 12.1, we can rewrite the formula for variance as

$$\hat{s}^2 = \frac{\Sigma(X - \overline{X})^2}{n - 1} \qquad (12.4)$$

Note that we introduced a new symbol $\hat{s}^2$. The caret (^) indicates that the statistic is an estimate, in this case it is the **unbiased estimate of the population variance.** We can apply the same mathematics to redefine the standard deviation. We also use the lowercase $n$ to indicate that the data represent a sample rather than a population.

$$\hat{s} = \sqrt{\frac{\Sigma(X - \overline{X})^2}{n - 1}} \qquad (12.5)$$

As a rule, when you want to *describe* the variance and standard deviation for a sample, divide the sum of squares by $N$. This procedure will calculate the descriptive statistics $s$ and $s^2$. When you want to *estimate* the population variance and standard deviation, divide the sum of squares by $n - 1$; you will calculate the statistics $\hat{s}^2$ and $\hat{s}$ that provide an estimate of the population parameters $\sigma^2$ and $\sigma$.

Let's review the status of our descriptive and inferential statistics. The arithmetic mean is an unbiased estimate of the population mean. Therefore, we can use the mean to describe the sample and estimate the value of the population mean. By contrast, $s^2$ and $s$ are biased estimates of the population variance and standard deviation. Consequently, we use $\hat{s}^2$ and $\hat{s}$ to estimate the population variance and standard deviation. Finally, the correlation coefficient, $r$, is a sample statistic that allows us to estimate a population parameter, $\rho$ (rho). The correlation coefficient $r$ is an unbiased estimate of the population parameter $\rho$. Table 12.1 summarizes how we can use these descriptive statistics to estimate population parameters.

# 12.3 / Degrees of Freedom

**A**s you already know, we call the numerator of the variance equation the sum of squares. The denominator of the equation also has a special name; we call it the **degrees of freedom.** As we venture into a more detailed analysis of inferential statistics, the concept of degrees of freedom will take on greater importance. We will begin with a general survey of the concept and then introduce more information as the need arises.

---

▨ **Unbiased Estimate of the Population Variance ($\hat{s}^2$):**

A form of variance that reduces the bias by which $s^2$ estimates the population variance, $\sigma^2$. The unbiased estimate of variance is the sum of squares divided by $n - 1$; $\hat{s}^2 = \frac{\Sigma(X - \overline{X})^2}{n - 1}$. The unbiased estimate of the population standard deviation is the square root of the unbiased variance, $\hat{s} = \sqrt{\hat{s}^2}$.

---

▨ **Degrees of Freedom:**

The number of values that are free to vary after specific restrictions are placed on the data. In estimates of variance, the degrees of freedom is the denominator of the variance equation and is always 1 less than the number of observations contributing to the variance estimate ($n - 1$).

**Table | 12.1**

**The Relation Between Sample Statistics as Estimates of Population Parameters**

| Statistic | Population Parameter |
|---|---|
| $\overline{X} = \dfrac{\Sigma X}{n}$ | $\rightarrow$ Unbiased estimate $\rightarrow \mu$ |
| $\hat{s}^2 = \dfrac{\Sigma(X - \overline{X})^2}{n - 1}$ | $\rightarrow$ Unbiased estimate $\rightarrow \sigma^2$ |
| $\hat{s} = \sqrt{\dfrac{\Sigma(X - \overline{X})^2}{n - 1}}$ | $\rightarrow$ Unbiased estimate $\rightarrow \sigma$ |
| $r = \dfrac{\Sigma z_X z_Y}{N}$ | $\rightarrow$ Unbiased estimate $\rightarrow \rho$ |
| $s^2 = \dfrac{\Sigma(X - \overline{X})^2}{N}$ | Describe sample variance |
| $s = \sqrt{\dfrac{\Sigma(X - \overline{X})^2}{N}}$ | Describe sample standard deviation |

The degrees of freedom refers to the number of observations that are free to vary after we place certain restrictions on the data. To illustrate, imagine that we have a sample with four numbers, 18, 23, 27, and 32. The sum is 100 and the mean is 25. If we subtract the mean from each score, the sum of the deviations *must* equal zero—remember that $\Sigma(X - \overline{X}) = 0$.

Assume that we drew these numbers randomly and independently from a population. Each observation is free to assume any value available in the population. The deviation scores are not free to vary, however. How is it that the observed scores are free to vary but the deviation scores are not? The answer lies in the fact that the definition of the mean requires the sum of the deviation scores to equal zero. Consequently, the mean restricts the values that the deviation scores can take. For example, if your sample size is $n = 1$, there are no degrees of freedom for the deviation score. If the raw score is 18, then the mean will be 18 and the deviation score *must* equal zero.

What happens when we begin to add scores to our sample? Adding a new score adds one degree of freedom because the mean is free to vary by the addition of a new score. Consider the example of the four scores. Once we impose the restriction that the deviations sum to zero, the values of only three deviations can vary. As soon as we determine the first three deviations, the fourth is fixed by the fact that its addition must make the sum of deviation scores equal zero. When we add a new number, the first four deviation scores can each change because the new score will, most likely, change the mean. The new deviation score is not free to vary, however.

In general, for any given sample the degrees of freedom will be $n - 1$. More broadly, the degrees of freedom is 1 less than the number of observations in the set. This generalization allows us to create an unbiased estimate of the population variance and standard deviation. Most statisticians abbreviate the degrees of freedom as *df*. For example, if we created a sample of $n = 25$, we would determine that $df = n - 1$. Therefore, $df = 25 - 1 = 24$. The concept of degrees of freedom is important and one that we will revisit in future chapters.

# 12.4

## Testing Statistical Hypotheses: Single Sample

W e can now bring together many of the skills and statistical techniques that we have introduced. Specifically, we will examine how to use descriptive statistics, probability, hypothesis testing, and inferential procedures to solve problems. You will learn how to use $z$-scores to test hypotheses. You will also learn about a new statistical test that is much like the $z$-score. Finally, we will show you how you can maximize the power of your statistical analysis.

The goal of a single sample inferential test is to determine what conclusions we can draw from a sample. As you learned in Chapter 11, there are several inferences we can make. First, we can use sample statistics to estimate population parameters. For example, we may want to know how well a sample mean estimates a population mean. Second, we can estimate how much a sample mean will vary if we repeatedly sample from the population. Finally, we can engage in hypothesis testing.

Hypothesis testing allows us to answer the question "How likely is it that the sample could be drawn from the population with these given parameters?" As you learned in Chapter 11, we create null and alternative hypotheses. If we fail to reject the null hypothesis we conclude that the sample mean is more likely than not to have come from a specified population. By contrast, if we reject the null hypothesis, we conclude that the sample is not representative of the population. The focus of this chapter, therefore, will be to show you how to use inferential statistics to conduct hypothesis testing.

Before we show you how to conduct the individual statistical tests, we want to introduce you to a conventional method for conducting inferential statistics. We find that these steps are good practice. Indeed, we use these steps for discussion of all inferential statistics reviewed in this book.

## Steps for Hypothesis Testing

**Step 1: State the Null Hypothesis** As you learned in the previous chapter, the null hypothesis, $H_0$, is the mathematical statement we want to reject. In this chapter, we examine statistical tests that compare a sample mean to the population mean. Therefore, the null hypothesis will state that the mean of the sampling distribution is representative of the population.

When you prepare the null hypothesis, you may select a nondirectional null hypothesis or a directional null hypothesis. To review, the nondirectional null hypothesis states that the mean of the sampling distribution, regardless of its size, comes from the population we specify. Symbolically, we state the null hypothesis as $H_0$: $\mu_{\overline{X}} = \mu_0$. The symbol $\mu_{\overline{X}}$ represents the mean of the sampling distribution of means, and $\mu_0$ represents the value of the mean of the hypothesized population.

There are two ways that you can write the directional null hypothesis. One version of the directional test is $H_0$: $\mu_{\overline{X}} \geq \mu_0$. This null condition states that the mean of sample means will be greater than or equal to the population mean. In other words, we would expect the difference between the sample and population means to be equal to or greater than 0. Specifically, $H_0$: $\mu_{\overline{X}} - \mu_0 \geq 0$.

The other version of the directional test is $H_0$: $\mu_{\overline{X}} \leq \mu_0$, which states that under the null condition the sample means will be less than or equal to the population mean. This hypothesis predicts that the difference between the mean of sample means and population mean will be negative. That is, $H_0$: $\mu_{\overline{X}} - \mu_0 \leq 0$.

**Step 2:** **State the Alternative Hypothesis** Once you state the null hypothesis, preparing the alternative is easy, just write the mathematical complement. To be specific, the alternative hypothesis for a nondirectional hypothesis is $H_1$: $\mu_{\overline{X}} \neq \mu_0$. When you use a directional hypothesis you use the greater than ($>$) or less than ($<$) sign that is opposite of the null hypothesis. Thus, if $H_0$: $\mu_{\overline{X}} \geq \mu_0$ then $H_1$: $\mu_{\overline{X}} < \mu_0$, if $H_0$: $\mu_{\overline{X}} \leq \mu_0$ then $H_1$: $\mu_{\overline{X}} > \mu_0$.

**Step 3:** **Identify the Appropriate Statistical Test** This step may seem obvious, but is often the downfall of many students and researchers. Part of the problem is that you can apply any statistical test to any set of data. One question you could ask is, "Can I use this statistic to analyze my data?" The answer will always be "Yes." Thus, the question is not very useful. For example, if you wanted to determine if a sample of fifth graders had greater reading ability than a sample of third graders, you would *not* correlate the third graders' scores with the fifth graders' scores. Indeed, if you had two random samples of children, any correlation among pairs of scores would probably be zero. More to the point, the correlation of scores says nothing about the difference between the means of the two groups.

We believe that a better question is, "Will this statistical test allow me to answer the question I posed in my hypothesis?" Therefore, your null and alternative hypotheses will, in part, determine the type of test you use. Other factors that influence the selection of the statistical test are the types of data you collect. Throughout this book, we will examine the types of answers that inferential statistics provide. We hope that you will recognize the differences and similarities among the uses of the various inferential statistics.

**Step 4:** **Determine the Significance Level** Determining the significance level is another important step that should not be taken lightly. As we showed you in the previous chapter, selecting a value for $\alpha$ affects the probability of Type I and Type II errors. As you decrease the $\alpha$-level (e.g., .05 to .01) the probability of a Type I error will decrease. At the same time, however, decreases in $\alpha$-level increase the probability of Type II errors. Most researchers set $\alpha = .05$ or $\alpha = .01$. Under some circumstances, however, researchers may use a smaller or larger $\alpha$. These circumstances are the exception, however, and not the rule.

**Step 5:** **Identify the Appropriate Sampling Distribution** Once you select a statistical test, the selection of the sampling distribution should be relatively clear. Again, we will make clear the relation between the statistical test and the appropriate sampling distribution.

**Step 6:  Determine the Critical Region for Rejection of $H_0$**
The critical region will allow you to determine the conditions under which you can reject $H_0$. The value for the critical region will reflect the type of null hypothesis you selected. In addition, the type of sampling distribution and the significance level will determine the critical region.

**Step 7:  Summarize and Analyze the Data** You are now ready to examine your data. We recommend that you always begin your analysis with exploratory data analysis. Using the exploratory data analysis techniques we first introduced in Chapter 3 will help you better interpret your data. For example, these techniques will help you see if the results you expected occurred. At the same time, exploratory data analysis will help you determine if there is anything unexpected in the data. Evidence of a bimodal distribution, skew, or extremely high or low scores may indicate that your data requires greater attention.

Once you collect your data and examine them using exploratory data analytic techniques, you are ready to engage in hypothesis testing. Following these steps is a useful habit to develop. We will follow and illustrate the use of these steps for each inferential statistic reviewed in the remainder of this book.

Let's practice these steps for hypothesis testing. In the remainder of the chapter we will use many examples to illustrate hypothesis testing for single sample tests.

## 12.5 / Hypothesis Testing: $\mu$ and $\sigma$ Known

In situations where you know $\mu$ and $\sigma$ for a population, you can describe the shape of the sample means randomly selected from the population, especially when the sample size, $n$, is large. The central limit theorem supports this statement. As you learned in Chapter 11, the sampling distribution of means will be approximately normal with a mean equal to the population mean (e.g., $\mu_{\overline{X}} = \mu$). In addition, the standard error of the mean is $\sigma_{\overline{X}} = \dfrac{\sigma}{\sqrt{N}}$. We can use the normal distribution to determine the probability values of means converted to $z$-scores. If the probability is sufficiently small, we can use that fact as evidence to reject the null hypothesis. Let's look at a concrete example.

### Example: $H_0$: $\mu_{\overline{X}} = \mu$

For the past semester, a high school psychology teacher tutored nine students in preparation for an advanced placement psychology test. According to national data, the average score is 40 with a standard deviation of 5. Thus, we know the population parameters, $\mu_0 = 40$ and $\sigma = 5$. The mean performance of the nine students is 44. Because we know the population parameters, we can use the z-score and the normal distribution. For this example, we will assume that the teacher will use a nondirectional hypothesis to compare the sample mean to the population mean. She uses a nondirectional hypothesis because she is interested in testing if the sample mean differs from the population mean—either higher or lower. If she were interested only in whether their scores *increased*, she would use a directional hypothesis.

**Null Hypothesis:** $H_0$: $\mu_{\overline{X}} = 40$. The mean of the population from which the sample was drawn equals 40.

**Alternative Hypothesis:** $H_1$: $\mu_{\overline{X}} \neq 40$. The mean of the population from which the sample was drawn does not equal 40.

**Statistical Test:** The z-statistic because we know $\sigma$.

**Significance Level:** $\alpha = .05$. If the difference between the sample mean and the specified population mean is sufficiently large that its associated probability under $H_0$ is equal to or less than .05, we shall reject $H_0$.

**Sampling Distribution:** The normal distribution.

**Critical Region for Rejecting $H_0$** $|z_{\text{critical}}| \geq |1.96|$. If $z_{\text{observed}}$ is less than $-1.96$ or greater than 1.96 we can reject $H_0$.

We can now proceed with our calculations. First, we use Equation 12.6 to convert the difference between the sample and population means to a z-score.

$$z = \frac{\overline{X} - \mu_0}{\dfrac{\sigma}{\sqrt{n}}} \tag{12.6}$$

According to the information provided previously, we know that

$$\overline{X} = 44 \qquad \mu_0 = 40 \qquad \sigma = 5 \qquad n = 9$$

Therefore,

$$z = \frac{44 - 40}{\dfrac{5}{\sqrt{9}}} = \frac{4}{1.6667} = 2.3999$$

$$z_{\text{observed}} = 2.40$$

The observed value of z is $z_{\text{observed}} = 2.40$. The critical value for this test is $z_{\text{critical}} = 1.96$. Because $z_{\text{observed}} > z_{\text{critical}}$ we can reject the null hypothesis that the students' average score of 44 represents a random sample from a population where $\mu_{\overline{X}} = 40$ and $\sigma = 5$.

Figure 12.1 represents the test we just conducted. The curve is a normal distribution and the X-axis represents the z-scores. The shaded areas represent the critical region. Because we used a nondirectional hypothesis, we must divide $\alpha$ in half. Each shaded area represents $\alpha/2 = .025$. Any z-score that falls in the shaded area allows us to reject the null hypothesis. If the z-score falls within the nonshaded area, we cannot reject the null hypothesis.

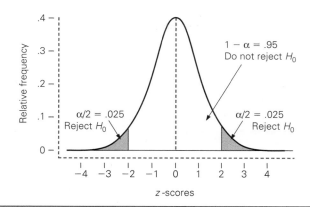

**Figure | 12.1**

The nondirectional or two-tailed test of significance. Because we predict that the sample mean can be either greater or less than the population mean, we divide α in half. The total of the extreme shaded regions equals α. In our example, $z_{observed} = 2.40$. Because the *z*-score falls in the shaded region, we can reject $H_0$.

## 12.6 / Student's *t*: μ and σ Unknown

As you saw in the previous example, Equation 12.6 works when you know the population parameters. The *z*-score is, therefore, a useful statistic that has many applications; however, it also has its limitations. First, we do not always know the population parameters and must estimate their values using sample statistics. Second, when we work with small sample sizes (e.g., $n < 30$), $\hat{s}$ is an inexact estimate of σ. As a generality, when *n* is less than 30, $\hat{s}$ will underestimate σ more than one-half the time. Consequently, the normal distribution does not accurately describe the sampling distribution of means when sample sizes are small. This is a particularly important problem in the behavioral sciences where many research projects routinely use fewer than 30 subjects in each group.

A young biologist named William Gossett solved the problem of small sample sizes and the relation between $\hat{s}$ and σ. Gossett worked for the Guinness Brewing Company during the early 1920s. His first research examined different strains of the yeast used to brew beer. Because of the type of research he conducted, he did not have large sample sizes. To resolve several statistical problems, Gossett developed a new set of sampling distributions that describe the distribution of means for small samples.

At the time, the Guinness Brewing Company forbade its employees from publishing their research. To get around the rule, Gossett published his work under the pseudonym "Student." Gossett's major contribution to statistics consisted of his description of the sampling distributions for small samples. Today, researchers call these distributions the **t-distributions** or Student's distributions. Many statisticians and historians (e.g., Stigler, 1986) consider Gossett's insights to be the most revolutionary contribution to modern statistics. As we will see in later chapters, Gossett's *t*-distribution and corresponding statistical analysis serve as the foundation of many of the most widely used statistical procedures.

▪ **t-Distributions:**

Theoretical symmetrical distributions with a mean of zero and a standard deviation that becomes smaller as the degrees of freedom (*df*) increase.

# Comparison of the Normal and *t*-Distributions

There are several similarities and important differences between the normal distribution and the *t*-distribution. Figure 12.2 presents the normal distribution and several *t*-distributions. Let's look at the two types of distribution in detail. First, how are the distributions similar?

The first similarity between the normal and the *t*-distributions is that they are sampling distributions. As you learned in our discussion of the central limit theorem, the distribution of randomly generated sample means from any population is normally distributed when the sample size is large. The *t*-distributions are also sampling distributions that reflect the expected sampling distribution for a specified sample size.

The second similarity is that the distributions are symmetrical and bell-shaped, therefore, much of what we have learned about interpreting the normal distribution applies directly to the *t*-distributions. For example, we can conduct either directional or nondirectional hypotheses using the *t*-distribution. Although the numbers are different, the procedures are the same as those used for the *z*-score.

Another similarity between the distributions is that they have a mean of zero. The fact that the mean of the distributions is zero indicates how we can use them. For the normal distribution, we use the *z*-score to determine the probability of obtaining a particular score. The greater the deviation between the mean and the observed score, the greater the absolute value of the *z*-score. The same is true of the *t*-distributions. Both the normal and the *t*-distributions allow us to determine the probability of obtaining a sample mean given its relative deviation from the population mean.

There are several noteworthy differences between the normal and *t*-distributions. The first difference is the fact that for the *t*-distributions there is a separate distribution to represent each *df*. For example, the distribution in Figure 12.2 representing $df = 1$ presents the *t*-distribution when $n = 2$. Similarly, when $df = 10$, the *t*-distribution represents the sampling distribution when $n = 11$.

As you can see in Figure 12.2, as the sample size increases, the *t*-distributions become more normal in shape. The largest discrepancies between the shape of the *t*-distribution and normal distribution occur when the sample size is small. The smaller the sample size, the more platykurtic, or flatter, the distribution.

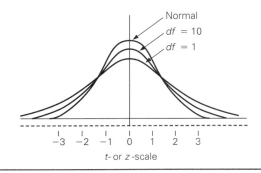

**Figure | 12.2**

The difference among *t*-distributions for *df* = 1, *df* = 10, and a normal distribution. Notice that the *t*-distributions are more spread out than the normal distribution, especially with small sample sizes.

## Hypothesis Testing

As noted previously, the $t$-distributions are applied when we do not have direct knowledge of the population parameters and must use sample statistics to estimate the population parameters. As you will see subsequently, we employ the same general logic used in the $z$-score tests when we use the $t$-distributions. The difference is that we call the statistic the $t$-ratio or Student's $t$ and use the $t$-distributions to determine whether to reject the null hypothesis.

The $t$-ratio for the single sample case is

$$t = \frac{\overline{X} - \mu_0}{\frac{\hat{s}}{\sqrt{n}}} \tag{12.7}$$

The $t$-ratio is, therefore, much like the $z$-score we just showed you in Equation 12.6. The major difference appears in the denominator. As you can see, we replaced $\sigma$ with $\hat{s}$ because we use $\hat{s}$ to estimate $\sigma$. We also use $n$ rather than $N$. Using the lowercase letter $n$ reminds us that we are using a sample of data to estimate population parameters. The $t$-ratio, then, is the ratio of the difference between the sample and population means to the standard error of the mean.

Before we move much further, we need to show you how to determine the critical region for the $t$-ratio. Table 12.2 is a partial reproduction of Table C in Appendix D. The table presents the critical values of the $t$-distribution required to reject the null hypothesis at various probability levels. This table presents a great deal of information in a small space; therefore, we need to examine how to use the table with care.

At the top of the table are two major headings that represent the type of hypothesis testing you want to use. The upper heading "Level of Significance of a One-Tailed, or Directional, Test" represents the significance levels of directional tests. Therefore, if you used $\leq$ or $\geq$ in your null hypothesis, you would use this heading as a guide for this table. In

**Table 12.2**

**Reproduction of a Portion of Table C from Appendix D**

For any given $df$, the table presents the values of $t$ corresponding to various levels of probability. The obtained $t$ is statistically significant at a given level of $\alpha$ if it is equal to or greater than the value shown in the table.

| | LEVEL OF SIGNIFICANCE OF A ONE-TAILED, OR DIRECTIONAL, TEST $H_0$: $\mu_1 - \mu_2 \leq 0$ OR $H_0$: $\mu_1 - \mu_2 \geq 0$ | | | | | |
|---|---|---|---|---|---|---|
| | .10 | .05 | .025 | .01 | .005 | .0005 |
| | LEVEL OF SIGNIFICANCE OF A TWO-TAILED, OR NONDIRECTIONAL, TEST $H_0$: $\mu_1 - \mu_2 = 0$ | | | | | |
| $df$ | .20 | .10 | .05 | .02 | .01 | .001 |
| 15 | 1.341 | 1.753 | 2.131 | 2.602 | 2.947 | 4.073 |
| 16 | 1.337 | 1.746 | 2.120 | 2.583 | 2.921 | 4.015 |

words, you use a directional test if you are interested in testing the significance of a difference in one direction, either higher or lower than the population parameter. The lower heading "Level of Significance of a Two-Tailed, or Nondirectional, Test," represents the significance levels of nondirectional tests. Use this heading if you have an = sign in your null hypothesis.

The numbers immediately below each heading represent conventional levels of $\alpha$. For the directional hypothesis, the $\alpha$-values range between .10 and .0005. The $\alpha$-levels for the nondirectional tests are always twice as great as the $\alpha$-levels for the directional test. The reason that both $\alpha$-levels share the same column is the simple fact that the nondirectional hypothesis splits $\alpha$ into two parts. For example, if we set $\alpha = .05$, then .025 will be in the upper and lower extremes of the $t$-distribution. By contrast, for the directional test, the entire $\alpha$ region is on one side of the $t$-distribution.

The *df* column represents $n - 1$ or the degrees of freedom. Our table has $t$-distributions that range in *df* from 1 to infinity ($\infty$). To determine the critical value to reject the null hypothesis, you will first need to set your null and alternative hypotheses. Next, confirm the $\alpha$-level that you will use. Finally, determine the degrees of freedom you have. For example, assume that a researcher conducted a study using 16 subjects. She decided to conduct a directional hypothesis test and set $\alpha = .05$. As you can see in Table 12.2, $t_{\text{critical}} = 1.753$. The researcher then compares the observed value of the $t$-ratio ($t_{\text{observed}}$) to the critical value of $t$, or ($t_{\text{critical}}$). If $t_{\text{observed}}$ is equal to or greater than $t_{\text{critical}}$, the researcher is able to reject the null hypothesis.

Many computer programs that perform statistical tests will automatically calculate the probability of the $t_{\text{observed}}$. This convenience saves you the step of having to thumb through the book to find the correct table in the appendix. The general rule is that if $p \leq \alpha$ you can reject $H_0$. Be careful, however. If you decide to use a directional hypothesis, you must ensure that the sign of your $t$-ratio matches the alternative hypothesis in order to reject $H_0$.

To determine whether to reject the null hypothesis you can use Table 12.3 which summarizes the decision rules.

You should take particular note of the directional hypothesis. When we use > in $H_1$, the observed $t$-ratio, ($t_{\text{observed}}$) must be positive and greater than or equal to $t_{\text{critical}}$. By contrast, when we use < in $H_1$, the $t_{\text{observed}}$ must be negative and less than or equal to $t_{\text{critical}}$ (remember that

**Table 12.3**

**Summary of Null and Alternative Hypotheses and Rules for When to Reject the Null Hypothesis**

| Nondirectional Hypotheses | | |
|---|---|---|
| $H_0$: $\mu_{\bar{X}} = \mu_0$ | If $\mid t_{\text{observed}} \mid \geq \mid t_{\text{critical}} \mid$ | Reject Null Hypothesis |
| $H_1$: $\mu_{\bar{X}} \neq \mu_0$ | If $p \leq \alpha$ | Reject Null Hypothesis |
| **Directional Hypotheses** | | |
| $H_0$: $\mu_{\bar{X}} \leq \mu_0$ | If $t_{\text{observed}} \geq t_{\text{critical}}$ | Reject Null Hypothesis |
| $H_1$: $\mu_{\bar{X}} > \mu_0$ | If $p \leq \alpha$ and $t_{\text{observed}}$ positive | Reject Null Hypothesis |
| $H_0$: $\mu_{\bar{X}} \geq \mu_0$ | If $t_{\text{observed}} \leq t_{\text{critical}}$ | Reject Null Hypothesis |
| $H_1$: $\mu_{\bar{X}} < \mu_0$ | If $p \leq \alpha$ and $t_{\text{observed}}$ negative | Reject Null Hypothesis |

$-1.964 < -1.753$). For the nondirectional hypothesis, the sign of the $t$-ratio is not important, only its magnitude. Therefore, we compare the absolute values of the $t$-ratios to determine whether to reject $H_0$.

## Example: $H_0$: $\mu_{\overline{X}} = \mu_0$

A psychologist wants to determine whether the answers for multiple-choice questions contain cues that indicate the correct response. To test this assumption, the psychologist randomly selected 16 college students and asked them to answer 100 multiple-choice questions from the reading section of a college aptitude test. The students did not read the corresponding essays, but rather, were asked to select the best answer based on reading the alternatives. Each question had five alternative answers. According to the results, $\overline{X} = 28$ and $\hat{s} = 12$. Because $n = 16$, $df = 15$.

The researcher assumed that if there were no cues, then students would be able to do no better than guessing. Because there were five items for each question, the researcher predicted that the average performance should be $\mu_0 = 20$ ($20 = 100 \times 1/5$).

How can we estimate $\sigma$? There is no way to know its value directly however, we can use $\hat{s}$ as an unbiased estimate of $\sigma$. Because $\sigma$ is unknown, we must use the $t$-distributions to determine whether to reject the null hypothesis. The researcher chose to use a nondirectional hypothesis.

***Null Hypothesis:*** $H_0$: $\mu_{\overline{X}} = 20$. The mean of the population from which the sample was drawn equals 20.

***Alternative Hypothesis:*** $H_1$: $\mu_{\overline{X}} \neq 20$. The mean of the population from which the sample was drawn does not equal 20.

***Statistical Test:*** We will use the $t$-ratio because $\sigma$ is estimated.

***Significance Level:*** $\alpha = .05$. If the difference between the sample mean and the specified population mean is sufficiently large that its associated probability under $H_0$ is equal to or less than .05, we shall reject $H_0$. If $p \leq \alpha$ then reject $H_0$.

***Sampling Distribution:*** The $t$-distribution with $df = 15$.

***Critical Region for Rejecting $H_0$:*** $|t_{\text{observed}}| \geq |2.131|$ If $t_{\text{observed}}$ is less than $-2.131$ or greater than 2.131 we can reject $H_0$.

According to the information provided previously, we know that

$$\overline{X} = 28 \qquad \mu_0 = 20 \qquad \hat{s} = 12 \qquad n = 16$$

Therefore,

$$t = \frac{28 - 20}{\dfrac{12}{\sqrt{16}}} \qquad = \frac{8}{3} \qquad = 2.6667$$

$$t_{\text{observed}} = 2.667$$

Because $t_{\text{observed}} > t_{\text{critical}}$ (e.g., $2.667 > 2.131$), we can reject the null hypothesis that the students' average score of 28 represents a random sample from a population where $\mu_{\overline{X}} = 20$. Stated from another perspective, given the null hypothesis, the probability of obtaining a $t$-ratio of at least $|2.667|$ is less than 5% (i.e., $\alpha = .05$). Because the probability of this event is remote, we are willing to reject the null hypothesis in favor of the alternative. The probability that we are making a Type I error is $\alpha = .05$.

If you used a computer program to perform your calculations, you may find that the computer prints a probability value next to the $t$-ratio. For example, the printout may contain the following information

$$t = 2.6667 \qquad\qquad df = 15$$

$$\underline{p}: \text{1-tailed} = .0088 \qquad \underline{p}: \text{2-tailed} = .0176$$

The computer calculated the $t$-ratio and the actual probabilities for the statistic. How should you interpret the probability values? First, you must decide your $\alpha$ level and if your hypothesis is directional (a one-tailed test) or nondirectional (a two-tailed test). Then if $p \leq \alpha$ you can reject the null hypothesis.

Many researchers in the behavioral sciences use the *Publication Manual of the American Psychological Association* (1994) when preparing their manuscripts for publication. The recommended format for reporting the results of the $t$-ratio is

$$\underline{t}\,(df) = \underline{t}_{\text{observed}}, \ \underline{p} = p \qquad \text{or} \qquad \underline{t}\,(df) = \underline{t}_{\text{observed}}, \ \underline{p} < \alpha$$

For this example we would report the $t$-ratio as

$$\underline{t}\,(15) = 2.67, \ \underline{p} = .018 \qquad \text{or} \qquad \underline{t}\,(15) = 2.67, \ \underline{p} < .05$$

## Computational Example: *t*-Ratio and Confidence Interval

The above example of the nondirectional hypothesis allows us to examine how to create a confidence interval using the $t$-distribution. As you will recall from the previous chapter, a confidence interval is a range of values above and below the mean. We use the confidence interval to estimate the potential values of additional sample means. In the last chapter we showed you how to use the $z$-score to create the confidence interval. We can use the same logic and the $t$-ratio to create a confidence interval when $\sigma$ is unknown.

We determine the critical interval using Equation 12.8.

$$CI = \overline{X} \pm t_{\text{critical}} \left( \frac{\hat{s}}{\sqrt{n}} \right) \tag{12.8}$$

In this equation, we use $t_{\text{critical}}$ to represent the criterion we wish to establish for the confidence interval. Let's use the last example to show the computational procedures. In this example, when $df = 15$ and $\alpha = .05$ for a two-tailed test, $t_{\text{critical}} = 2.131$. To calculate the 90% confidence interval, we set $\alpha = .10$. For degrees of freedom of 15, $t_{\text{critical}}$ for the 90% confidence interval is 1.753. For the 99% confidence interval we set $\alpha = .01$. For $df = 15$, $t_{\text{critical}} = 2.947$ for the 99% confidence interval. Table 12.4 presents the 90%, 95%, and 99% confidence intervals for $\overline{X} = 28$, $\hat{s} = 12$, and $n = 16$.

The interpretation of the confidence interval is straightforward. Consider the 95% confidence interval. According to our calculations, the confidence interval is $28 \pm 6.393$ or 21.607 to 34.393. This means that if the researcher were to continue to collect data in exactly the same manner, then 95% of the sample means would fall within this range.

**Table 12.4**

Three Confidence Intervals for a Mean of 28

| Confidence Interval | $t_{critical}$ | Lower Limit of CI | Upper Limit of CI |
|---|---|---|---|
| 90% | 1.753 | $22.741 = 28 - 1.753 \dfrac{12}{\sqrt{16}}$ | $33.259 = 28 + 1.753 \dfrac{12}{\sqrt{16}}$ |
| 95% | 2.131 | $21.607 = 28 - 2.131 \dfrac{12}{\sqrt{16}}$ | $34.393 = 28 + 2.131 \dfrac{12}{\sqrt{16}}$ |
| 99% | 2.947 | $19.159 = 28 - 2.947 \dfrac{12}{\sqrt{16}}$ | $36.841 = 28 + 2.947 \dfrac{12}{\sqrt{16}}$ |

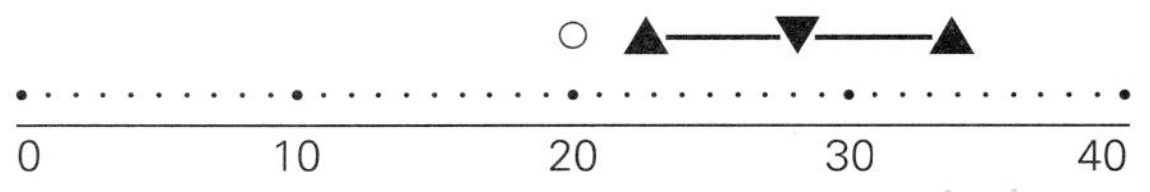

**Figure 12.3**

A dot chart of a mean of 28 with a 95% confidence interval as determined in Table 12.4. The ▼ represents the mean of 28. The lower and upper ends of the confidence interval are ► and ◄, respectively. The ○ represents the hypothetical location of the population mean, 20.

You do need to be careful in how you interpret the confidence interval. The confidence interval is a range of scores that we believe covers the population mean. The confidence interval does not establish the probability that our sample mean is the correct value. In other words, we cannot claim that the chances are 95% (or whatever confidence interval you select) that the population mean is 28. The critical value establishes the range of potential means that could occur if we continued to collect samples of the same size from the population. The reason we cannot be more decisive is that we estimate population parameters using sample statistics that may be influenced by sampling or random error. Indeed, each sample drawn from the population yields a slightly different mean and standard deviation. Therefore, the confidence interval should be used as an estimate of the magnitude of sampling variance.

Figure 12.3 is a simple dot-chart representation of the mean and the 95% confidence interval. Many researchers find it helpful to include the confidence interval in their graphs. Having the confidence interval about the location of the mean helps the reader visualize the magnitude of sampling variability. Figure 12.3 also demonstrates how a simple graph can relay much information without chartjunk.

## Example: $H_0$: $\mu_{\overline{X}} \geq \mu_0$

A college instructor believes that students should spend approximately 40 hours a week outside of class engaged in studying (e.g., reading assigned text, reviewing notes, preparing papers, and similar tasks). The instructor also suspects that students spend far less than 40 hours studying. To confirm her suspicions, she asks a random sample of 25 students to estimate the number of hours they study during a typical week. According to the results of the survey,

$$\overline{X} = 30 \qquad \mu_0 = 40 \qquad \hat{s} = 15 \qquad n = 25$$

**Null Hypothesis:** $H_0$: $\mu_{\bar{X}} \geq 40$. The mean of the population from which the sample was drawn is greater than or equal to 40.

**Alternative Hypothesis:** $H_1$: $\mu_{\bar{X}} < 40$. The mean of the population from which the sample was drawn is less than 40.

**Statistical Test:** We will use the $t$-ratio because $\sigma$ is unknown.

**Significance Level:** $\alpha = .05$. If the difference between the sample mean and the specified population mean is sufficiently large that its associated probability under $H_0$ is equal to or less than .05, we shall reject $H_0$.

**Sampling Distribution:** The $t$-distribution with $df = 24$.

**Critical Region for Rejecting $H_0$:** $t_{observed} \leq -1.711$. If $t_{observed}$ is less than $-1.711$ we can reject $H_0$. If $p \leq \alpha$ and $t_{observed}$ is negative then reject $H_0$.

Therefore,

$$ t = \frac{30 - 40}{\dfrac{15}{\sqrt{25}}} = \frac{-10}{3} = -3.333 $$

$$ t_{observed} = -3.33 $$

Because $t_{observed}$ is less than $t_{critical}$ ($-3.33 < -1.711$) we can reject the null hypothesis. In this example, the instructor can conclude that students study less than her ideal average of 40 hours a week.

What would have happened if $t_{observed}$ were a positive number? Could the researcher reject the null hypothesis? Because the alternative hypothesis stated that $\mu_{\bar{X}} < \mu_0$, the researcher can reject the null hypothesis only when the value of $t_{observed}$ is less than $t_{critical}$. Therefore, whenever you conduct a directional test, you must ensure that you pay attention to both the sign of the $t$-ratio and the relationship expressed in the hypothesis.

Let's look at another example. A psychology instructor is impressed by the quality of papers written by students in her Psychology 101 course. She believes that this sample of students has better than average writing skills. She also assumes that the class represents a random sample of college students because all students must take Psychology 101 as a part of their general education curriculum.

To test the hypothesis that her class of students has better than average writing abilities, she asks the students to report to her the grade they earned in their English composition course. According to the Records Office, the college-wide English composition grade is a B− or a 2.667. According to her students' self reports,

$$ \overline{X} = 3.333 \qquad \mu_0 = 2.667 \qquad \hat{s} = 0.937 \qquad n = 20 $$

**Null Hypothesis:** $H_0$: $\mu_{\bar{X}} \leq 2.667$. The mean of the population from which the sample was drawn is less than or equal to 2.667.

**Alternative Hypothesis:** $H_1$: $\mu_{\bar{X}} > 2.667$. The mean of the population from which the sample was drawn is greater than 2.667.

**Statistical Test:** We will use the $t$-ratio because $\sigma$ is estimated.

**Significance Level:** $\alpha = .05$. If the difference between the sample mean and the specified population mean is sufficiently large that its associated probability under $H_0$ is equal to or less than .05, we shall reject $H_0$.

**Sampling Distribution:**   The $t$-distribution with $df = 19$.

**Critical Region for Rejecting $H_0$:**   $t_{\text{observed}} \geq 1.729$. If $t_{\text{observed}}$ is greater than 1.729 we can reject $H_0$.

Therefore,

$$t = \frac{3.333 - 2.667}{\dfrac{0.937}{\sqrt{20}}} = \frac{0.666}{0.2095} = 3.179$$

$$t_{\text{observed}} = 3.179$$

Because $t_{\text{observed}}$ is greater than $t_{\text{critical}}$ (3.179 > 1.729), we can reject the null hypothesis. In this example, the instructor can conclude that the students in her class earned, on average, a higher grade in their English composition course than the average grade of 2.667.

## 12.7  Test of Significance for the Pearson $r$

In Chapter 8 we discussed the calculation of two statistics, the Pearson $r$ and the Spearman $r_S$. Recall that the correlation coefficient varies between $-1.00$ and 1.00, with $r = 0$ indicating the absence of a linear relation between the two variables. The correlation coefficient is a sample statistic that estimates the degree to which two populations are correlated. Specifically, the degree to which two variables are correlated is represented by the population parameter, $\rho$ (rho). The correlation coefficient is like any other descriptive statistic in that it is based on samples of data drawn randomly from the population. Thus, it is quite possible that a sample from a population where $\rho = 0$ may yield large positive or negative correlation coefficients by chance alone. In addition, the correlation coefficient has a sampling distribution. Therefore, we can apply the process of inferential statistical procedures to the analysis of a correlation coefficient.

The significance test for the correlation coefficient is complicated by the fact that the sampling distribution for $\rho$ is nonnormal, especially as $\rho$ approaches $+1.00$ or $-1.00$. Figure 12.4 presents an example of the sampling distribution for several correlations. When $\rho = 0$, the shape of the sampling distribution is symmetric. Indeed, the shape of the distribution conforms to the $t$-distributions. When $\rho = -.80$ or $\rho = .80$ the shape of the sampling distribution is skewed. In the following sections, we will examine how to use the logic of hypothesis testing to examine the magnitude of the correlation coefficient.

## $H_0: \rho = 0$

When testing the null hypothesis that the population correlation coefficient $\rho$ is zero, the observed correlation coefficient can be tested for significance with a $t$-ratio using Equation 12.9.

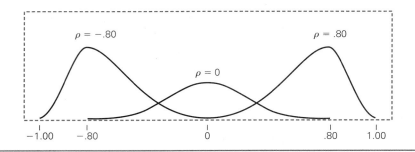

**Figure 12.4**

**Illustrative sample distribution of correlation coefficients when $\rho = -.80$, $\rho = 0$, and $\rho = +.80$.**

$$t = \frac{r\sqrt{n-2}}{\sqrt{1-r^2}}$$ (12.9)

In this equation, $r$ is the correlation coefficient obtained from your sample, and $n$ is the number of pairs of observations. Please note, the degrees of freedom for testing $r$ is $df = n - 2$. The degrees of freedom in this case are different from the single sample $t$-ratio because we obtain two scores from each subject. A degree of freedom is lost whenever we use a sample statistic to estimate a population parameter. The correlation involves the estimation of two parameters using the two variables we want to correlate.

Once you have the $t$-ratio, you can determine if the obtained $t$ is greater than $t_{critical}$ listed in Table C of Appendix D for the appropriate $\alpha$ level and degrees of freedom. An alternative is to use Table F of Appendix D. The layout of this table is similar to the table of critical values of the $t$-distributions. The obvious difference is that the values represent the critical values for Pearson's correlation coefficient.

Here is an illustrative example. A psychologist believes that people with higher levels of extroversion will be more likely to engage in risky behaviors. To test this idea, the psychologist asked a random sample of 25 students to complete a common measure of extroversion and a questionnaire indicating willingness to take risks. The correlation between the two measures is $r(23) = .462$.

> **Null Hypothesis:** $H_0$: $\rho = 0$. The correlation between the two variables of the population from which the sample was drawn equals 0.
>
> **Alternative Hypothesis:** $H_1$: $\rho \neq 0$. The correlation between the two variables of the population from which the sample was drawn does not equal 0.
>
> **Statistical Test:** Student's $t$-ratio or equivalent table for Pearson $r$.
>
> **Significance Level:** $\alpha = .05$. If the correlation between the variables is sufficiently large that its associated probability under $H_0$ is equal to or less than .05, we shall reject $H_0$.
>
> **Sampling Distribution:** The $df = n - 2 = 23$.
>
> **Critical Region for Rejecting $H_0$:** Using Table F, $|r_{observed}| \geq |.3961|$ If the absolute value of $r_{observed}$ is greater than or equal to .3961 we can reject $H_0$.

Because the observed correlation was larger than the criterion (e.g., .462 > .3961), we can reject the null hypothesis. With respect to the psychologist's hypothesis, there is evidence that people with higher levels of extroversion are more likely to indicate their willingness to take risks.

## $H_0$: $\rho_s = 0$

Determining the critical value for the Spearman Rank Order Correlation, $r_S$, follows the same procedures we just completed for the Pearson correlation. The obvious difference is that we must use a different sampling distribution. Table G of Appendix D presents the critical values for the Spearman correlation.

## Other Hypotheses Concerning $\rho$

When we wish to test a null hypothesis other than $\rho = 0$, for example the hypothesis that $\rho = .80$ or $\rho = .50$, we must use a different strategy. As you can see in Figure 12.4, when $\rho = -.80$ or $\rho = .80$, the sampling distributions are quite skewed and they do not conform to the *t*-distributions. In fact, whenever $\rho \neq 0$ the sampling distributions are skewed. The famous statistician Sir Ronald Fisher described a procedure for transforming sample *r*s into statistics $z_r$ that have sampling distributions that approximate the normal curve even for small sample sizes. Table H of Appendix D lists the correlations between 0 and 1 and the corresponding value of $z_r$. The value of $z_r$ can then be converted to a conventional *z*-score using Equation 12.10.

$$z = \frac{z_r - Z_r}{\sqrt{\dfrac{1}{(N-3)}}} \tag{12.10}$$

where $z_r$ is the transformed form of the sample *r* obtained from Table H, and $Z_r$ is the transformed value of the population correlation coefficient specified in $H_0$.

Here is an example. Assume that a researcher wants to determine whether a sample correlation of $r = .97$ is greater than a population correlation of $\rho = .50$ when the sample size is $N = 10$. Using Table H in Appendix D, we find that $z_r$ for $r = .97$ is $z_r = 2.092$. The $Z_r$ for the population correlation $\rho = .50$ is $Z_r = 0.549$.

**Null Hypothesis:** $H_0$: $\rho = .50$. The correlation between the two variables of the population from which the sample was drawn equals .50.

**Alternative Hypothesis:** $H_1$: $\rho \neq .50$. The correlation between the two variables of the population from which the sample was drawn does not equal .50.

**Statistical Test:** *z*-score.

**Significance Level:** $\alpha = .05$. If the correlation between the variables is sufficiently large that its associated probability under $H_0$ is equal to or less than .05, we shall reject $H_0$.

**Sampling Distribution:** Normal distribution.

**Critical Region for Rejecting $H_0$:** $|z_{observed}| \geq |1.960|$ If $z_{observed}$ is less than $-1.96$ or greater than 1.96 we can reject $H_0$.

Using Equation 12.10 we can convert the difference between the transformed correlations into a *z*-score.

$$z = \frac{2.092 - 0.549}{\sqrt{\dfrac{1}{(10 - 3)}}} = \frac{1.543}{0.3780} = 4.0820$$

$$z = 4.08$$

The $z$-score is evaluated in the same way we would evaluate any $z$-score, using the normal distribution. Because our $z$-score is greater than the critical value (e.g., $4.08 > 1.960$), we can reject the null hypothesis that $\rho = .50$.

## 12.8 The Power of a Test

As you may recall from the previous chapter, a Type II error occurs when we fail to reject a false null hypothesis. Researchers want to avoid Type II errors for obvious reasons. We conduct research because we want to discover interesting facts and relations among variables. If our statistical tools overlook these important findings, we will have wasted much time and energy. Therefore, researchers strive to increase the power of their statistical test when they conduct research. In this section of the chapter we will explore the concept of the **power of a statistical test** using the single sample $t$-ratio as a guide. The concepts that we explore in this section will apply in subsequent chapters as well.

For any statistical test, $\beta$ defines the probability of making a Type II Error. Power is the probability of correctly rejecting the null hypothesis. We represent power as $1 - \beta$. There are four factors that influence $1 - \beta$.

1. The size of the difference between the sample and population means: $\mu_{\overline{X}} - \mu_0$.
2. Sample size, $n$.
3. Variability in the population, $\sigma$.
4. Alpha ($\alpha$) level and directionality (directional vs. nondirectional) of the test.

Let's look at each of these in greater detail.

### $\mu_{\overline{X}} - \mu_0$

If the null hypothesis is false and the population mean is different from the hypothesized mean, we will have two sampling distributions similar to the ones presented in Figure 12.5. Each distribution represents sample means drawn from separate populations. The central limit theorem allows us to predict the shape of both distributions. The sampling distribution for the null hypothesis is a distribution of sample means for which $\mu_0 = 100$. The dark blue-gray area at the upper end of the scale represents the critical region for $\alpha = .05$ using a directional test. According to the null hypothesis, there is a 5% probability that any random sample will have a mean in the critical area.

The second distribution is a sampling distribution of means that would be obtained if samples of a given size were drawn from the population for which $\mu_{\overline{X}} = 103$. Clearly, there is a real difference between the two populations. Each curve represents a different population, one with a mean of 100 and another with a mean of 103.

▓ **Power of a Test:**

The probability that one will reject $H_0$ when it is a false statement. The power of a statistical analysis of a set of data is represented as $(1 - \beta)$ and is influenced by $\mu_{\overline{X}} - \mu_0$, $n$, $\sigma$, and $\alpha$.

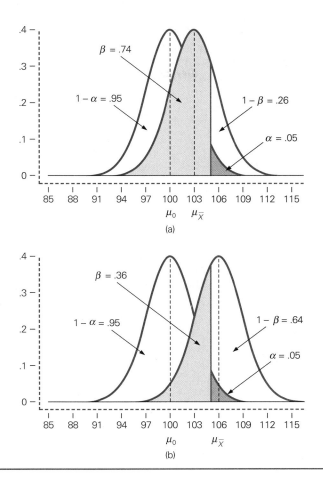

**Figure 12.5**

The effect on power of $(\mu_{\overline{X}} - \mu_0)$. In (a) the difference is 3. The difference in (b) is 6. For both pairs of distributions, the shaded areas represent the probabilities of committing a Type I error ($\alpha$) and a Type II error ($\beta$). The power of the statistic is $1 - \beta$. The lower graph represents greater power.

As you can see, the two distributions overlap, but not perfectly. The area shaded in the light blue-gray represents $\beta$, the probability of a Type II error. When we sample from the population with a mean of 103, some of the means will be less than the critical region and will not allow us to reject the null hypothesis. In our example, 74% ($\beta = .74$) of the curve is in the shaded area. The probability of committing a Type II error is 74% whereas the probability of rejecting the null hypothesis is a mere 26% ($1 - \beta = .26$). Therefore, the power of this statistic is 26%. Consequently, although the population means are different from each other, the chance that we will be able to discover this difference using sample statistics is only slightly better than 1 in 4.

Figure 12.5b presents a different set of conditions. Now the difference between the means is much greater ($\mu_{\overline{X}} - \mu_0 = 6$). Notice the differences between panels 12.5a and 12.5b. The obvious difference is that there is less overlap of the two variables. Because there is less overlap, the area representing $\beta$ decreases. Specifically, the probability of a Type II error is now 36% whereas the probability of correctly rejecting the null hypothesis is now 64%.

The obvious conclusion to draw from this example is that power increases as the difference between the two population means increases.

Here is a simple illustration. Let's set $\mu_0 = 100$ and $\hat{s} = 15$. Now imagine that we have two populations, one where $\mu_{\overline{X}} = 101$ and a second where $\mu_{\overline{X}} = 106$. Using the single-sample $t$-ratio we see that the larger difference in the numerator will produce a larger value of $t$.

$$t = \frac{101 - 100}{\dfrac{15}{\sqrt{25}}} = \frac{1}{3} = 0.333$$

$$t = \frac{106 - 100}{\dfrac{15}{\sqrt{25}}} = \frac{6}{3} = 2$$

How can you ensure that the difference between $\mu_{\overline{X}}$ and $\mu_0$ will be as large as possible? For the single-sample case, the best advice is to select your populations wisely. For example, if you wanted to examine the effects of alcohol abuse on memory, you would want to find people who have been habitual alcohol abusers for quite some time. Signs of serious decrease in memory function do not occur unless a person has been an abuser of alcohol for many years. Therefore, sampling from a population of 50-year-old alcoholics will produce more dramatic effects than selecting from a population of younger alcoholics.

If you wanted to examine the characteristics of people with an extroverted personality, it may be best to select from a population whose scores on conventional measures of extroversion are clearly high, indicating an unambiguous personality trait. Sampling from this population would produce a more powerful statistical test than if you selected anyone who had an above average extroversion score.

### Sample Size

As we have seen repeatedly, sample size is important in estimating population parameters. As sample size increases, the accuracy of our population estimates increases. Specifically, the spread of the sampling distribution decreases. Figure 12.6a presents the sampling distributions that would occur if one selected samples from two populations using a small sample size. Figure 12.6b shows the two distributions obtained when the sample size is larger. The difference in the shape of the two distributions is explained by the central limit theorem. Recall that sample size affects the variance of a sampling distribution. As a rule, as the sample size increases, the spread within the sampling distributions will get smaller. Thus, the degree of overlap of the two sampling distributions decreases and the corresponding power increases. A simple example will show how this principle applies. Notice that in the following equations everything is the same but the sample size. Also, when $n = 25$ the difference between the means is not statistically significant. By contrast, when $n = 100$ the same difference is statistically significant. In the following examples the difference between the two means is 5.0. The spread is $\hat{s} = 15.0$ and the sample size is 25 and 100. Clearly we have increased our power and are able to reject the null hypothesis when we use the larger sample.

$$t = \frac{55 - 50}{\dfrac{15}{\sqrt{25}}} = \frac{5}{3} = 1.667, p > .05$$

$$t = \frac{55 - 50}{\dfrac{15}{\sqrt{100}}} = \frac{5}{1.5} = 3.333, p < .05$$

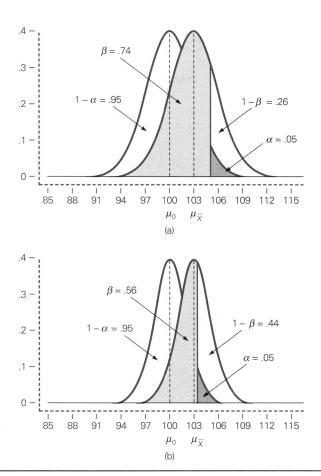

**Figure | 12.6**

The effect on power resulting from changes in sample size or changes in population variance. For both distributions, the shaded areas represent the probability of committing a Type I error ($\alpha$) and a Type II error ($\beta$). The power of the statistics is $1 - \beta$. The lower graph represents greater power.

Although it is true that increasing sample size will increase power, you need to be aware of the cost of this alternative. Increasing sample size sounds easy—you just collect more data. The solution can be a problem, however. Collecting data takes time and money. From the cost of purchasing materials to the time you must take out of your schedule, collecting data from each subject adds to the total cost of the research. In some cases, such as administering a set of questionnaires to students in their classes, there will be a minimal cost for collecting more data. In other cases, collecting the data from one subject will be time consuming and expensive. Therefore, we recommend that you consider all your options for increasing power before you jump to the conclusion that you just need to run more subjects through your study.

## Variability

If the population from which you are sampling has considerable variability, the sampling distribution will also have considerable variability. We can use Figure 12.6 again to represent the effects of population variance on power. The distributions in Figure 12.6a represent what would occur when the variance in the population is large. Consequently, there is considerable overlap of the two distributions and the relative power is small. Reducing the amount of variability in the population will produce a result similar to the one depicted in Figure 12.6b. Because the magnitude of $\sigma$ decreased, the overlap depicted in Figure 12.6b decreased and the power increased. Therefore, anything you can do to reduce sampling error will improve your ability to detect a statistically significant difference between the means.

Here is another computational example. Notice that decreasing $\sigma$ from 15 to 10 makes the statistic more powerful.

$$t = \frac{55 - 50}{\frac{15}{\sqrt{25}}} = \frac{5}{3} = 1.6667, \, p > .05$$

$$t = \frac{55 - 50}{\frac{10}{\sqrt{25}}} = \frac{5}{2} = 2.500, \, p < .05$$

Basically you can increase power by reducing sampling error. There are several ways to reduce sampling error. One is to ensure that your sample is homogeneous. You can help to make sure that your sample is homogeneous by carefully defining your population. Consider an obvious example. The population "children" is broad because any person younger than 18 years old could be in the population. By contrast, the population "3-year-olds" is a very specific and well-defined population. The chances are that the population "children" will have relatively more sampling error than the population "3-year-olds" for most dependent variables.

### Alpha

As you already know, the $\alpha$-level sets the probability of a Type I error. You also know that the smaller the $\alpha$ the less the probability of a Type I error. Unfortunately, lowering the $\alpha$-level will decrease the power of the statistical test. As the probability of the Type I error decreases, the probability of the Type II error increases. In other words, if you set a very stringent $\alpha$-level you are less likely to reject the null hypothesis, but you are more likely to make a Type II error. That is, you will conclude that you don't have a significant finding and you will be wrong. Look at Figure 12.7 for an illustration. The upper graph has $\alpha = .05$; the lower graph has $\alpha = .10$. All other aspects of the graph are identical. Note the differences between the power. When $\alpha = .10$, $\beta = .61$, and the power is $1 - \beta = .39$. Lowering the $\alpha$ to .05 decreases the power to $1 - \beta = .26$. In other words, all things being equal, the probability of a Type I error increases as $1 - \beta$ increases. Another way to say the same thing is that as $\alpha$ gets larger, power increases.

Your selection of a directional and nondirectional test will also influence power. As a generality, a directional test is more powerful than a nondirectional test. The reason for this difference is how we identify the critical region. This factor is easy to see visually. Look at the dark area indicating $\alpha$. The larger that area, the larger the area $1 - \beta$ and thus the greater the power. When we use the directional test, we place the critical region at one end of the distribution.

Let's consider a $t$-ratio with 15 degrees of freedom and $\alpha = .05$. In this example, $t_{\text{critical}}$ for the directional test is 1.753. When we conduct a nondirectional test, we split the criterion regions between the two extreme ends. Consequently, the $t$-ratio required to reject the null hypothesis is

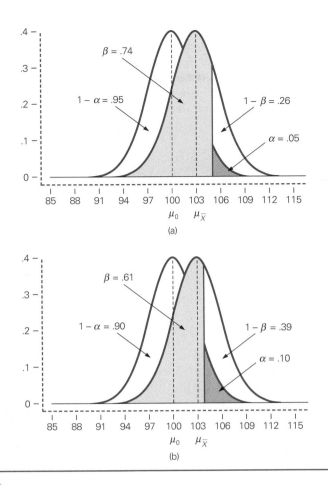

**Figure** | **12.7**

The effect on power caused by changes in $\alpha$. For both graphs, the difference between the means is 3. For the distributions in (a), $\alpha = .05$. For the distributions in (b), $\alpha$ is larger ($\alpha = .10$) and the power is greater. For both graphs, the probability of committing a Type I error ($\alpha$) and a Type II error ($\beta$) are represented by shaded areas. The power of the statistic is represented as $1 - \beta$.

larger than the comparable directional test. For the nondirectional test with 15 degrees of freedom $t_{\text{critical}} = 2.131$.

## 12.9
## Effect Size and Power

In the preceding examples, we showed you how to calculate the $t$-ratio and determine if its size justified rejecting the null hypothesis. Although calculating the $t$-ratio and hypothesis testing are important steps, there is additional information we can generate. Once we calculate the $t$-ratio we can determine the effect size. The effect size is extremely important for three reasons. First, we can use the effect size of a statistic to compare the results of one research project to the results of other projects. Second, knowing the effect size allows us to estimate the power of the statistic. Finally, we can use effect size to estimate the number of subjects we need in our research in order to maximize the chance of rejecting a false null hypothesis.

In this section of the chapter, we will introduce you to $d$, a common measure of effect size. We will then show you how to use $d$ to estimate the power of a statistic and how to use $d$ to determine the number of subjects you will need to maximize the power of your research.

### Effect Size, $d_1$

The $t$-ratio allows us to do one thing, determine whether to reject the null hypothesis. Similarly, the value of $p$ indicates the probability of obtaining at least the value of the $t_{observed}$ if $H_0$ were true. There are a few additional tools that will help us understand our data. An extremely useful statistic is the measure of effect size. For the single-sample $t$-ratio, the effect size is defined as

$$d_1 = \frac{\overline{X} - \mu_0}{\hat{s}} \sqrt{2} \tag{12.11}$$

We use the symbol $d_1$ to indicate that we are determining the effect size for a single-sample $t$-ratio. Notice that we take the difference between the sample and population mean and then divide the difference by the unbiased estimate of the standard deviation. The square root of 2 is 1.4142. This value is a constant that is part of the equation.

Technically speaking, the effect size is the ratio of the difference between the sample and population means to the unbiased estimate of the population standard deviation. Therefore, effect size is a ratio in the same way that the $z$-score is a ratio. As with the $z$-score, we can use the effect size to compare the results of different statistical tests.

Think back to when we first introduced you to the $z$-score. We noted that the score allows us to compare scores that come from samples with different means and standard deviations. Therefore, although the scores 20 and 275 are radically different numbers, we can say that they are equivalent if both convert to a $z$-score of 1.25. A $z$-score of 1.25 indicates that the score (20 or 275) is 1.25 standard deviations above the mean. The larger the absolute value of a $z$-score, the larger the relative difference between the mean and the score.

The same logic applies to the effect size. The effect size for a single sample $t$-ratio is a measure of the relative difference between the sample mean and the population mean. The larger the effect size, the greater the relative difference between the two means. This difference is evaluated relative to the variability of the sample. Because the effect size is a ratio, we can compare the $d_1$s from different studies. The larger the $d_1$ the greater the effect.

Look at Table 12.5. The numbers represent the results of four hypothetical studies. There are several things to notice. Can you see any interesting patterns?

Some people believe smaller values of $p$ automatically mean a stronger effect. In addition, some people believe that statistically significant effects with larger samples are more impressive than statistically significant effects with smaller samples. Inspection of the information in Table 12.5 indicates that these impressions are wrong. As an example, look at examples 2 and 4. As you can see, the effect size, as indicated by $d_1$, is extremely large in Example 2 although the $p$-value is .042. By contrast, the effect size for Example 4 is smaller although $p = .007$. In other words, the $p$-value is not an indication of effect size.

**Table** 12.5

**Example of Four Pairs of Means Used for a Single-Sample *t*-Ratio. Also Reported Are the Probability Levels of the *t*-Ratio and the Effect Size of Each Sample**

| Example | $\overline{X}$ | $\mu_0$ | $\hat{s}$ | $n$ | $t_{observed}$ | $p$ | $d_1$ |
|---------|-----|-------|-----|-----|------------|------|------|
| 1 | 13 | 10 | 2 | 8 | 4.24 | .003 | 2.12 |
| 2 | 13 | 10 | 4 | 10 | 2.37 | .042 | 1.06 |
| 3 | 15 | 10 | 10 | 25 | 2.50 | .020 | 0.71 |
| 4 | 16 | 10 | 15 | 50 | 2.83 | .007 | 0.57 |

Now look at examples 1 and 2. The differences between the means are identical for each example, but $\hat{s}$ is smaller for Example 1. The smaller the spread in the sample, the greater the effect size.

Example 1 has the greatest effect size and statistical power because the standard deviation is the smallest. Remember that whenever we can reduce the effect of random error, as estimated by $\hat{s}$, we can increase the power of a statistic. There is an important lesson to be learned here. You cannot judge the effect of the independent variable by examining the size of the *t*-ratio or the *p*-level. Similarly, you cannot compare one *t*-ratio with another in the hope of finding which represents "the more significant event." In order to evaluate the statistical results concerning magnitude of effect, you must calculate the effect size.

## Interpreting the Size of $d_1$

How big is big? How small is small? OK, this is not a philosophy course, but these are reasonable questions to ask when we examine the size of $d_1$. There are two ways to evaluate the magnitude of $d_1$. The first method is to compare values of $d_1$ to some preestablished standard. The second method is to compare values of $d_1$ to those found in a general line of research. We believe that both are useful. Let's start with the simpler of the two, the preestablished standard.

Cohen (1988) has suggested some general guidelines for interpreting $d_1$. Table 12.6 presents these guidelines. Although Cohen's guidelines are useful, different areas of research routinely produce different effect sizes. For example, psychologists who study perceptual processes may use three or four subjects in their research. The obvious implication is that the effect size of their research must be large. One reason the effect size is large is that research on perceptual processes typically occurs in laboratories where the researcher has control over the conditions of the experiment. Therefore, the amount of random error is minimal.

Other areas of psychology do not have the same level of control. For example, social psychologists who study complex human behavior in natural settings cannot control or keep constant all the variables that they study. As a consequence, there is more error and a need to use more subjects in order to detect a statistically significant effect.

Therefore, we should recognize the arbitrary nature of these guidelines and not apply them universally. Rather, we should examine what is the typical effect size in an area of research and use it as a point of comparison. We will return to this important topic in later chapters.

**Table 12.6**

**Cohen's (1988) Guidelines for Evaluating Effect Sizes**

| For Single-Sample $t$-Ratios | | |
|---|---|---|
| Small effect size | $d_1 = .20$ | Generally these differences are very small and difficult to detect without large sample sizes. Some researchers believe that when $d_1 \leq .10$, the effect is trivial. |
| Medium effect size | $d_1 = .50$ | A medium effect is sufficiently large to be seen by the eye when graphed. |
| Large effect size | $d_1 = .80$ | A large effect size is easily seen and requires few subjects to detect the effect. |

| For Pearson $rs$ | |
|---|---|
| Small effect size: | $r = .10$ |
| Medium effect size | $r = .30$ |
| Large effect size | $r = .50$ |

## Estimating Sample Size: Single Sample $t$-Ratio

How many subjects should you include in your sample? Great question. One way to ensure the power of your research is to have a sufficiently large sample. But how big is big enough? Too few subjects will result in inadequate power. Too many subjects may be too expensive and time consuming. Fortunately, we can use $d_1$ to estimate the number of subjects we will require.

Look at Table D of Appendix D, which is a table of power for single sample $t$-ratios. Along the left-most column are sample sizes ($n$). The columns represent values of $d_1$. As you can see, there are two versions of the table, one for directional tests and the other for nondirectional tests. Using the table is simple. Select an effect size that you believe represents your research. Then, determine the sample size you will need for a specific level of power. Some researchers believe that the power of $1 - \beta = .80$ is optimal. Others may want their power to be higher or lower.

Here is an example of the use of power to determine sample size. You want to measure the average number of fat grams students at your college consume during a typical day. How many subjects will you need to determine whether students eat more or fewer grams of fat than the national average? How should you proceed?

The implication of the example is that we will use a nondirectional test. Let's also presume that $\alpha = .05$ will be sufficient. Finally, let's assume that the effect size is medium, $d_1 \approx .50$. According to Table D, you will need approximately 65 subjects to have your power set at $1 - \beta = .81$. What would happen if you decided to collect data from 100 students. In that case, $1 - \beta = .94$. The larger sample size means that you will have a 94% chance of rejecting the null hypothesis if the difference between the fat consumption at your college is different from the national average.

## Using Effect Size to Estimate Sample Size: Pearson $r$

Table I of Appendix D presents the power estimates for various correlations and sample sizes. For example, assume that you want to examine the correlation between two variables. Based on previous research you believe that the effect size is medium, therefore, $r = .30$. You decide to use a nondirectional hypothesis with $\alpha = .05$. In order to have $1 - \beta = .80$ you will need about 84 subjects in your study.

## 12.10 / Putting It All Together

The instructor of a psychology class wants to impress upon his students that using elaborated study strategies will improve performance on exams. He tells the students how to use these techniques and that there will be a 20-question pop quiz some time within the next week. After seven days, the instructor administers both the pop quiz and a questionnaire concerning the student's study behavior. Higher scores on the questionnaire indicate that the student studied longer and used more of the elaboration techniques he recommended. Here are the data and the descriptive statistics.

| Student | Study Questionnaire | Quiz Score |
|---------|--------------------|-----------| 
| 1 | 82 | 16 |
| 2 | 77 | 15 |
| 3 | 60 | 15 |
| 4 | 85 | 17 |
| 5 | 70 | 14 |
| 6 | 79 | 16 |
| 7 | 73 | 14 |
| 8 | 87 | 17 |
| 9 | 69 | 17 |
| 10 | 71 | 15 |
| 11 | 71 | 17 |
| 12 | 75 | 16 |
| 13 | 98 | 18 |
| 14 | 71 | 15 |
| 15 | 64 | 15 |
| $\Sigma X$ | 1132.0 | 237.0 |
| $\Sigma X^2$ | 86726.0 | 3765.0 |
| $\overline{X}$ | 75.4667 | 15.8000 |
| $\hat{s}$ | 9.6278 | 1.2071 |

We can begin our analysis of the data using stem-and-leaf plots of the data. Figure 12.8 shows the plots of the two variables.

The data appear to be relatively normally distributed without any extremely high or low scores. No student earned less than a C on the quiz (14). The highest grade was an 18 or 90%. The instructor may want to determine if some of the questions are problematic. It seems strange that there are no perfect scores. Perhaps there are one or two questions that were a problem for most of the students or there was an error in the grading.

|   | Study Questionnaire |   | Quiz Score |
|---|---|---|---|
| 6 | 049 | 1 | 44 |
| 7 | 01113579 | 1 | 55555 |
| 8 | 257 | 1 | 666 |
| 9 | 8 | 1 | 7777 |
|   |   | 1 | 8 |

**Figure 12.8**

**Stem-and-leaf plots of the data.**

Let's assume that there is nothing wrong with the data. We can also use a scatterplot to examine the relation between the two variables. This graph will allow us to see the relative positions of the pairs of scores. Using the graph will help us visualize the data, ensure that there are no strange scores (e.g., outliers), and help us interpret the results. Figure 12.9 is a simple scatterplot of the data.

Looking at the graph, you should be able to see several things. First, there does appear to be a positive, linear relation between studying and the quiz score. Indeed, the correlation coefficient is $r = .6478$. We can also see that no one received a score greater than 18 or less than 14 on the quiz. There do not appear to be any odd scores in our data set. With this casual analysis of the data we can now proceed with the use of inferential statistics.

According to the instructor's records from past years, most students earn a 14.1 on this pop quiz. In addition, based on his records, most students score a 68 when asked to complete the questionnaire about their study habits. There are several questions that the instructor can address. They are:

1. Is the students' quiz average grade *greater* than the typical performance?
2. Is there evidence that the students studied *differently* during the past week?
3. Is there any relation between effort put into studying and quiz performance?

Let's look at each question in turn.

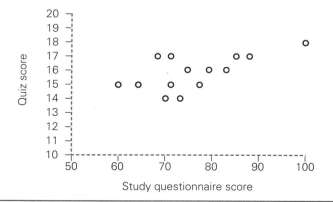

**Figure 12.9**

**Scatterplot of the relation between Study Questionnaire Score and Quiz Score.**

**1.** Is the students' quiz average grade *greater* than the typical performance?

***Null Hypothesis:*** $H_0$: 15.8 ≤ 14.1.

***Alternative Hypothesis:*** $H_1$: 15.8 > 14.1.

***Statistical Test:*** $t$-ratio—single sample

***Significance Level:*** $\alpha = .05.$

***Sampling Distribution:*** Student's $t$-distribution, $df = 14$

***Critical Region for Rejecting $H_0$:*** $t_{critical} \geq 1.761$

**Student's $t$-ratio**

$$t = \frac{15.8 - 14.1}{\frac{1.2071}{\sqrt{15}}} = \frac{1.70}{0.3117} = 5.45396$$

$t_{observed} = 5.45$, reject $H_0$.

**95% Confidence Interval**

$CI_{95} = 15.8 \pm (2.145 \times 0.3117)$      [Note the $t_{critical}$ is for $\alpha = .05$, two-tailed]

$CI_{95} = 15.8 \pm 0.6686$

$CI_{95} = 15.13$ to $16.47$

**Effect Size**

$$d_1 = \frac{15.8 - 14.1}{1.2071} \sqrt{2} = \frac{1.70}{1.2071} \times 1.4142 = 1.9917$$

$d_1 = 1.99$ A very large effect size.

**2.** Are the students' study questionnaire scores *different from* the typical performance?

***Null Hypothesis:*** $H_0$: 75.5 = 68.0

***Alternative Hypothesis:*** $H_1$: 75.5 ≠ 68.0

***Statistical Test:*** $t$-ratio—single sample

***Significance Level:*** $\alpha = .05$

***Sampling Distribution:*** Student's $t$-distribution, $df = 14$

***Critical Region for Rejecting $H_0$:*** $t_{critical} \geq 2.145$

**Student's $t$-ratio**

$$t = \frac{75.4667 - 68.0}{\frac{9.6278}{\sqrt{15}}} = \frac{7.4667}{2.4859} = 3.0036$$

$t_{observed} = 3.00$, reject $H_0$.

**95% Confidence Interval**

$CI_{95} = 75.5 \pm (2.145 \times 2.4859)$      [Note the $t_{critical}$ is for $\alpha = .05$, two-tailed]

$CI_{95} = 75.5 \pm 5.3322$

$CI_{95} = 70.17$ to $80.83$

**Effect Size**

$$d_1 = \frac{75.4667 - 68.0}{9.6278} \sqrt{2} = \frac{7.4667}{9.6278} \times 1.4142 = 1.0968$$

$d_1 = 1.10$ A very large effect size.

**3.** Is there any relation between effort put into studying and quiz performance?

***Null Hypothesis:*** $H_0$: .6478 = 0

***Alternative Hypothesis:*** $H_1$: .6478 ≠ 0

***Statistical Test:*** $t$-ratio—single sample or $r_{critical}$ distribution.

***Significance Level:*** $\alpha = .05$

***Sampling Distribution:*** Student's $t$- or $r_{critical}$ distribution, $df = 13 = n - 2$

***Critical Region for Rejecting $H_0$:*** $r_{critical} \geq .5748$

**Pearson Correlation Coefficient**

$r_{observed} = .648$, reject $H_0$.       [Recall that $r$ is the measure of effect size]

Given these results, the instructor can make several general conclusions. First, the students did do better on the quiz than had students in the past. Similarly, the instructor can assume that the students studied more and that there is a direct relation between studying and quiz grade. Although the students did do better on the quiz, we cannot be sure what caused the increase in performance. The instructor cannot be sure if it was the application of study techniques or just the simple fact that students were studying more. Because there is no control group or random assignment of subjects to different treatment conditions, we can not be sure what caused the increase in grades.

If the teacher wanted to replicate the study, how many students should he use? Based on the current data, we can assume that the effect is large. To be on the conservative side, we will set $d_1 = .80$. In order to have $1 - \beta = .80$, the instructor should use approximately 26 students.

## CHAPTER SUMMARY

Inferential statistics are the foundation of contemporary behavioral research. Any researcher who wishes to describe the population under study depends upon inferential statistics. In this chapter we introduced you to the essentials of inferential statistics. Each of the concepts learned and skills you mastered will be repeated and expanded upon in the subsequent chapters for this book. We can quickly chronicle your accomplishments and hint at how you will use these skills in the future.

The chapter began by reviewing methods of estimating the variance of a population using sample data. As a part of that discussion, we introduced you to the concept of degrees of freedom. The degrees of freedom are important for our calculations of variance and standard deviation. Specifically, they allow us to use sample data to estimate the variance and standard deviation of a population. We will continue to use estimates of variance and degrees of freedom as we examine more advanced statistics like the analysis of variance.

A major component of this chapter was the review of hypothesis testing. Hypothesis testing is really nothing more than a set of procedures for making decisions about probabilistic information. We focused on one of the first types of inferential statistics to be developed, the Student's *t*-ratio. Student's statistic is an extremely useful statistic and the intellectual foundation of a host of inferential statistics.

Although we showed you a step-by-step method for hypothesis testing, we hope you understand that hypothesis testing is merely a tool that we used to understand the data. As with all statistics, you must carefully consider how you will use and interpret a statistical test. There used to be a time when researchers focused only on whether or not they could reject the null hypothesis. During the past 20 years, however, researchers have begun to focus on broader issues, especially the power of their statistical tests.

This new perspective allows us to have a more meaningful discussion of the data. As you learned in this chapter, it is not enough to determine whether to reject the null hypothesis. Whenever we analyze the data, we need to examine the effect size of the data. Effect size is a method for describing the relative difference between the observed conditions and hypothesized conditions. In subsequent chapters, we will examine different methods of determining effect size for various statistical tests. Related to effect size is power. In essence, power is the probability that we will correctly decide to reject the null hypothesis. Knowing about power is essential in that it helps us use research designs that are efficient and effective.

In essence, each of the following chapters will introduce you to a new inferential statistic. Although the statistic will be new, its use will follow the same logic you mastered in this chapter.

## TERMS TO REMEMBER

| | |
|---|---|
| biased estimate | *t*-distributions |
| degrees of freedom (*df*) | unbiased estimate of the population |
| power of a test | variance ($\hat{s}^2$) |

## EXERCISES

1. Explain why the standard deviation of a sample usually underestimates the standard deviation of a population. Give an example.

2. Explain the difference between the following:
   **a.** $s^2$ and $\sigma^2$
   **b.** $\sigma^2$ and $\sigma_{\overline{X}}^2$
   **c.** $\mu$ and $\mu_{\overline{X}}$

3. Explain the difference among $\hat{s}$, $s_{\overline{X}}$, and $s$.

4. What statistics are used to describe the distribution of a sample? What ones are used to describe the distribution of sample statistics?

5a. Is $s^2$ an unbiased estimate of $\sigma^2$?

5b. Is $\hat{s}^2$ an unbiased estimate of $\sigma^2$?

6. When estimating the variance of a population using a single sample, the degrees of freedom is $(n - 1)$. However, when calculating the standard error of the estimate, the degrees of freedom is $(n - 2)$. When testing the significance of a correlation coefficient, the degrees of freedom is $(n - 2)$. Why?

7. Sometimes when testing the significance of a single mean, Equation 12.6 is used to calculate $z$. Other times when testing the significance of a single mean, Equation 12.7 is used to calculate $t$. When is it appropriate to use each?

8. Earlier in the text we calculated standard scores using the equation on the left. Compare this earlier formula with the one on the right used to evaluate the significance of a sample mean from a hypothesized mean. Describe how they are similar.

$$z = \frac{X - \mu}{\sigma} \qquad z = \frac{\overline{X} - \mu_0}{\sigma_{\overline{X}}}$$

9. In testing the significance of a single sample mean from a hypothesized population mean, what would $H_0$ and $H_1$ be for a nondirectional test?

10. What would $H_0$ and $H_1$ be for a directional test?

11. What are the critical values of $t$ using a nondirectional, two-tailed test $\alpha = .05$ and the following degrees of freedom: 10, 15, 20, and 25.

12. Based on Exercise 12, what generalization can be made regarding degrees of freedom and critical values of $t$?

13. Evaluate the following for significance.
    **a.** $t = 1.78$, $df = 15$, $\alpha = .05$, two-tailed
    **b.** $t = 2.18$, $df = 15$, $\alpha = .05$, two-tailed
    **c.** $t = 1.9$, $df = 15$, $\alpha = .05$, one-tailed
    **d.** $t = 1.9$, $df = 15$, $\alpha = .01$, one-tailed

14. A professor gives his class an examination that, as he knows from years of experience, yields $\mu = 78$ and $\sigma = 7$. His present class of 22 obtains a mean of 82. Is he correct in assuming that the performance of this class differs significantly from that of other classes? Employ $\alpha = .01$ and a two-tailed test.

15. A professor gives his class an examination that, as he knows from years of experience, yields $\mu = 78$. His present class of 22 obtains $\overline{X} = 82$ and $s = 7$. Is he correct in assuming that the performance of this class differs significantly from that of other classes? Employ $\alpha = .01$ and a two-tailed test.

16. Explain the difference between Exercises 15 and 16. What test statistic is employed in each case and why? Why is the decision different in each case?

17. Travis does research with a marine biology research team. His job is to catch lobsters, weigh them, tag them, and return them to the water. Over the years the team has determined that the average weight in pounds of the lobsters at a particular location is $\mu = 2.1$ and $\sigma = .5$. As part of an annual survey, Travis catches 27 lobsters with a mean weight of 3.1 pounds. Is he correct in assuming that the lobsters he caught are heavier than those usually found at this location? Employ $\alpha = .01$ and a one-tailed test.

**18.** If Travis had been interested in whether the lobsters simply differed in weight from those usually caught (i.e., were either heavier or lighter), would he have conducted a different type of test? What would he have done differently? Would his results have been different?

**19.** Overton University claims that because of its superior facilities and close faculty supervision, its students complete the Ph.D. program earlier than usual. They base this assertion on the fact that the national mean age for completion is 32.11, whereas the mean age of their 26 Ph.D.'s is 29.61 with $s = 6.00$. Test the validity of their assumption. Use $\alpha = .01$ and a one-tailed test.

**20.** How do the $t$-distributions differ from the normal distribution? Are they ever the same?

**21.** Professor Snyder administers two tests to a group of 10 research subjects. She then calculates a Pearson product moment correlation and obtains a coefficient of .31. Are her results statistically significant at the $\alpha = .05$ level?

**22.** What if Professor Snyder had used a larger sample, for example, 20, 30, or 40 subjects? Determine $r_{critical}$ for each sample size. Would her results have been statistically significant with a larger sample?

**23.** Based on the results for Exercise 22, what can be said about the significance of a correlation coefficient and the size of the sample?

**24.** It is axiomatic that when pairs of individuals are selected at random and the intelligence test scores of the first members of the pairs are correlated with the second members, $\rho = 0$.
  **a.** Thirty-nine pairs of siblings are randomly selected, and $r = .27$ is obtained between members of the pairs for intelligence. Are siblings more alike in intelligence than unrelated individuals? Use $\alpha = .05$, two-tailed.
  **b.** A study of 28 pairs of identical twins yields $r = .91$ on intelligence test scores. What do you conclude? Use $\alpha = .05$, two-tailed.

**25.** As a requirement for admission to Blue Chip University, a candidate must take a standardized entrance examination. The correlation between performance on this examination and college grades is $r = .43$.
  **a.** The director of admissions claims that a better way to predict college success is by using high school grade averages. To test her claim, she randomly selects 52 students and correlates their college grades with their high school averages. She obtains $r = .54$. What do you conclude? Use $\alpha = .05$, two-tailed.
  **b.** The director's assistant constructs a test that he claims is better for predicting college success than the one currently used. He randomly selects 67 students and correlates their grade point averages with performance on his test. He obtains $r = .61$. What do you conclude? Use $\alpha = .05$, two-tailed.

**26.** Matthew ranked the 17 waiters he supervises in terms of their speed and efficiency on the job. He correlated these ranks with the total amount of tips each of these waiters receive for a 1-week period and obtained $r_s = .438$. What do you conclude? Use $\alpha = .05$, two-tailed.

**27.** Graham, the owner of a car-leasing company, ranked 25 of his customers on their neatness and general care of their rented cars during a 3-month period. He correlated these ranks with the number of miles each customer drove during this same period. He obtained $r = -.397$. Employing $\alpha = .05$ and a two-tailed test, what do you conclude?

**28.** What degrees of freedom is used when testing the significance of a correlation coefficient? What degrees of freedom is used when testing the significance of the mean of a single sample? Do they differ? Explain why.

**29.** A researcher conducts a study in which he obtains a sample mean of 45.0 and a standard error of the mean of 2.2, with $df = 15$. Determine the confidence limits for the 95% confidence interval.

**30.** Using the same data described in Exercise 30, what are the 99% confidence limits? What conclusion can you draw about the effect of $\alpha$-level and the precision of a confidence interval?

**31.** Tim and Mark, two graduate students in psychology, are discussing their research. Mark is discouraged because after many hours of work on a research project his results are not statistically significant using $\alpha = .05$. His correlation is $r = .337$. Tim tells Mark that his conclusion is ridiculous! He says he has seen many studies in which correlations even smaller than .3 were statistically significant. He proves his point by showing Mark a journal article in which a correlation of $r = .21$ is statistically significant at $\alpha = .01$. Can both Mark and the author of the journal article be correct? Explain.

**32.** Name four factors that influence the power of a single-sample $t$-test. Describe in your own words the effects of each.

Instructions for questions 33–40. Each question represents an independent sample of data. For each sample, calculate the mean and unbiased estimate of the variance and standard deviation. For each mean, calculate the 95% confidence interval. Finally, for each sample, conduct a Student's $t$-test using the $\mu_0$ and test indicated for the item. Be sure that you identify the null and alternative hypothesis and the critical value for rejecting the null hypothesis.

| 33 | 34 | 35 | 36 | 37 |
|----|----|----|----|----|
| 13 | 28 | 20 | 19 | 28 |
| 7  | 23 | 18 | 6  | 27 |
| 11 | 23 | 12 | 9  | 27 |
| 9  | 23 | 12 | 13 | 23 |
| 10 | 26 | 14 | 13 | 23 |
| 10 | 26 | 14 | 12 | 24 |
|    | 26 | 15 | 12 | 24 |
|    |    |    |    | 24 |
| $\mu_0 = 12$ | $\mu_0 = 24$ | $\mu_0 = 20$ | $\mu_0 = 10$ | $\mu_0 = 23$ |
| $\alpha = .05$ | $\alpha = .05$ | $\alpha = .05$ | $\alpha = .05$ | $\alpha = .05$ |
| 1-tailed | 2-tailed | 2-tailed | 1-tailed | 2-tailed |

| 38 | 39 | 40 |
|---|---|---|
| 28 | 26 | 15 |
| 27 | 17 | 15 |
| 27 | 17 | 7 |
| 23 | 22 | 8 |
| 23 | 22 | 8 |
| 24 | 18 | 8 |
| 24 | 18 | 9 |
| 24 | 21 | 10 |
|  | 19 | 10 |
| $\mu_0 = 23$ | $\mu_0 = 17$ | $\mu_0 = 8$ |
| $\alpha = .05$ | $\alpha = .05$ | $\alpha = .05$ |
| 2-tailed | 1-tailed | 2-tailed |

Instructions for questions 41–47. For each of the questions, estimate the power for the *t*-test and the correlation coefficient, *r*.

|  | 41 | 42 | 43 | 44 |
|---|---|---|---|---|
| $N$ | 10 | 20 | 50 | 10 |
| $\alpha$ | .05 | .05 | .05 | .05 |
| Tails | 2 | 2 | 1 | 1 |
| Effect size | .2 | .2 | .5 | .8 |

|  | 45 | 46 | 47 |
|---|---|---|---|
| $N$ | 40 | 10 | 80 |
| $\alpha$ | .05 | .05 | .05 |
| Tails | 2 | 2 | 1 |
| Effect size | .2 | .2 | .2 |

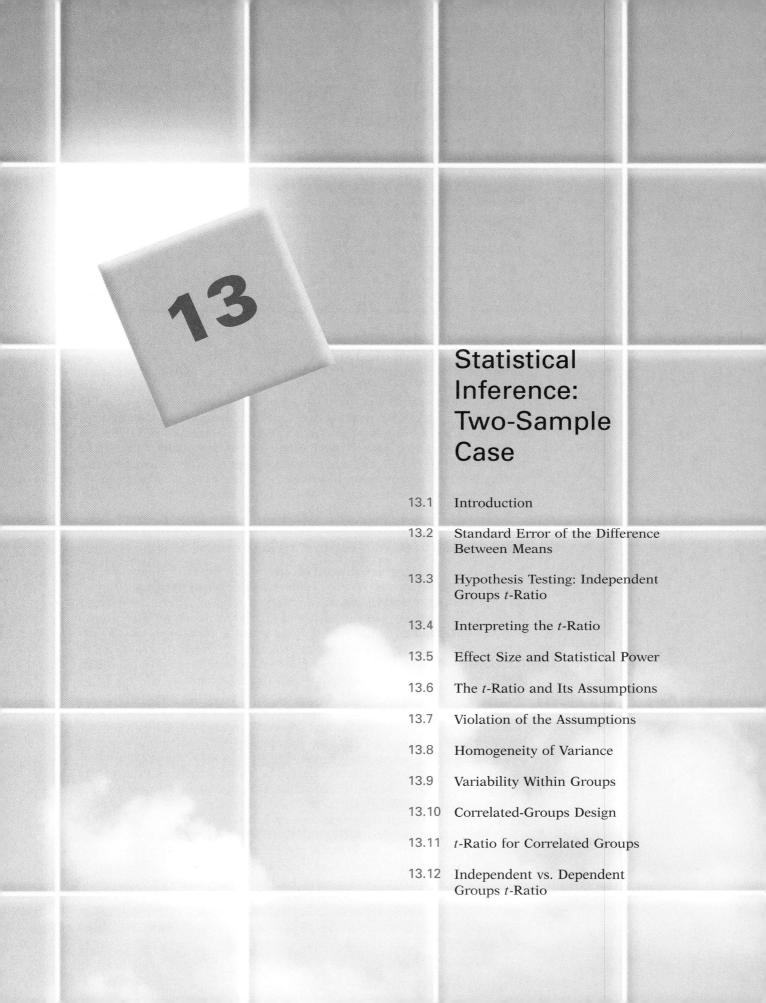

# 13

# Statistical Inference: Two-Sample Case

# 13.1 / Introduction

In Chapter 12 we introduced you to Student's *t*-ratio and the *t*-distributions. As you learned, *t*-distributions allow us to describe accurately the shape of the sampling distribution for small sample sizes (e.g., $n < 30$) and when we do not know the population parameters. Using the *t*-ratio and these sampling distributions, you learned how to conduct basic hypothesis testing to determine if the sample mean was significantly different from a hypothesized mean. In this chapter we will extend the use of *t*-distributions to a broader array of statistical applications. Specifically, we will show you how to apply inferential statistics to common research situations. In addition, we will examine several issues raised in the preceding chapters, including power and how to interpret the meaning of a statistically significant effect.

The primary focus of this chapter is how to compare two groups to one another. Let's begin by looking at some general research questions that represent two-group studies. As a group, who is better at math, men or women? Are children who spend their first 4 to 5 years in day care more or less developed emotionally than children who are raised by one of their parents at home? Are people more likely to make errors in remembering details about an important event if they are asked misleading questions?

We can answer each of these questions using empirical research. For instance, when we compare men's and women's abilities in English or math, we are comparing two populations. From each population we take a representative sample and measure the appropriate dependent variable (a standardized test of math, for example). If the difference between the sample means is greater than what we would expect from sampling error, we infer that there is a real difference between the populations.

## Intact Groups vs. True Experiments

There is also a major difference among the research questions we can ask. Some research questions represent *intact group designs*, and others represent *true experiments*. How can you tell the difference between the two? The answer is in the nature of the independent variable. Recall that the independent variable is the one that the researcher uses to describe and explain the results of the experiment. There are two types of independent variables, subject variables and manipulated variables. *Subject variables* are conditions over which the experimenter has no direct control such as the subject's sex, home environment, personality, age, smoking history, or intelligence. *Manipulated variables* are those conditions that the experimenter controls directly and to which he or she can *randomly assign* subjects. The type of independent variable and research design determines the type of inferences we can make from the data.

Specifically, the intact group design helps us understand the nature of the relation between the independent and dependent variables. Using an intact group design allows us to determine if the populations are different from one another, and to estimate the magnitude of the difference. We cannot use this design to infer cause and effect, however. For example, if we found a statistically significant difference in anxiety level between smokers and nonsmokers, we could not say that smoking causes the difference. There may be causes for the difference other than smoking. Indeed, it is possible that anxiety causes smoking. Therefore, the intact group design does allow us to determine if there is a statistically significant difference between the groups but does not allow us to determine the cause of the difference.

By contrast, when the experimenter randomly assigns subjects to the groups, he or she creates two hypothetical populations. One population represents the subjects in the control condition, and the second population represents subjects exposed to the treatment of interest. If the difference between the means is sufficiently large, we assume that the population parameters from which the samples were drawn are also different. We may also infer that the difference is the result of the manipulated independent variable.

## 13.2 / Standard Error of the Difference Between Means

Whenever you sample from a population there will be variability. For example, sample means, drawn from a population, will be different from each other. As you learned in the previous chapters, the standard error of the mean describes this variability. According to the central limit theorem, the distribution of sample means tends to be normally distributed with a standard deviation of $s_{\overline{X}} = \dfrac{\hat{s}}{\sqrt{n}}$.

We can use the same logic to describe the difference between means drawn from different populations. Imagine creating two samples, each from a different population. We can determine the difference between the means. If we repeat this process, we can create a sampling distribution of the difference between the means. To illustrate, imagine that we have two populations where $\mu_1 = 5.00$, $\sigma_1 = 1.00$ and $\mu_2 = 5.00$ and $\sigma_2 = 1.00$. We draw a random sample with $n = 2$ from each population. For the first sample, the scores might be 3 and 5. For the second sample, the scores may be 4 and 6. Therefore, $\overline{X}_1 = 4$ and $\overline{X}_2 = 5$. The difference between the means is $\overline{X}_1 - \overline{X}_2 = -1$. If we continue this sampling procedure, we can then create a sampling distribution of the difference between the means.

What would the distribution look like? The central limit theorem supplies the answer. Because we select pairs of samples at random from the populations with equal means, we expect a normal distribution with a mean of 0. Going one step further, we can describe the distribution of the difference between pairs of sample means even when these samples are not drawn from the same population. The distribution will be normally distributed with a mean of $\mu_{\overline{X}_1} - \mu_{\overline{X}_2}$. Specifically, the difference between the means of the two sampling distributions will equal the difference between the population means (i.e., $\mu_1 - \mu_2$). The distribution of sample mean differences has a standard deviation that we represent as $\sigma_{\overline{X}_1} - \overline{X}_2$ and that we call the **standard error of the difference between means**.

When we know the population parameters, we can use the $z$-score and normal distribution to describe the distribution of mean differences. Using Equation 13.1, we can compare the difference between two means. In the majority of cases, however, we do not know the parameters of the populations. Therefore, we must use sample statistics to estimate the parameters and Student's $t$-ratio and $t$-distributions to compare the difference between the means.

> ▨ **Standard Error of the Difference Between Means** $\sigma_{\overline{X}_1} - \overline{X}_2$:
>
> Standard deviation of the sampling distribution of the difference between means.

$$z = \frac{(\overline{X}_1 - \overline{X}_2) - (\mu_1 - \mu_2)}{\sigma_{\overline{X}_1} - \overline{X}_2}$$

(13.1)

## Estimating $\sigma_{\bar{X}_1 - \bar{X}_2}$

When the population parameters are unknown, the estimated standard error of the difference between means is

$$s_{\bar{X}_1 - \bar{X}_2} = \sqrt{s_{\bar{X}_1}^2 + s_{\bar{X}_2}^2} \qquad (13.2)$$

Unfortunately, this formula provides a biased estimate of $\sigma_{\bar{X}_1 - \bar{X}_2}$ whenever $n_1$ is not equal to $n_2$. If we create a sample of $n_1$ observations from a population with unknown variance and a second sample of $n_2$ observations from another population with unknown variance, Equation 13.3 provides an unbiased estimate of the standard error of the difference.

$$s_{\bar{X}_1 - \bar{X}_2} = \sqrt{\left(\frac{SS_1 + SS_2}{n_1 + n_2 - 2}\right)\left(\frac{1}{n_1} + \frac{1}{n_2}\right)} \qquad (13.3)$$

Equation 13.3 estimates $\sigma_{\bar{X}_1 - \bar{X}_2}$ by pooling the sum of squares and degrees of freedom of the two samples to obtain an estimate of the standard error of the difference between means.

Figure 13.1 presents the logic of $s_{\bar{X}_1 - \bar{X}_2}$. We begin with two independent populations from which we draw samples. Each sample has a mean and standard deviation. Using the standard deviation of the sample and the sample size, we can estimate the standard error of the mean for that population and sample size. When we combine, or pool, these variance estimates, we create an estimate of the standard error of the difference between means.

If the sample size for the two groups is equal, Equation 13.3 can be simplified to

$$s_{\bar{X}_1 - \bar{X}_2} = \sqrt{\left(\frac{SS_1 + SS_2}{N(N-1)}\right)} \qquad (13.4)$$

or

$$s_{\bar{X}_1 - \bar{X}_2} = \sqrt{\frac{\hat{s}_1^2}{n_1} + \frac{\hat{s}_2^2}{n_2}} \qquad (13.5)$$

Independent populations from which samples are drawn.

Population 1    Population 2

Samples selected from the populations.

$\bar{X}_1$    $\bar{X}_2$
$\hat{s}_1$    $\hat{s}_2$

Sample variance used to estimate the variance of the sampling distribution.

$s_{\bar{X}} = \sqrt{\dfrac{s^2}{n_1}}$    +    $s_{\bar{X}} = \sqrt{\dfrac{s^2}{n_2}}$

The two estimated variances are used to obtain the standard error of the difference between two means.

$s_{\bar{X}_1 - \bar{X}_2} = \sqrt{\dfrac{s_1^2}{n_1} + \dfrac{s_2^2}{n_2}}$

**Figure | 13.1**

**When the standard errors of the mean for two populations are combined, we obtain the standard error of the difference between means.**

In Equation 13.4, we use $N$ to represent the total number of observations. In other words, $N = n_1 + n_2$.

The sampling distribution for the difference between means is best described by Student's *t*-distributions when the variances of the two samples are relatively equal (i.e., $\sigma_1^2 \cong \sigma_2^2$) and sample sizes are equivalent. In other words, we can convert the difference between the means to a standard score using $s_{\overline{X}_1 - \overline{X}_2}$, and this standard score can then be converted to a probability using the *t*-distribution.

Many statisticians refer to $s_{\overline{X}_1 - \overline{X}_2}$ as the **error term.** The name refers to the fact that the primary function of $s_{\overline{X}_1 - \overline{X}_2}$ is to estimate the random error that occurs when we take samples from the population. We will discuss various forms of error in a subsequent section. At this point, recognize that $s_{\overline{X}_1 - \overline{X}_2}$ estimates the standard deviation of the sampling distribution for the difference between means. Using this information, we can turn our attention to hypothesis testing when we have two samples.

▨ **Error Term:**

Refers to the fact that $s_{\overline{X}_1 - \overline{X}_2}$ estimates the random error that occurs when taking samples from the population.

## 13.3 / Hypothesis Testing: Independent Groups *t*-Ratio

We use the familiar *t*-ratio for hypothesis testing when we do not know the population parameters. The purpose of this test is to evaluate the null hypothesis $H_0$ that $\mu_1 = \mu_2$ (we can also write $H_0: \mu_1 - \mu_2 = 0$). There are many ways to write the *t*-ratio. Perhaps the most frequently used form is

$$t = \frac{(\overline{X}_1 - \overline{X}_2) - (\mu_1 - \mu_2)}{s_{\overline{X}_1 - \overline{X}_2}}, \ df = (n_1 + n_2) - 2 \qquad (13.6)$$

Let's look at the logic of the statistic. The denominator of the equation is the standard error of the difference between means. The size of $s_{\overline{X}_1 - \overline{X}_2}$ depends on the variance within each group and the sample size. All else being equal, the larger the samples, the smaller $s_{\overline{X}_1 - \overline{X}_2}$. The variance of each population ($\sigma^2$) also affects the size of $s_{\overline{X}_1 - \overline{X}_2}$, therefore, the smaller the variance of the population, the smaller $s_{\overline{X}_1 - \overline{X}_2}$.

The numerator of the *t*-ratio is the difference between the means less the difference between population means. In most cases, we test the null hypothesis where we believe that $\mu_1 - \mu_2 = 0$. Therefore, the *t*-ratio is a comparison of the difference between the obtained sample means relative to the standard error. If the null hypothesis is true, we would expect the *t*-ratio to equal 0. If $H_0$ is a true statement, then any difference we see between the means must be due to sampling error. As we collect random samples from the population, the difference between the means will average 0. The standard error of the difference between the means will equal approximately $s_{\overline{X}_1 - \overline{X}_2}$.

We use the *t*-distributions to evaluate the *t*-ratio because we use $s_{\overline{X}_1 - \overline{X}_2}$ to estimate $\sigma_{\overline{X}_1 - \overline{X}_2}$. We use the same procedure you learned in the last chapter. We select a *t*-distribution that represents the degrees of freedom and determine the critical value needed to reject $H_0$. When we reject $H_0$, we assume that the probability of the result is too low to accept $H_0$ as correct. That is, we conclude that the difference between the means was influenced by some factor in addition to sampling error.

You will recall that Table C, in Appendix D, provides the critical values of *t* required for significance at various levels of $\alpha$. Because the degrees of freedom for each sample are $n_1 - 1$ and $n_2 - 1$, the total *df* in the two-sample case is $n_1 + n_2 - 2$.

| SEARCH | B | |
| :---: | :---: | :---: |
| | A E | OHOLENE |
| AND | DUMR | |
| Search high and low | Bermuda triangle | Hole in one |

**Figure** 13.2

**Examples of rebus problems used by Smith in his research. [Adapted from R. A. Fink, T. B. Ward, & S. M. Smith (1992). *Creative cognition: Theory, research, and applications,* Cambridge, MA: MIT Press.]**

## Computational Example

Let's look at an example of how the *t*-ratio can be used in a research context. Psychologists have long been interested in what is known as the incubation effect. The effect occurs when you appear to have a flash of insight into the solution of a problem. Steven M. Smith and his students have studied the incubation effect using rebuses. A rebus consists of scrambled words that can be interpreted as a phrase. Figure 13.2 presents some examples of the rebuses Smith used. For example, the first rebus where "search" is above "and" can be read as "search high and low."

For our experiment, we will show subjects five rebuses presented with misleading cues (e.g., the word "destroy" along with the "search high and low" rebus). We show the subjects each rebus for 30 seconds and tell the subjects that they must solve the rebus within the 30-second limit. Immediately after showing the last rebus, we retest half of the subjects using the same rebuses without the misleading cue. The other subjects work on a distracting task for 15 minutes before being retested.

Table 13.1 presents the data* along with a stem-and-leaf graph. From this display, it appears that the data confirm our expectation—the delayed testing group appears to have a higher average than the immediate group. We can now proceed with our hypothesis testing procedures.

**Null Hypothesis:** $H_0$: $\mu_1 = \mu_2$. The performance of the two groups is equivalent.

**Alternative Hypothesis:** $H_1$: $\mu_1 \neq \mu_2$. The performance of the two groups is not equivalent.

**Statistical Test:** We will use the *t*-ratio because we estimate $\sigma_{\overline{X}_1 - \overline{X}_2}$.

**Significance Level:** $\alpha = .05$ two-tailed

**Sampling Distribution:** The *t*-distribution with $df = (10 - 1) + (9 - 1) = 17$.

**Critical Region for Rejecting $H_0$:** $|t_{observed}| \geq |2.110|$ If $t_{observed}$ is less than $-2.110$ or greater than 2.110 we can reject $H_0$.

We can now use the *t*-ratio to test our hypothesis. For the sake of clarity and for practice, we will present a more elaborate form of the equation and show the intervening steps.

---

* The example is based loosely on one conducted by Smith and Blankenship (1989). We have taken the liberty of greatly simplifying the example for teaching purposes. Those interested in a more accurate and comprehensive account of incubation effects and related phenomena should consult the fine research conducted by Steven M. Smith and his associates.

**Table 13.1**

**Example of Data from a Two-Group Experiment in Which Mean Scores of Each Group Are Compared Using a *t*-Ratio**

| | Immediate Group 1 | Delayed Group 2 | Immediate | Delayed |
|---|---|---|---|---|
| | 3 | 2 | 11 | |
| | 2 | 2 | 222222 | 22 |
| | 2 | 3 | 33 | 33333 |
| | 1 | 3 | | 44 |
| | 2 | 3 | | |
| | 2 | 3 | | |
| | 3 | 4 | | |
| | 2 | 3 | | |
| | 2 | 4 | | |
| | 1 | | | |
| $n$ | 10 | 9 | | |
| $\Sigma X$ | 20 | 27 | | |
| $\Sigma X^2$ | 44 | 85 | | |
| $\overline{X}$ | 2.00 | 3.00 | | |
| $SS$ | 4.00 | 4.00 | | |
| $\hat{s}$ | 0.6667 | 0.7071 | | |

$$t = \frac{\overline{X}_1 - \overline{X}_2 - (\mu_1 - \mu_2)}{\sqrt{\frac{\Sigma X_1^2 - \frac{(\Sigma X_1)^2}{n_1} + \Sigma X_2^2 - \frac{(\Sigma X_2)^2}{n_2}}{n_1 + n_2 - 2}\left(\frac{1}{n_1} + \frac{1}{n_2}\right)}}$$

$$t = \frac{2.00 - 3.00 - (0)}{\sqrt{\frac{44 - \frac{(20)^2}{10} + 85 - \frac{(27)^2}{9}}{10 + 9 - 2}\left(\frac{1}{10} + \frac{1}{9}\right)}}$$

$$t = \frac{-1.00}{\sqrt{\frac{4.0 + 4.0}{17}(.10 + .1111)}}$$

$$t = \frac{-1.00}{\sqrt{\frac{8.0}{17}(.2111)}} \qquad t = \frac{-1.00}{\sqrt{(.4706)(.2111)}} \qquad t = \frac{-1.00}{\sqrt{.09934}} \qquad t = \frac{-1.00}{.3152}$$

$$t = -3.17$$

Because the absolute value of the obtained *t*-ratio exceeds the critical value ($t_{observed} > t_{critical}$), we can reject $H_0$. The probability of selecting at random two samples that differ this much or more is less than 5 times in 100 or $p < .05$.

If you used a computer to calculate the statistic, you may have obtained something like

$\underline{t}(17) = -3.17, \quad p$ one-tailed $= .002, \quad p$ two-tailed $= .004$

As you can see, the probability associated with this $t$-ratio is $p = .004$. Because $p < \alpha$, you can reject $H_0$.

The logic and procedures for hypothesis testing are similar to the ones presented in Chapter 12. Although calculation of the $t$-ratio includes a bit more information, its form is similar to that used for the $t$-ratio in the one-sample case. At this point we would like to pursue a different course of discussion. Specifically, we want to examine several important issues to consider whenever you use inferential statistics. The first is the appropriate way to interpret the $t$-ratio, the second is statistical power.

## 13.4 / Interpreting the $t$-Ratio

Once we calculate the $t$-ratio and its probability, we can determine whether to reject $H_0$. Although we have completed one important task, there are still many opportunities to analyze the results of our research. In this section we will examine several of the errors that many people make when interpreting the results of inferential statistics. We will also examine the inferences that can be made and several statistical procedures that can enhance our interpretation of inferential statistics.

### Cause and Effect

The $t$-ratio allows us to determine if there is a statistically significant difference between two groups. Before we can use a $t$-ratio to support conclusions of cause and effect, certain conditions must be met. First, the design of the research must be a true experiment. Therefore, the experimenter must have control over the independent variable, the subjects *must* have been randomly assigned to the two groups, and one of the groups must be a control or a different treatment group.

Intact group designs allow us to infer that the two groups are different from one another. Because we do not control the independent variable, however, we can not be sure if the difference is due to the independent variable or some other condition beyond our control.

### Common Errors

The following is a list of serious errors that some researchers make when interpreting inferential statistics. We present these errors because they are common. In addition, we believe that analyzing them will help you better understand how to interpret inferential statistics. For the most part, the greatest controversy surrounds the interpretation of the probability level associated with inferential statistics. Let's look at four common errors in statistical inference.

---

**Error 1:** Change $\alpha$ after analyzing the data.

---

Imagine that a researcher set $\alpha = .05$ before collecting the data. After analyzing the data the researcher finds that $p = .003$. Should he or she be able to revise $\alpha$ to $\alpha = .005$ to make the data look "more significant"? What if the researcher had set $\alpha = .01$ but the analysis of the data revealed $p = .03$. Can the researcher revise $\alpha$ to $\alpha = .05$ to say that there are statistically significant results? Shine (1980) argued that the answer to both questions is no! His rationale includes several points. The first problem with this type of revision is that it is *unethical*. Researchers should set $\alpha$ before analyzing their data. Revising $\alpha$ is not an honest practice and should not be done.

A second reason that $\alpha$ should not be revised is that the $p$-level cannot be considered a substitute for $\alpha$. The mathematical logic is beyond the scope of this text. For our purposes, however, we can state that we can use $p$ only to estimate the probability of obtaining at least the observed results if the null hypothesis is true. Because we estimate $p$ using sample statistics and because the null hypothesis may be false, we cannot work backward and use $p$ to revise $\alpha$.

Carver (1978) identified three additional errors that many researchers make when interpreting the results of an inferential statistic. We will examine each in turn.

---

**Error 2:** Assume that $p$ indicates the probability that the results are due to chance.

---

Carver (1978) calls this error the "odds-against-chance" error. Some researchers interpret $p$ to indicate the probability that the difference between the means is due to chance. For instance, a researcher may find that for a $t$-ratio $p = .023$ and conclude that the probability that the results were due to chance is 2.3% or less. This interpretation is incorrect because we begin our statistical test with an $H_0$ that states that *all differences are due to chance*. In other words, $H_0$ states that the probability of obtaining *any* difference between the means by chance is 1.00. The $p$-value merely indicates the probability of obtaining a specific or more extreme difference if $H_0$ is true. Because we do not know the real parameters of the populations from which the data were drawn, we cannot predict the probability that the results are due to chance.

A related error in the interpretation of the $p$-value is to assume that $p$ establishes the probability that we will commit a Type I error. If you found that $p = .023$, you could not conclude that the probability of committing a Type I error is 2.3%. The value of $\alpha$ determines the probability of a Type I error. As a rule, you should interpret the $p$-value to mean, "If $H_0$ is a true statement, the probability of obtaining results like these or more extreme is $p$. If the value of $p$ is small enough, I am willing to reject $H_0$ in favor of the alternative hypothesis. The probability of committing a Type I error is $\alpha$."

---

**Error 3:** Assume the size of $p$ indicates the validity of the results.

---

Many beginning researchers assume that the $p$-value indicates the probability that the research hypothesis is true. Again, the probability of the statistic does not allow us to determine the accuracy of the alternative hypothesis. Indeed, the ability to determine the validity of the research hypothesis is an extremely complicated issue that is beyond the mere discussion of statistics. As a simple generalization, the $p$-value cannot confirm the validity of the research hypothesis. The only function of the $p$-value is to determine if there is sufficient evidence to reject $H_0$.

Some researchers infer that a small value of $p$ indicates the degree to which there is a meaningful relation between the independent and dependent variables. For example, if $p = .001$, the researcher may conclude that the independent variable has a great effect upon the dependent variable. This inference is not true. As we will discuss subsequently, the value of $p$ cannot be used to make such a conclusion. We must use other statistical devices to determine the degree to which the independent and dependent variables are interrelated.

---

**Error 4:** Assume that $p$ establishes the probability that the
results can be replicated.

---

Some people assume that $(1 - p)$ indicates the probability that the experiment will yield the same result if repeated. If, for example, $p = .023$, a researcher may assume that the probability of replicating the experiment and rejecting $H_0$ is $1 - .023 = .977$. This is a false and misleading statement because the probability of correctly rejecting $H_0$ is not related to the value of $p$. As we will show later, the ability to replicate a given finding is determined by power and is dependent upon the difference between the means, the number of subjects, the amount of measurement error, and the level of $\alpha$. It is very possible to have a small level of $p$ (i.e., $p = .001$) and a low probability that the results can be directly replicated.

At this point you are probably wondering if there is anything that can be concluded from a statistically significant $t$-ratio. If you obtain a statistically significant $t$-ratio at $p \leq \alpha$, you may conclude that there is a statistically significant difference between the two groups. In addition, if your comparison is part of a true experiment, you may also conclude that the independent variable affects the dependent variable and that the probability that this conclusion is incorrect because of sampling error is $\alpha$.

## Omega Squared: $\omega^2$

As we reviewed in the previous section, the probability level of the $t$-ratio does not indicate the degree to which two variables are statistically associated with one another. Many factors contribute to the probability level, only one of which is the association between the two variables. The finding of a statistically significant $t$-ratio means that some degree of association exists between the independent and dependent variables. The presence of statistical significance does not automatically confer "importance" on a finding. Given a sufficiently large $n$, any difference, however trivial, may be found statistically significant.

One way to clarify the importance of a statistically significant $t$-ratio is to determine the extent to which variations in the independent variable account for variations in the dependent variable. In general, the higher the degree of relation, the greater the importance of the finding. One of the more popular measures of association is $\omega^2$ (omega squared). We calculate $\omega^2$ by

$$\omega^2 = \frac{t^2 - 1}{t^2 + n_1 + n_2 - 1} \tag{13.7}$$

■ **Omega Squared** $(\omega^2)$:

A statistical index of the degree to which the independent variable accounts for the variance in the dependent variable.

We can interpret $\omega^2$ in much the same way we interpret $r^2$. **Omega squared** is an index of the degree to which the variance in one variable accounts for the variance in another variable. There are some subtle differences between $\omega^2$ and $r^2$, however. Although the values of $r^2$ range between only 0 and 1, $\omega^2$ can assume positive and negative values. Specifically, when the absolute value of $t < 1.00$, $\omega^2$ will be negative. For practical purposes negative values of $\omega^2$ have little meaning. Indeed, we recommend that you follow this simple rule: Use $\omega^2$ only when $t$ is statistically significant.

We can apply the equation for $\omega^2$ to the data presented earlier about incubation effects. From that example, we know that $t = -3.17$, $n_1 = 10$, and $n_2 = 9$.

Therefore,      $\omega^2 = \dfrac{(-3.17)^2 - 1}{(-3.17)^2 + 10 + 9 - 1}$

$$\omega^2 = \dfrac{10,049 - 1}{10.049 + 18}$$

$$\omega^2 = \dfrac{9.049}{28.049}$$

$$\omega^2 = .323$$

Therefore, we may interpret $\omega^2$ to mean that the independent variable accounts for approximately 32% of the variance in the dependent variable. You may remember that when we discussed the interpretation of $r^2$, we said that whether we consider $r^2$ trivial or large is a matter of context. In some research contexts, accounting for 32% of the variance is a tremendous event and reflects a real advance in the science. In other contexts, 32% is barely worth considering. Consequently, you must use your own judgment to evaluate the size of this statistic. Your judgment will be based on your knowledge of the relevant literature and the results that other researchers have obtained.

Note that we cannot judge the magnitude of the association by merely looking at the value of the $t$-ratio or the probability level. For example, imagine that we had found the same $t$-ratio of $-3.17$ with 70 subjects in each group. The difference is clearly statistically significant. When the sample size was 10 per group, the probability of $t = -3.17$ was $p = .0017$. When the sample size is 70 per group, the probability for $t = -3.17$ is $p = .00052$. However,

$$\omega^2 = \dfrac{(-3.17)^2 - 1}{(-3.17)^2 + 70 + 70 - 1}$$

$$\omega^2 = .061$$

In this example we see that although the $t$-ratio remains the same, $\omega^2$ is much smaller. The differences in the independent variable are associated with approximately 6% of the variance in the dependent variable. The small size of $\omega^2$ suggests that the difference between the groups is trivial even though the $t$-ratio is statistically significant and the $p$-value is small. These calculations should reinforce the observation that neither the size of the $t$-ratio nor the size of the $p$-value can indicate the importance of the data. We hope that you will carefully review the claims of researchers who seem to imply that their results are of considerable significance merely because they rejected $H_0$. We also hope you remember our advice that many different techniques should be used to help you interpret your data.

## 13.5 / Effect Size and Statistical Power

In Chapter 12 we told you that the power of a statistical test is the probability of correctly rejecting a false $H_0$. Historically, researchers have been concerned more with avoiding Type I errors (false rejection of $H_0$) than with Type II errors (failure to reject a false $H_0$). More recently, however, researchers are more interested in power and the confidence intervals of their statistics.

We use $1 - \beta$ to represent statistical power. The power of a statistic depends upon the difference between the means, sample size, and $\alpha$. You may recall that we discussed these issues in Chapter 12. We can return to the topic of power with respect to a two-sample $t$-ratio.

In the last chapter, we introduced you to the statistic $d_1$, the effect size for the single sample $t$-ratio. Cohen (1988) devised a similar statistic for the two-sample $t$-ratio that we represent as $d_2$. For the nondirectional two-sample case,

$$d_2 = \frac{|\mu_1 - \mu_2|}{\sigma} \tag{13.8}$$

or for the directional (one-tailed) case,

$$d_2 = \frac{\mu_1 - \mu_2}{\sigma} \tag{13.9}$$

where

$d_2 =$ the effect size for the two-group $t$-ratio.

$\mu_1 - \mu_2 =$ The difference between the population means as estimated by the sample means.

$\sigma =$ common standard deviation of the populations estimated by $\hat{s}$. We estimate $\sigma$ as $\sigma = \dfrac{\hat{s}_1 + \hat{s}_2}{2}$ when $n_1 = n_2$.

We interpret the magnitude of $d_2$ in the same way we do $d_1$. Small effects are $d_2 = .20$ or less, medium effects range between .2 and .8, and large effects .8 or greater.

## Using $d_2$ to Predict Power

We can use our understanding of power to help us design our research. Specifically, we can determine the number of subjects needed to reject $H_0$. The procedures are much like those used in Chapter 12.

Suppose that you expect $\mu_1 - \mu_2 = 5$. Assume also that you have reason to believe that the population standard deviation will be 10. The effect size index for this hypothesis, $d_2$, is then $d_2 = 5/10 = .50$. How many subjects do you need in order to have a good chance of rejecting $H_0$?

Turn to Table E in Appendix D. Here we find the power of the test at $\alpha = .05$, two-tailed test, for varying sizes of $n$. In this illustration we will assume that the sample sizes are equal and that $n$ represents the size of each sample (i.e., if $n_1 = 10$ and $n_2 = 10$, $N = 20$). Reading down Column 1 ($n$) to 10 and across to $d_2 = .50$, we find the power of the test to be $1 - \beta = .17$. In other words, the probability of rejecting a false $H_0$ is about 17% when the sample size of each sample equals 10. Chances are you will not be able to reject $H_0$ because your power is low. Conducting such an experiment will be an act of futility because there is an 83% chance that you will get nonsignificant results.

How many subjects per group do you need in order to boost power to .80? Look down column .50 until you find approximately .80 in the body of the table. Now look at the $n$ column directly to the left. Here you see that the sample size for each group must be at least 60 subjects in each group (120 subjects total) to have an 80% chance, on average, of rejecting $H_0$ and asserting the alternative hypothesis is correct.

# 13.6

## The $t$-Ratio and Its Assumptions

$T$he $t$-ratio is known as a parametric test. A **parametric test** is a test that is based on a specified sampling distribution, or group of sampling distributions, when samples are drawn at random from the population (Siegel & Castellan, 1988).

■ **Parametric Test:**

An inferential statistic that makes specific assumptions about the population(s) from which the data are drawn.

The assumptions we make when performing a $t$-ratio concern the distribution of error. We assume that

1. Sampling error is distributed normally around $\mu$ in each treatment population.
2. The distribution of error is the same for each population, $\sigma_1 = \sigma_2$. This assumption is known as the homogeneity of variance.
3. The observations in each sample are independent of each other.

In other words, we assume that the scores we obtain from subjects will be normally distributed, the spread in the distributions will be the same, and the two groups are independent. To meet the requirements of these assumptions we should carefully consider the procedure we use to select subjects, to assign them to treatment groups, and to examine our data before we conduct analyses.

For example, when we use the $t$-ratio for independent means, we assume that the sampling distribution for the differences between the means is best described by Student's $t$-distributions. Indeed, whenever we use the $t$-ratio, we make many specific assumptions that we assume to be true. Specifically the assumptions for the $t$-ratio are as follows.

### Random Selection

Random selection is a critical procedure that we reviewed in Chapter 10. If each member of the population has an equal probability of being chosen, the sample is a random sample, and we have the basis for making inferences to the population. Without this critical element in our design, we would be unable to say that the results of our experiment can be generalized beyond the type of subjects in our study. To illustrate, consider the following simplified example.

Let's say we have developed a treatment for eating disorders, and we obtain our sample from a local clinic. We can conduct an experiment with a treatment and a control group and find our treatment highly successful. Are we able to generalize our findings to the population of patients with eating disorders? We can to the extent that the clients in the clinic are similar to the population of individuals with eating disorders. What if the clinic serves clients with severe disorders? What if the clinic has a clientele with only mild problems? Perhaps there are other characteristics of these people that set them apart from the population you are studying. In such cases we cannot generalize our results beyond the source of our subjects. Fortunately, other researchers, using clients from other settings, may be able to replicate our results. As the literature develops, we will have the opportunity for systematic replications. Specifically, different researchers will use different samples to test the effectiveness of the treatment. If the treatment is successful across many replications, we will have evidence of its effectiveness.

### Random Assignment

It is important that the observations in our treatment and control groups be independent of each other. This is sometimes called the

■ **Independent Groups:**

The researcher randomly assigns subjects to the treatment conditions. The behavior of subjects in one group has no effect on the behavior of subjects in the other group.

**independent groups** assumption. Without this important element, we would not know what portion of the difference between the means was due to the assignment procedure and what was due to the effects of the independent variable. Because we have discussed this topic before, we will not go into detail other than to reiterate that each subject should have an equal likelihood of being assigned to one of the two groups. Once the assignments are made, the treatment and data collection techniques should be identical for all subjects except for the manipulation of the independent variable.

### Normal Distribution of Error and $\sigma_1 = \sigma_2$

It is important that the distribution of error in the population be normally distributed and the same across treatment groups. Because we do not know the population parameters, we must use sample statistics to estimate them. Thus, it is the sample statistics that we use to determine if we have met the assumptions of the *t*-ratio. We look at the distribution for each group and ask: Is it normal? Is it skewed? Are there outliers or extreme values? We also look at the differences between the groups in terms of spread. We assume that both samples are drawn from populations whose variances are equal. Are the variances the same for the two groups or is one group much more variable than the other? If so, we may be violating the assumption of homogeneity of variance. Let's consider the consequences of violating this assumption.

## 13.7 / Violation of the Assumptions

What happens if you violate the assumptions of the *t*-ratio? Some violations are more critical than others. In general, we prefer that the data we collect match the assumptions of our statistical tests. In practice, however, the data do not always conform to our expectations. Sawilowsky & Blair (1992) examined what would happen to the *t*-ratio if the assumption of normality were violated. Sawilowsky and Blair tested the performance of the *t*-ratio using nonnormal populations commonly found in behavioral research (e.g., extreme asymmetry, multimodality, and platykurtic distributions). In brief, they found that the *t*-ratio is robust against violations of the assumptions. **Robust** is a statistical term that refers to the degree to which the assumptions of a test can be violated and still perform as expected. Specifically, statisticians want to determine if violations of the assumptions change the rate of Type I and Type II errors. A statistic is said to be "robust against violations of assumptions" when we violate the mathematical assumptions of a statistic and the rate of Type I and Type II errors remains constant. Although Sawilowsky and Blair found that the *t*-ratio is robust, they do offer a few points of warning.

■ **Robust:**

A term used to describe inferential statistics that preserve the rate of Type I and Type II errors when the assumptions of the test are violated.

They suggest that the *t*-ratio is most robust for equal sample sizes, large samples (e.g., 25 or more), and two-tailed tests. These requirements are relatively easy to meet. For example, you can, when you begin your research, plan to use plenty of subjects and to use subjects that will stay in the experiment. This does not mean that you can ignore the assumptions of the *t*-ratio. We want to point out that the *t*-ratio can be applied to many different situations that stray from ideal conditions. In the following sections we will examine steps you should take to ensure that the decisions you make are supported by the *t*-ratio and the alternate steps you should take when you believe that the assumptions of the *t*-ratio have been violated.

## 13.8 / Homogeneity of Variance

$\mathbf{A}$ simple test of the homogeneity of variance is the $F_{max}$ test. For the $t$-ratio, the $F_{max}$ is merely the larger variance divided by the smaller variance. Mathematically, the $F_{max}$ test is

$$F_{max} = \frac{\hat{s}^2 \text{larger variance}}{\hat{s}^2 \text{smaller variance}}, \qquad df = n - 1 \qquad (13.10)$$

We assume that the sample sizes are equal; when the sample sizes are not equal, take the average of the two groups and round up to the nearest whole number to obtain the degrees of freedom. Let's look at a few concrete examples. Imagine that a researcher conducted two related experiments. For both experiments the researcher wants to calculate a $t$-ratio for independent samples.

| **Experiment 1** | **Experiment 2** |
|---|---|
| $\hat{s}_1^2 = 5.00$ | $\hat{s}_1^2 = 1.00$ |
| $n_1 = 6$ | $n_1 = 9$ |
| $\hat{s}_2^2 = 3.00$ | $\hat{s}_2^2 = 5.00$ |
| $n_2 = 6$ | $n_2 = 12$ |

$$F_{max} = \frac{5}{3} \qquad\qquad F_{max} = \frac{5}{1}$$

$$F_{max} = 1.667 \qquad\qquad F_{max} = 5.00$$

$$df = 5 \qquad\qquad df = \frac{9 + 12}{2} - 1$$

$$= 10.5 - 1 = 11 - 1$$

$$df = 10$$

Table K of Appendix D, lists the critical values for the $F_{max}$ test. The columns represent the number of variances in the experiment. For the two-sample $t$-ratio, there are always two variances. Each row represents the degrees of freedom for the variance. In our example, the degrees of freedom are 5 and 10, respectively. The values in the body of the table are the critical values for the $F_{max}$ test. If the calculated $F_{max}$ test is greater than the tabled value, we must assume that $\sigma_1 \neq \sigma_2$. As you can see, the table includes critical values of $\alpha = .05$ and $\alpha = .01$. Let's see how we will use the table when we set $\alpha = .05$.

For Experiment 1, the $df = 5$. The critical value for the $F_{max}$ test is 7.2. Because 1.667 is less than 7.2, we can assume that the two variances are equivalent.

For Experiment 2, the $df = 10$. The critical value for the $F_{max}$ test is 3.7. Because 5.00 is greater than 3.7, we must assume that the two variances are not equal to each other.

### $t$-Ratio When $\sigma_1 \neq \sigma_2$

There are several options to follow when $\sigma_1 \neq \sigma_2$. One alternative is to use a $t$-ratio adjusted for the inequality of variances. The advantage of this statistic is that it accounts for the inequality of variances and the inequality of sample sizes. The corrected $t$-ratio (Li, 1964; Sachs, 1984) requires two equations, one for the $t$-ratio and one for the degrees of freedom.

$$\hat{t} = \frac{\overline{X}_1 - \overline{X}_2}{\sqrt{\left[\frac{1}{n_1}\left(\frac{SS_1}{n_1 - 1}\right)\right] + \left[\frac{1}{n_2}\left(\frac{SS_2}{n_2 - 1}\right)\right]}} \qquad (13.11)$$

$$df' = \frac{\left[\frac{1}{n_1}\left(\frac{SS_1}{n_1 - 1}\right) + \frac{1}{n_2}\left(\frac{SS_2}{n_2 - 1}\right)\right]^2}{\frac{\frac{1}{n_1}\left(\frac{SS_1}{n_1 - 1}\right)^2}{n_1 - 1} + \frac{\frac{1}{n_2}\left(\frac{SS_2}{n_2 - 1}\right)^2}{n_2 - 1}} \tag{13.12}$$

The corrected $t$-ratio provides a revised $t$-ratio and revised degrees of freedom. Let's look at an example. The data presented in Table 13.2 represent an experiment in which there are differences between the variances and the number of subjects in each group.

According to the data, $F_{max} = 5.782$. Looking at Table K in Appendix D, and using 7 degrees of freedom ($df = ((10 + 6)/2) - 1$) we find that the critical value for the $F_{max}$ test is 5.0. Because 5.781 is greater than 5.0, we must assume that we do not have homogeneity of variance and should proceed with the corrected $t$-ratio.

$$\hat{t} = \frac{2.00 - 3.167}{\sqrt{\left[\frac{1}{10}\left(\frac{4.00}{10 - 1}\right)\right] + \left[\frac{1}{6}\left(\frac{12.833}{6 - 1}\right)\right]}}$$

$$df' = \frac{\left[\frac{1}{10}\left(\frac{4.00}{10 - 1}\right) + \frac{1}{6}\left(\frac{12.833}{6 - 1}\right)\right]^2}{\frac{\frac{1}{10}\left(\frac{4.00}{10 - 1}\right)^2}{10 - 1} + \frac{\frac{1}{6}\left(\frac{12.833}{6 - 1}\right)^2}{6 - 1}}$$

$$\hat{t} = \frac{-1.167}{\sqrt{(0.0444) + (0.4278)}}$$

$$df' = \frac{(0.0444 + 0.4278)^2}{\frac{(0.0444)^2}{9} + \frac{(0.4278)^2}{5}}$$

$$\hat{t} = \frac{-1.167}{\sqrt{.4722}}$$

$$df' = \frac{(0.4722)^2}{\frac{0.0020}{9} + \frac{0.1830}{5}}$$

$$\hat{t} = \frac{-1.167}{0.6872}$$

$$df' = \frac{0.22297}{.0002 + .0366}$$

$$\hat{t} = -1.698$$

$$df' = \frac{0.22297}{.0368}$$

$$df' = 6.059$$

According to the corrected $t$-ratio, our results should be interpreted as $t(6) = -1.70, p > .05$. The critical $t$-ratio for 6 degrees of freedom with $\alpha = .05$, one-tailed, is 1.943. Therefore, we *cannot reject* $H_0$ with these data. Using a conventional $t$-ratio, we find that $t(14) = -2.061, p < .05$. This exercise should make clear that violation of the assumption of homogeneity of variance can greatly influence the final interpretation of the data. In this example, the conventional $t$-ratio led us to assume that a difference exists where one does not.

## Alternatives to the $t$-Ratio

Another alternative to the $t$-ratio are statistical tests based on ranks or ordinal scales. Chapter 18 presents these alternatives to the $t$-ratio. These statistics offer a useful alternative when you believe that it is not appropriate to analyze your data with parametric statistics.

**Table** 13.2

Example of Data Where $\hat{s}_1 \neq \hat{s}_2$ and $n_1 \neq n_2$

| Group 1 | Group 2 |
|---------|---------|
| 3 | 1 |
| 2 | 3 |
| 2 | 3 |
| 1 | 3 |
| 2 | 3 |
| 2 | 6 |
| 3 | |
| 2 | |
| 1 | |
| 2 | |

| | | | | |
|------|------|--------|-------|-------|
| $n$ | 10 | 6 | | |
| $\Sigma X$ | 20 | 19 | | |
| $\Sigma X^2$ | 44 | 73 | | |
| $\overline{X}$ | 2.00 | 3.167 | $F_{max}$ | $= \dfrac{2.567}{0.444}$ |
| $SS$ | 4.00 | 12.833 | $F_{max}$ | $= 5.782$ |
| $\hat{s}^2$ | 0.444 | 2.567 | | |
| $\hat{s}$ | 0.667 | 1.602 | | |

## 13.9 / Variability Within Groups

One of the problems behavioral researchers confront is the extreme variability of the data. Human and nonhuman behavior is extremely variable. This is the main reason why psychologists use inferential statistics. Because our data are variable, we need to examine the factors that influence the variability among subjects and seek ways to reduce this variability.

When we collect data in an experiment, two general factors influence the value of the observations, treatment effects and random effects. Treatment effects are the conditions created by the independent variable that may cause groups to differ from one another. For instance, in an experiment that examines the influence of a drug, we would expect the subjects exposed to the drug to have a different reaction or level of performance than subjects exposed to a placebo. When we examine treatment effects, we are looking for systematic differences between groups.

Random effects are a variety of factors that influence the differences among subjects. We can divide random effects into two additional categories, measurement error and individual differences. Measurement error refers to a broad class of errors that influence the value of an observation. There are many things that can affect the accuracy of measurement, including the accuracy of the measurement device, the time of day the data are collected, minor errors on the experimenter's part, chance events that distract the subject's attention, and a host of other factors. When you plan to conduct a research project, it is a good idea to examine all the factors that can contribute to measurement error and attempt to control for them. Although you can never remove all measurement error from an experiment, you can reduce the influence of measurement error by developing a well-controlled, practiced procedure. How to develop such plans is the focus of a research methods course.

Individual differences refer to characteristics of subjects that existed before the experiment and that can influence the results of the data. Some subjects may have an ability or proficiency in the basic task being used in the study, whereas others may not. For example, you may want to conduct a study that compares the effect of different types of aerobic training on overall fitness. Some of the subjects may already be in good condition when the experiment begins, whereas others may come to the experiment in poor condition. We have several ways to deal with individual differences. First, we could decide to work only with those subjects who are in poor condition. A potential shortcoming of this tactic is that we run the risk of having a small sample of subjects who may not be representative of the population we want to describe. Another alternative is to randomly assign subjects to the various treatment conditions. This is a good procedure to ensure that the groups are equivalent in terms of various factors. The problem is that large individual differences will create large estimates of error variance.

You should not be surprised that the subjects' earlier levels of fitness will influence their performance in the study. In many studies, the individual differences among subjects are typically the most significant factor contributing to the scores and the variability of scores on the dependent variable. Anything we can do to recognize this factor and "statistically remove" its effects will improve our ability to estimate the effects of the independent variable on the dependent variable. In the following sections we will examine several techniques used to control for and reduce variance within groups.

## 13.10 / Correlated-Groups Design

Previously, we discussed experimental designs in which we randomly assign subjects to the two groups. In this section we will examine the correlated-groups design, which is also known as the dependent groups design. In a correlated-groups design there is a direct correlation between the groups.

For the independent groups design, the standard error of the difference between means is

$$s_{\bar{X}_1 - \bar{X}_2} = \sqrt{s_{\bar{X}_1}^2 + s_{\bar{X}_2}^2} \tag{13.13}$$

However, the more general formula for the standard error of the difference is

$$s_{\bar{X}_1 - \bar{X}_2} = \sqrt{s_{\bar{X}_1}^2 + s_{\bar{X}_2}^2 - 2r(s_{\bar{X}_1})(s_{\bar{X}_2})} \tag{13.14}$$

The $r$ in the equation represents the correlation between the groups. In an independent groups design there should be no meaningful correlation between the two groups, as they are independent of one another. Consequently, the term $2r(s_{\bar{X}_1})(s_{\bar{X}_2}) = 0$ and we can drop it from the equation.

There are, however, many good experimental designs in which we do not randomly assign subjects to the experimental conditions. These designs are known as correlated-groups designs because there is an obvious relation between the two groups. There are two types of these designs, repeated-measures designs and matched-group designs.

## Repeated Measures Design

In a repeated-measures design, also known as a within-subjects design or before-after design, the same subject is tested on two or more occasions. The advantage of this design is that each subject serves as the control condition for measurements in the experimental condition. When we use the repeated-measures design, we expect that the performance of each individual will remain relatively consistent in comparison to the other subjects at each testing; thus, there will be a correlation between the score made by subjects during the first and second measurement periods.

Let's look at an example. Assume that you want to study the effects of practice on solving analogy problems. Students take a pretest consisting of 20 difficult analogy problems. A week later the students are retested with an equivalent form of the analogy test. We expect that among the students some will perform consistently better than others, and we also expect that most if not all the subjects will improve their scores. In other words, there will be a correlation of performance between the two conditions. This correlation is due to individual differences and can be measured. Because the variability due to individual differences has been identified and measured, we can remove this source of variance from our standard error of the differences between means. Specifically, $2r(s_{\overline{X}_1})(s_{\overline{X}_2})$ allows us to exercise *statistical control* over the variance created by individual differences. When we remove this variance created by individual differences, we increase the opportunity to observe the effects of our treatment.

Although the repeated measures design has many advantages, it suffers from one potential shortcoming, carryover effects. A *carryover effect* occurs when the first testing may affect the second testing. For example, if you use standardized tests, subjects may remember the questions and answers. Even if alternate forms are used, sometimes the first testing allows the subject to practice an unfamiliar skill, and consequently, the second testing is biased because of the effect of the first testing. Earlier in this chapter the example of the rebus study specifically examines the existence of the carryover effect. If a carryover effect presents a considerable threat to the validity of the study, you may need to consider an alternative design such as a matched-group design.

## Matched-Group Design

In this design you obtain measures for the subjects on the variable that you believe is related to the dependent variable and then match subjects in their assignment to the treatment conditions. The result is a set of paired subjects in which each member of the pair obtains approximately the same score on the matching variable. One member of the pair is randomly assigned to one condition, and the other is assigned to the other treatment condition.

A matched-group design can be used to test the effectiveness of a new antidepressant. The psychologist conducting the study may believe that the rate of improvement in symptoms of depression is dependent on the original condition of the patient. Subjects with severe depression may recover more slowly than those with mild depression. Therefore, the psychologist administers a reliable and valid measure of depression to all the subjects. Next, he or she rank-orders the subjects based on the test results and pairs them together so that each pair has similar scores on the depression test. Finally, the psychologist randomly assigns half of each pair to the drug condition and the remaining subjects to the placebo condition. One advantage of this design is that it ensures that the experimental groups are equivalent before the start of the experimental treatment. In addition, the design permits us to take advantage of the correlation based on the initial status of the subjects and allows us to remove a potentially important source of error from our measurements. Before deciding to use a matched-group design, the reader is advised to read further in the area and consider carefully the various sources of systematic error that are likely to affect the data.

## 13.11 / t-Ratio for Correlated Groups

When using one of the correlated-groups designs, we can define the $t$-ratio as

$$t = \frac{\overline{X}_1 - \overline{X}_2 - (\mu_1 - \mu_2)}{\sqrt{s_{\overline{X}_1}^2 + s_{\overline{X}_2}^2 - 2r(s_{\overline{X}_1})(s_{\overline{X}_2})}} \qquad (13.15)$$

The same result can be obtained by another method that permits direct calculation of the standard error of the difference. We refer to this method as the direct difference method and represent the standard error of the difference as $s_{\overline{D}}$.

In brief, the **direct difference method** consists of finding the differences between the scores obtained by each pair of correlated scores and treating these differences as if they were raw scores. In effect, the direct difference method transforms a two-sample case into a one-sample case. We find one sample mean and a standard error based on one standard deviation. In other words, we will conduct a single sample $t$-test on the mean of the differences. If $D$ represents the difference between two scores then $\overline{D} = \frac{\Sigma D}{n}$. The null hypothesis for the test takes the same form as a single sample $t$-test. We can compare the mean of the differences to any value. In most cases, we use the null hypothesis to say that there is no difference between the means. For a nondirectional test, the null hypothesis will be $H_0$: $\mu_{\overline{D}} = 0$. The $t$-ratio employed to test the hypothesis is

$$t = \frac{\overline{D}}{s_{\overline{D}}} \qquad (13.16)$$

You should note that $\overline{D} = \overline{X}_1 - \overline{X}_2$. In other words, this $t$-ratio tells us whether the difference between the means is large relative to the standard error of the difference.

$$s_{\overline{D}} = \sqrt{\frac{\Sigma D^2 - \frac{(\Sigma D)^2}{n}}{n(n-1)}} \qquad (13.17)$$

In this equation, $D$ represents the difference between each pair of numbers and $n$ represents the number of pairs in the sample. The practical equation for calculating the $t$-ratio is

■ **Direct Difference Method:**

A method of calculating the $t$-ratio for correlated groups using the difference between the pairs of scores.

$$t = \frac{\overline{D}}{\sqrt{\dfrac{\Sigma D^2 - \dfrac{(\Sigma D)^2}{n}}{n(n-1)}}}, \qquad df = n - 1 \qquad (13.18)$$

For correlated-groups designs, we based the degrees of freedom on the number of different scores obtained from <u>pairs</u> of observations. In other words, if we were conducting a matched-group design experiment using 20 subjects, 10 subjects would be placed in each group, 10 differences between the pairs would be calculated, and our degrees of freedom would be $10 - 1 = 9$.

## Worked Example

We can use a simple example to illustrate the *t*-ratio for correlated groups. Imagine that a researcher administers a 20-item anagram test to 10 students. One week later, the researcher administers another 20-item anagram test to the same students. How will students do the second time they take the quiz—better, worse, or the same? The data in Table 13.3 present the students' test scores.

*N = 10*

**Null Hypothesis:** $H_0$: $\mu_D = 0$. The performance of subjects in the two conditions is equivalent.

**Alternative Hypothesis:** $H_1$: $\mu_D \neq 0$. The performance of subjects in the two conditions is not equivalent.

**Statistical Test:** We will use the *t*-ratio for correlated groups.

**Significance Level:** $\alpha = .05$.

**Sampling Distribution:** The *t*-distribution with $df = (10 - 1) = 9$.

**Critical Region for Rejecting $H_0$:** $|t_{observed}| \geq |2.262|$ If $t_{observed}$ is less than $-2.262$ or greater than $2.262$ we can reject $H_0$.

Using the information in Table 13.3, we can conduct the *t*-ratio for the correlated groups.

**Table 13.3**

**Test Scores for 10 Students Taking the Same 20-Item Anagram Test on Separate Days**

| Student | Test 1 | Test 2 | $D$ = Test 2 − Test 1 | $D^2$ |
|---------|--------|--------|-----------------------|-------|
| 1 | 10 | 7 | −3 | 9 |
| 2 | 17 | 18 | 1 | 1 |
| 3 | 15 | 20 | 5 | 25 |
| 4 | 8 | 15 | 7 | 49 |
| 5 | 18 | 19 | 1 | 1 |
| 6 | 10 | 13 | 3 | 9 |
| 7 | 16 | 17 | 1 | 1 |
| 8 | 12 | 16 | 4 | 16 |
| 9 | 13 | 18 | 5 | 25 |
| 10 | 9 | 16 | 7 | 49 |
| | $\Sigma X_1 = 128$ | $\Sigma X_2 = 159$ | $\Sigma D = 31$ | $\Sigma D^2 = 185$ |
| | $\overline{X}_1$ 12.80 | $\overline{X}_2$ 15.90 | $\overline{D} = 3.10$ | |
| | $\hat{s}_1^2$ 12.62 | $\hat{s}_2^2$ 13.88 | | |

$$t = \frac{3.10}{\sqrt{\dfrac{185 - \dfrac{(31)^2}{10}}{10(10-1)}}} = \frac{3.10}{\sqrt{\dfrac{88.9}{90}}} = \frac{3.10}{\sqrt{.98778}} = \frac{3.10}{0.9939}$$

$$t = 3.119$$

Because $3.119 > 2.262$, we can reject $H_0$ and conclude that students did better on the second day. In other words, the average increase of 3.1 points is statistically significant.

## 13.12 / Independent vs. Dependent Groups $t$-Ratios

If we had ignored the fact that the preceding experiment involved correlated groups and used the conventional $t$-ratio based on independent samples, we would have obtained the following results:

$$t = \frac{15.9 - 12.8}{\sqrt{\dfrac{12.62}{10} + \dfrac{13.88}{10}}}, \qquad t = 1.904$$

Notice that the $t$-value of 1.904 obtained using this calculation is much smaller than the 3.12 we obtained using the direct difference method. The difference is due to the denominator of the $t$-ratio. For the independent groups $t$-ratio, the error term is 1.6279. For the correlated-groups $t$-ratio, the error term is 0.9939. The difference between the error terms comes from the fact that in the correlated-groups $t$-ratio, we remove the shared variance between the groups. By reducing variance associated with individual subjects, we were able to reduce the overall size of the error term. Therefore, the correlated groups $t$-ratio has a tendency to be more powerful than the independent groups $t$-ratio.

If you can identify and quantify the sources of individual differences that contribute to the error term, you can remove a source of error and increase the sensitivity of your design in detecting a statistically significant difference between the groups.

Although the correlated-groups design provides a potentially sensitive test for research, you should be aware of some inherent limitations. The greater sensitivity of the correlated-groups design arises from the fact that the error term removes the variance due to differences among individuals. When $r$ is large, the error term is correspondingly small. As $r$ approaches zero, the correlated-groups design can become a liability.

A potential drawback to the matched-groups design is that it requires testing or access to records that will provide information for pairing the subjects. The testing may require time, logistics, and economic resources that are beyond your means. Matching may also pose problems when subject dropout is high. Sometimes a subject does not or cannot complete an experiment. Therefore, you lose that subject and the other subject in the pair. Finally, it is not always possible to pair subjects without distorting the fit between the sample and the target population. In some instances, extreme cases may be dropped because there is no compatible subject to serve as a match. Selectively dropping subjects at the extremes of the distribution artificially lowers variability, thereby producing a spuriously low error term. Because a smaller difference in means is then required for significance, we may increase the risk of making a Type I error.

The point of this section was to highlight the advantages and disadvantages of the correlated-groups design. In some cases the design can allow you to discover difficult-to-find results in a cost-effective manner. In other cases, the correlated-groups design may create more problems than it solves. The moral of this section is that you must plan your experiment with considerable care before beginning to collect the data. Consider your many options and use the experimental design and statistical procedure that best meets your needs.

## CHAPTER SUMMARY

In this chapter we applied Student's $t$-ratio to research comparing the performance of two groups. We saw how the difference between the means has a sampling distribution whose variance is estimated by the standard error of the difference between means. Using the $t$-ratio for independent groups, we can compare two groups to determine whether the sample means were drawn from the same population or from different populations with different means.

We also spent much time examining the interpretation of the results of the $t$-ratio. One could say that we covered everything from $\alpha$ to $\omega^2$. Specifically, we examined four errors that some researchers make when interpreting the $p$-value of a $t$-ratio. We hope that you learned that $p$ merely represents the probability of obtaining the $t$-ratio if $H_0$ is true. Other interpretations of the $t$-ratio require different statistical procedures.

For example, you learned that $\omega^2$ is a measure of association that estimates the relationship between the independent variable and dependent variable. This statistic allows you to determine the degree to which the independent variable influences the dependent variable. You also learned that $\omega^2$, but not $p$, indicates the strength of the relation between the independent and dependent variables.

You also learned how to calculate the power of the $t$-ratio using the index of effect size, $d_2$, and Cohen's (1988) power tables. Using these power tables allows you to design research projects that increase the probability that you will reject a false $H_0$.

Another important topic we reviewed was the mathematical assumptions required to determine the $t$-ratio. You should recall that two essential assumptions are that subjects be randomly selected and that the two groups be independent of one another. We also showed you that the other assumptions are important to consider but that the $t$-ratio is robust against departures of normality and homogeneity of variance. The $F_{max}$ test can be used to determine if there is a severe violation of the assumption of homogeneity of variance. We suggested alternatives to the conventional $t$-ratio for cases in which homogeneity of variance cannot be assumed.

Finally, we introduced you to an alternative to independent groups designs called correlated-groups designs. The advantage of these designs is that they allow you to use subjects as their own control group or to equate groups for an important subject variable. The $t$-ratio for these designs can be more powerful than for independent group designs and requires fewer subjects.

**Table** 13.4

**Summary of Different Tests Using the *t*-Distribution, When the Test Should Be Used, the Formula, and Degrees of Freedom**

| Situation | *t*-Ratio | *df* |
|---|---|---|
| Compare single sample means to a hypothesized population mean | $t = \dfrac{\overline{X} - \mu_0}{s_{\overline{X}}}$ or $t = \dfrac{\overline{X} - \mu_0}{\sqrt{\dfrac{s}{n}}}$ | $df = n - 1$ |
| Test the significance of a correlation coefficient | $t = \dfrac{r\sqrt{n - 2}}{\sqrt{1 - r^2}}$ | $df = n - 2$ |
| Compare two independent groups $\sigma_1 = \sigma_2$ | $t = \dfrac{\overline{X}_1 - \overline{X}_2 - (\mu_1 - \mu_2)}{\sqrt{\left(\dfrac{SS_1 + SS_2}{n_1 + n_2 - 2}\right)\left(\dfrac{1}{n_1} + \dfrac{1}{n_2}\right)}}$ | $df = n_1 + n_2 - 2$ |
| Compare two independent groups $\sigma_1 \neq \sigma_2$ | $\hat{t} = \dfrac{\overline{X}_1 - \overline{X}_2 - (\mu_1 - \mu_2)}{\sqrt{\left[\dfrac{1}{n_1}\left(\dfrac{SS_1}{n_1 - 1}\right)\right] + \left[\dfrac{1}{n_2}\left(\dfrac{SS_2}{n_2 - 1}\right)\right]}}$ | $df' = \dfrac{\left[\left(\dfrac{1}{n_1}\dfrac{SS_1}{n_2 - 1}\right) + \left(\dfrac{1}{n_2}\dfrac{SS_2}{n_2 - 1}\right)\right]^2}{\dfrac{\left(\dfrac{1}{n_1}\dfrac{SS_1}{n_1 - 1}\right)^2}{n_1 - 1} + \dfrac{\left(\dfrac{1}{n_2}\dfrac{SS_2}{n_2 - 1}\right)^2}{n_2 - 1}}$ |
|  | $t = \dfrac{\overline{X}_1 - \overline{X}_2 - (\mu_1 - \mu)}{\sqrt{s_{\overline{X}_1}^2 + s_{\overline{X}_2}^2 - 2r(s_{\overline{X}_1})(s_{\overline{X}_2})}}$ |  |
| Compare two correlated groups | $t = \dfrac{\overline{D}}{\sqrt{\dfrac{\Sigma D^2 - \dfrac{(\Sigma D)^2}{n}}{n(n - 1)}}}$ | $df = n - 1$ |

## TERMS TO REMEMBER

direct difference method
error term
independent groups
omega squared ($\omega^2$)

parametric test
robust
standard error of the difference
   between means

## EXERCISES

1. Evaluate the following for significance.
   **a.** $t = 1.78$, $df = 15$, $\alpha = .05$, two-tailed
   **b.** $t = 2.18$, $df = 15$, $\alpha = .05$, two-tailed
   **c.** $t = 1.9$, $df = 15$, $\alpha = .05$, one-tailed
   **d.** $t = 1.9$, $df = 15$, $\alpha = .01$, one-tailed

2. Evaluate the following for significance.
   **a.** $t = 1.45$, $df = 12$, $\alpha = .05$, two-tailed
   **b.** $t = 2.9$, $df = 22$, $\alpha = .05$, two-tailed

**c.** $t = 2.6$, $df = 17$, $\alpha = .05$, one-tailed
**d.** $t = 1.7$, $df = 13$, $\alpha = .01$, one-tailed

3. Two statistics classes of 25 students each obtained the following results on the final examination. Employing $\alpha = .01$, two-tailed, test the hypothesis that the two classes are equal in ability.

|  | Class 1 | Class 2 |
|---|---|---|
| Mean | 82 | 77 |
| Sum of squares | 384.16 | 1536.64 |

4. In an experiment on the effect of a particular drug on the number of errors in the maze-learning behavior of rats, the following results were obtained:

| Drug Group | Placebo Group |
|---|---|
| $\Sigma X_1 = 324$ | $\Sigma X_2 = 256$ |
| $\Sigma X_1^2 = 6516$ | $\Sigma X_2^2 = 4352$ |
| $n_1 = 18$ | $n_2 = 16$ |

Set up this experiment in formal statistical terms, employing $\alpha = .05$, two-tailed, and draw the appropriate conclusions concerning the effect of the drug on the number of errors.

5. A researcher randomly presented a "target" on a computer screen. The subjects had to tap a key when they saw the target. The target was either 20 mm in diameter or 5 mm in diameter. The data show the number of correct responses out of 10 trials.

| Large Target | Small Target |
|---|---|
| 9 | 6 |
| 6 | 7 |
| 8 | 7 |
| 8 | 9 |
| 9 | 8 |

Set up this experiment in formal statistical terms, employing $\alpha = .05$, two-tailed, and draw the appropriate conclusions.

6. If we found a statistically significant difference between means at the 5% level of significance, it would follow that (true or false)
   **a.** this difference is statistically significant at the 1% level of significance.
   **b.** this difference is statistically significant at the 10% level of significance.
   **c.** the difference observed between means is the true difference.

7. In a study of workers suffering from repetitive strain disorder, subjects were randomly assigned to one of two treatment groups. The goal of the study was to evaluate the effectiveness of the treatments in terms of pain reduction. Before the study began subjects were asked to report the number of hours per week they spent relaxing or involved in recreational activities. The reports of the subjects are as follows.

| Group 1 | Group 2 |
|---|---|
| $\Sigma X_1 = 10371$ | $\Sigma X_2 = 20609$ |
| $\Sigma X_1^2 = 198503$ | $\Sigma X_2^2 = 427764$ |
| $n_1 = 582$ | $n_2 = 1052$ |

Using $\alpha = .05$, set up and test the null hypothesis that the two groups do not differ in terms of number of hours per week reported.

8. If the subjects in the study described in Exercise 7 were truly randomly assigned, is it possible that there are differences between the two groups in terms of their recreational habits? What effect might such a difference have on any conclusions that might be drawn or inferences made based on the experiment?

9. Following a 2-month treatment program the same patients described in Exercises 7 and 8 were asked to evaluate any pain they might still be experiencing. They were given a 5-point response scale that ranged from 1 (no pain or discomfort of any kind) to 5 (intense pain).

| Group 1 | Group 2 |
|---|---|
| $\Sigma X_1 = 1024$ | $\Sigma X_2 = 1694$ |
| $\Sigma X_1^2 = 2712$ | $\Sigma X_2^2 = 4318$ |
| $n_1 = 582$ | $n_2 = 1052$ |

Using $\alpha = .05$, set up and test the null hypothesis that the two groups do not differ in terms of reported pain.

10. Occasionally a researcher is fortunate enough to have available the population parameters and does not have to estimate them from sample data. In these cases we can use the $z$-score comparison for the difference between groups. Compare the $z$-score formula with the independent groups $t$-ratio used when the population parameters are estimated. In what way are the two formulas similar? In what way are they different?

11. Given are two normal populations with the following parameters:

| Population 1 | Population 2 |
|---|---|
| $\mu_1 = 80$ | $\mu_2 = 77$ |
| $\sigma_1 = 6$ | $\sigma_2 = 6$ |

If a sample of 36 cases is drawn from Population 1 and a sample of 36 cases from Population 2, what is the probability that
**a.** $\overline{X}_1 - \overline{X}_2 \geq 5$  **b.** $\overline{X}_1 - \overline{X}_2 \geq 0$  **c.** $\overline{X}_1 - \overline{X}_2 \leq 0$  **d.** $\overline{X}_1 - \overline{X}_2 \leq -5$

Hint: $\sigma_{\overline{X}_1} = \dfrac{\sigma_1}{\sqrt{n}}$

12. Assuming the same two populations as in Exercise 11, calculate the probability that $\overline{X}_1 - \overline{X}_2 \leq 0$ when
**a.** $n_1 = n_2 = 4$  **b.** $n_1 = n_2 = 9$  **c.** $n_1 = n_2 = 16$  **d.** $n_1 = n_2 = 25$

13. Consider the preceding probabilities as a function of $n$. Can you generalize about the probability of finding a difference in the correct direction between sample means (i.e., $\overline{X}_1 - \overline{X}_2 \geq 0$ when $\mu_1 > \mu_2$) as a function of sample size?

14. A publisher claims that students who receive instruction in mathematics based on his newly developed textbook will score at least 5 points higher on end-of-term grades than those instructed using the old

textbook. Thirty-six students are randomly assigned to two classes: The experimental group employs the new textbook for instruction, and the control group uses the old textbook. Students in the experimental group achieve $\overline{X}_1 = 83.05$ and $\hat{s}_1 = 6.04$ as final grades, whereas the controls obtain $\overline{X}_2 = 76.85$ and $\hat{s}_1 = 5.95$. Set up and test the appropriate null hypothesis employing $\alpha = .01$, one-tailed. [*Note*: Remember that the numerator in the test statistic is $(\overline{X}_1 - \overline{X}_2) - (\mu_1 - \mu_2)$.]

15. Professor Hennessey is planning a study in which he will evaluate the effect of exposure of patients at a clinic to one of two treatment plans. Previous research indicates that, in terms of the dependent measure, $\mu_1 - \mu_2 = 3.6$ with a standard deviation of approximately 6.0. Determine the probability of detecting a false null hypothesis when the sample size is 10, 20, and 30 subjects in each group. Use $\alpha = .05$, one-tailed test. Can you generalize about the effect of sample size on power?

16. Using the same data presented in Exercise 15, recalculate the power for sample sizes 10, 20, and 30 using a standard deviation of 4.5 for each group. Can you generalize about the effect of variability within treatment groups on the ability to reject a false null hypothesis?

17. Evaluate the following $F_{max}$-values to determine if two variances differ significantly. Use $\alpha = .05$ and Table K of Appendix D for you evaluations.

|   | $n_{larger}$ | $n_{smaller}$ |
|---|---|---|
| **a.** $F_{max} = 5.02$, | 12 | 12 |
| **b.** $F_{max} = 2.11$, | 10 | 10 |
| **c.** $F_{max} = 2.33$, | 10 | 7 |
| **d.** $F_{max} = 5.09$, | 10 | 8 |

18. A psychologist finds that the number of employee errors increases as the day progresses, reaching a peak between 3:00 and 5:00 P.M. He divides a sample of 20 employees into two groups. One group proceeds on the same work schedule as before, but the other group takes a 15-minute coffee break from 2:45 to 3:00. The subsequent number of errors made between 3:00 and 5:00 are

| No-break group | 5 | 6 | 7 | 4 | 8 | 9 | 6 | 5 | 7 | 6 |
|---|---|---|---|---|---|---|---|---|---|---|
| Break group | 2 | 3 | 4 | 3 | 4 | 4 | 3 | 1 | 5 | 4 |

Before evaluating the significance of the difference between the means of the two groups, it is important to determine whether the variances are homogeneous. Do the two variances differ significantly? Calculate the value of $F$ and test for significance using $\alpha = .05$.

19. Does it appear that the coffee break significantly affects the number of errors? Calculate the value of $t$ using $\alpha = .05$, two-tailed.

20. A telemarketing firm uses one of two training methods, A and B, to train 20 new employees. Later these employees are evaluated in terms of the number of sales they make during a single shift. The results are presented in the accompanying table. Determine if the variances are homogeneous. Calculate $F_{max}$.

| A | 19 | 20 | 20 | 21 | 18 | 20 | 19 | 21 | 23 | 17 |
|---|---|---|---|---|---|---|---|---|---|---|
| B | 26 | 24 | 25 | 23 | 25 | 24 | 22 | 26 | 27 | 25 |

21. Based on the data presented in Exercise 20, is there a statistically significant difference in the number of sales made? Set up the problem in formal terms and calculate the value of $t$ using $\alpha = .05$.

22. A company has just switched to a 4-day work week. It has measured the number of units produced per week for 10 employees before and after

the change. Set up the problem in formal terms and test the null hypothesis at $\alpha = .05$. (*Note*: If you are using a computer for your calculations, read the manual first to determine the appropriate format for entering your data. Remember, two measures were obtained for each subject.)

**NUMBER OF UNITS**

| Employee | Before | After |
|----------|--------|-------|
| 1 | 25 | 23 |
| 2 | 26 | 24 |
| 3 | 27 | 26 |
| 4 | 22 | 23 |
| 5 | 29 | 30 |
| 6 | 25 | 24 |
| 7 | 29 | 26 |
| 8 | 30 | 32 |
| 9 | 25 | 25 |
| 10 | 28 | 29 |

**23.** Referring to Exercises 18 and 19, assume that the two groups had been matched on their abilities before the coffee break was instituted. Assume that the pairs are in identical order for the two groups. Determine the standard error of the difference between the means and the value. Compare the obtained value with that found for Exercise 19.

**24.** A researcher showed men and women a humorous video clip. Half the subjects saw the video clip alone, the other half saw the clip after having seen a video clip from a horror film.
   **a.** In each of the two conditions (no horror vs. humor preceded by horror), combine the males and females into single groups of 20 subjects each. Test $H_0$: The mean difference in the ratings of pleasantness for the population(s) from which the two conditions were selected is equal to zero. Use $\alpha = .05$. Find $\omega^2$. What conclusion can you draw?
   **b.** Combine the male ratings for humor preceded by horror and humor not preceded by horror and the female ratings for both variables and administer a test of significance (males versus females) at $\alpha = .05$, two-tailed. Find $\omega^2$. What conclusion can you draw?

| HUMOR NOT PRECEDED BY HORROR | | HUMOR PRECEDED BY HORROR | |
|------|--------|------|--------|
| Male | Female | Male | Female |
| 17 | 9 | 17 | 10 |
| 24 | 12 | 11 | 15 |
| 13 | 20 | 25 | 14 |
| 13 | 18 | 20 | 7 |
| 24 | 23 | 6 | 10 |
| 18 | 18 | 10 | 13 |
| 21 | 21 | 6 | 6 |
| 28 | 32 | 31 | 6 |
| 12 | 12 | 8 | 11 |
| 9 | 12 | 17 | 14 |

# 14

# An Introduction
# to the Analysis
# of Variance

## 14.1 / Introduction

The classic research design consists of two groups, an experimental group and a control group. Both groups of subjects receive identical treatment except those subjects in the experimental group who receive the independent variable. We then use inferential statistics to determine whether both groups could have come from the same population. As you have learned in the last two chapters, the greater the difference between the means of the groups, the more willing we are to reject the null hypothesis that the samples represent the same population.

Although the design of the two-group experiment is the foundation for the true experiment, it has limitations. Because we psychologists study the wonderful complexity of human behavior, we often want to compare more than two groups. We rarely find that events in nature conveniently order themselves into two neat categories. More commonly, we ask questions that are more complex such as: Which of several conditions leads to the greatest frequency of altruistic acts? Which of five different methods of teaching the concepts of fractions to fourth graders facilitates the greatest comprehension? Which of four forms of psychotherapy leads to the fastest recovery from depression?

As we saw in Chapter 13, the $t$-test is quite useful for comparing two groups. What we need to examine now is a statistic that will allow us to simultaneously compare the effect of many conditions. Specifically, we want to answer such broad questions as: "Is there a meaningful and systematic relation between the independent variable and the dependent variable?" This question is broader than the more focused question "Is there a statistically significant difference between these two means?"

In this and the next two chapters we will introduce you to an extremely useful statistical technique known as the **analysis of variance** (often abbreviated as **ANOVA**). The great statistician, Sir Ronald Fisher, created this statistical procedure during the 1920s. Since then, the ANOVA has evolved into an elaborate collection of statistical procedures that are perhaps the most commonly used methods in contemporary behavioral research.

Although the ANOVA is a new statistical procedure for you, there is very little about the statistic that will be new. The ANOVA uses all the calculations we have practiced throughout the book. Indeed, the name of this statistic, "analysis of variance," should tell you that we will be using one of the most familiar statistical concepts presented in this book, variance. In other words, you will be putting the sum of squares to work again in another statistical procedure. Similarly, we will use the logic for hypothesis testing introduced with the $t$-ratio to establish the criteria for rejecting $H_0$ and accepting $H_1$. Finally, we will review the ability to infer causation from our research design and statistical analysis.

■ **Analysis of Variance (ANOVA):**

A statistical procedure developed by R. A. Fisher that allows one to compare simultaneously the difference between two or more means.

## 14.2 / Advantages of ANOVA

There are several advantages associated with the ANOVA as a statistical test. For our purposes we will consider two of the more important advantages.

## Omnibus Statistical Test

**Omnibus** means something that contains many different things or something that covers many situations at once. This is a useful description of the ANOVA because the statistic allows you to compare many different things and situations at once. Let's look at some examples.

Imagine that you are examining the relation between a new drug and its effect on behavior. One thing you may be interested in studying is the dose-response curve. For example, the data presented in Figure 14.1 represent the dose-response curves of a hypothetical drug. Curve A represents a linear dose-response curve. Within the range of dosages administered, gradual increases of the drug produce gradual increases in the response. Curves B and C represent nonlinear relations. For Curve B, a small dose of the drug is effective and larger dosages produce marginally diminishing returns. In contrast, Curve C illustrates that the drug is only effective in large doses.

The advantage of the ANOVA is that we can test a broad range of dosages in a single experiment. The results of the ANOVA will help us determine if there is a meaningful relation between the independent and dependent variable and the nature of that relation. With careful planning you will be able to learn much about the phenomenon you are studying with the ANOVA.

In this chapter we will focus on the analysis of a single-variable case. In a single-variable ANOVA, also known as a **one-way ANOVA,** we examine two or more levels of a single independent variable. In the drug example, our single independent variable would be the new drug. The levels of the independent variable are the dosages we use. In the next chapter we will examine a **two-way ANOVA.** That form of the ANOVA allows us to conduct experiments where we simultaneously examine the consequence of manipulating two independent variables. As you become familiar with the many variants of the ANOVA you will recognize that it is an invaluable tool for anyone who asks complex questions about behavior.

> **Omnibus Statistical Test:**
>
> A statistical test that permits one to compare simultaneously several variables or levels of a variable.

> **One-Way Analysis of Variance:**
>
> A form of ANOVA that allows one to compare the effects of different levels of a *single* independent variable.

> **Two-Way Analysis of Variance:**
>
> A form of ANOVA that allows one to compare simultaneously the effects of two independent variables.

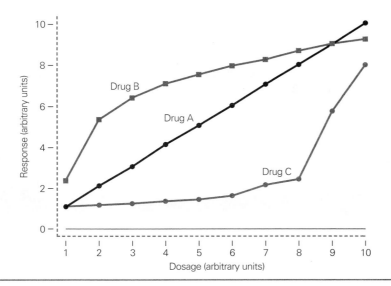

**Figure** | 14.1

Hypothetical data representing the dose-response curves for three drugs.

## Controls Experimentwise Error

You may be wondering what the possible advantage of the ANOVA is over the simple *t*-ratio. After all, you could collect the data for many samples and then use a series of *t*-ratios to compare the means. Such a procedure creates more problems than it solves. The problem with conducting *multiple nonindependent t-ratios* is that it greatly inflates the probability of committing a Type I error. Let's look at the problem more closely.

First, how many two-group comparisons are possible in an experiment with more than two groups? The answer comes from using an equation that calculates the total number of potential combinations:

$$C = \frac{k!}{2(k-2)!} \tag{14.1}$$

where
    $C$ = number of potential pairs
    $k$ = total number of groups
    ! = factorial of a number. The "!" directs you to multiply all
        the whole numbers between 1 and the number. For
        example, $5! = 5 \times 4 \times 3 \times 2 \times 1 = 120$. We set $0! = 1$.

We can apply this equation to an example where a psychologist wants to test the effects of 10 dosage levels of a drug. Using Equation 14.1, we find that

$$c = \frac{10!}{2(10-2)!} = \frac{3628800}{2 \times 40320} = 45$$

With 10 groups there are 45 pairs of means we can compare. These are a lot of *t*-ratios to conduct! Using a computer, we can calculate these tests in short order. The real problem is that conducting many *t*-ratios increases the probability of committing a Type I error. The researcher could cut the number of comparisons by examining only adjacent groups (e.g., Group 1 vs. Group 2, Group 2 vs. Group 3 . . . Group 9 vs. Group 10). This procedure will reduce the number of *t*-ratios to 9, but the risk of committing one or more Type I errors is still greater than $\alpha$.

When we conduct a *t*-ratio, we assume that the groups are independent of one another. When the groups are independent, we say that the probability of committing a Type I error for the pair is $\alpha$. Therefore, the probability of committing a Type I error for any comparison using the *t*-ratio will always be $\alpha$. Statisticians call this form of $\alpha$ the **pairwise comparison** $\alpha$.

The problem of inflated Type I error arises when we make many comparisons based on a single experiment with many groups. When we continually use the same means and variances for our calculations, we violate the assumption of independence and thereby inflate the probability of committing a Type I error. Consequently, if we were to compare three or more means from the sample experiment, the probability of committing a Type I error is greater than $\alpha$. Statisticians use Equation 14.2 to determine the probability of committing a Type I error under these conditions.

$$\alpha_{\text{experimentwise}} = 1 - (1 - \alpha)^c \tag{14.2}$$

■ **Pairwise Comparison** $\alpha$:

The probability of committing a Type I error when comparing any two means using a *t*-ratio. The pairwise comparison probability of a Type I error is established as $\alpha$.

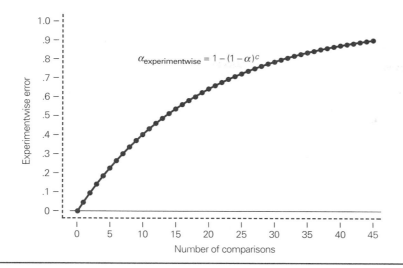

$$\alpha_{\text{experimentwise}} = 1 - (1 - \alpha)^c$$

**Figure | 14.2**

**The relation between the number of comparisons made and the experimentwise error when $\alpha = .05$**

where

$\alpha_{\text{experimentwise}}$ = experimentwise error

$\alpha$ = pairwise comparison $\alpha$

$c$ = number of comparisons made

The **experimentwise error** describes the probability of committing a Type I error when conducting multiple $t$-ratios from a single experiment.

Figure 14.2 represents the relation between the number of comparisons made and the experimentwise error rate for comparisons ranging between 1 and 45 with $\alpha = .05$. As you can see, $\alpha_{\text{experimentwise}}$ increases quickly as the number of comparisons increases. If the psychologist were to conduct 9 $t$-ratios, the $\alpha_{\text{experimentwise}}$ is approximately .40. The experimentwise error means that there is a 40% chance that one or more of the statistically significant $t$-ratios will represent the incorrect rejection of the null hypothesis. With 45 comparisons the experimentwise error rate increases to nearly .90.

You could attempt to lower $\alpha$ (e.g., from .05 to .01) in order to keep $\alpha_{\text{experimentwise}}$ to an acceptable level. The problem with this tactic is that the power for the individual comparisons will be so small that few if any of the $t$-ratios will reveal statistically significant results. For example, with 9 potential comparisons we would have to reduce the pairwise $\alpha$ to approximately* $\alpha = .0057$ to maintain $\alpha_{\text{experimentwise}}$ at .05. Setting $\alpha = .0057$ means that the power of the individual $t$-ratios will be so low that you may be better off not collecting the data.

Finally, the multiple $t$-ratio approach does not allow us to easily address the broader purpose of the experiment, to examine the relation between the independent variable and dependent variable. Although we will still rely upon the $t$-ratio for specific cases, we will use the ANOVA as an omnibus test of the relation among the variables in our research.

■ **Experimentwise Error** $\alpha_{\text{experimentwise}}$**:**

The probability of committing one or more Type I errors when conducting multiple $t$-ratios from a single experiment.

---

* Use the equation $\alpha = 1 - \sqrt[c]{1 - \alpha_{\text{experimentwise}}}$ to estimate the pairwise $\alpha$ required to control Type I error. To maintain the probability of a Type I error at .05 for 9 comparisons, the solution is $.00568 = 1 - \sqrt[9]{1 - .05}$.

In summary, the ANOVA is an elegant statistic that simultaneously compares the means of all groups in a single test. Consequently, the ANOVA is a convenient and powerful alternative to multiple *t*-ratios.

# 14.3 The General Linear Model

**Partition:**

A statistical procedure where the total variance is divided into separate components.

**Factor:**

A term used in the analysis to describe the independent variable.

**Levels:**

The different values or conditions within an independent variable that are analyzed in an ANOVA.

The analysis of variance gets its name because it takes the entire variance in a set of data and **partitions,** or divides, the sources of variance into different components. It may be useful to remind you of the steps of a true experiment as they relate to our discussion of the ANOVA. Figure 14.3 is a representation of the components of an experimental design.

In the true experiment we begin by selecting subjects from a population with a mean of $\mu$ and a standard deviation of $\sigma$. Next, we randomly assign the subjects to the specific treatment groups. For the analysis of variance we call the independent variable the **factor.** The factor in the experiment will have several **levels.** For example, if we study the effects of an antidepressant drug, our factor would be the drug under study. The levels of the factor would represent the different dosage levels we are testing.

Using sampling theory, we predict that each group represents the same population before the start of the experiment. In other words, before the experiment begins we assume that the means of the groups are equivalent and representative of the population mean. Therefore, any difference among the group means represents sampling error. We also assume that the variances of the groups are equivalent and representative of the population variance, and that the variance among subjects in each group represents random error. More specifically, we assume that the variance within each group represents individual differences among the subjects. Because we use random selection and assignment, we assume that the variances among subjects are randomly distributed with a mean effect of 0.

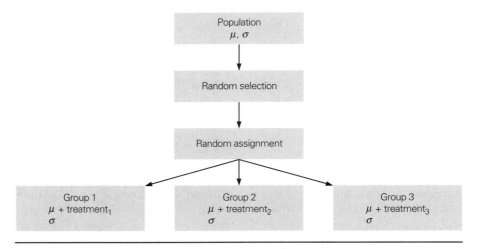

**Figure 14.3**

Representational model of an experiment with three levels of one factor. All subjects are drawn from a common population and are randomly assigned to a treatment condition. The effects of this condition, represented as "treatment," influence the size of the sample mean.

In an experiment, we expose the subjects in each group to a specific level of the factor. In Figure 14.3 we use *treatment_j* to represent the effect of a specific level of the independent variable. We can also represent the treatment effect as $\alpha_j$.* The effect of the factor can be 0 (as we would assume for the control group), positive, or negative. Consequently, the means of the groups will represent the population mean, the effect of treatment, and the sampling error.

When we collect a set of data for an experiment we assume that each score is described by the following equation:

$$X_{ij} = \mu + \alpha_j + \epsilon_{ij} \qquad (14.3)$$

where
- $X_{ij}$ = an observation within a specific treatment condition. The *i* in the subscript represents the individual subject, the *j* represents the group. For example $X_{2,3}$ represents the second subject in the third group.
- $\mu$ = population mean for the base population.
- $\alpha_j$ = the effects of a specific treatment condition which may be 0, positive, or negative.
- $\epsilon_{ij}$ = undifferentiated error that is assumed to be random with a mean effect of 0 and a standard deviation equal to $\sigma$, the population standard deviation.

Equation 14.3 is known as the **general linear model.** The model may be read as: "Any individual score is the sum of the mean of the population, the effects of the treatment, and random error."

Figure 14.4 presents how we can interpret the general linear model. As you can see, there are four normal curves; one drawn with a bold line, the other three drawn with lighter lines. The normal curve with the bold line represents the base population from which the subjects were drawn. For our example, the mean of the base population is $\mu = 50$. The other three curves represent the distribution of scores for three separate treatment conditions. The means of these groups are 35, 45, and 70.

According to the general linear model, all observations are the sum of the effect due to treatment and effect due to error. In Figure 14.4 we identified an observation from the third treatment group as an example. The difference between the base population mean ($\mu = 50$) and the group mean ($\overline{X}_3 = 70$) represents the effect of the treatment used in that group ($\alpha_3$). The difference between the individual score ($X_{i3} = 81$) and the group mean ($\overline{X}_3 = 70$) represents the effects of random error ($\epsilon$).

## Components of Variance

When we conduct a one-way ANOVA we estimate three forms of variance. We can begin with the most familiar form of variance, the total variance. The **total variance** is nothing more than the variance of all subjects regardless of the experimental group to which they were assigned. For example, if we conducted an experiment in which 30 subjects were randomly assigned to one of three treatment conditions, we could calculate the variance of all 30 subjects.

Figure 14.5 presents such a situation. The three normal distributions drawn with a light line represent the distributions of scores for the three

■ **General Linear Model:**

A conceptual mathematical model that describes an observed score as the sum of the population mean, the treatment effect for a specific level of a factor, and random error. For the one-way ANOVA the general linear model is $X_{ij} = \mu + \alpha_j + \epsilon_{ij}$.

■ **Total Variance:**

The variance of all scores in the data set regardless of experimental group.

* Do not confuse $\alpha$, which we use to represent the treatment condition, with $\alpha$, which we have used to represent our $\alpha$ level, the probability of making a Type I error.

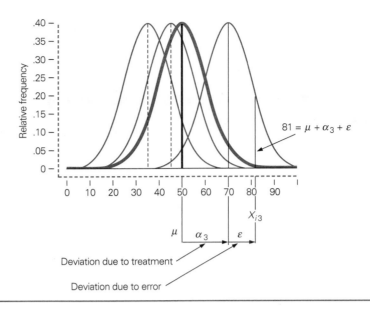

**Figure | 14.4**

A representation of the different sources of variance in an experiment with three groups. The normal curve drawn with a bold line represents the population from which all subjects were drawn. The three other normal curves represent the populations for each of the treatment conditions. See the text for detailed comments.

individual groups. The normal distribution drawn with the bold line represents the total variance. Specifically, this distribution represents the distribution of all observations collected in the experiment. If you look carefully, you should see that the total variation is greater than the variance in the individual groups. The definitional equation for the total variance is

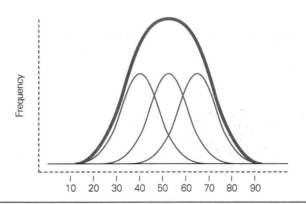

**Figure | 14.5**

An illustration of the total variance. The distribution drawn with a bold line represents the distribution of all observations in the study considered as a single group. The variance among all of these scores represents the total variation. The other three distributions represent treatment groups.

$$\hat{s}^2_{\text{total}} = \frac{\Sigma(X_{ij} - \overline{\overline{X}})^2}{N - 1} \tag{14.4}$$

where

$\overline{\overline{X}}$ = the grand mean, the mean of all the data.

$N$ = the total number of subjects in all groups.

We can now partition, or divide, the total variance into smaller components—the variance between the group means and the variance within each group. You already did something like this in Chapter 9 when we examined the regression equation. In Chapter 9 we wanted to determine how much of the total variance of the dependent variable could be accounted for by variance in the independent variable and how much of the total variance was due to random error. As you recall, the total sum of squares equaled the sum of squares for the regression model and the sum of squares for error.

We do the same thing with the ANOVA. Specifically, we partition the total variance into two smaller components: the **between-groups variance** and the **within-groups variance.** The between-groups variance is an index of differences among the group means produced by the independent variable and random error. The within-groups variance is an index of the degree to which random error causes the differences among the subjects within the individual groups.

In each of the following sections we will examine how to estimate each component of the ANOVA. Please note that in these sections we will show you the definitional equations for the variance terms. In a subsequent section we will show you the computational procedures for the ANOVA.

**Within-Groups Variance ($\sigma^2_{\text{within}}$):** The within-groups variance represents differences among the subjects caused by random error and factors not controlled by the researcher. We assume that this variance is randomly distributed and has a mean of 0. Because the mean of random error is 0, we believe that over the long run, the random error adds to or takes away nothing from the population mean. Random error does, however, have a variance. Therefore, random error causes individual scores to be greater than or less than the group mean.

The within-groups variance represents the average variation of observations within each group. As we show in Figure 14.6, the within-groups variation represents the variation of observations within each of the three distributions of scores.

We can estimate the within-groups variance as

$$\hat{s}^2_{\text{within}} = \frac{\Sigma\left(\dfrac{\Sigma(X_{ij} - \overline{X}_j)^2}{n_j - 1}\right)}{k} \tag{14.5}$$

In this equation, $n_j$ represents the number of subjects in the $j$th group and $k$ represents the number of groups.

When we use the ANOVA we assume that the variances of each group are equal or homogeneous. Specifically, **homogeneity of variance** means that $\sigma^2_1 = \sigma^2_2 = \sigma^2_3 = \ldots \sigma^2_j$. This is an important assumption because $\hat{s}^2_{\text{within}}$ is an unbiased estimate of the population variance, $\sigma^2$. In the ANOVA, the $\hat{s}^2_{\text{within}}$ is the average of the variance in each group. Therefore, if one or more group variances are much larger or smaller than the other variances, our estimate of the population variance will not be accurate. As you can see, Equation 14.5 is just an elaborate equation for the mean of variances. The numerator is the total of the variances in

■ **Between-Groups Variance:**

Estimate of variance between group means.

■ **Within-Groups Variance:**

Estimate of the average variance within each group.

■ **Homogeneity of Variance:**

The assumption that the variance of the groups are equivalent to each other,

$\sigma^2_1 = \sigma^2_2 = \sigma^2_3 = \ldots \sigma^2_j$.

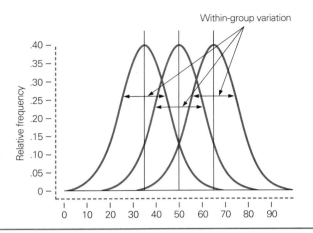

**Figure** | **14.6**

The three distributions represent three independent groups. Each group contains scores that vary from the group mean. The within-group variance represents the average of the group variances.

each group and the denominator is the number of groups. What are we doing with this equation? First, we calculate the variance ($\hat{s}_j^2$) of each group. These variances are then added together and the total is divided by the number of groups.

**Between-Groups Variance ($\hat{s}_{\text{between}}^2$)** The between-groups variance represents the variance between* the group means. Specifically, we treat each group mean as if it were an individual score and calculate the variance between the means. Figure 14.7 illustrates the basis of the between-groups variance. As you can see, each distribution of scores has a mean. The between-groups variance estimates the variance between the three means. The difference between the between-groups variance and the within-groups variance is that the between-groups variance estimates the variance *between the group means* whereas the within-groups variance estimates the average variance of *scores within each group*.

Symbolically, the between-groups variance is expressed as

$$\hat{s}_{\text{between}}^2 = \frac{\Sigma n_j(\overline{X}_j - \overline{\overline{X}})^2}{k - 1}$$

(14.6)

where
$\overline{X}_j$ = the mean of observations in one group.
$n_j$ = the number of subjects in the $j$th group.
$\overline{\overline{X}}$ = the mean of all observations.
$k$ = the number of means.

Here is an example. Imagine that we conducted an experiment with 4 groups and 4 subjects in each group. The means of the groups are 2.5, 4.5, 5.5, and 6.0. The grand mean is 4.625. Applying Equation 14.6, we can estimate $\sigma_{\text{between}}^2$ using

---

* We apologize to those sensitive to English grammar and usage. The correct preposition is "among" as we are talking about the contrast of more than two things. However, statisticians always talk about the variance *between* the means. In order to avoid confusion, we will take license with our usage.

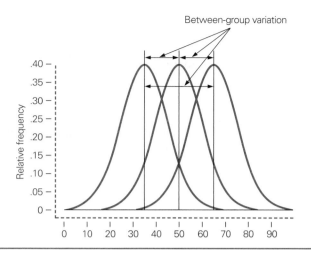

Between-group variation

**Figure** | **14.7**

**The three distributions represent three independent groups. Each group can be represented by its mean. The between-group variance represents the variance among the three group means.**

$$\hat{s}^2_{between} = \frac{4(2.5 - 4.625)^2 + 4(4.5 - 4.625)^2 + 4(5.5 - 4.625)^2 + 4(6.0 - 4.625)^2}{4 - 1}$$

$$\hat{s}^2_{between} = \frac{18.062 + 0.062 + 3.062 + 7.562}{3}$$

$$\hat{s}^2_{between} = \frac{28.75}{3}$$

$$\hat{s}^2_{between} = 9.58$$

There are two sources of variance that contribute to the size of $\hat{s}^2_{between}$, **error variance** and **treatment variance.** The error variance, which is estimated by $\hat{s}^2_{within}$, represents uncontrolled and unpredictable events that create differences among individual scores. The treatment variance is the effect of the different levels of the independent variable on the data. Therefore, we can say that $\hat{s}^2_{between}$ = error variance + treatment variance.

To summarize, we have just looked at three types of variance, the total variance, the between-groups variance, and the within-groups variance. The total variance represents the variance among all subjects. We then divide the total variance into the variance between the groups and the variance within groups. The variance between the groups is the variation due to the independent variable and random error. The within-groups variance consists of variation in performance of the subjects within each treatment group. Consequently, the within-groups variance is an estimate of the amount of random error in the data and reflects such factors as individual differences and sampling error. Because the within-groups variance estimates the amount of variance that cannot be accounted for, it is often known as the error variance. Likewise, because the between-groups variance is an estimate of the variance associated with the treatment variable, it is often known as the treatment variance.

The role of the ANOVA is to help us determine the proportion of between-groups variance that is due to error and the proportion due to treatment. Stated another way, the ANOVA helps us determine if the

■ **Error Variance:**

Uncontrolled and unpredicted differences among individual scores. The within-group variance estimates the error variance.

■ **Treatment Variance:**

The variance among group means that is due to the effects of the independent variable.

difference among the means is due to random variation or whether we can infer that the amount of difference among the means is greater than chance alone would produce. We use the **F-ratio** to answer this question.

## The *F*-Ratio

In the previous section we stated that the between-groups variance represents the influence of error variance and treatment variance. If this is true, how do we go about determining the variance due to the treatment? The answer comes in the form of the standardized ratio, the *F*-ratio. The title of the ratio is given in honor of Sir Ronald Fisher who developed the original version of the statistic. There are several ways we can express the *F*-ratio:

$$F = \frac{\text{treatment variance} + \text{error variance}}{\text{error variance}} \tag{14.7a}$$

or as

$$F = \frac{\text{between-groups variance}}{\text{within-groups variance}} \tag{14.7b}$$

or as

$$F = \frac{\sigma^2_{\text{between}}}{\sigma^2_{\text{within}}} \tag{14.7c}$$

The *F*-ratio uses the same logic as the *z*-score or the *t*-ratio. The *F*-ratio creates a standardized score that compares the size of the between-groups variance relative to the within-groups variance. We can use Equation 14.7a to look further into the meaning of the *F*-ratio.

**No Treatment Effect**  Let's assume that our independent variable has no influence on the dependent variable. If this were true, what would the variance between the groups look like? Would all the means be equal to one another? If you said "No" you are correct. The means would probably not be equal to one another because sampling error, or random error, causes each sample mean to be slightly different from the population mean. We would expect, however, that the means would be relatively close to one another. More to the point, the variance between the means would, theoretically, equal the variance within the groups. Figure 14.8a presents an example of such a situation. For the sake of the example, we will assume the variance within groups is 5.0 and that the variance due to the independent variable is 0.0. Therefore,

$$F = \frac{0.0 + 5.0}{5.0} = 1.00$$

In words, the variance between-groups is the same relative size as the variance within-groups. Thus, we would interpret this *F*-ratio to indicate that the variance we observe between the group means is due to random factors. As you can see in Figure 14.8a, there is variance between the group means. There is, however, considerable overlap among the distributions. Based on these data and the *F*-ratio, we should consider the differences between the group means to be due to random effects or sampling error. In other words, the independent variable had no detectable effect on the dependent variable.

■ **F-Ratio:**

The ratio of the between-groups variance divided by the within-groups variance.

*F-tests are always two tailed*

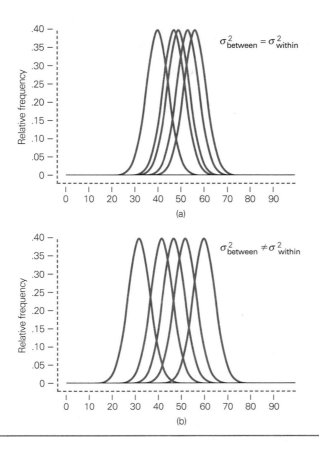

**Figure** | **14.8**

Two graphs representing hypothetical data for a one-way ANOVA. In both graphs the within-group variation is 5. In (a) the between-group variation (the variance between the group means) is also 5. Therefore, the ratio of the between-group variance to the within-group variance is 1.00. We could interpret these data as reflecting random effects and suggesting that there is no systematic relation between the independent and dependent variables. In (b) the between-group variance is twice as large as the within-group variance. Such data may be interpreted to indicate that the differences among the means represents random error and a treatment effect. The *F*-ratio for such data would be 2.00. We could interpret these data as suggesting that there is a systematic relationship between the independent and dependent variables.

**Treatment Effect Present**   What happens to the *F*-ratio when there is an effect due to the independent variable? As you saw in Figure 14.3, and in the general linear model, the treatment effect adds a constant to the observations of each group. Therefore, the effect of the independent variable may cause the mean of the sample to be greater or less than the population mean. If this is the case, the between-groups variance will be larger than the within-groups variance. Figure 14.8b represents what could occur if there is a statistically significant treatment effect. Compare this figure with Figure 14.8a. Notice that in Figure 14.8b the differences between the means appear to be greater than in Figure 14.8a. Using Equation 14.7a we indicate that

$$F = \frac{5.0 + 5.0}{5.0} = 2.00$$

We can interpret this ratio to indicate that the variance between the group means is twice as large as the variance within groups. Going a step further, we are able to conclude that the presence of different levels of the independent variable creates greater variability between the means than would be expected from random variation. In other words, we may have statistical evidence that the independent variable influences the dependent variable.

## $H_0$ and $H_1$

The null and alternative hypotheses for the ANOVA are similar in form and logic to the null and alternative hypotheses used to test the $t$-ratio. Specifically, the null hypothesis specifies that the independent variable has no effect on the dependent variable. In the case of a non-experimental design (e.g., intact group design), the null hypothesis states that there are no differences between the groups. Specifically, we write the null hypothesis as

$$H_0 : \mu_1 = \mu_2 = \mu_3 \cdots = \mu_k$$

We used a similar null hypothesis for the $t$-ratio. The only difference is that with the ANOVA we compare simultaneously more than two means. The interpretation of the null hypothesis is simply that all groups represent the same population and that any observed differences between the means is due to random factors, or sampling errors.

Because the ANOVA is an omnibus test, we do not make specific statements about how the means will be different from one another in the alternative hypothesis. Remember that the primary purpose of the ANOVA is to determine whether or not there are any systematic differences between the means. Because we do not specify the relation between the means in the ANOVA, we write the alternative hypothesis as

$$H_1: \text{Not } H_0$$

The alternative hypothesis for the $F$-ratio is a nondirectional hypothesis because we do not specify how the means will be different from one another, only that they will be different from one another.

We will have more to say about the interpretation of the $F$-ratio in a subsequent section. One point we want to highlight now is that the $F$-ratio does not specify which means are different from other means. All the alternative hypothesis allows us to conclude is that the difference between the means is great enough for us to reject the null hypothesis. Once we reject the null hypothesis in favor of the alternative, we can then use a special form of $t$-ratio to make specific comparisons between the means.

## $F$-Ratio Sampling Distribution

Just as Student developed a family of sampling distributions for the $t$-ratio, Fisher developed a family of sampling distributions for the $F$-ratio. The concept of the sampling distributions for the $F$-ratio is the same as for other sampling distributions. Specifically, the sampling distributions represent the probability of various $F$-ratios when the null hypothesis is true.

Two types of degrees of freedom determine the shape of the distribution. The first degrees of freedom represent the between-groups variance. You may remember that when we defined the degrees of freedom we said that the degrees of freedom always equals 1 less than the number of observations that contribute to the variance we are estimating. Because we estimate the variance between the group means, the degrees of freedom between-groups is the number of means less 1. For the between-groups variance, the degrees of freedom are

$$df_{\text{between}} = k - 1 \tag{14.8}$$

where $k$ is the number of groups compared in the variance term. If we conducted an experiment with 4 groups we would have 3 degrees of freedom for the between-groups variance.

The second degrees of freedom represent the within-groups variance. As we noted previously, the within-groups is really an average of the variances of each of the groups. We define these degrees of freedom as

$$df_{\text{within}} = \Sigma(n_j - 1) \tag{14.9}$$

where $n_j$ represents the number of observations in each group. Imagine that we conducted an experiment with 4 groups. The number of observations in the groups are 6, 5, 7, 6. Therefore the degrees of freedom are

$$df_{\text{between}} = 4 - 1 \quad df_{\text{within}} = (6 - 1) + (5 - 1) + (7 - 1) + (6 - 1)$$

$$\textbf{\textit{df}}_{\textbf{between}} = \textbf{3} \qquad df_{\text{within}} = 5 + 4 + 6 + 5$$

$$\textbf{\textit{df}}_{\textbf{within}} = \textbf{20}$$

Figure 14.9 represents the sampling distribution for the $F$-ratio when the degrees of freedom are 3 and 20. As you can see, the distribution is highly skewed with the greatest proportion of the distribution being close to 1.00. Because we want to determine if $F$ is greater than 1.00, we place $\alpha$ on the extreme right of the distribution. This procedure allows us to determine the $F_{\text{critical}}$ required to reject the null hypothesis.

Table J of Appendix D lists the critical values of $F$. Table 14.1 is a facsimile of this table. As you can see the numbers are organized in specific rows and columns. The columns represent the degrees of freedom for the numerator of the $F$-ratio—the between-groups variance. The rows represent the degrees of freedom for the denominator of the $F$-ratio—

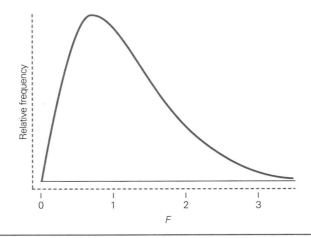

**Figure** | **14.9**

**Sampling distribution for *F* with 3, 20 *df*.**

**Table** | **14.1**

**Excerpts from Table J: Critical Values of _F_. The Obtained _F_ Is Significant at a Given Level If It Is Equal to or Greater Than the Value Shown in the Table— $\alpha = .05$ (Light Numbers) and $\alpha = .01$ (Dark Numbers)**

<table>
<tr><th rowspan="2">Degrees of freedom for denominator</th><th colspan="8">Degrees of freedom for numerator</th></tr>
<tr><th>1</th><th>2</th><th>3</th><th>4</th><th>5</th><th>6</th><th>7</th><th>8</th></tr>
<tr><td>1</td><td>161<br>**4052**</td><td>200<br>**4999**</td><td>216<br>**5403**</td><td>225<br>**5625**</td><td>230<br>**5764**</td><td>234<br>**5859**</td><td>237<br>**5928**</td><td>239<br>**5981**</td></tr>
<tr><td>2</td><td>18.51<br>**98.49**</td><td>19.00<br>**99.01**</td><td>19.16<br>**99.17**</td><td>19.25<br>**99.25**</td><td>19.30<br>**99.30**</td><td>19.33<br>**99.33**</td><td>19.36<br>**99.34**</td><td>19.37<br>**99.36**</td></tr>
<tr><td>3</td><td>10.13<br>**34.12**</td><td>9.55<br>**30.81**</td><td>9.28<br>**29.46**</td><td>9.12<br>**28.71**</td><td>9.01<br>**28.24**</td><td>8.94<br>**27.91**</td><td>8.88<br>**27.67**</td><td>8.84<br>**27.49**</td></tr>
<tr><td>4</td><td>7.71<br>**21.20**</td><td>6.94<br>**18.00**</td><td>6.59<br>**16.69**</td><td>6.39<br>**15.98**</td><td>6.26<br>**15.52**</td><td>6.16<br>**15.21**</td><td>6.09<br>**14.98**</td><td>6.04<br>**14.80**</td></tr>
<tr><td>5</td><td>6.61<br>**16.26**</td><td>5.79<br>**13.27**</td><td>5.41<br>**12.06**</td><td>5.19<br>**11.39**</td><td>5.05<br>**10.97**</td><td>4.95<br>**10.67**</td><td>4.88<br>**10.45**</td><td>4.82<br>**10.27**</td></tr>
<tr><td>⋮</td><td>. . .</td><td>. . .</td><td>. . .</td><td>. . .</td><td>. . .</td><td>. . .</td><td>. . .</td><td>. . .</td></tr>
<tr><td>18</td><td>4.41<br>**8.28**</td><td>3.55<br>**6.01**</td><td>3.16<br>**5.09**</td><td>2.93<br>**4.58**</td><td>2.77<br>**4.25**</td><td>2.66<br>**4.01**</td><td>2.58<br>**3.85**</td><td>2.51<br>**3.71**</td></tr>
<tr><td>19</td><td>4.38<br>**8.18**</td><td>3.52<br>**5.93**</td><td>3.13<br>**5.01**</td><td>2.90<br>**4.50**</td><td>2.74<br>**4.17**</td><td>2.63<br>**3.94**</td><td>2.55<br>**3.77**</td><td>2.48<br>**3.63**</td></tr>
<tr><td>20</td><td>4.35<br>**8.10**</td><td>3.49<br>**5.85**</td><td>3.10<br>**4.94**</td><td>2.87<br>**4.43**</td><td>2.71<br>**4.10**</td><td>2.60<br>**3.87**</td><td>2.52<br>**3.71**</td><td>2.45<br>**3.56**</td></tr>
<tr><td>21</td><td>4.32<br>**8.02**</td><td>3.47<br>**5.78**</td><td>3.07<br>**4.87**</td><td>2.84<br>**4.37**</td><td>2.68<br>**4.04**</td><td>2.57<br>**3.81**</td><td>2.49<br>**3.65**</td><td>2.42<br>**3.51**</td></tr>
<tr><td>22</td><td>4.30<br>**7.94**</td><td>3.44<br>**5.72**</td><td>3.05<br>**4.82**</td><td>2.82<br>**4.31**</td><td>2.66<br>**3.99**</td><td>2.55<br>**3.76**</td><td>2.47<br>**3.59**</td><td>2.40<br>**3.45**</td></tr>
</table>

the within-groups variance. In the current example, the degrees of freedom are 3 and 20. Looking down the $df = 3$ _column_ and over on the $df = 20$ _row_ we find that $F_{\text{critical}} = 3.10$ when $\alpha = .05$, and $F_{\text{critical}} = 4.94$ when $\alpha = .01$.

## The _F_-Ratio and $\omega^2$

All the rules you learned about interpreting the _t_-ratio apply to the interpretation of the _F_-ratio. Specifically, the size of the _F_-ratio and _p_-value indicate only whether we can reject the null hypothesis given the value selected for $H_0$. In order to evaluate the degree to which the independent variable is associated with the dependent variable, we need to convert the _F_-ratio to $\omega^2$. For the _F_-ratio, $\omega^2$ is

$$\omega^2 = \frac{df_{\text{between}}(F - 1)}{df_{\text{between}}(F - 1) + N}$$

(14.10)

In this equation $N$ represents all subjects in the experiment. The size of $\omega^2$ indicates the degree of association between the independent and dependent variables. When we introduced you to $\omega^2$ in Chapter 13, we

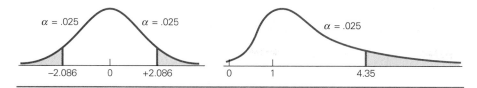

**Figure | 14.10**

> **Sampling distributions for the *t*-ratio and the *F*-ratio. The degrees of freedom for the *t*-ratio are 20. The degrees of freedom for the *F*-ratio are 1 and 20. The critical regions ($\alpha = .05$) for both distributions are shaded.**

suggested that $\omega^2$ be calculated only if the statistic is statistically significant. The same is true for the *F*-ratio. It is good practice to calculate $\omega^2$ only after you have established that the *F*-ratio is statistically significant.

### *t*-Ratio vs. *F*-Ratio

When we use the ANOVA to compare the means of two groups we have a special case of the *t*-ratio. Specifically, statisticians have shown that $t^2 = F$ when $k = 2$. This means that if you wanted to compare two means, you could use the ANOVA or a *t*-ratio with a nondirectional hypothesis and obtain the same statistical conclusion. This raises a few questions from you such as, "Why even study the *t*-ratio?" and "Why is the ANOVA a test of a nondirectional hypothesis?"

The answer to the first question is that the *t*-ratio is an essential statistic for comparing means when the researcher has a logically derived hypothesis to test. In other words, the *t*-ratio, and not the *F*-ratio, allows us to make directional comparisons between means.

The answer to the second question comes to us from how the sampling distribution for the *F*-ratio is constructed when $k = 2$. Figure 14.10 presents the sampling distribution for the *t*-ratio for 20 degrees of freedom and the sampling distribution for the *F*-ratio when the degrees of freedom are 1 and 20. For the *t*-ratio, the critical region for $\alpha$ is divided on both ends of the distribution. The sampling distribution for the *F*-ratio represents the same characteristics. The shapes of the distributions are different because the sampling distribution for *t* is based on the distribution of mean differences, whereas the sampling distribution for *F* is based on the distribution of variances between means. The differences between means can be negative, consequently the *t*-distribution is symmetrical. Variances can only be positive, thus the *F*-distribution always has a positive skew.

## 14.4 / Assumptions of ANOVA

Like the *t*-test, the ANOVA is a parametric statistic that makes basic assumptions about the data. We assume that

1. The sampling error is distributed normally around $\mu$ in each treatment population. Therefore, the data should be normally distributed within each group.
2. There is homogeneity of variance, specifically $\sigma_1 = \sigma_2 = \sigma_3 \ldots \sigma_k$.

**3.** The observations in each sample are independent of each other. That is, there is no systematic relation between pairs of scores for each group.

How important are these assumptions? What happens if we violate some or all of these conditions? We call a statistic robust if we can violate its assumptions and retain its integrity. More specifically, a test is robust if the levels of Type I and Type II errors are not affected by violations of the assumptions. There is some controversy among statisticians about how robust the ANOVA is against violations of the homogeneity of variance and normal distribution assumptions. For example, Milligan, Wong, and Thompson (1987) demonstrated that the ANOVA is not robust when variances and sample sizes are radically different. Their study, however, examined extreme violations of homogeneity and used large differences in sample size. As a generality, the ANOVA is robust to violations of homogeneity of variance and normal distribution if the sample sizes are equal and large. Therefore, when you collect data for your research, you should attempt to place a premium on collecting as many subjects as possible and ensuring that each group has the same number of subjects.

Violation of the third assumption is a real problem. In order to make fair inferences from the one-way ANOVA the data must be independent. There are several ways that you can ensure independence of the data. For a true experiment, you can randomly assign subjects to the different levels of the independent variable. If you use an intact group design, then you will need to ensure that your measurement of subjects in one group does not affect the measurement of subjects in the other groups.

## 14.5 / Obtaining Variance Estimates

We return to our familiar sum of squares to estimate the variance for each of the components of the ANOVA. As we progress, we will introduce you to special symbols and conventions for presenting information about the ANOVA.

### Total Variance

The total variance for all the data represents the variance among all subjects regardless of their placement in a treatment group. We can begin with the sum of squares:

$$SS_{\text{total}} = \Sigma X_{ij}^2 - \frac{(\Sigma X_{ij})^2}{N} \tag{14.11}$$

This form of sum of squares is no different than the sum of squares we showed you in Chapter 5. The only difference is that we have embellished the subscripts for $X$.

The degrees of freedom are

$$df_{\text{total}} = N - 1 \tag{14.12}$$

In the ANOVA, $N$ represents the total number of subjects used in the experiment. We will use the symbol $n_j$ to represent the number of subjects in a specific treatment group. As a rule, $N = \Sigma n_j$. Finally, we can estimate the total variance as

$$MS_{\text{total}} = \frac{SS_{\text{total}}}{df_{\text{total}}} \tag{14.13}$$

Mean Squares, MS, is a term used interchangeably with the term, *estimated variance.* We call it the mean squares because it is the mean or average of the sum of squared deviations. Because this term is used to estimate a population variance it is also called estimated variance or variance estimate.

## Between-Groups Variance

To estimate the variance between groups we begin with the sum of squares:

$$SS_{\text{between}} = \Sigma \frac{(X_{\bullet j})^2}{n_j} - \frac{(\Sigma X_{ij})^2}{N} \tag{14.14}$$

The variable $X_{\bullet j}$ is a shorthand symbol for the sum of all the observations in a group. The dot ($\bullet$) in the subscript indicates summation and takes the place of a $\Sigma$. Specifically, the dot represents the summation of observations for that subscript. For example $X_{\bullet 1}$ is the total of all scores in Group 1 and $X_{\bullet 4}$ is the sum of all scores in Group 4, and $X_{\bullet j}$ indicates the sum of all scores in each of the individual $j$ groups.

Figure 14.11 presents our subscript system. The first subscript for any variable represents the subject number. The second subscript represents the group number for the subject. For example, $X_{2,3}$ represents the second subject in Group 3, whereas $X_{25,2}$ represents the 25th subject in Group 2.

The degrees of freedom are

$$df_{\text{between}} = k - 1$$

The estimate of the between-groups variance, $\sigma^2_{\text{between}}$, is

$$MS_{\text{between}} = \frac{SS_{\text{between}}}{df_{\text{between}}} \tag{14.15}$$

## Within-Groups Variance

The last variance term we need to estimate is the $\sigma^2_{\text{within}}$. The Sum of Squares Within is

**Figure 14.11**

A representation of the subscript notation for a one-way ANOVA. The first subscript represents the subject, and the second subscript represents the level of the factor. A dot ($\cdot$) represents summation across that index. For example $X_{\cdot 1} = \Sigma X_{i1}$.

$$SS_{\text{within}} = \Sigma X_{ij}^2 - \Sigma \frac{(X_{\bullet j})^2}{n_j} \tag{14.16}$$

The degrees of freedom are

$$df_{\text{within}} = \Sigma(n_j - 1) \tag{14.17}$$

The estimate of the within-groups variance is, therefore,

$$MS_{\text{within}} = \frac{SS_{\text{within}}}{df_{\text{within}}} \tag{14.18}$$

## 14.6 Worked Example

One of the well-known effects in psychology is the partial reinforcement extinction effect. Stated simply, a person who has been reinforced on a random, or partial, basis will be more persistent than subjects continuously reinforced (Pittenger & Pavlik, 1989). The effect can be applied to a variety of settings.

Imagine that a teacher wants to study the effects of partial reinforcement on children's persistence. The teacher wants students to work on hard math problems without much supervision; she wants them to be persistent. She selects 16 children from a fifth grade class and randomly assigns them to one of four treatment conditions. In Group 1 the subjects receive a reinforcer (e.g., a token that can be cashed in for time with a video game) for each math problem they solve. In Group 2 the subjects receive a reinforcer for a random 80% of the problems. In Groups 3 and 4, the subjects receive a reinforcer for a random 60% or 50% of the problems, respectively.

After a week of this training, the teacher witholds all reinforcement. The teacher gives the students 12 math problems to solve and counts the number of problems they solve before quitting. The data for the four groups are presented on page 377. Please note that this example is much simplified for teaching purposes. Before conducting a study of this type, one would want to estimate the statistical power of the research design.

We can begin the analysis of these data by establishing the null and alternative hypotheses.

**Null Hypothesis:** $H_0$: $\mu_1 = \mu_2 = \mu_3 = \mu_4$. The differences between the means are due to sampling error. The percentage of reinforcement has no particular effect on the persistence of the children.

**Alternative Hypothesis:** $H_1$: Not $H_0$: The differences between the means are too large to be due simply to sampling error. The percentage of reinforcement creates changes in the persistence of the children.

**Statistical Test:** We use the $F$-ratio because we are simultaneously comparing more than two groups. We assume that the data are normally distributed and that the variances of the groups are equal.

**Significance Level:** $\alpha = .05$. If the size of the $F$-ratio is sufficiently large, we will reject the null hypothesis in favor of the alternative hypothesis.

***Sampling Distribution:***   The degrees of freedom for the ANOVA are:

$$df_\text{between} = 4 - 1 \quad df_\text{within} = (4 - 1) + (4 - 1) + (4 - 1) + (4 - 1)$$
$$df_\text{between} = 3 \quad df_\text{within} = 12$$

We will use the $F$-distribution.

The Numerator Degrees of Freedom = $df_\text{between} = 3$, the Denominator Degrees of Freedom = $df_\text{within} = 12$.

***Critical Region for Rejection of $H_0$:***   $F_\text{critical} \geq 3.49$. A critical region is that portion of the area under the $F$-distribution that includes those values of a statistic that leads to rejection of $H_0$. If the $F$-ratio is equal to or larger than 3.49 we will reject $H_0$.

Our first step will be to calculate the sum of squares for each of the three terms.

| Group 1<br>100% | Group 2<br>80% | Group 3<br>60% | Group 4<br>40% | |
|---|---|---|---|---|
| $X_{1,1} = 4$ | $X_{1,2} = 6$ | $X_{1,3} = 4$ | $X_{1,4} = 5$ | |
| $X_{2,1} = 2$ | $X_{2,2} = 3$ | $X_{2,3} = 5$ | $X_{2,4} = 8$ | |
| $X_{3,1} = 1$ | $X_{3,2} = 5$ | $X_{3,3} = 7$ | $X_{3,4} = 6$ | |
| $X_{4,1} = 3$ | $X_{4,2} = 4$ | $X_{4,3} = 6$ | $X_{4,4} = 5$ | |
| $X_{\bullet 1} = 10$ | $X_{\bullet 2} = 18$ | $X_{\bullet 3} = 22$ | $X_{\bullet 4} = 24$ | $\Sigma X_{ij} = 74$ |
| $n_1 = 4$ | $n_2 = 4$ | $n_3 = 4$ | $n_4 = 4$ | $N = 16$ |
| $\overline{X} = 2.5$ | $\overline{X} = 4.5$ | $\overline{X} = 5.5$ | $\overline{X} = 6.0$ | $\overline{\overline{X}} = 4.62$ |
| $\Sigma X_{i1}^2 = 30$ | $\Sigma X_{i2}^2 = 86$ | $\Sigma X_{i3}^2 = 126$ | $\Sigma X_{i4}^2 = 150$ | $\Sigma X_{ij}^2 = 392$ |
| $\hat{s}_1^2 = 1.67$ | $\hat{s}_2^2 = 1.67$ | $\hat{s}_3^2 = 1.67$ | $\hat{s}_4^2 = 2.00$ | |

Stem-and-Leaf Presentation of Data

Group 1    <u>1234</u>

Group 2    <u>  3456</u>

Group 3    <u>    4567</u>
                  5
Group 4    <u>    56 8</u>

Examining the stem-and-leaf plots of the data indicates that there appear to be no outliers or exceptional scores. The variances of the four groups also appear to be equivalent. To be sure that we have homogeneity of variance, we need to conduct the $F_\text{max}$ test. As you recall from the last chapter, $F_\text{max}$ is the largest variance divided by the smallest variance. For these data,

$$F_\text{max} = \frac{2.00}{1.67}, \quad F_\text{max} = 1.198$$

Use Table K from Appendix D to determine the critical value for the $F_\text{max}$ test. For this study there are four variances in the study; the degrees of freedom for the samples is 4. Therefore, the critical value for the $F_\text{max}$ test is 20.60 for $\alpha = .05$. Because 1.198 is much less than 20.60, we can assume that the variances among the groups are equivalent. Consequently, we can progress with our analysis of the data.

**Step 1** **Sum of Squares**

**Sum of Squares Total**     **Sum of Squares Within Groups**

$$SS_{total} = \Sigma X_{ij}^2 - \frac{(\Sigma X_{ij})^2}{N} \qquad SS_{within} = \Sigma X_{ij}^2 - \Sigma \frac{(X_{\bullet j})^2}{n_j}$$

$$SS_{total} = 392 - \frac{(74)^2}{16} \qquad SS_{within} = 392 - 371$$

$$\qquad\qquad\qquad\qquad\qquad SS_{within} = 21.00$$

$$SS_{total} = 392 - 342.25$$

$$SS_{total} = 49.75$$

**Sum of Squares Between Groups**

$$SS_{between} = \Sigma \frac{(X_{\bullet j})^2}{n_j} - \frac{(\Sigma X_{ij})^2}{N}$$

$$SS_{between} = \frac{(10)^2}{4} + \frac{(18)^2}{4} + \frac{(22)^2}{4} + \frac{(24)^2}{4} - \frac{(74)^2}{16}$$

$$SS_{between} = 25 + 81 + 121 + 144 - 342.25$$

$$SS_{between} = 371 - 342.25$$

$$SS_{between} = 28.75$$

If you are using a hand calculator, we recommended that you to make extensive and neat notes. Due to the number of steps required, you need to be able to have complete notes to look for and find potential errors in calculation. When you are done with sum of squares, all values should be positive and $SS_{total} = SS_{between} + SS_{within}$.

**Step 2** **Degrees of Freedom**

**Degrees of Freedom Total**     **Degrees of Freedom Between Groups**

$$df_{total} = N - 1 \qquad\qquad df_{between} = k - 1$$

$$df_{total} = 16 - 1 \qquad\qquad df_{between} = 4 - 1$$

$$df_{total} = 15 \qquad\qquad\quad df_{between} = 3$$

**Degrees of Freedom Within Groups**

$$df_{within} = \Sigma(n_j - 1)$$

$$df_{within} = (4 - 1) + (4 - 1) + (4 - 1) + (4 - 1)$$

$$df_{within} = 12$$

As with the sum of squares, the $df_{total} = df_{between} + df_{within}$.

**Step 3** **Mean Squares**

Because our interest is only in the relation of the between-groups variance to the within-groups variance we need only to calculate the variance for those terms.

### *Mean Squares Between Groups*

$$MS_{between} = \frac{SS_{between}}{df_{between}}$$

$$MS_{between} = \frac{28.75}{3}$$

$$MS_{between} = 9.583$$

### *Mean Squares Within Groups*

$$MS_{within} = \frac{SS_{within}}{df_{within}}$$

$$MS_{within} = \frac{21.00}{12}$$

$$MS_{within} = 1.75$$

**Step 4  F-ratio**

Our last step is to calculate the *F*-ratio

$$F = \frac{MS_{between}}{MS_{within}}$$

$$F = \frac{9.583}{1.75}$$

$$F = 5.48$$

## ANOVA Summary Table

It is a common practice to report the sum of squares, degrees of freedom, mean squares, and the *F*-ratio in an ANOVA summary table. This common practice has been used by several generations of statisticians and is now common in the printout of computer programs that perform statistical analyses. The basic format of the summary table is as follows:

| Source | SS | df | MS | F |
|---|---|---|---|---|
| Between-groups | 28.75 | 3 | 9.583 | 5.48 |
| Within-groups | 21.00 | 12 | 1.750 | |
| Total | 49.75 | 15 | | |

Because the calculated $F_{observed}$ is greater than the $F_{critical}$ (5.48 > 3.49), we can reject the null hypothesis and conclude that the schedule of reinforcement did influence the student's persistence at the math task.

Many researchers in the behavioral sciences use the *Publication Manual of the American Psychological Association* (1994) when preparing papers and reporting the results of their research. The recommended format for reporting the results of an *F*-test is:

$$\underline{F}(df_N, \ df_D) = F_O, \ \underline{p} = p \quad or \quad \underline{F}(df_N, \ df_D) = F_O, \ \underline{p}, \ \alpha$$

For this example we would report the *F*-ratio as

$$\underline{F}(3, \ 12) = 5.48, \ \underline{p} \ 5 \ .013^* \quad or \quad \underline{F}(3, \ 12) = 5.48, \ \underline{p} < .05$$

Notice that $df_N$ refers to the numerator degrees of freedom, the degrees of freedom for the between-groups effect. The $df_D$ refers to the denominator degrees of freedom, the degrees of freedom for within-group effect.

---

\* This probability was calculated by a computer program. Many statistical software packages will calculate the exact probability level for you. If you are not using a computer to do your calculations, you will need to use Table J of Appendix D to determine whether or not to reject the null hypothesis.

## 14.7 Interpreting the *F*-Ratio

When we reject the null hypothesis for the ANOVA we conclude that the difference between the group means is large enough to infer that $H_0$ is false. Specifically, we accept the alternative hypothesis that states that $H_1: \sigma^2_{between} \neq \sigma^2_{within}$. Although the *F*-ratio allowed us to take a significant step forward, we need to continue the analysis of our data to learn more about the relation between the treatment and the results.

### Omega Squared, $\omega^2$

The first question we can examine is the degree of association between the two variables, which is accomplished using $\omega^2$:

$$\omega^2 = \frac{df_{between}(F-1)}{df_{between}(F-1) + N}$$

$$\omega^2 = \frac{3(5.48 - 1)}{3(5.48 - 1) + 16}$$

$$\omega^2 = \frac{3(4.48)}{3(4.48) + 16}$$

$$\omega^2 = \frac{13.44}{29.44}$$

$$\omega^2 = .457$$

Therefore we can conclude that approximately 45.7% of the differences among the scores of the dependent variable can be accounted for by the differences in the independent variable.

### Effect Size and Power

Cohen (1988) developed a measure of effect size for the *F*-ratio. The effect size for the *F*-ratio is symbolized by **f** and is interpreted in the same way $d$ is interpreted for the *t*-ratio. We calculate **f** using

$$\mathbf{f} = \sqrt{\frac{\eta^2}{1 - \eta^2}} \tag{14.19}$$

where $\eta^2$ (eta squared)

$$\eta^2 = \frac{df_{between}(F)}{df_{between}(F) + df_{within}} \quad \text{or} \quad \eta^2 = \frac{SS_{between}}{SS_{total}} \tag{14.20}$$

For our experiment:

$$\eta^2 = \frac{28.75}{49.75} = .578$$

and

$$\mathbf{f} = \sqrt{\frac{.578}{1 - .578}} = 1.170$$

According to Cohen (1988), effect sizes for the ANOVA can be classified into one of three categories:

Small effect size **f** = .10

Medium effect size **f** = .25

Large effect size **f** = .40

Obviously, the effect size for this hypothetical experiment is much larger than what Cohen calls a large effect size. The magnitude of the effect size results from our desire to create an obvious example so you can see differences between the group means.

Effect sizes must be interpreted with caution and humility. When an effect size is small, the relationship between the independent and dependent variables may also be small. However, a small effect size may still be considered an extremely important effect in social science research. For example, when studying a complex social behavior in a natural environment, one has little direct control over the environment and the treatment of the subjects. Furthermore, in this situation, and many others, the dependent variable may be measured with a procedure or instrument that has much inherent error. Therefore, we need to always remember to interpret effect size within a broader context. Sometimes a "small" effect size can represent a major breakthrough in a program of research (Abelson, 1985). Sometimes a "small" effect size is small and the data are soon forgotten.

According to Cohen (1988) effect sizes greater than .50 are rare in the behavioral sciences. Why is **f** "small" for the behavioral sciences? The problem may arise from several factors related to random error. First, most of the phenomena studied by behavioral scientists are complex behaviors that have many causes. In other words, people are complex. Although behavioral research is becoming more sophisticated, many of the critical variables that influence a person's behavior are still being identified and studied. Another problem is the inherent differences among humans. Even in a highly controlled laboratory experiment, each subject walks into the experiment with his or her life experiences. These experiences create differences among subjects that the experimenter cannot control. Finally, measurement in the behavioral sciences contains much error. No questionnaire, attitude survey, or observation technique is free of measurement error. These uncontrolled sources of error combine to reduce the overall effect size of an experiment. The successful researcher recognizes the presence of these inherent sources of error and attempts to improve the quality of the research procedure. In time, small effect sizes become progressively larger as the discipline matures.

Cohen's book (1988) provides many (65 pages worth) power tables that allow you to determine the power of an experiment. These tables can also be used to plan experiments. Specifically, one can use the tables and an estimated effect size to determine the number of subjects required thereby maximizing the power of the study. A condensed version of the power tables for the ANOVA is presented in Table M of Appendix D. Table 14.2 presents a portion of those tables.

The table contains several pieces of information. The first step is selecting the correct table. We selected this table because our experiment has 3 degrees of freedom in the numerator (the $df_{between}$). The table also includes the three conventional alpha levels, (.01, .05, and .10). The column labeled "$n$" represents the number of subjects in each treatment condition, and the column marked $F_c$ represents the critical *F*-ratio required for the specified degrees of freedom. The three other columns of

Table | 14.2

**An Example of a Power Table for the One-Way ANOVA. The $F_C$ Column Represents the Critical Value of $F$ for the Degrees of Freedom. The f Columns Represent the Small, Medium, and Large Effect Sizes.**

**DEGREES OF FREEDOM NUMERATOR = 3**

| | $\alpha = .01$ | | | | $\alpha = .05$ | | | | $\alpha = .10$ | | | |
|---|---|---|---|---|---|---|---|---|---|---|---|---|
| $n$ | $F_c$ | f 0.10 | f 0.25 | f 0.40 | $F_c$ | f 0.10 | f 0.25 | f 0.40 | $F_c$ | f 0.10 | f 0.25 | f 0.40 |
| 5 | 5.292 | .01 | .03 | .08 | 3.239 | .06 | .12 | .24 | 2.462 | .12 | .20 | .37 |
| 10 | 4.377 | .01 | .07 | .25 | 2.866 | .07 | .21 | .51 | 2.243 | .14 | .33 | .64 |
| 15 | 4.152 | .02 | .13 | .46 | 2.769 | .08 | .32 | .71 | 2.184 | .16 | .45 | .82 |
| 20 | 4.050 | .02 | .20 | .65 | 2.725 | .10 | .43 | .85 | 2.157 | .18 | .56 | .91 |
| 25 | 3.992 | .03 | .28 | .79 | 2.699 | .11 | .53 | .93 | 2.142 | .20 | .65 | .96 |
| 30 | 3.955 | .03 | .36 | .88 | 2.683 | .13 | .61 | .96 | 2.132 | .22 | .73 | .98 |
| 35 | 3.929 | .04 | .45 | .94 | 2.671 | .14 | .69 | .98 | 2.124 | .24 | .79 | .99 |
| 40 | 3.910 | .04 | .53 | .97 | 2.663 | .16 | .76 | .99 | 2.119 | .26 | .84 | .** |
| 45 | 3.895 | .05 | .60 | .98 | 2.656 | .17 | .81 | .** | 2.115 | .28 | .88 | .** |
| 50 | 3.883 | .06 | .67 | .99 | 2.651 | .19 | .85 | .** | 2.112 | .30 | .91 | .** |
| 100 | 3.831 | .16 | .97 | .** | 2.627 | .36 | .99 | .** | 2.098 | .49 | .** | .** |

numbers represent the small (.10), medium (.25), and large (.40) effect sizes. We can use this table to estimate the power of our experiment and to plan our future research projects.

The results of the hypothetical persistence study suggest that there is a very large effect size. If these were data from a real experiment, we could conclude that we have a very powerful effect and that the chances for replicating the study are good.

Let's look at how you can use the table to plan an experiment. Assume that you want to conduct a study where you believe the effect size is moderate, **f** = .25. You use four levels of the independent variable and set $\alpha$ = .05. How many subjects do you need in order to have to have an 80% chance of rejecting the null hypothesis? Looking at Table 14.2, you can see that you will need at least 45 subjects in each group (a total of $45 \times 4 = 180$ subjects) to have sufficient power to reject the null hypothesis.

### Cause and Effect

Can the $F$-ratio be used as a piece of evidence to demonstrate a causal link between the independent and dependent variables? By now you should have a reflexive answer for this question: "It depends on whether or not the subjects were randomly assigned to the treatment conditions in which the independent variable was manipulated." If you use the ANOVA to analyze data collected from a true experiment you may be able to infer a causal link between the two variables if the $F$-ratio is statistically significant.

There are many instances where you may want to use the ANOVA to make comparisons among multiple intact groups. For example you may want to see if there are systematic differences among the age groups with respect to attitude toward specific political topics. You may, for example, find that younger people tend to be more willing to endorse "conservative" attitudes whereas older voters are more likely to represent more "liberal" attitudes. Although there may be sizable differences between the age groups you studied, you cannot assume that growing older causes people to become more liberal in their politics. It may well be that the older group of subjects represents a generation that experienced certain political events that shaped their political views. Therefore, it is not the growing older that created the political ideology, but the political experiences that one has had.

## 14.8 / Multiple Comparisons of the Means

When we reject the null hypothesis tested by the ANOVA, we can only conclude that the variance between the means is greater than sampling error. The *F*-ratio does not specify where the statistically significant differences among the groups may occur. To determine which means are statistically different from one another, we must return to the logic of the *t*-ratio to compare individual means.

You may be wondering why we would return to the *t*-ratio after demonstrating the problems with conducting multiple *t*-ratios at the start of the chapter. The answer is that we will be using a variant of the *t*-ratio to conduct this analysis. Before we turn to that technique, we need to introduce a few new topics.

### Planned vs. Unplanned Comparisons

When we construct the alternative hypothesis for the *F*-ratio we do not make specific statements about the differences between the means other than they will be different. In some cases the researcher does not want to predict the nature of the differences between the groups or is not capable of predicting which means will be equal and which will be different. When such cases arise, the researcher uses the *F*-ratio as an omnibus test to determine if there is evidence to suggest that there are differences between the means. If the *F*-ratio is statistically significant, the researcher can then conduct additional *a posteriori* comparisons.

The term *a posteriori* means "after the fact." Applied to statistics, an *a posteriori* comparison is a statistical test that is created after the data are collected and analyzed. The hallmark of the *a posteriori* comparison is that the null and alternative hypotheses are created after one has examined the data. The *a posteriori* comparisons are an extremely popular set of comparisons used by many behavioral scientists.

There are other situations where the researcher is interested in testing results in which the means differ in a particular direction or is able to predict the specific relations between the means prior to conducting the experiment. Because the researcher states these hypotheses before the data are collected and analyzed, these specific comparisons are known as *a priori* comparisons. The term *a priori* means "before the fact." For statisticians, *a priori* means that the hypotheses for the multiple comparisons were stated before the start of the data analysis.

There are several important points of similarity and difference between the *a posteriori* and *a priori* multiple comparisons. Both procedures are similar in that they allow us to directly compare means, or groups of means, and both protect against inflated experimentwise error. There are two important differences, however.

First, *a posteriori* comparisons can be made only after we have successfully rejected the null hypothesis with the *F*-ratio. The *a priori* comparisons can be made without having conducted an ANOVA.

Second, the *a priori* comparisons control the experimentwise error rate using the number of comparisons made. In contrast, the *a posteriori* tests control the experimentwise error rate by using the potential number of comparisons regardless of the number of comparisons actually made. Consequently, the *a priori* tests tend to have greater statistical power.

Although both *a priori* and *a posteriori* tests are important, we will focus only on the *a posteriori* test. Our decision is based on the observation that behavioral scientists are more likely to conduct an ANOVA without any prior hypotheses. Furthermore, if a researcher does have prior hypotheses, the ANOVA is, in some respects, redundant. If you want to learn more about *a priori* tests, we highly recommend several advanced and specialized texts including Kirk (1982), Miller, (1981), and Toothaker (1991).

### A *Posteriori* Comparisons: Tukey's HSD

When we conduct *a posteriori* comparisons we need to balance opposing goals. On the one side, we need to protect against the inflation of $\alpha$ created by multiple unplanned comparisons. On the other side we need to have a comparison with sufficient power to detect differences among means that will help us understand our data. Many statisticians have devised various forms of *a posteriori* multiple comparison (see Kirk (1982), Miller (1981), and Toothaker (1991) for technical reviews of these procedures). The multiple comparison procedure that strikes a reasonable balance between these opposing goals is Tukey's HSD (Honestly Significant Difference) procedure (Jaccard, Becker, & Wood, 1984).

Tukey (1953) developed the HSD to compare all possible pairs of means after one has rejected the null hypothesis using the ANOVA. The difference between two means is statistically significant at a given level of $\alpha$ if it equals or exceeds HSD, which is

$$\text{HSD} = q_{\text{critical}} \sqrt{\frac{MS_{\text{within}}}{n}} \qquad (14.21)$$

where

$\quad$ HSD = critical difference required to consider the means statistically different.

$\quad q_{\text{critica}}$ = tabled value for a given $\alpha$ level for number of means and $df_w$.

$\quad MS_{\text{within}}$ = mean square within groups.

$\quad n$ = number of subjects in each group.

If the number of subjects in each group is not equal, $n'$ is defined as

$$n' = \frac{\text{Number of Means}}{\Sigma\left(\frac{1}{n_j}\right)} \qquad (14.22)$$

For example, if we had four groups with sample sizes of 5, 4, 5, 4, the corrected sample size would be

$$n' = \frac{4}{\frac{1}{5} + \frac{1}{4} + \frac{1}{4} + \frac{1}{5}} = \frac{4}{.20 + .25 + .25 + .20} = \frac{4}{.90} = 4.44$$

**Table** 14.3

**Comparison of All the Differences Between All Pairs of Means Using the Tukey HSD Test.**

| | | REINFORCEMENT GROUP | | | |
|---|---|---|---|---|---|
| Reinforcement Group | $\overline{X}$ | 100% 2.5 | 80% 4.5 | 60% 5.5 | 50% 6.0 |
| 100% | 2.5 | — | 2.0 | 3.0* | 3.5* |
| 80% | 4.5 | — | — | 1.0 | 1.5 |
| 60% | 5.5 | — | — | — | .5 |
| 50% | 6.0 | — | — | — | — |

The * indicates that the difference is statistically significant at the $\alpha = .05$ level.

We can use the data from our example of partial reinforcement and persistence to examine the use of Tukey's HSD. We know that the number of groups is 4, $df_{within} = 12$, and $MS_{within} = 1.75$. Table L in Appendix D presents the values of $q_{critical}$. The columns represent the number of means and the rows represent $df_{within}$. Looking down the column for $k = 4$ and across the row for $df_{within} = 12$, we find that $q_{critical} = 4.20$. Therefore, HSD equals

$$HSD = 4.20 \sqrt{\frac{1.75}{4}}$$

$$HSD = 4.20 \ (0.6614)$$

$$HSD = 2.78$$

Any difference between means that is 2.78 or greater will be considered statistically significant at $\alpha = .05$. We can create a matrix of the differences between the means to determine which are statistically different with respect to HSD as we did in Table 14.3.

We placed the asterisk (*) by those differences that are statistically different according to the HSD. As you can see, 60% and 50% reinforcement created greater persistence than did the 100% reinforcement. The 80% reinforcement condition created a level of persistence that appears to be intermediate between the 100% and the 60% and 50% conditions. Using data such as these, we may conclude that partial reinforcement at a rate of 60% or less created greater persistence in the children when they did not receive reinforcement for completing the math problems.

## 14.9 / Putting It All Together

Before we close the chapter, let's look at another complete example of the one-way ANOVA. Maria wanted to study the effects of elaborated rehearsal on memory. To conduct the experiment she created four independent treatment groups to which the subjects were randomly assigned. All subjects received a list of 10 words to read. The independent variable was the instruction the subjects received for reading the words. Maria told

4 groups
6 per group 2 who
minus failed

subjects in the Control Group to just read the list as many times as they wanted. The subjects in the Sound Group received instructions to examine the sounds of the words. Subjects in the Meaning Group were told to examine the meaning of the words. Subjects in the Self-Reference Group were told to examine how the words related to them. Later, all subjects read the list of words and received a surprise recall test. Although Maria tried to use 6 people in each group, 2 people did not cooperate with the instructions; Maria removed their data. With her data, Maria can now proceed with an analysis of the data.

**Null Hypothesis:** $H_0$: $\mu_1 = \mu_2 = \mu_3 = \mu_4$

**Alternative Hypothesis:** $H_1$: Not $H_0$

**Statistical Test:** Maria may use the $F$-ratio because she is simultaneously comparing more than two groups. She assumes that the data are normally distributed and that the variances of the groups are equal.

**Significance Level:** $\alpha = .05$.

**Sampling Distribution:** The degrees of freedom for the ANOVA are:

$$df_{between} = 4 - 1 \qquad df_{within} = (6 - 1) + (5 - 1) + (6 - 1) + (5 - 1)$$
$$df_{between} = 3 \qquad df_{within} = 18$$

We will use the $F$-distribution.

**Critical Region for Rejection of $H_0$:** $F_{critical} \geq 3.16$.

| | Control | Sound | Meaning | Self-Reference | | |
|---|---|---|---|---|---|---|
| | 5 | 6 | 5 | 10 | | |
| | 6 | 7 | 7 | 9 | | |
| | 3 | 7 | 8 | 10 | | |
| | 6 | 4 | 5 | 7 | | |
| | 3 | 4 | 8 | 7 | | |
| | 3 | | 5 | | | |
| $X_{\bullet j}$ | 26 | 28 | 38 | 43 | $\Sigma X_{ij} =$ | 135 |
| $n_j$ | 6 | 5 | 6 | 5 | $N =$ | 22 |
| $\overline{X}_j$ | 4.33 | 5.60 | 6.33 | 8.60 | $\overline{\overline{X}} =$ | 6.14 |
| $\Sigma X_{ij}^2$ | 124 | 166 | 252 | 379 | $\Sigma X_{in}^2 =$ | 921 |
| $(X_{\bullet j})^2$ | 676 | 784 | 1444 | 1849 | $\Sigma (X_{\bullet j})^2 =$ | 4753 |
| $\dfrac{(X_{\bullet j})^2}{n_j}$ | 112.6667 | 156.8000 | 240.6667 | 369.8000 | $\Sigma \dfrac{(X_{\bullet j})^2}{n_j} =$ | 879.9333 |
| $\hat{s}_j^2$ | 2.2667 | 2.30 | 2.2667 | 2.30 | | |

$$F_{max} = \frac{2.3000}{2.2667} \qquad F_{max} = 1.0147, \text{ degrees of freedom } k = 4, n = 6$$

$$F_{max\ critical} = 10.4$$

Because $1.0147 < 10.40$ we can conclude that variances are homogeneous.

$$SS_{total} = \Sigma X_{ij}^2 - \frac{(\Sigma X_{ij})^2}{N} \qquad SS_{between} = \Sigma \frac{(X_{\bullet j})^2}{n_j} - \frac{(\Sigma X_{ij})^2}{N} \qquad SS_{within} = \Sigma X_{ij}^2 - \Sigma \frac{(X_{\bullet j})^2}{n_j}$$

$$SS_{total} = 921 - \frac{(135)^2}{22} \qquad SS_{between} = 879.9333 - \frac{(135)^2}{22} \qquad SS_{within} = 921 - 879.9333$$

| $SS_{total} = 92.5909$ | $SS_{between} = 51.5242$ | $SS_{within} = 41.0667$ |
|---|---|---|
| $df_{total} = N - 1$ | $df_{between} = k - 1$ | $df_{within} = \Sigma(n_j - 1)$ |
| $df_{total} = 21$ | $df_{between} = 3$ | $df_{within} = 18$ |
| | $MS_{between} = \dfrac{SS_{between}}{df_{between}}$ | $MS_{within} = \dfrac{SS_{within}}{df_{within}}$ |
| | $MS_{between} = \dfrac{51.5242}{3}$ | $MS_{within} = \dfrac{41.0667}{18}$ |
| | $MS_{between} = 17.1747$ | $MS_{within} = 2.2815$ |
| $F = \dfrac{MS_{between}}{MS_{within}}$ | $F = \dfrac{17.1747}{2.2815}$ | $F = 7.5278$ |
| $\omega^2 = \dfrac{df_{between}(F-1)}{df_{between}(F-1)+N}$ | $\omega^2 = \dfrac{3(7.5278-1)}{3(7.5278-1)+22}$ | $\omega^2 = .4709$ |
| $\eta^2 = \dfrac{SS_{between}}{SS_{total}}$ | $\eta^2 = \dfrac{51.5242}{92.5909}$ | $\eta^2 = .5565$ |
| $\mathbf{f} = \sqrt{\dfrac{\eta^2}{1-\eta^2}}$ | $\mathbf{f} = \sqrt{\dfrac{.5565}{1-.5565}}$ | $\mathbf{f} = 1.1202$ |

| Source | SS | df | MS | F |
|---|---|---|---|---|
| Between-groups | 51.52 | 3 | 17.17 | 7.53 |
| Within-groups | 41.07 | 18 | 2.28 | |
| Total | 92.59 | 21 | | |

Because $F_{observed}$ is greater than $F_{critical}$ (7.53 > 3.16), Maria can reject the null hypothesis. She can now examine the specific differences among the means using Tukey's HSD test.

***Null Hypothesis:*** $H_0$: $\mu = \mu'$

***Alternative Hypothesis:*** $H_1$: $\mu \neq \mu'$

***Statistical Test:*** Maria may use Tukey's HSD because she found a statistically significant $F$-ratio and now wishes to examine the means using *a posteriori* procedures.

***Significance Level:*** $\alpha = .05$.

***Sampling Distribution:*** The degrees of freedom for the ANOVA are as follows:

$HSD = q_{crit}\sqrt{\dfrac{MS_{within}}{n}}$

$k = 4$

$df_{within} = 18$

$q_{critical} = 3.61$

$n' = \dfrac{4}{\frac{1}{6}+\frac{1}{5}+\frac{1}{6}+\frac{1}{5}} = \dfrac{4}{.1667+.20+.1667+.20} = \dfrac{4}{.7334} = 5.4540$

$HSD = 4.00\sqrt{\dfrac{2.28}{5.454}}$

$HSD = 2.59$

*HSD=2.59*

Using the results of this analysis, Maria could write the following brief results section.

**Table 14.4**

**Comparison of All Differences Between All Pairs of Means Using the Tukey HSD Test**

| | | INSTRUCTION GROUPS | | | |
| Instruction Groups | $\overline{X}$ | Control 4.33 | Sound 5.60 | Meaning 6.33 | Self-Reference 8.60 |
| --- | --- | --- | --- | --- | --- |
| Control | 4.33 | — | 1.27 | 2.00 | 4.27* |
| Sound | 5.60 | — | — | 0.73 | 3.00* |
| Meaning | 6.33 | — | — | — | 2.27 |
| Self-reference | 8.60 | — | — | — | — |

The * indicates that the difference is statistically significant at the $\alpha = .05$ level.

Recall 4

Figure 1 presents the average number of words re-called for each of the four groups. By far, the high-est level of recall occurs in the Self-Reference group. A one-way ANOVA reveals that there are statistically significant differences among the means $\underline{F}(3, 18) = 7.53$, p < .05, $\omega^2 = 47$. Subsequent analysis using Tukey's HSD indicates that mean recall for the Self-Reference con-dition ($\underline{M} = 8.60$, $\underline{SD} = 1.52$) was significantly larger than the mean recall for the Sound condition ($\underline{M} = 5.60$, $\underline{SD} = 1.52$) and the Control condition ($\underline{M} = 4.33$, $\underline{SD} = 1.51$). All other differences were not statistically significant.

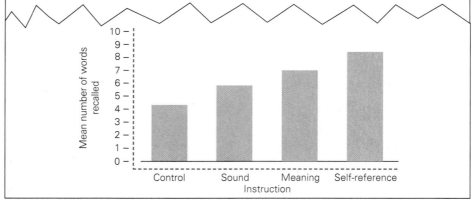

## TERMS TO REMEMBER

analysis of variance (ANOVA)

between-groups variance

error variance

experimentwise error ($\alpha_{experimentwise}$)

F-ratio

factor

general linear model

homogeneity of variance

levels of a factor
omnibus statistical test
one-way ANOVA
pairwise comparison $\alpha$
partition

total variance
treatment variance
two-way ANOVA
within-groups variance

# E XERCISES

**1.** For each of the following $F_{observed}$, determine $F_{critical}$ and indicate whether the $F_{observed}$ justifies rejection of the null hypothesis.

| $F_{observed}$ | $F_{critical}$ $\alpha = .05$ | Reject $H_0$? | $F_{critical} = .01$ | Reject $H_0$? |
|---|---|---|---|---|
| **a.** $F(3, 23) = 3.56$ | _____ | _____ | _____ | _____ |
| **b.** $F(5, 40) = 4.12$ | _____ | _____ | _____ | _____ |
| **c.** $F(2, 4) = 5.23$ | _____ | _____ | _____ | _____ |
| **d.** $F(3, 12) = 4.16$ | _____ | _____ | _____ | _____ |

**2.** For each of the following $F_{observed}$, determine $F_{critical}$ and indicate whether the $F_{observed}$ justifies rejection of the null hypothesis.

| $F_{observed}$ | $F_{critical}$ $\alpha = .05$ | Reject $H_0$? | $F_{critical} = .01$ | Reject $H_0$? |
|---|---|---|---|---|
| **a.** $F(4, 46) = 3.56$ | _____ | _____ | _____ | _____ |
| **b.** $F(8, 125) = 2.82$ | _____ | _____ | _____ | _____ |
| **c.** $F(1, 22) = 6.23$ | _____ | _____ | _____ | _____ |
| **d.** $F(4, 34) = 4.45$ | _____ | _____ | _____ | _____ |

**3.** The accompanying table is a summary table for an analysis of variance. Some of the information has been left out. Fill in the missing material and then continue with the following questions.

| Source | SS | df | MS | F |
|---|---|---|---|---|
| Between-groups | _____ | 3 | _____ | 6.25 |
| Within-groups | _____ | 16 | 2.114 | |
| Total | | _____ | _____ | |

   **a.** How many levels of the independent variable are there?
   **b.** Assuming equal sample sizes, how many subjects were in each treatment condition?
   **c.** What are the degrees of freedom for the $F$-ratio?
   **d.** If $\alpha = .05$, what is the critical value of $F$ required to reject the null hypothesis?
   **e.** Given the data reported in the summary table, can the null hypothesis be rejected?
   **f.** Assume that the researcher wants to report the result of this analysis, how should the $F$-ratio be reported according to APA style?
   **g.** What is the $\omega^2$ for this experiment? How should it be interpreted?
   **h.** What is the effect size, **f,** for this experiment? How should this value be interpreted?

**4.** The accompanying table is a summary table for an analysis of variance. Some of the information has been left out. Fill in the missing material and then continue with the following questions.

| Source | SS | df | MS | F |
|---|---|---|---|---|
| Between-groups | 12.450 | ___ | 6.225 | ___ |
| Within-groups | ___ | 27 | ___ | |
| Total | 60.609 | 29 | | |

a. How many levels osf the independent variable are there?
b. Assuming equal sample sizes, how many subjects were in each treatment condition?
c. What are the degrees of freedom for the $F$-ratio?
d. If $\alpha = .05$, what is the critical value of $F$ required to reject the null hypothesis?
e. Given the data reported in the summary table, can the null hypothesis be rejected?
f. Assume that the researcher wants to report the result of this analysis, how should the $F$-ratio be reported according to APA style?
g. What is the $\omega^2$ for this experiment? How should it be interpreted?
h. What is the effect size, **f,** for this experiment? How should this value be interpreted?
i. Assume that **f** = .40. If you wanted to do this experiment, what is the approximate probability that will permit you to reject the null hypothesis?
j. Assume that **f** = .40. If you wanted to conduct this experiment, how many subjects should there be in each group to have an 80% or greater chance of rejecting the null hypothesis?

5. The accompanying table is a summary table for an analysis of variance. Some of the information has been left out. Fill in the missing material and then continue with the following questions.

| Source | SS | df | MS | F |
|---|---|---|---|---|
| Between-groups | 42.596 | ___ | 10.649 | ___ |
| Within-groups | 162.450 | ___ | 3.610 | |
| Total | ___ | ___ | | |

a. How many levels of the independent variable are there?
b. Assuming equal sample sizes, how many subjects were in each treatment condition?
c. What are the degrees of freedom for the $F$-ratio?
d. If $\alpha = .05$, what is the critical value of $F$ required to reject the null hypothesis?
e. Given the data reported in the summary table, can the null hypothesis be rejected?
f. Assume that the researcher wants to report the result of this analysis, how should the $F$-ratio be reported according to APA style?
g. What is the $\omega^2$ for this experiment? How should it be interpreted?
h. What is the effect size, **f,** for this experiment? How should this value be interpreted?

6. The accompanying table is a summary table for an analysis of variance. Some of the information has been left out. Fill in the missing material and then continue with the following questions.

| Source | SS | df | MS | F |
|---|---|---|---|---|
| Between-groups | _____ | _____ | 3.570 | _____ |
| Within-groups | _____ | 95 | 0.127 | |
| Total | _____ | 99 | | |

a. How many levels of the independent variable are there?
b. Assuming equal sample sizes, how many subjects were in each treatment condition?
c. What are the degrees of freedom for the F-ratio?
d. If $\alpha = .05$, what is the critical value of F required to reject the null hypothesis?
e. Given the data reported in the summary table, can the null hypothesis be rejected?
f. Assume that the researcher wants to report the result of this analysis, how should the F-ratio be reported according to APA style?
g. What is the $\omega^2$ for this experiment? How should it be interpreted?
h. What is the effect size, **f,** for this experiment? How should this value be interpreted?
i. Assume that **f** = .40. If you wanted to do this experiment, what is the approximate probability that will permit you to reject the null hypothesis?
j. Assume that **f** = .40. If you wanted to conduct this experiment, how many subjects should there be in each group to have an 80% or greater chance of rejecting the null hypothesis?

7. A psychologist wants to test the effects of cognitive dissonance on decision making. The researcher randomly assigns subjects to one of three experimental groups. The first group of subjects are told that they will receive $50 for completing the requirements of the experiment, and the second group of subjects are told that they will receive extra credit in their general psychology course. The last group of subjects are told nothing about cash or extra credits for completing the experiment. All subjects are asked to read a long, boring essay. After the subjects read the essay, they are asked to write a persuasive statement that the essay was quite interesting and that other college students would find the reading entertaining. The subjects then indicate on a scale of 1 to 10 (with 10 being the highest) how much they really liked the essay. According to cognitive dissonance theory, the smaller the reward, the greater the likelihood that subjects will say that they like the essay. Here are the scores for all subjects in the experiment.

| | $50 | Extra Credit | No Reward | |
|---|---|---|---|---|
| | 0 | 7 | 10 | |
| | 7 | 7 | 3 | |
| | 0 | 1 | 3 | |
| | 4 | 1 | 7 | |
| | 4 | 4 | 7 | |
| $X_{\bullet j}$ | 15 | 20 | 30 | $\Sigma X_{ij} = 65$ |
| $X_{\bullet j}^2$ | 81 | 116 | 216 | $\Sigma X_{ij}^2 = 413$ |

a. Draw a stem-and-leaf diagram of these data. Do the data appear to confirm the researcher's hypothesis?

**b.** Draw a histogram of the three means of the groups. Does this representation of the data appear to confirm the researcher's hypothesis?

**c.** What are the researcher's null and alternative hypotheses?

**d.** Use these data to conduct an analysis of variance. Report the final summary table.

**e.** Assume the researcher set $\alpha = .05$. Is the researcher justified in rejecting the null hypothesis? What is the relation between the payoff and the subject's rating of the task?

**f.** What is $\omega^2$ for this experiment? How should this statistic be described?

**g.** Calculate the effect size for these data. How would you describe the effect size of the results of this experiment?

**h.** Use Tukey's HSD to compare the individual means. Are the differences among the means consistent with the psychologist's hypotheses?

**8.** The Stroop effect is a classic phenomenon in experimental psychology. It is created when there is conflicting information. For example, the word "red" is printed in green ink and the subject must name the color of the ink. A student studied the Stroop effect by randomly assigning subjects to one of four groups. Subjects in Group 1 were shown colored rectangles and required to identify the color. Subjects in Group 2 were shown color adjectives printed in the corresponding color ("red" printed in red) and required to identify the color. Subjects in Groups 3 and 4 saw a mixed combination of noncorresponding words and colors. Subjects in Group 3 were required to say the word, whereas subjects in Group 4 were told to identify the color. The dependent variable was the time required to make the correct response. All subjects responded to 10 items, and the averages of the reaction times were recorded. The data are shown in the accompanying table.

|  | Group 1 | Group 2 | Group 3 | Group 4 |  |
|---|---|---|---|---|---|
|  | 0.37 | 0.40 | 1.06 | 1.26 |  |
|  | 0.27 | 0.28 | 0.95 | 1.24 |  |
|  | 0.28 | 0.36 | 0.96 | 1.16 |  |
|  | 0.35 | 0.32 | 1.01 | 1.18 |  |
|  | 0.34 | 0.34 | 1.01 | 1.18 |  |
|  | 0.31 | 0.34 | 1.01 | 1.18 |  |
| $X_{\bullet j}$ | 1.9200 | 2.0400 | 6.0000 | 7.2000 | $\Sigma X_{ij} = 17.16$ |
| $X_{\bullet j}^2$ | 0.6224 | 0.7016 | 6.0080 | 8.6480 | $\Sigma X_{ij}^2 = 15.98$ |

**a.** Draw a histogram of the four means of the groups. Does this representation of the data appear to confirm the researcher's hypothesis?

**b.** What are the researcher's null and alternative hypotheses?

**c.** Use these data to conduct an analysis of variance. Report the final summary table.

**d.** Assume the researcher set $\alpha = .05$. Is the researcher justified in rejecting the null hypothesis?

**e.** What is $\omega^2$ for this experiment? How should this statistic be described?

**f.** Use Tukey's HSD to compare the individual means. Does the Stroop effect require more time to solve?

**9.** A psychologist wanted to determine if an artificial sweetener would increase a rat's motivation to press a bar. The researcher randomly assigned rats to one of 5 groups. Rats received a small amount of water mixed at specific concentrations (0%, 4%, 8%, 16%, or 32%) of artificial sweetener for pressing the bar 10 times. After a 3-day training period, the researcher recorded the number of times each rat pressed the bar during a 20-minute period. Due to random equipment error, the data from 3 subjects were lost.

| Group 1 0% | Group 2 4% | Group 3 8% | Group 4 16% | Group 5 32% |
|---|---|---|---|---|
| 16 | 21 | 20 | 54 | 56 |
| 5 | 11 | 15 | 54 | 45 |
| 13 | 19 | 22 | 46 | 46 |
| 7 | 14 | 27 | 46 | 51 |
| 9 | 15 | 26 | 50 | 51 |
| 10 | | | | 51 |

a. Draw a line graph of the five means of the groups. Does this representation of the data appear to confirm the researcher's hypothesis?
b. What are the researcher's null and alternative hypotheses?
c. Use these data to conduct an analysis of variance. Report the final summary table.
d. Assume the researcher set $\alpha = .05$. Is the researcher justified in rejecting the null hypothesis?
e. What is $\omega^2$ for this experiment? How should this statistic be described?
f. Use Tukey's HSD to compare the individual means. How does the concentration of the sweetener affect the rat's performance?

10. Phobias are irrational fears. The fear can be severe enough that it will greatly affect a person's life. A clinical psychologist wants to determine which type of psychotherapy best helps people overcome their fear. The psychologist randomly assigns clients with a fear of heights to one of four forms of psychotherapy or a control condition. Each client in the treatment condition receives 10 sessions with a trained psychotherapist. Clients in the control condition receive no treatment. All clients are then taken to the 15th floor of an office building and asked to stand next to a floor to ceiling window and rate their anxiety on a 20-point scale (20 = strongest fear; 0 = no fear).

| Group 1 Control | Group 2 Gestalt | Group 3 Psychoanalysis | Group 4 Rational Emotive | Group 5 Behavior Modification |
|---|---|---|---|---|
| 20 | 20 | 20 | 18 | 15 |
| 14 | 10 | 9 | 7 | 5 |
| 18 | 11 | 10 | 15 | 6 |
| 16 | 18 | 15 | 9 | 13 |
| 17 | 17 | 15 | 11 | 12 |
| 17 | 14 | 15 | 12 | 9 |

a. Draw a histogram of the five means of the groups. Does this representation of the data appear to confirm the researcher's hypothesis?
b. What are the researcher's null and alternative hypotheses for the ANOVA? Report the final summary table.
c. Use these data to conduct an analysis of variance. Report the final summary table.
d. Assume the researcher set $\alpha = .05$. Is the researcher justified in rejecting the null hypothesis?
e. What is $\omega^2$ for this experiment? How should this statistic be described?
f. Use Tukey's HSD to compare the individual means. How do the treatment conditions compare to each other?

11. Tracy wants to repeat an experiment that was reported in a research journal. The author of the article noted that the results were statistically sig-

nificant. Specifically, the researcher wrote, "The results of a one-way ANOVA were statistically significant, $F(2, 19) = 3.75$, $p < .05$." Use this information to answer the following questions.

a. How many levels of the independent variable were there?

b. In total, how many subjects did the experimenter use?

c. What was the $\omega^2$ for this experiment? How should this statistic be interpreted?

d. Calculate the effect size for these data. According to Cohen's criteria, is the effect size small, medium, or large?

e. Tracy wants to repeat the experiment. Can Tracy assume that the probability that the effect will be replicated will be $1 - \alpha$, or $1 - .05 = .95$? Explain your answer.

f. Assume that $\mathbf{f} = .40$ for this experiment. Using the power tables, how many subjects will Tracy have to use to have at least an 80% chance of repeating the experiment with statistically significant results?

12. Margaret is a senior psychology major and is planning to do an independent research project. Her advisor tells her to conduct a power analysis to determine the number of subjects she will need in order to obtain statistically significant results. Margaret wants to use five levels of the independent variable and believes that there is a medium effect size ($\mathbf{f} = .25$). How many subjects should she run if she wants

a. better than a 50% chance of obtaining statistically significant results?

b. better than an 80% chance of obtaining statistically significant results?

Assume that Margaret decides to make the experiment simpler by using only three experimental groups? How many subjects should she run if she wants

c. better than a 50% chance of obtaining statistically significant results?

d. better than an 80% chance of obtaining statistically significant results?

13. Here are data from an experiment where a researcher used two groups. Use the $t$-ratio for independent groups and the analysis of variance to analyze the data.

| $X_1$ | $X_2$ |
|-----|-----|
| 6 | 5 |
| 8 | 4 |
| 14 | 3 |
| 9 | 7 |
| 10 | 4 |
| 4 | 2 |
| 7 | 1 |
| 3 | |

a. Verify that in the two-group condition, $F = t^2$.

14. Here are data from an experiment where a researcher used two groups. Use the $t$-ratio for independent groups and the analysis of variance to analyze the data.

| $X_1$ | $X_2$ |
|-----|-----|
| 10 | 21 |
| 5 | 9 |
| 6 | 17 |
| 13 | 13 |
| 12 | 15 |
| 9 | 15 |

a. Verify that in the two-group condition, $F = t^2$.

# 15

# The Two-Factor Analysis of Variance

## 15.1 / Introduction

As we saw in Chapter 14, the analysis of variance (ANOVA) is an extremely useful statistic because it allows us to study the effects of many levels of one independent variable on the dependent variable. We use the one-way ANOVA when we want to compare a number of groups that represent different levels of a single independent variable. Specifically, we saw how the ANOVA partitions the total variance into the variance caused by systematic differences in the independent variable and variance caused by random effects. Furthermore, we saw how the one-way ANOVA frees us from the limitations of the two-group experiment (e.g., experimental vs. control group design) and the use of many *t*-ratios for one set of data.

In this chapter we will introduce you to an advanced form of ANOVA with additional advantages. These advantages include (1) the ability to examine the effects of more than one independent variable at a time; (2) the ability to examine the possible interaction between the independent variables; and (3) the ability to conduct research that is an efficient use of time and effort. The focus of this chapter is the **two-factor** or the **two-way** analysis of variance.

As you may recall, a factor is another term for an independent variable. Consequently, a two-factor ANOVA is a statistical technique that allows us to examine simultaneously the effects of two independent variables on a specific behavior. The beauty of this technique is that it allows us to examine the complex conditions that influence behavior. Many of the fascinating phenomena we study in the behavioral sciences are influenced by a number of factors. Therefore, conducting an experiment that includes several independent variables may help us learn more about the behavior we study.

As you will see in the following pages, the basic principles you learned about the one-way ANOVA apply to the two-way ANOVA. The primary statistic calculated in the two-factor ANOVA is the *F*-ratio. This statistic serves the same function in the two-way ANOVA that it did in the one-way ANOVA; it allows us to determine the probability that the difference between means is due to chance or to the effects of treatment. The new material that we will cover refers to the fact we can simultaneously examine two factors (or variables) within one experiment. We will show you how you can estimate the effects of each factor on the dependent variable. In addition, we will introduce you to a new statistical concept known as an interaction.

■ **Two-Factor ANOVA:**

An analysis of variance used to examine research designs with two independent variables. The two-factor or two-way analysis of variance examines the unique effects of each independent variable and the interaction of the two variables.

## 15.2 / The Logic of the Two-Way ANOVA

The logic of the two-way ANOVA is similar to the one-way ANOVA. The primary difference is that the two-way ANOVA allows us to examine the relation between two independent variables and the dependent variable. Specifically, the two-way ANOVA allows us to determine how much each independent variable, by itself, accounts for the total variance. In addition, the test determines how much the combination of the variables accounts for the total variance.

In the two-way ANOVA, the factors may be either qualitative or quantitative. Recall that *qualitative* variables differ in kind. For example, we may want to know which of several teaching methods is most effective for helping illiterate adults learn to read, or which type of psychotherapy is most effective for the treatment of men who batter their spouses. *Quantitative* variables differ in "how much." If we were testing the effects of a new drug, we could vary the dosage and examine the rate of recovery.

To understand the utility and logic of the two-factor ANOVA, we find it helpful to examine a concrete example. In the following sections we use a common example to present different aspects of the two-way ANOVA. Once we review the concept of the two-way ANOVA, we examine how to perform the calculations to obtain the statistic. Let's begin, as most researchers do, with a set of questions about behavior that we can answer using empirical research.

Why is it that some people, when faced with a difficult problem, work hard at solving the problem whereas other people seem to give up quickly? You may have noticed that some people seem to work by the motto, "If at first you don't succeed, try, try again," whereas others seem to work by the motto, "Never throw good money after bad." In other words, we want to know why some people are more persistent than others. What are some of the factors that influence how persistent a person will be? Chances are that you can think of many factors that will influence a person's persistence. There may be characteristics of the task (hard vs. easy), the skill level of the task (skill vs. luck is required), and the outcome of completing the task (much reward vs. little reward) that influence the person's persistence. Personality factors may also influence persistence. Some people may find the task interesting whereas others find it boring. Some people may believe that they have a particular skill that will allow them to succeed whereas others may believe that they are not qualified to complete the task.

Sandelands, Brocker, and Glynn (1988) conducted an experiment that examined persistence. For the experiment, they had subjects attempt to complete a long list of anagrams (e.g., WOREP is POWER). Some of the anagrams had solutions; the others were impossible to solve. The dependent variable was the amount of time spent on the unsolvable anagrams. Sandelands, Brocker, and Glynn used two independent variables in their study. The first variable was the self-esteem of the subjects. The researchers selected subjects with either high or low self-esteem to participate in the study. The second variable was the type of instructions the subjects received. They told half the subjects that each anagram had a solution and that persistence was a good strategy. The researchers told the other subjects that some of the anagrams had no solution and that giving up on occasion was a good strategy.

This experiment has two factors, Factor A and Factor B. The first factor is subject's self-esteem. There are two levels of self-esteem: (1) Low and (2) High. The second factor is the Type of Instruction. There are two levels of instruction: (1) Persist and (2) Don't Persist.

You should not be surprised to learn that the subjects differed in terms of how much time they spent on each unsolvable anagram. Some subjects devoted much time to working on each anagram whereas others spent much less time trying to solve each problem. The variability among the scores of *all* subjects in *all* groups represents the total variation. Using a two-way ANOVA, we can determine how much the independent variables systematically affect the total variance.

Table 15.1 illustrates the two factors and the assignment of the subjects to the treatment groups. For the entire experiment, there are 60 subjects. Half of the subjects are identified as "Low Self-Esteem" whereas

**Table 15.1**

**Illustration of a Two-Way ANOVA and the Assignment of Subjects to Treatment Conditions**

| Factor B (Type of Instruction) | FACTOR A (SELF-ESTEEM) | | Raw Totals— Factor B |
|---|---|---|---|
| | Low | High | |
| **Persist** | Low self-esteem subjects instructed to persist; $n_{11} = 15, X_{\bullet 11}$ | High self-esteem subjects instructed to persist; $n_{21} = 15, X_{\bullet 21}$ | Subjects instructed to persist; $n_{\bullet 1} = 30, X_{\bullet \bullet 1}$ |
| **Don't persist** | Low self-esteem subjects instructed not to persist; $n_{12} = 15, X_{\bullet 12}$ | High self-esteem subjects instructed not to persist; $n_{22} = 15, X_{\bullet 22}$ | Subjects instructed not to persist; $n_{\bullet 2} = 30, X_{\bullet \bullet 2}$ |
| **Column Totals— Factor A** | Subjects with low self-esteem; $n_{1\bullet} = 30, X_{\bullet 1 \bullet}$ | Subjects with high self-esteem; $n_{2\bullet} = 30, X_{\bullet 2 \bullet}$ | $N = 60, X_{\bullet \bullet \bullet}$ |

the other half are classified as "High Self-Esteem." In addition, half of all subjects are told to persist whereas the other subjects are told not to persist. You should notice several things about the design of a two-way ANOVA. First, the design of the experiment allows us to look at all possible combinations of the variables we chose to study. That is, we study subjects with high or low self-esteem under conditions of instructions either to persist or not to persist.

A second important feature of the two-way ANOVA is that we can use different types of independent variables. Self-esteem is a *subject* variable. The Type of Instruction is a *manipulated* variable. Using the two-way ANOVA we can combine any pattern of independent variables. In this experiment, we combined a subject and a manipulated variable. For a two-way ANOVA we can have combination of quantitative and qualitative independent variables. Be sure that you recognize, however, that the *dependent* variable must always represent an interval or ratio scale.

Figure 15.1 illustrates the logic of the steps we will take with the two-way analysis of variance. As you can see, the ANOVA partitions the Total Variation among subjects into two general components, the Between-Groups Variation and the Within-Groups Variation. The Within-Groups variation represents the variation among subjects that cannot be predicted or explained by the independent variables. Therefore, the Within-Groups Variation represents sampling error.

The Between-Groups Variation represents variance that is caused by systematic differences in the independent variables. Specifically, the Between-Groups Variation consists of the effects due to each of the independent factors and the interaction of these factors.

We can use the general linear model, introduced in Chapter 14, to represent the logic of the two-way ANOVA. Specifically,

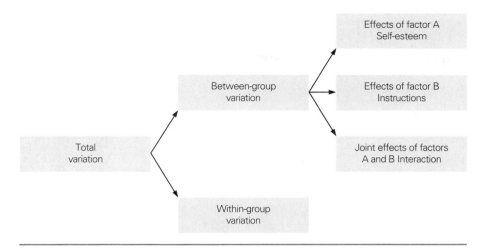

**Figure | 15.1**

Illustration of the two-factor analysis of variance. The total variation is partitioned into two general categories, between-group variation and within-group variation. The between-group variation is further subdivided into the effects due to factor A, factor B, and the interaction of factors A and B.

$$X_{ijk} = \mu + \alpha_j + \beta_k + \alpha\beta_{jk} + \epsilon_{ijk} \tag{15.1}$$

where

$X_{ijk}$ = individual observation within a specific treatment condition. The $i$ in the subscript represents the individual observation, the $j$ represents the level of the first factor, and the $k$ represents the level of the second factor.

$\mu$ = population mean for the base population.

$\alpha_j$ = the effects of a specific level of the first treatment factor.

$\beta_k$ = the effects of a specific level of the second treatment factor.

$\alpha\beta_{jk}$ = the effects of the interaction of the two factors at specific levels.

$\epsilon_{ijk}$ = undifferentiated error that is assumed to be random with a mean effect of 0.

This equation is much like the one you learned in Chapter 14. Again, an individual score is the sum of several components. Equation 15.1 identifies more things that influence the individual scores. The two-way ANOVA allows us to estimate the degree to which persistence is influenced by self-esteem (represented as $\alpha_j$ in the equation), type of instruction (represented as $\beta_k$ in the equation), and the interaction of these two variables (represented as $\alpha\beta_{jk}$). Figure 15.2 provides further help in understanding the subscript notation.

## 15.3 / Advantages of the Two-Way ANOVA

There are several distinct advantages of the two-way ANOVA over the one-way ANOVA. To examine these advantages let's consider what would happen to the Sandelands, Brocker, and Glynn

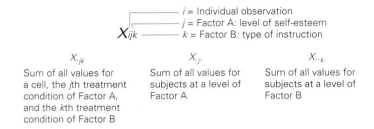

$X_{ijk}$ — $i$ = Individual observation
$j$ = Factor A: level of self-esteem
$k$ = Factor B: type of instruction

| $X_{.jk}$ | $X_{.j.}$ | $X_{..k}$ |
|---|---|---|
| Sum of all values for a cell, the $j$th treatment condition of Factor A, and the $k$th treatment condition of Factor B | Sum of all values for subjects at a level of Factor A | Sum of all values for subjects at a level of Factor B |

**Figure** | **15.2**

**A representation of the subscript notation for a two-way ANOVA.**

(1988) study if we used two one-way ANOVAs. One of the studies would compare the difference in persistence of people with low or high self-esteem. The second study would compare the difference created by the instructions. Assume for a moment that a power analysis of these experiments indicated that we need 30 subjects in each treatment condition to have the sufficient statistical power (e.g., $1 - \beta = .80$). As you can see in Figure 15.3, we will need 60 subjects for each experiment, or 120 subjects total for both experiments. Now consider what would happen if we combined the two experiments.

As you can see Figure 15.3, Experiment 3 (the two-way ANOVA), contains the elements of each of the two one-way designs and the

Experiment 1 One-way ANOVA comparison of low and high self-esteem where Sample size $N = 60$:

| Low Self-Esteem | High Self-Esteem | Total |
|---|---|---|
| $n = 30$ | $n = 30$ | $N = 60$ |

Experiment 2 One-way ANOVA comparison of instructions to persist or not where Sample size $N = 60$:

| Persist | Don't Persist | Total |
|---|---|---|
| $n = 30$ | $n = 30$ | $N = 60$ |

Experiment 3 Two-way ANOVA comparing levels of self-esteem and instructions where Sample size $N = 60$:

| Factor B (Instructions) | Factor A (Self-Esteem) Low | High | Row Total |
|---|---|---|---|
| Persist | $n = 15$ | $n = 15$ | $n = 30$ |
| Don't persist | $n = 15$ | $n = 15$ | $n = 30$ |
| Column total | $n = 30$ | $n = 30$ | $N = 60$ |

**Figure** | **15.3**

**Representation of the advantages of the two-way ANOVA. Experiments represent simple one-way ANOVAs for each factor, self-esteem and instructions. Together, both experiments require 60 subjects. In contrast, Experiment 3 requires only 60 subjects and allows one to examine each main effect and the joint effects of the two variables.**

number of subjects has also been maintained—there are 30 subjects with low self-esteem and 30 subjects with high self-esteem. By combining the two experiments, we require half as many subjects than if we conducted two separate experiments. Therefore, one two-way ANOVA is more cost effective than two one-way ANOVAs and it provides more information.

Another advantage of the two-way ANOVA is that it provides a greater opportunity to study the simultaneous manipulation of two factors that we think influence the dependent variable. Specifically, in the two-way ANOVA we can see how each variable and combinations of the variables influence persistence. As we will review below, we can use the two-way ANOVA to examine main effects and interactions. Specifically, the results of such an experiment have greater generality because we are testing the subjects under a greater variety of conditions.

A third advantage of the two-way ANOVA is an increase in power. We have defined the within-group variance as a form of variation that represents random and unidentified sources of error. Any time we can identify, or isolate, a factor that systematically contributes to the total variance, we effectively reduce the size of the error term. In other words, by adding more factors to our statistical design, we will be able to do a better job of explaining the differences among the observations. Indeed, if we select the correct variables to measure or manipulate, we can increase the statistical power of the experiment.

## 15.4 / Factorial Designs: Factors, Levels, and Cells

When researchers talk about the two-way design, they often refer to concepts such as factorial designs, main effects, and the interaction. These terms refer to the design of the experiment and to the specific components of the General Linear Model of the two-way ANOVA. Before we continue, you need to understand the meaning of these terms. We can use our experiment on persistence to help us understand these important concepts.

### The Concept of a Treatment Combination

One of the advantages of the two-way ANOVA is that it allows us to examine simultaneously the effects of two independent variables and their combined effects. When we design a two-factor experiment, we select the number of levels that we want to use for each factor. Because we combine the two factors into one experimental design, we are creating a factorial design. In a factorial design, each treatment condition represents the combination of each factor. The number of treatment conditions equals all the possible combinations of the factors.

We can represent our experiment as a $2 \times 2$ **factorial design.** When we multiply the number of levels for each factor, we have the factorial or the number of treatment conditions. In this experiment there are $2 \times 2 = 4$ treatment combinations. Table 15.2 represents a model for our data.

As you can see, there are four cells or treatment combinations in the table. Each cell represents a different treatment combination. For example, cell $a_1b_1$ represents the treatment combination of Low Self-esteem

■ **Factorial Design:**

Refers to studies in which the researcher uses two or more independent variables. The study contains a treatment condition for every possible combination of levels of the variables. The number of treatment conditions is the product of the levels of the variables.

Table | 15.2

| Model of a 2 × 2 Factorial Design

|  | **FACTOR A** (Subject's Self-esteem) | | |
| --- | --- | --- | --- |
| **Factor B (Instructions** | **Low ($a_1$)** | **High ($a_2$)** | |
|  | $a_1b_1$ | $a_2b_1$ | |
| Persist ($b_1$) | $X_{111}$ | $X_{121}$ | |
|  | $X_{211}$ | $X_{221}$ | |
|  | $X_{311}$ | $X_{321}$ | |
|  | $X_{411}$ | $X_{421}$ | |
|  | ••• | ••• | |
|  | $X_{n11}$ | $X_{n21}$ | |
|  | $X_{\bullet11}$ | $X_{\bullet21}$ | $X_{\bullet\bullet1}$ |
|  | $a_1b_2$ | $a_2b_2$ | |
| Don't persist ($b_2$) | $X_{112}$ | $X_{122}$ | |
|  | $X_{212}$ | $X_{222}$ | |
|  | $X_{312}$ | $X_{322}$ | |
|  | $X_{412}$ | $X_{422}$ | |
|  | ••• | ••• | |
|  | $X_{n12}$ | $X_{n22}$ | |
|  | $X_{\bullet12}$ | $X_{\bullet22}$ | $X_{\bullet\bullet2}$ |
|  | $X_{\bullet1\bullet}$ | $X_{\bullet2\bullet}$ | $X_{\bullet\bullet\bullet}$ |

and Instructions to Persist whereas cell $a_2b_2$ represents the treatment combination of High Self-esteem and Instructions Not to Persist. Therefore, a cell represents a specific treatment combination of the factors used in the experiment.

Factorial designs can vary in complexity from the very simple 2 × 2 design to more complex designs such as a 3 × 5 or a 4 × 6 factorial. Indeed, the ANOVA allows us to create many variations of this design. The common feature of all factorial designs is that the experiment contains all possible combinations of the variables.

Because this is an introductory text, we will not consider designs more complex than the two-factor model. If you need to use a more complex form of the ANOVA we recommend Hayes, (1981), Kirk (1982), and Winer, Brown, and Michels (1991) as comprehensive references.

## 15.5

## Treatment Combinations: Main Effects and Interaction

The whole purpose of the two-way ANOVA is to examine how the two variables combine and possibly interact with one another to produce the effects of the experiment. In this section, we will examine the potential outcomes for a two-way ANOVA and describe how to interpret the results. Specifically, we will examine **main effects** and **interactions.** As a brief preview, a main effect represents conditions wherein one or both of the factors have a statistically significant effect on the dependent variable. An interaction represents a condition where both factors have an effect on the dependent variable, but the effect differs across the treatment combinations.

In the following sections, we will examine various combinations of main effects and interaction. For the sake of clarity, we will continue to use the same experimental design and variables. Each scenario, however, will have a completely different interpretation. In other words, each of the following examples can be considered to be hypothetical outcomes for that the experiment. After we have reviewed the different possible outcomes, we will examine an example that represents what Sandelands, Brocker, and Glynn (1988) found in their experiment.

■ **Main Effect:**

The effect of a single independent variable independent of the other factor and the interaction.

■ **Interaction:**

Differences among the group means that cannot be explained by the simple main effects or random variation alone.

## Main Effects

When we speak of the *main effects,* we refer to the effect of one of the factors without regard to the other factor and the interaction. Specifically, the main effect represents the means of all subjects exposed to a common level of a factor. In all two-way ANOVAs, there are two main effects. In the current example, one main effect represents the subject's self-esteem; the other main effect represents the instructions. Each main effect can be either statistically significant or not statistically significant. Consequently, we can have four potential patterns of results: (1) A statistically significant main effect for Factor A, (2) A statistically significant main effect for Factor B, (3) A simultaneous statistically significant main effect for Factors A and B, and (4) no statistically significant main effect for Factors A and B. Let's look at each of these patterns in turn.

Each of the following figures presents the means for all four cells of the experiment. Each of these figures is different from one another. As you read through the following sections, remember that we are showing you what the data might look like if the experiment produced specific results. We will present the actual results of the study later in the chapter. The points along the X-axis represent Factor A, self-esteem. The two lines on the graph represent Factor B, the instructions. Along with the graph is a table of the cell means and the means for each level of the factors.

**Significant Main Effect for Factor A: Self-Esteem**  Figure 15.4 represents data where there is a statistically significant difference between levels of self-esteem. There is no statistically significant difference between the Persist and Don't Persist instruction conditions, and there is no interaction between the variables. Simply stated, people with lower self-esteem spent less time on the task (an average of 20 seconds) than people with high self-esteem (an average of 40 seconds). The type of instruction had no influence on the results. Subjects told to persist worked as long on the task (30 seconds) as people told to give up and move along (also 30 seconds). We would conclude from these data that the differences in persistence among subjects are due primarily to differences in self-esteem.

**Significant Main Effect for Factor B: Instructions**  The data presented in Figure 15.5 represent a condition where there is a statistically significant main effect for the type of instructions but no main effect for self-esteem or interaction. Specifically, these data would suggest that

Hypothetical mean scores in each cell for this figure:

|  | Self-Esteem | | |
| Instruction | Low ($a_1$) | High ($a_2$) | $\overline{X}$ |
| --- | --- | --- | --- |
| Persist ($b_1$) | 20 | 40 | 30 |
| Don't persist ($b_2$) | 20 | 40 | 30 |
| $\overline{X}$ | 20 | 40 | 30 |

**Figure | 15.4**

**An example of a significant main effect for Factor A. Note that in the data and in the graph mean time in $a_1$ is consistently lower than in $a_2$. There are no differences between subjects in conditions $b_1$ and $b_2$.**

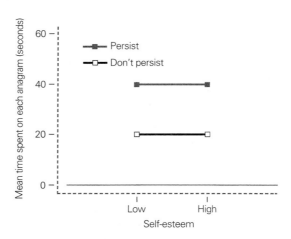

Hypothetical mean scores in each cell for this figure:

|  | Self-Esteem | | |
| Instruction | Low ($a_1$) | High ($a_2$) | $\overline{X}$ |
| --- | --- | --- | --- |
| Persist ($b_1$) | 40 | 40 | 40 |
| Don't persist ($b_2$) | 20 | 20 | 20 |
| $\overline{X}$ | 30 | 30 | 30 |

**Figure | 15.5**

**An example of a significant main effect for Factor B. Note that in the data and in the graph mean time in $b_1$ is consistently lower than in $b_2$. There are no differences between subjects in conditions $a_1$ and $a_2$.**

people were less persistent when told that moving on to the next problem is the best strategy and worked longer when told that persistence is the best strategy. The subject's self-esteem had no apparent influence on the persistence of the subjects.

**Significant Main Effect for Factor A and Factor B**   With this scenario, you can begin to see the utility of the two-way ANOVA. The data presented in Figure 15.6 represent a condition where both main effects are statistically significant and there is no interaction.

If you look at the figure you see that overall, high self-esteem subjects are more persistent than low self-esteem subjects. Furthermore, the subjects told to persist were more persistent than subjects told not to persist. Because the difference between the low and high self-esteem subjects is consistent across the two sets of instructions, we say that the effects of instructions are consistent for each personality characteristic. In other words, there is no interaction.

In this example, both main effects are statistically significant. Therefore, we can conclude that both variables contributed to the overall persistence of the subjects. Notice that the lines in the graph are parallel. This indicates that there is no interaction and that the two variables are independent of each other. Statisticians call this type of condition an **additive effect** because each variable "adds" a constant effect to the total variance of the data. A quick way to tell if there is an additive effect is to look at a graph of the data. If the lines are reasonably parallel, then there is an additive effect but no interaction. Let's look at the additive effect in detail.

■ **Additive Effect:**

Refers to the consistent effect of one variable on another variable in a two-factor analysis of variance. Each variable adds a constant effect to the total variance of the data.

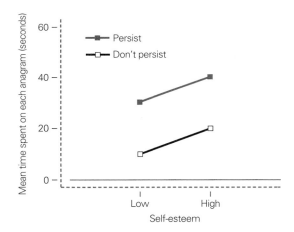

Hypothetical mean scores in each cell for this figure:

| Instruction | Self-Esteem | | $\overline{X}$ |
| --- | --- | --- | --- |
| | Low (a₁) | High (a₂) | |
| Persist (b₁) | 30 | 40 | 35 |
| Don't persist (b₂) | 10 | 20 | 15 |
| $\overline{X}$ | 20 | 30 | 25 |

**Figure** | **15.6**

An example of a significant main effect for Factors A and B. Note that in the data and in the graph mean time in a₁ is consistently lower than in a₂. In addition there are differences between subjects in conditions b₁ and b₂. The differences between the groups are consistent, however. Therefore, there is no interaction.

What is the difference between the Persist and Don't Persist conditions for each level of self-esteem? For both levels of self-esteem, the difference is 20 ($30 - 10 = 20$, and $40 - 20 = 20$). We can interpret this consistent difference to indicate that, in general, high self-esteem subjects are more persistent than low self-esteem subjects. In other words, having higher self-esteem consistently added approximately 20 seconds to the subjects' persistence on the task.

Is there a consistent effect across types of instruction? To answer this question we need to compare levels of self-esteem for the two instruction conditions. The difference between the "Persist" conditions ($40 - 30 = 10$) is the same difference for the "Don't Persist" conditions ($20 - 10 = 10$). Therefore, we can conclude that regardless of the subject's self-esteem, the instructions to persist add approximately 10 seconds to the time subjects spend on task.

The main point to recognize for this scenario is that differences between the conditions remained constant. Specifically, the effects of the instructions were consistent across levels of self-esteem. Likewise, the effect of self-esteem was consistent across the instructions conditions. When the effect of a variable is not consistent across levels of the other variables, we conclude that the variables interact.

## The Concept of the Interaction

Two factors interact when the effect of one variable on some measure of behavior depends on either the presence or the amount of a second variable. The finding of a statistically significant interaction is of great importance to our interpretation of the data. An interaction means that we cannot claim that the effect of one variable is the same at all levels of a second variable. Indeed, we must look at each level of each variable to interpret our results. In other words, you cannot explain the interaction by merely describing the separate effects of the independent variable. Instead, you must examine the unique combinations created by the data.

Let's look at some everyday examples of interaction before we return to our example of self-esteem, instructions, and persistence. Which is more important to use when describing why a person acts a certain way, the situation or their personality? Chances are you find that both are important because the situation influences a person's behavior just as personality influences their behavior. That is, you may recognize that neither the situation nor the person's personality, by themselves, provide a complete explanation of the person's behavior. To provide a complete account of their behavior, you have to describe both conditions and the interplay between the two variables. We accomplish this with a statistical interaction. We recognize that both variables are important to explain the behavior we are studying, but that neither variable, by itself, provides a complete explanation of the phenomenon we are studying.

With this brief introduction to the interaction, we return to our example and the potential outcomes that could occur. Each of the following hypothetical scenarios illustrates the presence of an interaction. Each example illustrates the information that would have been lost if we used just a one-way ANOVA. One of the important things to recognize about each of the following examples is that the interaction is interpreted using the question, "What effect occurred in the experiment that cannot be explained by simply describing each of the main effects alone?"

**Significant Main Effect for Factor A and an Interaction**   Figure 15.7 represents why a two-factor ANOVA is such an important statistic. A one-

Hypothetical mean scores in each cell for this figure:

| Instruction | Self-Esteem | | $\overline{X}$ |
| --- | --- | --- | --- |
| | Low ($a_1$) | High ($a_2$) | |
| Persist ($b_1$) | 30 | 30 | 30 |
| Don't persist ($b_2$) | 45 | 15 | 30 |
| $\overline{X}$ | 37.5 | 22.5 | 30 |

**Figure | 15.7**

An example of a main effect for Factor A and an interaction. Note that in the data and in the graph there are significant differences between subjects in conditions $a_1$ and $a_2$. These differences are not consistent however. Therefore, there is an interaction. There appears to be no effect of self-esteem when the subjects were told to persist. In contrast, when the subjects were told not to persist, low self-esteem subjects were very persistent whereas high self-esteem subjects were less persistent.

way design would not detect the interaction of two variables presented in this figure. Interactions can be more difficult to interpret than simple main effects, but the reward is that we will end up learning more about the behavior we are studying.

One of the most important things to remember about a two-factor ANOVA is that an interaction indicates that the results cannot be explained by merely describing the effects of the main effects alone. By definition, an interaction is not an additive effect. Indeed, as we will show in the following examples, an interaction indicates that the effects of the independent variables are not consistent across all treatment conditions. Consequently, our description of the data must reflect a review of the effects of the statistically significant main effects and how they interact with the other variables in the study.

One cue that we have an interaction is that the lines are not parallel to one another. That the lines are not parallel suggests that the effects of the two variables do not produce similar results as their levels change. Look at the data in Figure 15.7 more closely. Clearly, low self-esteem subjects as a group spent more time, on average, on each task than the high self-esteem subjects (e.g., 37.5 seconds vs. 22.5 seconds). In addition, it is clear that subjects given the "Persist" instructions, regardless of their level of self-esteem, spent, on average, as much time on each problem as the "Don't Persist" subjects. These statements, however, do not accurately describe the complete picture. As you can see, the "Persist" instructions

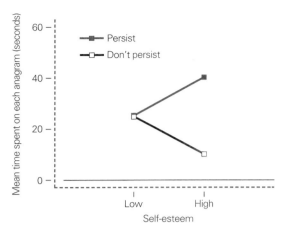

Hypothetical mean scores in each cell for this figure:

| Instruction | Self-Esteem | | $\overline{X}$ |
| --- | --- | --- | --- |
| | Low ($a_1$) | High ($a_2$) | |
| Persist ($b_1$) | 25 | 40 | 32 |
| Don't persist ($b_2$) | 25 | 10 | 17 |
| $\overline{X}$ | 25 | 25 | 25 |

**Figure** | **15.8**

An example of a main effect for Factor B and an interaction. Note that in the data and in the graph there are significant differences between subjects in conditions $b_1$ and $b_2$. These differences are not consistent however. Therefore, there is an interaction. Low-self-esteem subjects are not influenced by the instructions they receive, they are equally persistent under both conditions. High-self-esteem subjects are influenced by the instructions. When told to persist, they are very persistent. When told not to persist, they stop the task quickly.

appear to have no differing effect on either high or low self-esteem subjects; the scores are equal. What happened when subjects were told not to persist? It appears that there are opposite effects for low and high self-esteem subjects. According to these hypothetical data, low self-esteem subjects become more persistent at the task whereas high self-esteem subjects become far less persistent. Finding such an interesting result would surely require one to conclude that the phenomenon of persistence is more than a simple combination of personality and instruction.

**Significant Main Effect for Factor B and an Interaction** The data in Figure 15.8 also represent an interaction. As you can see the lines are not parallel to one another, therefore we can conclude that there are inconsistent effects across the treatment conditions. Specifically, it appears that instructions did not influence the subjects with low self-esteem; they spent the same average amount of time (25 seconds) on the anagrams regardless of the instructions. There is a different pattern for subjects with high self-esteem. Subjects with high self-esteem spent much time on each problem (40 seconds) when told to persist and little time on task when told not to persist (10 seconds).

**Significant Main Effects for A and B and an Interaction** This is an interesting type of interaction because all the effects are statistically significant. Figure 15.9 represents an example of this condition. In essence,

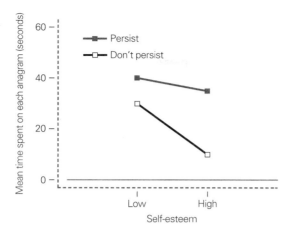

Hypothetical mean scores in each cell for this figure:

| Instruction | Self-Esteem | | |
| --- | --- | --- | --- |
| | Low ($a_1$) | High ($a_2$) | $\overline{X}$ |
| Persist ($b_1$) | 40 | 35 | 37.5 |
| Don't persist ($b_2$) | 30 | 10 | 20 |
| $\overline{X}$ | 35 | 22.5 | 28.75 |

**Figure** | **15.9**

An example of significant main effects for Factors A and B and for the interaction. Note that in the data and in the graph both the personality and the instructions influence the results. In general, low-self-esteem subjects are more persistent than high-self-esteem subjects. Also, instructions to persist create greater persistence than instructions not to persist. The pattern of results is not consistent, however. Note that effects of the instructions not to persist is greater for the high-self-esteem subjects than the other conditions. This difference represents the interaction.

we find three things are true of the data. First, we find that subjects with high self-esteem are less persistent than subjects with low self-esteem. Second, subjects told to persist are more persistent than subjects told not to persist. Finally, there is an interaction between the two variables that suggests that the instruction not to persist has a greater effect on subjects with high self-esteem than subjects with low self-esteem.

When we find data such as these, it is important to explain the data from the vantage point of the interaction. In this example, we would stress that subjects with high self-esteem appear to be more influenced by the instructions than subjects with low self-esteem. Compared to subjects with low self-esteem, subjects with high self-esteem persist more when the instructions recommend persistence and are less persistent when the instructions recommend not to persist.

**A Significant Interaction and No Main Effects** The last illustration for this section represents results where there are no main effects but there is a statistically significant interaction (see Figure 15.10). This is a particularly interesting type of outcome because it suggests that there are no statistically significant main effects for either variable. The reason for this observation is that the treatment conditions have opposite effects on each other. As you can see in the graph and the data, the instruction to persist created much persistence in the low self-esteem subjects but not in the high self-esteem subjects. In contrast, the instructions

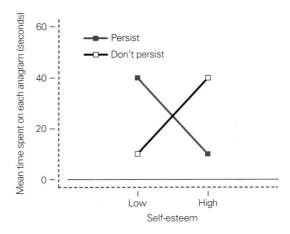

Hypothetical mean scores in each cell for this figure:

| Instruction | Self-Esteem | | $\bar{X}$ |
| --- | --- | --- | --- |
| | Low ($a_1$) | High ($a_2$) | |
| Persist ($b_1$) | 40 | 10 | 25 |
| Don't persist ($b_2$) | 10 | 40 | 25 |
| $\bar{X}$ | 25 | 25 | 25 |

**Figure | 15.10**

An example of a significant interaction but no significant main effects. These data indicate that high- and low-self-esteem subjects react in opposite ways when given instructions to either persist or not persist.

not to persist created great persistence in the high self-esteem subjects but not the low self-esteem subjects.

## 15.6 / Partitioning the Sum of Squares

The estimates of variance for the two-way ANOVA are generated the same way as they are for the one-way ANOVA. Specifically, we identify the variance associated with each of the main effects, the interaction term, and the within-group variance. We also identify the variance associated with error variance. When we finish, we will have partitioned the total sum of squares into individual components. For the two-way ANOVA, we find that

$$SS_{\text{total}} = SS_A + SS_B + SS_{AB} + SS_{\text{within}} \tag{15.2}$$

As you can see, we use a new form of subscript. The capital letters for each sum of squares represent the variance source. Therefore, $SS_A$ represents the sum of squares for the main effect of Factor A, and $SS_{AB}$ represents the main effect for the interaction of Factors A and B.

As with the one-way ANOVA, we will calculate a variance estimate for those components of the general linear model that contribute to the total variance. Because the two-way model is more complex, we will have to calculate more variance terms. Specifically, we will generate a variance estimate for Factor A, Factor B, the interaction of AB, and the within-groups term. We then create separate *F*-ratios for the effect of Factor A, Factor B, and the interaction of AB by dividing each of these variance terms by the error variance. The *F*-ratios consist, therefore, of the ratio of variance attributable to the independent variables relative to the error variance.

We can show how to create the two-way ANOVA summary table by showing how the total sum of squares are partitioned into the individual components and how each variance estimate is calculated. You will notice that we continue to use the dot notation for our equations. As a quick reminder, remember that a dot (•) represents summation across that indicator.

## Between-Groups Variance: Factor A

To estimate the variance between the groups for Factor A we begin with the sum of squares for that factor.

$$SS_A = \Sigma\frac{(X_{\bullet j\bullet})^2}{n_{j\bullet}} - \frac{(\Sigma X_{ijk})^2}{N} \tag{15.3}$$

Be careful that you use the correct number for $n_j$. Remember that you are adding the scores across all the levels for Factor B. In our example, we are asking how much variation there is between the high and low self-esteem subjects, regardless of the type of instruction they received.

The degrees of freedom for Factor A are

$$df_A = j - 1 \tag{15.4}$$

where *j* represents the number of levels for Factor A.

The Mean Square or variance estimate for Factor A is

$$MS_B = \frac{SS_A}{df_A} \tag{15.5}$$

## Between-Groups Variance: Factor B

We can repeat the logic to calculate the sum of squares for Factor B. Now we ignore the grouping created by Factor A and examine the variation associated with the levels of Factor B, the two types of instructions given the subjects. Specifically,

$$SS_B = \Sigma\frac{(X_{\bullet\bullet k})^2}{n_{\bullet k}} - \frac{(\Sigma X_{ijk})^2}{N} \tag{15.6}$$

The degrees of freedom for Factor B are

$$df_B = k - 1 \tag{15.7}$$

where *k* represents the number of levels of Factor B.

The Mean Square for Factor B is

$$MS_b = \frac{SS_B}{df_B} \tag{15.8}$$

### Interaction Variance

The sum of squares is a bit more complex. Let's look at the equation first. The sum of squares for the interaction is calculated as

$$SS_{AB} = \Sigma \frac{(X_{\bullet jk})^2}{n_{jk}} - \frac{(\Sigma X_{ijk})^2}{N} - (SS_A + SS_B) \qquad (15.9)$$

Notice that we calculate the sum of squares for all the cell means first and then subtract the sum of squares due to Factor A and Factor B. We do this because of our definition of the interaction. Specifically, we want to determine the variance among the cell means that the main effects cannot account for.

The degrees of freedom for interaction is

$$df_{AB} = (j - 1)(k - 1) \qquad (15.10)$$

The Mean Square for the interaction is

$$MS_{AB} = \frac{SS_{AB}}{df_{AB}} \qquad (15.11)$$

### Within-Groups Variance

The estimate of the error variation within all groups is

$$SS_{\text{within}} = \Sigma X_{ijk}^2 - \Sigma \frac{(X_{\bullet jk})^2}{n_{jk}} \qquad (15.12)$$

The degrees of freedom for within-groups variance is

$$df_{\text{within}} = \Sigma(n_{jk} - 1) \qquad (15.13)$$

The Mean Square for the within-groups variance is

$$MS_{\text{within}} = \frac{SS_{\text{within}}}{df_{\text{within}}} \qquad (15.14)$$

### Total Variance

$$SS_{\text{total}} = \Sigma X_{ijk}^2 - \frac{(\Sigma X_{ijk})^2}{N} \qquad (15.15)$$

The degrees of freedom for total variance is

$$df_{\text{total}} = N - 1 \qquad (15.16)$$

### The *F*-Ratios for the Two-Way ANOVA

As you have seen, we use the two-way ANOVA to partition the total variance into four sources of variance. The first three sources represent the two main effects and the interaction. The fourth source of variance represents the random error that is common to the entire experiment. We will use the *F*-ratio to determine if the variance associated with a treatment condition is significantly greater than that which would occur by chance alone. Table 15.3 presents the three *F*-ratios that we calculate when we conduct a two-way ANOVA.

**Table 15.3**

*F*-Ratios for a Two-Way ANOVA and the Estimated *F*-Ratios When $H_0$ Is True and When $H_0$ Is False

| | | ESTIMATED EFFECTS | |
|---|---|---|---|
| **Effect** | **F-Ratio** | $H_0$: "True" | $H_0$: "False" |
| Factor A | $F_A = \dfrac{MS_A}{MS_{\text{within}}}$ | $\sigma_\alpha^2 = 0.0$  $F_A \approx \dfrac{\sigma_\alpha^2 + \sigma_\epsilon^2}{\sigma_\epsilon^2} = 1$ | $\sigma_\alpha^2 > 0.0$  $F_A \approx \dfrac{\sigma_\alpha^2 + \sigma_\epsilon^2}{\sigma_\epsilon^2} > 1$ |
| Factor B | $F_B = \dfrac{MS_B}{MS_{\text{within}}}$ | $\sigma_\beta^2 = 0.0$  $F_B \approx \dfrac{\sigma_\beta^2 + \sigma_\epsilon^2}{\sigma_\epsilon^2} = 1$ | $\sigma_\beta^2 > 0.0$  $F_B \approx \dfrac{\sigma_\beta^2 + \sigma_\epsilon^2}{\sigma_\epsilon^2} > 1$ |
| Factor AB | $F_{AB} = \dfrac{MS_{AB}}{MS_{\text{within}}}$ | $\sigma_{\alpha\beta}^2 = 0.0$  $F_{AB} \approx \dfrac{\sigma_{\alpha\beta}^2 + \sigma_\epsilon^2}{\sigma_\epsilon^2} = 1$ | $\sigma_{\alpha\beta}^2 > 0.0$  $F_{AB} \approx \dfrac{\sigma_{\alpha\beta}^2 + \sigma_\epsilon^2}{\sigma_\epsilon^2} > 1$ |

Note that when the null hypothesis is true that $\omega_\alpha^2 = 0$. Consequently, the *F*-ratio represents the error variance divided by itself.

The logic of the *F*-ratios for the two-way ANOVA is the same as for the one-way ANOVA. We assume that the Mean Square for each effect (e.g., Factor A, Factor B, and Factor AB) represents the variance due to the treatment conditions plus the variance due to random error. The Mean Square Within-Groups represents the variance due to random error.

If the null hypothesis is true, then we assume that the there is no systematic variance between the groups. For example, if there is no effect for Factor A, we assume that $\sigma_\alpha^2 = 0$. Consequently, the *F*-ratio is $F_A \approx \dfrac{\sigma_\alpha^2 + \sigma_\epsilon^2}{\sigma_\epsilon^2} = 1.0$. If the null hypothesis is false, then $\sigma_\alpha^2 > 0$ and the *F*-ratio can be represented as $F_A \approx \dfrac{\sigma_\alpha^2 + \sigma_\epsilon^2}{\sigma_\epsilon^2} > 1.0$. Therefore, if the *F*-ratio is not significantly greater than 1.0 we must assume that the treatment effect had no statistically significant effect on the data. By contrast, if the *F*-ratio is greater than 1.0 we assume that part of the variance in the data is due to random effects, but that a greater part is due to the treatment effect.

## 15.7 A Worked Example

Now that we have examined the difference between main effects and interactions, we can turn our attention to the actual calculations. We will continue to use the experiment conducted by Sandelands, Brocker, and Glynn (1988) as our model.*

* The data we use are hypothetical to help make the calculations easier to understand. They are, however, based on the data reported by Sandelands, Brocker, and Glynn (1988). We highly recommend this fine article if you are interested in learning more about their data and the interpretation they provided.

We can begin the analysis of these data by establishing the null and alternative hypotheses. Because we are using a two-way ANOVA, we will need to create a null and alternative hypothesis for each effect—the two main effects and the interaction.

### Null Hypotheses:

$H_0: \sigma_\alpha^2 + \sigma_\epsilon^2 = \sigma_\epsilon^2$:   There is no main effect for self-esteem.

$H_0: \sigma_\beta^2 + \sigma_\epsilon^2 = \sigma_\epsilon^2$:   There is no main effect for instructions.

$H_0: \sigma_{\alpha\beta}^2 + \sigma_\epsilon^2 = \sigma_\epsilon^2$:   There is no interaction for self-esteem and instructions.

### Alternative Hypotheses:

$H_1: \sigma_\alpha^2 + \sigma_\epsilon^2 \neq \sigma_\epsilon^2$:   There is a main effect for self-esteem.

$H_1: \sigma_\beta^2 + \sigma_\epsilon^2 \neq \sigma_\epsilon^2$:   There is a main effect for instructions.

$H_1: \sigma_{\alpha\beta}^2 + \sigma_\epsilon^2 \neq \sigma_\epsilon^2$:   There is an interaction for self-esteem and instructions.

***Statistical Test:***   We use the two-way ANOVA because we are simultaneously comparing the effects of two independent variables. We assume that the data are normally distributed and that the variances of the groups are equal.

***Significance Level:***   $\alpha = .05$. If the size of the $F$-ratio is sufficiently large, we will reject the null hypothesis in favor of the alternative hypothesis.

***Sampling Distribution:***   $F$-distribution

| Effect | $df_N$ | $df_D$ | $F_{critical}$ |
|--------|--------|--------|----------------|
| A | 1 | 16 | 4.49 |
| B | 1 | 16 | 4.49 |
| AB | 1 | 16 | 4.49 |

If the $F_{observed}$ is equal to or larger than $F_{critical}$, we will reject $H_0$.

Before we begin our analysis, let us look at the data in Table 15.4. Look carefully at the values contained in the data set. Are there any extreme scores or outliers? Are the values accurate or are they the result of typographical errors (keystroke errors)? Next, draw a graph of the means and attempt to describe the results as was done in Figure 15.11. The first fact you should notice is that the lines are not parallel. This suggests that there may be an interaction between the two variables. If we find that there is a statistically significant interaction, then we will not be able to explain the data by merely describing the effects of the independent variables.

Before we begin with our analysis of the data, we should ensure that the variances are homogeneous using the $F_{max}$ test.

$$F_{max} = \frac{0.073}{0.027}$$

$$F_{max} = 2.7037$$

$$F_{max-critical} \; k = 4, \, n = 5 = 20.60$$

**Table 15.4**

**Hypothetical Data for Example**

| | FACTOR A (SELF-ESTEEM) | | |
|---|---|---|---|
| **Factor B (Instructions)** | **Low ($a_1$)** | **High ($a_2$)** | |
| | $a_1b_1$ | $a_2b_1$ | |
| Persist ($b_1$) | $X_{111} = 2.6$ | $X_{121} = 3.5$ | |
| | $X_{211} = 2.9$ | $X_{221} = 3.0$ | |
| | $X_{311} = 2.5$ | $X_{321} = 2.8$ | |
| | $X_{411} = 2.8$ | $X_{421} = 3.1$ | |
| | $X_{511} = 2.3$ | $X_{521} = 2.9$ | |
| | $X_{\bullet11} = 13.1$ | $X_{\bullet21} = 15.3$ | $X_{\bullet\bullet1} = 28.4$ |
| | $n_{11} = 5$ | $n_{21} = 5$ | $n_{\bullet1} = 10$ |
| | $\overline{X}_{11} = 2.62$ | $\overline{X}_{21} = 3.06$ | $\overline{X}_{\bullet1} = 2.84$ |
| | $a_1b_2$ | $a_2b_2$ | |
| Don't persist ($b_2$) | $X_{112} = 2.5$ | $X_{122} = 2.0$ | |
| | $X_{212} = 2.3$ | $X_{222} = 1.9$ | |
| | $X_{312} = 2.4$ | $X_{322} = 1.8$ | |
| | $X_{412} = 1.9$ | $X_{422} = 2.2$ | |
| | $X_{512} = 2.2$ | $X_{522} = 1.7$ | |
| | $X_{\bullet12} = 11.3$ | $X_{\bullet22} = 9.6$ | $X_{\bullet\bullet2} = 20.9$ |
| | $n_{12} = 5$ | $n_{22} = 5$ | $n_{\bullet1} = 10$ |
| | $\overline{X}_{12} = 2.26$ | $\overline{X}_{22} = 1.92$ | $\overline{X}_{\bullet2} = 2.09$ |
| | $X_{\bullet1\bullet} = 24.4$ | $X_{\bullet2\bullet} = 24.9$ | $X_{\bullet\bullet\bullet} = 49.3$ |
| | $n_{1\bullet} = 10$ | $n_{2\bullet} = 10$ | $n_{\bullet\bullet} = 20$ |
| | $\overline{X}_{1\bullet} = 2.44$ | $\overline{X}_{2\bullet} = 2.49$ | $\overline{X}_{\bullet\bullet} = 2.465$ |
| | | | $\Sigma X_{ijk} = 49.3$ |
| | | | $\Sigma X_{ijk}^2 = 125.99$ |

Because $F_{max} = 2.7037 < F_{max-critical} = 20.60$ we can assume that the variances are equivalent. We are now ready to analyze the data.

**Step 1** Calculate Sum of Squares for Factor A

$$SS_A = \Sigma \frac{(X_{\bullet j\bullet})^2}{n_{j\bullet}} - \frac{(\Sigma X_{ijk})^2}{N}$$

$$SS_A = \frac{(24.4)^2}{10} + \frac{(24.9)^2}{10} - \frac{(49.3)^2}{20}$$

$$SS_A = 59.536 + 62.001 - 121.524$$

$$SS_A = 121.537 - 121.524$$

$$SS_A = 0.013$$

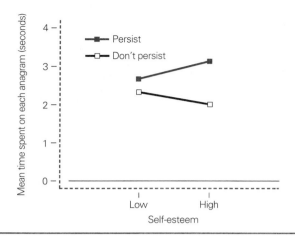

**Figure** | **15.11**

| **Graph of data presented in Table 15.4.**

**Step 2** Calculate Degrees of Freedom for Factor A

$$df_A = j - 1$$
$$df_A = 2 - 1$$
$$df_A = 1$$

**Step 3** Calculate Mean Square for Factor A

$$MS_A = \frac{SS_A}{df_A}$$
$$MS_A = \frac{0.013}{1}$$
$$MS_A = 0.013$$

**Step 4** Calculate Sum of Squares for Factor B

$$SS_B = \Sigma \frac{(X_{\bullet\bullet k})^2}{n_{\bullet k}} - \frac{(\Sigma X_{ijk})^2}{N}$$
$$SS_B = \frac{(28.4)^2}{10} + \frac{(20.9)^2}{10} - \frac{(49.3)^2}{20}$$
$$SS_B = 80.656 + 43.681 - 121.524$$
$$SS_B = 124.337 - 121.524$$
$$SS_B = 2.813$$

**Step 5** Calculate Degrees of Freedom for Factor B

$$df_B = k - 1$$
$$df_B = 2 - 1$$
$$df_B = 1$$

**Step 6** Calculate Mean Square for Factor B

$$MS_B = \frac{SS_B}{df_B}$$

$$MS_B = \frac{2.813}{1}$$

$$MS_B = 2.813$$

**Step 7**   Calculate Sum of Squares of Interaction of AB

$$SS_{AB} = \Sigma\frac{(X_{\bullet jk})^2}{n_{jk}} - \frac{(\Sigma X_{ijk})^2}{N} - (SS_A + SS_B)$$

$$SS_{AB} = \frac{(13.1)^2}{5} + \frac{(11.3)^2}{5} + \frac{(15.3)^2}{5} + \frac{(9.6)^2}{5} - \frac{(49.3)^2}{20} - (0.013 + 2.813)$$

$$SS_{AB} = 34.322 + 25.538 + 46.818 + 18.432 - 121.524 - 2.826$$

$$SS_{AB} = 125.11 - 124.35$$

$$SS_{AB} = 0.76$$

**Step 8**   Calculate the Degrees of Freedom for Interaction of AB

$$df_{AB} = (j - 1)(k - 1)$$

$$df_{AB} = (2 - 1)(2 - 1)$$

$$df_{AB} = (1)(1)$$

$$df_{AB} = 1$$

**Step 9**   Calculate the Mean Square for Interaction of AB

$$MS_{AB} = \frac{SS_{AB}}{df_{AB}}$$

$$MS_{AB} = \frac{0.760}{1}$$

$$MS_{AB} = 0.760$$

**Step 10** Calculate the Sum of Squares for the Within-Groups Error

$$SS_{within} = \Sigma X_{ijk}^2 - \Sigma\frac{(X_{\bullet jk})^2}{n_{jk}}$$

$$SS_{within} = 125.990 - \left(\frac{(13.1)^2}{5} + \frac{(11.3)^2}{5} + \frac{(15.3)^2}{5} + \frac{(9.6)^2}{5}\right)$$

$$SS_{within} = 125.990 - 125.11$$

$$SS_{within} = 0.880$$

**Step 11** Calculate the Degrees of Freedom for the Within-Groups Error

$$df_{within} = \Sigma(n_{jk} - 1)$$

$$df_{within} = (5 - 1) + (5 - 1) + (5 - 1) + (5 - 1)$$

$$df_{within} = 4 + 4 + 4 + 4$$

$$df_{within} = 16$$

**Step 12** Calculate the Mean Square for the Within-Groups Error

$$MS_{within} = \frac{SS_{within}}{df_{within}}$$

$$MS_{\text{within}} = \frac{0.880}{16}$$

$$MS_{\text{within}} = 0.055$$

**Step 13** Calculate the Total Sum of Squares

$$SS_{\text{total}} = \Sigma^2_{ijk} - \frac{(\Sigma X_{ijk})^2}{N}$$

$$SS_{\text{total}} = 125.990 - \frac{(49.3)^2}{20}$$

$$SS_{\text{total}} = 125.990 - 121.524$$

$$SS_{\text{total}} = 4.466$$

As a check of your work, the total of the other sum of squares must equal the $SS_{\text{total}}$.

$$SS_{\text{total}} = SS_A + SS_B + SS_{AB} + SS_W$$

$$SS_{\text{total}} = 0.013 + 2.813 + 0.760 + 0.880$$

$$SS_{\text{total}} = 4.466$$

**Step 14** Calculate the Degrees of Freedom for the Total

$$df_{\text{total}} = N - 1$$

$$df_{\text{total}} = 20 - 1$$

$$df_{\text{total}} = 19$$

**Step 15** Calculate the *F*-ratio for each treatment effect

Factor A $\qquad F_A = \dfrac{MS_A}{MS_{\text{within}}} \qquad F_A = \dfrac{0.013}{0.055} = 0.236$

Factor B $\qquad F_B = \dfrac{MS_B}{MS_{\text{within}}} \qquad F_B = \dfrac{2.813}{0.055} = 51.145$

Factor AB $\qquad F_{AB} = \dfrac{MS_{AB}}{MS_{\text{within}}} \qquad F_{AB} = \dfrac{0.760}{0.055} = 13.818$

Summary table for data presented in Table 15.4:

| Source | SS | df | MS | F |
|---|---|---|---|---|
| A | 0.013 | 1 | 0.013 | 0.236 |
| B | 2.813 | 1 | 2.813 | 51.145 |
| AB | 0.760 | 1 | 0.760 | 13.818 |
| Within-groups | 0.880 | 16 | 0.055 | |
| Total | 4.466 | 19 | | |

From this summary table we can see that there is a statistically significant main effect for Factor B, instructions $F(1, 16) = 51.145$, $p < .05$, a statistically significant interaction $F(1, 16) = 13.818$, $p < .05$, but that the effect for self-esteem is not statistically significant $F(1, 16) = 0.236$, $p > .05$. Before we begin to describe the results, it will be helpful to obtain more information. Although we have tested each of the effects for significance, we now need to look at the relation between the independent and dependent variables. As we have seen previously, even very small effects may be statistically significant if the sample size is sufficiently large. Specifically, we should calculate $\omega^2$ for each of the statistically significant $F$-ratios. You will recall from Chapter 14 that $\omega^2$ is defined as:

$$\omega^2 = \frac{df_{effect}\,(F_{effect} - 1)}{df_{effect}\,(F_{effect} - 1) + N}$$

Therefore, the $\omega^2$ for the effect of the instructions is:

$$\omega^2 = \frac{1(51.145 - 1)}{1(51.45 - 1) + 20}$$

$$\omega^2 = \frac{50.145}{70.145}$$

$$\omega^2 = .715$$

The $\omega^2$ for the interaction is:

$$\omega^2 = \frac{1(13.827 - 1)}{1(13.827 - 1) + 20}$$

$$\omega^2 = \frac{12.827}{32.827}$$

$$\omega^2 = .391$$

We can interpret the results as follows: The instructions that subjects received accounted for approximately 71.5% of the total difference among subjects. The interaction between self-esteem and the instructions accounted for 39.1% of the variance that cannot be explained by either levels of self-esteem or type of instruction. The instructions not to persist caused subjects with high self-esteem to spend less time on each problem but caused subjects with low self-esteem to spend more time on each problem.

In their review of the results, Sandelands, Brocker, and Glynn (1988) admitted that they found the results "a bit more puzzling." (p. 214) They then reviewed the relevant literature that appears to offer a reasonable account of the data. After providing a potential account of their results, they conclude that "the accuracy of these speculative remarks must await further research." (p. 214)

Their concluding remark is important for several reasons. First, they admitted that they had not anticipated the interaction and are trying to explain the finding after the fact. Therefore, they recognized that in order to verify the accuracy of their explanation, they should replicate the effect. This is the hallmark of good research. The researchers discovered an interesting effect, attempted to explain why the effect occurred, and then continued with more research to understand the effect.

## 15.8 / Power Calculations

We can also revisit the issue of statistical power. If you wanted to replicate the effect, how many subjects should you use? Should you use their methods, or spend the time to invent new methods? Using the hypothetical data presented above, what is the power of the experiment? More specifically, we need to know the power of the interaction because that is the effect we want to replicate. As you recall from Chapter 14, the effect size of a $F$-ratio is **f.** We calculate **f** using

$$\mathbf{f} = \sqrt{\frac{\eta^2_{\text{effect}}}{1.0 - \eta^2_{\text{effect}}}}$$

where

$$\eta^2 = \frac{df_{\text{effect}}\,F_{\text{effect}}}{df_{\text{effect}}F_{\text{effect}} + df_{\text{within}}} \qquad \text{or} \qquad \eta^2 = \frac{SS_{\text{effect}}}{SS_{\text{total}}}$$

For our experiment the power of the interaction is:

$$\eta^2 = \frac{0.760}{4.466} = 0.170$$

$$\mathbf{f} = \sqrt{\frac{0.170}{1.0 - 0.170}} = 0.453$$

According to these data and Cohen's (1988) guidelines the effect size for the interaction is large. How many subjects should you use in each cell in order to have power equal to .80? We can use Table M in Appendix D to answer this question.

The first step will be to calculate an adjusted sample size. The adjustment reflects that the two-way ANOVA uses the same denominator degrees of freedom for all $F$-ratios in the test. Specifically,

$$n' = \frac{\Sigma(n_{ij} - 1)}{df_{\text{effect}} + 1} + 1$$

What would our power be if we attempted to repeat the experiment with 5 subjects in each treatment cell?

$$n' = \frac{(5 - 1) + (5 - 1) + (5 - 1) + (5 - 1)}{1 + 1} + 1$$

$$n' = \frac{16}{2} + 1$$

$$n' = 9$$

For the sake of simplicity, we will round $n'$ to 10.* Now look at Table M in the Appendix. We use the section titled "Degrees of Freedom Numerator = 1" because the interaction will have 1 degree of freedom. Next, we use the set of columns labeled $\alpha = .05$. Finally, we select the column labeled .40 because that value is closest to the actual effect size. According to this table, there is a 40% chance that the effect can be replicated if the experiment is repeated. What would happen if we used 15 subjects in each treatment condition? According to our calculations,

---

* We rounded here because we want to estimate the power of an experiment. You should remember that the purpose of estimation is not to produce exact figures, but to estimate what the final answer should or could be.

$$n' = \frac{(15 - 1) + (15 - 1) + (15 - 1) + (15 - 1)}{1 + 1} + 1$$

$$n' = \frac{56}{2} + 1$$

$$n' = 29$$

Rounding $n'$ to 30 and following the same steps as above, we find that the power is .87. Therefore, if you were to replicate this experiment with 15 subjects in each of the treatment conditions, you will have a high probability of replicating the effect and rejecting the null hypothesis.

## 15.9 / Other Two-Factor ANOVA Designs

In this chapter we spent most of our time examining a basic 2 × 2 ANOVA. You can use the procedures with any experimental design where there are two independent variables, each with two or more levels. For example, you could conduct an experiment that has two levels of Factor A and 3 levels of Factor B; a 2 × 3 design. Again, you would want to know how Factors A, B and the interaction of A and B influence the data.

A statistically significant main effect suggests that there are statistically significant differences among the levels of the factor. When the interaction is statistically significant, we interpret it to suggest that the effects of the two factors are not consistent across all levels of the treatment conditions. The graphs in Figure 15.12 represent different patterns that could occur in a 2 × 3 study.

The top two graphs represent the existence of only a simple main effect with no interaction. In the upper left graph, there is a main effect for Factor A. That is, across all levels of Factor B, $A_1$ is greater than $A_2$. In the upper right graph, there is a main effect for Factor B. Specifically, for both levels of Factor A, $B_1 < B_2 < B_3$. The second row of graphs represents statistically significant main effects for factors A and B, but no interaction. Notice that in both these graphs, the differences between $A_1$ and $A_2$ is constant for each level of Factor B.

Finally, in the last row of graphs, are interactions between the two factors. As you can see, the effects of the two variables are not consistent across all treatment conditions. Therefore, our explanation of these data must include an account of the effects of each main effect and the interaction of the two variables.

## 15.10 / Putting It All Together: A 2 × 3 ANOVA

Have you ever noticed that some people don't seem to work as hard as they should when they are in a group? Social psychologists call this phenomenon "social loafing." The phenomenon describes the fact that for some tasks people work hard when they are alone, but work less hard when

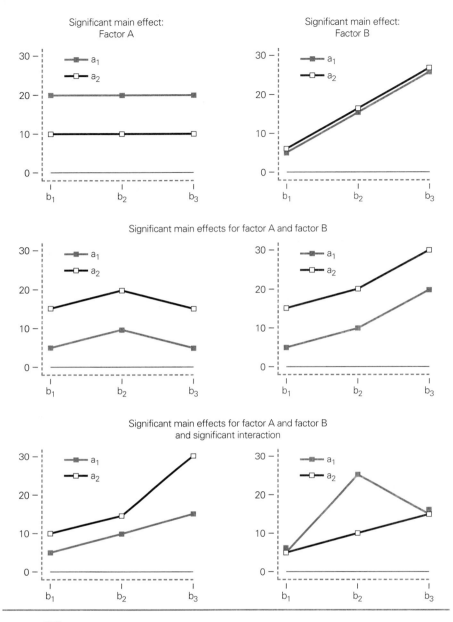

**Figure** | **15.12**

**Examples of main effects and interaction for a 2 × 3 factorial experiment.**

they are in a group. For our example, let's assume that a psychologist decided to conduct an experiment to study social loafing.

The researcher decided to use a boring task to examine social loafing. Specifically, when the subject arrived at the laboratory, the researcher asked him or her to read a 20-page manuscript on the history of the Byzantine empire and to identify spelling and grammar errors. The dependent variable was the number of errors the subject found.

The psychologist decided to control two independent variables. The first variable was whether the person worked in a real group or a pseudo group. In the real group condition, the subject worked in a room with other people. In the pseudo group condition, the experimenter told the subject that he or she was working as a part of a team and that the other team members were working independently in different rooms. The second variable was the number of people in the group. The subjects in the experiment learned that they were working on the task alone, with one other person, or with five other people.

The design of this research is a 2 × 3 factorial design. The first variable has two levels (*real* group vs. *p*seudo group). The second variable has three levels (0, 1, or 5 additional workers). Six unique treatment conditions represent the different combinations of the independent variable. Table 15.5 presents the results of the experiment.

### Null Hypotheses:

$H_1: \sigma_\alpha^2 + \sigma_\epsilon^2 = \sigma_\epsilon^2$:   There is no main effect for group type.

$H_1: \sigma_\beta^2 + \sigma_\epsilon^2 = \sigma_\epsilon^2$:   There is no main effect for group size.

$H_1: \sigma_{\alpha\beta}^2 + \sigma_\epsilon^2 = \sigma_\epsilon^2$:   There is no interaction for group type and group size.

### Alternative Hypotheses:

$H_0: \sigma_\alpha^2 + \sigma_\epsilon^2 \neq \sigma_\epsilon^2$:   There is a main effect for group type.

$H_0: \sigma_\beta^2 + \sigma_\epsilon^2 \neq \sigma_\epsilon^2$:   There is a main effect for group size.

$H_0: \sigma_{\alpha\beta}^2 + \sigma_\epsilon^2 \neq \sigma_\epsilon^2$:   There is an interaction for group type and group size.

***Statistical Test:***   We use the two-way ANOVA because we are simultaneously comparing the effects of two independent variables. We assume that the data are normally distributed and that the variances of the groups are equal.

***Significance Level:***   $\alpha = .05$. If the size of the $F$-ratio is sufficiently large, we will reject the null hypothesis in favor of the alternative hypothesis.

**Table | 15.5a**

**Hypothetical Data for a 2 × 3 ANOVA**

|        | $a_1$ |    | $a_2$ |    |
| ------ | ----- | -- | ----- | -- |
|        | $a_1b_1$ | | $a_2b_1$ | |
|        | 15 | 14 | 22 | 14 |
|        | 18 | 17 | 17 | 17 |
| $b_1$  | 18 | 18 | 16 | 17 |
|        | 17 | 20 | 21 | 18 |
|        | $a_1b_2$ | | $a_2b_2$ | |
|        | 12 | 16 | 12 | 15 |
|        | 16 | 16 | 10 | 14 |
| $b_2$  | 15 | 19 | 14 | 16 |
|        | 13 | 12 | 13 | 14 |
|        | $a_1b_3$ | | $a_2b_3$ | |
|        | 9  | 18 | 12 | 15 |
|        | 16 | 14 | 10 | 14 |
| $b_3$  | 14 | 11 | 14 | 16 |
|        | 11 | 14 | 13 | 14 |

**Table 15.5b**

**Summary Statistics for Data in Table 15.5a**

|  | $a_1$ | $a_2$ |  |
|---|---|---|---|
| $b_1$ | $X_{\bullet 11} = 137$ <br> $n_{11} = 8$ <br> $\overline{X}_{11} = 17.12$ <br> $\hat{s}_{11}^2 = 3.55$ | $X_{\bullet 21} = 142$ <br> $n_{21} = 8$ <br> $\overline{X}_{21} = 17.75$ <br> $\hat{s}_{12}^2 = 6.79$ | $X_{\bullet\bullet 1} = 279$ <br> $n_{\bullet 1} = 16$ <br> $\overline{X}_{\bullet 1} = 17.49$ |
| $b_2$ | $X_{\bullet 12} = 119$ <br> $n_{12} = 8$ <br> $\overline{X}_{12} = 14.88$ <br> $\hat{s}_{12}^2 = 5.84$ | $X_{\bullet 22} = 108$ <br> $n_{22} = 8$ <br> $\overline{X}_{22} = 13.50$ <br> $\hat{s}_{22}^2 = 3.43$ | $X_{\bullet\bullet 2} = 227$ <br> $n_{\bullet 2} = 16$ <br> $\overline{X}_{\bullet 2} = 14.19$ |
| $b_3$ | $X_{\bullet 13} = 107$ <br> $n_{13} = 8$ <br> $\overline{X}_{13} = 13.38$ <br> $\hat{s}_{13}^2 = 8.55$ | $X_{\bullet 23} = 71$ <br> $n_{23} = 8$ <br> $\overline{X}_{23} = 8.88$ <br> $\hat{s}_{23}^2 = 2.98$ | $X_{\bullet\bullet 3} = 178$ <br> $n_{\bullet 3} = 16$ <br> $\overline{X}_{\bullet 3} = 11.12$ |
|  | $X_{\bullet 1 \bullet} = 363$ <br> $n_{1 \bullet} = 24$ <br> $\overline{X}_{1 \bullet} = 15.13$ | $X_{\bullet 2 \bullet} = 321$ <br> $n_{2 \bullet} = 24$ <br> $\overline{X}_{2 \bullet} = 13.38$ | $X_{\bullet\bullet\bullet} = 684$ <br> $N = 48$ <br> $\overline{\overline{X}} = 14.25$ <br> $\Sigma X_{ijk}^2 = 10374$ |

*Sampling Distribution:*   *F*-distribution

| **Effect** | $df_N$ | $df_D$ | $F_{\text{critical}}$ |
|---|---|---|---|
| A | 1 | 42 | 4.07 |
| B | 2 | 42 | 3.22 |
| AB | 2 | 42 | 3.22 |

If the $F_{\text{observed}}$ is equal to or larger than $F_{\text{critical}}$ we will reject $H_0$.

Let's begin by drawing a graph of the data. Figure 15.13 presents such a graph. The data appear to confirm the existence of the social loafing phenomenon. When people worked alone, they found many errors. By contrast, when there other people in the group, the average number of errors found decreased. From the graph we can see that there appears to be an interaction. Specifically, the presence of other people in the room seems to have a greater effect on social loafing than the pseudo group condition.

All we need to do now is to ensure homogeneity of variance.

$$F_{\max} = \frac{8.55}{2.98}$$

$$F_{\max} = 2.8691$$

$$F_{\max-\text{critical}}\ 9.03,\ k = 6,\ n = 8$$

Because $F_{\max} = 2.8691 < F_{\max-\text{critical}} = 9.03$, we can assume that the variances are equivalent. We are now ready to analyze the data.

We can begin our formal analysis of the data by calculating the sum of squares for each estimate of variance.

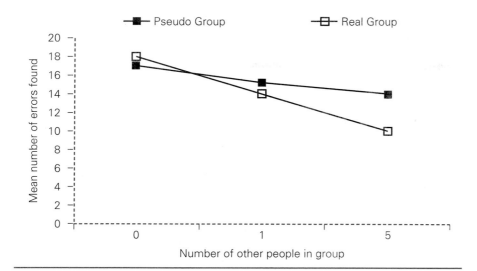

**Figure** 15.13

$$SS_A = \Sigma \frac{(X_{\bullet j\bullet})^2}{n_{j\bullet}} - \frac{(\Sigma X_{ijk})^2}{N}$$

$$SS_A = \frac{(363)^2}{24} + \frac{(321)^2}{24} - \frac{(684)^2}{48}$$

$$SS_A = 5490.3750 + 4293.375 - 9747.0$$

$$SS_A = 36.75$$

$$df_A = j - 1 \qquad MS_A = \frac{SS_A}{df_A}$$

$$df_A = 2 - 1 \qquad MS_A = \frac{36.75}{1}$$

$$df_A = 1 \qquad MS_A = 36.75$$

$$SS_B = \Sigma \frac{(X_{\bullet\bullet k})^2}{n_{\bullet k}} - \frac{(\Sigma X_{ijk})^2}{N}$$

$$SS_B = \frac{(279)^2}{16} + \frac{(227)^2}{16} + \frac{(178)^2}{16} - \frac{(684)^2}{48}$$

$$SS_B = 4865.0625 + 3220.5625 + 1980.25 - 9747.0$$

$$SS_B = 318.875$$

$$df_B = j - 1 \qquad MS_B = \frac{SS_B}{df_B}$$

$$df_B = 3 - 1 \qquad MS_B = \frac{318.875}{2}$$

$$df_B = 2 \qquad MS_B = 159.437$$

$$SS_{AB} = \Sigma \frac{(X_{\bullet jk})^2}{n_{jk}} - \frac{(\Sigma X_{ijk})^2}{N} - (SS_A + SS_B)$$

$$SS_{AB} = \frac{(137)^2}{8} + \frac{(119)^2}{8} + \frac{(107)^2}{8} +$$

$$\frac{(142)^2}{8} + \frac{(108)^2}{8} + \frac{(71)^2}{8} - \frac{(684)^2}{48} - (36.750 + 318.875)$$

$$SS_{AB} = 2346.125 + 1770.125 + 1431.135 + 2520.50 + \\ 1458.0 + 630.125 - 9747.0 - 355.625$$

$$SS_{AB} = 53.375$$

$$df_{AB} = (j - 1)(k - 1) \qquad MS_{AB} = \frac{SS_{AB}}{df_{AB}}$$

$$df_{AB} = (2 - 1)(3 - 1) \qquad MS_{AB} = \frac{53.375}{2}$$

$$df_{AB} = 2 \qquad MS_{AB} = 26.687$$

$$SS_{\text{within}} = \Sigma X_{ijk}^2 - \Sigma \frac{(X_{\bullet jk})^2}{n_{jk}}$$

$$SS_{\text{within}} = 10374.0 - 10156.0$$

$$SS_{\text{within}} = 218.0$$

$$df_{\text{within}} = \Sigma(n_{ij} - 1) \qquad MS_{AB} = \frac{SS_{AB}}{df_{AB}}$$

$$df_{\text{within}} = (8 - 1) + (8 - 1) + (8 - 1) + MS_{AB} = \frac{218.0}{42} \\ (8 - 1) + (8 - 1) + (8 - 1)$$

$$df_{\text{within}} = 42 \qquad MS_{AB} = 5.190$$

$$SS_{\text{total}} = \Sigma X_{ijk}^2 - \frac{(\Sigma X_{ijk})^2}{N}$$

$$SS_{\text{total}} = 10374.0 - \frac{(684.0)^2}{48}$$

$$SS_{\text{total}} = 627.0$$

$$df_{\text{total}} = N - 1$$

$$df_{\text{total}} = 48 - 1$$

$$df_{\text{total}} = 47$$

Summary table for data presented in Table 15.5:

| Source | SS | df | MS | F | $\omega^2$ |
|--------|--------|----|---------|--------|------|
| A | 36.750 | 1 | 36.759 | 7.080 | .169 |
| B | 318.875 | 2 | 159.438 | 30.720 | .665 |
| AB | 53.385 | 2 | 26.687 | 5.142 | .216 |
| Within | 218.000 | 42 | 5.190 | | |
| Total | 327.000 | 47 | | | |

As you can see, each $F$-ratio is greater than the $F_{\text{critical}}$ for the appropriate degrees of freedom. Because the interaction is statistically significant, we will need to examine the individual means in detail. We can conduct this analysis using the multiple comparison procedure we taught you in Chapter 14.

## Multiple Comparisons

The multiple comparison procedure for a two-way ANOVA follows the same procedure that we used for the one-way ANOVA. The procedure is a bit more complicated because there are many different ways that we can analyze the data. With the two-way ANOVA we can examine the differences among means due to the two main effects as well as the interaction. Let's review some guidelines that will help make using the multiple comparison procedures easier to understand.

First, we will still need to protect the $\alpha$ level using an *a posteriori* test. The Tukey HSD is a good test to use to examine the main effects and the interaction.

Second, we can use the Tukey HSD to compare means only when the $F$-ratio for the effect is statistically significant. In our example, all three effects are statistically significant. If, however, the main effect for Factor B was the only statistically significant result, we would restrict our analysis to the means for that factor.

Finally, you will have to determine a separate critical value for each set of comparisons. We must do this because each $F$-ratio represents a different group of means. Specifically, Factor A represents two means, Factor B represents three means, and the interaction represents six means. Let's now look at each multiple comparison test in turn.

**Factor A**   There are two means for this factor. Technically, we do not need to do any additional testing on this factor. The $F$-ratio is statistically significant. Therefore, we can assume that 13.38 is less than 15.13. For the sake of practice, however, we will show you how to apply the Tukey HSD test.

**Null Hypothesis:**   $\mu_j = \mu_j{}'$

**Alternative Hypothesis:**   $\mu_j \neq \mu_j{}'$

**Statistical Test:**   Tukey's HSD

**Significance Level:**   $\alpha = .05$.

**Sampling Distribution:** Studentized Range Test. Number of means = 2, $df_{within} = 42$. Therefore $q_{critical} = 2.86$.

**Critical Value:**   $\text{HSD} = q_{critical} \sqrt{\dfrac{MS_{within}}{n_{j\bullet}}}$

$$\text{HSD} = 2.86 \sqrt{\dfrac{5.190}{24}}$$

$$\text{HSD} = 1.33$$

Because the difference between the means is greater than the HSD (e.g., $15.125 - 13.375 = 1.75 > 1.33$), we can again conclude that people in the Real Group treatment condition detected fewer errors on average than the people in the Pseudo Group condition.

**Factor B**   There are three means for this factor, and the $F$-ratio is statistically significant. Therefore, we can compare each of the main effect means.

**Null Hypothesis:**   $\mu_k = \mu_k{}'$

**Alternative Hypothesis:**   $\mu_k = \mu_k{}'$

**Statistical Test:**   Tukey's HSD

***Significance Level:***   $\alpha = .05$.

***Sampling Distribution:***   Studentized Range Test. Number of means = 3, $df_{within} = 42$. Therefore $q_{critical} = 3.44$.

***Critical Value:***   $HSD = q_{critical} \sqrt{\dfrac{MS_{within}}{n_{\bullet k}}}$

$$HSD = 3.55 \sqrt{\dfrac{5.190}{16}}$$

$$HSD = 2.02$$

Because there are three means, there are three possible comparisons.

$$17.438 - 11.125 = 6.313,\, p < .05$$
$$17.438 - 14.188 = 3.250,\, p < .05$$
$$14.188 - 11.125 = 3.063,\, p < .05$$

As you can see, each mean is different from the other means. In other words, as the number of people in the group increased, the number of errors detected decreased. Therefore, social loafing increased as the size of the group increased.

**Factor AB**   Comparing the means for the interaction is a bit more difficult. Recall that the interaction represents the variance among the individual cell means less the influence of the main effects. Therefore, when you compare the individual cell means, you must remember that the difference will represent the interaction as well as the main effect. Also, because of the large number of means represented by the interaction there are many potential comparisons. For example, with six means in this study, we can make 15 comparisons. Although all these differences may be interesting, we can save time by focusing on those differences that make sense given the purpose of the research.

***Null Hypothesis:***   $\mu_{jk} = \mu_{jk}{}'$

***Alternative Hypothesis:***   $\mu_{jk} \neq \mu_{jk}{}'$

***Statistical Test:***   Tukey's HSD

***Significance Level:***   $\alpha = .05$.

***Sampling Distribution:***   Studentized Range Test. Number of means = 6, $df_{within} = 42$. Therefore $q_{critical} = 4.23$.

***Critical Value:***   $HSD = q_{critical} \sqrt{\dfrac{MS_{within}}{n_{jk}}}$

$$HSD = 4.23 \sqrt{\dfrac{5.190}{8}}$$

$$HSD = 3.41$$

Let's think about the comparisons that make the most sense. First, how do the types of groups differ given the group sizes? Table 15.6 represents these comparisons

As you can see, none of the differences between the pairs of means is statistically significant. Therefore, we can tentatively conclude that the degree of social loafing increased at approximately the same rate for the two types of group.

**Table** 15.6

Difference Between Specified Pairs of Means for 2 × 3 ANOVA

|  | 0 | 1 | 5 |
|---|---|---|---|
| Pseudo group vs. Real group | 17.125 − 17.750 = −0.375 | 14.875 − 14.188 = 0.687 | 13.375 − 11.125 = 2.25 |

Table 15.7 presents an interesting perspective of the data. Look at the comparisons for the 0 vs. 1 people and 0 vs. 5 people conditions for the Pseudo and Real groups. As is clear, the greatest amount of social loafing occurred when there were 5 other people. In the Pseudo Group condition, the difference between 0 and 1 person is not statistically significant whereas the difference is statistically significant for the Real Group condition. In addition, the difference between 1 and 5 other people is statistically significant for the Real Group condition but not the Pseudo Group condition. This pattern of results leads us to conclude that social loafing increases as the size of the group increases, but that the effects are more striking when everyone is in the same room.

Using the results of this analysis, the researcher could write the following brief results section.

**Table** 15.7

Difference Between Specified Pairs of Means for 2 × 3 ANOVA

|  | 0 vs. 1 | 0 vs. 5 | 1 vs. 5 |
|---|---|---|---|
| Pseudo group | 17.125 − 14.875 = 2.25 | 17.125 − 13.375 = 3.75* | 14.875 − 13.375 = 1.50 |
| Real group | 17.750 − 14.188 = 3.562* | 17.750 − 11.125 = 6.625* | 14.188 − 11.125 = 3.063* |

Note: * $p < .05$.

---

Social Loafing   5

Figure 1 presents the average number of errors found for each of the treatment conditions. As expected, the number of errors decreased as sample group increased. The greatest amount of social loafing appeared to occur in the Real Group condition. Specifically, the decrease in error detection was greatest for the 1 and 5 Others conditions in the Real Group condition.

Using a 2 × 3 (Group Type × Number of Others) ANOVA revealed a statistically significant main effect for Group Type, $F(1, 42) = 7.080$, $p = .011$, $\omega^2 = .169$. Overall, participants in the Real Group conditions detected fewer errors on average than participants in the Pseudo Group conditions. There is also a main effect for Number of Others, $F(2, 42) = 30.720$, $p < .001$, $\omega^2 = .665$. Subsequent analysis of this main effect using Tukey's HSD indicated that each treatment mean was significantly different than the other treatment means (all $ps < .05$). There is also a statistically significant interaction, $F(2, 42) = 5.142$, $p = .01$, $\omega^2 = .216$

Further analysis of the interaction using Tukey's HSD revealed several interesting findings. For the Pseudo Groups condition, there was a statistically significant difference between the 0 Others condition and the 1 and 5 Others conditions; however, there were no statistically significant difference between the 1 and 5 Others conditions. For the Real Groups condition, each group size condition was significantly different from the other conditions (all ps < .05).

## CHAPTER SUMMARY

In this chapter we took the general logic of the one-way ANOVA and expanded it to include a second independent variable. There are many advantages of conducting this more complex statistic including: (1) The two-way ANOVA allows us to examine the effects of more than one independent variable on the dependent variable; (2) the two-way ANOVA is more cost effective than multiple one-way ANOVAs; (3) the two-way ANOVA tends to increase power and improve the generalizability of the data; and (4) the two-way ANOVA allows us to look for the presence of an interaction between independent variables.

You learned that the two-way ANOVA partitions the total variance among observations into two general components—main effects and interaction. Each of the two main effects represents the effect that the variable alone has on the variance of the observations. The interaction represents differences among the treatment conditions that the main effects

**Table 15.8**

**Summary Table for Two-Factor ANOVA**

| Sum of Squares | Degrees of Freedom | Mean Square | F-Ratio |
|---|---|---|---|
| $SS_A = \Sigma \frac{(X_{\bullet j \bullet})^2}{n_{j \bullet}} - \frac{(\Sigma X_{ijk})^2}{N}$ | $df_A = j - 1$ | $MS_A = \frac{SS_A}{df_A}$ | $F_A = \frac{MS_A}{MS_{within}}$ |
| $SS_B = \Sigma \frac{(X_{\bullet \bullet k})^2}{n_{\bullet k}} - \frac{(\Sigma X_{ijk})^2}{N}$ | $df_B = k - 1$ | $MS_B = \frac{SS_B}{df_B}$ | $F_B = \frac{MS_B}{MS_{within}}$ |
| $SS_{AB} = \Sigma \frac{(X_{\bullet jk})^2}{n_{jk}} - \frac{(\Sigma X_{ijk})^2}{N} -$ | | | |
| $(SS_A + SS_B)$ | $df_{AB} = (j - 1)(k - 1)$ | $MS_{AB} = \frac{SS_{AB}}{df_{AB}}$ | $F_{AB} = \frac{MS_{AB}}{MS_{within}}$ |
| $SS_{within} = \Sigma X_{ijk}^2 - \Sigma \frac{(X_{\bullet jk})^2}{n_{jk}}$ | $df_{within} = \Sigma(n_{jk} - 1)$ | $MS_{within} = \frac{SS_{within}}{df_{within}}$ | |
| $SS_{total} = \Sigma X_{ijk}^2 - \frac{(\Sigma X_{ijk})^2}{N}$ | $df_{total} = N - 1$ | | |

Omega Squared:

$$\omega^2 = \frac{df_{effect}(F_{effect} - 1)}{df_{effect}(F_{effect} - 1) + N}$$

Effect size:

$$f_{effect} = \sqrt{\frac{\eta^2}{1 - \eta^2}}$$

$$\eta^2 = \frac{df_{effect}\, F_{effect}}{df_{effect}\, F_{effect} +} \quad \text{or } \eta^2 = \frac{SS_{effect}}{SS_{total}}$$

alone cannot explain. In this chapter we spent much time examining the meaning of an interaction and the need to explain the interaction.

We also examined how we can apply the formulae for $\omega^2$ and Cohen's effect size to help us interpret the data. Specifically, $\omega^2$ estimates the percentage of the total variance that can be accounted for by the factor, holding all other factors constant. Using **f** we can estimate the effect size of the factor and determine the power associated with the statistic. We also showed you how to use Tukey's HSD to examine the main effects and the interaction.

Finally, we concluded that the same procedures for calculating the $2 \times 2$ ANOVA are applied to other designs such as a $2 \times 3$ design. Although the design of the ANOVA is different, the interpretation of the main effects and interaction is the same as the simple $2 \times 2$ design.

**TERMS TO** R E M E M B E R

| | |
|---|---|
| additive effect | main effect |
| factorial design | two-factor or two-way ANOVA |
| interaction | |

E X E R C I S E S

1. In the accompanying summary table for an analysis of variance some of the information has been left out. Fill in the missing material and then continue with the following questions.

| Source | SS | df | MS | F |
|--------|------|------|--------|------|
| A | 160.0 | _____ | 160.00 | _____ |
| B | 372.1 | _____ | 372.10 | _____ |
| AB | 3.6 | _____ | 3.60 | _____ |
| Within | 1221.1 | _____ | 33.92 | _____ |
| Total | _____ | 39 | | |

a. How many levels of Factor A were there?
b. How many levels of Factor B were there?
c. Assuming equal sample sizes, how many subjects were in each treatment condition?
d. What are the degrees of freedom for each $F$-ratio?
e. If $\alpha = .05$, what is the critical value of $F$ required to reject the null hypothesis for each $F$-ratio?
f. Given the data reported in the summary table, which null hypothesis should be rejected?

2. In the accompanying summary table for an analysis of variance some of the information has been left out. Fill in the missing material and then continue with the following questions.
a. How many levels of Factor A were there?
b. How many levels of Factor B were there?
c. Assuming equal sample sizes, how many subjects were in each treatment condition?
d. What is the degrees of freedom for each $F$-ratio?
e. If $\alpha = .05$, what is the critical value of $F$ required to reject the null hypothesis for each $F$-ratio?

| Source | SS | df | MS | F |
|--------|------|------|------|------|
| A | _____ | 3 | _____ | 3.13 |
| B | 53.67 | 2 | _____ | _____ |
| AB | _____ | 6 | 3.54 | _____ |
| Within | 237.72 | | 2.83 | |
| Total | _____ | 95 | | |

**f.** Given the data reported in the summary table, which null hypothesis should be rejected?

**3.** In the accompanying summary table for an analysis of variance some of the information has been left out. Fill in the missing material and then continue with the following questions.

| Source | SS | df | MS | F |
|--------|---------|------|-------|------|
| A | 162.60 | _____ | 54.20 | _____ |
| B | 251.09 | _____ | 62.77 | _____ |
| AB | 704.87 | _____ | 58.74 | _____ |
| Within | 2016.80 | | | |
| Total | _____ | 99 | | |

**a.** How many levels of Factor A were there?
**b.** How many levels of Factor B were there?
**c.** Assuming equal sample sizes, how many subjects were in each treatment condition?
**d.** What is the degrees of freedom for each $F$-ratio?
**e.** If $\alpha = .05$, what is the critical value of $F$ required to reject the null hypothesis for each $F$-ratio?
**f.** Given the data reported in the summary table, which null hypothesis should be rejected?

**4.** In the accompanying summary table for an analysis of variance some of the information has been left out. Fill in the missing material and then continue with the following questions.

| Source | SS | df | MS | F |
|--------|---------|------|------|------|
| A | 178.99 | 2 | _____ | _____ |
| B | 106.39 | 2 | _____ | _____ |
| AB | 242.01 | _____ | _____ | _____ |
| Within | | | | |
| Total | 1561.00 | 49 | | |

**a.** How many levels of Factor A were there?
**b.** How many levels of Factor B were there?
**c.** Assuming equal sample sizes, how many subjects were in each treatment condition?
**d.** What is the degrees of freedom for each $F$-ratio?
**e.** If $\alpha = .05$, what is the critical value of $F$ required to reject the null hypothesis for each $F$-ratio?
**f.** Given the data reported in the summary table, which null hypothesis should be rejected?

**5.** Use the following figure to complete the questions that follow.
**a.** What are the means associated with each level of Factor A (assume equal sample sizes).

**b.** What are the means associated with each level of Factor B (assume equal sample sizes).

**c.** Does there appear to be an interaction? What about these data would lead you to make this conclusion?

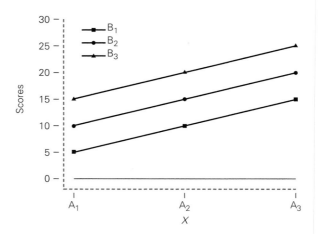

**6.** Use the following figure to complete the questions that follow.

**a.** What are the means associated with each level of Factor A (assume equal sample sizes).

**b.** What are the means associated with each level of Factor B (assume equal sample sizes).

**c.** Does there appear to be an interaction? What about these data would lead you to make this conclusion?

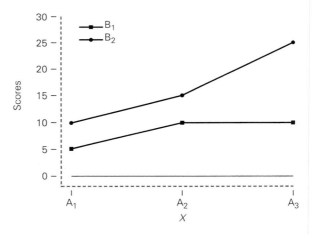

**7.** Does one's mood influence how well things are remembered? To conduct the research, a psychologist decides to use two factors. Factor A represents the emotional condition under which the subjects are required to learn a list of words. Subjects are made to feel either happy ($a_1$) or sad ($a_2$). Factor B represents the emotional condition under which the subjects' memory is tested. Subjects are made to feel either happy ($b_1$) or sad ($b_2$) before they are told to recall the words. The data appear in the accompanying table.

**a.** Draw a graph of these data and describe the results. Does there appear to be a main effect for Factor A? Does there appear to be a main effect for Factor B? Does there appear to be an interaction of the two factors?

**b.** Conduct a two-way ANOVA on these data and prepare a summary table.

**c.** Is there a statistically significant interaction between these two factors?

| | EMOTION EXPERIENCED WHEN LEARNING LIST | |
|---|---|---|
| **Emotion Experienced During Recall of List** | **Sad ($a_1$)** | **Happy ($a_2$)** |
| **Sad ($b_1$)** | 70 | 48 |
| | 77 | 41 |
| | 79 | 47 |
| | 77 | 49 |
| | 78 | 44 |
| **Happy ($b_2$)** | 39 | 85 |
| | 40 | 83 |
| | 40 | 88 |
| | 36 | 88 |
| | 38 | 86 |

**d.** Calculate $\omega^2$ for each main effect and the interaction.

**e.** Write a brief description of these results based on the analysis conducted.

**8.** A researcher examined two factors that he believed would affect how hard a person would work on a task. For the experiment, the researcher had subjects attempt to complete a collection of 70 anagrams. Forty-two of the anagrams could be solved whereas the remaining 28 were impossible to solve. The researcher told all subjects that they could quit the task at any time. The dependent variable was the number of anagrams the person attempted to complete before quitting.

The researcher manipulated two variables. The first variable was expectancy. The researcher told the subjects in the High Expectancy groups

| | EXPECTANCY | |
|---|---|---|
| **Warning About Impossible-to-Solve Anagrams** | **High ($a_1$)** | **Low ($a_2$)** |
| **Warning ($b_1$)** | 40 | 27 |
| | 30 | 17 |
| | 38 | 25 |
| | 32 | 24 |
| | 36 | 20 |
| | 36 | 20 |
| | 34 | 21 |
| | 34 | 22 |
| | 35 | 22 |
| **No Warning ($b_2$)** | 26 | 27 |
| | 26 | 19 |
| | 18 | 26 |
| | 18 | 26 |
| | 24 | 20 |
| | 20 | 25 |
| | 22 | 21 |
| | 22 | 21 |
| | 22 | 22 |

that their score on an anagram pretest was one of the best scores observed. The subjects in the Low Expectancy groups learned that their pretest scores were extremely low. The second variable was a Warning that some of the anagrams could not be solved. Half the subjects were warned that the test contained some unsolvable anagrams whereas the other subjects were not warned. Here are the data.

**a.** Draw a graph of these data and describe the results. Does there appear to be a main effect for Factor A? Does there appear to be a main effect for Factor B? Does there appear to be an interaction of the two factors?

**b.** Conduct a two-way ANOVA on these data and prepare a summary table.

**c.** Is there a statistically significant interaction between these two factors?

**d.** Calculate $\omega^2$ for each main effect and the interaction.

**e.** Write a brief description of these results based on the analysis conducted.

**9.** Several social psychologists (Helmrich, Aronson, & LeFan, 1970) examined the effects of seeing a person commit a social blunder. The subjects were divided into three conditions on the basis of their self-esteem scores ($a_1$ = low, $a_2$ = medium, $a_3$ = high). Some subjects in each self-esteem group saw a competent person accidentally spill a cup of coffee on the floor ($b_1$). The other subjects saw the competent person in the same situation but not spilling the coffee ($b_2$). All subjects were then asked to indicate how much they liked the person on a 20-point scale (20 = like a lot). Some data based on that study appear in the following table.

|  | Low ($a_1$) | Medium ($a_2$) | High ($a_3$) |
|---|---|---|---|
| **Spill Coffee ($b_1$)** | 6 | 13 | 10 |
|  | 4 | 15 | 8 |
|  | 7 | 14 | 11 |
|  | 8 | 11 | 12 |
| **No Spill ($b_2$)** | 12 | 9 | 13 |
|  | 10 | 11 | 11 |
|  | 13 | 8 | 14 |
|  | 14 | 7 | 15 |

**a.** Draw a graph of these data and describe the results. Does there appear to be a main effect for Factor A? Does there appear to be a main effect for Factor B? Does there appear to be an interaction of the two factors?

**b.** Conduct a two-way ANOVA on these data and prepare a summary table.

**c.** Is there a statistically significant interaction between these two factors?

**d.** Calculate $\omega^2$ for each main effect and the interaction.

# 16

# Analysis of Variance With Correlated Samples

## 16.1 / Introduction

The real advantage of the ANOVA is its ability to partition the total variance into its constituent parts. As you learned in the previous chapters, we can use the ANOVA to identify between-groups variance and within-groups variance. In Chapter 15 you learned how to examine the data when there are two independent variables. As you saw, adding a second independent variable had many advantages, one of which was the increase of statistical power. In this chapter we examine another variant of the ANOVA. Specifically, we will show you how to apply the ANOVA to research where we use either a repeated-measures design or a matched-groups design. Under some circumstances, these designs and ANOVAs offer the researcher the opportunity to conduct experiments that have considerable statistical power.

### Logic of the Correlated Samples ANOVA

Many factors contribute to the random variability of scores in behavioral research. Among the most important of these factors are individual differences among the subjects. Individual differences refer to the natural variation that occurs among people. Each person who participates in an experiment is different from every other person and brings to the experiment an additional source of variance. Although the independent variable will have the same general effect on each person, it may have a greater effect on some people and less of an effect on others.

In the conventional independent groups ANOVA, the variance due to individual differences is part of the error term for the ANOVA. In other words, the $MS_{within}$ represents variance due to random error and to individual differences among subjects. If we can partition out the variance due to individual differences, we can reduce the size of $MS_{within}$ and thereby increase the size of the $F$-ratio. Therefore, a correlated groups design has the potential of being more powerful than an independent groups design.

In Chapter 13 we taught you how to use the correlated groups $t$-ratio. As you saw, we used the correlation between observations in the two groups to reduce the size of the standard error of the difference between means. We do something similar with the correlated samples ANOVA. Specifically, we treat differences among the subjects as a variable. This research tactic helps us reduce $MS_{within}$. There are a number of ways we can use the correlated samples design to our advantage. Specifically, we can examine a simple repeated-measures design or a matched-groups design.

### Repeated-Measures Designs

In the simple repeated-measures design we collect the data from the same subjects on a series of occasions to determine if there are systematic changes in the subjects as time progresses. As an example of a simple repeated-measures design, imagine that we want to study the process of forgetting. To conduct our study we collect a group of subjects and have them memorize a long list of words until they can repeat the list without error. We then test the subjects every 24 hours for the next 4 days to determine how much of the list they can recall. Using this tactic allows us to use each person as his or her own control condition. Therefore, the repeated-measures design allows us to better examine how the independent variable affects the dependent variable.

Repeated measurement of the same subject can introduce unwanted effects in some cases. For example, a subject may get tired or bored if repeatedly tested under different conditions. We use the phrase **carryover effect** to describe situations where experience in one testing condition affects the subject's performance in the following conditions. Because carryover effects are not part of the purpose of the experiment, they confound the interpretation of our results.

We can reduce the amount of the carryover effect by randomly changing the sequence of testing for each subject. For example, if you wanted to test the effects of three dosages of a drug on the same subjects, you would shuffle the order in which each subject receives the different dosages. One subject would receive the pattern 1, 2, 3 whereas another subject may receive the pattern 3, 1, 2. Researchers call this shuffling procedure **counterbalancing.** Research designs that use specific sequencing procedures have names, such as Latin Square designs. These experiments require advanced ANOVA procedures that are beyond the scope of this text.

In summary, if you are looking at how a behavior changes over time, then a simple repeated-measures design will work. We conduct such experiments to specifically examine how subjects change over time. If you are conducting an experiment that requires multiple testing, but the order of the testing is not important, then you need to consult an advanced text on research methods and statistics for guidance.

### Matched-Group Design

In the matched-group design we may believe that a particular characteristic of the subjects may influence the results of our study. Therefore, we measure that characteristic and assign subjects to groups based on the subject's score. Imagine that we want to test the effectiveness of four different types of psychotherapy for the treatment of depression. We believe that the initial severity of the person's depression will influence his or her success in psychotherapy. Therefore, we administer a standard test of depression to all subjects. We then take the 4 subjects with the lowest scores and randomly assign them to one of the four treatment groups. We do this for all subjects in order to ensure that each group is matched with respect to initial levels of depression. Again, because we are not using simple randomization procedures our treatment groups will lack the independence found in our earlier example. The matched-groups design will allow us to use the information we have to match subjects to further analyze our components of variance.

### The Logic of the Correlated Samples Design

For the conventional between-subjects design we saw that the total sum of squares is partitioned into two parts, the sum of squares for between-groups variance and the sum of squares for within-groups variance.

$$SS_{total} = SS_{between} + SS_{within}$$

Using the correlated groups design, we can partition additional variance information from $SS_{within}$. Specifically, we can identify that variance that is due to differences among subjects. Therefore, we can partition the total sum of squares into three components.

$$SS_{total} = SS_{between} + SS_{subjects} + SS_{within}$$

**■ Carryover Effect:**

Refers to research when the researcher tests the same subjects on more than one occasion. The effects of previous measurements may affect the subject's behavior on subsequent trials.

**■ Counterbalancing**

A technique used to reduce the effects of carryover effect. The order of treatment conditions is shuffled among the subjects.

The sum of squares for subjects, $SS_{\text{subjects}}$, represents the systematic differences among subjects across groups. If there is a strong individual-differences component to the experiment, then $SS_{\text{subjects}}$ will be a relatively large number. Consequently, $SS_{\text{within}}$ will be smaller than if the individual-differences were not identified. If, however, there is no individual-differences component, the $SS_{\text{subjects}}$ will be small or equal 0. The consequence of a relatively small $SS_{\text{subjects}}$ will be that the power of the ANOVA will be low.

## 16.2 / Single Factor Correlated Groups ANOVA

Table 16.1 presents the equations for sum of squares and degrees of freedom for the single factor correlated groups ANOVA. To determine the mean square, divide the sum of squares by the corresponding degrees of freedom. The $F$-ratio is the $MS_{\text{between}}$ divided by the $MS_{\text{within}}$.

We will use an example to help us explain how to estimate the different sources of variance. For our experiment, we will assume that we are using a matched-groups design. The same calculations will apply to a simple repeated-measures design, however.

Imagine that we wish to evaluate three different methods for teaching students basic algebra. We have twenty-one 12-year-old students who have taken a math achievement test. Based on their scores, we can rank the students from highest to lowest math ability. The three students with the best math score are each randomly assigned to one of the three training programs. When we are done distributing subjects to the treatment conditions, each training condition will have the sample proportion of the better and less able students. Specifically, the first subject in each group will have the highest math test score.

After the training, the subjects are tested again using a 20-item math test. The data in Table 16.2 provide the basis for our example.

The first step to take is to ensure the homogeneity of variance.

$$F_{\text{max}} = \frac{82.86}{49.43}$$

$$F_{\text{max}} = 1.68$$

**Table** | **16.1**

**Computational Equations for the Sum of Squares and Degrees of Freedom for the Single Factor Correlated Groups Design**

| | | |
|---|---|---|
| $SS_{\text{between}} = \dfrac{\Sigma X_{\bullet j}^2}{n_j} - \dfrac{(\Sigma X_{ij})^2}{N}$ | $df_{\text{between}} = j - 1$ | (16.1) |
| $SS_{\text{subjects}} = \dfrac{\Sigma X_{i\bullet}^2}{j} - \dfrac{(\Sigma X_{ij})^2}{N}$ | $df_{\text{subjects}} = n - 1$ | (16.2) |
| $SS_{\text{within}} = \Sigma X_{ij}^2 - \dfrac{\Sigma X_{i\bullet}^2}{j} - \dfrac{\Sigma X_{\bullet j}^2}{n} + \dfrac{(\Sigma X_{ij})^2}{N}$ | $df_{\text{within}} = (j-1)(n-1)$ | (16.3) |
| $SS_{\text{total}} = \Sigma X_{ij}^2 - \dfrac{(\Sigma X_{ij})^2}{N}$ | $df_{\text{total}} = N - 1$ | (16.4) |

**Table** 16.2

Hypothetical Data for a Matched-Group Design

| Subject | $X_1$ | $X_2$ | $X_3$ | $X_{i\bullet}$ |
|---------|-------|-------|-------|----------------|
| 1 | $X_{1\,1} = 15$ | $X_{1\,2} = 13$ | $X_{1\,3} = 11$ | $X_{1\bullet} = 39$ |
| 2 | $X_{2\,1} = 13$ | $X_{2\,2} = 9$ | $X_{2\,3} = 10$ | $X_{2\bullet} = 32$ |
| 3 | $X_{3\,1} = 12$ | $X_{3\,2} = 10$ | $X_{3\,3} = 9$ | $X_{3\bullet} = 31$ |
| 4 | $X_{4\,1} = 11$ | $X_{4\,2} = 13$ | $X_{4\,3} = 12$ | $X_{4\bullet} = 36$ |
| 5 | $X_{5\,1} = 9$ | $X_{5\,2} = 5$ | $X_{5\,3} = 7$ | $X_{5\bullet} = 21$ |
| 6 | $X_{6\,1} = 8$ | $X_{6\,2} = 6$ | $X_{6\,3} = 4$ | $X_{6\bullet} = 18$ |
| 7 | $X_{7\,1} = 7$ | $X_{7\,2} = 5$ | $X_{7\,3} = 2$ | $X_{7\bullet} = 14$ |

$$X_{\bullet 1} = 75 \qquad X_{\bullet 2} = 61 \qquad X_{\bullet 3} = 55$$
$$\Sigma X_{i1}^2 = 853 \qquad \Sigma X_{i2}^2 = 605 \qquad \Sigma X_{i3}^2 = 515$$
$$\overline{X}_1 = 10.71 \qquad \overline{X}_2 = 8.71 \qquad \overline{X}_3 = 7.86$$
$$\hat{s}_1^2 = 8.24 \qquad \hat{s}_2^2 = 12.24 \qquad \hat{s}_3^2 = 13.81$$

$$X_{\bullet\bullet} = 191$$
$$\Sigma X_{ij}^2 = 1973$$

**Stem-and-Leaf Presentation of the Data**

| Group 1 | | Group 2 | | Group 3 | |
|---------|-----|---------|------|---------|-----|
| 0* | | 0* | | 0* | 24 |
| 0• | 789 | 0• | 5569 | 0• | 79 |
| 1* | 123 | 1* | 033 | 1* | 012 |
| 1• | 5 | 1• | | 1• | |

**Histogram of the data presented in Table 16.2:**

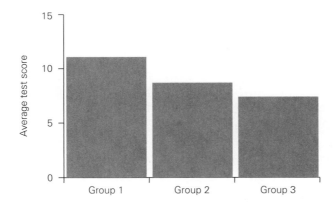

The $F_{max}$ is well below the critical value for $j = 3$ and $n = 7$ $F_{\text{critical}} = 8.38$. Therefore, we can assume homogeneity of variance and continue with our analysis.

As with all our inferential statistics, we need to present our rationale for conducting the appropriate statistic and making an inference about the significance of the results.

**Null Hypothesis:** $H_0$: $\sigma^2_{\text{between}} = \sigma^2_{\text{within}}$: The differences among the means are due to sampling error and other random events.

**Alternative Hypothesis:** $H_1$: $\sigma^2_{\text{between}} \neq \sigma^2_{\text{within}}$: The differences among the means are too large to be due simply to sampling error.

**Statistical Test:** The $F$-ratio for a correlated groups design.

**Significance Level:** $\alpha = .05$. If the size of the $F$-ratio is sufficiently large, we will reject the null hypothesis in favor of the alternative hypothesis.

**Sampling Distribution:** The $F$-distribution with $df$ of $df_N = 2$, $df_D = 12$.

**Critical Region for Rejection of $H_0$:** $F_{\text{critical}} = 3.88$. If the $F$-ratio is equal to or larger than 3.88 we will reject $H_0$.

With this analysis we must introduce you to some additional uses of the dot notation. As you can see, the sum of the rows and the columns contains dots ($\bullet$). For example, $X_{\bullet j}$ indicates that all the data have been totaled in the jth group. In Table 16.2, $X_{\bullet 1} = 75$, the total of all subjects in the first treatment group. When we sum across treatment groups we use the notation $\Sigma X_{ij}$. Because the correlated group ANOVA allows us to estimate the variance among subjects, we need to determine the total for each subject. For the sum across subjects, we use $X_{j \bullet}$. For example, $X_{1 \bullet} = 39$ is the total of the scores for the first subject in each condition. Using this notation, we can now estimate the variances components for the ANOVA.

### Total Variance

$$SS_{\text{total}} = \Sigma X_{ij}^2 - \frac{(\Sigma X_{ij})^2}{N} \qquad\qquad df_{\text{total}} = N - 1$$

$$SS_{\text{total}} = 1973 - \frac{(191)^2}{21} = 1973 - 1737.1905 \qquad df_{\text{total}} = 21 - 1$$

$$SS_{\text{total}} = 235.8095 \qquad\qquad df_{\text{total}} = 20$$

### Between-Groups Variance

$$SS_{\text{between}} = \frac{\Sigma X_{\bullet j}^2}{n_j} - \frac{(\Sigma X_{ij})^2}{N} \qquad\qquad df_{\text{between}} = j - 1$$

$$SS_{\text{between}} = \frac{75^2 + 61^2 + 55^2}{7} - \frac{(191)^2}{21}$$

$$SS_{\text{between}} = \frac{12371}{7} - \frac{36481}{21}$$

$$SS_{\text{between}} = 1767.2857 - 1737.1905 \qquad df_{\text{between}} = 3 - 1$$

$$SS_{\text{between}} = 30.0952 \qquad\qquad df_{\text{between}} = 2$$

### Subjects Variance

$$SS_{\text{subjects}} = \frac{\Sigma X_{i \bullet}^2}{j} - \frac{(\Sigma X_{ij})^2}{N} \qquad\qquad df_{\text{subjects}} = n - 1$$

$$SS_{\text{subjects}} = \frac{39^2 + 32^2 + 31^2 + 36^2 + 21^2 + 18^2 + 14^2}{3} - 1737.1905$$

$$SS_{\text{subjects}} = \frac{5763}{3} - 1732.1905$$

$$SS_{\text{subjects}} = 1921 - 1732.1905 \qquad\qquad df_{\text{subjects}} = 7 - 1$$

$$SS_{\text{subjects}} = 183.8095 \qquad\qquad df_{\text{subjects}} = 6$$

**Table 16.3**

**The ANOVA Summary Table for a Single Factor ANOVA with Repeated Measures**

| Source | SS | df | MS | F |
|---|---|---|---|---|
| Between-groups | 30.10 | 2 | 15.05 | 8.27 |
| Subjects | 183.81 | 6 | 30.64 | 16.84 |
| Within-groups | 21.90 | 12 | 1.82 | |
| Total | 235.81 | 20 | | |

### Within-Groups Variance

$$SS_{within} = \Sigma X_{ij}^2 - \frac{\Sigma X_{i\bullet}^2}{j} - \frac{\Sigma X_{\bullet j}^2}{n} + \frac{(\Sigma X_{ij})^2}{N} \quad df_{within} = (j-1)(n-1)$$

$$SS_{within} = 1973 - 1767.2857 - 1921 + 1737.1905 \quad df_{within} = (2)(6)$$

$$SS_{within} = 21.9007 \quad\quad\quad\quad\quad\quad\quad df_{within} = 12$$

As a quick check of our work, we should find that $SS_{total} = SS_{between} + SS_{subjects} + SS_{within}$. According to the calculations: $235.81 = 30.10 + 183.81 + 21.90$. Therefore, we have done our work correctly.

We can use these calculations to create our summary table as shown in Table 16.3.

Because $F_{observed}$ is greater than $F_{critical}$ ($8.27 > 3.88$), we can reject $H_0$ in favor of $H_1$. We can interpret the between-groups $F$-ratio the same way we have for the conventional ANOVA. The statistic is an omnibus score that indicates that the variance between the means is greater than would be expected by random variation. The same cautions about over-interpretation of any inferential statistic apply to this form of the ANOVA.

## $\omega^2$ for Correlated-Samples ANOVA

When we use $\omega^2$ for the one-way correlated samples ANOVA, we must use a different equation than the one presented earlier for the independent groups design. The version of $\omega^2$ presented here allows us to represent the degree to which our independent variable influences the dependent variable, less the effect of the individual differences between subjects.

$$\omega^2 = \frac{df_{between}(F_{between} - 1)}{df_{between}(F_{between} - 1) + F_{subjects}(n) + j(n)} \quad (16.5)$$

$$\omega^2 = \frac{2(8.26 - 1)}{2(8.26 - 1) + 16.84(7) + 3(7)}$$

$$\omega^2 = \frac{14.52}{14.52 + 117.88 + 21}$$

$$\omega^2 = \frac{14.52}{153.40}$$

$$\omega^2 = .095$$

We can conclude that approximately 9.5% of the difference among the three training groups was due to the teaching method the children received. The rest of the differences between subjects were due to the student's general ability at math and random error.

Many people may find this equation daunting. As an alternative, a quick estimate of the association between the independent variable and the dependent variables is given by $\eta^2$ where

$$\eta^2 = \frac{SS_{\text{between}}}{SS_{\text{total}}} \tag{16.6}$$

For this example we find that $\eta^2 = 30.10/235.81 = .128$. Using $\eta^2$ we can also calculate the effect size for the training programs. Specifically,

$$\mathbf{f} = \sqrt{\frac{\eta^2}{1 - \eta^2}} \tag{16.7}$$

$$\mathbf{f} = \sqrt{\frac{.128}{1 - .128}}$$

$$\mathbf{f} = \sqrt{\frac{.128}{.872}}$$

$$\mathbf{f} = \sqrt{0.146}$$

$$\mathbf{f} = .383.$$

Therefore, we can conclude that we have a moderate to large effect size for this variable. What is the power of our statistic? Because we are using the same subjects on several occasions, we need to adjust the size of $n$ by counting the total number of observations that contributed to the $F$-ratio. In this example, we have 21 subjects, therefore $n = 21$. We can round down to 20 for the purposes of estimation. Look at Table M in Appendix D under the category Degrees of Freedom Numerator = 2. We can assume that $\alpha = .05$, and we can round the effect size from .383 to .40. Using these values, we can estimate the power to be: $1 - \beta = .78$. Therefore, the chance that we could replicate these findings using 7 subjects is large. If we attempted to replicate the study with 30 subjects (10 in each group) the power would be .93.

## Applying Tukey's HSD Test

Recall that Tukey's HSD test may be applied to individual comparisons when the overall $F$-ratio is statistically significant. Because the between-groups $F$-ratio is statistically significant, we can proceed with a comparison of the three means.

Referring to Table L of Appendix D, we find that $q_{\text{critical}} = 3.77$ for $k = 3$, $df_{\text{within}} = 12$, and $\alpha = .05$. We find that

$$\text{HSD} = q_{\text{critical}} \sqrt{\frac{MS_{\text{within}}}{n}}$$

$$\text{HSD} = 3.77 \sqrt{\frac{1.82}{7}}$$

$$\text{HSD} = 1.92$$

From the table of comparisons shown in Table 16.4, we can conclude that students in Group 1 had higher average scores than subjects in Groups 2 and 3.

**Table** 16.4

**The Differences Among the Means for the Data Presented in Table 16.2**

| | | TREATMENT GROUPS | | |
| --- | --- | --- | --- | --- |
| | | Group 1 10.71 | Group 2 8.71 | Group 3 7.86 |
| Treatment Groups | 10.71 | — | 2.00* | 2.85* |
| | 8.71 | — | — | 0.85 |
| | 7.86 | — | — | — |

## 16.3 Mixed-Model ANOVA

As you might have guessed, we can continue to apply the logic of the ANOVA to various research applications. In this section we will examine how to conduct a mixed-model ANOVA. The mixed-model ANOVA gets its name because there are two types of variables, a between-subjects variable and a within-subjects variable.

A **between-subjects** variable is an independent variable to which the researcher randomly assigns the subjects. In other words, for each level of a between-subjects variable there is a different and independent group of subjects. The essential characteristic of a between-subjects variable is that subjects experience only one level of the variable. For example, if the researcher randomly assigns subjects to only one level of the variable, it is a between-subjects variable. If the researcher uses a subject variable (e.g., men vs. women, depressed vs. not depressed) then the variable is also a between-subjects variable. The term, between-subjects, refers to the fact that the ANOVA compares the differences between independent groups of different subjects.

By contrast, a **within-subjects** variable is a correlated groups variable. Therefore, if a factor represents a repeated measures variable or matched groups variable, we call it a within-subjects variable. The essential characteristic of a within-subjects variable is that we collect data from the same subject on different occasions or under different treatment conditions. We also use within-subjects to describe the matched groups research design.

■ **Between-subjects Variable:**

A treatment variable to which subjects are randomly assigned. The groups are independent of each other and the subjects experience only one level of the independent variable.

■ **Within-Subjects Variable:**

A variable for which the subjects are tested under multiple conditions.

### Equations for the Mixed-Models ANOVA

Table 16.5 presents the equations for the sum of squares and degrees of freedom for the mixed models ANOVA. There are several things to note. There are two special sum of squares we use to estimate error variance. First, the $SS_{subjects}$ estimates the variance that can be attributed to the differences among subjects. Therefore, when we examine the difference among the means for Factor A (the between-subjects factor), we will use $SS_{subjects}$ to estimate error. When we examine the differences among the means for Factor B (the within-subjects factor), we use $SS_{B \times subjects}$ to estimate error. As always, we determine the mean square by dividing the sum of squares by the matching degrees of freedom.

**Table 16.5**

**Notation for the Sum of Squares and Degrees of Freedom for the Mixed-Models ANOVA**

$$SS_A = \frac{\Sigma(X_{\bullet j \bullet})^2}{nk} - \frac{(\Sigma X_{ijk})^2}{N} \qquad\qquad df_A = j - 1 \qquad\qquad (16.8)$$

$$SS_{\text{subjects}} = \frac{\Sigma(X_{i \bullet \bullet})^2}{k} - \frac{\Sigma(X_{\bullet j \bullet})^2}{nk} \qquad\qquad df_{\text{subjects}} = j(n - 1) \qquad\qquad (16.9)$$

$$SS_B = \frac{\Sigma(X_{\bullet \bullet k})^2}{nj} - \frac{(\Sigma X_{ijk})^2}{N} \qquad\qquad df_B = k - 1 \qquad\qquad (16.10)$$

$$SS_{AB} = \frac{\Sigma(X_{\bullet ij})^2}{n} - \frac{(\Sigma X_{ijk})^2}{N} - SS_A - SS_B \qquad\qquad df_{AB} = (j - 1)(k - 1) \qquad\qquad (16.11)$$

$$SS_{B \times \text{subjects}} = \Sigma X_{ijk}^2 - \frac{\Sigma(X_{\bullet ij})^2}{n} + \frac{\Sigma(X_{\bullet j \bullet})^2}{nk} \qquad\qquad df_{B \times \text{subjects}} = j(n - 1)(k - 1) \qquad\qquad (16.12)$$

$$SS_{\text{total}} = \Sigma X_{ijk}^2 - \frac{\Sigma(X_{ijk})^2}{N} \qquad\qquad df_{\text{total}} = N - 1 \qquad\qquad (16.13)$$

## A Numerical Example

Let's look at a simple experiment to demonstrate how to use a mixed-model ANOVA. A psychology major wanted to study the effect of reinforcement on rats' maze learning behavior for a class project. For the research she used a large maze that contained many alleys. The student designated one corner of the maze to be the "start box" and the other corner to be the "goal box."

The student selected 10 rats from the department's animal facilities and randomly divided them into two groups. The first group received no reinforcement (food) while they were in the maze. The student merely put the rat in the maze for 10 minutes and counted the number of times they changed direction in the maze. The second group of rats received reinforcement when they reached the goal box. Again, the researcher counted the number of times the rats changed direction before reaching the goal box. She repeated this procedure for 4 days. Table 16.6 presents the data.

As always, we do a quick check for homogeneity of variance using the $F_{\max}$ test.

$$F_{\max} = \frac{4.3}{1.3}$$

$$F_{\max} = 3.3$$

The $F_{\max}$ is well below the critical value for $j = 8$ and $n = 5$ $F_{\text{critical}} = 33.6$. Therefore, we can continue with our analysis.

### Null Hypothesis:

Factor A      $H_0$: $\sigma_\alpha^2 + \sigma_{\text{subjects}}^2 = \sigma_{\text{subjects}}^2$

Factor B      $H_0$: $\sigma_\beta^2 + \sigma_{\beta \times \text{subjects}}^2 = \sigma_{\beta \times \text{subjects}}^2$

Factor AB      $H_0$: $\sigma_{\alpha\beta}^2 + \sigma_{B \times \text{subjects}}^2 = \sigma_{\beta \times \text{subjects}}^2$

### Alternative Hypothesis:

Factor A      $H_1$: $\sigma_\alpha^2 + \sigma_{\text{subjects}}^2 \neq \sigma_{\text{subjects}}^2$

**Table 16.6**

**Hypothetical Data for An Experiment Examining the Effects of Reinforcement on Maze Learning over a 4-Day Period**

| | Subject | Day 1 | Day 2 | Day 3 | Day 4 | |
|---|---|---|---|---|---|---|
| | 1 | 10 | 9 | 10 | 10 | 39 |
| No | 2 | 12 | 12 | 12 | 12 | 48 |
| Reinforcement | 3 | 9 | 9 | 10 | 12 | 40 |
| | 4 | 8 | 9 | 8 | 7 | 32 |
| | 5 | 11 | 11 | 10 | 10 | 42 |
| | $X_{\bullet 1k}$ | 50 | 50 | 50 | 51 | $X_{\bullet 1 \bullet} = 201$ |
| | $\hat{s}^2_{1k}$ | 2.5 | 2.0 | 2.0 | 4.2 | |
| | 6 | 12 | 3 | 9 | 3 | 27 |
| | 7 | 11 | 4 | 4 | 2 | 21 |
| Reinforcement | 8 | 8 | 7 | 3 | 4 | 22 |
| | 9 | 9 | 6 | 6 | 5 | 26 |
| | 10 | 10 | 8 | 10 | 4 | 32 |
| | $X_{\bullet 2k}$ | 50 | 28 | 32 | 18 | $X_{\bullet 2 \bullet} = 128$ |
| | $\hat{s}^2_{2k}$ | 2.5 | 4.3 | 3.05 | 1.3 | |
| | $X_{\bullet\bullet k}$ | 100.0 | 78.0 | 82.0 | 69.0 | $X_{\bullet\bullet\bullet} = 329$ |

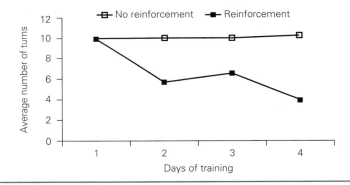

**Figure 16.1**

**Graph of the data presented in Table 16.6.**

Factor B      $H_1: \sigma^2_{\beta} + \sigma^2_{\beta \times \text{subjects}} \neq \sigma^2_{\beta \times \text{subjects}}$

Factor AB     $H_1: \sigma^2_{\alpha\beta} + \sigma^2_{B \times \text{subjects}} \neq \sigma^2_{\beta \times \text{subjects}}$

***Statistical Test:***  The $F$-ratio for a correlated groups design.

***Significance Level:***  $\alpha = .05$.

***Sampling Distribution:***

Factor A      The $F$-distribution with $df$ of 1, 8.

Factor B      The $F$-distribution with $df$ of 3, 24.

Factor AB     The $F$-distribution with $df$ of 3, 24.

***Critical Region for Rejection of $H_0$:***

Factor A      $F_{\text{critical}} = 5.32$

Factor B      $F_{\text{critical}} = 3.01$

Factor AB     $F_{\text{critical}} = 3.01$

### Between-Subjects Variable Variance: Factor A

$$SS_A = \frac{\Sigma(X_{\bullet j \bullet})^2}{nk} - \frac{(\Sigma X_{ijk})^2}{N} \qquad\qquad df_A = j - 1$$

$$SS_A = \frac{201^2 + 128^2}{5(4)} - \frac{(329)^2}{40} \qquad\qquad df_A = 2 - 1$$

$$SS_A = \frac{56785}{20} - \frac{108241}{40}$$

$$SS_A = 2839.25 - 2706.025$$

$$SS_A = 133.225 \qquad\qquad df_A = 1$$

$$MS_A = \frac{133.225}{1}$$

$$MS_A = 133.225$$

### Variance Due to Subjects Across Factor A

$$SS_{\text{subjects}} = \frac{\Sigma(X_{i \bullet \bullet})^2}{k} - \frac{\Sigma(X_{\bullet j \bullet})^2}{nk} \qquad\qquad df_{\text{subjects}} = j(n - 1)$$

$$SS_{\text{subjects}} = \frac{39^2 + 48^2 + 40^2 + \cdots 26^2 + 32^2}{4} - \frac{201^2 + 128^2}{5(4)}$$
$$df_{\text{subjects}} = 2(5 - 1)$$

$$SS_{\text{subjects}} = \frac{11567}{4} - \frac{56785}{20} \qquad\qquad df_{\text{subjects}} = 2(4)$$

$$SS_{\text{subjects}} = 2891.75 - 2839.25$$

$$SS_{\text{subjects}} = 52.50 \qquad\qquad df_{\text{subjects}} = 8$$

$$MS_{\text{subjects}} = \frac{52.5}{8}$$

$$MS_{\text{subjects}} = 6.5625$$

### Within-Subjects Variable Variance: Factor B

$$SS_B = \frac{\Sigma(X_{\bullet \bullet k})^2}{nj} - \frac{(\Sigma X_{ijk})^2}{N} \qquad\qquad df_B = k - 1$$

$$SS_B = \frac{100^2 + 78^2 + 82^2 + 69^2}{5(2)} - \frac{(329)^2}{40} \qquad\qquad df_B = 4 - 1$$

$$SS_B = \frac{27569}{10} - \frac{108241}{40}$$

$$SS_B = 2756.9 - 2706.025$$

$$SS_B = 50.875 \qquad\qquad df_B = 3$$

$$MS_B = \frac{50.875}{3}$$

$$MS_B = 16.9583$$

### Interaction Variance

$$SS_{AB} = \frac{\Sigma(X_{\bullet ij})^2}{n} - \frac{(\Sigma X_{ijk})^2}{N} - SS_A - SS_B \qquad df_{AB} = (kj - 1)(k - 1)$$

$$SS_{AB} = \frac{50^2 + 50^2 + \cdots 32^2 + 18^2}{5} - \frac{(329)^2}{40} - 133.225 - 50.875$$

$$df_{AB} = (2 - 1)(4 - 1)$$

$$SS_{AB} = \frac{14733}{5} - \frac{108241}{40} - 133.225 - 50.875 \qquad df_{AB} = (1)(3)$$

$$SS_{AB} = 2946.6 - 2706.025 - 133.225 - 50.875$$

$$SS_{AB} = 56.475 \qquad\qquad df_{AB} = 3$$

$$MS_{AB} = \frac{56.475}{3}$$

$$MS_{AB} = 18.825$$

### Factor B × Subjects Variance

$$SS_{B\times\text{subjects}} = \Sigma X_{ijk}^2 - \frac{\Sigma(X_{\bullet ij})}{n} - \frac{\Sigma(X_{i\bullet\bullet})^2}{k} + \frac{\Sigma(X_{\bullet j\bullet})^2}{nk}$$

$$df_{B\times\text{subjects}} = j(n - 1)(k - 1)$$

$$SS_{B\times\text{subjects}} = 3059 - 2946.6 - 2891.75 + 2839.25$$

$$df_{B\times\text{subjects}} = 2(5 - 1)(4 - 1)$$

$$SS_{B\times\text{subjects}} = 59.900 \qquad df_{B\times\text{subjects}} = 24$$

$$MS_{B\times\text{subjects}} = \frac{59.900}{24}$$

$$MS_{B\times\text{subjects}} = 2.4958$$

### Total Sum of Squares

$$SS_{\text{total}} = \Sigma X_{ijk}^2 - \frac{(\Sigma X_{ijk})^2}{N} \qquad df_{\text{total}} = N - 1$$

$$SS_{\text{total}} = 3059 - 2706.025$$

$$SS_{\text{total}} = 352.975 \qquad df_{\text{total}} = 39$$

As a check, the $SS_{\text{total}}$ must equal the sum of the other sum of squares: $SS_{\text{total}} = SS_A + SS_B + SS_{AB} + SS_{\text{subjects}} + SS_{B\times\text{subjects}}$. According to our calculations, $352.975 = 133.225 + 50.875 + 56.475 + 52.50 + 59.90$.

These calculations allow us to create our ANOVA summary table as shown in Table 16.7. As you can see, for each $F$-ratio, $F_{\text{observed}}$ is greater than $F_{\text{critical}}$. The interpretation of these results is obvious. The interaction between reinforcement conditions and days indicates that those rats receiv-

**Table** 16.7

**The ANOVA Summary Table for a Mixed-Model ANOVA**

| Source | SS | df | MS | F |
|--------|------|-----|--------|--------|
| A | 133.225 | 1 | 133.225 | 20.301 |
| Subjects | 52.500 | 8 | 6.563 | 2.629 |
| B | 50.875 | 3 | 16.958 | 6.795 |
| AB | 56.475 | 3 | 18.825 | 7.543 |
| B×subjects | 59.900 | 24 | 2.496 | |
| Total | 352.975 | 39 | | |

ing food learned how to solve the maze and improved their performance on each day. The rats not receiving food showed no change in their behavior.

## Tukey's HSD

As with the other forms of the ANOVA, we can now apply our *a posteriori* analysis techniques to the data. Let's focus on using Tukey's HSD test to compare the individual means.

When we use the Tukey HSD for the mixed-model ANOVA, it is critical that we use the correct $MS_{within}$. Because of the mixed-model design, this step can be a bit tricky. Here are the explicit steps we need to follow for the main effects and the interaction.

***Factor A***   The $HSD_A$ uses the $MS_{subjects}$ and $n(k)$ to determine the critical values for the differences among the means. For our example,

$$HSD_A = q_{critical}\sqrt{\frac{MS_{subjects}}{n(k)}} \tag{16.14}$$

$$HSD_A = 2.86\sqrt{\frac{6.563}{5(4)}}$$

$$HSD_A = 1.638$$

Obviously, the difference between the reinforcement and nonreinforcement groups is statistically significant (e.g., $10.0 - 6.4 = 3.60$). If there were more than two groups, we could use $HSD_A$ to compare all possible combinations of means.

***Factor B***   The $HSD_B$ uses the $MS_{within}$ and $n(j)$ to determine the critical values for the differences between the means. Although we do not calculate $MS_{within}$ for the ANOVA summary table, we can find its value relatively easily. Remember that the mixed-model ANOVA partitions the within-groups variance to variance due to subjects and variance due to error. Therefore, to reconstruct the within-groups variance we use the following equation

$$MS_{within} = \frac{SS_{subjects} + SS_{B \times subjects}}{df_{subjects} + df_{B \times subjects}} \tag{16.15}$$

For these data,

$$MS_{within} = \frac{52.50 + 59.9}{8 + 24}$$

$$MS_{within} = \frac{112.4}{32}$$

$$MS_{within} = 3.512$$

With this information we can proceed to determine the HSD for Factor B and the interaction.

$$HSD_B = q_{critical}\sqrt{\frac{MS_{within}}{n(j)}} \tag{16.16}$$

$$HSD_B = 3.44\sqrt{\frac{3.512}{5(2)}}$$

$$HSD_B = 2.039$$

**Table 16.8**

**The Difference Between Means for Factor B**

|      | 10.0 | 8.2 | 7.8 | 6.9  |
|------|------|-----|-----|------|
| 10.0 | —    | 1.8 | 2.2* | 3.1* |
| 8.2  | —    | —   | 0.4 | 1.3  |
| 7.8  | —    | —   | —   | 0.9  |
| 6.9  | —    | —   | —   | —    |

Note: *, $p < .05$

Comparing the differences among the main effect means reveals that the average performance for days 2 and 4 were significantly less than Day 1. The other differences are not statistically significant, however. Because there is a statistically significant interaction, we will need to examine the data in detail (see Table 16.8).

***Factor AB*** To determine the HSD for the interaction we use

$$\text{HSD}_{AB} = q_{\text{critical}} \sqrt{\frac{MS_{\text{within}}}{n}}$$

$$\text{HSD}_{AB} = 4.52 \sqrt{\frac{4.3231}{5}}$$

$$\text{HSD}_{AB} = 4.2029$$

The means for the interaction are shown in Table 16.9.

As you can see in Table 16.9 and Figure 16.1, the interaction appears to be due to the fact that the averages for the No Reinforcement Group do not change across the 4 days. By contrast, the averages for the Reinforcement Group do decrease across the 4 days. For example, on the second day, there is a statistically significant difference between the two groups. The fact that the difference between the two groups on Day 3 is not statistically significant is a bit odd, especially given the difference on Day 4. The lack of a statistically significant difference on Day 3 could represent an error in recording, chance factors, or both. The HSD does, however, confirm our inspection of the data: Rats receiving no reinforcement showed no change in their behavior whereas rats receiving reinforcement quickly learned to navigate the maze.

## $\omega^2$ for Mixed-Model ANOVA

To calculate $\omega^2$ for the mixed-model ANOVA we need to apply a more complex formula for our work (Dodd & Schultz, 1973). The first step is to calculate a common denominator for each $\omega^2$.

**Table 16.9**

**The Means for the Interaction of the Data Presented in Table 16.6**

|                 | DAY  |     |     |     |
|-----------------|------|-----|-----|-----|
|                 | 1    | 2   | 3   | 4   |
| No reinforcement | 10.0 | 10.0 | 10.0 | 10.2 |
| Reinforcement   | 10.0 | 5.6 | 6.4 | 3.6 |

$$F_A(j - 1) + F_s(n - 1) + f_B(k - 1) + F_{AB}((j - 1)(k - 1)) + \\ (n - 1)(jk - 1) \qquad (16.17)$$

$$20.301(2 - 1) + 2.629(5 - 1) + 6.795(4 - 1) + \\ 7.543((2 - 1)(4 - 1)) + (5 - 1)(2(4) - 1)$$

$$20.301 + 10.516 + 20.385 + 22.629 + 28$$

$$101.831$$

The numerators for the three $\omega^2$s are

$$A = (F_A - 1)(j - 1) = (20.301 - 1)(2 - 1) = 19.301 \qquad (16.18)$$

$$B = (F_B - 1)(k - 1) = (6.795 - 1)(4 - 1) = 17.386 \qquad (16.19)$$

$$AB = (F_{AB} - 1)(j - 1)(k - 1) = (7.543 - 1)(2 - 1)(4 - 1) \\ = 19.269 \qquad (16.20)$$

Therefore, the three values of $\omega^2$ are

$$\omega_A^2 = \frac{19.301}{101.831} \qquad \omega_A^2 = .1895$$

$$\omega_B^2 = \frac{17.386}{101.831} \qquad \omega_B^2 = .1707$$

$$\omega_{AB}^2 = \frac{19.269}{101.831} \qquad \omega_{AB}^2 = .1892$$

## Effect Size for Mixed-Model ANOVA

Determining the effect size for the mixed-model is relatively simple. First, we use the basic equation for determining $\eta^2$ and then determine the effect size, **f**. Specifically, we use the equations,

$$\eta_{\text{effect}}^2 = \frac{SS_{\text{effect}}}{SS_{\text{total}}}$$

and

$$\mathbf{f}_{\text{effect}} = \sqrt{\frac{\eta_{\text{effect}}^2}{1 - \eta_{\text{effect}}^2}}$$

For the current data, we can determine the effect size of the main effects and the interaction.

$$\eta_A^2 = \frac{133.225}{352.975} \qquad \eta_A^2 = .377 \qquad f_A = \sqrt{\frac{.377}{1 - .377}} \qquad f_A = .78$$

$$\eta_B^2 = \frac{50.875}{352.975} \qquad \eta_B^2 = .144 \qquad f_B = \sqrt{\frac{.144}{1 - .144}} \qquad f_B = .41$$

$$\eta_{AB}^2 = \frac{56.475}{352.975} \qquad \eta_{AB}^2 = .160 \qquad f_{AB} = \sqrt{\frac{.160}{1 - .160}} \qquad f_{AB} = .44$$

The effect size for each factor is large, especially the effect size for Factor A, the reinforcement versus the nonreinforcement conditions.

## CHAPTER SUMMARY

The goal was to introduce you to another advanced from of the analysis of variance. Specifically, we showed you how to calculate the ANOVA when the research design calls for correlated groups. A correlated groups design refers to the fact that we believe that there is a meaningful correlation among the groups for one factor. We create this correlation by using a matched-groups design or a repeated-measures design. The primary advantage of the correlated groups ANOVA is that it provides greater power. The increase in power comes from the fact that we can determine how much variance among the subjects causes the random variation among the scores. A specific advantage of the repeated measures design is that it requires fewer subjects. Because we measure each subject under a number of treatment conditions, each subject serves as the control condition.

Correlated groups designs should be used with care, however. In some cases, the effects of one treatment condition can influence the behavior of the subject in another condition. This carryover effect is a potential confound that must be examined. In some cases, we can reduce the carryover effect using random sequence of treatments. Statisticians call these sequences Latin Squares. There are other situations where no methodological procedure will adequately remove the effects of the carryover effect. In these cases, the correlated groups ANOVA should not be used. The suitable alternative would be a conventional ANOVA where all the variables represent independent groups.

## TERMS TO REMEMBER

between-subjects variable          counterbalancing
carryover effect                   within-subjects variable

## EXERCISES

1. Juliana wants to conduct a study in which people view videotaped interactions between two people. After each presentation, the subject will be asked a series of questions.
   **a.** Explain how a carryover effect could effect Juliana's results.
   **b.** What advice would you offer to Juliana concerning the design of the research?
   **c.** Why is a repeated-measures design desirable for Juliana's research?

2. Explain why a single factor correlated groups ANOVA may have greater power than a comparable between-groups experiment.

3. How can you distinguish between a between-subjects factor and a within-subjects factor?

4. Some people say that for within-subjects factors, each subject serves as his or her own control condition. Explain why this statement is accurate.

5. A well-known phenomenon in experimental psychology is the forgetting curve. A psychology major conducted a study to replicate the effect. The student recruited 5 students from an introductory psychology course and

asked them to memorize 60 simple words consisting of 3 to 4 letters. After 8 hours, the researcher called each student and asked him or her to recite the list. The researcher then called the students again at the same time of day for the next 5 days and recorded the number of words they recalled. Here are the data.

| Subject | 1 | 2 | 3 | 4 | 5 | 6 |
|---------|----|----|----|----|----|----|
| 1 | 47 | 45 | 32 | 32 | 26 | 27 |
| 2 | 51 | 45 | 37 | 35 | 30 | 31 |
| 3 | 52 | 46 | 40 | 36 | 33 | 29 |
| 4 | 50 | 45 | 41 | 37 | 30 | 35 |
| 5 | 49 | 43 | 38 | 39 | 28 | 31 |

**a.** Draw a stem-and-leaf diagram of these data. What preliminary conclusions can you draw from these data?
**b.** What are the researcher's null and alternative hypotheses?
**c.** Use these data to conduct an analysis of variance. Report the final summary table.
**d.** Assume the researcher set $\alpha = .05$. Is the researcher justified in rejecting the null hypothesis?
**e.** What is $\omega^2$ for this experiment? How should this statistic be described?
**f.** Use Tukey's HSD to compare the individual means. Use the results to describe the change in the subject's memory of the list.

**6.** The following data represent the results of a hypothetical experiment. As you can see, there is one factor with four levels.

| Subject | 1 | 2 | 3 | 4 |
|---------|---|---|---|---|
| 1 | 2 | 4 | 6 | 8 |
| 2 | 3 | 4 | 5 | 7 |
| 3 | 4 | 5 | 8 | 9 |
| 4 | 3 | 4 | 7 | 7 |
| 5 | 3 | 4 | 7 | 7 |
| 6 | 4 | 5 | 8 | 8 |
| 7 | 2 | 4 | 5 | 5 |
| 8 | 2 | 4 | 6 | 7 |

**a.** Use the data to calculate the single factor correlated groups design. Calculate $\omega^2$ and $\eta^2$.
**b.** Use the same data to calculate a conventional between-groups one-way ANOVA (see Chapter 14). Calculate $\omega^2$ and $\eta^2$.
**c.** Compare the $SS_{total}$ for the two ANOVAs. Are they the same or different? Why?
**d.** Compare $SS_{within}$ for the two ANOVAs. Are they the same or different? Why?
**e.** Compare the $SS_{between}$ for the two ANOVAs. Are they the same or different? Why?

**7.** Do men and women use different ethical principles to resolve moral dilemmas? A researcher randomly selected 10 subjects (5 men and 5 women). She then had them explain how they would resolve four separate moral dilemmas. Two of the dilemmas stressed circumstances involving legal issues and social norms. The other dilemmas stressed circumstances that involved the care and well being of other people. The order of the dilemmas was randomly arranged for each subject. A trained reader scored each subject's responses using a 100-point scale where low scores represent a greater concern for following rules and high scores represent a greater concern for the welfare for others. Here are the data.

|  | Subject | 1 | 2 | 3 | 4 |
|---|---|---|---|---|---|
| **Men** | 1 | 26 | 34 | 60 | 70 |
|  | 2 | 47 | 51 | 71 | 98 |
|  | 3 | 24 | 36 | 57 | 59 |
|  | 4 | 39 | 49 | 66 | 89 |
|  | 5 | 44 | 54 | 67 | 73 |
| **Woman** | 6 | 32 | 49 | 86 | 65 |
|  | 7 | 37 | 49 | 73 | 69 |
|  | 8 | 47 | 47 | 70 | 51 |
|  | 9 | 37 | 45 | 53 | 82 |
|  | 10 | 33 | 43 | 53 | 57 |

a. Draw a graph of the data. What preliminary conclusions can you draw from the data?
b. Use these data to conduct an analysis of variance? Report the final summary table.
c. Assume the researcher set $\alpha = .05$. Is the researcher justified in rejecting the null hypotheses?
d. What is $\omega^2$ for each effect? How should this statistic be described?

# 17

# Analysis of Categorical Data: $\chi^2$ and Binomial Tests

## 17.1 / Introduction

In the previous chapters we examined a number of statistical procedures based on Student's $t$-ratio and Fisher's analysis of variance. Although these are extremely useful statistics, we cannot use them for every research project. Specifically, we may use the $t$-ratio and ANOVA when we want to compare group means. There are many times, however, when the dependent variable is a categorical variable or a nominal scale. As we will show you in this chapter, there are several useful statistical tests that we can use to analyze these data.

Before we jump into examining these statistical tests, we should review background information. As you should recall, a nominal scale consists of a set of mutually exclusive classes. We then count the number of items that fit within each class. For example, you can ask a random sample of students to tell you their major. The data will indicate the number of accounting, economics, philosophy, education, and psychology majors. Because the data are nominal, it does not make sense to calculate an average. Indeed, what would it tell you to say that the average major is a 3.473? We can, however, ask questions about the frequency of different events. For example, assume that 12 students in your sample said that they were philosophy majors. Using the $\chi^2$ (chi-square) test, we can determine if this number is high, low, or normal.

Karl Pearson, the statistician who proposed the correlation coefficient ($r$), also devised a statistical test we call the $\chi^2$ test. There are many uses of this test. In general, the **$\chi^2$ test** is an inferential statistic that allows us to determine whether the number of observations within mutually exclusive classes differs significantly from hypothetical conditions. In this chapter we will examine several general uses of the $\chi^2$ test including the goodness-of-fit test and the test of independence.

A second statistical test that we will examine is the binomial test. The binomial test is another popular inferential statistic that researchers use when analyzing categorical data. Specifically, we will show you how to use the binomial test to conduct hypothesis testing on proportions.

Although the $\chi^2$ and binomial test are new statistical procedures for you, they follow the familiar logic of hypothesis testing. For both tests, we prepare null and alternative hypotheses, select a sampling distribution, determine a critical value for rejecting the null hypothesis, and then perform the necessary computations. With this brief introduction, let's begin by examining the goodness-of-fit test.

### ■ Chi-Square $\chi^2$ Test:

An inferential statistic used to examine the frequencies of categorical, mutually exclusive classes. The statistic determines whether the observed frequencies equal hypothesized frequencies.

### ■ Goodness-of-Fit Test:

A version of the $\chi^2$ test that determines whether a statistically significant difference exists between observed frequencies and expected frequencies within mutually exclusive classes.

## 17.2 / Goodness-of-Fit Test

The purpose of the **goodness-of-fit $\chi^2$ test** is to determine whether the frequencies of different mutually exclusive categories match or fit the hypothesized population. Let's use a simple example to illustrate how this version of the $\chi^2$ test works.

At the end of their sophomore year, all students at a college must declare a major. The chair of the social sciences program is interested in the number of students who have just declared one of the social sciences as their major. For the sake of this example, assume that the college does not allow students to double major. This assumption ensures that the groups are truly mutually exclusive. Table 17.1 presents the current year's class by the major they selected.

**Table 17.1**

Hypothetical Data of the Number of Students Who Identified a Major Within the Social Science Division at the End of Their Sophomore Year

| Major | Observed Frequency |
|---|---|
| Anthropology | $O_1 = 3$ |
| Economics | $O_2 = 45$ |
| Political Science | $O_3 = 77$ |
| Psychology | $O_4 = 90$ |
| Sociology | $O_5 = 85$ |
| Total | $T = 300$ |

For the $\chi^2$ test we use $O_i$ to indicate the observed frequency within each class. The symbol $T$ represents the total of all observations. For this example, 300 students selected a major within the social sciences. Of these students, 90 selected psychology as their major.

What can we make of these data? By observation, it is clear that psychology is the most popular major and anthropology the least popular. How do these data compare to national trends? In other words, the chair wants to know whether the current data match the national pattern.

In Table 17.2, we present the observed frequencies along with the expected frequencies. The column titled "Proportions" represents the hypothetical data based on the national sample. Specifically, in this sample, 25% of the social science majors are psychology majors. The "Expected" column represents the frequency that would be observed if the sample followed the population parameters. Specifically, if this college is like the national average, 75 social science majors should be psychology majors.

Looking at Table 17.2, you can see that there is a difference between the observed frequencies and the expected frequencies. For example, there appear to be fewer than expected anthropology and economics majors, and more than expected political science, psychology, and sociology majors. We can now ask the obvious question, do these differences represent random variation or are the differences statistically significant? To answer that question, we will turn to the $\chi^2$ test of goodness-of-fit.

$$\chi^2 = \Sigma \frac{(O_i - E_i)^2}{E_i} \tag{17.1}$$

**Table 17.2**

An Extension of the Data Presented in Table 17.1

| Major | Observed | Proportions Based on National Data | Expected = $p_i \times T_i$ Frequencies |
|---|---|---|---|
| Anthropology | $O_1 = 3$ | $p_1 = .05$ | $E_1 = .05 \times 300 = 15$ |
| Economics | $O_2 = 45$ | $p_2 = .30$ | $E_2 = .30 \times 300 = 90$ |
| Political Science | $O_3 = 77$ | $p_3 = .25$ | $E_3 = .25 \times 300 = 75$ |
| Psychology | $O_4 = 90$ | $p_4 = .25$ | $E_4 = .25 \times 300 = 75$ |
| Sociology | $O_5 = 85$ | $p_5 = .15$ | $E_5 = .15 \times 300 = 45$ |
| Total | $T = 300$ | 1.00 | $E_\bullet = 300$ |

The proportions represent data based on national data. The expected values ($E_i$) equal the hypothetical proportion multiplied by the total number of observations $T$.

Equation 17.1 defines the $\chi^2$ test. The numerator is the squared difference between the observed ($O_i$) and expected ($E_i$) scores. The denominator is the expected value for the same class. If the differences between the observed and expected scores are due to chance, then the $\chi^2$ will be relatively small. By contrast, $\chi^2$ will be large if there is a nonrandom difference between the observed and expected scores.

As with the other inferential statistics you have learned to use, the $\chi^2$ test has its own family of sampling distributions. The shape of the $\chi^2$ sampling distribution is determined by the degrees of freedom. The degrees of freedom for the $\chi^2$ test is one less the number of classes. Stated mathematically, the degrees of freedom for the goodness-of-fitness test is

$$df = k - 1 \tag{17.2}$$

In our example, there are five majors, therefore the degrees of freedom are $df = 4$ ($df = 5 - 1$). Table Q of Appendix D lists the critical values for the $\chi^2$ test.

Like the ANOVA, the $\chi^2$ is a nondirectional and omnibus test. This means that the $\chi^2$ will indicate whether the pattern of observed frequencies deviates from the expected frequencies. It does not, however, indicate whether one particular difference is significantly greater or less than the expected value.

## Assumptions of the Goodness-of-Fit Test

There are several assumptions that must be met in order for the goodness-of-fit $\chi^2$ to provide valid results. These assumptions include (1) mutually exclusive categories, (2) independence of observations, and (3) sufficient sample size.

We have already examined the requirement of mutually exclusive categories. In summary, each subject must be placed in one, and only one, category. Examples of mutually exclusive events include one's sex, political party, and marital status. In other cases, we must ensure that we use procedures that prohibit double counting of the subjects. If the college allowed students to double major, then $T$ would be artificially inflated because some students would be counted twice. In our current example, we prohibited double majors. Therefore, we have met the assumption of mutually exclusive categories.

The independence of observations means that the classification of subjects into one category has no effect on other categories. For example, if students must have a 3.0 cumulative GPA in order to declare Economics as a major, then the distribution of majors is not independent. To meet the independence requirement, there must be equivalent criteria for entry into each category. The special admission requirement means that some majors may be easier to enter than others. This practice violates the independence rule because not all students would be freely able to select that major.

The final requirement is that sample size be sufficiently large. The general rule for this requirement is that none of the expected frequencies be less than 5. If the expected frequencies are too small, the $\chi^2$ will be more likely to produce erroneous results.

## Worked Examples

In our example, we see we have met all the requirements of the $\chi^2$ test. The groups are mutually exclusive, the classification of the students is independent, and the sample size is sufficiently large. Therefore, we can proceed with the test. We begin by defining the null and

**Table** | **17.3**

An Extension of the Data Presented in Tables 17.1 and 17.2. This Table Shows
How One Calculates $\chi^2$.

| Major | O | E | $O_i - E_i$ | $(O_i - E_i)^2$ | $\dfrac{(O_i - E_i)^2}{E_i}$ |
|---|---|---|---|---|---|
| Anthropology | 3 | 15 | −12 | 144 | 9.6000 |
| Economics | 45 | 90 | −45 | 2025 | 22.5000 |
| Political Science | 77 | 75 | 2 | 4 | 0.0533 |
| Psychology | 90 | 75 | 15 | 225 | 3.0000 |
| Sociology | 85 | 45 | 40 | 1600 | 35.5556 |
| Total | 300 | 300 | 0 | | $\chi^2 = 70.7089$ |

alternative hypotheses and determining the criteria for rejecting $\chi^2$. Our
calculations are presented in Table 17.3.

**Null Hypothesis:**   $H_0$: The observed frequencies match the expected
frequencies defined by the population.

**Alternative Hypothesis:**   $H_1$: The observed frequencies do not match
the expected frequencies defined by the population.

**Statistical Test:**   The $\chi^2$ goodness-of-fit test.

**Significance Level:**   $\alpha = .05$. If the size of $\chi^2$ is sufficiently large, we
will reject the null hypothesis in favor of the alternative hypothesis.

**Sampling Distribution:**

$\chi^2$ Distribution with $df = 5 - 1 = 4$
$\chi^2_{critical} = 9.488$

If the $\chi^2_{observed}$ is equal to or greater than $\chi^2_{critical}$, we will reject $H_0$.

Obviously, the value of $\chi^2_{observed}$ is much greater than $\chi^2_{critical}$ ($70.709 >$
$9.488$). Therefore, we can reject the null hypothesis that the enrollment pattern at this college matches the national average. Based on the differences
between the observed and expected frequencies, it appears that Sociology
and Psychology are more popular majors at this college than national trends.

In this example, we used empirical data to determine the values of
the expected frequencies. This tactic allowed us to determine if the selection at this college differed from national trends. There are cases where
we want to determine if the data are evenly distributed across a set of
categories. Let's consider an example.

A social worker wants to know if the rate of depressive episodes differs by the time of year. Using the data collected by a large hospital, the
social worker records the number of first-time admissions for depression that occurred during the past 5 years. The social worker divides the
year into the four seasons (e.g., Winter = December, January, and Feb-
ruary). Table 17.4 presents the data.

In this case, the researcher may want to know whether the frequency
of severe depression varies with the time of year. The simplest null hypothesis to propose is that the rate of admission for depression is equal
throughout the year. Therefore, the researcher determined that the expected number of admissions in each season should be equal. In other
words, the expected frequency for each season is $517.5 = 2070/4$. The remainder of the test follows the same procedures listed above.

**Table 17.4**

**Hypothetical Data Representing the Number of People Admitted to a Hospital for Depression During Different Seasons Over a 5-Year Interval**

| Season | O | E | $O_i - E_i$ | $(O_i - E_i)^2$ | $\dfrac{(O_i - E_i)^2}{E_i}$ |
|--------|-----|-------|-------|----------|---------|
| Spring | 495 | 517.5 | −22.5 | 506.25 | 0.9783 |
| Summer | 503 | 517.5 | −14.5 | 210.25 | 0.4063 |
| Autumn | 491 | 517.5 | −26.5 | 702.25 | 1.3570 |
| Winter | 581 | 517.5 | 63.5 | 4032.25 | 7.7918 |
| Total | 2070 | 2070 | 0 | | $\chi^2 = 10.5334$ |

With $df = 3$ and $\alpha = .05$, $\chi^2_{critical} = 7.815$. Because the observed value of $\chi^2$ is greater than the critical value, we may assume that the distribution of admissions for depression does deviate from the expected hypothesized values. By casual inspection of the data, it appears that there is an increase of admissions during the winter months.

## 17.3 / The $\chi^2$ Test of Independence

We can now extend the logic of the $\chi^2$ to cases where we have two categorical variables. The question that we want to address is whether these variables are independent of each other. Let's look at a simple example to help illustrate how to use the $\chi^2$ **test of independence.**

Are people more willing to help people like themselves or are people willing to be helpful regardless of the person in need of help? We can answer this question by conducting an experiment. A social psychologist recruits students for a research project. When they arrive, the researcher tells the subjects that they have the opportunity to help another person by loaning them $50. In the Similar condition, the subjects learn that they have much in common with the person receiving the loan. In the Not Similar condition, the subjects learn that they have little in common with the person receiving the loan. Table 17.5 presents the hypothetical data.

The $\chi^2$ test allows us to determine if helping behavior is related to the perceived similarity between the person offering help and the person receiving help. If the two variables are independent of each other, then the rate of helping behavior will have nothing to do with the experimental condition. By contrast, if similarity does affect helping behavior, then we should observe a nonrandom pattern in the data.

■ $\chi^2$ **Test of Independence:**

A version of the $\chi^2$ test that determines whether the distribution of frequencies for two categorical variables is independent.

**Table 17.5**

**Hypothetical Data From an Experiment Examining the Degree to Which People Are Likely to Lend a Stranger $50 If the Stranger Is Perceived as Similar or Not Similar to the Subject**

| | EXPERIMENTAL CONDITION | | |
|--------------|---------|-------------|-----------|
| | Similar | Not Similar | Row Total |
| Helped | 35 | 10 | 45 |
| No help | 15 | 40 | 55 |
| Column total | 50 | 50 | 100 |

**Table** 17.6

**An Extension of the Data Presented in Table 17.5. This Table Illustrates How One Calculates the Expected Values for Each Cell.**

| | EXPERIMENTAL CONDITION | | |
|---|---|---|---|
| | **Similar** | **Not Similar** | **Row Total** |
| Helped | $O_{1\,1} = 35$ $E_{1\,1} = \dfrac{45 \times 50}{100}$ $E_{1\,1} = 22.5$ | $O_{1\,2} = 10$ $E_{1\,2} = \dfrac{45 \times 50}{100}$ $E_{1\,2} = 22.5$ | $R_1 = \ \ 45$ |
| No Help | $O_{2\,1} = 15$ $E_{2\,1} = \dfrac{55 \times 50}{100}$ $E_{2\,1} = 27.5$ | $O_{2\,2} = 40$ $E_{2\,2} = \dfrac{55 \times 50}{100}$ $E_{2\,2} = 27.5$ | $R_2 = \ \ 55$ |
| Column total | $C_1 = 50$ | $C_2 = 50$ | $T = 100$ |

As with the goodness-of-fit test, we need to determine the expected value for each cell in the table. We determine the expected frequencies using Equation 17.3.

$$E_{ij} = \frac{R_i C_j}{T} \tag{17.3}$$

In this equation, $R_i$ and $C_j$ represent the row and column totals for each category and $T$ represents the total number of observations. Table 17.6 presents the expected values for the data.

In all cases, the sum of the expected values will always equal the row, column, and grand total of observations. Mathematically, $\Sigma E_{i\bullet} = R_i$, $\Sigma E_{\bullet j} = C_j$, and $\Sigma E_{ij} = T$.

If there is no relation between the two conditions, then the overall difference between the observed and expected frequencies should be minimal. If the differences between the observed and expected frequencies are large, however, then we can infer that the variables are related to each other. For this example, a statistically significant $\chi^2$ would allow us to assume that perceived similarity and helping behavior are interrelated.

$$\chi^2 = \sum_{i=1}^{r} \sum_{j=1}^{c} \frac{(O_{ij} - E_{ij})^2}{E_{ij}} \tag{17.4}$$

Equation 17.4 presents the method for calculating $\chi^2$. As you can see, the equation is much like the goodness-of-fit test. The obvious difference is that we need to calculate a ratio for each cell in the matrix. The number of rows, $r$, and the number of columns, $c$, determine the degrees of freedom. Specifically,

$$df = (r - 1)(c - 1) \tag{17.5}$$

With this information, we can now proceed to our calculations.

***Null Hypothesis:*** $H_0$: The observed frequencies match the expected frequencies.

***Alternative Hypotheses:*** $H_1$: The observed frequencies do not match the expected frequencies.

**Table | 17.7**

**An Extension of the Data Presented in Table 17.6. This Table Illustrates How One Calculates the $\chi^2$ Test of Independence.**

| | EXPERIMENTAL CONDITION | | |
|---|---|---|---|
| | **Similar** | **Not Similar** | **Row Total** |
| Helped | $O_{1\,1} = 35$<br>$E_{1\,1} = 22.5$<br>$6.944 = \dfrac{(35 - 22.5)^2}{22.5}$ | $O_{1\,2} = 10$<br>$E_{1\,2} = 22.5$<br>$6.944 = \dfrac{(10 - 22.5)^2}{22.5}$ | $R_1 = 45$ |
| No Help | $O_{2\,1} = 15$<br>$E_{2\,1} = 27.5$<br>$5.682 = \dfrac{(15 - 27.5)^2}{27.5}$ | $O_{2\,2} = 40$<br>$E_{2\,2} = 27.5$<br>$5.682 = \dfrac{(40 - 27.5)^2}{27.5}$ | $R_2 = 55$ |
| Column total | $C_1 = 50$ | $C_2 = 50$ | $T = 100$ |

$\chi^2 = 6.944 + 6.944 + 5.682 + 5.682$
$\chi^2 = 25.252$

*Statistical Test:* The $\chi^2$ test of independence.

*Significance Level:* $\alpha = .05$. If the size of $\chi^2$ is sufficiently large, we will reject the null hypothesis in favor of the alternative hypothesis.

*Sampling Distribution:*

$\chi^2$ Distribution with $df = (2 - 1)(2 - 1) = 1$

$\chi^2_{\text{critical}} = 3.841$

If the $\chi^2_{\text{observed}}$ is equal to or greater than $\chi_{\text{critical}}{}^2$ we will reject $H_0$.

As you can see in Table 17.7, $\chi^2_{\text{observed}}$ is much greater than $\chi^2_{\text{critical}}$ (25.252 > 3.841), therefore we are justified in rejecting the null hypothesis. These data allow the researcher to infer that perceived similarity influences the degree to which one person is willing to help another person. Looking at the differences between the observed and expected values, you can see what should be an obvious effect: The greater helping occurred in the Similar condition, and the least helping occurred in the Not Similar condition.

The style guide published by the American Psychological Association (1994) recommends that we report $\chi^2$ as

$$\chi^2(1, \underline{N} = 100) = 25.252, \underline{p} < .05$$

The recommended format has you report the degrees of freedom and the number of subjects used in the study. You also indicate whether the probability level associated with the statistic is greater than or less than the $\alpha$-level selected for the study.

## Assumptions of the $\chi^2$ Test

In order for the interpretation of $\chi^2$ to be valid, we must ensure that several specific assumptions of the $\chi^2$ test have been met. These assumptions are similar to the ones we reviewed for the goodness-of-fit test. Specifically, the categories must be mutually exclusive and independent, the data must represent frequencies, and the sample size must be sufficiently large.

Regarding sample size, many authors offer general guidelines for the $\chi^2$ test of independence. For example, Siegel and Castellan (1988) noted that when either the number of rows or the number of columns is greater than 2, "no more than 20% of the cells should have an expected frequency of less than 5, and no cell should have an expected frequency less than 1." (p. 199) Some researchers, however, have found that the $\chi^2$ test is robust against violations of this assumption. For example Good, Grover, and Mitchell (1977) suggested that expected values could be as low as 0.33 with no change in the probability of committing a Type I error.

Although the test appears to be robust with small frequencies, we should not forget the issue of power. As with all inferential statistics, the probability of correctly rejecting the null hypothesis increases as the sample size increases. Therefore, although $\chi^2$ may be valid when the sample size is small, the power may be insufficient to detect an effect. Cohen (1988) provides a good review of issues surrounding the power of $\chi^2$.

## 17.4 / Further Analysis of the $\chi^2$

Although the $\chi^2$ test allows us to determine whether to reject the null hypothesis, the result provides no information for determining the strength of the relation between the variables. In the next two sections, we will show you how to determine the degree to which the variables are related to each other and to examine the differences observed within each cell.

### Cramér's Coefficient $\phi$

In Chapter 8 we reviewed the Pearson product moment correlation coefficient. The Pearson $r$ is a statistic used to indicate the degree of association between two variables. The larger the absolute value of $r$, the greater the association between the two variables. **Cramér's coefficient, $\phi$,** serves the same purpose as $r$; it indicates the degree of association between two variables analyzed using the $\chi^2$ statistic. There is an important difference between $\phi$ and $r$. Specifically, whereas $r$ can range between –1 and 1, $\phi$ can only have values equal to or greater than 0.

■ **Cramér's Coefficient $\phi$:**

A descriptive statistic used with the $\chi^2$ test of independence to quantify the degree of association between the two categorical variables.

$$\phi = \sqrt{\frac{\chi^2}{T(S-1)}} \tag{17.6}$$

Equation 17.6 presents Cramér's $\phi$. In the equation, $T$ represents the total number of observations and $S$ represents the smaller value of number of rows or number of columns. The $\phi$ coefficient is a descriptive statistic. Because the size of $\phi$ depends upon the value of $\chi^2$, we can infer that if $\chi^2$ is statistically significant, the same is true of $\phi$.

We can use the data from Table 17.7 to illustrate how to calculate Cramér's $\phi$.

$$\phi = \sqrt{\frac{25.252}{100(2-1)}} \qquad \phi = \sqrt{\frac{25.252}{100}} \qquad \phi = \sqrt{0.25252}$$

$$\phi = .50$$

Therefore, we can conclude that there is a moderate to strong relation between the two variables.

## Post Hoc Analysis of $\chi^2$

You may recall from our discussion of the analysis of variance that the ANOVA is an omnibus test because it allows us to conclude that there is a relation between several variables, but it does not tell us which specific conditions are significantly different from the others. For the ANOVA, we recommend that you use Tukey's HSD to compare specific means.

A similar situation arises for the $\chi^2$ test. We can use the $\chi^2$ test to reject the hypothesis that the two conditions are independent of one another, but we cannot determine from the test which condition or conditions contributed to the statistically significant result. One technique that many researchers use is to convert the differences between the observed and expected values to a statistic called the **standardized residual, e.** Equation 17.7 presents the method of calculating $e$.

■ **Standardized Residual, e:**

A descriptive statistic that indicates the relative difference between the observed and expected scores for a single condition in the $\chi^2$ test of independence.

$$e_{ij} = \frac{O_{ij} - E_{ij}}{\sqrt{E_{ij}}} \tag{17.7}$$

We can also use the data from the table to estimate a special form of variance for the residual. Equation 17.8 (Haberman, 1973; Delucchi, 1993) presents the method of calculating the variance for each cell.

$$v_{ij} = \left(1 - \frac{C_i}{T}\right)\left(1 - \frac{R_j}{T}\right) \tag{17.8}$$

**Table 17.8**

An Extension of the Data Presented in Table 17.6. This Table Illustrates How One Calculates the Standardized Residual, *e*, and the Adjusted Residual, *ê*.

| | EXPERIMENTAL CONDITION | | |
|---|---|---|---|
| | **Similar** | **Not Similar** | **Row Total** |
| Helped | $O_{1\,1} = 35$ | $O_{1\,2} = 10$ | $R_1 = 45$ |
| | $E_{1\,1} = 22.5$ | $E_{1\,2} = 22.5$ | |
| | $e_{1\,1} = \dfrac{35 - 22.5}{\sqrt{22.5}}$ | $e_{1\,2} = \dfrac{10 - 22.5}{\sqrt{22.5}}$ | |
| | $e_{1\,1} = 2.635$ | $e_{1\,2} = -2.635$ | |
| | $v_{1\,1} = .275$ | $v_{1\,2} = .275$ | $.55 = 1 - \dfrac{45}{100}$ |
| | $\hat{e}_{1\,1} = \dfrac{2.635}{\sqrt{.275}}$ | $\hat{e}_{1\,2} = \dfrac{-2.635}{\sqrt{.275}}$ | |
| | $\hat{e}_{1\,1} = 5.02$ | $\hat{e}_{1\,2} = -5.03$ | |
| No help | $O_{2\,1} = 15$ | $O_{2\,2} = 40$ | $R_2 = 55$ |
| | $E_{2\,1} = 27.5$ | $E_{2\,2} = 27.5$ | |
| | $e_{2\,1} = \dfrac{15 - 27.5}{\sqrt{27.5}}$ | $e_{2\,2} = \dfrac{40 - 27.5}{\sqrt{27.5}}$ | |
| | $e_{2\,1} = {}^-2.384$ | $e_{2\,2} = 2.384$ | |
| | $v_{1\,1} = .225$ | $v_{1\,2} = .225$ | $.45 = 1 - \dfrac{55}{100}$ |
| | $\hat{e}_{2\,1} = \dfrac{-2.384}{\sqrt{.225}}$ | $\hat{e}_{2\,2} = \dfrac{2.384}{\sqrt{.225}}$ | |
| | $\hat{e}_{2\,1} = {}^-5.03$ | $\hat{e}_{2\,2} = 5.03$ | |
| Column total | $C_1 = 50$ | $C_2 = 50$ | $T = 100$ |
| | $.50 = 1 - \dfrac{50}{100}$ | $.50 = 1 - \dfrac{50}{100}$ | |

Finally, Equation 17.9 presents the method for calculating the **adjusted residual, $\hat{e}_{ij}$.**

$$\hat{e}_{ij} = \frac{e_{ij}}{\sqrt{v}} \qquad (17.9)$$

As a generality, $\hat{e}$ is normally distributed with a mean of 0 and a standard deviation of 1. Therefore, we can treat $\hat{e}$ as if it were a $z$-score. If the absolute value of $\hat{e}$ is sufficiently large, we can assume that the difference between the observed and expected values is statistically significant. For example, $z = \pm1.96$ represents the critical value for $\alpha = .05$, two-tailed. In other words, if $\hat{e} \leq 1.96$ or $\hat{e} \geq 1.96$, we can assume that the difference between $O$ and $E$ is statistically significant.

Table 17.8 presents the calculations for $e$, $v$, and $\hat{e}$. From this work, we can conclude that each observed value is statistically significant from the expected value.

## 17.5 / Cohen's Kappa

There are many instances when researchers use observational techniques to collect data. In the simplest case, a researcher observes a person and then classifies or categorizes the behavior. For example, a clinical psychologist may render a diagnosis of a client. The classifications could be Normal, Depressed, Bipolar, or Schizophrenic. As another example, a developmental psychologist may observe a child while a stranger enters the room. The psychologist may use a rating scale that classifies the child's behavior as Intense Fear, Fearful, Withdrawn, Inquisitive, or Engaging.

Researchers who use observational techniques want to ensure that the measurement technique is reliable. One of the more popular techniques to ensure reliability is to have two well-trained observers independently rate the behavior. The greater the level of interrater reliability, the greater confidence the researcher can have in the reliability of the data.

Cohen (1960) developed a statistic that allows us to quantify the degree of interrater reliability. This statistic, known as **Cohen's Kappa,** uses the same procedures used in the $\chi^2$ test of independence. Here is an example of how one might use Kappa.

Imagine that a researcher wanted to study the effectiveness of different forms of treatment for different psychological disorders. In order to have good data, it is critical for the researcher that clients be correctly diagnosed. Therefore, the researcher hires two clinical psychologists to diagnose potential subjects for the research. Table 17.9 presents hypothetical data for this example.

Casual inspection reveals that the psychologists agree on many of the diagnoses. For example, both agreed that 68 of the clients were depressed and 48 were schizophrenic. There were, however, disagreements. Psychologist 1, for example, labeled 6 clients depressed that Psychologist 2 diagnosed as having borderline personality disorder. We can use $\kappa$ to quantify the degree of agreement.

Cohen (1960) found that the following equation defines the degree of interrater reliability for nominal data.

$$\kappa = \frac{\Sigma O_{ii} - \Sigma E_{ii}}{T - \Sigma E_{ii}} \qquad (17.10)$$

**■ Adjusted Residual, $\hat{e}$:**

An enhancement of $e$ that is adjusted to fit the normal distribution.

**■ Cohen's Kappa, $\kappa$:**

A descriptive statistic that quantifies the interrater reliability of categorical variables.

**Table** 17.9

**Hypothetical Data Illustrating the Calculation of Cohen's Kappa. Two Clinical Psychologists Independently Diagnose 200 Clients Who Seek Psychotherapy at a Clinic.**

|  | PSYCHOLOGIST 1 | | | |
|---|---|---|---|---|
| **PSYCHOLOGIST 2** | **Depressed** | **Borderline** | **Bipolar** | **Schizophrenic** |
| Depressed | 68 | 5 | 2 | 2 |
| Borderline | 6 | 15 | 1 | 4 |
| Bipolar | 3 | 4 | 23 | 2 |
| Schizophrenic | 2 | 7 | 8 | 48 |

We can also estimate the standard deviation of $\kappa$. The utility of calculating this standard deviation is that we will be able to determine the confidence interval for $\kappa$.

$$\sigma_\kappa = \sqrt{\frac{\Sigma O_{ii}(T - \Sigma O_{ii})}{T(T - \Sigma E_{ii})^2}} \qquad (17.11)$$

For this equation, $O_{ii}$ and $E_{ii}$ represent the numbers along the main diagonal in the table. In Table 17.10 we highlighted the numbers we use in the equation. As a quick review, the values of $O_{ii}$ represent the observed agreement between the two psychologists. The values of $E_{ii}$ represent the expected agreement that could have occurred at chance levels.

According to the data presented in Table 17.10:

$$\Sigma O_{ii} = 68 + 15 + 23 + 48 \qquad \Sigma O_{ii} = 154$$
$$\Sigma E_{ii} = 30.415 + 4.03 + 5.44 + 18.20 \qquad \Sigma E_{ii} = 58.085$$

**Table** 17.10

**Extension of Table 17.9. This Table Presents Information Needed to Calculate Cohen's Kappa.**

|  | PSYCHOLOGIST 1 | | | | |
|---|---|---|---|---|---|
| **PSYCHOLOGIST 2** | **Depressed** | **Borderline** | **Bipolar** | **Schizophrenic** | $R_i$ |
| Depressed | $O_{11} = 68$<br>$E_{11} = 30.415$ | 5 | 2 | 2 | 77 |
| Borderline | 6 | $O_{22} = 15$<br>$E_{22} = 4.03$ | 1 | 4 | 26 |
| Bipolar | 3 | 4 | $O_{33} = 23$<br>$E_{33} = 5.44$ | 2 | 32 |
| Schizophrenic | 2 | 7 | 8 | $O_{44} = 48$<br>$E_{44} = 18.20$ | 65 |
| $C_j$ | 79 | 31 | 34 | 56 | $T = 200$ |

Therefore,

$$\kappa = \frac{154 - 58.085}{200 - 58.085} \qquad \kappa = \frac{95.915}{141.915} \qquad \kappa = .676$$

$$\sigma_\kappa = \sqrt{\frac{154(200 - 154)}{200(200 - 58.085)^2}} \quad \sigma_\kappa = \sqrt{\frac{7084}{4027973.4}} \quad \sigma_\kappa = 0.0419$$

The data allow us to assume that the degree of interrater reliability is moderate to high. To determine the 95% confidence interval, multiply the $z$-score of 1.96 by the standard deviation of $\kappa(\sigma_k = .082 = 0.0419 \times 1.96)$. Therefore, the 95% confidence interval for $\kappa$ is .594—.676—.758.

## 17.6 / The Binomial Test

There are many occasions when a researcher will use a two-category or dichotomous variable for a research project. A dichotomous variable is the simplest form of nominal variable because there are two categories. In some cases, the data being collected are already dichotomous. For example, people are male or female, employed or unemployed, and give either the correct or incorrect answer to a question. In other cases, the researcher may take a variable and reduce it to a dichotomous variable. A researcher may, for example, convert reading level to literate vs. illiterate. Similarly, a psychologist may classify people as depressed or not depressed.

The results of such research projects can be examined using the binomial distribution. As you may recall from our review in Chapter 10, the binomial distribution describes sampling distributions where the data represent dichotomous outcomes.

When the number of subjects is fewer than 50, we can use Table N of Appendix D to determine the critical values required to reject the null hypothesis. Let's look at a practical example to see how the **binomial test** works.

The dean of students at a college claims that since the sale of cigarettes was prohibited on campus, the proportion of students who smoke has dropped to 30%. In other words $P_0 = .30$ and $Q_0 = .70$ represent the number of students who smoke or do not smoke, respectively. Research at other colleges, however, suggests that banning the sale of cigarettes has had little effect on students' smoking behavior. Is the dean of students correct to assume that the level of smoking among students is close to 30%? To answer that question, we will need to collect data and analyze them using statistics.

Assume that we randomly sample 20 students and ask if they smoke. Table 17.11 presents the hypothetical data for this survey. In the table, we use $A$ to represent the number of people who smoke and *not A* for the number of people who do not smoke. Dividing $A$ and *not A* by the total converts them to $P$ and $Q$, respectively.

There appears to be a conflict between what the dean of students claims and the results from the sample. Specifically, the dean claimed that the level of smoking should be 30%, but the sample data suggest that the percentage of smoking is 60%. Is it possible that only 30% of the students actually smoke and that the discrepancy between these proportions is due to chance—or is there a substantive difference between these proportions that is beyond what we consider to be due to chance?

■ **Binominal Test:**

An inferential statistic used to determine whether a proportion differs significantly from a hypothesized value. The test uses the binomial distribution to determine the probability of an event.

**Table** | **17.11**

Hypothetical Data Representing the Number of Students Who Smoke Cigarettes

|  | Smoke | Do Not Smoke | Total |
|---|---|---|---|
|  | $A = 12$ | not $A = 8$ | 20 |
|  | $P = \dfrac{A}{N}$ | $Q = \dfrac{not\ A}{N}$ |  |
|  | $.60 = \dfrac{12}{20}$ | $.40 = \dfrac{8}{20}$ |  |
| Sample proportions | $P = .60$ | $Q = .40$ | 1.0 |
| Dean's claim | $P_0 = .30$ | $Q_0 = .70$ | 1.0 |

Table N in Appendix D* is a comprehensive table of values we can use for hypothesis testing using the binomial distribution. The first column, labeled $N$, consists of the number of subjects in the sample. The values range between 2 and 49. The $P$ and $Q$ rows represent the hypothesized population proportions between $P = .10$ and $P = .50$. In our example, $N = 20$ and the population parameters are predicted to be $P_0 = .30$ and $Q_0 = .70$. At the intersection of the row-column are the numbers 10 and 12. These are the critical values associated with $\alpha = .05$ and $\alpha = .01$, respectively. In other words, the probability of obtaining 10 or more smokers from a population where $P_0 = .30$ is less than 5%. The probability of obtaining 12 or more smokers from the population where $P_0 = .30$ is less than 1%. Using this information, we can now test the accuracy of the dean's claim about smoking on campus.

**Null Hypotheses:** $H_0$: The population proportion of students who smoke is equal to or less than .30 ($P_0 \leq .30$).

**Alternative Hypotheses:** $H_1$: The proportion of students who smoke is greater than .30 ($P_0 > .30$).

**Statistical Test:** The binomial test.

**Significance Level:** $\alpha = .05$, one tailed.

**Sampling Distribution:**

Binomial distribution with $P = .30$, $Q = .70$, and $N = 20$
$A_{critical} = 10$
If the $A_{observed}$ is equal to or greater than $A_{critical}$, we will reject $H_0$.

Because $A_{observed} > A_{critical}$ ($12 > 10$) we can reject the null hypothesis and infer that more students are smoking than predicted by the dean.

## Large $N$ Binomial Test

When $P = .50$ and $N \geq 50$, the binomial distribution approaches the normal distribution. As a generality, when $N \times P \times Q \geq 9$, the binomial distribution will be normally distributed. For all binomial distributions, $\mu = N \times P$ and $\sigma = \sqrt{NPQ}$. We can use this information to create a $z$-score using the binomial distribution. Specifically,

$$z = \frac{A - NP}{\sqrt{NPQ}} \tag{17.12}$$

*When $P = Q = .5$ and $N < 50$, use Table $N_1$.

To determine whether to reject the null hypothesis, just compare the $z$-score to the critical value taken from the table of the normal distribution. Here is a concrete example.

Assume that you create a random sample of 50 students. You know that in the population there are equal numbers of men and women. In your sample, there are 30 men. Is there something wrong with your sample—have you selected a greater proportion of men than you would expect by chance? We can use Equation 17.12 to answer that question.

**Null Hypothesis:** $H_0$: The population proportion of males is .50 ($P_0 = .50$).

**Alternative Hypothesis:** $H_1$: The proportion of males is not .50 ($P_0 \neq .50$).

**Statistical Test:** The binomial test, $z$-score version.

**Significance Level:** $\alpha = .05$, two tailed.

**Sampling Distribution:**

Normal distribution: $z_{\text{critical}} = 1.96$
If the absolute value of $z_{\text{observed}}$ is greater than $z_{\text{critical}}$ we will reject $H_0$.

$$z = \frac{30 - 50(.50)}{\sqrt{50(.50)(.50)}} \qquad z = \frac{30 - 25}{\sqrt{12.5}} \qquad z = \frac{5}{3.5355}$$

$$z = 1.4142$$

Because $z_{\text{observed}}$ is less than $z_{\text{critical}}$, we cannot reject the null hypothesis. Therefore, we can conclude that the difference between the observed frequency of 30 men and the expected frequency of 25 men is due to random factors.

# 17.7 / Putting It All Together

A researcher is interested in the link between alcohol abuse and various psychological disorders. More specifically, the researcher believes that people who abuse alcohol will be more likely to suffer a form of psychological disorder. To test this hypothesis, the researcher randomly selects clients of a community mental health center. The researcher evaluated the primary diagnoses for each of the clients. The data are presented in Table 17.12.

**Null Hypothesis:** $H_0$: The observed frequencies match the expected frequencies.

**Alternative Hypothesis:** $H_1$: The observed frequencies do not match the expected frequencies.

**Statistical Test:** The $\chi^2$ test of independence.

**Significance Level:** $\alpha = .05$. If the size of $\chi^2$ is sufficiently large, we will reject the null hypothesis in favor of the alternative hypothesis.

**Sampling Distribution:**

$\chi^2$ distribution with $df = (4 - 1)(2 - 1) = 3$
$\chi^2_{\text{critical}} = 7.815$
If the $\chi^2_{\text{observed}}$ is equal to or greater than $\chi^2_{\text{critical}}$, we will reject $H_0$.

**Table 17.12**

**Hypothetical Data Representing the Frequency of Various Psychological Disorders and the Presence or Absence of Alcohol Abuse**

| | PSYCHOLOGICAL DIAGNOSIS | | | | |
| --- | --- | --- | --- | --- | --- |
| | **Depression** | **Borderline** | **Schizophrenia** | **Other** | **Total** |
| **Alcohol Abuse** $\dfrac{(O_{ij} - E_{ij})^2}{E_{ij}}$ | $O_{11} = 40$ $E_{11} = 26.510$ 6.865 $e_{11} = 2.620$ $v_{11} = .3986$ $\hat{e}_{11} = 4.15^*$ | $O_{12} = 10$ $E_{12} = 10.604$ 0.034 $e_{12} = -0.1855$ $v_{12} = .5723$ $\hat{e}_{12} = -0.25$ | $O_{13} = 7$ $E_{13} = 11.540$ 1.786 $e_{13} = -1.3364$ $v_{13} = .5621$ $\hat{e}_{13} = -1.78$ | $O_{14} = 6$ $E_{14} = 14.347$ 4.856 $e_{14} = -2.2036$ $v_{14} = .5314$ $\hat{e}_{14} = -3.02^*$ | $R_1 = 63$ $p(R_1) = .3119$ $1 - p(R_1) = .6881$ |
| **No Alcohol Abuse** $\dfrac{(O_{ij} - E_{ij})^2}{E_{ij}}$ | $O_{21} = 45$ $E_{32} = 58.490$ 3.111 $e_{21} = -1.7639$ $v_{21} = .1806$ $\hat{e}_{21} = -4.15^*$ | $O_{22} = 24$ $E_{22} = 23.396$ 0.016 $e_{22} = 0.125$ $v_{s2} = .2594$ $\hat{e}_{22} = 0.25$ | $O_{23} = 30$ $E_{23} = 25.460$ 0.810 $e_{23} = 0.8997$ $v_{s3} = .2548$ $\hat{e}_{23} = 1.78$ | $O_{24} = 40$ $E_{24} = 31.653$ 2.210 $e_{24} = 1.4836$ $v_{14} = .2409$ $\hat{e}_{24} = -3.02^*$ | $R_2 = 139$ $p(R_2) = .6881$ $1 - p(R_2) = .3119$ |
| | $C_1 = 85$ $p(C_i)$ .4208 $1 - p(C_i)$ .5792 | $C_s = 34$ .1683 .8317 | $C_3 = 37$ .1832 .8168 | $C_4 = 46$ .2277 .7723 | $T = 202$ |

Notes:

$^*p < .05,$

$$e_{ij} = \frac{O_{ij} - E_{ij}}{\sqrt{E_{ij}}} \qquad v = \left(1 - \frac{C_i}{T}\right)\left(1 - \frac{R_j}{T}\right) \qquad \hat{e}_{ij} = \frac{e_{ij}}{\sqrt{v}}$$

$$\chi^2 = 6.865 + 0.034 + 1.786 + 4.856 + 3.111 + 0.016 + 0.810 + 2.201 = 19.679$$

$$\phi = \sqrt{\frac{19.679}{202(2 - 1)}} \qquad \phi = .312$$

For these data, if $\chi^2_{observed}$ is greater than $\chi^2_{critical}$, the researcher can reject the null hypothesis that the presence of alcohol abuse and psychological pathology are independent of each other. $\chi^2_{observed} = 19.679$ and $\chi^2_{critical}$ is 7.815. The null hypothesis is rejected. Further analysis of the data reveals that $\phi = .312$, which means that the degree of association between alcohol abuse and psychological diagnosis is moderate. Finally, the researcher calculated the standardized residuals for the individual cells. This analysis indicated that patients who are diagnosed as depressed are more likely to abuse alcohol.

Of course, the researcher needs to interpret the data with caution. First, the data do not represent the entire population of people who abuse alcohol or who have a severe behavioral or emotional dysfunction. The sample consisted of persons seeking treatment at a community mental health center. Therefore, the researcher should ensure that his or her generalizations to a broader population be guarded. Second, the data do not allow us to infer cause and effect. We cannot know which came first, the depression or the alcohol abuse.

If the researcher were to report the results of the study in a journal, the results section may look like the following example.

---

Social Loafing      5

Of the 202 subjects sampled, 63 (31.2%) had an additional diagnosis of alcohol abuse. Within the alcohol abuse diagnosis, 40 (63.5%) had a dual diagnosis of depression. Analysis of the data reveals a statistically significant relation between psychological diagnosis and alcohol abuse, $\chi^2(3, \underline{N} = 202) = 19.679$, $\underline{p} >, .05$, $\phi = .312$. Analysis of the residuals revealed that frequency of clients with the dual diagnosis of alcohol abuse and depression was greater than expected by chance, $\underline{z} = 4.15$, $\underline{p} >, .05$.

---

## TERMS TO R EMEMBER

adjusted residual
binomial test
chi-square $\chi^2$
$\chi^2$ test of independence
Cohen's Kappa
Cramér's coefficient
goodness-of-fit test
standardized residual

## E XERCISES

1. For the following values of $\chi^2$, determine if the obtained value is statistically significant using $\alpha = .01$.
   a. $\chi^2 = 4.12$, $df = 1$
   b. $\chi^2 = 3.94$, $df = 2$
   c. $\chi^2 = 7.99$, $df = 3$
   d. $\chi^2 = 7.99$, $df = 1$

2. Evaluate the $\chi^2$ values presented in Exercise 1 using $\alpha = .05$.

3. A student conducted a study in which three groups of rats (5 per group) were reinforced under three different schedules of reinforcement (100%, 50%, and 25%). The number of bar-pressing responses obtained during extinction are as follows: 100%, 615; 50%, 843; 25%, 545. Criticize the use of the chi-square as the appropriate statistical technique.

4. Neil is conducting research on memory. He asks 50 subjects to think about their earliest memory of their father and their earliest one of their mother. Then he asks them to evaluate each memory as to whether it is positive or negative. He obtains the results listed in the accompanying table.

|          | Memory of Mother | Memory of Father |
|----------|:----------------:|:----------------:|
| Positive | 35               | 31               |
| Negative | 15               | 19               |

Neil plans to analyze his data using $\chi^2$. Do you think such an analysis is appropriate? Explain.

5. The World Series may last from four to seven games. During the period 1922 to 1989, the distribution of the number of games played per series was

| Number of games | 4 | 5 | 6 | 7 |
|---|---|---|---|---|
| Frequency of occurrence | 11 | 15 | 13 | 29 |

For these data, test the hypothesis that each number of games is equally likely to occur.

6. Bill believes that the current generation of students are much different than students in the 1960s. He asks a sample of students at his college the following question:

Which of the following best describes your reason for attending college (pick only one alternative)?
a. Develop a philosophy of life.
b. Learn more about the world around me.
c. Obtain a good paying job.
d. Unsure of reason.

This same question was asked of students at the college in 1965. Here are the results of the two surveys.

| | 1965 | 1998 |
|---|---|---|
| Develop a philosophy of life | 15 | 8 |
| Learn more about the world around me | 53 | 48 |
| Obtain a good paying job | 25 | 57 |
| Unsure of reason | 27 | 47 |

Is Bill justified in concluding that there is a difference between the current class of students and students in 1965?

7. Erin is the chair of the psychology department. She sent a questionnaire to all students who graduated from the program during the past 10 years. One question asked whether the student attended a graduate program, and the type of program attended. Of the students returning questionnaires, 88 indicated that they were in or had completed a Ph.D. program.

| Program | Number of Students |
|---|---|
| Clinical | 12 |
| Counseling | 23 |
| Developmental | 8 |
| Experimental | 7 |
| Industrial/Organizational | 15 |
| Physiological | 5 |
| Social | 18 |

Can Erin assume that graduates of the department equally attended each of the seven programs?

8. Jackie conducted a study in which she compared the helping behavior of passersby under two conditions. What can you conclude from the results shown in the accompanying table?

|  | Condition A | Condition B |
|---|---|---|
| Helped | 75 | 45 |
| Did not help | 40 | 80 |

Set up this study in formal statistical terms and draw appropriate conclusions.

9. In a study concerned with preferences for four different types of checking accounts offered by a bank, 100 people in a high-income group and 200 people in a lower-income group were interviewed. The results of their choices are shown in the accompanying table.

| Preference | Upper-Income Group | Low-Income Group |
|---|---|---|
| Account A | 36 | 84 |
| Account B | 39 | 51 |
| Account C | 16 | 44 |
| Account D | 9 | 21 |

Set up this study in formal statistical terms and draw appropriate conclusions.

10. The accompanying table shows the number of female subjects helping an attractive or an unattractive male applicant.

|  | CHARACTERISTICS OF TARGET | | |
|---|---|---|---|
| **Helping Response** | **Attractive** | **Unattractive** | **Total** |
| Helped | 17 | 13 | 30 |
| Did not help | 24 | 27 | 51 |

Set up this study in formal statistical terms and draw appropriate conclusions.

11. Two friends love to watch and classify movies. They decide to determine how much they agree with each other's ratings of movies. Their rating system is 👍👍 = Great Movie, 👍 Good Movie, 0 Passable Movie, 👎 Bad Movie, 👎👎 Horrible Movie. Here are their independent ratings of 213 movies. How well do the friends agree?

|  |  | RATER A | | | | |
|---|---|---|---|---|---|---|
|  |  | 👍👍 | 👍 | **0** | 👎 | 👎👎 |
|  | XX | 12 | 7 | 1 | 0 | 0 |
|  | X | 8 | 25 | 9 | 0 | 0 |
| Rater B | 0 | 3 | 12 | 45 | 8 | 1 |
|  | X | 1 | 3 | 6 | 23 | 19 |
|  | XX | 0 | 2 | 1 | 15 | 12 |

12. A small corporation wants to examine its hiring practices. Traditionally, applicants meet with the two members of the personnel office. Each interviewer rates the applicant as Superior, Adequate, Marginal, or Inadequate. Only applicants with a rating of Adequate or Superior from both raters are considered for employment. Here are the results for the rater's

performance. How reliable are the two raters? Do you believe that this hiring practice should be continued?

| | | RATER A | | | |
|---|---|---|---|---|---|
| | | **Superior** | **Adequate** | **Marginal** | **Inadequate** |
| | Superior | 15 | 17 | 21 | 10 |
| | Adequate | 11 | 12 | 14 | 8 |
| Rater B | Marginal | 12 | 17 | 9 | 12 |
| | Inadequate | 9 | 13 | 8 | 6 |

13. A radio station claims that 40% of its audience listens to the station more than 30 hours per week. A potential advertiser questions the validity of the claim and decides to conduct a telephone survey of listeners. Presented below are sample sizes and numbers in the sample reporting that they listen at least 30 hours per week. For each case determine if the obtained value lies in the critical region, provide the critical value, and indicate if the results are statistically significant at $\alpha = .05$.
   a. $N = 20$, 10 reported 30+ hours
   b. $N = 20$, 14 reported 30+ hours
   c. $N = 24$, 14 reported 30+ hours
   d. $N = 24$, 18 reported 30+ hours

14. For each case presented in Exercise 13, evaluate each obtained value, provide the critical value, and indicate if the results are statistically significant at $\alpha = .01$.

15. In polling 46 interviewees drawn at random from a specified population, we find that 28 favor and 18 oppose building a mental health center in their neighborhood. Test the hypothesis that the sample was drawn from a population in which $P = Q = 1/2$. Use $\alpha = 0.05$, two-tailed test.

16. Jamie works at a large market research firm that has been hired to evaluate two checking account plans offered by one of their clients. They conduct in-depth interviews during which a sample of customers are asked to choose one of two checking account options. Presented below are the sample sizes and number choosing the first option. Test the hypothesis that the sample was drawn from a population in which $P = Q = 1/2$. Provide the critical value using $\alpha = 0.05$, two-tailed test and indicate if the results are statistically significant.
   a. $N = 20$, 10
   b. $N = 20$, 14
   c. $N = 24$, 20
   d. $N = 24$, 22

17. Evaluate the data presented in Exercise 16 using $\alpha = .01$, two-tailed.

# 18

# Statistical Inference: Ordinally Scaled Variables

## 18.1 Introduction: Ordinally Scaled Variables

In Chapter 13 we examined different versions of Student's $t$-ratio. As a generality, Student's $t$-ratio is a powerful and robust inferential statistic that many researchers use. In spite of its utility, the $t$-ratio does have its limitations. Many researchers prefer not to use the $t$-ratio when the data violate its mathematical assumptions, especially the assumptions of normality and homogeneity of variance. Furthermore, some researchers do not like to use the $t$-ratio to analyze data measured on an ordinal scale. Consequently, these researchers turn to alternatives to the $t$-ratio. These alternatives use the ranks of scores for the statistical test. In this chapter we will briefly review three alternatives to the conventional $t$-ratio. As you will see, these alternatives allow you to analyze data for independent groups as well as correlated groups.

Each of these statistics works by examining the rank of the data. In other words, the statistics treat the measurement scale as if it is an ordinal scale. As you may recall from Chapter 2, we can convert any interval or ratio scale into an ordinal scale. For example, a teacher can convert test scores to rankings. The student with the highest grade has a rank of $X = 1$. The student with the next highest grade has a rank of $X = 2$. The teacher would repeat this process until each student's test score is converted to a rank. As you may recall from Chapter 2, you can rank order scores in either direction. In this example, high scores have a low rank. We could have just as easily given the high score the high ranks. In the following sections, be sure that you follow the ranking procedures advocated for the test.

■ **Mann-Whitney *U*-Test:**

An alternative inferential statistic to Student's $t$-ratio used when the data violate the assumptions of the Student's $t$-ratio. The test works by comparing the ranks of the scores observed in two independent groups.

## 18.2 Independent Groups: Mann-Whitney *U*-Test

The **Mann-Whitney *U*-test** is a popular alternative to Student's $t$-ratio. Many researchers use the Mann-Whitney $U$-test when the data represent an ordinal scale or when the data violate the assumption that the populations are normally distributed and that $\sigma_1 = \sigma_2$. The test is popular because it uses most of the quantitative information in the data. Let's examine the application of this technique to some hypothetical data.

Suppose we conducted a study to determine the effects of a drug on the reaction time to a visual stimulus. The researcher randomly assigned eight subjects to the experimental condition and seven to the control condition. The dependent measure is reaction time in milliseconds. Typically, reaction time and related measures (such as latency, time to solve an anagram, etc.) are positively skewed. The data are skewed because it is impossible to have a reaction time less than 0 and because it is possible to have extremely long reaction times. Because these data are skewed, the researcher selected the Mann-Whitney $U$-test as an alternative to Student's $t$-ratio. The results of this hypothetical study and the procedures for calculating the test statistic, $U$ or $U'$, are shown in Table 18.1.

The first step is to combine the scores of the two conditions and rank order the combined group from lowest to highest score. The lowest score receives a rank of 1 and the highest score receives a rank of 15. You then sum the ranks of each group separately: $R_1$ equals the sum of the

**Table 18.1**

**Calculation of Mann-Whitney *U* Employing Formula 18.1**

| EXPERIMENTAL | | CONTROL | | |
|---|---|---|---|---|
| Time (ms) | Rank | Time (ms) | Rank | |
| 140 | 4 | 130 | 1 | |
| 147 | 6 | 135 | 2 | |
| 153 | 8 | 138 | 3 | $U = N_1 N_2 + \dfrac{N_1(N_1 + 1)}{2} - R_1$ |
| 160 | 10 | 144 | 5 | $U = 8(7) + \dfrac{8(8 + 1)}{2} - 81$ |
| 165 | 11 | 148 | 7 | $U = 56 + \dfrac{72}{2} - 81$ |
| 170 | 13 | 155 | 9 | $U = 56 + 36 - 81$ |
| 171 | 14 | 168 | 12 | $U = 11$ |
| 193 | 15 | | | |
| | $R_1 = 81$ | | $R_2 = 39$ | |
| | $N_1 = 8$ | | $N_2 = 7$ | |

experimental condition in which $N_1 = 8$ and $R_2$ equals the sum of the control condition with $N_2 = 7$.

There are two test statistics, $U$ and $U'$, either of which can be used to test the null hypothesis. They are:

$$U = N_1 N_2 + \frac{N_1(N_1 + 1)}{2} - R_1 \tag{18.1}$$

$$U' = N_1 N_2 + \frac{N_2(N_2 + 1)}{2} - R_2 \tag{18.2}$$

The null hypothesis for the Mann-Whitney $U$ is that $U = U'$. In other words, if the ranks are equally distributed across the two groups, then $U = U'$, and we must assume that there is no systematic difference between the groups. If, however, more of the lower ranking scores are in one group then we will find that $U \neq U'$. When we reject the null hypothesis, we conclude that one group has more low-ranking scores than expected and that the other group has more high-ranking scores than expected.

Table R of Appendix D, provides the critical values of $U$ necessary to reject the null hypothesis. You should note that we constructed Table R so that you only have to calculate $U$. For any given $N_1$ and $N_2$, at a specific $\alpha$-level, the tabled values represent the critical upper and lower limits of the critical region. Therefore, the value of $U$ must be greater than or less than these limits to reject the null hypothesis.

Given the data in Table 18.1, we can proceed with the hypothesis testing.

***Null Hypothesis:*** $H_0$: $U = U'$: The differences between the groups' ranks are due to chance.

***Alternative Hypothesis:*** $H_1$: $U \neq U'$: The differences between the groups' ranks are not random.

***Statistical Test:*** The Mann-Whitney $U$-Test.

*Significance Level:* $\alpha = .05$.

*Sampling Distribution:* The Mann-Whitney $U$: $N_1 = 8$, $N_2 = 7$.

*Critical Region for Rejection of $H_0$:* $U \leq 10$ or $U \geq 46$. If the $U$ is beyond these limits, we will reject $H_0$.

Because the $U_{\text{observed}} = 11$, which is within the critical region for the null hypothesis, we cannot reject the null hypothesis. If we had found a statistically significant result, we would report the statistic as:

$$\underline{U} \ (\underline{N}_1 = 8, \ \underline{N}_2 = 7) = 8, \ \underline{p} < .05$$

## Mann-Whitney $U$-Test with Tied Ranks

A problem that often arises with data is that several scores may be the same. Although there should be no ties if we use a sufficiently sensitive measuring instrument, we do, in fact, occasionally obtain ties. The procedures for converting tied scores to ranks are the same ones we used with the Spearman $r_S$, (see Chapter 8). We assign the mean of the tied ranks to each of the tied scores, with the next rank in the array receiving the rank that is normally assigned to it.

Using the Mann-Whitney $U$-test becomes problematic when ties occur between two or more observations that involve both groups. Specifically, ties increase the probability of a Type II error (failing to reject the null hypothesis when it is actually false). Unfortunately, the procedures for dealing with ties are rather involved and are beyond the scope of this textbook (see Siegel and Castellan, 1988, for a review of these procedures).

In the event that several ties occur, we recommend that you calculate the Mann-Whitney $U$ without correcting for ties. If the uncorrected $U$ approaches but does not achieve the $\alpha$-level we have set for rejecting the null hypothesis, consult Siegel and Castellan (1988) and recalculate the Mann-Whitney $U$, correcting for ties.

## Mann-Whitney $U$ for Large Samples

Table R of Appendix D provides critical values of $U$ for sample sizes up to and including $N_1 = 20$ and $N_2 = 20$. As with many other statistics, the sampling distribution for the Mann-Whitney $U$ approaches normality as the sample size becomes larger. As long as both $N$s are approximately equal and the $N$ for one group is greater than 20, the normal curve and the $z$-statistic may be used to evaluate the significance of the difference between ranks. The $z$ statistic takes on the following form:

$$z = \frac{U_1 - U_E}{s_U} \tag{18.3}$$

where
$U_I$ = sum of ranks in Group 1
$U_E$ = sum of ranks expected under $H_0$
$$U_E = \frac{N_1(N_1 + N_2 + 1)}{2} \tag{18.4}$$
$s_U$ = standard error of the $U$-statistic
$$s_U = \sqrt{\frac{N_1 N_2(N_1 + N_2 + 1)}{12}} \tag{18.5}$$

Imagine that an investigator completed a study in which $N_1 = 22$ and $N_2 = 22$. The sum of the ranks in Group 1 is 630. At $\alpha = .05$, test the null hypothesis that both groups were drawn from a population with the same mean rank. The critical value of $z = \pm 1.96$.

The standard error of the ranks is

$$s_U = \sqrt{\frac{22 \times 22(22 \times 22 + 1)}{12}}$$

$$s_U = \sqrt{\frac{21780}{12}}$$

$$s_U = \sqrt{1815}$$

$$s_U = 42.60$$

The expected rank under $H_0$ is

$$U_E = \frac{22(22 + 22 + 1)}{2}$$

$$U_E = \frac{990}{2}$$

$$U_E = 495$$

The test statistic $z$ becomes

$$z = \frac{630 - 495}{42.60}$$

$$z = 3.17$$

Because our obtained $z$ of 3.17 exceeds the critical value of 1.96, we may reject the null hypothesis and assert that the experimental treatment produced a statistically significant difference between conditions.

# 18.3 / Correlated Samples Tests

In Chapter 13, when discussing Student's $t$-ratio for correlated samples, we noted the advantages of employing correlated samples wherever feasible. Two tests allow one to examine the ranks of correlated groups. Specifically, we will examine the sign test and the Wilcoxon signed-rank test.

## The Sign Test

Suppose we conduct an experiment in which we wish to determine if specific training in leadership leads to superior performance over a control condition for which leadership is not the focus. Because we believe that intelligence correlates with leadership, we use a matched groups procedure, using intelligence as the matching variable. In other words, one member of each pair of correlated subjects is randomly assigned to the experimental condition and the remaining member is assigned to the control condition. Upon completion of the leadership course and the control course, independent observers are asked to rank the leadership qualities of each subject on a 50-point scale. The results are shown in Table 18.2.

**Table** 18.2

Ratings on Leadership Qualities of Two Groups of Subjects Matched on Intelligence (Hypothetical Data)

| | LEADERSHIP SCORE | | SIGN OF DIFFERENCE |
| Matched Pair | Experimental | Control | (E–C) |
|---|---|---|---|
| 1 | 47 | 40 | + |
| 2 | 43 | 38 | + |
| 3 | 36 | 42 | − |
| 4 | 38 | 25 | + |
| 5 | 30 | 29 | + |
| 6 | 22 | 26 | − |
| 7 | 25 | 16 | + |
| 8 | 21 | 18 | + |
| 9 | 14 | 8 | + |
| 10 | 12 | 4 | + |
| 11 | 5 | 7 | − |
| 12 | 9 | 3 | + |
| 13 | 5 | 5 | (0) |

■ **Sign Test:**

An alternative inferential statistic to Student's *t*-ratio for correlated groups. The test compares the sign of the difference between of scores.

The **sign test** examines only the sign of the difference, not the magnitude of the difference. Therefore, the test treats the difference between 47 and 40 as equivalent to the difference between 30 and 29. Therefore, the test does lose information by ignoring the magnitude of the difference. Although there is a loss of information, the test is still useful because it is a quick way to determine if there are systematic differences among the groups. The test also makes few assumptions concerning the data collected. Therefore, the sign test is a useful tool when the data violate the many assumptions that Student's *t*-ratio imposes upon the data.

There are 13 pairs of observations in Table 18.2. Because pair 13 is tied, there is no indication of a difference one way or the other. Consequently, we drop this pair of observations. Of the remaining 12 pairs, we would expect, on the basis of the null hypothesis, about half the changes to be in a positive direction and about half in the negative direction. In other words, under $H_0$ the probability of any difference being positive is equal to the probability to its being negative.

Because we are dealing with a two-category population (positive differences and negative differences), we can use the binomial distribution as the sampling distribution for our statistic. As you recall from Chapter 10, we use the binomial distribution to describe the potential outcomes of events that have only two outcomes. We use $P$ to represent the probability of a positive outcome and $Q$ to represent the probability of a negative outcome. Because $P$ and $Q$ are complementary, $Q = (1 − P)$. We express $H_0$ as $P = Q = .5$.

Out of 12 comparisons showing a difference ($N = 12$) in the present example, 9 are positive and 3 are negative. Therefore, $f(A) = 9$ $f(not\ A) = 3$. Because we assume that $P = Q = .5$, therefore, we refer to Table N1 in Appendix D under $f(A) = 9$, $N = 12$, and find that the critical value at $\alpha = .05$, two-tailed test, is 10. Because obtained $f(A)$ is less than 10, we fail to reject $H_0$.

**Table** 18.3

**Ratings and Ranking of Differences in Ratings of Two Groups of Subjects Matched on Qualities of Leadership (Hypothetical Data)**

| Matched Pair | LEADERSHIP SCORE | | | Rank of Difference | RANKS | |
|---|---|---|---|---|---|---|
| | Experimental | Control | Difference | | Negative | Positive |
| 1 | 47 | 40 | +7 | 9 | | 9 |
| 2 | 43 | 38 | +5 | 5 | | 5 |
| 3 | 36 | 42 | −6 | (−) 7 | (−) 7 | |
| 4 | 38 | 25 | +13 | 12 | | 12 |
| 5 | 30 | 29 | +1 | 1 | | 1 |
| 6 | 22 | 26 | −4 | (−) 4 | (−) 4 | |
| 7 | 25 | 16 | +9 | 11 | | 11 |
| 8 | 21 | 18 | +3 | 3 | | 3 |
| 9 | 14 | 8 | +6 | 7 | | 7 |
| 10 | 12 | 4 | +8 | 10 | | 10 |
| 11 | 5 | 7 | −2 | (−) 2 | (−) 2 | |
| 12 | 9 | 3 | +6 | 7 | | 7 |
| 13 | 5 | 5 | (0) | | | |
| | | | | | (−)13 | 65 |
| | | | | | $T_W = 13$ | |

## Wilcoxon Matched-Pairs Signed-Rank Test

We have seen that the sign test simply uses information concerning the direction of the differences between pairs. If the *magnitude* as well as the *direction* of these differences may be considered, a more powerful test is available. The **Wilcoxon matched-pairs signed-rank test** achieves greater power by using the quantitative information that is inherent in the *ranking* of the differences.

For illustrative purposes, let us return to the data in Table 18.2 and make a different assumption about the scale of measurement employed. Suppose the rating scale is not so crude as we had imagined; that is, not only do the measurements achieve nominal scaling, but also the differences between measures achieve ordinality. Table 18.3 reproduces these data, with additional columns indicating the rank of the difference and the sum of the ranks with the smallest value.

We first determine the difference between the experimental and control groups and then rank the absolute difference scores. When there are ties, we report the average of the tied rank. For example, note that pairs 3, 9, and 12 are tied. The ranks for the next three numbers are 6, 7, and 8. Therefore, the tied rank is 7. The next ranked score, the data for Pair 1, receives a rank of 9. We placed the negative sign in parentheses so that we can keep track of the differences bearing positive and negative signs. Note that we dropped pair 13 from our calculations because a zero difference in scores cannot be considered either a positive or negative change. Now, if the null hypothesis were correct, we would expect the sum of the positive and negative ranks to balance each other. The more the sums of the ranks are preponderantly negative or positive, the more likely we are to reject the null hypothesis.

■ **Wilcoxon Matched-Pairs Signed-Rank Test:**

An alternative inferential statistic to Student's *t*-ratio for correlated groups. The test compares both the sign of the difference between pairs of scores as well as the magnitude of the difference.

The statistic $T_W$ is the absolute value of the sum of the ranks with the smallest value. In this problem, the sum of the ranks for positive differences is 65; the sum of the ranks for negative differences is –13. Consequently, $T_W = 13$. Table S in Appendix D presents the critical values of $T_W$ for sample sizes up to 50 pairs. All entries are for the absolute value of $T_W$. In the present example, we find that a $T_W$ of 13 or less is required for statistical significance at the .05 level, two-tailed test, when $N = 12$. Because our obtained $T_W$ was 13, we may reject the null hypothesis. We may conclude that the leadership training produced higher ratings for the experimental subjects.

You will recall that the sign test was applied to the same data and did not lead to the rejection of the null hypothesis. Why was this so? The reason should be apparent. We were not taking advantage of all the information inherent in our data when we employed the sign test.

### Assumptions Underlying the Wilcoxon Matched-Pairs Signed-Rank Test

One assumption involved in the use of the Wilcoxon signed-rank test is that the scale of measurement is ordinal in nature. In other words, the assumption is that the scores permit ordering the data in relationships of greater than and less than. Another assumption of the signed-rank test, which may rule it out for some potential applications, is that the differences in scores also constitute an ordinal scale. It is not always clear whether or not this assumption is valid for a given set of data. Take, for example, a personality scale purported to measure "manifest anxiety" in a testing situation. Can we validly claim that a difference between matched pairs of, say, 5 points on one part of the scale is greater than a difference of 4 points on another part of the scale? If we cannot validly make this claim, we should use another form of statistical analysis, even if we move to a less sensitive and less powerful test of significance. Again, our basic conservatism as scientists makes us more willing to risk a Type II than a Type I error.

## CHAPTER Summary

In this chapter, we have looked at three tests for ordinally scaled variables that are commonly used to replace their parametric counterparts whenever there are serious doubts concerning the validity of meeting the assumptions of the parametric tests. Table 18.4 summarizes the conditions under which each of these tests might be used.

**Table 18.4**

**Three Ordinal Tests That May Be Used to Replace Indicated Statistical Tests When the Validity of the Assumptions of the Parametric Tests Are Questionable**

| Test of Significance | Experimental Design | Number of Conditions | Test Statistic | Test Replaced |
|---|---|---|---|---|
| Mann-Whitney $U$ | Independent samples | 2 | $U$ or $U'$ | Student's $t$-ratio for independent samples |
| Sign Test | Correlated samples | 2 | Binomial | Student's $t$-ratio and Wilcoxon's signed-rank test |
| Wilcoxon's Signed-Rank test | Correlated samples | 2 | $T_W$ | Student's $t$-ratio for correlated samples |

Mann-Whitney $U$-test
sign test
Wilcoxon matched-pairs signed-rank test

E XERCISES

**1.** The data in the accompanying table represent the number of stolen bases in two leagues. From these data, determine whether there is a statistically significant difference in the number of stolen bases between the two leagues using
  **a.** the sign test.
  **b.** the Wilcoxon matched-pairs test.
  **c.** the Mann-Whitney $U$-test.
  **d.** Which is the best statistical test for these data? Why?

| | NUMBER OF STOLEN BASES | |
|---|---|---|
| **Team Standing** | **League 1** | **League 2** |
| 1 | 91 | 81 |
| 2 | 46 | 51 |
| 3 | 108 | 63 |
| 4 | 99 | 51 |
| 5 | 110 | 46 |
| 6 | 105 | 45 |
| 7 | 191 | 66 |
| 8 | 57 | 64 |
| 9 | 34 | 90 |
| 10 | 81 | 28 |

**2.** In a study to determine the effect of a drug on aggressiveness, Group A received a drug and Group B received a placebo. A test of aggressiveness was applied following the drug administration. The scores obtained are shown in the accompanying table (the higher the score, the greater the aggressiveness).

| **Group A** | **Group B** |
|---|---|
| 10 | 12 |
| 8 | 15 |
| 12 | 20 |
| 16 | 18 |
| 5 | 13 |
| 9 | 14 |
| 7 | 9 |
| 11 | 16 |
| 6 | |

  **a.** What do you believe the null and alternative hypotheses are for this study?
  **b.** Draw a graph that best represents these data.
  **c.** Which test do you believe is appropriate for analyzing these data?
  **d.** Apply the statistic you selected to these data.

**e.** Is there sufficient evidence to reject the null hypothesis assuming $\alpha = .05$? How should these data be interpreted?

**3.** The personnel director at a large insurance office claims that insurance agents trained in personal-social relations make a more favorable impression on prospective clients. To test this hypothesis, 22 individuals are randomly selected from among those recently hired, and half are assigned to a personal-social relations course. The remaining 11 individuals constitute the control group. Following the training period, all 22 individuals are observed in a simulated interview with a client and rated on a 20-point scale (1 to 20) for their ease in establishing relationships. The higher the score, the better the rating. The data are listed in the accompanying table.

| Personal-Social Training | Control Group |
|:---:|:---:|
| 18 | 12 |
| 15 | 13 |
| 9 | 9 |
| 10 | 8 |
| 14 | 1 |
| 16 | 2 |
| 11 | 7 |
| 13 | 5 |
| 19 | 3 |
| 20 | 2 |
| 6 | 4 |

**a.** What do you believe the null and alternative hypotheses are for this study?
**b.** Draw a graph that best represents the data.
**c.** Which test do you believe is appropriate for analyzing these data?
**d.** Apply the statistic you selected to these data.
**e.** Is there sufficient evidence to reject the null hypothesis assuming $\alpha = .05$? How should these data be interpreted? What would the interpretation of the data be if $\alpha = .01$?

**4.** Assume that the subjects in Exercise 3 were matched on a variable known to be correlated with the criterion variable. Employ the appropriate test and repeat Exercise 3 (d) and (e).

**5.** Fifteen husbands and their wives were administered an opinion scale to assess their attitudes about a particular political issue. These results are shown in the accompanying table (the higher the score, the more favorable the attitude).

| Husband | | Wife | |
|:---:|:---:|:---:|:---:|
| 37 | 32 | 33 | 46 |
| 46 | 35 | 44 | 32 |
| 59 | 39 | 48 | 29 |
| 17 | 37 | 30 | 45 |
| 41 | 36 | 56 | 29 |
| 36 | 45 | 30 | 48 |
| 29 | 40 | 35 | 35 |
| 38 | | 38 | |

a. What do you believe the null and alternative hypotheses are for this study?
b. Draw a graph that best represents the data.
c. Which test do you believe is appropriate for analyzing these data?
d. Apply the statistic you selected to these data.
e. Is there sufficient evidence to reject the null hypothesis assuming $\alpha =$ .05? How should these data be interpreted? What would the interpretation of the data be if $\alpha = .01$?

6. Suppose that during the last track season there was no difference in the mean running speeds of the runners from two schools. Assume that the same people are on the teams this year. Runners from School A train as usual; however, the coach from School B introduces bicycle work as a part of the training cycle. During a meet, the times were recorded (in seconds) for the runners from the two schools in the 50-yard dash and are listed in the accompanying table.

| School A | School B |
|----------|----------|
| 10.2 | 9.9 |
| 11.1 | 10.3 |
| 10.5 | 11.0 |
| 10.0 | 10.1 |
| 9.7 | 9.8 |
| 12.0 | 9.5 |
| 10.7 | 10.8 |
| 10.9 | 10.6 |
| 11.5 | 9.6 |
| 10.4 | 9.4 |

a. What do you believe the null and alternative hypotheses are for this study?
b. Which test do you believe is appropriate for analyzing these data?
c. Apply the statistic you selected to these data.
d. Is there sufficient evidence to reject the null hypothesis assuming $\alpha =$ .05? How should these data be interpreted? What would be the interpretation of the data if $\alpha = .01$?

7. Suppose that in Exercise 6 the people on each team had been previously matched on running speed for the 50-yard dash. The matches are as listed in Exercise 6. Using the sign test and the Wilcoxon matched-pairs signed-rank test, set up and test the null hypothesis.

8. An investigator wanted to measure the effectiveness of an advertisement promoting his brand of toothpaste. He matched subjects (none of whom had ever bought this brand of toothpaste) according to the number of tubes of toothpaste they usually buy in 6 months. He then divided the sample into two groups and showed one group the advertisement. The accompanying table lists the number of tubes of this brand of toothpaste sold during the next 6 months.

| Advertisement | No Advertisement |
|:---:|:---:|
| 4 | 1 |
| 4 | 2 |
| 3 | 0 |
| 1 | 2 |
| 2 | 0 |
| 0 | 1 |
| 1 | 0 |
| 0 | 1 |

a. What do you believe the null and alternative hypotheses are for this study?
b. Which test do you believe is appropriate for analyzing these data?
c. Apply the statistic you selected to these data.
d. Is there sufficient evidence to reject the null hypothesis assuming $\alpha$ = .05? How should these data be interpreted? What would be the interpretation of the data if $\alpha$ = .01?

# Review of Basic Mathematics

## INTRODUCTION

The math skills needed to work through the material in this book are rather basic. This section reviews the arithmetic and algebra that you will need to succeed using statistics.

We assume that you will use a calculator for many of your homework assignments. Your instructor may also allow you to use a calculator for exams and quizzes. Although calculators make many tedious tasks easier, and help to reduce the chance of minor errors, you must still understand the foundation of mathematics to ensure that you use the correct procedures to solve specific tasks.

## ARITHMETIC OPERATIONS

You already know that "+" represents addition, "−" represents subtraction, "×" represents multiplication, and that "/" or "÷" represents division. Sometimes, however, people forget the rules concerning these basic operations. Let's review some of the basic mathematical symbols.

| | Symbol | Function | Example |
|---|---|---|---|
| **Relation** | | | |
| | $=$ | Equal | $12 = 12$ |
| | $\neq$ | Not equal | $12 \neq 15$ |
| | $>$ | Greater than | $12 > 10$ |
| | $\geq$ | Greater than or equal | $11 \geq 11$ |
| | $<$ | Less than | $12 < 14$ |
| | $\leq$ | Less than or equal | $14 \leq 14$ |
| **Operations** | | | |
| | $+$ | Addition | $12 + 10 = 22$ |
| | $-$ | Subtraction | $12 - 10 = 2$ |
| | / or ÷ | Division | $12 \div 2 = 6$ |
| | $\pm$ | Add and subtract | $10 \pm 2 = 8, 12$ |
| | $\times$ or $X(Y)$ | Multiplication | $2 \times 2 = 4$ |
| | | | $2(2) = 4$ |
| | $X^2$ | Square | $2^2 = 4$ |
| | $\sqrt{\phantom{x}}$ | Square root | $\sqrt{4} = 2$ |

## ADDITION AND SUBTRACTION

When adding numbers, the order has no influence on the sum. Therefore, $2 + 5 + 3 = 10$ regardless of the order of the numbers in the equation. Similarly, when adding positive and negative numbers, the order of the numbers has no effect. You can also break the numbers into three steps that include: (1) add all the positive numbers, (2) add all the negative numbers, (3) add the sum of the first two steps. For example,

$$
\begin{aligned}
-2 + 3 + 5 - 4 + 2 + 1 - 8 &= \\
3 + 5 + 2 + 1 &= \quad 11 \\
-2 - 4 - 8 &= -14 \\
&= \quad -3
\end{aligned}
$$

## MULTIPLICATION

The order of numbers has no effect on the product of numbers. For example, $2 \times 3 \times 4 = 3 \times 2 \times 4 = 4 \times 3 \times 2$; each equation produces 24.

When multiplying by a fraction, be sure to observe the correct location of the decimal place. Consider the following examples.

$$
\begin{array}{r}
8.0 \\
\times 5.0 \\
\hline
40.0
\end{array}
\qquad
\begin{array}{r}
8.0 \\
\times 0.5 \\
\hline
4.0
\end{array}
$$

Students often misplace the decimal point. Many things can cause this error, therefore, be sure that you keep neat notes of your work and be sure that you double-check each step for accuracy.

## DIVISION

The division operation involves two numbers. The order of the numbers is critical! For example, $4/2 \neq 2/4$. In most cases, we present division as

$$
\frac{12}{2} = 6
$$

The name for the number in the top part of the equation is the *numerator*. The name for the number in the bottom part of the equation is the *denominator*. In our example, the numerator is 12 and the denominator is 2.

Be careful when there are decimal numbers in the numerator. Look at the following examples.

$$
\frac{12.0}{2.0} = 6.0
\qquad
\frac{12}{0.2} = 60.0
$$

Many students get the wrong answer because they misplace the decimal point. Again, be sure that you double-check your work.

## EXPONENTIATION AND SQUARE ROOT

Exponentiation means raising a number to a specified power. The most common form of exponentiation is squaring a number. For example, $3^2 = 3 \times 3 = 9$. The number in the superscript indicates the number of times that a number is multiplied against itself. Here are three common examples.

$$2^2 = 2 \times 2 \qquad\qquad = 4$$
$$2^3 = 2 \times 2 \times 2 \qquad = 8$$
$$2^4 = 2 \times 2 \times 2 \times 2 = 16$$

The square root is the reverse of the squaring function. Almost all calculators allow you to calculate square roots.

$$\sqrt{4} = 2 \qquad\qquad\qquad \sqrt{351} = 18.734994$$

## ABSOLUTE VALUES

Whenever you see a number within two vertical lines, it means that you convert the number to a positive number. For example,

$$|-12| = 12 \qquad\qquad |45| = 45$$

## RULES OF PRIORITY

Many statistical equations have numerous steps in a single equation. It is vital that you remember the rules of priority for interpreting a mathematical equation. Here are the general rules that apply to all mathematical operations:

1. Work from the left to the right of the equation.
2. Perform all operations *inside* the parenthesis before performing those *outside* the parenthesis.
3. Some mathematical operations have precedence over others. Table A.1 presents the order of priority for common mathematical operations.

Here are some examples of multi-step problems. When you come to problems like these, make sure that you show each step. Our experience is that most students make mistakes because they try to skip steps and make an error in the process.

### Example 1

$$X = (49 - (28 \times 5) + 23)$$
$$X = (49 - 140 + 23)$$
$$X = 49 - 117$$
$$X = -68$$

### Example 2

$$X = (49 - (-7 + 4) + 8 - (-15))$$
$$X = (49 - (^-3) + 8 + 15)$$
$$X = (49 + 3 + 8 + 15)$$
$$X = 75$$

**Table A.1**

**Rules of Priority for Mathematical Operations**

| Operator | Equation Format | Example |
|---|---|---|
| 1. Exponentiation and square root | | |
|     Exponentiation | $X^2$ | $5^2 = 25$ |
|     Square root | $\sqrt{X}$ | $\sqrt{25} = 5$ |
| 2. Negation | $-X$ | $-(15) = -15$ |
| 3. Multiplication and division | | |
|     Multiplication | $X(Y)$ | $3(4) = 12$ |
| | $X \times Y$ | $3 \times 4 = 12$ |
|     Division | $X/Y$ | $12/4 = 3$ |
| | $\dfrac{X}{Y}$ | $\dfrac{12}{3} = 4$ |
| 4. Addition and subtraction | $X + Y$ | $3 + 4 = 7$ |
| | $X - Y$ | $12 - 4 = 8$ |

The Table Lists the Order of Priority from Highest (1) to Lowest (4).

## ALGEBRAIC OPERATIONS

The most common algebra problem encountered in statistics is solving for an unknown. The following are the types of algebraic operations you will need to use.

### Transposition

Transposing refers to the operation where we move a term from one side of an equation to another. To transpose, change the sign of the term and place it on the other side of the equation. All of the following mathematical statements are equivalent.

$$a + b = c$$
$$a = c - b$$
$$b = c - a$$
$$0 = c - a - b$$
$$0 = c - (a + b)$$

We can use this rule to solve for unknowns. Consider the problem

$$12 + X = 3$$

To solve for the equation, move the 12 to the other side of the equation and then solve using arithmetic.

$$X = 3 - 12$$
$$X = -9$$

To check your work, replace $X$ with $-9$

$$12 + -9 = 3$$

### Solving Equations Containing Fractions

Perhaps the most complex form of algebra you will encounter when doing statistics is solving for an unknown when division is involved in the equation. The following are three common examples.

**Problem 1**   The first example is the simplest.

$$X = \frac{10 - 5}{2}$$

For this problem, complete the equation.

$$X = \frac{5}{2}$$
$$X = 2.5$$

**Problem 2**   In this problem, we must solve for the missing denominator.

$$12 = \frac{6 - 3}{X}$$

The first step would be to work through part of the equation

$$12 = \frac{3}{X}$$

Next, we need to transpose the numbers so that $X$ is on the left side of the equation. We do that by multiplying both sides of the equation by $X/12$, which produces

$$\frac{X}{12} \times 12 = \frac{3}{X} \times \frac{X}{12}$$

Notice that the 12s cancel out on the left of the equation and that the $X$s cancel out on the right of the equation leaving

$$X = \frac{3}{12}$$
$$X = 0.25$$

**Problem 3**   For the last problem of transposition, we will solve for $X$ when it is part of the numerator. Here is an example

$$5 = \frac{X - 2}{12}$$

The first step will be to multiply both sides of the equation by 12.

$$12 \times 5 = \frac{X - 2}{12} \times 12$$

This operation reduces the equation to

$$60 = X - 2$$

We can now add 2 to both sides of the equation to solve for $X$.

$$62 = X$$

## MATHEMATICAL OPERATIONS

| Symbol | Definition | Page Reference |
|---|---|---|
| $\neq$ | Not equal to | 489 |
| $>$ | Greater than | 489 |
| $<$ | Less than | 489 |
| $\leq$ | Less than or equal to | 489 |
| $\geq$ | Greater than or equal to | 428 |
| $\approx$ | Approximately equal to | 28 |
| $X^2$ | $X$ squared | 28 |
| $X^a$ | $X$ raised to the $a$th power | 28 |
| $\sqrt{X}$ | Square root of $X$ | 28 |
| $X!$ | Factorial of $X$; multiply all integers between 1 and $X$. $4! = 1 \times 2 \times 3 \times 4 = 24$ | 28 |
| $\Sigma X$ | Sum of all the numbers in the set $X$ | 27 |
| $\Sigma X^2$ | Sum of squared scores | 29 |
| $(\Sigma X)^2$ | Sum of scores, quantity squared | 29 |
| $-X$ | Negative value of $X$ | 28 |
| $XY$, $X(Y)$, $X \times Y$ | Multiplication | 28 |
| $X/Y$, $\dfrac{X}{Y}$ | Division | 28 |

## GREEK LETTERS

| Symbol | Definition | Page Reference |
|---|---|---|
| $\alpha$ | Probability of Type I error, probability of rejecting $H_0$ when it is true | 285 |
| $\alpha_j$ | Effect of Factor A in the General Linear Model of the ANOVA | 363 |
| $1 - \alpha$ | Probability of correct decision not to reject $H_0$ | 287 |
| $\alpha_{experimentwise}$ | Experimentwise error | 361 |
| $\alpha\beta$ | Interaction effect used in the General Linear Model of the ANOVA | 399 |
| $\beta$ | Probability of a Type II error; probability of accepting $H_0$ when it is false | 286 |
| $1 - \beta$ | Power or the probability of correctly rejecting $H_0$ | 287 |
| $\beta_k$ | Effect of Factor B in the General Linear Model of the ANOVA | 399 |
| $\epsilon_{ij}$ | Sampling error in the General Linear Model of the ANOVA | 363 |
| $\eta^2$ | Eta squared; measure of association used with the ANOVA | 368 |
| $\chi^2$ | Chi-square | 358 |
| $\mu$ | Population mean | 264 |
| $\mu_0$ | Population mean under $H_0$ | 297 |
| $\mu_{\bar{X}}$ | Mean of the distribution of sample means | 297 |
| $\sigma^2$ | Sigma squared; population variance | 264 |
| $\sigma$ | Sigma; population standard deviation | 264 |
| $\sigma_{\bar{X}} = \dfrac{\sigma}{\sqrt{N}}$ | Standard error of the mean | 275 |
| $\sigma_{\bar{X}_1 - \bar{X}_2}$ | Standard error of the difference between means | 332 |
| $\omega^2$ | Omega squared; measure of association used with the $t$-ratio and the ANOVA | 372 |
| $\phi$ | Phi; Cramer's measure of association used with $\chi^2$ test | 465 |
| $\rho$ | Rho; population correlation | 308 |

## ENGLISH LETTERS

| Symbol | Definition | Page Reference |
|---|---|---|
| $a$ | Constant or the intercept in a regression equation | 204 |
| $b_Y$ | Slope of a line relating values of $Y$ to values of $X$ | 204 |
| $c$ | Number of columns in a contingency table | 463 |
| $C$ | Number of potential combinations | 360 |
| $CI^{\bar{x}}$ | Confidence interval of a mean | 276 |
| cum $f$ | Cumulative frequency | 60 |
| cum $\%$ | Cumulative percentage | 60 |
| $d_1$ and $d_2$ | Effect size for the $t$-ratio; 1-sample and 2-sample | 316 |
| $d$ | Standard normal deviate calculated for the $\chi^2$ test | 466 |
| $D$ | Difference in ranks for $X$-variable and $Y$-variable for Spearman's correlation coefficient | 187 |
| $\bar{D}$ | Mean of differences | 348 |
| $df$ | Degrees of freedom | 293 |
| $e$ | Used to calculate the standard normal deviate | 466 |
| $E_i$ | Expected number in a given category | 463 |
| $F$ | The ratio of two variances | 368, 379 |
| $f$ | Effect size for the $F$-ratio | 381 |
| $f(X)$ | Frequency of a number | 80 |
| $fX$ | Frequency of a number times itself | 80 |
| $H_0$ | Null hypothesis | 281 |
| $H_1$ | Alternative hypothesis | 291 |
| $HSD$ | Tukey's honestly significant difference | 384 |
| $\kappa$ | Coefficient kappa | 467 |
| $MS_{\text{between}}$ | Mean square between groups | 375 |
| $MS_{\text{within}}$ | Mean square within groups | 376 |
| $n$ | Sample size | 293 |
| $N$ | Sample size | 28 |
| $n'$ | Sample size average for ANOVA when sample sizes are not equal | 385 |
| $O_i$ | Observed frequency in a given category | 463 |
| $p$ | Probability | 236 |
| $p(A)$ | Probability of event $A$ | 236 |
| $p(\text{not } A)$ | Probability of not event $A$ | 236 |
| $p(B|A)$ | Probability of $B$ given the presence of $A$ | 244 |
| $P$ | Proportion of cases in one class in a two-category population | 268 |
| $Q$ | Proportion of cases in the other class in a two-category population. $Q = 1 - P$ | 268 |
| $Q_1$ | First quartile, 25th percentile | 61 |
| $Q_2$ | Median, 50th percentile | 61 |
| $Q_3$ | Third quartile, 75th percentile | 61 |
| $r$ | Pearson product-moment correlation coefficient | 167-168 |
| $r$ | Number of rows in a contingency table | 463 |
| $r^2$ | Coefficient of determination | 177 |
| $1 - r^2$ | Coefficient of nondetermination | 178 |
| $r_S$ | Spearman rank-order correlation coefficient | 186-187 |
| $R_1$ | Sum of ranks assigned to the groups with a sample size of $N_1$ for the Mann-Whitney $U$-test | 479 |
| $R_2$ | Sum of ranks assigned to the groups with a sample size of $N_2$ for the Mann-Whitney $U$-test | 479 |
| Range | Difference between highest and lowest | 97 |

## ENGLISH LETTERS *(continued)*

| Symbol | Definition | Page Reference |
|:---:|:---|:---:|
| $s^2 = \dfrac{SS}{N}$ | Variance of a sample | 101 |
| $\hat{s}^2 = \dfrac{SS}{n-1}$ | Unbiased estimate of the population variance | 293 |
| $s = \sqrt{\dfrac{SS}{N}}$ | Standard deviation of a sample | 101 |
| $\hat{s} = \sqrt{\dfrac{SS}{n-1}}$ | Unbiased estimate of the population standard deviation | 293 |
| $s^3$ | Skew of a distribution | 107 |
| $s^4$ | Kurtosis of a distribution | 108 |
| $s_{\bar{X}} = \dfrac{\hat{s}}{\sqrt{N}}$ | Estimated standard error of mean | 275 |
| $s_{\bar{X}_1 - \bar{X}_2}$ | Estimated standard error of the difference between means | 332 |
| $\hat{s}_D$ | Standard deviation of the difference scores | 348 |
| $s_{\bar{D}}$ | Estimated deviation of the difference between means | 348 |
| $s^2_{\text{between}}$ | Between-group variance estimate | 375 |
| $s^2_{\text{within}}$ | Within-group variance estimate | 376 |
| $s_{\text{est } Y}$ | Standard error of estimate when predicting $Y$ from $X$ | 215 |
| $SS = \Sigma(X - \overline{X})^2$ | Sum of squares | 100 |
| $SIR = \dfrac{Q_3 - Q_1}{2}$ | Semi-interquartile range | 98 |
| $SS_{\text{total}}$ | Sum of squares total | 374 |
| T | Transformed Scores | 127 |
| $T$ | Sum of ranks | 484 |
| $T$ | Sum of observations in a contingency table | 466 |
| $t$ | Student's $t$-ratio | 301, 308 |
| $\hat{t}$ | Adjusted $t$-ratio when $N_1 \neq N_2$ and $\sigma_1 \neq \sigma_2$ | 343 |
| $U, U'$ | Statistics calculated for the Mann-Whitney $U$-test | 479 |
| $v$ | Used to calculate the standard normal deviate | 466 |
| $X, Y$ | Variables | 27 |
| $X_i, Y_i$ | Specific quantities indicated by the subscript, $i$ | 27 |
| $\overline{X}$ | Arithmetic mean | 78, 79 |
| $(X - \overline{X})$ | Deviation score | 98 |
| $\Sigma X^2$ | Sum of squared raw scores | 28 |
| $(\Sigma X)^2$ | Sum of scores squared | 28 |
| $Z$ | Standard Deviate | 116 |

# Handbook of Fundamental Statistics

---

## MEASURES OF CENTRAL TENDENCY

## MODE: $M_O$

$M_O$ = Most frequently occurring score or scores in data set.

**Example:**

$X$    {18   10   11   13   8   11   6   10   3   10}

**Step 1**   Rank order the numbers from lowest to highest.

$X$    {3   6   8   10   10   10   11   11   13   18}

**Step 2**   Find the most frequently occurring score.

$M_O$ = 10

The mode is easy to determine and a useful tool to express the location of a cluster of high frequency scores. The statistic is also useful when there are several "peaks" in the data. In such cases, we describe the data as bimodal (two modes) or multi-modal.

## MEDIAN: $M_D$

$M_D$ or $Q_2$ = Score that divides the ranked data in half.

**Example:**

$X$    {18   10   11   13   8   11   6   10    3   10}
$Y$    {18   17   4   6   6   13   7   9   10}

**Step 1**   Rank order the numbers from lowest to highest.

$X$    {3   6   8   10   10   10   11   11   13   18}
$Y$    {4   6   6   7   9   10   13   17   18}

**Step 2** Add 1 to $N$ and then divide by 2.

$X$  $5.5 = (10 + 1)/2$

$Y$  $5.0 = (9 + 1)/2$

**Step 3** Starting with the lowest score, count up to the value from Step 2.

$X$  {3  6  8  10  10___10  11  11  13  18}

$Y$  {4  6  6  7  9  10  13  17  18}

**Step 4** If the midpoint falls between the two numbers, add them and divide by 2.

$X$   $M_D = 10.0 = (10 + 10)/2$

$Y$   $M_D = 9.0$

The median is a useful descriptive statistic especially for skewed distributions of data. The median, unlike the arithmetic mean, is not affected by the presence of outliers (one or two extremely high or low scores).

## ARITHMETIC MEAN: $\overline{X}$

Arithmetic mean or $\overline{X} = \dfrac{\Sigma X}{N}$

**Example:**

$X$  {18  10  11  13  8  11  6  10  3  10}

$Y$  {18  17  4  6  6  13  7  9  10}

**Step 1** Calculate the sum of all numbers in the set.

$\Sigma X = 18 + 10 + 11 + 13 + 8 + 11 + 6 + 10 + 3 + 10 = 100.0$

$\Sigma Y = 18 + 17 + 4 + 6 + 6 + 13 + 7 + 9 + 10 \quad\quad = 90.0$

**Step 2** Divide by the sum of numbers by the sample size, $N$.

$$\overline{X} = \frac{100.0}{10} = 10.0 \qquad\qquad \overline{Y} = \frac{90.0}{9} = 10.0$$

---

## MEASURES OF VARIABILITY

## SIMPLE RANGE

$Range = X_{highest} - X_{lowest}$

Like the mode, the range is easy to determine, however, it is greatly affected by outliers. Therefore, most researchers use it only as a general descriptive tool.

*Example:*

$X$    {18   10   11   13   8   11   6   10   3   10}

$Y$    {18   17   4   6   6   13   7   9   10}

**Step 1**   Rank the scores from lowest to highest.

$X$    {3   6   8   10   10   10   11   11   13   18}

$Y$    {4   6   6   7   9   10   13   17   18}

**Step 2**   Determine the difference between the highest and lowest scores.

$Range_X = 15.0 = 18 - 3$

$Range_Y = 14.0 = 18 - 4$

## SEMI-INTERQUARTILE RANGE

$$SIR = \frac{Q_3 - Q_1}{2}$$

*Example:*

$X$    {18   10   11   13   8   11   6   10   3   10}

$Y$    {18   17   4   6   6   13   7   9   10}

**Step 1**   Rank the scores from lowest to highest.

$X$    {3   6   8   10   10   10   11   11   13   18}

$Y$    {4   6   6   7   9   10   13   17   18}

**Step 2**   Add 1 to the sample size and divide by 4.

$X$    2.75    $= (10 + 1)/4$

$Y$    2.50    $= (9 + 1)/4$

**Step 3**   Convert the naumbers in Step 2 into the location for $Q_1$ and $Q_3$.

$X: Q_1 = 2.75$            $Q_3 = 8.25 = 2.75 \times 3$

$Y: Q_1 = 2.50$            $Q_3 = 7.50 = 2.50 \times 3$

**Step 4**   Using numbers from the previous step, determine $Q_1$ and $Q_3$. If the location of $Q_1$ or $Q_3$ falls between two numbers, take the average of the two.

$X$    {3   6__8   10   10   10   11   11__13   18}

$Y$    {4   6__6   7   9   10   13__17   18}

$X$   $Q_1 = 7.0 = (6 + 8)/2$    $Q_3 = 12.0 = (11 + 13)/2$

$Y$   $Q_1 = 6.0 = (6 + 6)/2$    $Q_3 = 15.0 = (13 + 17)/2$

Step 5  Calculate *SIR*.

$$SIR_X = 2.5 = (12 - 7)/2$$

$$SIR_Y = 4.5 = (15 - 6)/2$$

Like the median, extreme scores do not affect the semi-interquartile range. Therefore, researchers often use the statistic to described skewed data.

## VARIANCE AND STANDARD DEVIATION

### DEFINITIONAL FORMULAS

| Sample statistic | Unbiased estimate of population |
|---|---|

Variance

$$s^2 = \frac{\Sigma(X - \overline{X})^2}{N} \qquad\qquad \hat{s}^2 = \frac{\Sigma(X - \overline{X})^2}{n - 1}$$

Standard Deviation

$$s = \sqrt{\frac{\Sigma(X - \overline{X})^2}{N}} \qquad\qquad \hat{s} = \sqrt{\frac{\Sigma(X - \overline{X})^2}{n - 1}}$$

The difference between the sample statistic and the unbiased estimate of the population is an important one. Use the sample statistic when the data represent the population. Use the unbiased estimate of the population when the data represent a sample used to estimate the population variance and standard deviation.

### COMPUTATIONAL FORMULAS

| Sample statistic | Unbiased estimate of population |
|---|---|

Variance

$$s^2 = \frac{\Sigma X^2 - \frac{(\Sigma X)^2}{N}}{N} \qquad\qquad \hat{s}^2 = \frac{\overline{z}X^2 - \frac{(\Sigma X)^2}{n}}{n - 1}$$

Standard Deviation

$$s = \sqrt{\frac{\Sigma X^2 - \frac{(\Sigma X)^2}{n}}{N}} \qquad\qquad \hat{s} = \sqrt{\frac{\Sigma X^2 - \frac{(\Sigma X)^2}{n}}{n - 1}}$$

*Example:*

$$X \quad \{18 \quad 10 \quad 11 \quad 13 \quad 8 \quad 11 \quad 6 \quad 10 \quad 3 \quad 10\}$$

Step 1  Determine the sum of the data.

$$\Sigma X = 18 + 10 + 11 + 13 + 8 + 11 + 6 + 10 + 3 + 10 = 100.0$$

Step 2  Square each score and add together for the sum of squared scores.

$$\Sigma X^2 = 324 + 100 + 121 + 169 + 64 + 121 + 36 + 100 + 9 + 100 = 1144.0$$

**Step 3**   Complete the equations.

| Sample statistic | Unbiased estimate of population |
|---|---|

$$s^2 = \dfrac{\Sigma X^2 - \dfrac{(\Sigma X)^2}{n}}{N} \qquad\qquad \hat{s}^2 = \dfrac{\Sigma X^2 - \dfrac{(\Sigma X)^2}{n}}{n-1}$$

a.  $\quad s^2 = \dfrac{1144 - \dfrac{(100)^2}{10}}{10} \qquad\qquad \hat{s}^2 = \dfrac{1144 - \dfrac{(100)^2}{10}}{10-1}$

b.  $\quad s^2 = \dfrac{1144 - \dfrac{10000}{10}}{10} \qquad\qquad \hat{s}^2 = \dfrac{1144 - \dfrac{10000}{10}}{9}$

c.  $\quad s^2 = \dfrac{1144 - 1000}{10} \qquad\qquad \hat{s}^2 = \dfrac{1144 - 1000}{9}$

d.  $\quad s^2 = \dfrac{144}{10} \qquad\qquad\qquad\quad \hat{s}^2 = \dfrac{144}{9}$

e.  $\quad s^2 = 14.40 \qquad\qquad\qquad\quad \hat{s}^2 = 16.00$

f.  $\quad s = \sqrt{s^2} \qquad\qquad\qquad\quad \hat{s} = \sqrt{\hat{s}^2}$

g.  $\quad s = \sqrt{14.4} \qquad\qquad\qquad \hat{s} = \sqrt{16.0}$

h.  $\quad s = 3.7947 \qquad\qquad\qquad \hat{s} = 4.00$

## STANDARD NORMAL DISTRIBUTION: $z$-SCORE

### *Purpose:*

The $z$-score allows us to convert observed scores, $X$, to standard scores or $z$-scores. If we assume that the normal distribution represents the data, we can use the $z$-score to convert the observed score to a percentile. Because the two forms of the $z$-score are functionally equivalent, we will use $\hat{s}$ in the denominator for the following examples.

$$z = \dfrac{(X - \overline{X})}{s} \quad \text{or} \quad z = \dfrac{(X - \overline{X})}{\hat{s}}$$

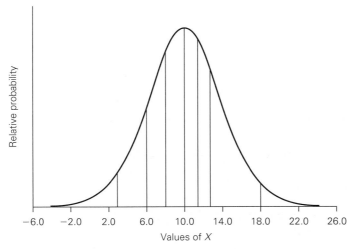

Illustration of the normal curve. The vertical lines represent the location of values of $X$ presented in the following table.

*Example:*

| X | z | AREA BELOW*<br>z-score | AREA ABOVE*<br>z-score |
|---|---|---|---|
| 3 | $-1.75 = (3 - 10.0)/4.0$ | .0401 | $.9599 = .4599 + .5000$ |
| 6 | $-1.00 = (6 - 10.0)/4.0$ | .1587 | $.8413 = .3413 + .5000$ |
| 8 | $-0.50 = (8 - 10.0)/4.0$ | .3085 | $.6915 = .1915 + .5000$ |
| 10 | $0.00 = (10 - 10.0)/4.0$ | .5000 | .5000 |
| 10 | $0.00 = (10 - 10.0)/4.0$ | .5000 | .5000 |
| 10 | $0.00 = (10 - 10.0)/4.0$ | .5000 | .5000 |
| 11 | $0.25 = (11 - 10.0)/4.0$ | $.5987 = .5000 + .0987$ | .4013 |
| 11 | $0.25 = (11 - 10.0)/4.0$ | $.5987 = .5000 + .0987$ | .4013 |
| 13 | $0.75 = (13 - 10.0)/4.0$ | $.7734 = .5000 + .2734$ | .2266 |
| 18 | $2.00 = (18 - 10.0)/4.0$ | $.9772 = .5000 + .4772$ | .0228 |

$\overline{X} = 10.0$    $\Sigma z = 0.00$
$\hat{s} = 4.0$
*From Table A.

## T-SCORES

The *T*-score allows us to use the *z*-score to convert data from one scale to another.

$$T = \overline{T} + s(z)$$

Where $\overline{T}$ is the mean of the new scale, $s$ is the standard deviation of the new scale, and $z$ is the *z*-score transformation of the original score, $X$.

*Example:*

Convert the following data ($\overline{X} = 10.0$, $\hat{s} = 4.0$) to a new scale when $\overline{T} = 50$ and $s = 5$

| X | z | $T = 50 + 5(z)$ |
|---|---|---|
| 3 | $-1.75$ | $41.25 = 50 + 5(-1.75)$ |
| 6 | $-1.00$ | $45.00 = 50 + 5(-1.00)$ |
| 8 | $-0.50$ | $47.50 = 50 + 5(-0.50)$ |
| 10 | $0.00$ | $50.00 = 50 + 5(\ 0.00)$ |
| 10 | $0.00$ | $50.00 = 50 + 5(\ 0.00)$ |
| 10 | $0.00$ | $50.00 = 50 + 5(\ 0.00)$ |
| 11 | $0.25$ | $51.25 = 50 + 5(\ 0.25)$ |
| 11 | $0.25$ | $51.25 = 50 + 5(\ 0.25)$ |
| 13 | $0.75$ | $53.75 = 50 + 5(\ 0.75)$ |
| 18 | $2.00$ | $60.00 = 50 + 5(\ 2.00)$ |

## z-SCORE: SAMPLE MEAN VS. POPULATION MEAN

### Purpose:

This test determines if the difference between a sample mean ($\overline{X}$) and a population mean ($\mu_0$) is statistically significant. For this equation, we assume that we know the mean ($\mu_0$) and variance ($\sigma^2$) of the population.

### Hypothesis:

Nondirectional

$$H_0: \mu_{\bar{X}} = \mu_0$$

$$H_1: \mu_{\bar{X}} \neq \mu_0$$

If $|z_{observed}| \geq |z_{critical}|$ then reject $H_0$.

Directional

$H_0: \mu_{\bar{X}} \geq \mu_0$     $H_0: \mu_{\bar{X}} \leq \mu_0$

$H_1: \mu_{\bar{X}} < \mu_0$     $H_1: \mu_{\bar{X}} > \mu_0$

If $z_{observed} \leq z_{critical}$ then reject $H_0$.   If $z_{observed} \geq z_{critical}$ then reject $H_0$.

$z_{critical}$ will be a negative number.   $z_{critical}$ will be a positive number.

### Equation:

$$z = \frac{\bar{X} - \mu_0}{\frac{\sigma}{\sqrt{n}}}$$

**Sampling Distribution:** Standard Normal Distribution—Table A

To determine $z_{critical}$, establish the level of $\alpha$ and the type of hypothesis to use. Using the column labeled "*Area beyond z-score,*" find the value that equals $\alpha$ and use the corresponding $z$-score. For example, if $\alpha = .05$, then $z_{critical} = 1.96$ for a nondirectional test. Note that if you use a directional hypothesis, you must convert the sign of $z_{critical}$ to conform to the test.

### Example:

$\bar{X} = 15.0$          $\mu_0 = 13.0$

$n = 25$          $\sigma = 5.0$

$$z = \frac{\bar{X} - \mu_0}{\frac{\sigma}{\sqrt{n}}} \qquad z = \frac{150.0 - 13.0}{\frac{5.0}{\sqrt{25}}} \qquad z = \frac{2.0}{\frac{5.0}{5}} \qquad z = \frac{2.0}{1.0}$$

$z = 2.00$

|  | One-tailed | Two-tailed |
|---|---|---|
| $\alpha = .05$ | $z_{critical} = 1.65$ <br> Reject $H_0$ | $z_{critical} = \pm 1.96$ <br> Reject $H_0$ |

## $z$-SCORE: DIFFERENCE BETWEEN TWO SAMPLE MEANS

### Purpose:

This test determines if the difference between two sample means is statistically significant. For this equation, we assume that we know the means and variances of the populations.

### Hypothesis:

Nondirectional

$$H_0: \mu_1 = \mu_2$$
$$H_1: \mu_1 = \mu_2$$

If $|z_{observed}| \geq |z_{critical}|$ then reject $H_0$.

Directional

$$H_0: \mu_1 \geq \mu_2 \qquad\qquad\qquad H_0: \mu_1 \leq \mu_2$$
$$H_1: \mu_1 < \mu_2 \qquad\qquad\qquad H_1: \mu_1 > \mu_2$$

If $z_{observed} \leq z_{critical}$ then reject $H_0$.  If $z_{observed} \geq z_{critical}$ then reject $H_0$.

$z_{critical}$ will be a negative number.   $z_{critical}$ will be a positive number.

### Equation:

$$z = \frac{(\overline{X}_1 - \overline{X}_2) - (\mu_1 - \mu_2)}{\sqrt{\dfrac{\sigma_1^2}{n_1} + \dfrac{\sigma_2^2}{n_2}}}$$

For most situations, $(\mu_1 - \mu_2) = 0$. Therefore, the test examines the simple difference between the means. One can, however, set $(\mu_1 - \mu_2)$ to a value that does not equal 0. Doing so allows one to test if the difference between the sample means is greater than the hypothesized difference.

### Sampling Distribution: Standard Normal Distribution—Table A

To determine $z_{critical}$, establish the level of $\alpha$ and the type of hypothesis to use. Using the column labeled "*Area beyond z-score*," find the value that equals $\alpha$ and use the corresponding z-score. For example, if $\alpha = .05$, then $z_{critical} = 1.96$ for a nondirectional test. Note that if you use a directional hypothesis, then you must convert the sign of $z_{critical}$ to conform to the test.

### Example:

$$\overline{X}_1 = 15.0 \qquad\qquad \sigma_1 = 10.0 \qquad\qquad N_1 = 16$$
$$\overline{X}_2 = 13.0 \qquad\qquad \sigma_2 = \phantom{0}5.0 \qquad\qquad N_2 = 25$$

$$z = \frac{(\overline{X}_1 - \overline{X}_2) - (\mu_1 - \mu_2)}{\sqrt{\dfrac{\sigma_1^2}{N_1} + \dfrac{\sigma_2^2}{N_2}}} \qquad z = \frac{(15.0 - 13.0) - (0)}{\sqrt{\dfrac{100.0}{16} + \dfrac{25.0}{25}}} \qquad z = \frac{2.0}{\sqrt{6.25 + 1}}$$

$$z = \frac{2.0}{\sqrt{7.25}} \qquad\qquad\qquad z = \frac{2.0}{2.6926} \qquad\qquad\qquad z = 0.7428$$

| | One-tailed | Two-tailed |
|---|---|---|
| $\alpha = .05$ | $z_{critical} = 1.65$ <br> Fail to reject $H_0$ | $z_{critical} = \pm 1.96$ <br> Fail to reject $H_0$ |

## $z$-SCORE: SAMPLE VS. POPULATION PROPORTION

### *Purpose:*

This test determines if the difference between a sample proportion ($p$) and a population proportion ($P_0$) is statistically significant.

### *Hypothesis:*

Nondirectional

$$H_0: p = P_0$$
$$H_1: p \neq P_0$$

If $|z_{observed}| \geq |z_{critical}|$ then reject $H_0$.

Directional

$$H_0: p \geq P_0 \qquad\qquad H_0: p \leq P_0$$
$$H_1: p < P_0 \qquad\qquad H_1: p > P_0$$

If $z_{observed} \leq z_{critical}$ then reject $H_0$. If $z_{observed} \geq z_{critical}$ then reject $H_0$.

$z_{critical}$ will be a negative number.   $z_{critical}$ will be a positive number.

### *Equation:*

$$z = \frac{p - P_0}{\sqrt{\dfrac{P_0(1 - P_0)}{N}}}$$

### *Sampling Distribution:* Standard Normal Distribution—Table A

To determine $z_{critical}$, establish the level of $\alpha$ and the type of hypothesis to use. Using the column labeled *"Area beyond z-score,"* find the value that equals $\alpha$ and use the corresponding $z$-score. For example, if $\alpha = .05$, then $z_{critical} = 1.96$ for a nondirectional test. Note that if you use a directional hypothesis, then you must convert the sign of $z_{critical}$ to conform to the test.

### *Example:*

$$p = .80 \qquad\qquad P_0 = .50$$
$$N = 25$$

$$z = \frac{.80 - .50}{\sqrt{\dfrac{.50(1 - .50)}{25}}} \qquad z = \frac{.30}{\sqrt{\dfrac{.50(.50)}{25}}} \qquad z = \frac{.30}{\sqrt{\dfrac{.25}{25}}}$$

$$z = \frac{.30}{\sqrt{.01}} \qquad\qquad z = \frac{.30}{.10} \qquad\qquad z = 3.00$$

|  | One-tailed | Two-tailed |
|---|---|---|
| $\alpha = .05$ | $z_{critical} = 1.65$ <br> Reject $H_0$ | $z_{critical} = \pm 1.96$ <br> Reject $H_0$ |

*Additional Test:*

**Standard Error of *p*:** This statistic describes the potential range of proportions that could occur if one continues to sample from the population under identical conditions.

$$SE_p = \frac{\sqrt{p(1 - p)}}{\sqrt{N}}$$

$$SE_p = \frac{\sqrt{.80(1 - .80)}}{\sqrt{25}} \qquad SE_p = \frac{\sqrt{.80(.20)}}{5} \qquad SE_p = \frac{\sqrt{.16}}{5} \qquad SE_p = \frac{.40}{5}$$

$$SE_p = 0.08$$

**Confidence Interval:** This statistic allows one to estimate the range of potential proportions given continual sampling from the population.

$$CI = \boldsymbol{p} \pm z_\alpha \, (SE_p)$$

Where $z_\alpha$ is the $z$-score corresponding to the nondirectional (or two-tailed) level of $\alpha$.

95% Confidence interval:
$$CI_{95} = .80 \pm 1.96 \, (0.08)$$

$$CI_{95} = .80 \pm 0.1568$$

$$CI_{95} = .6432 \text{---} .9568$$

---

## $z$-SCORE: DIFFERENCE BETWEEN TWO PROPORTIONS

### *Purpose:*

This test determines if the difference between two sample proportions is statistically significant.

### *Hypothesis:*

Nondirectional

$$H_0: p_1 = p_2$$
$$H_1: p_1 \neq p_2$$

If $|z_{\text{observed}}| \geq |z_{\text{critical}}|$ then reject $H_0$.

Directional

$$H_0: p_1 \geq p_2 \qquad\qquad\qquad H_0: p_1 \leq p_2$$
$$H_1: p_1 < p_2 \qquad\qquad\qquad H_1: p_1 > p_2$$

If $z_{\text{observed}} \leq z_{\text{critical}}$ then reject $H_0$. If $z_{\text{observed}} \geq z_{\text{critical}}$ then reject $H_0$.

$z_{\text{critical}}$ will be a negative number. $\qquad$ $z_{\text{critical}}$ will be a positive number.

### *Equation:*

$$z = \frac{(p_1 - p_2)}{\sqrt{P(1 - P)\left(\dfrac{1}{n_1} + \dfrac{1}{n_2}\right)}} \quad \text{where} \quad P = \frac{p_1 n_1 + p_2 n_2}{n_1 + n_2}$$

**Sampling Distribution:** Standard Normal Distribution—Table A

To determine $z_{critical}$, establish the level of $\alpha$ and the type of hypothesis to use. Using the column labeled *"Area beyond z-score,"* find the value that equals $\alpha$ and use the corresponding z-score. For example, if $\alpha = .05$, then $z_{critical} = 1.96$ for a nondirectional test. Note that if you use a directional hypothesis, then you must convert the sign of $z_{critical}$ to conform to the test.

**Example:**

$$p_1 = .60 \qquad\qquad p_2 = .40$$

$$n_1 = 40 \qquad\qquad n_2 = 50$$

$$P = \frac{p_1 n_1 + p_2 n_2}{n_1 + n_2} \quad P = \frac{.60(40) + .40(50)}{40 + 50} \quad P = \frac{24 + 20}{90} \quad P = \frac{44}{90} \quad P = .4889$$

$$z = \frac{(p_1 - p_2)}{\sqrt{P(1 - P)\left(\dfrac{1}{n_1} + \dfrac{1}{n_2}\right)}} \quad z = \frac{(.60 - .40)}{\sqrt{.4889(1 - .4889)\left(\dfrac{1}{40} + \dfrac{1}{50}\right)}}$$

$$z = \frac{20}{\sqrt{.4889(.5111)(.025 + .020)}} \quad z = \frac{.20}{\sqrt{(.2499)(.045)}} \quad z = \frac{.20}{\sqrt{.0112}} \quad z = \frac{.20}{.1058}$$

$$z = 1.8898$$

|  | One-tailed | Two-tailed |
|---|---|---|
| $\alpha = .05$ | $z_{critical} = 1.65$ <br> Reject $H_0$ | $z_{critical} = \pm 1.96$ <br> Fail to reject $H_0$ |

---

# *t*-RATIO: SAMPLE MEAN VS. POPULATION MEAN

**Purpose:**

This test determines if the difference between a sample mean ($\overline{X}$) and a population mean ($\mu_0$) is statistically significant. For this equation, we estimate the mean ($\mu_0$) and variance ($\sigma^2$) of the population using $\overline{X}$ and $\hat{s}^2$.

**Hypothesis:**

Nondirectional

$$H_0: \mu_{\overline{X}} = \mu_0$$

$$H_1: \mu_{\overline{X}} = \mu_0$$

If $|t_{observed}| \geq |t_{critical}|$ then reject $H_0$.

Directional

$$H_0: \mu_{\overline{X}} \geq \mu_0 \qquad\qquad H_0: \mu_{\overline{X}} \leq \mu_0$$

$$H_1: \mu_{\overline{X}} < \mu_0 \qquad\qquad H_1: \mu_{\overline{X}} > \mu_0$$

If $t_{observed} \leq t_{critical}$ then reject $H_0$.    If $t_{observed} \geq t_{critical}$ then reject $H_0$.

$t_{critical}$ will be a negative number.    $t_{critical}$ will be a positive number.

*Equation:*

$$t = \frac{\overline{X} - \mu_0}{\frac{\hat{s}}{\sqrt{n}}}, \, df = n - 1$$

*Assumptions:*

Data are normally distributed.

*Sampling Distribution:* Student's $t$-distribution—Table C

To determine $t_{\text{critical}}$, establish the level of $\alpha$ and type of hypothesis, and calculate the degrees of freedom. Use Table B to find the degrees of freedom (rows) and appropriate $\alpha$ level (columns). For example, if $\alpha = .05$ one-tailed and $df = 15$, $t_{\text{critical}} = 1.753$. Note that if you use a directional hypothesis, then you must convert the sign of $t_{\text{critical}}$ to conform to the test.

*Example:*

$$\overline{X} = 15.0 \qquad \mu_0 = 13.0$$

$$n = 25 \qquad \hat{s} = 5.0$$

$$t = \frac{\overline{X} - \mu_0}{\frac{\hat{s}}{\sqrt{n}}} \quad t = \frac{15.0 - 13.0}{\frac{5.0}{\sqrt{25}}} \quad t = \frac{2.0}{\frac{5.0}{5}} \quad t = \frac{2.0}{1.0} \quad df = 24 = 25 - 1$$

$$t = 2.00, \, df = 24$$

| | One-tailed | Two-tailed |
|---|---|---|
| $\alpha = .05$ | $t_{critical} = 1.711$ <br> Reject $H_0$ | $t_{critical} = \pm\, 2.064$ <br> Fail to reject $H_0$ |

*Additional Test:*

**Effect Size ($d_1$)** is an index of the relative difference between the means. The index is similar to a $z$-score in that it converts the difference between the means into standard deviation units.

$$d_1 = \frac{\overline{X} - \mu_0}{\hat{s}}\sqrt{2}$$

$$d_1 = \frac{15.0 - 13.0}{5.0}\sqrt{2} \quad d_1 = \left(\frac{2.0}{5.0}\right)1.4142$$

$$d_1 = 0.566$$

**Cohen's (1988) guidelines for evaluating effect sizes**

| **Small effect size:** | $d_1 = .20$ | Generally these difference are very small and difficult to detect without large sample sizes. Some researchers believe that when $d_1 \leq 0.10$, the effect is trivial. |
|---|---|---|
| **Medium effect size** | $d_1 = .50$ | A medium effect is sufficiently large to be seen by the naked eye when graphed. |

**Large effect size**   $d_1 = .80$   A large effect size is easily seen and requires few subjects to detect the effect.

## CONFIDENCE INTERVAL ABOUT A MEAN

### Purpose:

This test determines the range of potential means created if one were to continue to sample from the population under identical conditions.

### Equation:

$$CI = \overline{X} \pm t_{\text{critical}}\left(\frac{\hat{s}}{\sqrt{n}}\right), df = n - 1$$

**Sampling Distribution:** Student's $t$-distribution—Table C

To determine $t_{\text{critical}}$, establish the level of $\alpha$ two-tailed for the confidence interval. Use Table C to find the sample size (rows) and appropriate $\alpha$ level (columns). For example, if $\alpha = .05$ $n = 15$, $t_{\text{critical}} = 2.145$.

### Example:

$\overline{X} = 15.0$

$n = 25$ $\qquad\qquad$ $df = 24$

$\hat{s} = \;\;5.0$ $\qquad$ $t_{.05}(24) = \;\;2.064$

$$CI = 15.0 \pm 2.064\left(\frac{5.0}{\sqrt{25}}\right) \quad CI = 15.0 \pm 2.064\left(\frac{5.0}{5}\right) \quad CI = 15.0 \pm 2.064$$

$CI = 12.936 \text{—} 15.000 \text{—} 17.064$

## $t$-RATIO: DIFFERENCE BETWEEN TWO SAMPLE MEANS— VARIANCES AND SAMPLE SIZES EQUIVALENT

### Purpose:

This test determines if the difference between two sample means is statistically significant.

### Hypothesis:

Nondirectional

$H_0: \mu_1 = \mu_2$

$H_1: \mu_1 \neq \mu_2$

If $|t_{\text{observed}}| \geq |t_{\text{critical}}|$ then reject $H_0$.

Directional

$H_0: \mu_1 \geq \mu_2$ $\qquad\qquad\qquad\qquad$ $H_0: \mu_1 \leq \mu_2$

$H_1: \mu_1 < \mu_2$ $\qquad\qquad\qquad\qquad$ $H_1: \mu_1 > \mu_2$

If $t_{\text{observed}} \leq t_{\text{critical}}$ then reject $H_0$. $\quad$ If $t_{\text{observed}} \geq t_{\text{critical}}$ then reject $H_0$.

$t_{\text{critical}}$ will be a negative number. $\qquad$ $t_{\text{critical}}$ will be a positive number.

*Equation:*

$$t = \frac{\overline{X}_1 - \overline{X}_2 - (\mu_1 - \mu_2)}{\sqrt{\dfrac{\Sigma X_1^2 - \dfrac{(\Sigma X_1)^2}{n_1} + \Sigma X_2^2 - \dfrac{(\Sigma X_2)^2}{n_2}}{n_1 + n_2 - 2}\left(\dfrac{1}{n_1} + \dfrac{1}{n_2}\right)}} \ , \ df = (n_1 - 1) + (n_2 - 1)$$

For most situations, $(\mu_1 - \mu_2) = 0$. Therefore, the test examines the simple difference between the means. One can, however, set $(\mu_1 - \mu_2)$ to a value that does not equal 0. Doing so allows one to test if the difference between the sample means is greater than the hypothesized difference.

*Assumptions:*

Data are normally distributed.
Data in each group are independent of data in the other group.
$\sigma_1 = \sigma_2$

*Sampling Distribution:* Student's $t$-distribution—Table C

To determine $t_{critical}$, establish the level of $\alpha$ and type of hypothesis, and calculate the degrees of freedom. Use Table C to find the degrees of freedom (rows) and appropriate $\alpha$ level (columns). For example, if $\alpha = .05$ one-tailed and $df = 15$, $t_{critical} = 1.753$. Note that if you use a directional hypothesis, then you must convert the sign of $t_{critical}$ to conform to the test.

*Example:*

| | | |
|---|---|---|
| $\overline{X}_1 = 18.0$ | $\overline{X}_2 = 13.0$ | $(\mu_1 - \mu_2) = 0$ |
| $SS_1 = 1600.0$ | $SS_2 = 1825.0$ | |
| $n_1 = 23$ | $n_2 = 25$ | $df = 23 + 25 - 2 = 46$ |

$$t = \frac{18.0 - 13.0 - (0)}{\sqrt{\dfrac{1600 + 1825}{23 + 25 - 2}\left(\dfrac{1}{23} + \dfrac{1}{25}\right)}} \qquad t = \frac{5.00}{\sqrt{\dfrac{3425}{48 - 2}(0.0435 + 0.0400)}}$$

$$t = \frac{5.0}{\sqrt{\dfrac{3425}{46}(0.0835)}} \qquad t = \frac{5.0}{\sqrt{6.2171}} \qquad t = \frac{5.0}{2.4934}$$

$$t = 2.0053$$

| | One-tailed | Two-tailed |
|---|---|---|
| $\alpha = .05$ | $t_{critical} = 1.678*$ <br> Reject $H_0$ | $t_{critical} = \pm 2.011*$ <br> Reject $H_0$ |

\* Determined by interpolation

### Additional Tests

**Omega Squared ($\omega^2$)** is a measure of association that estimates the degree to which the independent variable shares common variance with the dependent variable. The larger the value of $\omega^2$ the greater the relation.

$$\omega^2 = \frac{t^2 - 1}{t^2 + n_1 + n_2 - 1}$$

$$\omega^2 = \frac{2.0053^2 - 1}{2.0053^2 + 23 + 25 - 1} \qquad \omega^2 = \frac{4.0212 - 1}{4.0212 + 47} \qquad \omega^2 = \frac{3.0212}{51.0212}$$

$$\omega^2 = 0.0592$$

The independent variable accounts for approximately 5.92% of the variance in the dependent variable.

**Effect Size ($d_2$)** is an index of the relative difference between the means. The index is similar to a $z$-score in that statistics converts the difference between the means into standard deviation units.

$$d_2 = \frac{|\mu_1 - \mu_2|}{\sigma}, \quad \sigma = \frac{\hat{s}_1 + \hat{s}_2}{2} \text{ when } n_1 = n_2.$$

Do not use this equation if $n_1 \neq n_2$.

**Cohen's (1988) guidelines for evaluating effect sizes**

**Small effect size:** $d_2 = .20$    Generally these differences are very small and difficult to detect without large sample sizes. Some researchers believe that when $d_1 \leq 0.10$, the effect is trivial.

**Medium effect size** $d_2 = .50$    A medium effect is sufficiently large to be seen by the naked eye when graphed.

**Large effect size** $d_2 = .80$    A large effect size is easily seen and requires few subjects to detect the effect.

$$d_2 = \frac{|\mu_1 - \mu_2|}{\sigma} \qquad\qquad \sigma = \frac{\hat{s}_1 + \hat{s}_2}{2}$$

$$.5798 = \frac{|18.0 - 13.0|}{8.6241} \qquad\qquad 8.6241 = \frac{8.528 + 8.7202}{2}$$

## $t$-RATIO: DIFFERENCE BETWEEN TWO SAMPLE MEANS—VARIANCES AND SAMPLE SIZES NOT EQUIVALENT

### Purpose:

This test determines if the difference between two sample means is statistically significant. Use this test when there are large differences between the variances of two groups. As a generality, when $\hat{s}^2_{\text{larger}}/\hat{s}^2_{\text{smaller}} > 3.00$ the protected $t$-ratio is a more accurate test.

### Hypothesis:

Nondirectional

$$H_0: \mu_1 = \mu_2$$
$$H_1: \mu_1 \neq \mu_2$$

If $|t_{\text{observed}}| \geq |t_{\text{critical}}|$ then reject $H_0$.

Directional

$H_0: \mu_1 \geq \mu_2$          $H_0: \mu_1 \leq \mu_2$

$H_1: \mu_1 < \mu_2$          $H_1: \mu_1 > \mu_2$

If $t_{observed} \leq t_{critical}$ then reject $H_0$.    If $t_{observed} \geq t_{critical}$ then reject $H_0$.

$t_{critical}$ will be a negative number.    $t_{critical}$ will be a positive number.

***Equation:***

$$\hat{t} = \frac{\overline{X}_1 - \overline{X}_2}{\sqrt{\left[\frac{1}{n_1}\left(\frac{SS_1}{n_1 - 1}\right)\right] + \left[\frac{1}{n_2}\left(\frac{SS_2}{n_2 - 1}\right)\right]}} \qquad df' = \frac{\left[\frac{1}{n_1}\left(\frac{SS_1}{n_1 - 1}\right) + \frac{1}{n_2}\left(\frac{SS_2}{n_2 - 1}\right)\right]^2}{\frac{\frac{1}{n_1}\left(\frac{SS_1}{n_1 - 1}\right)^2}{n_1 - 1} + \frac{\frac{1}{n_2}\left(\frac{SS_2}{n_2 - 1}\right)^2}{n_2 - 1}}$$

***Sampling Distribution:*** Student's $t$-Distribution—Table C

To determine $t_{critical}$, establish the level of $\alpha$ and type of hypothesis, and calculate the degrees of freedom. Use the table to find the degrees of freedom (rows) and appropriate $\alpha$ level (columns). For example, if $\alpha = .05$ one-tailed and $df = 15$, $t_{critical} = 1.753$. Note that if you use a directional hypothesis, then you must convert the sign of $t_{critical}$ to conform to the test.

***Example:***

| | $\overline{X}$ | 2.00 | 3.167 |
|---|---|---|---|
| | $SS$ | 4.00 | 12.833 |
| | $n$ | 10 | 6 |

$$\hat{t} = \frac{\overline{X}_1 - \overline{X}_2}{\sqrt{\left[\frac{1}{n_1}\left(\frac{SS_1}{n_1 - 1}\right)\right] + \left[\frac{1}{n_2}\left(\frac{SS_2}{n_2 - 1}\right)\right]}} \qquad df' = \frac{\left[\frac{1}{n_1}\left(\frac{SS_1}{n_1 - 1}\right) + \frac{1}{n_2}\left(\frac{SS_2}{n_2 - 1}\right)\right]^2}{\frac{\frac{1}{n_1}\left(\frac{SS_1}{n_1 - 1}\right)^2}{n_1 - 1} + \frac{\frac{1}{n_2}\left(\frac{SS_2}{n_2 - 1}\right)^2}{n_2 - 1}}$$

$$\hat{t} = \frac{2.00 - 3.167}{\left[\frac{1}{10}\left(\frac{4.00}{10 - 1}\right)\right] + \left[\frac{1}{6}\left(\frac{12.833}{6 - 1}\right)\right]} \qquad df' = \frac{\left[\frac{1}{10}\left(\frac{4.00}{10 - 1}\right) + \frac{1}{6}\left(\frac{12.833}{6 - 1}\right)\right]^2}{\frac{\frac{1}{10}\left(\frac{4.00}{10 - 1}\right)^2}{10 - 1} + \frac{\frac{1}{6}\left(\frac{12.833}{6 - 1}\right)^2}{6 - 1}}$$

$$\hat{t} = \frac{-1.167}{\sqrt{(0.0444) + (0.4278)}} \qquad df' = \frac{(0.0444 + 0.4278)^2}{\frac{(0.0444)^2}{9} + \frac{(0.4278)^2}{5}}$$

$$\hat{t} = \frac{-1.167}{\sqrt{.4722}} \qquad df' = \frac{(0.4722)^2}{\frac{0.0020}{9} + \frac{0.1830}{5}}$$

$$\hat{t} = \frac{-1.167}{0.6872} \qquad df' = \frac{0.22297}{.0002 + .0366}$$

$$df' = \frac{0.22297}{.0368}$$

$$df' = 6.059$$

$$\hat{t} = -1.698 \qquad df' = 6$$

|  | **One-tailed** | **Two-tailed** |
|---|---|---|
| $\alpha = .05$ | $t_{critical} = 1.943$ <br> Do not reject $H_0$ | $t_{critical} = \pm 2.447$ <br> Do not reject $H_0$ |

## $t$-RATIO: DIFFERENCE BETWEEN TWO CORRELATED SAMPLE MEANS

### Purpose:

This test determines if the difference between two sample means is statistically significant when there is a correlation between the groups. The correlation arises because the researcher uses the same subjects under two conditions or the subjects are matched to the groups based on a common variable.

### Hypothesis:

Nondirectional

$H_0: \mu_1 = \mu_2$

$H_1: \mu_1 \neq \mu_2$

If $|t_{observed}| \geq |t_{critical}|$ then reject $H_0$.

Directional

$H_0: \mu_1 \geq \mu_2$  $\qquad\qquad$  $H_0: \mu_1 \leq \mu_2$

$H_1: \mu_1 < \mu_2$  $\qquad\qquad$  $H_1: \mu_1 > \mu_2$

If $t_{observed} \leq t_{critical}$ then reject $H_0$.  If $t_{observed} \geq t_{critical}$ then reject $H_0$.

$t_{critical}$ will be a negative number.  $t_{critical}$ will be a positive number.

### Equation:

$$t = \frac{\overline{D}}{\sqrt{\dfrac{\Sigma D - \dfrac{(\Sigma D)^2}{N}}{N(N-1)}}}, \qquad df = n - 1$$

Where $\overline{D}$ is the average difference between pairs of scores and $D$ represents the difference between pairs.

### Assumption:

Data are normally distributed.

### Sampling Distribution: Student's $t$-Distribution—Table C

To determine $t_{critical}$, establish the level of $\alpha$ and type of hypothesis, and calculate the degrees of freedom. Use Table C to find the degrees of freedom (rows) and appropriate $\alpha$ level (columns). For example, if $\alpha = .05$ one-tailed and $df = 15$, $t_{critical} = 1.753$. Note that if you use a directional hypothesis, then you must convert the sign of $t_{critical}$ to conform to the test.

*Example:*

| Subject | $X_1$ | $X_2$ | $D$ | $D^2$ |
|---------|-------|-------|-----|-------|
| 1 | 10 | 7 | −3 | 9 |
| 2 | 17 | 18 | 1 | 1 |
| 3 | 15 | 20 | 5 | 25 |
| 4 | 8 | 15 | 7 | 49 |
| 5 | 18 | 19 | 1 | 1 |
| 6 | 10 | 13 | 3 | 9 |
| 7 | 16 | 17 | 1 | 1 |
| 8 | 12 | 16 | 4 | 16 |
| 9 | 13 | 18 | 5 | 25 |
| 10 | 9 | 16 | 7 | 49 |

$$\Sigma X_1 = 128 \quad \Sigma X_2 = 159 \quad \Sigma D = 31 \quad \Sigma D^2 = 185$$

$$\overline{X}_1 = 12.80 \quad \overline{X}_2 = 15.90 \quad \overline{D} = 3.10$$

$$\hat{s}_1^2 = 12.62 \quad \hat{s}_2^2 = 13.88$$

$$n = 10 \quad df = 9$$

$$t = \frac{\overline{D}}{\sqrt{\dfrac{\Sigma D - \dfrac{(\Sigma D)^2}{N}}{N(N-1)}}} \quad t = \frac{3.1}{\sqrt{\dfrac{185 - \dfrac{(31)^2}{10}}{10(10-1)}}} \quad t = \frac{3.1}{\sqrt{\dfrac{88.9}{90}}} \quad t = \frac{3.1}{\sqrt{.98778}} \quad t = \frac{3.1}{0.9939}$$

$$t = 3.119$$

|  | **One-tailed** | **Two-tailed** |
|---|---|---|
| $\alpha = .05$ | $t_{critical} = 1.833$ <br> Reject $H_0$ | $t_{critical} = \pm 2.262$ <br> Reject $H_0$ |

## PEARSON PRODUCT MOMENT CORRELATION COEFFICIENT

*Purpose:*

The Pearson product moment correlation coefficient, or Pearson's $r$, is a descriptive statistic that indicates the degree of relation between two variables. The values of $r$ can range between −1.00 and 1.00. Correlations close to 0 represent no linear relation between the two variables. Correlations close to −1.0 or 1.0 represent large linear relations. To use this equation, the data should be normally distributed and both variables should represent interval or ratio data.

*Equation:*

$$r = \frac{\Sigma XY - \dfrac{(\Sigma X)(\Sigma Y)}{N}}{\left(\Sigma X^2 - \dfrac{(\Sigma X)^2}{N}\right)\left(\Sigma Y^2 - \dfrac{(\Sigma Y)^2}{N}\right)}$$

*Example:*

| Subject | $X$ | $X^2$ | $Y$ | $Y^2$ | $XY$ |
|---|---|---|---|---|---|
| 1 | 90 | 8100 | 3.5 | 12.25 | 315 |
| 2 | 85 | 7225 | 3.0 | 9.00 | 255 |
| 3 | 80 | 6400 | 3.5 | 12.25 | 280 |
| 4 | 75 | 5625 | 3.0 | 9.00 | 225 |
| 5 | 70 | 4900 | 2.5 | 6.25 | 175 |
| 6 | 70 | 4900 | 2.0 | 4.00 | 140 |
| 7 | 70 | 4900 | 2.0 | 4.00 | 140 |
| 8 | 60 | 3600 | 1.5 | 2.25 | 90 |
| 9 | 60 | 3600 | 1.5 | 2.25 | 90 |
| 10 | 50 | 2500 | 1.5 | 2.25 | 75 |
| $\Sigma$ | 710 | 51750 | 24.0 | 63.50 | 1785 |

$$r = \frac{1785 - \frac{(710)(24)}{10}}{\sqrt{\left(51750 - \frac{(710)^2}{10}\right)\left(63.5 - \frac{(24.0)^2}{10}\right)}}$$

$$r = \frac{1785 - \frac{17040}{10}}{\sqrt{\left(51750.0 - \frac{504100}{10}\right)\left(63.5 - \frac{576}{10}\right)}} \qquad r = \frac{1785 - 1704.0}{\sqrt{(51750.0 - 50410.0)(63.5 - 57.6)}}$$

$$r = \frac{81.0}{\sqrt{(1340)(5.9)}} \qquad r = \frac{81.0}{\sqrt{7906}} \qquad r = \frac{81.0}{88.9157}$$

$$r = .91$$

## Additional Tests:

**Regression Analysis:** Upon calculating the correlation coefficient, one can determine the equation that defines the linear relation between $X$ and $Y$. The linear equation has an intercept ($a_Y$) and a slope ($b_Y$).

**Slope**

$$b_Y = r\left(\frac{s_Y}{s_X}\right)$$

**Intercept**

$$a_Y = \overline{Y} - b_Y(\overline{X})$$

**Regression Equation:**

$$Y' = a_Y + b_Y(X)$$

*Example:*

$$b_Y = r\left(\frac{s_Y}{s_X}\right) \qquad b_Y = .91\left(\frac{0.7681}{11.5758}\right) \qquad b_Y = .91(0.0664)$$

$$b_Y = 0.0604$$

$$a_Y = \overline{Y} - b_Y(\overline{X}) \quad a_Y = 2.40 - 0.0604(71.0) \quad a_Y = 2.40 - 4.2884$$

$$a_Y = -1.8884$$

$$Y' = -1.8884 + 0.0604(X)$$

**Standard Error of Estimate:** The regression line is an estimate of probable values of $Y$ given $X$. The accuracy of the prediction depends upon the value of the correlation between the two variables. In addition, the variances of the two variables affect the range of potential scores for the estimate. The standard error of estimate allows us to predict the range of potential scores given the regression equation.

$$Y_T = Y' \pm s_{estY}\sqrt{1 + \frac{1}{N} + \frac{(X - \overline{X})^2}{\Sigma X^2 - \frac{(\Sigma X)^2}{N}}} \quad \text{where} \quad s_{estY} = s_Y\sqrt{\frac{N(1 - r^2)}{N - 2}}$$

*Example:*

$$\overline{X} = 71.0 \qquad N = 10 \qquad \overline{Y} = 2.40$$

$$s_X = 11.58 \qquad r = .91 \qquad s_Y = 0.7681$$

$$s_{estY} = .7681\sqrt{\frac{10(1 - .91^2)}{10 - 2}} \quad s_{estY} = .7681\sqrt{\frac{10(1 - .8281)}{8}} \quad s_{estY} = .7681\sqrt{\frac{10(0.1719)}{8}}$$

$$s_{estY} = .7681\sqrt{\frac{1.719}{8}} \qquad s_{estY} = .7681\sqrt{0.2149} \qquad s_{estY} = .7681(0.4635)$$

$$s_{estY} = 0.3560$$

$$X = 80.0$$

$$Y' = 6(80) \qquad\qquad Y' = -0.866 + 3.68$$

$$Y' = 2.814$$

$$Y_T = 2.814 \pm 0.2734\sqrt{1 + \frac{1}{10} + \frac{(80.0 - 71.0)^2}{51750 - \frac{(710)^2}{10}}} \qquad Y_T = 2.814 \pm 0.2734\sqrt{1.10 + \frac{81}{1340}}$$

$$Y_T = 2.814 \pm 0.2734\sqrt{1 + .10 + \frac{81}{51750 - 50410}} \qquad Y_T = 2.814 \pm 0.2734\sqrt{1.1604}$$

$$Y_T = 2.814 \pm 0.2734\sqrt{1.10 + 0.0604} \qquad Y_T = 2.814 \pm 0.2945$$

$$Y_T = 2.814 \pm 0.2734(1.0772)$$

$$Y_T = 2.5195\text{---}3.1085$$

$$Y_T = 2.814 \pm 0.2734\sqrt{1 + \frac{1}{10} + \frac{(9.0)^2}{51750 - \frac{504100}{10}}}$$

## t-RATIO: SINGLE CORRELATION COEFFICIENT, *r*

### *Purpose:*

This test determines if a correlation coefficient, $r$, is statistically different from 0. The test works by converting the correlation coefficient into a $t$-ratio.

*Hypothesis:*

Nondirectional

$H_0$: $\rho = 0.0$

$H_1$: $\rho \neq 0.0$

If $|t_{observed}| \geq |t_{critical}|$ then reject $H_0$.

Directional

| | |
|---|---|
| $H_0$: $\rho \geq 0.0$ | $H_0$: $\rho \leq 0.0$ |
| $H_1$: $\rho < 0.0$ | $H_1$: $\rho > 0.0$ |

If $t_{observed} \leq t_{critical}$ then reject $H_0$.  If $t_{observed} \geq t_{critical}$ then reject $H_0$.

$t_{critical}$ will be a negative number.  $t_{critical}$ will be a positive number.

*Equation:*

$$t = \frac{r\sqrt{n-2}}{\sqrt{1-r^2}} \qquad df = n - 2$$

*Sampling Distribution:* Student's $t$-Distribution—Table C

To determine $t_{critical}$, establish the level of $\alpha$ and type of hypothesis, and calculate the degrees of freedom. Use Table B to find the degrees of freedom (rows) and appropriate $\alpha$ level (columns). For example, if $\alpha = .05$ one-tailed and $df = 15$, $t_{critical} = 1.753$. Note that if you use a directional hypothesis, then you must convert the sign of $t_{critical}$ to conform to the test.

*Example:*

$r = .90$

$n = 10$

$$t = \frac{.90\sqrt{10-2}}{\sqrt{1-.90^2}} \qquad t = \frac{.90\sqrt{8}}{\sqrt{1-.81}} \qquad t = \frac{.90(2.8284)}{\sqrt{19}} \qquad t = \frac{2.5456}{0.4359}$$

$t = 5.8399$, $df = 8$

| | One-tailed | Two-tailed |
|---|---|---|
| $\alpha = .05$ | $t_{critical} = 1.860$<br>Reject $H_0$ | $t_{critical} = \pm 2.306$<br>Reject $H_0$ |

## $z$-SCORE: COMPARISON OF CORRELATION COEFFICIENTS TO POPULATION VALUE

*Purpose:*

This test allows one to determine if the difference between an observed correlation and a population value is statistically significant. The test works by converting the individual $r$s to $z$-scores and the difference to a $z$-score.

*Hypothesis:*

Nondirectional

$H_0: \rho_1 = \rho_0$

$H_1: \rho_1 \neq \rho_0$

If $|z_{observed}| \geq |z_{critical}|$ then reject $H_0$.

Directional

$H_0: \rho_1 \geq \rho_0$            $H_0: \rho_1 \leq \rho_0$

$H_1: \rho_1 < \rho_0$            $H_1: \rho_1 > \rho_0$

If $z_{observed} \leq z_{critical}$ then reject $H_0$.    If $z_{observed} \geq z_{critical}$ then reject $H_0$.

$z_{critical}$ will be a negative number.    $z_{critical}$ will be a positive number.

*Equation:*

$$z = \frac{z_r - Z_r}{\sqrt{\dfrac{1}{n-3}}}$$

where $z_r$ represents the $z$-score for the observed correlation.
where $Z_r$ represents the $z$-score for the hypothesized population correlation.
Use Table H to convert the correlations to $z$-scores.

*Sampling Distribution:* Standard Normal Distribution—Table A

To determine $z_{critical}$, establish the level of $\alpha$ and the type of hypothesis to use. Using the column labeled "*Area beyond* z-*score*," find the value that equals $\alpha$ and use the corresponding $z$-score. For example, if $\alpha = .05$, then $z_{critical} = 1.96$ for a nondirectional test. Note that if you use a directional hypothesis, then you must convert the sign of $z_{critical}$ to conform to the test.

*Example:*

$r = .97 \quad \rho = .50 \quad N = 10$

For $r = .97$, $z_r = 2.092$

For $\rho_0 = .50$, $Z_r$ 0.549

$$z = \frac{z_r - Z_r}{\sqrt{\dfrac{1}{N-3}}} \quad z = \frac{2.092 - 0.549}{\sqrt{\dfrac{1}{(10\text{-}3)}}} \quad z = \frac{1.543}{\sqrt{\dfrac{1}{7}}} \quad z = \frac{1.543}{\sqrt{.1429}} \quad z = \frac{1.543}{0.3780}$$

$z = 4.08$

| | One-tailed | Two-tailed |
|---|---|---|
| $\alpha = .05$ | $z_{critical} = 1.65$ <br> Reject $H_0$ | $z_{critical} = \pm 1.96$ <br> Reject $H_0$ |

# SPEARMAN RANK-ORDER CORRELATION COEFFICIENT

## Purpose:

The Spearman rank-order correlation coefficient, or Spearman's $r_S$, is a descriptive statistic that indicates the degree of relation between two variables. The values of $r_S$ can range between $-1.00$ and $1.00$. Correlations close to 0 represent no linear relation between the two variables. Correlations close to $\pm 1.0$ represent large linear relations. The statistic can be used with ordinal data.

## Equation:

$$r_S = 1 - \frac{6\Sigma D_i^2}{n(n^2 - 1)}$$

## Hypothesis:

Nondirectional: Two-Tailed

$H_0$: $r_S = 0$
$H_1$: $r_S \neq 0$
If $r_S$ observed $\geq r_S$ critical then reject $H_0$.

Directional: One-Tailed

$H_0$: $r_S \leq 0$
$H_1$: $r_S > 0$
If $r_S$ observed $\geq r_S$ critical then reject $H_0$.

## Sampling Distribution: Spearman Rank-Order Correlation—Table G

To determine $r_S$ critical, establish the level of $\alpha$ and the type of hypothesis to use. Use the number of pairs to determine the critical value.

## Example:

| | | | | | RANK$_X$ − RANK$_Y$ | |
|---|---|---|---|---|---|---|
| Subject | X | Rank | Y | Rank | D | $D^2$ |
| 1 | 90 | 10 | 3.10 | 8 | 2 | 4 |
| 2 | 85 | 9 | 3.50 | 9 | 0 | 0 |
| 3 | 80 | 8 | 3.55 | 10 | −2 | 4 |
| 4 | 75 | 7 | 3.00 | 7 | 0 | 0 |
| 5 | 71 | 4 | 2.50 | 6 | −2 | 4 |
| 6 | 73 | 6 | 2.10 | 4 | 2 | 2 |
| 7 | 72 | 5 | 2.40 | 5 | 0 | 0 |
| 8 | 64 | 2 | 1.90 | 3 | −1 | 1 |
| 9 | 66 | 3 | 1.10 | 1 | 2 | 4 |
| 10 | 50 | 1 | 1.20 | 2 | −1 | 1 |
| | | | | | | Σ 20 |

$$r_S = 1 - \frac{6\Sigma D_i^2}{N(N^2 - 1)} \qquad r_S = 1 - \frac{6(20)}{10(10^2 - 1)} \qquad r_S = 1 - \frac{120}{10(100 - 1)} \qquad r_S = 1 - \frac{120}{990}$$

$$r_S = 1 - .1212$$

$$r_S = .8788$$

| | One-tailed | Two-tailed |
|---|---|---|
| $\alpha = .05$ | $r_{S\text{ critical}} = .564$<br>Reject $H_0$ | $r_{S\text{ critical}} = .648$<br>Reject $H_0$ |

## $F$-MAX TEST

### Purpose:

This test allows us to determine if the variances among two or more groups are equivalent. This test is commonly used for the Student's $t$-test and the ANOVA to ensure homogeneity of variance.

### Hypothesis:

$$H_0: \sigma^2_{\text{smallest}} = \sigma^2_{\text{largest}}$$
$$H_1: \sigma^2_{\text{smallest}} \neq \sigma^2_{\text{largest}}$$

### Equations:

$$F_{\text{max}} = \frac{\hat{s}^2_{\text{largest}}}{\hat{s}^2_{\text{smallest}}}$$

**Sampling Distribution:** Distribution for $F_{\text{max}}$ statistic—Table K

To determine $F_{\text{critical}}$, establish the level of $\alpha$. The two critical variables are $k$ the number of variances in the data and the degrees of freedom for $\hat{s}^2$, $(n-1)$.

### Example:

| | Group 1 | Group 2 | Group 3 | Group 4 |
|---|---|---|---|---|
| $\hat{s}^2$ | 12.0 | 14.0 | 24.0 | 10.0 |
| $n$ | 10 | 10 | 10 | 10 |

$$F_{\text{max}} = \frac{\hat{s}^2_{\text{largest}}}{\hat{s}^2_{\text{smallest}}} \qquad F_{\text{max}} = \frac{24.0}{10.0} \qquad F_{\text{max}} = 2.40$$

$$k = 4, \, df = 9, \, \boldsymbol{\alpha} = .05$$

$F_{\text{max critical}} = 6.31$, do not reject $H_0$.

## $F$-RATIO: ONE-WAY ANALYSIS OF VARIANCE

### Purpose:

This test determines if the difference among a group of independent means is greater than that expected by chance. Each group represents a different level of the independent variable. The statistic may be used for two or more groups.

### Hypothesis:

$$H_0: \mu_1 = \mu_2 = \ldots \mu_k$$
$$H_1: \text{Not } H_0$$

If $F_{observed} \geq F_{critical}$ then reject $H_0$.

## Equations:

| Sum of Squares | Degrees of Freedom | Mean Square | F-Ratio |
|---|---|---|---|
| $SS_{between} = \Sigma \dfrac{(X_{\bullet j})^2}{n_j} - \dfrac{(\Sigma X_{ij})^2}{N}$ | $j - 1$ | $MS_{between} = \dfrac{SS_{between}}{df_{between}}$ | $F = \dfrac{MS_{between}}{MS_{within}}$ |
| $SS_{within} = \Sigma X_{ij}^2 - \Sigma \dfrac{(X_{\bullet j})^2}{n_j}$ | $\Sigma(n_j - 1)$ | $MS_{within} = \dfrac{SS_{within}}{df_{within}}$ | |
| $SS_{total} = \Sigma X_{ij}^2 - \dfrac{(\Sigma X_{ij})^2}{N}$ | $N - 1$ | | |

## Assumptions:

Data are normally distributed.
Data in each group are independent of data in other groups.
$\sigma_1 = \sigma_2 = \ldots = \sigma_j$

## Sampling Distribution: Fisher's F-Distribution—Table J

To determine $F_{critical}$, establish the level of $\alpha$ and calculate the degrees of freedom. The F-distribution has two degrees of freedom. The numerator degrees of freedom $(df_N)$ is the degrees of freedom associated with the between-groups variance. The denominator degrees of freedom $(df_D)$ is the degrees of freedom associated with the within-groups variance. For example, if $\alpha = .05$ and $df_N = 3$ and $df_D = 6$ $F_{critical} = 4.76$.

| Group 1 | Group 2 | Group 3 | Group 4 | |
|---|---|---|---|---|
| $X_{1,1} = 4$ | $X_{1,2} = 6$ | $X_{1,3} = 4$ | $X_{1,4} = 5$ | |
| $X_{2,1} = 2$ | $X_{2,2} = 3$ | $X_{2,3} = 5$ | $X_{2,4} = 8$ | |
| $X_{3,1} = 1$ | $X_{3,2} = 5$ | $X_{3,3} = 7$ | $X_{3,4} = 6$ | |
| $X_{4,1} = 3$ | $X_{4,2} = 4$ | $X_{4,3} = 6$ | $X_{4,4} = 5$ | |
| $X_{\bullet 1} = 10$ | $X_{\bullet 2} = 18$ | $X_{\bullet 3} = 22$ | $X_{\bullet 4} = 24$ | $\Sigma X_{ij} = 74$ |
| $n_1 = 4$ | $n_2 = 4$ | $n_3 = 4$ | $n_4 = 4$ | $N = 16$ |
| $\overline{X}_1 = 2.5$ | $\overline{X}_2 = 4.5$ | $\overline{X}_3 = 5.5$ | $\overline{X}_4 = 6.0$ | $\overline{X} = 4.625$ |
| $\Sigma X_{i1}^2 = 30$ | $\Sigma X_{i2}^2 = 86$ | $\Sigma X_{i3}^2 = 126$ | $\Sigma X_{i4}^2 = 150$ | $\Sigma X_{ij}^2 = 392$ |
| $\hat{s}_1^2 = 1.67$ | $\hat{s}_2^2 = 1.67$ | $\hat{s}_3^2 = 1.67$ | $\hat{s}_4^2 = 2.00$ | |

## Sum of Squares

## Sum of Squares Total

$$SS_{total} = \Sigma X_{ij}^2 - \frac{\Sigma(X_{ij})^2}{N} \qquad SS_{total} = 392 - \frac{(74)^2}{16} \qquad SS_{total} = 392 - 342.25$$

$$SS_{total} = 49.75$$

## Sum of Squares Between-Groups

$$SS_{between} = \Sigma \frac{(X_{\bullet j})^2}{n_j} - \frac{(\Sigma X_{ij})^2}{N} \qquad SS_{between} = \frac{(10)^2}{4} + \frac{(18)^2}{4} + \frac{(22)^2}{4} + \frac{(24)^2}{4} - \frac{(74)^2}{16}$$

$$SS_{\text{between}} = 25 + 81 + 121 + 144 - 342.25 \quad SS_{\text{between}} = 371 - 342.25$$

$$SS_{\text{between}} = 28.75$$

### Sum of Squares Within-Groups

$$SS_{\text{within}} = \Sigma X_{ij}^2 - \Sigma \frac{(X_{\bullet j})^2}{n_j} \qquad SS_{\text{within}} = 392 - 371$$

$$SS_{\text{within}} = 21.00$$

### Degrees of Freedom
### Degrees of Freedom Total

$$df_{\text{total}} = N - 1 \qquad df_{\text{total}} = 16 - 1$$

$$df_{\text{total}} = 15$$

### Degrees of Freedom Between-Groups

$$df_{\text{between}} = k - 1 \qquad df_{\text{between}} = 4 - 1$$

$$df_{\text{between}} = 3$$

### Degrees of Freedom Within-Groups

$$df_{\text{within}} = \Sigma(n_j - 1) \qquad df_{\text{within}} = (4 - 1) + (4 - 1) + (4 - 1) + (4 - 1)$$

$$df_{\text{within}} = 12$$

### Mean Square
### Mean Squares Between-Groups

$$MS_{\text{between}} = \frac{SS_{\text{between}}}{df_{\text{between}}} \qquad MS_{\text{between}} = \frac{28.75}{3}$$

$$MS_{\text{between}} = 9.583$$

### Mean Squares Within-Groups

$$MS_{\text{within}} = \frac{SS_{\text{within}}}{df_{\text{within}}} \qquad MS_{\text{within}} = \frac{21.0}{12}$$

$$MS_{\text{within}} = 1.75$$

## F-ratio:

$$F = \frac{MS_{between}}{MS_{within}}$$

$$F = \frac{9.583}{1.75}$$

$$F = 5.48$$

**ANOVA Summary Table**

| Source | SS | df | MS | F |
|---|---|---|---|---|
| Between-groups | 28.75 | 3 | 9.583 | 5.48 |
| Within-groups | 21.00 | 12 | 1.750 | |
| Total | 49.75 | 15 | | |

$$F_{critical} (3, 12) = 3.49, \alpha = .05; \text{ Reject } H_0$$

## Additional Tests:

**Omega squared ($\omega^2$)** is a measure of the degree of association between the independent and dependent variables.

$$\omega^2 = \frac{df_{between}(F - 1)}{df_{between}(F - 1) + N}$$

$$\omega^2 = \frac{3(5.48 - 1)}{3(5.48 - 1) + 16} \qquad \omega^2 = \frac{3(4.48)}{3(4.48) + 16} \qquad \omega^2 = \frac{13.44}{29.44}$$

$$\omega^2 = .456$$

**Effect size** is symbolized by **f** and is interpreted in the same way **d** is interpreted for the *t*-ratio.

$$\mathbf{f} = \sqrt{\frac{\eta^2}{1 - \eta^2}} \quad \text{where} \quad \eta^2 = \frac{df_{between}(F)}{df_{between}(F) + df_{within}} \quad \text{or} \quad \eta^2 = \frac{SS_{between}}{SS_{total}}$$

$$\eta^2 = \frac{28.75}{49.75} = 0.578$$

$$\mathbf{f} = \sqrt{\frac{.578}{1 - .578}} = 1.170$$

**Cohen's (1988) guidelines for evaluating effect sizes**

**Small effect size**     **f = .10**

**Medium effect size**   **f = .25**

**Large effect size**     **f = .40**

## F-RATIO: TWO-WAY ANALYSIS OF VARIANCE

### Purpose:

This test determines the effects of two independent variables on the dependent variable. Each group represents a different combination of levels of the independent variables. The statistic examines the effect of each independent variable. These comparisons are the main effects. The statistic also examines the interaction between the two independent variables. The interaction accounts for variance in the dependent variable that cannot be accounted for by either independent variable by itself.

### Hypothesis:

### Null Hypotheses

$H_0$: $\sigma_a^2 + \sigma_\epsilon^2 = \sigma_\epsilon^2$: There is no main effect for Factor A.

$H_0$: $\sigma_\beta^2 + \sigma_\epsilon^2 = \sigma_\epsilon^2$:  There is no main effect for Factor B.

$H_0$: $\sigma_{\alpha\beta}^2 + \sigma_\epsilon^2 = \sigma_\epsilon^2$: There is no interaction between Factors A and B.

### Alternative Hypotheses:

$H_0$: $\sigma_a^2 + \sigma_\epsilon^2 \neq \sigma_\epsilon^2$: There is a main effect for Factor A.

$H_0$: $\sigma_\beta^2 + \sigma_\epsilon^2 \neq \sigma_\epsilon^2$:  There is a main effect for Factor B.

$H_0$: $\sigma_{\alpha\beta}^2 + \sigma_\epsilon^2 \neq \sigma_\epsilon^2$: There is an interaction for Factors A and B.

If $F_{\text{observed}} \geq F_{\text{critical}}$ then reject $H_0$.

### Equations:

| Sum of Squares | Degrees of Freedom | Mean Square | F-ratio |
|---|---|---|---|
| $SS_A = \Sigma \dfrac{(X_{\bullet j \bullet})^2}{n_{j\bullet}} - \dfrac{(\Sigma X_{ijk})^2}{N}$ | $df_A = j - 1$ | $MS_A = \dfrac{SS_A}{df_A}$ | $F_A = \dfrac{MS_A}{MS_{\text{within}}}$ |
| $SS_B = \Sigma \dfrac{(X_{\bullet\bullet k})^2}{n_{\bullet k}} - \dfrac{(\Sigma X_{ijk})^2}{N}$ | $df_B = k - 1$ | $MS_B = \dfrac{SS_B}{df_B}$ | $F_B = \dfrac{MS_B}{MS_{\text{within}}}$ |
| $SS_{AB} = \Sigma \dfrac{(X_{\bullet jk})^2}{n_{jk}} - \dfrac{(\Sigma X_{ijk})^2}{N} - (SS_A + SS_B)$ | $df_{AB} = (j-1)(k-1)$ | $MS_{AB} = \dfrac{SS_{AB}}{df_{AB}}$ | $F_{AB} = \dfrac{MS_{AB}}{MS_{\text{within}}}$ |
| $SS_{\text{within}} = \Sigma X_{ijk}^2 - \Sigma \dfrac{(X_{\bullet jk})^2}{n_{jk}}$ | $df_{\text{within}} = \Sigma(n_{ij} - 1)$ | $MS_{\text{within}} = \dfrac{SS_{\text{within}}}{df_{\text{within}}}$ | |
| $SS_{\text{total}} = \Sigma X_{ijk}^2 - \dfrac{(\Sigma X_{ijk})^2}{N}$ | $df_{\text{total}} = N - 1$ | | |

### Assumptions:

Data are normally distributed.
Data in each group are independent of data in other groups.
$\sigma_1 = \sigma_2 = \ldots = \sigma_k$

### Sampling Distribution: Fisher's F-Distribution—Table J

To determine $F_{\text{critical}}$, establish the level of $\alpha$ and calculate the degrees of freedom. The $F$-distribution has two degrees of freedom. The numerator degrees of freedom ($df_N$) is the degrees of freedom associated with the between groups variance. The denominator degrees of freedom ($df_D$) is the degrees of freedom associated with the within-groups variance. For example, if $\alpha = .05$ and $df_N = 3$ and $df_D = 6$ then $F_{\text{critical}} = 4.76$. Note that there is a separate $F_{\text{critical}}$ for each main effect and the interaction.

|  | $a_1$ | | $a_2$ | |
|---|---|---|---|---|
|  | $a_1b_1$ | | $a_2b_1$ | |
| $b_1$ | 15 | 14 | 22 | 14 |
|  | 18 | 17 | 17 | 17 |
|  | 18 | 18 | 16 | 17 |
|  | 17 | 20 | 21 | 18 |
|  | $a_1b_2$ | | $a_2b_2$ | |
| $b_2$ | 12 | 16 | 12 | 15 |
|  | 14 | 19 | 10 | 14 |
|  | 14 | 15 | 14 | 16 |
|  | 12 | 17 | 13 | 14 |
|  | $a_1b_3$ | | $a_2b_3$ | |
| $b_3$ | 9 | 18 | 10 | 11 |
|  | 16 | 14 | 9 | 8 |
|  | 14 | 11 | 8 | 6 |
|  | 11 | 14 | 8 | 11 |

Summary statistics of previous table

|  | $a_1$ | $a_2$ | |
|---|---|---|---|
| $b_1$ | $X_{\bullet 11} = 137$<br>$n_{11} = 8$<br>$\overline{X}_{11} = 17.12$<br>$\hat{s}^2_{11} = 3.55$ | $X_{\bullet 21} = 142$<br>$n_{21} = 8$<br>$\overline{X}_{21} = 17.75$<br>$\hat{s}^2_{21} = 6.79$ | $X_{\bullet\bullet 1} = 279$<br>$n_{\bullet 1} = 16$<br>$\overline{X}_{\bullet 1} = 17.49$ |
| $b_2$ | $X_{\bullet 12} = 119$<br>$n_{12} = 8$<br>$\overline{X}_{12} = 14.88$<br>$\hat{s}^2_{12} = 5.84$ | $X_{\bullet 22} = 108$<br>$n_{22} = 8$<br>$\overline{X}_{22} = 13.50$<br>$\hat{s}^2_{22} = 3.43$ | $X_{\bullet\bullet 2} = 227$<br>$n_{\bullet 2} = 16$<br>$\overline{X}_{\bullet 2} = 14.19$ |
| $b_3$ | $X_{\bullet 13} = 107$<br>$n_{13} = 8$<br>$\overline{X}_{13} = 13.38$<br>$\hat{s}^2_{13} = 8.55$ | $X_{\bullet 23} = 71$<br>$n_{23} = 8$<br>$\overline{X}_{23} = 8.88$<br>$\hat{s}^2_{23} = 2.98$ | $X_{\bullet\bullet 3} = 178$<br>$n_{\bullet 3} = 16$<br>$\overline{X}_{\bullet 3} = 11.12$ |
|  | $X_{\bullet 1\bullet} = 363$<br>$n_{1\bullet} = 24$<br>$X_{1\bullet} = 15.13$ | $X_{\bullet 2\bullet} = 321$<br>$n_{2\bullet} = 24$<br>$X_{2\bullet} = 13.38$ | $\Sigma X_{ijk} = 684$<br>$N = 48$<br>$\overline{X} = 14.25$<br>$\Sigma X^2_{ijk} = 10374$ |

$$SS_A = \Sigma \frac{(X_{\bullet j \bullet})^2}{n_{j\bullet}} - \frac{(\Sigma X_{ijk})^2}{N}$$

$$SS_A = \frac{(363)^2}{24} + \frac{(321)^2}{24} - \frac{(684)^2}{48} \qquad SS_A = 5490.3750 + 4293.375 - 9747.0$$

$$SS_A = 36.75$$

$$df_A = j - 1 \qquad\qquad MS_A = \frac{SS_A}{df_A}$$

$$df_A = 2 - 1 \qquad\qquad MS_A = \frac{36.75}{1}$$

$$df_A = 1 \qquad\qquad MS_A = 36.75$$

$$SS_B = \Sigma \frac{(X_{\cdot\cdot k})^2}{n_{\cdot k}} - \frac{(\Sigma X_{ijk})^2}{N}$$

$$SS_B = \frac{(279)^2}{16} + \frac{(227)^2}{16} + \frac{(178)^2}{16} - \frac{(684)^2}{48}$$

$$SS_B = 4865.0625 + 3220.5625 + 1980.25 - 9747.0$$

$$SS_B = 318.875$$

$$df_B = j - 1 \qquad\qquad MS_B = \frac{SS_B}{df_B}$$

$$df_B = 3 - 1 \qquad\qquad MS_B = \frac{318.875}{2}$$

$$df_B = 2 \qquad\qquad MS_B = 159.437$$

---

$$SS_{AB} = \frac{(X_{\cdot jk})^2}{n_{jk}} - \frac{(\Sigma X_{ijk})^2}{N} - (SS_A + SS_B)$$

$$SS_{AB} = \frac{(137)^2}{8} + \frac{(119)^2}{8} + \frac{(107)^2}{8} + \frac{(142)^2}{8} + \frac{(108)^2}{8} + \frac{(71)^2}{8} - \frac{(684)^2}{8} - (36.750 + 318.875)$$

$$SS_{AB} = 2346.125 + 1770.125 + 1431.125 + 2520.50 + 1458.0 + 630.125 - 9747.0 - 355.625$$

$$SS_{AB} = 53.375$$

$$df_{AB} = (j - 1)(k - 1) \qquad MS_{AB} = \frac{SS_{AB}}{df_{AB}}$$

$$df_{AB} = (2 - 1)(3 - 1) \qquad MS_{AB} = \frac{53.375}{2}$$

$$df_{AB} = 2 \qquad\qquad MS_{AB} = 26.687$$

---

$$SS_{within} = \Sigma X_{ijk}^2 - \Sigma \frac{(X_{\cdot jk})^2}{n_{jk}}$$

$$SS_{within} = 10374.0 - 2346.125 + 1770.125 + 1431.125 + 2520.50 + 1458.0 + 630.125$$

$$SS_{within} = 10374.0 - 10156$$

$$SS_{within} = 218.00$$

$$df_{within} = \Sigma(n_{ij} - 1) \qquad\qquad MS_{within} = \frac{SS_{within}}{df_{within}}$$

$$df_{within} = (8 - 1) + (8 - 1) + (8 - 1) + (8 - 1) + (8 - 1) + (8 - 1) \qquad MS_{AB} = \frac{218.0}{42}$$

$$df_{within} = 42 \qquad\qquad MS_{AB} = 5.190$$

---

$$SS_{total} = \Sigma X_{ijk}^2 - \frac{(\Sigma X_{ijk})^2}{N}$$

$$SS_{total} = 10374.0 - \frac{(684)^2}{48}$$

$$SS_{total} = 627.0$$

$$df_{total} = N - 1$$

$$df_{total} = 48 - 1$$

$$df_{total} = 47$$

**ANOVA Summary Table**

| Source | SS | df | MS | F |
|--------|------|----|--------|--------|
| A | 36.750 | 1 | 36.759 | 7.080 |
| B | 318.875 | 2 | 159.437 | 30.717 |
| AB | 53.385 | 2 | 26.687 | 5.142 |
| Within | 218.000 | 42 | 5.190 | |
| Total | 327.000 | 47 | | |

## Additional Tests:

### Omega squared:

$$\omega^2 = \frac{df_{\text{effect}}(F_{\text{effect}} - 1)}{df_{\text{effect}}(F_{\text{effect}} - 1) + N}$$

### Effect size:

$$\mathbf{f} = \sqrt{\frac{\eta^2_{\text{effect}}}{1.0 - \eta^2_{\text{effect}}}} \quad \text{where} \quad \eta^2 = \frac{df_{\text{effect}}F_{\text{effect}}}{df_{\text{effect}}F_{\text{effect}} + df_{\text{within}}} \quad \text{or} \quad \eta^2 = \frac{SS_{\text{effect}}}{SS_{\text{total}}}$$

## F-RATIO: ONE-WAY ANALYSIS OF VARIANCE— CORRELATED GROUPS DESIGN

### Purpose:

This test determines the effects of one independent variable on the dependent variable in a correlated-groups design. The design of the study may represent a repeated-measures design, wherein the researcher uses the same subject in each measurement condition. The design of the study may also represent a matched-group design. For a matched-group design, the researcher uses a criterion for assessing a subject variable and then assigning the subject to the groups so that each group has an equal proportion of high-and low-scoring subjects.

### Hypothesis:

### Null Hypotheses

$$H_0: \sigma^2_\alpha + \sigma^2_\epsilon = \sigma^2_\epsilon$$

### Alternative Hypotheses:

$$H_1: \sigma^2_\alpha + \sigma^2_\epsilon \neq \sigma^2_\epsilon$$
If $F_{\text{observed}} \geq F_{\text{critical}}$ then reject $H_0$.

### Equations:

| Sum of Squares | Degrees of Freedom | Mean Square | F-ratio |
|----------------|--------------------|--------------|---------|
| $SS_{\text{between}} = \frac{\Sigma X^2_{\bullet j}}{n_j} - \frac{(\Sigma X_{ij})^2}{N}$ | $df_{\text{between}} = j - 1$ | $MS_{\text{between}} = \frac{SS_{\text{between}}}{df_{\text{between}}}$ | $F_{\text{between}} = \frac{MS_{\text{between}}}{}$ |
| $SS_{\text{subjects}} = \frac{\Sigma X^2_{i\bullet}}{j} - \frac{(\Sigma X_{ij})^2}{N}$ | $df_{\text{subjects}} = n - 1$ | $MS_{\text{subjects}} = \frac{SS_{\text{subjects}}}{df_{\text{subjects}}}$ | $F_{\text{subjects}} = \frac{MS_{\text{between}}}{MS_{\text{within}}}$ |
| $SS_{\text{within}} = \Sigma X^2_{ij} - \frac{\Sigma X^2_{i\bullet}}{j} - \frac{\Sigma X^2_{\bullet j}}{n} + \frac{(\Sigma X_{ij})^2}{N}$ | $df_{\text{within}} = (j - 1)(n - 1)$ | $MS_{\text{within}} = \frac{SS_{\text{within}}}{df_{\text{within}}}$ | |
| $SS_{\text{total}} = \Sigma X^2_{ij} - \frac{(\Sigma X_{ij})^2}{N}$ | $df_{\text{total}} = N - 1$ | | |

### Assumptions:

Data are normally distributed.

$$\sigma_1 = \sigma_2 = \ldots = \sigma_k$$

### Sampling Distribution: Fisher's $F$-Distribution—Table J

To determine $F_{\text{critical}}$, establish the level of $\alpha$ and calculate the degrees of freedom. The $F$-distribution has two degrees of freedom. The numerator degrees of freedom ($df_N$) is the degrees of freedom associated with the between-groups variance. The denominator degrees of freedom ($df_D$) is the degrees of freedom associated with the within-groups variance. For example, if $\alpha = .05$ one-tailed and $df_N = 3$ and $df_D = 6$ $F_{\text{critical}} = 4.76$. Note that there is a separate $F_{\text{critical}}$ for each main effect and the interaction.

### Example:

| Subject | $X_1$ | $X_2$ | $X_3$ | $X_{i\bullet}$ |
|---------|-------|-------|-------|----------------|
| 1 | $X_{1\,1} = 15$ | $X_{1\,2} = 13$ | $X_{1\,3} = 11$ | $X_{1\bullet} = 39$ |
| 2 | $X_{2\,1} = 13$ | $X_{2\,2} = 9$ | $X_{2\,3} = 10$ | $X_{2\bullet} = 32$ |
| 3 | $X_{3\,1} = 12$ | $X_{3\,2} = 10$ | $X_{3\,3} = 9$ | $X_{3\bullet} = 31$ |
| 4 | $X_{4\,1} = 11$ | $X_{4\,2} = 13$ | $X_{4\,3} = 12$ | $X_{4\bullet} = 36$ |
| 5 | $X_{5\,1} = 9$ | $X_{5\,2} = 5$ | $X_{5\,3} = 7$ | $X_{5\bullet} = 21$ |
| 6 | $X_{6\,1} = 8$ | $X_{6\,2} = 6$ | $X_{6\,3} = 4$ | $X_{6\bullet} = 18$ |
| 7 | $X_{7\,1} = 7$ | $X_{7\,2} = 5$ | $X_{7\,3} = 2$ | $X_{7\bullet} = 14$ |
| | $X_{\bullet 1} = 75$ | $X_{\bullet 2} = 61$ | $X_{\bullet 3} = 55$ | $\Sigma X_{ij} = 191$ |
| | $\Sigma X_{i1}^2 = 853$ | $\Sigma X_{i2}^2 = 605$ | $\Sigma X_{i3}^2 = 515$ | $\Sigma X_{ij}^2 = 1973$ |
| | $\overline{X}_1 = 10.71$ | $\overline{X}_2 = 8.71$ | $\overline{X}_3 = 7.86$ | $\overline{X} = 9.10$ |
| | $\hat{s}_1^2 = 8.24$ | $\hat{s}_2^2 = 12.34$ | $\hat{s}_3^2 = 13.81$ | |

### Between-Groups Variance

$$SS_{\text{between}} = \frac{\Sigma X_{\bullet j}^2}{n_j} - \frac{(\Sigma X_{ij})^2}{N} \qquad df_{\text{between}} = j - 1$$

$$SS_{\text{between}} = \frac{75^2 + 61^2 + 55^2}{7} - \frac{(191)^2}{21}$$

$$SS_{\text{between}} = \frac{12371}{7} - \frac{36481}{21}$$

$$SS_{\text{between}} = 1767.2857 - 1737.1905 \qquad df_{\text{between}} = 3 - 1$$

$$SS_{\text{between}} = 30.0952 \qquad df_{\text{between}} = 2$$

### Subjects Variance

$$SS_{\text{subjects}} = \frac{\Sigma X_{i\bullet}^2}{j} - \frac{(\Sigma X_{ij})^2}{N} \qquad df_{\text{subjects}} = n - 1$$

$$SS_{\text{subjects}} = \frac{39^2 + 32^2 + 31^2 + 36^2 + 21^2 + 18^2 + 14^2}{3} - 1737.1904$$

$$SS_{\text{subjects}} = \frac{5763}{3} - 1737.1905$$

$$SS_{\text{subjects}} = 1921 - 1737.1905 \qquad df_{\text{subjects}} = 7 - 1$$

$$SS_{\text{subjects}} = 183.8095 \qquad df_{\text{subjects}} = 6$$

### Within-Groups Variance

$$SS_{within} = \Sigma X_{ij}^2 - \frac{\Sigma X_{i\bullet}^2}{j} - \frac{\Sigma X_{\bullet j}^2}{n} + \frac{\Sigma(X_{ij})^2}{N} \qquad df_{within} = (j-1)(n-1)$$

$$SS_{within} = 1973 - 1767.2857 - 1921 + 1737.1905 \qquad df_{within} = (2)(6)$$

$$SS_{within} = 21.9048 \qquad\qquad\qquad\qquad\qquad df_{within} = 12$$

### Total Variance

$$SS_{total} = \Sigma X_{ij}^2 - \frac{\Sigma(X_{ij})^2}{N} \qquad\qquad\qquad df_{total} = N - 1$$

$$SS_{total} = 1973 - \frac{(191)^2}{21} = 1973 - 1737.1905 \qquad df_{total} = 21 - 1$$

$$SS_{total} = 235.8095 \qquad\qquad\qquad\qquad\qquad df_{total} = 20$$

| Source | SS | df | MS | F |
|--------|-----|-----|------|------|
| Between-groups | 30.0952 | 2 | 15.05 | 8.22 |
| Subjects | 183.8095 | 6 | 30.63 | 16.74 |
| Within-groups | 21.9048 | 12 | 1.83 | |
| Total | 235.8095 | 20 | | |

### Additional Tests:

#### Omega Squared:

$$\omega^2 = \frac{df_{between}(F_{between} - 1)}{df_{between}(F_{between} - 1) + F_{subjects}(n) + j(n)}$$

## F-RATIO: TWO-WAY ANALYSIS OF VARIANCE— CORRELATED-GROUPS DESIGN

### Purpose:

This test determines the effects of two factors on the dependent variable. One factor is a between-subjects variable. The second factor is a correlated-groups factor. The statistic examines the effect of each variable. These comparisons are the main effects. The statistic also examines the interaction between the two independent variables. The interaction accounts for variance in the dependent variable that cannot be accounted for by either independent variable by itself.

### Hypotheses:

### Null Hypothesis:

Factor A  $H_0$: $\sigma_A^2 + \sigma_{subjects}^2 = \sigma_{subjects}^2$

Factor B  $H_0$: $\sigma_B^2 + \sigma_{B \times subjects}^2 = \sigma_{B \times subjects}^2$

Factor AB  $H_0$: $\sigma_{AB}^2 + \sigma_{B \times subjects}^2 = \sigma_{B \times subjects}^2$

### Alternative Hypothesis:

Factor A  $H_0$: $\sigma_A^2 + \sigma_{subjects}^2 \; \sigma_{subjects}^2$

Factor B  $H_0$: $\sigma_B^2 + \sigma_{B \times subjects}^2 \neq \sigma_{B \times subjects}^2$

Factor AB $H_0$: $\sigma^2_{AB} + \sigma^2_{B \times \text{subjects}} \neq \sigma^2_{B \times \text{subjects}}$

If $F_{\text{observed}} \geq F_{\text{critical}}$ then reject $H_0$.

$$SS_A = \frac{\Sigma(X_{\bullet j \bullet})^2}{nk} - \frac{(\Sigma X_{ijk})^2}{N} \qquad df_A = j - 1 \qquad MS_A = \frac{SS_A}{df_{\text{subjects}}} \qquad F_A = \frac{MS_A}{MS_{\text{subjects}}}$$

$$SS_{\text{subjects}} = \frac{\Sigma(X_{i \bullet \bullet})^2}{k} - \frac{\Sigma(X_{\bullet j \bullet})^2}{nk} \qquad df_{\text{subjects}} = j(n - 1)$$

$$SS_B = \frac{\Sigma(X_{\bullet \bullet k})^2}{nj} - \frac{(\Sigma X_{ijk})^2}{N} \qquad df_B = k - 1 \qquad MS_B = \frac{SS_B}{df_{B \times \text{subjects}}} \qquad F_B = \frac{MS_B}{MS_{B \times \text{subjects}}}$$

$$SS_{AB} = \frac{\Sigma(X_{\bullet ij})^2}{n} - \frac{\Sigma(X_{ijk})^2}{N} - SS_A - SS_B \qquad df_{AB} = (j - 1)(k - 1) \qquad MS_{AB} = \frac{SS_{AB}}{df_{B \times \text{subjects}}} \qquad F_{AB} = \frac{MS_{AB}}{MS_{B \times \text{subjects}}}$$

$$SS_{B \times \text{subjects}} = \Sigma X_{ijk}^2 - \frac{\Sigma(X_{\bullet ij})^2}{n} - \frac{\Sigma(X_{i \bullet \bullet})^2}{k} + \frac{\Sigma(X_{\bullet j \bullet})^2}{nk}$$

$$df_{B \times \text{subjects}} = j(n - 1)(k - 1)$$

$$SS_{\text{total}} = \Sigma X_{ijk}^2 - \frac{(\Sigma X_{ijk})^2}{N} \qquad df_{\text{total}} = N - 1$$

*Assumptions:*

Data are normally distributed.

$\sigma_1 = \sigma_2 = \ldots = \sigma_k$

*Sampling Distribution:* Fisher's $F$-Distribution—Table J

To determine $F_{\text{critical}}$, establish the level of $\alpha$ and calculate the degrees of freedom. The $F$-distribution has two degrees of freedom. The numerator degrees of freedom ($df_N$) is the degrees of freedom associated with the between-groups variance. The denominator degrees of freedom ($df_D$) is the degrees of freedom associated with the within-groups variance. For example, if $\alpha = .05$ one-tailed and $df_N = 3$ and $df_D = 6$ $F_{\text{critical}} = 4.76$. Note that there is a separate $F_{\text{critical}}$ for each main effect and the interaction.

*Example:*

|        | Subject | Day 1 | Day 2 | Day 3 | Day 4 | $X_{i \bullet \bullet}$ |
|--------|---------|-------|-------|-------|-------|-----------|
|        | 1       | 10    | 9     | 10    | 10    | 39        |
|        | 2       | 12    | 12    | 12    | 12    | 48        |
| $TX_1$ | 3       | 9     | 9     | 10    | 12    | 40        |
|        | 4       | 8     | 9     | 8     | 7     | 32        |
|        | 5       | 11    | 11    | 10    | 10    | 42        |
|        | $X_{\bullet 1k}$ | 50 | 50 | 50 | 51 | $X_{\bullet 1 \bullet} = 201$ |
|        | 6       | 12    | 3     | 9     | 3     | 27        |
|        | 7       | 11    | 4     | 4     | 2     | 21        |
| $TX_2$ | 8       | 8     | 7     | 3     | 4     | 22        |
|        | 9       | 9     | 6     | 6     | 5     | 26        |
|        | 10      | 10    | 8     | 10    | 4     | 32        |
|        | $X_{\bullet 2k}$ | 50 | 28 | 32 | 18 | $X_{\bullet 2 \bullet} = 128$ |
|        | $X_{\bullet \bullet k}$ | 100 | 78 | 82 | 69 | $X_{\bullet \bullet \bullet} = 329$ |

### Between-Subjects Variable Variance: Factor A

$$SS_A = \frac{\Sigma(X_{\bullet j \bullet})^2}{nk} - \frac{(\Sigma X_{ijk})^2}{Nk} \qquad\qquad df_A = j - 1$$

$$SS_A = \frac{201^2 + 128^2}{5(4)} - \frac{(329)^2}{40} \qquad\qquad df_A = 2 - 1$$

$$SS_A = \frac{56785}{20} - \frac{108241}{40}$$

$$SS_A = 2839.25 - 2706.025$$

$$SS_A = 133.225 \qquad\qquad df_A = 1$$

$$MS_A = \frac{133.225}{1}$$

$$MS_A = 133.225$$

### Variance Due to Subjects Across Factor A

$$SS_{\text{subjects}} = \frac{\Sigma(X_{i \bullet \bullet})^2}{k} - \frac{\Sigma(X_{\bullet j \bullet})^2}{nk}$$

$$df_{\text{subjects}} = j(n - 1)$$

$$SS_{\text{subjects}} = \frac{39^2 + 48^2 + 40^2 + \cdots 26^2 + 32^2}{4} - \frac{201^2 + 128^2}{5(4)}$$

$$df_{\text{subjects}} = 2(5 - 1)$$

$$SS_{\text{subjects}} = \frac{11567}{4} - \frac{56785}{20}$$

$$df_{\text{subjects}} = 2(4)$$

$$SS_{subject} = 2891.75 - 2839.25$$

$$SS_{\text{subjects}} = 52.50$$

$$df_{\text{subjects}} = 8$$

$$MS_{\text{subjects}} = \frac{52.5}{8}$$

$$MS_{\text{subjects}} = 6.5625$$

### Within-Subjects Variable Variance: Factor B

$$SS_B = \frac{\Sigma(X_{\bullet \bullet k})^2}{nj} - \frac{(\Sigma X_{ijk})^2}{N} \qquad\qquad df_B = k - 1$$

$$SS_B = \frac{100^2 + 78^2 + 82^2 + 69^2}{5(2)} - \frac{(329)^2}{40} \qquad\qquad df_B = 4 - 1$$

$$SS_B = \frac{27569}{10} - \frac{108241}{40}$$

$$SS_B = 2756.9 - 2706.025$$

$$SS_B = 50.875 \qquad\qquad df_B = 3$$

$$MS_B = \frac{50.875}{3}$$

$$MS_B = 16.9583$$

## Interaction Variance

$$SS_{AB} = \frac{\Sigma(X_{\bullet ij})}{n} - \frac{(\Sigma X_{ijk})^2}{N} - SS_A - SS_B \qquad\qquad df_{AB} = (j-1)(k-1)$$

$$SS_{AB} = \frac{50^2 + 50^2 + \cdots 32^2 + 18^2}{5} - \frac{(329)^2}{40} - 133.225 - 50.875 \quad df_{AB} = (2-1)(4-1)$$

$$SS_{AB} = \frac{14733}{5} - \frac{108241}{40} - 133.225 - 50.875 \qquad\qquad df_{AB} = (1)(3)$$

$$SS_{AB} = 2946.6 - 2706.025 - 133.225 - 50.875$$

$$SS_{AB} = 56.475 \qquad\qquad df_{AB} = 3$$

$$MS_{AB} = \frac{56.475}{3}$$

$$MS_{AB} = 18.825$$

## Factor B × Subjects Variance

$$SS_{B \times \text{subjects}} = \Sigma X_{ijk}^2 - \frac{\Sigma(X_{\bullet ij})}{n} - \frac{\Sigma(X_{i \bullet \bullet})^2}{k} + \frac{\Sigma(X_{\bullet j \bullet})^2}{nk} \qquad df_{B \times \text{subjects}} = j(n-1)(k-1)$$

$$SS_{B \times \text{subjects}} = 3059 - 2946.6 - 2891.75 + 2839.25 \qquad df_{B \times \text{subjects}} = 2(5-1)(4-1)$$

$$SS_{B \times \text{subjects}} = 59.900 \qquad\qquad df_{B \times \text{subjects}} = 24$$

$$MS_{B \times \text{subjects}} = \frac{59.900}{24}$$

$$MS_{B \times \text{subjects}} = 2.4958$$

$$SS_{\text{total}} = \Sigma X_{ijk}^2 - \frac{\Sigma(X_{ijk})^2}{N} \qquad\qquad df_{\text{total}} = N - 1$$

$$SS_{\text{total}} = 3059 - 2706.025$$

$$SS_{\text{total}} = 352.975 \qquad\qquad df_{\text{total}} = 39$$

| Source | SS | df | MS | F |
|---|---|---|---|---|
| A | 133.225 | 1 | 133.225 | 20.301 |
| Subjects | 52.500 | 8 | 6.563 | 2.629 |
| B | 50.875 | 3 | 16.958 | 6.795 |
| AB | 56.475 | 3 | 18.825 | 7.543 |
| B×subjects | 59.900 | 24 | 2.496 | |
| Total | 352.975 | 39 | | |

### Omega Squared

The first step is to calculate a common denominator for each $\omega^2$.

$$F_A(j-1) + F_s(n-1) + F_B(k-1) + F_{AB}((j-1)(k-1)) + (n-1)(jk-1) \quad 16.17$$

$$20.301(2-1) + 2.629(5-1) + 6.795(4-1) + 7.543((2-1)(4-1)) + (5-1)(2(4)-1)$$

$$20.301 + 10.516 + 20.385 + 22.629 + 28$$

$$101.831$$

The numerators for the three $\omega^2$s are:

| | | | |
|---|---|---|---|
| $A = (F_A - 1)(j - 1)$ | $= (20.301 - 1)(2 - 1)$ | $= 19.301$ | 16.18 |
| $B = (F_B - 1)(k - 1)$ | $= (6.795 - 1)(4 - 1)$ | $= 17.386$ | 16.19 |
| $AB = (F_{AB} - 1)(j - 1)(k - 1)$ | $= (7.543 - 1)(2 - 1)(4 - 1)$ | $= 19.269$ | 16.20 |

Therefore, the three values of $\omega^2$ are

$$\omega_A^2 = \frac{19.301}{101.831} \qquad\qquad \omega_A^2 = .1895$$

$$\omega_B^2 = \frac{17.386}{101.831} \qquad\qquad \omega_B^2 = .1707$$

$$\omega_{AB}^2 = \frac{19.269}{101.831} \qquad\qquad \omega_{AB}^2 = .1892$$

---

## TUKEY'S HONEST SIGNIFICANT DIFFERENCE

### Purpose:

Tukey's HSD is a test used in conjunction with the ANOVA to examine the differences between means. The test protects against inflated experimentwise errors. One uses the test to compare means only if there is a significant $F$-ratio.

### Equations:

$$HSD = q_{critical} \sqrt{\frac{MS_{within}}{n}}$$

where
   HSD = Critical difference required to consider the means statistically different.
   $q_{critical}$ = Tabled value for a given $\alpha$ level for number of means and $df_w$.
   MSW = Mean square within groups.
   $n$ = Number of subjects in each group.

If the number of subjects in each group is not equal, $n'$ is defined as

$$n' = \frac{Number\ of\ Means}{\Sigma\left(\dfrac{1}{n_j}\right)}$$

For example, if we had four groups with sample sizes of 5, 4, 5, 4, the corrected sample size would be

$$n = \frac{4}{\dfrac{1}{5} + \dfrac{1}{4} + \dfrac{1}{4} + \dfrac{1}{5}} = \frac{4}{.20 + .25 + .25 + .20} = \frac{4}{.90} = 4.44$$

**Sampling Distribution:** Studentized Range

|  | Group 1 | Group 2 | Group 3 | Group 4 |
|---|---|---|---|---|
| $\overline{X}$ | 2.50 | 4.5 | 5.5 | 6.0 |

$k = 4$, $df_{\text{within}} = 12$, and $MS_{\text{within}} = 1.75$, $\alpha = .05$

$q_{\text{critical}} = 4.20$.

$$\text{HSD} = 4.20 \sqrt{\frac{1.75}{4}}$$

$$\text{HSD} = 4.24(0.6614)$$

$$\text{HSD} = 2.78$$

|  |  | Group 1 | Group 2 | Group 3 | Group 4 |
|---|---|---|---|---|---|
|  | $\overline{X}$ | 2.50 | 4.5 | 5.5 | 6.0 |
| Group 1 | 2.5 | — | 2.0 | 3.0* | 3.5* |
| Group 2 | 4.5 | | — | 1.0 | 1.5 |
| Group 3 | 5.5 | | | — | .5 |
| Group 4 | 6.0 | | | | — |

*$p < .05$

### Tukey for Two-Factor Mixed-Model ANOVA

When we use the Tukey HSD for the mixed-model ANOVA, it is critical that we use the correct $MS_{\text{within}}$.

### Factor A

The $HSD_A$ uses the $MS_{\text{subjects}}$ and $n(k)$ to determine the critical values for the differences among the means.

$$\text{HSD}_A = q_{\text{critical}} \sqrt{\frac{MS_{\text{subjects}}}{n(k)}}$$

### Factor B

The $\text{HSD}_B$ uses the $MS_{\text{within}}$ and $n(j)$ to determine the critical values for the differences among the means.

$$MS_{\text{within}} = \frac{SS_{\text{subjects}} + SS_{B \times \text{subjects}}}{df_{\text{subjects}} + df_{B \times \text{subjects}}}$$

$$HSD_B = q_{\text{critical}} \sqrt{\frac{MS_{\text{within}}}{n(j)}}$$

### Factor AB

To determine the HSD for the interaction we use

$$HSD_{AB} = q_{\text{critical}} \sqrt{\frac{MS_{\text{within}}}{n}}$$

# $\chi^2$ GOODNESS-OF-FIT TEST

### Purpose:

The $\chi^2$ test determines if the difference between observed and expected frequencies is greater than expected by chance. The expected frequencies can be determined empirically or on the basis of population estimates.

### Hypotheses:

### Null Hypothesis:

$H_0$: The observed frequencies match the expected frequencies defined by the population.

### Alternative Hypothesis:

$H_1$: The observed frequencies do not match the expected frequencies defined by the population.

If $\chi^2_{\text{observed}} \geq \chi^2_{\text{observed}}$ then reject $H_0$.

### Equations:

$$\chi^2 = \Sigma \frac{(O_i - E_i)^2}{E_i}, \, df = k - 1$$

where
$O$ is the observed frequency.
$E$ is the expected frequency. $E$ may represent a population estimate or determined empirically. Note that $\Sigma O = \Sigma E$.
$k$ is the number of categories

### Assumptions:

Mutually exclusive categories
Independence of observations
Sufficient sample size—all values of $E$ should be greater than 5.

### Sampling Distribution: $\chi^2$-distribution—Table Q

To determine $\chi^2_{\text{critical}}$, establish the level of $\alpha$ and calculate the degrees of freedom.

### Example:

| Major | O | E | $O_i - E_i$ | $(O_i - E_i)^2$ | $\dfrac{(O_i - E_i)^2}{E_i}$ |
|---|---|---|---|---|---|
| Anthropology | 3 | 15 | -12 | 144 | 9.6000 |
| Economics | 45 | 90 | -45 | 2025 | 22.5000 |
| Political Science | 77 | 75 | 2 | 4 | 0.0533 |
| Psychology | 90 | 75 | 15 | 225 | 3.0000 |
| Sociology | 85 | 45 | 40 | 1600 | 35.5556 |
| **Total** | **300** | **300** | **0** | | $\chi^2 = \mathbf{70.7089}$ |

$df = 4 = 5 - 1$      $\chi^2_{\text{critical}} = 9.488$, Reject $H_0$

## THE $\chi^2$ TEST OF INDEPENDENCE

### Purpose:

The $\chi^2$ test determines if the difference between observed and expected frequencies is greater than expected by chance.

### Hypotheses:

### Null Hypothesis:

$H_0$: The observed frequencies match the expected frequencies.

### Alternative Hypothesis:

$H_1$: The observed frequencies do not match the expected frequencies. If $\chi^2_{observed} \geq \chi^2_{critical}$ then reject $H_0$.

### Equations:

$$\chi^2 = \sum_{i=1}^{r} \sum_{j=1}^{c} \frac{(O_{ij} - E_{ij})^2}{E_{ij}}, \, df = (r - 1)(c - 1)$$

where
$O_{ij}$ = Observed frequency
$E_{ij} = \dfrac{R_i C_j}{T}$
$R_i$ = Row total
$C_{ij}$ = Column total
$T$ = Total of all observations
$r$ = Number of rows
$c$ = Number of columns

### Assumptions:

Mutually exclusive categories
Independence of observations
Sufficient sample size—At least 80% of the cells should have an expected frequency of greater than 5 and no cell should have an expected frequency less than 1.

### Sampling Distribution: $\chi^2$-distribution

To determine $\chi^2_{critical}$, establish the level of $\alpha$ and calculate the degrees of freedom. The $\chi^2$-distribution has one degree of freedom. Use Table X to determine the critical value of $\chi^2$.

## *Example:*

**Experimental Condition**

| | $A_1$ | $A_2$ | Row total |
|---|---|---|---|
| $B_1$ | $O_{11} = 35$ <br> $E_{11} = \dfrac{45 \times 50}{100}$ <br><br> $E_{11} = 22.5$ <br><br> $6.944 = \dfrac{(35 - 22.5)^2}{22.5}$ | $O_{12} = 10$ <br> $E_{12} = \dfrac{45 \times 50}{100}$ <br><br> $E_{12} = 22.5$ <br><br> $6.944 = \dfrac{(10 - 22.5)^2}{22.5}$ | $R_1 = 45$ |
| $B_2$ | $O_{21} = 15$ <br> $E_{21} = \dfrac{55 \times 50}{100}$ <br><br> $E_{21} = 27.5$ <br><br> $5.682 = \dfrac{(15 - 27.5)^2}{27.5}$ | $O_{22} = 40$ <br> $E_{22} = \dfrac{55 \times 50}{100}$ <br><br> $E_{21} = 27.5$ <br><br> $5.682 = \dfrac{(40 - 27.5)^2}{27.5}$ | $R_2 = 55$ |
| **Column total** | $C_1 = 50$ | $C_2 = 50$ | $T = 100$ |

$$\chi^2 = 6.944 + 6.944 + 5.682 + 5.682$$
$$\chi^2 = 25.252$$

## *Additional Tests:*

***Cramér's Coefficient $\phi$:*** The $\phi$ coefficient is a measure of association between the two variables. Like the correlation coefficient, $\phi$ indicates the degree to which the two variables relate to each other.

$$\phi = \sqrt{\frac{\chi^2}{N(S - 1)}}$$

Where $N$ is the number of observations and $S$ is the smaller number or rows or columns.

$$\phi = \sqrt{\frac{25.252}{100(2 - 1)}} \qquad \phi = \sqrt{\frac{25.252}{100}} \qquad \phi = \sqrt{0.25252}$$

$$\phi = .50$$

**Post Hoc Analysis of $\chi^2$:** The $\chi^2$ is an omnibus test that examines the overall hypothesis of the independence between the two variables. The test does not indicate which cell or cells contribute to the significant $\chi^2$. The statistic, $\hat{e}_{ij}$ is a residual that is normally distributed. Therefore, it may be interpreted as a $z$-score

$$e_{ij} = \frac{O_{ij} - E_{ij}}{\sqrt{E_{ij}}}$$

$$v_{ij} = \left(1 - \frac{C_i}{T}\right)\left(1 - \frac{R_j}{T}\right)$$

$$\hat{e}_{ij} = \frac{e_{ij}}{\sqrt{v}}$$

**Experimental Condition**

| | $A_1$ | $A_2$ | Row total |
|---|---|---|---|
| $B_1$ | $O_{11} = 35$<br>$E_{11} = 22.5$<br>$e_{11} = \dfrac{35 - 22.5}{\sqrt{22.5}}$<br>$e_{11} = 2.635$<br><br>$v_{11} = .275$<br><br>$\hat{e}_{11} = \dfrac{2.635}{\sqrt{275}}$<br>$\hat{e}_{11} = 5.03$ | $O_{12} = 10$<br>$E_{12} = 22.5$<br>$e_{12} = \dfrac{35 - 22.5}{\sqrt{22.5}}$<br>$e_{12} = 2.635$<br><br>$v_{12} = .275$<br><br>$\hat{e}_{12} = \dfrac{-2.635}{\sqrt{.275}}$<br>$\hat{e}_{12} = -5.03$ | $R_1 = 45$<br><br><br><br>$.55 = 1 - \dfrac{45}{100}$ |
| $B_2$ | $O_{21} = 15$<br>$E_{21} = 27.5$<br>$e_{21} = \dfrac{15 - 27.5}{\sqrt{27.5}}$<br>$e_{21} = -2.383$<br><br>$v_{11} = .225$<br><br>$\hat{e}_{21} = \dfrac{-2.383}{\sqrt{225}}$<br>$\hat{e}_{21} = -5.02$ | $O_{22} = 40$<br>$E_{22} = 27.5$<br>$e_{22} = \dfrac{40 - 27.5}{\sqrt{27.5}}$<br>$e_{22} = 2.383$<br><br>$v_{12} = .225$<br><br>$\hat{e}_{21} = \dfrac{2.383}{\sqrt{.225}}$<br>$\hat{e}_{22} = 5.02$ | $R_2 = 55$<br><br><br><br>$.45 = 1 - \dfrac{55}{100}$ |
| Column total | $C_1 = 50$<br>$.50 = 1 - \dfrac{50}{100}$ | $C_2 = 50$<br>$.50 = 1 - \dfrac{50}{100}$ | $T = 100$ |

## McNEMAR CHANGE TEST

### Purpose:

This test determines if the difference between two correlated sample proportions is statistically significant. Researchers use this test when comparing the proportion of an event sampled on two occasions.

### Hypothesis:

$H_0$: $p_1 = p_2$

$H_1$: $p_1 \neq p_2$

If $\chi^2_{observed} \geq \chi^2_{critical}$ then reject $H_0$.

### Equation:

$$\chi^2 = \frac{(|a - d| - 1)^2}{a + d}, \, df = 1$$

$a, b, c,$ and $d$ represent frequencies in a $2 \times 2$ table.

### Sampling Distribution: $\chi^2$ distribution—Table Q

To determine $\chi^2_{critical}$ establish the level of $\alpha$ and then find the critical value of $\chi^2$ associated with 1 degree of freedom. For example, with $\alpha = .05$ $\chi^2 = 3.84$

*Example:*

| | RESPONSE, TIME 1 | |
|---|---|---|
| | **A** | **B** |
| Response, Time 2 A | $a = 90$ | $b = 40$ |
| Response, Time 2 B | $c = 27$ | $d = 153$ |
| | | $N = 310$ |

$$\chi^2 = \frac{(|a - d| - 1)^2}{a + d} \qquad \chi^2 = \frac{(|90 - 153| - 1)^2}{90 + 153} \qquad \chi^2 = \frac{(63 - 1)^2}{243}$$

$$\chi^2 = \frac{(62)^2}{243} \qquad \chi^2 = \frac{3844}{243}$$

$$\chi^2 = 15.8189$$

## COHEN'S KAPPA

*Purpose:*

Cohen's kappa is a descriptive statistic that indicates the degree of interrater reliability between two independent observers. The statistic takes into consideration the frequency of the different categories. One can calculate both the $\kappa$ coefficient and the standard error of the statistic ($\sigma_\kappa$).

*Equations:*

$$\kappa = \frac{\Sigma O_{ii} - \Sigma E_{ii}}{T - \Sigma E_{ii}} \qquad \sigma_\kappa = \sqrt{\frac{\Sigma O_{ii}(T - \Sigma O_{ii})}{T(T - \Sigma E_{ii})^2}}$$

where
$O_{ii} =$ Observed frequency
$E_{ii} = \dfrac{R_i C_i}{T}$
$R_i =$ Row total
$C_i =$ Column total
$T =$ Total of all observations

| | OBSERVER 1 | | | | |
|---|---|---|---|---|---|
| **Observer 2** | **A** | **B** | **C** | **D** | $R_i$ |
| A | $O_{11} = 68$ $E_{11} = 30.415$ | 5 | 2 | 2 | 77 |
| B | 6 | $O_{22} = 15$ $E_{22} = 4.03$ | 1 | 4 | 26 |
| C | 3 | 4 | $O_{33} = 23$ $E_{33} = 5.44$ | 2 | 32 |
| D | 2 | 7 | 8 | $O_{44} = 48$ $E_{44} = 18.20$ | 65 |
| $C_j$ | 79 | 31 | 34 | 56 | $T = 200$ |

$$\Sigma O_{ii} = 68 + 15 + 23 + 48 \qquad \Sigma O_{ii} = 154$$

$$\Sigma E_{ii} = 30.415 + 4.03 + 5.44 + 18.20 \qquad \Sigma E_{ii} = 58.085$$

$$\kappa = \frac{154 - 58.085}{200 - 58.085} \qquad \kappa = \frac{95.915}{141.915}$$

$$\kappa = .678$$

$$\sigma_\kappa = \sqrt{\frac{154(200 - 154)}{200(200 - 58.085)^2}} \qquad \sigma_\kappa = \sqrt{\frac{7084}{4027973.445}}$$

$$\sigma_\kappa = 0.0419$$

---

## MANN-WHITNEY *U*-TEST

### *Purpose:*

The Mann-Whitney *U*-Test is an alternative to the Student's *t*-ratio for comparing two groups. Many researchers prefer to use the *U*-test when the data do not fit the assumptions of the *t*-ratio.

### *Hypotheses:*

**Null Hypothesis:** $H_0: U = U'$: The differences between the groups' ranks are due to chance.

**Alternative Hypothesis:** $H_1: U \neq U'$: The differences between the groups' ranks are not random.

**Sampling Distribution:** The Mann-Whitney *U*-Test—Table R

### *Equations:*

$$U = N_1 N_2 + \frac{N_1(N_1 + 1)}{2} - R_1 \qquad U' = N_1 N_2 + \frac{N_2(N_2 + 1)}{2} - R_2$$

Where $N$ represents the sample sizes and $R$ represents the sum of ranks for each group. To calculate $R$ for each group, rank all the data from lowest to highest. Assign the ranks and then return the observed scores and their ranks to the original groups.

### *Example:*

| EXPERIMENTAL | | CONTROL | |
|---|---|---|---|
| Time (ms) | Rank | Time (ms) | Rank |
| 140 | 4 | 130 | 1 |
| 147 | 6 | 135 | 2 |
| 153 | 8 | 138 | 3 |
| 160 | 10 | 144 | 5 |
| 165 | 11 | 148 | 7 |
| 170 | 13 | 155 | 9 |
| 171 | 14 | 168 | 12 |
| 193 | 15 | | |

$$R_1 = 81 \qquad\qquad\qquad\qquad R_1 = 39$$

$$N_1 = 8 \qquad\qquad\qquad\qquad N_1 = 7$$

$$U = N_1 N_2 + \frac{N_1(N_1 + 1)}{2} - R_1$$

$$U = 8(7) + \frac{8(8 + 1)}{2} - 81 \quad U = 56 + \frac{72}{2} - 81 \quad U = 56 + 36 - 81 \quad U = 11$$

|  | One-tailed | Two-tailed |
|---|---|---|
| $\alpha = .05$ | $U_{critical} = 13$<br>Reject $H_0$ | $U_{critical} = 10$<br>Fail to reject $H_0$ |

## WILCOXON MATCHED-PAIRS SIGNED-RANK TEST

### Purpose:

The Wilcoxon Matched-Pairs test is an alternative to the correlated-groups Student's $t$-ratio. Many researchers prefer to use the $U$-test when the data do not fit the assumptions of the $t$-ratio.

### Hypotheses:

**Null Hypothesis:**   $H_0$: The differences between the groups' ranks are due to chance.

**Alternative Hypothesis:**   $H_1$: The differences between the groups' ranks are not random.

**Sampling Distribution:**   Wilcoxon Matched-Pairs Test.

### Equations:

$$T_W$$

Where $T_W$ is the smaller sum of the total of positive and negative differences. To determine $T_W$:

1. Determine the difference between each pair in the data set.
2. Rank order the differences and apply the sign of the difference to the rank.
3. Create separate totals for the negative and positive ranks.
4. $T_W$ equals the smaller of the two sums.

*Example:*

| | | | | | RANKS | |
|:---:|:---:|:---:|:---:|:---:|:---:|:---:|
| Pair | A | B | Difference | Rank of Difference | Negative | Positive |
| 1 | 47 | 40 | +7 | 9 | | 9 |
| 2 | 43 | 38 | +5 | 5 | | 5 |
| 3 | 36 | 42 | −6 | (−) 7 | **(−) 7** | |
| 4 | 38 | 25 | +13 | 12 | | 12 |
| 5 | 30 | 29 | +1 | 1 | | 1 |
| 6 | 22 | 26 | −4 | (−) 4 | **(−) 4** | |
| 7 | 25 | 16 | +9 | 11 | | 11 |
| 8 | 21 | 18 | +3 | 3 | | 3 |
| 9 | 14 | 8 | +6 | 7 | | 7 |
| 10 | 12 | 4 | +8 | 10 | | 10 |
| 11 | 5 | 7 | −2 | (−) 2 | **(−) 2** | |
| 12 | 9 | 3 | +6 | 7 | | 7 |
| 13 | 5 | 5 | (0) | | | |
| | | | | | **(−)13** | **65** |
| | | | | | $T_W = 13$ | |

There is one tied pair, therefore $df = 12 = N - 1$
$\alpha = .05$, two tailed, $T_{w\ critical} = 13$, reject $H_0$.

| | One-tailed | Two-tailed |
|:---|:---:|:---:|
| $\alpha = .05$ | $T_{w\ critical} = 17$ | $T_{w\ critical} = 13$ |
| | Fail to Reject $H_0$ | Reject $H_0$ |

# Table of Contents

# Statistical Tables

**Table** **A**

**Proportions of Area Under the Normal Curve**

The use of Table A requires that you convert the raw score to a $z$-score. The $z$-score is a standard deviate that allows you to use standard normal distribution. This distribution has a mean of 0.0, a standard deviation of 1.0, and a total area equal to 1.0.

The values in Table A represent the proportion of area in the standard normal curve. The table contains $z$-scores between 0.0 and 4.00 with .01 increments. Because the normal distribution is symmetrical, the table represents $z$-scores ranging between $-4.00$ and 4.00.

Column A of the table represents the $z$-score. Column B represents the proportion of the curve between the mean and the $z$-score. Column C represents the proportion of the curve that extends from the $z$-score to $\infty$.

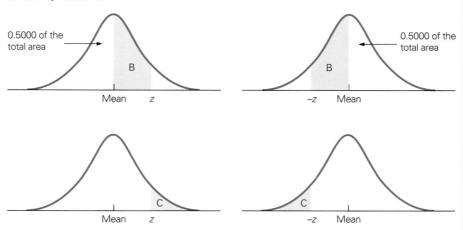

## Example

$z$-score = 1.30

|  | **Column B** | **Column C** |  |
|---|---|---|---|
| **Positive z-scores** |  |  |  |
| Area between mean and $+z$ | .4032 |  | 40.32% of curve |
| Area greater than $+z$ |  | .0968 | 9.68% of curve |
| **Negative z-scores** |  |  |  |
| Area between mean and $-z$ | .4032 |  | 40.32% of curve |
| Area less than $-z$ |  | .0968 | 9.68% of curve |
| Area between $-z$ and $+z$ | .4032 + .4032 = .8064 or 80.64% of curve | | |
| Area beyond $-z$ and beyond $+z$ | .0968 + .0968 = .1936 or 19.36% of curve | | |

In the following examples, we add .5000 to the area between the mean and $z$-score. The .5000 represents the proportion of the curve on the complementary half of the normal curve.

| Area at and below $+z$ | .5000 + .4032 = .9032 or 90.32% of curve |
|---|---|
| Area at and above $-z$ | .4032 + .5000 = .9032 or 90.32% of curve |

## Table A

| (A) z | (B) area between mean and z | (C) area beyond z | (A) z | (B) area between mean and z | (C) area beyond z | (A) z | (B) area between mean and z | (C) area beyond z |
|---|---|---|---|---|---|---|---|---|
| 0.00 | .0000 | .5000 | 0.55 | .2088 | .2912 | 1.10 | .3643 | .1357 |
| 0.01 | .0040 | .4960 | 0.56 | .2123 | .2877 | 1.11 | .3665 | .1335 |
| 0.02 | .0080 | .4920 | 0.57 | .2157 | .2843 | 1.12 | .3686 | .1314 |
| 0.03 | .0120 | .4880 | 0.58 | .2190 | .2810 | 1.13 | .3708 | .1292 |
| 0.04 | .0160 | .4840 | 0.59 | .2224 | .2776 | 1.14 | .3729 | .1271 |
| 0.05 | .0199 | .4801 | 0.60 | .2257 | .2743 | 1.15 | .3749 | .1251 |
| 0.06 | .0239 | .4761 | 0.61 | .2291 | .2709 | 1.16 | .3770 | .1230 |
| 0.07 | .0279 | .4721 | 0.62 | .2324 | .2676 | 1.17 | .3790 | .1210 |
| 0.08 | .0319 | .4681 | 0.63 | .2357 | .2643 | 1.18 | .3810 | .1190 |
| 0.09 | .0359 | .4641 | 0.64 | .2389 | .2611 | 1.19 | .3830 | .1170 |
| 0.10 | .0398 | .4602 | 0.65 | .2422 | .2578 | 1.20 | .3849 | .1151 |
| 0.11 | .0438 | .4562 | 0.66 | .2454 | .2546 | 1.21 | .3869 | .1131 |
| 0.12 | .0478 | .4522 | 0.67 | .2486 | .2514 | 1.22 | .3888 | .1112 |
| 0.13 | .0517 | .4483 | 0.68 | .2517 | .2483 | 1.23 | .3907 | .1093 |
| 0.14 | .0557 | .4443 | 0.69 | .2549 | .2451 | 1.24 | .3925 | .1075 |
| 0.15 | .0596 | .4404 | 0.70 | .2580 | .2420 | 1.25 | .3944 | .1056 |
| 0.16 | .0636 | .4364 | 0.71 | .2611 | .2389 | 1.26 | .3962 | .1038 |
| 0.17 | .0675 | .4325 | 0.72 | .2642 | .2358 | 1.27 | .3980 | .1020 |
| 0.18 | .0714 | .4286 | 0.73 | .2673 | .2327 | 1.28 | .3997 | .1003 |
| 0.19 | .0753 | .4247 | 0.74 | .2704 | .2296 | 1.29 | .4015 | .0985 |
| 0.20 | .0793 | .4207 | 0.75 | .2734 | .2266 | 1.30 | .4032 | .0968 |
| 0.21 | .0832 | .4168 | 0.76 | .2764 | .2236 | 1.31 | .4049 | .0951 |
| 0.22 | .0871 | .4129 | 0.77 | .2794 | .2206 | 1.32 | .4066 | .0934 |
| 0.23 | .0910 | .4090 | 0.78 | .2823 | .2177 | 1.33 | .4082 | .0918 |
| 0.24 | .0948 | .4052 | 0.79 | .2852 | .2148 | 1.34 | .4099 | .0901 |
| 0.25 | .0987 | .4013 | 0.80 | .2881 | .2119 | 1.35 | .4115 | .0885 |
| 0.26 | .1026 | .3974 | 0.81 | .2910 | .2090 | 1.36 | .4131 | .0869 |
| 0.27 | .1064 | .3936 | 0.82 | .2939 | .2061 | 1.37 | .4147 | .0853 |
| 0.28 | .1103 | .3897 | 0.83 | .2967 | .2033 | 1.38 | .4162 | .0838 |
| 0.29 | .1141 | .3859 | 0.84 | .2995 | .2005 | 1.39 | .4177 | .0823 |
| 0.30 | .1179 | .3821 | 0.85 | .3023 | .1977 | 1.40 | .4192 | .0808 |
| 0.31 | .1217 | .3783 | 0.86 | .3051 | .1949 | 1.41 | .4207 | .0793 |
| 0.32 | .1255 | .3745 | 0.87 | .3078 | .1922 | 1.42 | .4222 | .0778 |
| 0.33 | .1293 | .3707 | 0.88 | .3106 | .1894 | 1.43 | .4236 | .0764 |
| 0.34 | .1331 | .3669 | 0.89 | .3133 | .1867 | 1.44 | .4251 | .0749 |
| 0.35 | .1368 | .3632 | 0.90 | .3159 | .1841 | 1.45 | .4265 | .0735 |
| 0.36 | .1406 | .3594 | 0.91 | .3186 | .1814 | 1.46 | .4279 | .0721 |
| 0.37 | .1443 | .3557 | 0.92 | .3212 | .1788 | 1.47 | .4292 | .0708 |
| 0.38 | .1480 | .3520 | 0.93 | .3238 | .1762 | 1.48 | .4306 | .0694 |
| 0.39 | .1517 | .3483 | 0.94 | .3264 | .1736 | 1.49 | .4319 | .0681 |
| 0.40 | .1554 | .3446 | 0.95 | .3289 | .1711 | 1.50 | .4332 | .0668 |
| 0.41 | .1591 | .3409 | 0.96 | .3315 | .1685 | 1.51 | .4345 | .0655 |
| 0.42 | .1628 | .3372 | 0.97 | .3340 | .1660 | 1.52 | .4357 | .0643 |
| 0.43 | .1664 | .3336 | 0.98 | .3365 | .1635 | 1.53 | .4370 | .0630 |
| 0.44 | .1700 | .3300 | 0.99 | .3389 | .1611 | 1.54 | .4382 | .0618 |
| 0.45 | .1736 | .3264 | 1.00 | .3413 | .1587 | 1.55 | .4394 | .0606 |
| 0.46 | .1772 | .3228 | 1.01 | .3438 | .1562 | 1.56 | .4406 | .0594 |
| 0.47 | .1808 | .3192 | 1.02 | .3461 | .1539 | 1.57 | .4418 | .0582 |
| 0.48 | .1844 | .3156 | 1.03 | .3485 | .1515 | 1.58 | .4429 | .0571 |
| 0.49 | .1879 | .3121 | 1.04 | .3508 | .1492 | 1.59 | .4441 | .0559 |
| 0.50 | .1915 | .3085 | 1.05 | .3531 | .1469 | 1.60 | .4452 | .0548 |
| 0.51 | .1950 | .3050 | 1.06 | .3554 | .1446 | 1.61 | .4463 | .0537 |
| 0.52 | .1985 | .3015 | 1.07 | .3577 | .1423 | 1.62 | .4474 | .0526 |
| 0.53 | .2019 | .2981 | 1.08 | .3599 | .1401 | 1.63 | .4484 | .0516 |
| 0.54 | .2054 | .2946 | 1.09 | .3621 | .1379 | 1.64 | .4495 | .0505 |

**Table** **A** *(continued)*

| (A) z | (B) area between mean and z | (C) area beyond z | (A) z | (B) area between mean and z | (C) area beyond z | (A) z | (B) area between mean and z | (C) area beyond z |
|---|---|---|---|---|---|---|---|---|
| 1.65 | .4505 | .0495 | 2.22 | .4868 | .0132 | 2.79 | .4974 | .0026 |
| 1.66 | .4515 | .0485 | 2.23 | .4871 | .0129 | 2.80 | .4974 | .0026 |
| 1.67 | .4525 | .0475 | 2.24 | .4875 | .0125 | 2.81 | .4975 | .0025 |
| 1.68 | .4535 | .0465 | 2.25 | .4878 | .0122 | 2.82 | .4976 | .0024 |
| 1.69 | .4545 | .0455 | 2.26 | .4881 | .0119 | 2.83 | .4977 | .0023 |
| 1.70 | .4554 | .0446 | 2.27 | .4884 | .0116 | 2.84 | .4977 | .0023 |
| 1.71 | .4564 | .0436 | 2.28 | .4887 | .0113 | 2.85 | .4978 | .0022 |
| 1.72 | .4573 | .0427 | 2.29 | .4890 | .0110 | 2.86 | .4979 | .0021 |
| 1.73 | .4582 | .0418 | 2.30 | .4893 | .0107 | 2.87 | .4979 | .0021 |
| 1.74 | .4591 | .0409 | 2.31 | .4896 | .0104 | 2.88 | .4980 | .0020 |
| 1.75 | .4599 | .0401 | 2.32 | .4898 | .0102 | 2.89 | .4981 | .0019 |
| 1.76 | .4608 | .0392 | 2.33 | .4901 | .0099 | 2.90 | .4981 | .0019 |
| 1.77 | .4616 | .0384 | 2.34 | .4904 | .0096 | 2.91 | .4982 | .0018 |
| 1.78 | .4625 | .0375 | 2.35 | .4906 | .0094 | 2.92 | .4982 | .0018 |
| 1.79 | .4633 | .0367 | 2.36 | .4909 | .0091 | 2.93 | .4983 | .0017 |
| 1.80 | .4641 | .0359 | 2.37 | .4911 | .0089 | 2.94 | .4984 | .0016 |
| 1.81 | .4649 | .0351 | 2.38 | .4913 | .0087 | 2.95 | .4984 | .0016 |
| 1.82 | .4656 | .0344 | 2.39 | .4916 | .0084 | 2.96 | .4985 | .0015 |
| 1.83 | .4664 | .0336 | 2.40 | .4918 | .0082 | 2.97 | .4985 | .0015 |
| 1.84 | .4671 | .0329 | 2.41 | .4920 | .0080 | 2.98 | .4986 | .0014 |
| 1.85 | .4678 | .0322 | 2.42 | .4922 | .0078 | 2.99 | .4986 | .0014 |
| 1.86 | .4686 | .0314 | 2.43 | .4925 | .0075 | 3.00 | .4987 | .0013 |
| 1.87 | .4693 | .0307 | 2.44 | .4927 | .0073 | 3.01 | .4987 | .0013 |
| 1.88 | .4699 | .0301 | 2.45 | .4929 | .0071 | 3.02 | .4987 | .0013 |
| 1.89 | .4706 | .0294 | 2.46 | .4931 | .0069 | 3.03 | .4988 | .0012 |
| 1.90 | .4713 | .0287 | 2.47 | .4932 | .0068 | 3.04 | .4988 | .0012 |
| 1.91 | .4719 | .0281 | 2.48 | .4934 | .0066 | 3.05 | .4989 | .0011 |
| 1.92 | .4726 | .0274 | 2.49 | .4936 | .0064 | 3.06 | .4989 | .0011 |
| 1.93 | .4732 | .0268 | 2.50 | .4938 | .0062 | 3.07 | .4989 | .0011 |
| 1.94 | .4738 | .0262 | 2.51 | .4940 | .0060 | 3.08 | .4990 | .0010 |
| 1.95 | .4744 | .0256 | 2.52 | .4941 | .0059 | 3.09 | .4990 | .0010 |
| 1.96 | .4750 | .0250 | 2.53 | .4943 | .0057 | 3.10 | .4990 | .0010 |
| 1.97 | .4756 | .0244 | 2.54 | .4945 | .0055 | 3.11 | .4991 | .0009 |
| 1.98 | .4761 | .0239 | 2.55 | .4946 | .0054 | 3.12 | .4991 | .0009 |
| 1.99 | .4767 | .0233 | 2.56 | .4948 | .0052 | 3.13 | .4991 | .0009 |
| 2.00 | .4772 | .0228 | 2.57 | .4949 | .0051 | 3.14 | .4992 | .0008 |
| 2.01 | .4778 | .0222 | 2.58 | .4951 | .0049 | 3.15 | .4992 | .0008 |
| 2.02 | .4783 | .0217 | 2.59 | .4952 | .0048 | 3.16 | .4992 | .0008 |
| 2.03 | .4788 | .0212 | 2.60 | .4953 | .0047 | 3.17 | .4992 | .0008 |
| 2.04 | .4793 | .0207 | 2.61 | .4955 | .0045 | 3.18 | .4993 | .0007 |
| 2.05 | .4798 | .0202 | 2.62 | .4956 | .0044 | 3.19 | .4993 | .0007 |
| 2.06 | .4803 | .0197 | 2.63 | .4957 | .0043 | 3.20 | .4993 | .0007 |
| 2.07 | .4808 | .0192 | 2.64 | .4959 | .0041 | 3.21 | .4993 | .0007 |
| 2.08 | .4812 | .0188 | 2.65 | .4960 | .0040 | 3.22 | .4994 | .0006 |
| 2.09 | .4817 | .0183 | 2.66 | .4961 | .0039 | 3.23 | .4994 | .0006 |
| 2.10 | .4821 | .0179 | 2.67 | .4962 | .0038 | 3.24 | .4994 | .0006 |
| 2.11 | .4826 | .0174 | 2.68 | .4963 | .0037 | 3.25 | .4994 | .0006 |
| 2.12 | .4830 | .0170 | 2.69 | .4964 | .0036 | 3.30 | .4995 | .0005 |
| 2.13 | .4834 | .0166 | 2.70 | .4965 | .0035 | 3.35 | .4996 | .0004 |
| 2.14 | .4838 | .0162 | 2.71 | .4966 | .0034 | 3.40 | .4997 | .0003 |
| 2.15 | .4842 | .0158 | 2.72 | .4967 | .0033 | 3.45 | .4997 | .0003 |
| 2.16 | .4846 | .0154 | 2.73 | .4968 | .0032 | 3.50 | .4998 | .0002 |
| 2.17 | .4850 | .0150 | 2.74 | .4969 | .0031 | 3.60 | .4998 | .0002 |
| 2.18 | .4854 | .0146 | 2.75 | .4970 | .0030 | 3.70 | .4999 | .0001 |
| 2.19 | .4857 | .0143 | 2.76 | .4971 | .0029 | 3.80 | .4999 | .0001 |
| 2.20 | .4861 | .0139 | 2.77 | .4972 | .0028 | 3.90 | .49995 | .00005 |
| 2.21 | .4864 | .0136 | 2.78 | .4973 | .0027 | 4.00 | .49997 | .00003 |

Table B

**Random Numbers**

| Row number | | | | | | | | | | |
|---|---|---|---|---|---|---|---|---|---|---|
| 00000 | 10097 | 32533 | 76520 | 13586 | 34673 | 54876 | 80959 | 09117 | 39292 | 74945 |
| 00001 | 37542 | 04805 | 64894 | 74296 | 24805 | 24037 | 20636 | 10402 | 00822 | 91665 |
| 00002 | 08422 | 68953 | 19645 | 09303 | 23209 | 02560 | 15953 | 34764 | 35080 | 33606 |
| 00003 | 99019 | 02529 | 09376 | 70715 | 38311 | 31165 | 88676 | 74397 | 04436 | 27659 |
| 00004 | 12807 | 99970 | 80157 | 36147 | 64032 | 36653 | 98951 | 16877 | 12171 | 76833 |
| 00005 | 66065 | 74717 | 34072 | 76850 | 36697 | 36170 | 65813 | 39885 | 11199 | 29170 |
| 00006 | 31060 | 10805 | 45571 | 82406 | 35303 | 42614 | 86799 | 07439 | 23403 | 09732 |
| 00007 | 85269 | 77602 | 02051 | 65692 | 68665 | 74818 | 73053 | 85247 | 18623 | 88579 |
| 00008 | 63573 | 32135 | 05325 | 47048 | 90553 | 57548 | 28468 | 28709 | 83491 | 25624 |
| 00009 | 73796 | 45753 | 03529 | 64778 | 35808 | 34282 | 60935 | 20344 | 35273 | 88435 |
| 00010 | 98520 | 17767 | 14905 | 68607 | 22109 | 40558 | 60970 | 93433 | 50500 | 73998 |
| 00011 | 11805 | 05431 | 39808 | 27732 | 50725 | 68248 | 29405 | 24201 | 52775 | 67851 |
| 00012 | 83452 | 99634 | 06288 | 98033 | 13746 | 70078 | 18475 | 40610 | 68711 | 77817 |
| 00013 | 88685 | 40200 | 86507 | 58401 | 36766 | 67951 | 90364 | 76493 | 29609 | 11062 |
| 00014 | 99594 | 67348 | 87517 | 64969 | 91826 | 08928 | 93785 | 61368 | 23478 | 34113 |
| 00015 | 65481 | 17674 | 17468 | 50950 | 58047 | 76974 | 73039 | 57186 | 40218 | 16544 |
| 00016 | 80124 | 35635 | 17727 | 08015 | 45318 | 22374 | 21115 | 78253 | 14385 | 53763 |
| 00017 | 74350 | 99817 | 77402 | 77214 | 43236 | 00210 | 45521 | 64237 | 96286 | 02655 |
| 00018 | 69916 | 26803 | 66252 | 29148 | 36936 | 87203 | 76621 | 13990 | 94400 | 56418 |
| 00019 | 09893 | 20505 | 14225 | 68514 | 46427 | 56788 | 96297 | 78822 | 54382 | 14598 |
| 00020 | 91499 | 14523 | 68479 | 27686 | 46162 | 83554 | 94750 | 89923 | 37089 | 20048 |
| 00021 | 80336 | 94598 | 26940 | 36858 | 70297 | 34135 | 53140 | 33340 | 42050 | 82341 |
| 00022 | 44104 | 81949 | 85157 | 47954 | 32979 | 26575 | 57600 | 40881 | 22222 | 06413 |
| 00023 | 12550 | 73742 | 11100 | 02040 | 12860 | 74697 | 96644 | 89439 | 28707 | 25815 |
| 00024 | 63606 | 49329 | 16505 | 34484 | 40219 | 52563 | 43651 | 77082 | 07207 | 31790 |
| 00025 | 61196 | 90446 | 26457 | 47774 | 51924 | 33729 | 65394 | 59593 | 42582 | 60527 |
| 00026 | 15474 | 45266 | 95270 | 79953 | 59367 | 83848 | 82396 | 10118 | 33211 | 59466 |
| 00027 | 94557 | 28573 | 67897 | 54387 | 54622 | 44431 | 91190 | 42592 | 92927 | 45973 |
| 00028 | 42481 | 16213 | 97344 | 08721 | 16868 | 48767 | 03071 | 12059 | 25701 | 46670 |
| 00029 | 23523 | 78317 | 73208 | 89837 | 68935 | 91416 | 26252 | 29663 | 05522 | 82562 |
| 00030 | 04493 | 52494 | 75246 | 33824 | 45862 | 51025 | 61962 | 79335 | 65337 | 12472 |
| 00031 | 00549 | 97654 | 64051 | 88159 | 96119 | 63896 | 54692 | 82391 | 23287 | 29529 |
| 00032 | 35963 | 15307 | 26898 | 09354 | 33351 | 35462 | 77974 | 50024 | 90103 | 39333 |
| 00033 | 59808 | 08391 | 45427 | 26842 | 83609 | 49700 | 13021 | 24892 | 78565 | 20106 |
| 00034 | 46058 | 85236 | 01390 | 92286 | 77281 | 44077 | 93910 | 83647 | 70617 | 42941 |
| 00035 | 32179 | 00597 | 87379 | 25241 | 05567 | 07007 | 86743 | 17157 | 85394 | 11838 |
| 00036 | 69234 | 61406 | 20117 | 45204 | 15956 | 60000 | 18743 | 92423 | 97118 | 96338 |
| 00037 | 19565 | 41430 | 01758 | 75379 | 40419 | 21585 | 66674 | 36806 | 84962 | 85207 |
| 00038 | 45155 | 14938 | 19476 | 07246 | 43667 | 94543 | 59047 | 90033 | 20826 | 69541 |
| 00039 | 94864 | 31994 | 36168 | 10851 | 34888 | 81553 | 01540 | 35456 | 05014 | 51176 |
| 00040 | 98086 | 24826 | 45240 | 28404 | 44999 | 08896 | 39094 | 73407 | 35441 | 31880 |
| 00041 | 33185 | 16232 | 41941 | 50949 | 89435 | 48581 | 88695 | 41994 | 37548 | 73043 |
| 00042 | 80951 | 00406 | 96382 | 70774 | 20151 | 23387 | 25016 | 25298 | 94624 | 61171 |
| 00043 | 79752 | 49140 | 71961 | 28296 | 69861 | 02591 | 74852 | 20539 | 00387 | 59579 |
| 00044 | 18633 | 32537 | 98145 | 06571 | 31010 | 24674 | 05455 | 61427 | 77938 | 91936 |
| 00045 | 74029 | 43902 | 77557 | 32270 | 97790 | 17119 | 52527 | 58021 | 80814 | 51748 |
| 00046 | 54178 | 45611 | 80993 | 37143 | 05335 | 12969 | 56127 | 19255 | 36040 | 90324 |
| 00047 | 11664 | 49883 | 52079 | 84827 | 59381 | 71539 | 09973 | 33440 | 88461 | 23356 |
| 00048 | 48324 | 77928* | 31249 | 64710 | 02295 | 36870 | 32307 | 57546 | 15020 | 09994 |
| 00049 | 69074 | 94138 | 87637 | 91976 | 35584 | 04401 | 10518 | 21615 | 01848 | 76938 |
| 00050 | 09188 | 20097 | 32825 | 39527 | 04220 | 86304 | 83389 | 87374 | 64278 | 58044 |
| 00051 | 90045 | 85497 | 51981 | 50654 | 94938 | 81997 | 91870 | 76150 | 68476 | 64659 |
| 00052 | 73189 | 50207 | 47677 | 26269 | 62290 | 64464 | 27124 | 67018 | 41361 | 82760 |
| 00053 | 75768 | 76490 | 20971 | 87749 | 90429 | 12272 | 95375 | 05871 | 93823 | 43178 |
| 00054 | 54016 | 44056 | 66281 | 31003 | 00682 | 27398 | 20714 | 53295 | 07706 | 17813 |
| 00055 | 08358 | 69910 | 78542 | 42785 | 13661 | 58873 | 04618 | 97553 | 31223 | 08420 |
| 00056 | 28306 | 03264 | 81333 | 10591 | 40510 | 07893 | 32604 | 60475 | 94119 | 01840 |
| 00057 | 53840 | 86233 | 81594 | 13628 | 51215 | 90290 | 28466 | 68795 | 77762 | 20791 |
| 00058 | 91757 | 53741 | 61613 | 62669 | 50263 | 90212 | 55781 | 76514 | 83483 | 47055 |
| 00059 | 89415 | 92694 | 00397 | 58391 | 12607 | 17646 | 48949 | 72306 | 94541 | 37408 |

## Table C

### Critical Values of the *t*-Ratio

For any given *df*, the table shows the values of $t_{critical}$ corresponding to various levels of probability. The $t_{observed}$ is statistically significant at a given level when it is equal to or greater than the value shown in the table.

For the single sample *t*-ratio, $df = n - 1$.

For the two sample *t*-ratio, $df = (n_1 - 1) + (n_2 - 1)$.

## Examples

Nondirectional Hypothesis:

$H_0: \mu - \mu = 0$ 　　　$H_1: \mu - \mu \neq 0$ 　　$\alpha = .05 \; df = 30$

$t_{critical} = \pm 2.042$ 　　If $|t_{observed}| \geq |t_{critical}|$ then Reject $H_0$

Directional Hypothesis:

$H_0: \mu - \mu \leq 0$ 　　　$H_1: \mu - \mu > 0$ 　　$\alpha = .05 \; df = 30$

$t_{critical} = +1.697$ 　　If $t_{observed} \geq t_{critical}$ then Reject $H_0$

$H_0: \mu - \mu \geq 0$ 　　　$H_1: \mu - \mu < 0$ 　　$\alpha = .05 \; df = 30$

$t_{critical} = -1.697$ 　　If $t_{observed} \leq t_{critical}$ then Reject $H_0$

| | Level of Significance of a One-Tailed or Directional Test $H_0: \mu - \mu \leq 0$ or $H_0: \mu - \mu \geq 0$ | | | | | |
| | .1 | .05 | .025 | .01 | .005 | .0005 |
| | Level of Significance of a Two-Tailed or Nondirectional Test $H_0: \mu - \mu = 0$ | | | | | |
| *df* | .2 | .1 | .05 | .02 | .01 | .001 |
|---|---|---|---|---|---|---|
| 1 | 3.078 | 6.314 | 12.706 | 31.821 | 63.657 | 636.619 |
| 2 | 1.886 | 2.920 | 4.303 | 6.965 | 9.925 | 31.598 |
| 3 | 1.638 | 2.353 | 3.182 | 4.541 | 5.841 | 12.941 |
| 4 | 1.533 | 2.132 | 2.776 | 3.747 | 4.604 | 8.610 |
| 5 | 1.476 | 2.015 | 2.571 | 3.365 | 4.032 | 6.859 |
| 6 | 1.440 | 1.943 | 2.447 | 3.143 | 3.707 | 5.959 |
| 7 | 1.415 | 1.895 | 2.365 | 2.998 | 3.499 | 5.405 |
| 8 | 1.397 | 1.860 | 2.306 | 2.896 | 3.355 | 5.041 |
| 9 | 1.383 | 1.833 | 2.262 | 2.821 | 3.250 | 4.781 |
| 10 | 1.372 | 1.812 | 2.228 | 2.764 | 3.169 | 4.587 |
| 11 | 1.363 | 1.796 | 2.201 | 2.718 | 3.106 | 4.437 |
| 12 | 1.356 | 1.782 | 2.179 | 2.681 | 3.055 | 4.318 |
| 13 | 1.350 | 1.771 | 2.160 | 2.650 | 3.012 | 4.221 |
| 14 | 1.345 | 1.761 | 2.145 | 2.624 | 2.977 | 4.140 |
| 15 | 1.341 | 1.753 | 2.131 | 2.602 | 2.947 | 4.073 |
| 16 | 1.337 | 1.746 | 2.120 | 2.583 | 2.921 | 4.015 |
| 17 | 1.333 | 1.740 | 2.110 | 2.567 | 2.898 | 3.965 |
| 18 | 1.330 | 1.734 | 2.101 | 2.552 | 2.878 | 3.922 |
| 19 | 1.328 | 1.729 | 2.093 | 2.539 | 2.861 | 3.883 |
| 20 | 1.325 | 1.725 | 2.086 | 2.528 | 2.845 | 3.850 |
| 21 | 1.323 | 1.721 | 2.080 | 2.518 | 2.831 | 3.819 |
| 22 | 1.321 | 1.717 | 2.074 | 2.508 | 2.819 | 3.792 |
| 23 | 1.319 | 1.714 | 2.069 | 2.500 | 2.807 | 3.767 |
| 24 | 1.318 | 1.711 | 2.064 | 2.492 | 2.797 | 3.745 |
| 25 | 1.316 | 1.708 | 2.060 | 2.485 | 2.787 | 3.725 |
| 26 | 1.315 | 1.706 | 2.056 | 2.479 | 2.779 | 3.707 |
| 27 | 1.314 | 1.703 | 2.052 | 2.473 | 2.771 | 3.690 |
| 28 | 1.313 | 1.701 | 2.048 | 2.467 | 2.763 | 3.674 |
| 29 | 1.311 | 1.699 | 2.045 | 2.462 | 2.756 | 3.659 |
| 30 | 1.310 | 1.697 | 2.042 | 2.457 | 2.750 | 3.646 |
| 40 | 1.303 | 1.684 | 2.021 | 2.423 | 2.704 | 3.551 |
| 60 | 1.296 | 1.671 | 2.000 | 2.390 | 2.660 | 3.460 |
| 120 | 1.289 | 1.658 | 1.980 | 2.358 | 2.617 | 3.373 |
| ∞ | 1.282 | 1.645 | 1.960 | 2.326 | 2.576 | 3.291 |

Table C is taken from Table III (page 46) of Fisher and Yates, *Statistical Tables for Biological, Agricultural, and Medical Research*, 6th ed., published by Longman Group Ltd., 1974. London (previously published by Oliver and Boyd, Edinburgh), and by permission of the authors and publishers.

**Table** D

**Power of Student's Single-Sample *t*-Ratio**

The power of the single-sample *t*-ratio given effect size, sample size (*n*), $\alpha$ and directionality of the test. The ** indicates that $1 - \beta > .99$.

**POWER TABLE: SINGLE SAMPLE *t*-RATIO**

| *n* | $\alpha$ = .05 one-tailed | | | | | $\alpha$ = .05 two-tailed | | | | |
|-----|------|------|------|------|------|------|------|------|------|------|
|     | 0.20 | 0.50 | 0.80 | 1.10 | 1.40 | 0.20 | 0.50 | 0.80 | 1.10 | 1.40 |
| 10  | .15 | .42 | .77 | .95 | ** | .08 | .28 | .62 | .88 | .98 |
| 11  | .16 | .46 | .81 | .97 | ** | .09 | .31 | .67 | .92 | ** |
| 12  | .17 | .51 | .85 | .98 | ** | .09 | .34 | .72 | .95 | ** |
| 13  | .17 | .52 | .88 | ** | ** | .10 | .37 | .76 | .96 | ** |
| 14  | .18 | .55 | .9 | ** | ** | .10 | .4 | .8 | .98 | ** |
| 15  | .18 | .58 | .92 | ** | ** | .11 | .43 | .83 | .98 | ** |
| 16  | .19 | .61 | .94 | ** | ** | .11 | .46 | .86 | ** | ** |
| 17  | .20 | .63 | .95 | ** | ** | .11 | .48 | .89 | ** | ** |
| 18  | .20 | .66 | .96 | ** | ** | .12 | .51 | .91 | ** | ** |
| 19  | .21 | .68 | .97 | ** | ** | .12 | .54 | .92 | ** | ** |
| 20  | .22 | .71 | .98 | ** | ** | .13 | .56 | .94 | ** | ** |
| 21  | .22 | .73 | .98 | ** | ** | .13 | .59 | .95 | ** | ** |
| 22  | .23 | .75 | ** | ** | ** | .14 | .61 | .96 | ** | ** |
| 23  | .23 | .77 | ** | ** | ** | .14 | .63 | .97 | ** | ** |
| 24  | .24 | .78 | ** | ** | ** | .15 | .65 | .98 | ** | ** |
| 25  | .25 | .8 | ** | ** | ** | .15 | .67 | .98 | ** | ** |
| 26  | .25 | .82 | ** | ** | ** | .16 | .69 | .98 | ** | ** |
| 27  | .26 | .83 | ** | ** | ** | .16 | .71 | ** | ** | ** |
| 28  | .26 | .85 | ** | ** | ** | .16 | .73 | ** | ** | ** |
| 29  | .27 | .86 | ** | ** | ** | .17 | .75 | ** | ** | ** |
| 30  | .28 | .87 | ** | ** | ** | .17 | .76 | ** | ** | ** |
| 31  | .28 | .88 | ** | ** | ** | .18 | .78 | ** | ** | ** |
| 32  | .29 | .89 | ** | ** | ** | .18 | .8 | ** | ** | ** |
| 33  | .29 | .9 | ** | ** | ** | .19 | .81 | ** | ** | ** |
| 34  | .30 | .91 | ** | ** | ** | .19 | .82 | ** | ** | ** |
| 35  | .31 | .92 | ** | ** | ** | .20 | .84 | ** | ** | ** |
| 36  | .31 | .92 | ** | ** | ** | .20 | .85 | ** | ** | ** |
| 37  | .32 | .93 | ** | ** | ** | .21 | .86 | ** | ** | ** |
| 38  | .32 | .94 | ** | ** | ** | .21 | .87 | ** | ** | ** |
| 39  | .33 | .94 | ** | ** | ** | .22 | .88 | ** | ** | ** |
| 40  | .34 | .95 | ** | ** | ** | .22 | .89 | ** | ** | ** |
| 45  | .36 | .97 | ** | ** | ** | .24 | .92 | ** | ** | ** |
| 50  | .39 | .98 | ** | ** | ** | .27 | .95 | ** | ** | ** |
| 60  | .45 | ** | ** | ** | ** | .32 | .98 | ** | ** | ** |
| 70  | .50 | ** | ** | ** | ** | .36 | ** | ** | ** | ** |
| 80  | .55 | ** | ** | ** | ** | .41 | ** | ** | ** | ** |
| 90  | .60 | ** | ** | ** | ** | .45 | ** | ** | ** | ** |
| 100 | .64 | ** | ** | ** | ** | .50 | ** | ** | ** | ** |
| 200 | .90 | ** | ** | ** | ** | .82 | ** | ** | ** | ** |
| 300 | .98 | ** | ** | ** | ** | .95 | ** | ** | ** | ** |
| 400 | ** | ** | ** | ** | ** | ** | ** | ** | ** | ** |
| 500 | ** | ** | ** | ** | ** | ** | ** | ** | ** | ** |

**Table** | **E**

**Power of Student's Two-Sample *t*-Ratio**

The power of the two-sample *t*-ratio given effect size, sample size (*n*), $\alpha$ and directionality of the test. The ** indicates that $1 - \beta > .99$.

### POWER TABLE: TWO SAMPLE *t*-RATIO

| *n* | $\alpha = .05$ one-tailed | | | | | $\alpha = .05$ two-tailed | | | | |
|---|---|---|---|---|---|---|---|---|---|---|
|  | 0.20 | 0.50 | 0.80 | 1.10 | 1.40 | 0.20 | 0.50 | 0.80 | 1.10 | 1.40 |
| 10 | .13 | .28 | .53 | .78 | .93 | .07 | .17 | .38 | .65 | .86 |
| 11 | .13 | .30 | .57 | .82 | .95 | .07 | .19 | .42 | .70 | .89 |
| 12 | .13 | .32 | .60 | .85 | .97 | .07 | .20 | .46 | .74 | .92 |
| 13 | .14 | .33 | .64 | .88 | .98 | .07 | .22 | .51 | .78 | .94 |
| 14 | .14 | .35 | .67 | .90 | ** | .08 | .23 | .52 | .81 | .96 |
| 15 | .14 | .37 | .70 | .92 | ** | .08 | .25 | .56 | .84 | .97 |
| 16 | .15 | .39 | .73 | .94 | ** | .08 | .26 | .59 | .87 | .98 |
| 17 | .15 | .41 | .75 | .95 | ** | .08 | .28 | .62 | .89 | ** |
| 18 | .15 | .42 | .78 | .96 | ** | .09 | .29 | .65 | .91 | ** |
| 19 | .16 | .44 | .80 | .97 | ** | .09 | .31 | .67 | .93 | ** |
| 20 | .16 | .46 | .82 | .98 | ** | .09 | .32 | .70 | .94 | ** |
| 21 | .16 | .47 | .84 | .98 | ** | .09 | .34 | .72 | .95 | ** |
| 22 | .16 | .51 | .85 | ** | ** | .09 | .35 | .75 | .96 | ** |
| 23 | .17 | .51 | .87 | ** | ** | .10 | .37 | .77 | .97 | ** |
| 24 | .17 | .52 | .88 | ** | ** | .10 | .38 | .79 | .98 | ** |
| 25 | .17 | .54 | .90 | ** | ** | .10 | .40 | .81 | .98 | ** |
| 26 | .18 | .55 | .91 | ** | ** | .10 | .41 | .82 | .98 | ** |
| 27 | .18 | .57 | .92 | ** | ** | .10 | .42 | .84 | ** | ** |
| 28 | .18 | .58 | .93 | ** | ** | .11 | .44 | .85 | ** | ** |
| 29 | .19 | .60 | .94 | ** | ** | .11 | .45 | .87 | ** | ** |
| 30 | .19 | .61 | .94 | ** | ** | .11 | .47 | .88 | ** | ** |
| 31 | .19 | .62 | .95 | ** | ** | .11 | .52 | .89 | ** | ** |
| 32 | .20 | .64 | .96 | ** | ** | .12 | .51 | .90 | ** | ** |
| 33 | .20 | .65 | .96 | ** | ** | .12 | .51 | .91 | ** | ** |
| 34 | .20 | .66 | .97 | ** | ** | .12 | .52 | .92 | ** | ** |
| 35 | .21 | .67 | .97 | ** | ** | .12 | .53 | .93 | ** | ** |
| 36 | .21 | .69 | .97 | ** | ** | .12 | .55 | .94 | ** | ** |
| 37 | .21 | .70 | .98 | ** | ** | .13 | .56 | .94 | ** | ** |
| 38 | .21 | .71 | .98 | ** | ** | .13 | .57 | .95 | ** | ** |
| 39 | .22 | .72 | .98 | ** | ** | .13 | .58 | .95 | ** | ** |
| 40 | .22 | .73 | .98 | ** | ** | .13 | .60 | .96 | ** | ** |
| 45 | .24 | .78 | ** | ** | ** | .15 | .65 | .98 | ** | ** |
| 50 | .25 | .82 | ** | ** | ** | .16 | .70 | ** | ** | ** |
| 60 | .28 | .88 | ** | ** | ** | .18 | .79 | ** | ** | ** |
| 70 | .31 | .93 | ** | ** | ** | .20 | .85 | ** | ** | ** |
| 80 | .34 | .95 | ** | ** | ** | .23 | .90 | ** | ** | ** |
| 90 | .37 | .97 | ** | ** | ** | .25 | .93 | ** | ** | ** |
| 100 | .40 | .98 | ** | ** | ** | .27 | .96 | ** | ** | ** |
| 200 | .64 | ** | ** | ** | ** | .50 | ** | ** | ** | ** |
| 300 | .81 | ** | ** | ** | ** | .69 | ** | ** | ** | ** |
| 400 | .91 | ** | ** | ** | ** | .82 | ** | ** | ** | ** |
| 500 | .96 | ** | ** | ** | ** | .90 | ** | ** | ** | ** |

Table | F

| Critical Values for Pearson's Correlation Coefficient

For any given *df,* the table shows the values of *r* corresponding to various levels of probability. The $r_{observed}$ is statistically significant at a given level when it is equal to or greater than the value shown in the table.

## Examples

Nondirectional Hypothesis:

$H_0$: $\rho = 0$ $\qquad$ $H_1$: $\rho \neq 0$ $\qquad$ $\alpha = .05$ $df = 30$
$r_{critical} = \pm.3494$ $\qquad$ If $|r_{observed}| \geq |r_{critical}|$ then Reject $H_0$

Directional Hypothesis:

$H_0$: $\rho \leq 0$ $\qquad$ $H_1$: $\rho > 0$ $\qquad$ $\alpha = .05$ $df = 30$
$r_{critical} = +.2560$ $\qquad$ If $r_{observed} \geq r_{critical}$ then Reject $H_0$

$H_0$: $\rho \geq 0$ $\qquad$ $H_1$: $\rho < 0$ $\qquad$ $\alpha = .05$ $df = 30$
$r_{critical} = -.2560$ $\qquad$ If $r_{observed} \leq r_{critical}$ then Reject $H_0$

Note: $r_c = \dfrac{t_c}{\sqrt{(n-2)t_c^2}}$

| | Level of Significance of a One-Tailed or Directional Test $H_0$: $r \leq 0$ or $H_0$: $r \geq 0$ | | | | | |
| --- | --- | --- | --- | --- | --- | --- |
| | .1 | .05 | .025 | .01 | .005 | .0005 |
| | Level of Significance of a Two-Tailed or Nondirectional Test $H_0$: $r = 0$ | | | | | |
| *df* | .2 | .1 | .05 | .02 | .01 | .001 |
| 1 | .9511 | .9877 | .9969 | .9995 | .9999 | 1.0000 |
| 2 | .8000 | .9000 | .9500 | .9800 | .9900 | .9990 |
| 3 | .6870 | .8054 | .8783 | .9343 | .9587 | .9911 |
| 4 | .6084 | .7293 | .8114 | .8822 | .9172 | .9741 |
| 5 | .5509 | .6694 | .7545 | .8329 | .8745 | .9509 |
| 6 | .5067 | .6215 | .7067 | .7887 | .8343 | .9249 |
| 7 | .4716 | .5822 | .6664 | .7498 | .7977 | .8983 |
| 8 | .4428 | .5494 | .6319 | .7155 | .7646 | .8721 |
| 9 | .4187 | .5214 | .6021 | .6851 | .7348 | .8470 |
| 10 | .3981 | .4973 | .5760 | .6581 | .7079 | .8233 |
| 11 | .3802 | .4762 | .5529 | .6339 | .6835 | .8010 |
| 12 | .3646 | .4575 | .5324 | .6120 | .6614 | .7800 |
| 13 | .3507 | .4409 | .5140 | .5923 | .6411 | .7604 |
| 14 | .3383 | .4259 | .4973 | .5742 | .6226 | .7419 |
| 15 | .3271 | .4124 | .4821 | .5577 | .6055 | .7247 |
| 16 | .3170 | .4000 | .4683 | .5425 | .5897 | .7084 |
| 17 | .3077 | .3887 | .4555 | .5285 | .5751 | .6932 |
| 18 | .2992 | .3783 | .4438 | .5155 | .5614 | .6788 |
| 19 | .2914 | .3687 | .4329 | .5034 | .5487 | .6652 |
| 20 | .2841 | .3598 | .4227 | .4921 | .5368 | .6524 |
| 21 | .2774 | .3515 | .4132 | .4815 | .5256 | .6402 |
| 22 | .2711 | .3438 | .4044 | .4716 | .5151 | .6287 |
| 23 | .2653 | .3365 | .3961 | .4622 | .5052 | .6178 |
| 24 | .2598 | .3297 | .3882 | .4534 | .4958 | .6074 |
| 25 | .2546 | .3233 | .3809 | .4451 | .4869 | .5974 |

| 30 | .2327 | .2960 | .3494 | .4093 | .4487 | .5541 |
|---|---|---|---|---|---|---|
| 35 | .2156 | .2746 | .3246 | .3810 | .4182 | .5189 |
| 40 | .2018 | .2573 | .3044 | .3578 | .3932 | .4896 |
| 50 | .1806 | .2306 | .2732 | .3218 | .3542 | .4432 |
| 60 | .1650 | .2108 | .2500 | .2948 | .3248 | .4079 |
| 70 | .1528 | .1954 | .2319 | .2737 | .3017 | .3798 |
| 80 | .1430 | .1829 | .2172 | .2565 | .2830 | .3568 |
| 90 | .1348 | .1726 | .2050 | .2422 | .2673 | .3375 |
| 100 | .1279 | .1638 | .1946 | .2301 | .2540 | .3211 |
| 150 | .1045 | .1339 | .1593 | .1886 | .2084 | .2643 |
| 300 | .0740 | .0948 | .1129 | .1338 | .1480 | .1884 |
| 500 | .0573 | .0735 | .0875 | .1038 | .1149 | .1464 |
| 1000 | .0405 | .0520 | .0619 | .0735 | .0813 | .1038 |

## Table G

### Critical Values for Spearman's Correlation Coefficient

A given value of $r_s$ is statistically significant if it equals or exceeds the tabled value at the designated $\alpha$-level at a given $N$. To interpolate, sum the critical values above and below the $N$ of interest and divide by 2. Thus, the critical value at $\alpha = 0.05$, two-tailed test, when $N = 21$, is $(0.450 + 0.428)/2 = 0.439$.

| | Level of significance for one-tailed test | | | |
|---|---|---|---|---|
| | .05 | .025 | .01 | .005 |
| | Level of significance for two-tailed test | | | |
| $N^*$ | .10 | .05 | .02 | .01 |
| 5 | .900 | 1.000 | 1.000 | -- |
| 6 | .829 | .886 | .943 | 1.000 |
| 7 | .714 | .786 | .893 | .929 |
| 8 | .643 | .738 | .833 | .881 |
| 9 | .600 | .683 | .783 | .833 |
| 10 | .564 | .648 | .746 | .794 |
| 12 | .506 | .591 | .712 | .777 |
| 14 | .456 | .544 | .645 | .715 |
| 16 | .425 | .506 | .601 | .665 |
| 18 | .399 | .475 | .564 | .625 |
| 20 | .377 | .450 | .534 | .591 |
| 22 | .359 | .428 | .508 | .562 |
| 24 | .343 | .409 | .485 | .537 |
| 26 | .329 | .392 | .465 | .515 |
| 28 | .317 | .377 | .448 | .496 |
| 30 | .306 | .364 | .432 | .478 |

$^*N$ = number of pairs.

Note that when $N > 30$ we can convert the $r_S$ to a $t$-ratio and then use Table C for hypothesis testing.

$$t = r_S \sqrt{\frac{N-2}{1-r_S^2}}$$

For example, $r_S = .60$, $N = 42$

$$t = .60 \sqrt{\frac{42-2}{1-.60^2}} \quad t = .60 \sqrt{\frac{40}{.64}} \quad t = .60\sqrt{62.5}$$

$$t = 4.74, \ df = 40$$

**Table** **H**

**Transformation of r to z_r**

| r | zr | r | zr | r | zr |
|---|---|---|---|---|---|
| .01 | .010 | .34 | .354 | .67 | .811 |
| .02 | .020 | .35 | .366 | .68 | .829 |
| .03 | .030 | .36 | .377 | .69 | .848 |
| .04 | .040 | .37 | .389 | .70 | .867 |
| .05 | .050 | .38 | .400 | .71 | .887 |
| .06 | .060 | .39 | .412 | .72 | .908 |
| .07 | .070 | .40 | .424 | .73 | .929 |
| .08 | .080 | .41 | .436 | .74 | .950 |
| .09 | .090 | .42 | .448 | .75 | .973 |
| .10 | .100 | .43 | .460 | .76 | .996 |
| .11 | .110 | .44 | .472 | .77 | 1.020 |
| .12 | .121 | .45 | .485 | .78 | 1.045 |
| .13 | .131 | .46 | .497 | .79 | 1.071 |
| .14 | .141 | .47 | .510 | .80 | 1.099 |
| .15 | .151 | .48 | .523 | .81 | 1.127 |
| .16 | .161 | .49 | .536 | .82 | 1.157 |
| .17 | .172 | .50 | .549 | .83 | 1.188 |
| .18 | .181 | .51 | .563 | .84 | 1.221 |
| .19 | .192 | .52 | .577 | .85 | 1.256 |
| .20 | .203 | .53 | .590 | .86 | 1.293 |
| .21 | .214 | .54 | .604 | .87 | 1.333 |
| .22 | .224 | .55 | .618 | .88 | 1.376 |
| .23 | .234 | .56 | .633 | .89 | 1.422 |
| .24 | .245 | .57 | .648 | .90 | 1.472 |
| .25 | .256 | .58 | .663 | .91 | 1.528 |
| .26 | .266 | .59 | .678 | .92 | 1.589 |
| .27 | .277 | .60 | .693 | .93 | 1.658 |
| .28 | .288 | .61 | .709 | .94 | 1.738 |
| .29 | .299 | .62 | .725 | .95 | 1.832 |
| .30 | .309 | .63 | .741 | .96 | 1.946 |
| .31 | .321 | .64 | .758 | .97 | 2.092 |
| .32 | .332 | .65 | .775 | .98 | 2.298 |
| .33 | .343 | .66 | .793 | .99 | 2.647 |

**Table** I

**Power of Pearson's Correlation Coefficient**

The power of the Pearson Correlation Coefficient given effect size, sample size ($n$), and $\alpha$ and directionality of the test. Note that ** indicates that $1 - \beta > .99$.

| | $\alpha = .05$ one-tailed | | | | | | $\alpha = .05$ one-tailed | | | | |
|---|---|---|---|---|---|---|---|---|---|---|---|
| | Effect size: $r$ | | | | | | Effect size: $r$ | | | | |
| $n$ | 0.10 | 0.30 | 0.50 | 0.70 | 0.95 | $n$ | 0.10 | 0.30 | 0.50 | 0.70 | 0.95 |
| 10 | .07 | .19 | .42 | .75 | .98 | 10 | 0.03 | 0.11 | 0.29 | 0.63 | ** |
| 11 | .07 | .21 | .46 | .80 | ** | 11 | 0.03 | 0.12 | 0.33 | 0.69 | ** |
| 12 | .08 | .23 | .50 | .83 | ** | 12 | 0.04 | 0.14 | 0.37 | 0.74 | ** |
| 13 | .08 | .24 | .54 | .87 | ** | 13 | 0.04 | 0.15 | 0.40 | 0.78 | ** |
| 14 | .08 | .26 | .57 | .89 | ** | 14 | 0.04 | 0.16 | 0.44 | 0.82 | ** |
| 15 | .09 | .27 | .60 | .91 | ** | 15 | 0.04 | 0.17 | 0.47 | 0.85 | ** |
| 16 | .09 | .29 | .63 | .93 | ** | 16 | 0.04 | 0.19 | 0.50 | 0.88 | ** |
| 17 | .09 | .31 | .66 | .94 | ** | 17 | 0.05 | 0.20 | 0.53 | 0.90 | ** |
| 18 | .09 | .32 | .69 | .96 | ** | 18 | 0.05 | 0.21 | 0.56 | 0.92 | ** |
| 19 | .10 | .33 | .71 | .96 | ** | 19 | 0.05 | 0.22 | 0.59 | 0.93 | ** |
| 20 | .10 | .35 | .73 | .97 | ** | 20 | 0.05 | 0.24 | 0.61 | 0.94 | ** |
| 21 | .10 | .36 | .75 | .98 | ** | 21 | 0.05 | 0.25 | 0.64 | 0.95 | ** |
| 22 | .10 | .38 | .77 | .98 | ** | 22 | 0.05 | 0.26 | 0.66 | 0.96 | ** |
| 23 | .11 | .39 | .79 | .98 | ** | 23 | 0.06 | 0.27 | 0.69 | 0.97 | ** |
| 24 | .11 | .40 | .81 | ** | ** | 24 | 0.06 | 0.28 | 0.71 | 0.97 | ** |
| 25 | .11 | .42 | .82 | ** | ** | 25 | 0.06 | 0.30 | 0.73 | 0.98 | ** |
| 26 | .11 | .43 | .84 | ** | ** | 26 | 0.06 | 0.31 | 0.75 | 0.98 | ** |
| 27 | .12 | .44 | .85 | ** | ** | 27 | 0.06 | 0.32 | 0.76 | 0.98 | ** |
| 28 | .12 | .46 | .86 | ** | ** | 28 | 0.06 | 0.33 | 0.78 | ** | ** |
| 29 | .12 | .47 | .88 | ** | ** | 29 | 0.06 | 0.34 | 0.80 | ** | ** |
| 30 | .12 | .48 | .89 | ** | ** | 30 | 0.07 | 0.35 | 0.81 | ** | ** |
| 31 | .12 | .49 | .89 | ** | ** | 31 | 0.07 | 0.37 | 0.83 | ** | ** |
| 32 | .13 | .50 | .90 | ** | ** | 32 | 0.07 | 0.38 | 0.84 | ** | ** |
| 33 | .13 | .52 | .91 | ** | ** | 33 | 0.07 | 0.39 | 0.85 | ** | ** |
| 34 | .13 | .53 | .92 | ** | ** | 34 | 0.07 | 0.40 | 0.86 | ** | ** |
| 35 | .13 | .54 | .93 | ** | ** | 35 | 0.07 | 0.41 | 0.87 | ** | ** |
| 36 | .13 | .55 | .93 | ** | ** | 36 | 0.07 | 0.42 | 0.88 | ** | ** |
| 37 | .14 | .56 | .94 | ** | ** | 37 | 0.08 | 0.43 | 0.89 | ** | ** |
| 38 | .14 | .57 | .94 | ** | ** | 38 | 0.08 | 0.44 | 0.90 | ** | ** |
| 39 | .14 | .58 | .95 | ** | ** | 39 | 0.08 | 0.45 | 0.91 | ** | ** |
| 40 | .14 | .59 | .95 | ** | ** | 40 | 0.08 | 0.46 | 0.91 | ** | ** |
| 50 | .17 | .69 | .98 | ** | ** | 50 | 0.09 | 0.56 | 0.96 | ** | ** |
| 60 | .18 | .75 | ** | ** | ** | 60 | 0.11 | 0.64 | 0.98 | ** | ** |
| 70 | .20 | .81 | ** | ** | ** | 70 | 0.12 | 0.71 | ** | ** | ** |
| 80 | .22 | .85 | ** | ** | ** | 80 | 0.13 | 0.77 | ** | ** | ** |
| 90 | .23 | .89 | ** | ** | ** | 90 | 0.15 | 0.82 | ** | ** | ** |
| 100 | .25 | .92 | ** | ** | ** | 100 | 0.16 | 0.86 | ** | ** | ** |
| 200 | .40 | ** | ** | ** | ** | 200 | 0.28 | ** | ** | ** | ** |
| 300 | .53 | ** | ** | ** | ** | 300 | 0.40 | ** | ** | ** | ** |
| 400 | .63 | ** | ** | ** | ** | 400 | 0.51 | ** | ** | ** | ** |
| 500 | .72 | ** | ** | ** | ** | 500 | 0.60 | ** | ** | ** | ** |

# Table J

## Critical Values of the F-Ratio

The obtained $F$ is significant at a given level if it is equal to or *greater than* the value shown in the table. 0.05 (light row) and 0.01 (dark row) points for the distribution of $F$.

The values shown are the right tail of the distribution obtained by dividing the larger variance estimate by the smaller variance estimate. To find the complementary left or lower tail for a given df and α-level, reverse the degrees of freedom and find the reciprocal of that value in the $F$-table. For example, the value cutting off the top 5% of the area for 7 and 12 $df$ is 2.92. To find the cutoff point of the bottom 5% of the area, find the tabled value of the $\alpha = 0.05$ level for 12 and 7 $df$. This value is 3.57. The reciprocal is 1/3.57 = 0.28. Thus 5% of the area falls *at or below an* $F = 0.28$.

Degrees of freedom for numerator (each cell: 0.05 level / 0.01 level)

| df (denom) | 1 | 2 | 3 | 4 | 5 | 6 | 7 | 8 | 9 | 10 | 11 | 12 | 14 | 16 | 20 | 24 | 30 | 40 | 50 | 75 | 100 | 200 | 500 | ∞ |
|---|---|---|---|---|---|---|---|---|---|---|---|---|---|---|---|---|---|---|---|---|---|---|---|---|
| 1 | 161 / 4052 | 200 / 4999 | 216 / 5403 | 225 / 5625 | 230 / 5764 | 234 / 5859 | 237 / 5928 | 239 / 5981 | 241 / 6022 | 242 / 6056 | 243 / 6082 | 244 / 6106 | 245 / 6142 | 246 / 6169 | 248 / 6208 | 249 / 6234 | 250 / 6258 | 251 / 6286 | 252 / 6302 | 253 / 6323 | 253 / 6334 | 254 / 6352 | 254 / 6361 | 254 / 6366 |
| 2 | 18.51 / 98.49 | 19.00 / 99.01 | 19.16 / 99.17 | 19.25 / 99.25 | 19.30 / 99.30 | 19.33 / 99.33 | 19.36 / 99.34 | 19.37 / 99.36 | 19.38 / 99.36 | 19.39 / 99.40 | 19.40 / 99.41 | 19.41 / 99.42 | 19.42 / 99.43 | 19.43 / 99.44 | 19.44 / 99.45 | 19.45 / 99.46 | 19.46 / 99.47 | 19.47 / 99.48 | 19.47 / 99.48 | 19.48 / 99.49 | 19.49 / 99.49 | 19.49 / 99.49 | 19.50 / 99.50 | 19.50 / 99.50 |
| 3 | 10.13 / 34.12 | 9.55 / 30.81 | 9.28 / 29.46 | 9.12 / 28.71 | 9.01 / 28.24 | 8.94 / 27.91 | 8.88 / 27.67 | 8.84 / 27.49 | 8.81 / 27.34 | 8.78 / 27.23 | 8.76 / 27.13 | 8.74 / 27.05 | 8.71 / 26.92 | 8.69 / 26.83 | 8.66 / 26.69 | 8.64 / 26.60 | 8.62 / 26.50 | 8.60 / 26.41 | 8.58 / 26.30 | 8.57 / 26.27 | 8.56 / 26.23 | 8.54 / 26.18 | 8.54 / 26.14 | 8.53 / 26.12 |
| 4 | 7.71 / 21.20 | 6.94 / 18.00 | 6.59 / 16.69 | 6.39 / 15.98 | 6.26 / 15.52 | 6.16 / 15.21 | 6.09 / 14.98 | 6.04 / 14.80 | 6.00 / 14.66 | 5.96 / 14.54 | 5.93 / 14.45 | 5.91 / 14.37 | 5.87 / 14.24 | 5.84 / 14.15 | 5.80 / 14.02 | 5.77 / 13.93 | 5.74 / 13.83 | 5.71 / 13.74 | 5.70 / 13.69 | 5.68 / 13.61 | 5.66 / 13.57 | 5.65 / 13.52 | 5.64 / 13.48 | 5.63 / 13.46 |
| 5 | 6.61 / 16.26 | 5.79 / 13.27 | 5.41 / 12.06 | 5.19 / 11.39 | 5.05 / 10.97 | 4.95 / 10.67 | 4.88 / 10.45 | 4.82 / 10.27 | 4.78 / 10.15 | 4.74 / 10.05 | 4.70 / 9.96 | 4.68 / 9.89 | 4.64 / 9.77 | 4.60 / 9.68 | 4.56 / 9.55 | 4.53 / 9.47 | 4.50 / 9.38 | 4.46 / 9.29 | 4.44 / 9.24 | 4.42 / 9.17 | 4.40 / 9.13 | 4.38 / 9.07 | 4.37 / 9.04 | 4.36 / 9.02 |
| 6 | 5.99 / 13.74 | 5.14 / 10.92 | 4.76 / 9.78 | 4.53 / 9.15 | 4.39 / 8.75 | 4.28 / 8.47 | 4.21 / 8.26 | 4.15 / 8.10 | 4.10 / 7.98 | 4.06 / 7.87 | 4.03 / 7.79 | 4.00 / 7.72 | 3.96 / 7.60 | 3.92 / 7.52 | 3.87 / 7.39 | 3.84 / 7.31 | 3.81 / 7.23 | 3.77 / 7.14 | 3.75 / 7.09 | 3.72 / 7.02 | 3.71 / 6.99 | 3.69 / 6.94 | 3.68 / 6.90 | 3.67 / 6.88 |
| 7 | 5.59 / 12.25 | 4.74 / 9.55 | 4.35 / 8.45 | 4.12 / 7.85 | 3.97 / 7.46 | 3.87 / 7.19 | 3.79 / 7.00 | 3.73 / 6.84 | 3.68 / 6.71 | 3.63 / 6.62 | 3.60 / 6.54 | 3.57 / 6.47 | 3.52 / 6.35 | 3.49 / 6.27 | 3.44 / 6.15 | 3.41 / 6.07 | 3.38 / 5.98 | 3.34 / 5.90 | 3.32 / 5.85 | 3.29 / 5.78 | 3.28 / 5.75 | 3.25 / 5.70 | 3.24 / 5.67 | 3.23 / 5.65 |
| 8 | 5.32 / 11.26 | 4.46 / 8.65 | 4.07 / 7.59 | 3.84 / 7.01 | 3.69 / 6.63 | 3.58 / 6.37 | 3.50 / 6.19 | 3.44 / 6.03 | 3.39 / 5.91 | 3.34 / 5.82 | 3.31 / 5.74 | 3.28 / 5.67 | 3.23 / 5.56 | 3.20 / 5.48 | 3.15 / 5.36 | 3.12 / 5.28 | 3.08 / 5.20 | 3.05 / 5.11 | 3.03 / 5.06 | 3.00 / 5.00 | 2.98 / 4.96 | 2.96 / 4.91 | 2.94 / 4.88 | 2.93 / 4.86 |
| 9 | 5.12 / 10.56 | 4.26 / 8.02 | 3.86 / 6.99 | 3.63 / 6.42 | 3.48 / 6.06 | 3.37 / 5.80 | 3.29 / 5.62 | 3.23 / 5.47 | 3.18 / 5.35 | 3.13 / 5.26 | 3.10 / 5.18 | 3.07 / 5.11 | 3.02 / 5.00 | 2.98 / 4.92 | 2.93 / 4.80 | 2.90 / 4.73 | 2.86 / 4.64 | 2.82 / 4.56 | 2.80 / 4.51 | 2.77 / 4.45 | 2.76 / 4.41 | 2.73 / 4.36 | 2.72 / 4.33 | 2.71 / 4.31 |
| 10 | 4.96 / 10.04 | 4.10 / 7.56 | 3.71 / 6.55 | 3.48 / 5.99 | 3.33 / 5.64 | 3.22 / 5.39 | 3.14 / 5.21 | 3.07 / 5.06 | 3.02 / 4.95 | 2.97 / 4.85 | 2.94 / 4.78 | 2.91 / 4.71 | 2.86 / 4.60 | 2.82 / 4.52 | 2.77 / 4.41 | 2.74 / 4.33 | 2.70 / 4.25 | 2.67 / 4.17 | 2.64 / 4.12 | 2.61 / 4.05 | 2.59 / 4.01 | 2.56 / 3.96 | 2.55 / 3.93 | 2.54 / 3.91 |
| 11 | 4.84 / 9.65 | 3.98 / 7.20 | 3.59 / 6.22 | 3.36 / 5.67 | 3.20 / 5.32 | 3.09 / 5.07 | 3.01 / 4.88 | 2.95 / 4.74 | 2.90 / 4.63 | 2.86 / 4.54 | 2.82 / 4.46 | 2.79 / 4.40 | 2.74 / 4.29 | 2.70 / 4.21 | 2.65 / 4.10 | 2.61 / 4.02 | 2.57 / 3.94 | 2.53 / 3.86 | 2.50 / 3.80 | 2.47 / 3.74 | 2.45 / 3.70 | 2.42 / 3.66 | 2.41 / 3.62 | 2.40 / 3.60 |
| 12 | 4.75 / 9.33 | 3.88 / 6.93 | 3.49 / 5.95 | 3.26 / 5.41 | 3.11 / 5.06 | 3.00 / 4.82 | 2.92 / 4.65 | 2.85 / 4.50 | 2.80 / 4.39 | 2.76 / 4.30 | 2.72 / 4.22 | 2.69 / 4.16 | 2.64 / 4.05 | 2.60 / 3.98 | 2.54 / 3.86 | 2.50 / 3.78 | 2.46 / 3.70 | 2.42 / 3.61 | 2.40 / 3.56 | 2.36 / 3.49 | 2.35 / 3.46 | 2.32 / 3.41 | 2.31 / 3.38 | 2.30 / 3.36 |
| 13 | 4.67 / 9.07 | 3.80 / 6.70 | 3.41 / 5.74 | 3.18 / 5.20 | 3.02 / 4.86 | 2.92 / 4.62 | 2.84 / 4.44 | 2.77 / 4.30 | 2.72 / 4.19 | 2.67 / 4.10 | 2.63 / 4.02 | 2.60 / 3.96 | 2.55 / 3.85 | 2.51 / 3.78 | 2.46 / 3.67 | 2.42 / 3.59 | 2.38 / 3.51 | 2.34 / 3.42 | 2.32 / 3.37 | 2.28 / 3.30 | 2.26 / 3.27 | 2.24 / 3.21 | 2.22 / 3.18 | 2.21 / 3.16 |
| 14 | 4.60 / 8.86 | 3.74 / 6.51 | 3.34 / 5.56 | 3.11 / 5.03 | 2.96 / 4.69 | 2.85 / 4.46 | 2.77 / 4.28 | 2.70 / 4.14 | 2.65 / 4.03 | 2.60 / 3.94 | 2.56 / 3.86 | 2.53 / 3.80 | 2.48 / 3.70 | 2.44 / 3.62 | 2.39 / 3.51 | 2.35 / 3.43 | 2.31 / 3.34 | 2.27 / 3.26 | 2.24 / 3.21 | 2.21 / 3.14 | 2.19 / 3.11 | 2.16 / 3.06 | 2.14 / 3.02 | 2.13 / 3.00 |
| 15 | 4.54 / 8.68 | 3.68 / 6.36 | 3.29 / 5.42 | 3.06 / 4.89 | 2.90 / 4.56 | 2.79 / 4.32 | 2.70 / 4.14 | 2.64 / 4.00 | 2.59 / 3.89 | 2.55 / 3.80 | 2.51 / 3.73 | 2.48 / 3.67 | 2.43 / 3.56 | 2.39 / 3.48 | 2.33 / 3.36 | 2.29 / 3.29 | 2.25 / 3.20 | 2.21 / 3.12 | 2.18 / 3.07 | 2.15 / 3.00 | 2.12 / 2.97 | 2.10 / 2.92 | 2.08 / 2.89 | 2.07 / 2.87 |

Degrees of freedom of denominator

**Table J** *(continued)*

Degrees of freedom for numerator (top value in each cell = .05, bottom value = .01)

| Degrees of freedom for denominator | 1 | 2 | 3 | 4 | 5 | 6 | 7 | 8 | 9 | 10 | 11 | 12 | 14 | 16 | 20 | 24 | 30 | 40 | 50 | 75 | 100 | 200 | 500 | ∞ |
|---|---|---|---|---|---|---|---|---|---|---|---|---|---|---|---|---|---|---|---|---|---|---|---|---|
| 16 | 4.49/8.53 | 3.63/6.23 | 3.24/5.29 | 3.01/4.77 | 2.85/4.44 | 2.74/4.20 | 2.66/4.03 | 2.59/3.89 | 2.54/3.78 | 2.49/3.69 | 2.45/3.61 | 2.42/3.55 | 2.37/3.45 | 2.33/3.37 | 2.28/3.25 | 2.24/3.18 | 2.20/3.10 | 2.16/3.01 | 2.13/2.96 | 2.09/2.89 | 2.07/2.86 | 2.04/2.80 | 2.02/2.77 | 2.01/2.75 |
| 17 | 4.45/8.40 | 3.59/6.11 | 3.20/5.18 | 2.96/4.67 | 2.81/4.34 | 2.70/4.10 | 2.62/3.93 | 2.55/3.79 | 2.50/3.68 | 2.45/3.59 | 2.41/3.52 | 2.38/3.45 | 2.33/3.35 | 2.29/3.27 | 2.23/3.16 | 2.19/3.08 | 2.15/3.00 | 2.11/2.92 | 2.08/2.86 | 2.04/2.79 | 2.02/2.76 | 1.99/2.70 | 1.97/2.67 | 1.96/2.65 |
| 18 | 4.41/8.28 | 3.55/6.01 | 3.16/5.09 | 2.93/4.58 | 2.77/4.25 | 2.66/4.01 | 2.58/3.85 | 2.51/3.71 | 2.46/3.60 | 2.41/3.51 | 2.37/3.44 | 2.34/3.37 | 2.29/3.27 | 2.25/3.19 | 2.19/3.07 | 2.15/3.00 | 2.11/2.91 | 2.07/2.83 | 2.04/2.78 | 2.00/2.71 | 1.98/2.68 | 1.95/2.62 | 1.93/2.59 | 1.92/2.57 |
| 19 | 4.38/8.18 | 3.52/5.93 | 3.13/5.01 | 2.90/4.50 | 2.74/4.17 | 2.63/3.94 | 2.55/3.77 | 2.48/3.63 | 2.43/3.52 | 2.38/3.43 | 2.34/3.36 | 2.31/3.30 | 2.26/3.19 | 2.21/3.12 | 2.15/3.00 | 2.11/2.92 | 2.07/2.84 | 2.02/2.76 | 2.00/2.70 | 1.96/2.63 | 1.94/2.60 | 1.91/2.54 | 1.90/2.51 | 1.88/2.49 |
| 20 | 4.35/8.10 | 3.49/5.85 | 3.10/4.94 | 2.87/4.43 | 2.71/4.10 | 2.60/3.87 | 2.52/3.71 | 2.45/3.56 | 2.40/3.45 | 2.35/3.37 | 2.31/3.30 | 2.28/3.23 | 2.23/3.13 | 2.18/3.05 | 2.12/2.94 | 2.08/2.86 | 2.04/2.77 | 1.99/2.69 | 1.96/2.63 | 1.92/2.56 | 1.90/2.53 | 1.87/2.47 | 1.85/2.44 | 1.84/2.42 |
| 21 | 4.32/8.02 | 3.47/5.78 | 3.07/4.87 | 2.84/4.37 | 2.68/4.04 | 2.57/3.81 | 2.49/3.65 | 2.42/3.51 | 2.37/3.40 | 2.32/3.31 | 2.28/3.24 | 2.25/3.17 | 2.20/3.07 | 2.15/2.99 | 2.09/2.88 | 2.05/2.80 | 2.00/2.72 | 1.96/2.63 | 1.93/2.58 | 1.89/2.51 | 1.87/2.47 | 1.84/2.42 | 1.82/2.38 | 1.81/2.36 |
| 22 | 4.30/7.94 | 3.44/5.72 | 3.05/4.82 | 2.82/4.31 | 2.66/3.99 | 2.55/3.76 | 2.47/3.59 | 2.40/3.45 | 2.35/3.35 | 2.30/3.26 | 2.26/3.18 | 2.23/3.12 | 2.18/3.02 | 2.13/2.94 | 2.07/2.83 | 2.03/2.75 | 1.98/2.67 | 1.93/2.58 | 1.91/2.53 | 1.87/2.46 | 1.84/2.42 | 1.81/2.37 | 1.80/2.33 | 1.78/2.31 |
| 23 | 4.28/7.88 | 3.42/5.66 | 3.03/4.76 | 2.80/4.26 | 2.64/3.94 | 2.53/3.71 | 2.45/3.54 | 2.38/3.41 | 2.32/3.30 | 2.28/3.21 | 2.24/3.14 | 2.20/3.07 | 2.14/2.97 | 2.10/2.89 | 2.04/2.78 | 2.00/2.70 | 1.96/2.62 | 1.91/2.53 | 1.88/2.48 | 1.84/2.41 | 1.82/2.37 | 1.79/2.32 | 1.77/2.28 | 1.76/2.26 |
| 24 | 4.26/7.82 | 3.40/5.61 | 3.01/4.72 | 2.78/4.22 | 2.62/3.90 | 2.51/3.67 | 2.43/3.50 | 2.36/3.36 | 2.30/3.25 | 2.26/3.17 | 2.22/3.09 | 2.18/3.03 | 2.13/2.93 | 2.09/2.85 | 2.02/2.74 | 1.98/2.66 | 1.94/2.58 | 1.89/2.49 | 1.86/2.44 | 1.82/2.36 | 1.80/2.33 | 1.76/2.27 | 1.74/2.23 | 1.73/2.21 |
| 25 | 4.24/7.77 | 3.38/5.57 | 2.99/4.68 | 2.76/4.18 | 2.60/3.86 | 2.49/3.63 | 2.41/3.46 | 2.34/3.32 | 2.28/3.21 | 2.24/3.13 | 2.20/3.05 | 2.16/2.99 | 2.11/2.89 | 2.06/2.81 | 2.00/2.70 | 1.96/2.62 | 1.92/2.54 | 1.87/2.45 | 1.84/2.40 | 1.80/2.32 | 1.77/2.29 | 1.74/2.23 | 1.72/2.19 | 1.71/2.17 |
| 26 | 4.22/7.72 | 3.37/5.53 | 2.98/4.64 | 2.74/4.14 | 2.59/3.82 | 2.47/3.59 | 2.39/3.42 | 2.32/3.29 | 2.27/3.17 | 2.22/3.09 | 2.18/3.02 | 2.15/2.96 | 2.10/2.86 | 2.05/2.77 | 1.99/2.66 | 1.95/2.58 | 1.90/2.50 | 1.85/2.41 | 1.82/2.36 | 1.78/2.28 | 1.76/2.25 | 1.72/2.19 | 1.70/2.15 | 1.69/2.13 |
| 27 | 4.21/7.68 | 3.35/5.49 | 2.96/4.60 | 2.73/4.11 | 2.57/3.79 | 2.46/3.56 | 2.37/3.39 | 2.30/3.26 | 2.25/3.14 | 2.20/3.06 | 2.16/2.98 | 2.13/2.93 | 2.08/2.83 | 2.03/2.74 | 1.97/2.63 | 1.93/2.55 | 1.88/2.47 | 1.84/2.38 | 1.80/2.33 | 1.76/2.25 | 1.74/2.21 | 1.71/2.16 | 1.68/2.12 | 1.67/2.10 |
| 28 | 4.20/7.64 | 3.34/5.45 | 2.95/4.57 | 2.71/4.07 | 2.56/3.76 | 2.44/3.53 | 2.36/3.36 | 2.29/3.23 | 2.24/3.11 | 2.19/3.03 | 2.15/2.95 | 2.12/2.90 | 2.06/2.80 | 2.02/2.71 | 1.96/2.60 | 1.91/2.52 | 1.87/2.44 | 1.81/2.35 | 1.78/2.30 | 1.75/2.22 | 1.72/2.18 | 1.69/2.13 | 1.67/2.09 | 1.65/2.06 |
| 29 | 4.18/7.60 | 3.33/5.42 | 2.93/4.54 | 2.70/4.04 | 2.54/3.73 | 2.43/3.50 | 2.35/3.33 | 2.28/3.20 | 2.22/3.08 | 2.18/3.00 | 2.14/2.92 | 2.10/2.87 | 2.05/2.77 | 2.00/2.68 | 1.94/2.57 | 1.90/2.49 | 1.85/2.41 | 1.80/2.32 | 1.77/2.27 | 1.73/2.19 | 1.71/2.15 | 1.68/2.10 | 1.65/2.06 | 1.64/2.03 |
| 30 | 4.17/7.56 | 3.32/5.39 | 2.92/4.51 | 2.69/4.02 | 2.53/3.70 | 2.42/3.47 | 2.34/3.30 | 2.27/3.17 | 2.21/3.06 | 2.16/2.98 | 2.12/2.90 | 2.09/2.84 | 2.04/2.74 | 1.99/2.66 | 1.93/2.55 | 1.89/2.47 | 1.84/2.38 | 1.79/2.29 | 1.76/2.24 | 1.72/2.16 | 1.69/2.13 | 1.66/2.07 | 1.64/2.03 | 1.62/2.01 |
| 32 | 4.15/7.50 | 3.30/5.34 | 2.90/4.46 | 2.67/3.97 | 2.51/3.66 | 2.40/3.42 | 2.32/3.25 | 2.25/3.12 | 2.19/3.01 | 2.14/2.94 | 2.10/2.86 | 2.07/2.80 | 2.02/2.70 | 1.97/2.62 | 1.91/2.51 | 1.86/2.42 | 1.82/2.34 | 1.76/2.25 | 1.74/2.20 | 1.69/2.12 | 1.67/2.08 | 1.64/2.02 | 1.61/1.98 | 1.59/1.96 |
| 34 | 4.13/7.44 | 3.28/5.29 | 2.88/4.42 | 2.65/3.93 | 2.49/3.61 | 2.38/3.38 | 2.30/3.21 | 2.23/3.08 | 2.17/2.97 | 2.12/2.89 | 2.08/2.82 | 2.05/2.76 | 2.00/2.66 | 1.95/2.58 | 1.89/2.47 | 1.84/2.38 | 1.80/2.30 | 1.74/2.21 | 1.71/2.15 | 1.67/2.08 | 1.64/2.04 | 1.61/1.98 | 1.59/1.94 | 1.57/1.91 |

Degrees of freedom for denominator

**Table J** (continued)

Degrees of freedom for numerator

| Degrees of freedom for denominator | 1 | 2 | 3 | 4 | 5 | 6 | 7 | 8 | 9 | 10 | 11 | 12 | 14 | 16 | 20 | 24 | 30 | 40 | 50 | 75 | 100 | 200 | 500 | ∞ |
|---|---|---|---|---|---|---|---|---|---|---|---|---|---|---|---|---|---|---|---|---|---|---|---|---|
| 36 | 4.11 / 7.39 | 3.26 / 5.25 | 2.86 / 4.38 | 2.63 / 3.89 | 2.48 / 3.58 | 2.36 / 3.35 | 2.28 / 3.18 | 2.21 / 3.04 | 2.15 / 2.94 | 2.10 / 2.86 | 2.06 / 2.78 | 2.03 / 2.72 | 1.98 / 2.62 | 1.93 / 2.54 | 1.87 / 2.43 | 1.82 / 2.35 | 1.78 / 2.26 | 1.72 / 2.17 | 1.69 / 2.12 | 1.65 / 2.04 | 1.62 / 2.00 | 1.59 / 1.94 | 1.56 / 1.90 | 1.55 / 1.87 |
| 38 | 4.10 / 7.35 | 3.25 / 5.21 | 2.85 / 4.34 | 2.62 / 3.86 | 2.46 / 3.54 | 2.35 / 3.32 | 2.26 / 3.15 | 2.19 / 3.02 | 2.14 / 2.91 | 2.09 / 2.82 | 2.05 / 2.75 | 2.02 / 2.69 | 1.96 / 2.59 | 1.92 / 2.51 | 1.85 / 2.40 | 1.80 / 2.32 | 1.76 / 2.22 | 1.71 / 2.14 | 1.67 / 2.08 | 1.63 / 2.00 | 1.60 / 1.97 | 1.57 / 1.90 | 1.54 / 1.86 | 1.53 / 1.84 |
| 40 | 4.08 / 7.31 | 3.23 / 5.18 | 2.84 / 4.31 | 2.61 / 3.83 | 2.45 / 3.51 | 2.34 / 3.29 | 2.25 / 3.12 | 2.18 / 2.99 | 2.12 / 2.88 | 2.07 / 2.80 | 2.04 / 2.73 | 2.00 / 2.66 | 1.95 / 2.56 | 1.90 / 2.49 | 1.84 / 2.37 | 1.79 / 2.29 | 1.74 / 2.20 | 1.69 / 2.11 | 1.66 / 2.05 | 1.61 / 1.97 | 1.59 / 1.94 | 1.55 / 1.88 | 1.53 / 1.84 | 1.51 / 1.81 |
| 42 | 4.07 / 7.27 | 3.22 / 5.15 | 2.83 / 4.29 | 2.59 / 3.80 | 2.44 / 3.49 | 2.32 / 3.26 | 2.24 / 3.10 | 2.17 / 2.96 | 2.11 / 2.86 | 2.06 / 2.77 | 2.02 / 2.70 | 1.99 / 2.64 | 1.94 / 2.54 | 1.89 / 2.46 | 1.82 / 2.35 | 1.78 / 2.26 | 1.73 / 2.17 | 1.68 / 2.08 | 1.64 / 2.02 | 1.60 / 1.94 | 1.57 / 1.91 | 1.54 / 1.85 | 1.51 / 1.80 | 1.49 / 1.78 |
| 44 | 4.06 / 7.24 | 3.21 / 5.12 | 2.82 / 4.26 | 2.58 / 3.78 | 2.43 / 3.46 | 2.31 / 3.24 | 2.23 / 3.07 | 2.16 / 2.94 | 2.10 / 2.84 | 2.05 / 2.75 | 2.01 / 2.68 | 1.98 / 2.62 | 1.92 / 2.52 | 1.88 / 2.44 | 1.81 / 2.32 | 1.76 / 2.24 | 1.72 / 2.15 | 1.66 / 2.06 | 1.63 / 2.00 | 1.58 / 1.92 | 1.56 / 1.88 | 1.52 / 1.82 | 1.50 / 1.78 | 1.48 / 1.75 |
| 46 | 4.05 / 7.21 | 3.20 / 5.10 | 2.81 / 4.24 | 2.57 / 3.76 | 2.42 / 3.44 | 2.30 / 3.22 | 2.22 / 3.05 | 2.14 / 2.92 | 2.09 / 2.82 | 2.04 / 2.73 | 2.00 / 2.66 | 1.97 / 2.60 | 1.91 / 2.50 | 1.87 / 2.42 | 1.80 / 2.30 | 1.75 / 2.22 | 1.71 / 2.13 | 1.65 / 2.04 | 1.62 / 1.98 | 1.57 / 1.90 | 1.54 / 1.86 | 1.51 / 1.80 | 1.48 / 1.76 | 1.46 / 1.72 |
| 48 | 4.04 / 7.19 | 3.19 / 5.08 | 2.80 / 4.22 | 2.56 / 3.74 | 2.41 / 3.42 | 2.30 / 3.20 | 2.21 / 3.04 | 2.14 / 2.90 | 2.08 / 2.80 | 2.03 / 2.71 | 1.99 / 2.64 | 1.96 / 2.58 | 1.90 / 2.48 | 1.86 / 2.40 | 1.79 / 2.28 | 1.74 / 2.20 | 1.70 / 2.11 | 1.64 / 2.02 | 1.61 / 1.96 | 1.56 / 1.88 | 1.53 / 1.84 | 1.50 / 1.78 | 1.47 / 1.73 | 1.45 / 1.70 |
| 50 | 4.03 / 7.17 | 3.18 / 5.06 | 2.79 / 4.20 | 2.56 / 3.72 | 2.40 / 3.41 | 2.29 / 3.18 | 2.20 / 3.02 | 2.13 / 2.88 | 2.07 / 2.78 | 2.02 / 2.70 | 1.98 / 2.62 | 1.95 / 2.56 | 1.90 / 2.46 | 1.85 / 2.39 | 1.78 / 2.26 | 1.74 / 2.18 | 1.69 / 2.10 | 1.63 / 2.00 | 1.60 / 1.94 | 1.55 / 1.86 | 1.52 / 1.82 | 1.48 / 1.76 | 1.46 / 1.71 | 1.44 / 1.68 |
| 55 | 4.02 / 7.12 | 3.17 / 5.01 | 2.78 / 4.16 | 2.54 / 3.68 | 2.38 / 3.37 | 2.27 / 3.15 | 2.18 / 2.98 | 2.11 / 2.85 | 2.05 / 2.75 | 2.00 / 2.66 | 1.97 / 2.59 | 1.93 / 2.53 | 1.88 / 2.43 | 1.83 / 2.35 | 1.76 / 2.23 | 1.72 / 2.15 | 1.67 / 2.06 | 1.61 / 1.96 | 1.58 / 1.90 | 1.52 / 1.82 | 1.50 / 1.78 | 1.46 / 1.71 | 1.43 / 1.66 | 1.41 / 1.64 |
| 60 | 4.00 / 7.08 | 3.15 / 4.98 | 2.76 / 4.13 | 2.52 / 3.65 | 2.37 / 3.34 | 2.25 / 3.12 | 2.17 / 2.95 | 2.10 / 2.82 | 2.04 / 2.72 | 1.99 / 2.63 | 1.95 / 2.56 | 1.92 / 2.50 | 1.86 / 2.40 | 1.81 / 2.32 | 1.75 / 2.20 | 1.70 / 2.12 | 1.65 / 2.03 | 1.59 / 1.93 | 1.56 / 1.87 | 1.50 / 1.79 | 1.48 / 1.74 | 1.44 / 1.68 | 1.41 / 1.63 | 1.39 / 1.60 |
| 65 | 3.99 / 7.04 | 3.14 / 4.95 | 2.75 / 4.10 | 2.51 / 3.62 | 2.36 / 3.31 | 2.24 / 3.09 | 2.15 / 2.93 | 2.08 / 2.79 | 2.02 / 2.70 | 1.98 / 2.61 | 1.94 / 2.54 | 1.90 / 2.47 | 1.85 / 2.37 | 1.80 / 2.30 | 1.73 / 2.18 | 1.68 / 2.09 | 1.63 / 2.00 | 1.57 / 1.90 | 1.54 / 1.84 | 1.49 / 1.76 | 1.46 / 1.71 | 1.42 / 1.64 | 1.39 / 1.60 | 1.37 / 1.56 |
| 70 | 3.98 / 7.01 | 3.13 / 4.92 | 2.74 / 4.08 | 2.50 / 3.60 | 2.35 / 3.29 | 2.23 / 3.07 | 2.14 / 2.91 | 2.07 / 2.77 | 2.01 / 2.67 | 1.97 / 2.59 | 1.93 / 2.51 | 1.89 / 2.45 | 1.84 / 2.35 | 1.79 / 2.28 | 1.72 / 2.15 | 1.67 / 2.07 | 1.62 / 1.98 | 1.56 / 1.88 | 1.53 / 1.82 | 1.47 / 1.74 | 1.45 / 1.69 | 1.40 / 1.62 | 1.37 / 1.56 | 1.35 / 1.53 |
| 80 | 3.96 / 6.96 | 3.11 / 4.88 | 2.72 / 4.04 | 2.48 / 3.56 | 2.33 / 3.25 | 2.21 / 3.04 | 2.12 / 2.87 | 2.05 / 2.74 | 1.99 / 2.64 | 1.95 / 2.55 | 1.91 / 2.48 | 1.88 / 2.41 | 1.82 / 2.32 | 1.77 / 2.24 | 1.70 / 2.11 | 1.65 / 2.03 | 1.60 / 1.94 | 1.54 / 1.84 | 1.51 / 1.78 | 1.45 / 1.70 | 1.42 / 1.65 | 1.38 / 1.57 | 1.35 / 1.52 | 1.32 / 1.49 |
| 100 | 3.94 / 6.90 | 3.09 / 4.82 | 2.70 / 3.98 | 2.46 / 3.51 | 2.30 / 3.20 | 2.19 / 2.99 | 2.10 / 2.82 | 2.03 / 2.69 | 1.97 / 2.59 | 1.92 / 2.51 | 1.88 / 2.43 | 1.85 / 2.36 | 1.79 / 2.26 | 1.75 / 2.19 | 1.68 / 2.06 | 1.63 / 1.98 | 1.57 / 1.89 | 1.51 / 1.79 | 1.48 / 1.73 | 1.42 / 1.64 | 1.39 / 1.59 | 1.34 / 1.51 | 1.30 / 1.46 | 1.28 / 1.43 |
| 125 | 3.92 / 6.84 | 3.07 / 4.78 | 2.68 / 3.94 | 2.44 / 3.47 | 2.29 / 3.17 | 2.17 / 2.95 | 2.08 / 2.79 | 2.01 / 2.65 | 1.95 / 2.56 | 1.90 / 2.47 | 1.86 / 2.40 | 1.83 / 2.33 | 1.77 / 2.23 | 1.72 / 2.15 | 1.65 / 2.03 | 1.60 / 1.94 | 1.55 / 1.85 | 1.49 / 1.75 | 1.45 / 1.68 | 1.39 / 1.59 | 1.36 / 1.54 | 1.31 / 1.46 | 1.27 / 1.40 | 1.25 / 1.37 |
| 150 | 3.91 / 6.81 | 3.06 / 4.75 | 2.67 / 3.91 | 2.43 / 3.44 | 2.27 / 3.13 | 2.16 / 2.92 | 2.07 / 2.76 | 2.00 / 2.62 | 1.94 / 2.53 | 1.89 / 2.44 | 1.85 / 2.37 | 1.82 / 2.30 | 1.76 / 2.20 | 1.71 / 2.12 | 1.64 / 2.00 | 1.59 / 1.91 | 1.54 / 1.83 | 1.47 / 1.72 | 1.44 / 1.66 | 1.37 / 1.56 | 1.34 / 1.51 | 1.29 / 1.43 | 1.25 / 1.37 | 1.22 / 1.33 |
| 200 | 3.89 / 6.76 | 3.04 / 4.71 | 2.65 / 3.88 | 2.41 / 3.41 | 2.26 / 3.11 | 2.14 / 2.90 | 2.05 / 2.73 | 1.98 / 2.60 | 1.92 / 2.50 | 1.87 / 2.41 | 1.83 / 2.34 | 1.80 / 2.28 | 1.74 / 2.17 | 1.69 / 2.09 | 1.62 / 1.97 | 1.57 / 1.88 | 1.52 / 1.79 | 1.45 / 1.69 | 1.42 / 1.62 | 1.35 / 1.53 | 1.32 / 1.48 | 1.26 / 1.39 | 1.22 / 1.33 | 1.19 / 1.28 |
| 400 | 3.86 / 6.70 | 3.02 / 4.66 | 2.62 / 3.83 | 2.39 / 3.36 | 2.23 / 3.06 | 2.12 / 2.85 | 2.03 / 2.69 | 1.96 / 2.55 | 1.90 / 2.46 | 1.85 / 2.37 | 1.81 / 2.29 | 1.78 / 2.23 | 1.72 / 2.12 | 1.67 / 2.04 | 1.60 / 1.92 | 1.54 / 1.84 | 1.49 / 1.74 | 1.42 / 1.64 | 1.38 / 1.57 | 1.32 / 1.47 | 1.28 / 1.42 | 1.22 / 1.32 | 1.16 / 1.24 | 1.13 / 1.19 |
| 1000 | 3.85 / 6.66 | 3.00 / 4.62 | 2.61 / 3.80 | 2.38 / 3.34 | 2.22 / 3.04 | 2.10 / 2.82 | 2.02 / 2.66 | 1.95 / 2.53 | 1.89 / 2.43 | 1.84 / 2.34 | 1.80 / 2.26 | 1.76 / 2.20 | 1.70 / 2.09 | 1.65 / 2.01 | 1.58 / 1.89 | 1.53 / 1.81 | 1.47 / 1.71 | 1.41 / 1.61 | 1.36 / 1.54 | 1.30 / 1.44 | 1.26 / 1.38 | 1.19 / 1.28 | 1.13 / 1.19 | 1.08 / 1.11 |
| ∞ | 3.84 / 6.64 | 2.99 / 4.60 | 2.60 / 3.78 | 2.37 / 3.32 | 2.21 / 3.02 | 2.09 / 2.80 | 2.01 / 2.64 | 1.94 / 2.51 | 1.88 / 2.41 | 1.83 / 2.32 | 1.79 / 2.24 | 1.75 / 2.18 | 1.69 / 2.07 | 1.64 / 1.99 | 1.57 / 1.87 | 1.52 / 1.79 | 1.46 / 1.69 | 1.40 / 1.59 | 1.35 / 1.52 | 1.28 / 1.41 | 1.24 / 1.36 | 1.17 / 1.25 | 1.11 / 1.15 | 1.00 / 1.00 |

## Table K

### Critical Values for the $F_{max}$ Test

To use this table, divide the largest variance by the smallest variance to create $F_{max}$. The column labeled $n$ represents the number of subjects in each group. If the sample sizes for the two groups are not equal, determine the average $n$ and round up. The other columns of numbers represent the number of treatment conditions in the study. If the observed value of $F_{max}$ is less than the tabled value, then you may assume that the variances are homogeneous, $\sigma_{smallest} = \sigma_{largest}$.

| $n$ | $\alpha$ | NUMBER OF VARIANCES IN STUDY | | | | | | | | |
|---|---|---|---|---|---|---|---|---|---|---|
| | | 2 | 3 | 4 | 5 | 6 | 7 | 8 | 9 | 10 |
| 4 | .05 | 9.6 | 15.5 | 20.6 | 25.2 | 29.5 | 33.6 | 37.5 | 41.4 | 44.6 |
| | .01 | 23.2 | 37.0 | 49.0 | 59.0 | 69.0 | 79.0 | 89.0 | 97.0 | 106.0 |
| 5 | .05 | 7.2 | 10.8 | 13.7 | 16.3 | 18.7 | 20.8 | 22.9 | 24.7 | 26.5 |
| | .01 | 14.9 | 22.0 | 28.0 | 33.0 | 38.0 | 42.0 | 46.0 | 50.0 | 54.0 |
| 6 | .05 | 5.8 | 8.4 | 10.4 | 12.1 | 13.7 | 15.0 | 16.3 | 17.5 | 18.6 |
| | .01 | 11.1 | 15.5 | 19.1 | 22.0 | 25.0 | 27.0 | 30.0 | 32.0 | 34.0 |
| 7 | .05 | 5.0 | 6.9 | 8.4 | 9.7 | 10.8 | 11.8 | 12.7 | 13.5 | 14.3 |
| | .01 | 8.9 | 12.1 | 14.5 | 16.5 | 18.4 | 20.0 | 22.0 | 23.0 | 24.0 |
| 8 | .05 | 4.4 | 6.0 | 7.2 | 8.1 | 9.0 | 9.8 | 10.5 | 11.1 | 11.7 |
| | .01 | 7.5 | 9.9 | 11.7 | 13.2 | 14.5 | 15.8 | 16.9 | 17.9 | 18.9 |
| 9 | .05 | 4.0 | 5.3 | 6.3 | 7.1 | 7.8 | 8.4 | 8.9 | 9.5 | 9.9 |
| | .01 | 6.5 | 8.5 | 9.9 | 11.1 | 12.1 | 13.1 | 13.9 | 14.7 | 15.3 |
| 10 | .05 | 3.7 | 4.9 | 5.7 | 6.3 | 6.9 | 7.4 | 7.9 | 8.3 | 8.7 |
| | .01 | 5.9 | 7.4 | 8.6 | 9.6 | 10.4 | 11.1 | 11.8 | 12.4 | 12.9 |
| 12 | .05 | 3.3 | 4.2 | 4.8 | 5.3 | 5.7 | 6.1 | 6.4 | 6.7 | 7.0 |
| | .01 | 4.9 | 6.1 | 6.9 | 7.6 | 8.2 | 8.7 | 9.1 | 9.5 | 9.9 |
| 15 | .05 | 2.7 | 3.5 | 4.0 | 4.4 | 4.7 | 4.9 | 5.2 | 5.4 | 5.6 |
| | .01 | 4.1 | 4.9 | 5.5 | 6.0 | 6.4 | 6.7 | 7.1 | 7.3 | 7.5 |
| 20 | .05 | 2.5 | 2.9 | 3.3 | 3.5 | 3.7 | 3.9 | 4.1 | 4.2 | 4.4 |
| | .01 | 3.3 | 3.8 | 4.3 | 4.6 | 4.9 | 5.1 | 5.3 | 5.5 | 5.6 |
| 30 | .05 | 2.1 | 2.4 | 2.6 | 2.8 | 2.9 | 3.0 | 3.1 | 3.2 | 3.3 |
| | .01 | 2.6 | 3.0 | 3.3 | 3.4 | 3.6 | 3.7 | 3.8 | 3.9 | 4.0 |
| 60 | .05 | 1.7 | 1.9 | 1.9 | 2.0 | 2.1 | 2.2 | 2.2 | 2.3 | 2.3 |
| | .01 | 2.0 | 2.2 | 2.3 | 2.4 | 2.4 | 2.5 | 2.5 | 2.6 | 2.6 |
| $\infty$ | .05 | 1.0 | 1.0 | 1.0 | 1.0 | 1.0 | 1.0 | 1.0 | 1.0 | 1.0 |
| | .01 | 1.0 | 1.0 | 1.0 | 1.0 | 1.0 | 1.0 | 1.0 | 1.0 | 1.0 |

**Table L**

**Critical Values for the Studentized Range Test**

| Error df | α | \(k\) = number of means or number of steps between ordered means | | | | | | | | | |
|---|---|---|---|---|---|---|---|---|---|---|---|
| | | 2 | 3 | 4 | 5 | 6 | 7 | 8 | 9 | 10 | 11 |
| 5 | .05 | 3.64 | 4.60 | 5.22 | 5.67 | 6.03 | 6.33 | 6.58 | 6.80 | 6.99 | 7.17 |
| | .01 | 5.70 | 6.98 | 7.80 | 8.42 | 8.91 | 9.32 | 9.67 | 9.97 | 10.24 | 10.48 |
| 6 | .05 | 3.46 | 4.34 | 4.90 | 5.30 | 5.63 | 5.90 | 6.12 | 6.32 | 6.49 | 6.65 |
| | .01 | 5.24 | 6.33 | 7.03 | 7.56 | 7.97 | 8.32 | 8.61 | 8.87 | 9.10 | 9.30 |
| 7 | .05 | 3.34 | 4.16 | 4.68 | 5.06 | 5.36 | 5.61 | 5.82 | 6.00 | 6.16 | 6.30 |
| | .01 | 4.95 | 5.92 | 6.54 | 7.01 | 7.37 | 7.68 | 7.94 | 8.17 | 8.37 | 8.55 |
| 8 | .05 | 3.26 | 4.04 | 4.53 | 4.89 | 5.17 | 5.40 | 5.60 | 5.77 | 5.92 | 6.05 |
| | .01 | 4.75 | 5.64 | 6.20 | 6.62 | 6.96 | 7.24 | 7.47 | 7.68 | 7.86 | 8.03 |
| 9 | .05 | 3.20 | 3.95 | 4.41 | 4.76 | 5.02 | 5.24 | 5.43 | 5.59 | 5.74 | 5.87 |
| | .01 | 4.60 | 5.43 | 5.96 | 6.35 | 6.66 | 6.91 | 7.13 | 7.33 | 7.49 | 7.65 |
| 10 | .05 | 3.15 | 3.88 | 4.33 | 4.65 | 4.91 | 5.12 | 5.30 | 5.46 | 5.60 | 5.72 |
| | .01 | 4.48 | 5.27 | 5.77 | 6.14 | 6.43 | 6.67 | 6.87 | 7.05 | 7.21 | 7.36 |
| 11 | .05 | 3.11 | 3.82 | 4.26 | 4.57 | 4.82 | 5.03 | 5.20 | 5.35 | 5.49 | 5.61 |
| | .01 | 4.39 | 5.15 | 5.62 | 5.97 | 6.25 | 6.48 | 6.67 | 6.84 | 6.99 | 7.13 |
| 12 | .05 | 3.08 | 3.77 | 4.20 | 4.51 | 4.75 | 4.95 | 5.12 | 5.27 | 5.39 | 5.51 |
| | .01 | 4.32 | 5.05 | 5.50 | 5.84 | 6.10 | 6.32 | 6.51 | 6.67 | 6.81 | 6.94 |
| 13 | .05 | 3.06 | 3.73 | 4.15 | 4.45 | 4.69 | 4.88 | 5.05 | 5.19 | 5.32 | 5.43 |
| | .01 | 4.26 | 4.96 | 5.40 | 5.73 | 5.98 | 6.19 | 6.37 | 6.53 | 6.67 | 6.79 |
| 14 | .05 | 3.03 | 3.70 | 4.11 | 4.41 | 4.64 | 4.83 | 4.99 | 5.13 | 5.25 | 5.36 |
| | .01 | 4.21 | 4.89 | 5.32 | 5.63 | 5.88 | 6.08 | 6.26 | 6.41 | 6.54 | 6.66 |
| 15 | .05 | 3.01 | 3.67 | 4.08 | 4.37 | 4.59 | 4.78 | 4.94 | 5.08 | 5.20 | 5.31 |
| | .01 | 4.17 | 4.84 | 5.25 | 5.56 | 5.80 | 5.99 | 6.16 | 6.31 | 6.44 | 6.55 |
| 16 | .05 | 3.00 | 3.65 | 4.05 | 4.33 | 4.56 | 4.74 | 4.90 | 5.03 | 5.15 | 5.26 |
| | .01 | 4.13 | 4.79 | 5.19 | 5.49 | 5.72 | 5.92 | 6.08 | 6.22 | 6.35 | 6.46 |
| 17 | .05 | 2.98 | 3.63 | 4.02 | 4.30 | 4.52 | 4.70 | 4.86 | 4.99 | 5.11 | 5.21 |
| | .01 | 4.10 | 4.74 | 5.14 | 5.43 | 5.66 | 5.85 | 6.01 | 6.15 | 6.27 | 6.38 |
| 18 | .05 | 2.97 | 3.61 | 4.00 | 4.28 | 4.49 | 4.67 | 4.82 | 4.96 | 5.07 | 5.17 |
| | .01 | 4.07 | 4.70 | 5.09 | 5.38 | 5.60 | 5.79 | 5.94 | 6.08 | 6.20 | 6.31 |
| 19 | .05 | 2.96 | 3.59 | 3.98 | 4.25 | 4.47 | 4.65 | 4.79 | 4.92 | 5.04 | 5.14 |
| | .01 | 4.05 | 4.67 | 5.05 | 5.33 | 5.55 | 5.73 | 5.89 | 6.02 | 6.14 | 6.25 |
| 20 | .05 | 2.95 | 3.58 | 3.96 | 4.23 | 4.45 | 4.62 | 4.77 | 4.90 | 5.01 | 5.11 |
| | .01 | 4.02 | 4.64 | 5.02 | 5.29 | 5.51 | 5.69 | 5.84 | 5.97 | 6.09 | 6.19 |
| 24 | .05 | 2.92 | 3.53 | 3.90 | 4.17 | 4.37 | 4.54 | 4.68 | 4.81 | 4.92 | 5.01 |
| | .01 | 3.96 | 4.55 | 4.91 | 5.17 | 5.37 | 5.54 | 5.69 | 5.81 | 5.92 | 6.02 |
| 30 | .05 | 2.89 | 3.49 | 3.85 | 4.10 | 4.30 | 4.46 | 4.60 | 4.72 | 4.82 | 4.92 |
| | .01 | 3.89 | 4.45 | 4.80 | 5.05 | 5.24 | 5.40 | 5.54 | 5.65 | 5.76 | 5.85 |
| 40 | .05 | 2.86 | 3.44 | 3.79 | 4.04 | 4.23 | 4.39 | 4.52 | 4.63 | 4.73 | 4.82 |
| | .01 | 3.82 | 4.37 | 4.70 | 4.93 | 5.11 | 5.26 | 5.39 | 5.50 | 5.60 | 5.69 |
| 60 | .05 | 2.83 | 3.40 | 3.74 | 3.98 | 4.16 | 4.31 | 4.44 | 4.55 | 4.65 | 4.73 |
| | .01 | 3.76 | 4.28 | 4.59 | 4.82 | 4.99 | 5.13 | 5.25 | 5.36 | 5.45 | 5.53 |
| 120 | .05 | 2.80 | 3.36 | 3.68 | 3.92 | 4.10 | 4.24 | 4.36 | 4.47 | 4.56 | 4.64 |
| | .01 | 3.70 | 4.20 | 4.50 | 4.71 | 4.87 | 5.01 | 5.12 | 5.21 | 5.30 | 5.37 |
| ∞ | .05 | 2.77 | 3.31 | 3.63 | 3.86 | 4.03 | 4.17 | 4.29 | 4.39 | 4.47 | 4.55 |
| | .01 | 3.64 | 4.12 | 4.40 | 4.60 | 4.76 | 4.88 | 4.99 | 5.08 | 5.16 | 5.23 |

**Table** | **M**

| **Power of ANOVA**

This table presents the power for the $F$-ratio. Each section represents the degrees of freedom for the numerator (e.g., the degrees of freedom for the effect or $k - 1$). Power is presented for sample sizes of 5 to 100, $\alpha$ levels of $\alpha = .01$, $\alpha = .05$, and $\alpha = .10$; and for effect sizes of $\mathbf{f} = .1$ (small effect), $\mathbf{f} = .25$ (medium effect), and $\mathbf{f} = .40$ (large effect). The $F_c$ column represents the critical value of $F$ required to reject the null hypothesis.

To use the table, locate the section that represents the appropriate degrees of freedom. Next select the column that represents the $\alpha$ level you plan to use and the effect size you predict. That column of values represents the power for the sample size indicated for each row. For example, if you plan to conduct an ANOVA wherein the degrees of freedom in the numerator are 5, $\alpha = .05$, $\mathbf{f} = .25$, and $n = 20$, then the predicted power is .52.

The entry .** represents a value of power greater than .99.

### DEGREES OF FREEDOM NUMERATOR = 1

| | $\alpha = .01$ | | | | $\alpha = .05$ | | | | $\alpha = .10$ | | | |
|---|---|---|---|---|---|---|---|---|---|---|---|---|
| $n$ | $F_c$ | .10 | .25 | .40 | $F_c$ | .10 | .25 | .40 | $F_c$ | .10 | .25 | .40 |
| 5 | 11.259 | .01 | .03 | .06 | 5.318 | .06 | .11 | .20 | 3.458 | .11 | .19 | .32 |
| 10 | 8.285 | .01 | .05 | .17 | 4.414 | .06 | .18 | .40 | 3.007 | .13 | .30 | .55 |
| 15 | 7.636 | .01 | .09 | .30 | 4.196 | .07 | .26 | .57 | 2.894 | .15 | .39 | .70 |
| 20 | 7.353 | .02 | .14 | .44 | 4.098 | .09 | .34 | .70 | 2.842 | .16 | .48 | .81 |
| 25 | 7.194 | .02 | .19 | .57 | 4.043 | .10 | .42 | .80 | 2.813 | .18 | .56 | .88 |
| 30 | 7.093 | .02 | .24 | .67 | 4.007 | .11 | .49 | .87 | 2.794 | .20 | .62 | .93 |
| 35 | 7.023 | .03 | .30 | .76 | 3.982 | .12 | .55 | .92 | 2.781 | .22 | .68 | .96 |
| 40 | 6.971 | .03 | .35 | .83 | 3.963 | .14 | .61 | .95 | 2.771 | .24 | .73 | .97 |
| 45 | 6.932 | .04 | .40 | .88 | 3.949 | .15 | .66 | .97 | 2.763 | .25 | .77 | .98 |
| 50 | 6.901 | .05 | .46 | .92 | 3.938 | .16 | .71 | .98 | 2.757 | .27 | .81 | .99 |
| 100 | 6.765 | .11 | .83 | .** | 3.889 | .29 | .94 | .** | 2.731 | .42 | .97 | .** |

### DEGREES OF FREEDOM NUMERATOR = 2

| | $\alpha = .01$ | | | | $\alpha = .05$ | | | | $\alpha = .10$ | | | |
|---|---|---|---|---|---|---|---|---|---|---|---|---|
| $n$ | $F_c$ | .10 | .25 | .40 | $F_c$ | .10 | .25 | .40 | $F_c$ | .10 | .25 | .40 |
| 5 | 6.927 | .01 | .03 | .07 | 3.885 | .06 | .11 | .22 | 2.807 | .12 | .20 | .34 |
| 10 | 5.488 | .01 | .06 | .21 | 3.354 | .07 | .20 | .45 | 2.511 | .13 | .31 | .59 |
| 15 | 5.149 | .02 | .11 | .38 | 3.220 | .08 | .29 | .64 | 2.434 | .15 | .42 | .76 |
| 20 | 4.998 | .02 | .17 | .55 | 3.159 | .09 | .38 | .78 | 2.398 | .17 | .52 | .87 |
| 25 | 4.913 | .02 | .23 | .69 | 3.124 | .10 | .47 | .87 | 2.376 | .19 | .60 | .93 |
| 30 | 4.858 | .03 | .30 | .80 | 3.101 | .12 | .55 | .93 | 2.365 | .21 | .68 | .96 |
| 35 | 4.819 | .03 | .37 | .87 | 3.085 | .13 | .62 | .96 | 2.355 | .23 | .74 | .98 |
| 40 | 4.791 | .04 | .44 | .92 | 3.074 | .15 | .68 | .98 | 2.348 | .25 | .79 | .99 |
| 45 | 4.770 | .05 | .50 | .95 | 3.065 | .16 | .74 | .99 | 2.343 | .26 | .83 | .** |
| 50 | 4.752 | .05 | .56 | .97 | 3.058 | .18 | .79 | .99 | 2.339 | .28 | .87 | .** |
| 100 | 4.677 | .13 | .92 | .** | 3.026 | .32 | .98 | .** | 2.321 | .45 | .99 | .** |

### DEGREES OF FREEDOM NUMERATOR = 3

| n | $\alpha = .01$ $F_c$ | .10 | .25 | .40 | $\alpha = .05$ $F_c$ | .10 | .25 | .40 | $\alpha = .10$ $F_c$ | .10 | .25 | .40 |
|---|---|---|---|---|---|---|---|---|---|---|---|---|
| 5 | 5.292 | .01 | .03 | .08 | 3.239 | .06 | .12 | .24 | 2.462 | .12 | .20 | .37 |
| 10 | 4.377 | .01 | .07 | .25 | 2.866 | .07 | .21 | .51 | 2.243 | .14 | .33 | .64 |
| 15 | 4.152 | .02 | .13 | .46 | 2.769 | .08 | .32 | .71 | 2.184 | .16 | .45 | .82 |
| 20 | 4.050 | .02 | .20 | .65 | 2.725 | .10 | .43 | .85 | 2.157 | .18 | .56 | .91 |
| 25 | 3.992 | .03 | .28 | .79 | 2.699 | .11 | .53 | .93 | 2.142 | .20 | .65 | .96 |
| 30 | 3.955 | .03 | .36 | .88 | 2.683 | .13 | .61 | .96 | 2.132 | .22 | .73 | .98 |
| 35 | 3.929 | .04 | .45 | .94 | 2.671 | .14 | .69 | .98 | 2.124 | .24 | .79 | .99 |
| 40 | 3.910 | .04 | .53 | .97 | 2.663 | .16 | .76 | .99 | 2.119 | .26 | .84 | .** |
| 45 | 3.895 | .05 | .60 | .98 | 2.656 | .17 | .81 | .** | 2.115 | .28 | .88 | .** |
| 50 | 3.883 | .06 | .67 | .99 | 2.651 | .19 | .85 | .** | 2.112 | .30 | .91 | .** |
| 100 | 3.831 | .16 | .97 | .** | 2.627 | .36 | .99 | .** | 2.098 | .49 | .** | .** |

### DEGREES OF FREEDOM NUMERATOR = 4

| n | $\alpha = .01$ $F_c$ | .10 | .25 | .40 | $\alpha = .05$ $F_c$ | .10 | .25 | .40 | $\alpha = .10$ $F_c$ | .10 | .25 | .40 |
|---|---|---|---|---|---|---|---|---|---|---|---|---|
| 5 | 4.431 | .01 | .03 | .09 | 2.866 | .06 | .12 | .26 | 2.249 | .12 | .21 | .39 |
| 10 | 3.787 | .01 | .08 | .30 | 2.579 | .07 | .23 | .56 | 2.074 | .14 | .36 | .69 |
| 15 | 3.600 | .02 | .15 | .54 | 2.503 | .08 | .36 | .78 | 2.027 | .16 | .49 | .86 |
| 20 | 3.523 | .02 | .24 | .74 | 2.467 | .10 | .47 | .90 | 2.005 | .18 | .61 | .94 |
| 25 | 3.480 | .03 | .33 | .86 | 2.447 | .12 | .58 | .96 | 1.992 | .21 | .70 | .98 |
| 30 | 3.451 | .03 | .43 | .93 | 2.434 | .13 | .67 | .98 | 1.984 | .23 | .78 | .99 |
| 35 | 3.431 | .04 | .52 | .97 | 2.425 | .15 | .75 | .99 | 1.978 | .25 | .84 | .** |
| 40 | 3.417 | .05 | .61 | .99 | 2.418 | .17 | .81 | .** | 1.974 | .27 | .89 | .** |
| 45 | 3.406 | .06 | .68 | .** | 2.413 | .19 | .86 | .** | 1.971 | .30 | .92 | .** |
| 50 | 3.397 | .07 | .75 | .** | 2.408 | .21 | .90 | .** | 1.968 | .32 | .94 | .** |
| 100 | 3.357 | .19 | .99 | .** | 2.390 | .40 | .** | .** | 1.956 | .53 | .** | .** |

### DEGREES OF FREEDOM NUMERATOR = 5

| n | $\alpha = .01$ $F_c$ | .10 | .25 | .40 | $\alpha = .05$ $F_c$ | .10 | .25 | .40 | $\alpha = .10$ $F_c$ | .10 | .25 | .40 |
|---|---|---|---|---|---|---|---|---|---|---|---|---|
| 5 | 3.895 | .01 | .03 | .10 | 2.621 | .06 | .13 | .29 | 2.103 | .12 | .22 | .42 |
| 10 | 3.377 | .01 | .09 | .35 | 2.386 | .07 | .25 | .61 | 1.957 | .14 | .38 | .73 |
| 15 | 3.243 | .02 | .17 | .62 | 2.323 | .09 | .39 | .83 | 1.917 | .16 | .52 | .90 |
| 20 | 3.182 | .02 | .27 | .81 | 2.294 | .10 | .52 | .93 | 1.898 | .19 | .65 | .96 |
| 25 | 3.147 | .03 | .38 | .91 | 2.277 | .12 | .63 | .98 | 1.888 | .21 | .75 | .99 |
| 30 | 3.124 | .04 | .49 | .97 | 2.266 | .14 | .73 | .99 | 1.881 | .24 | .82 | .** |
| 35 | 3.108 | .05 | .59 | .99 | 2.258 | .16 | .80 | .** | 1.876 | .26 | .88 | .** |
| 40 | 3.096 | .05 | .68 | .** | 2.253 | .18 | .86 | .** | 1.872 | .29 | .92 | .** |
| 45 | 3.087 | .06 | .75 | .** | 2.248 | .20 | .90 | .** | 1.869 | .31 | .95 | .** |
| 50 | 3.080 | .07 | .81 | .** | 2.245 | .22 | .93 | .** | 1.857 | .34 | .96 | .** |
| 100 | 3.048 | .21 | .** | .** | 2.229 | .44 | .** | .** | 1.857 | .57 | .** | .** |

## DEGREES OF FREEDOM NUMERATOR = 6

| | $\alpha = .01$ | | | $\alpha = .05$ | | | $\alpha = .10$ | | |
| --- | --- | --- | --- | --- | --- | --- | --- | --- | --- | --- |
| $n$ | $F_c$ | .10 | .25 | .40 | $F_c$ | .10 | .25 | .40 | $F_c$ | .10 | .25 | .40 |
| 5 | 3.528 | .01 | .04 | .12 | 2.445 | .06 | .13 | .31 | 1.996 | .12 | .23 | .45 |
| 10 | 3.103 | .01 | .10 | .40 | 2.246 | .07 | .27 | .66 | 1.870 | .14 | .40 | .77 |
| 15 | 2.992 | .02 | .20 | .68 | 2.193 | .09 | .42 | .86 | 1.835 | .17 | .56 | .92 |
| 20 | 2.940 | .03 | .31 | .86 | 2.167 | .11 | .56 | .95 | 1.819 | .19 | .68 | .98 |
| 25 | 2.911 | .03 | .43 | .95 | 2.153 | .13 | .68 | .99 | 1.809 | .22 | .78 | .99 |
| 30 | 2.892 | .04 | .55 | .98 | 2.143 | .15 | .77 | .** | 1.803 | .25 | .86 | .** |
| 35 | 2.878 | .05 | .65 | .99 | 2.137 | .17 | .84 | .** | 1.799 | .28 | .91 | .** |
| 40 | 2.868 | .06 | .74 | .** | 2.132 | .19 | .89 | .** | 1.796 | .30 | .94 | .** |
| 45 | 2.861 | .07 | .81 | .** | 2.128 | .21 | .93 | .** | 1.793 | .33 | .96 | .** |
| 50 | 2.855 | .08 | .87 | .** | 2.125 | .24 | .96 | .** | 1.791 | .36 | .98 | .** |
| 100 | 2.828 | .24 | .** | .** | 2.112 | .47 | .** | .** | 1.783 | .60 | .** | .** |

## DEGREES OF FREEDOM NUMERATOR = 7

| | $\alpha = .01$ | | | $\alpha = .05$ | | | $\alpha = .10$ | | |
| --- | --- | --- | --- | --- | --- | --- | --- | --- | --- | --- |
| $n$ | $F_c$ | .10 | .25 | .40 | $F_c$ | .10 | .25 | .40 | $F_c$ | .10 | .25 | .40 |
| 5 | 3.258 | .01 | .04 | .13 | 2.313 | .06 | .14 | .33 | 1.913 | .12 | .24 | .47 |
| 10 | 2.898 | .02 | .11 | .45 | 2.140 | .08 | .29 | .70 | 1.802 | .14 | .42 | .80 |
| 15 | 2.803 | .02 | .22 | .74 | 2.092 | .09 | .45 | .90 | 1.771 | .17 | .59 | .94 |
| 20 | 2.759 | .03 | .35 | .90 | 2.070 | .11 | .60 | .97 | 1.757 | .20 | .72 | .99 |
| 25 | 2.734 | .04 | .48 | .97 | 2.057 | .13 | .72 | .99 | 1.748 | .23 | .82 | .** |
| 30 | 2.717 | .04 | .60 | .99 | 2.049 | .16 | .81 | .** | 1.743 | .26 | .88 | .** |
| 35 | 2.705 | .05 | .71 | .** | 2.043 | .18 | .88 | .** | 1.739 | .29 | .93 | .** |
| 40 | 2.697 | .07 | .79 | .** | 2.039 | .20 | .92 | .** | 1.736 | .32 | .96 | .** |
| 45 | 2.690 | .08 | .86 | .** | 2.036 | .23 | .95 | .** | 1.734 | .35 | .98 | .** |
| 50 | 2.685 | .09 | .90 | .** | 2.033 | .25 | .97 | .** | 1.732 | .37 | .99 | .** |
| 100 | 2.662 | .27 | .** | .** | 2.021 | .51 | .** | .** | 1.724 | .63 | .** | .** |

## DEGREES OF FREEDOM NUMERATOR = 8

| | $\alpha = .01$ | | | $\alpha = .05$ | | | $\alpha = .10$ | | |
| --- | --- | --- | --- | --- | --- | --- | --- | --- | --- | --- |
| $n$ | $F_c$ | .10 | .25 | .40 | $F_c$ | .10 | .25 | .40 | $F_c$ | .10 | .25 | .40 |
| 5 | 3.052 | .01 | .04 | .14 | 2.208 | .06 | .15 | .35 | 1.847 | .12 | .25 | .49 |
| 10 | 2.739 | .02 | .12 | .49 | 2.055 | .08 | .31 | .73 | 1.747 | .15 | .44 | .83 |
| 15 | 2.655 | .02 | .24 | .78 | 2.013 | .10 | .48 | .92 | 1.719 | .18 | .61 | .96 |
| 20 | 2.617 | .03 | .38 | .93 | 1.993 | .12 | .63 | .98 | 1.706 | .21 | .75 | .99 |
| 25 | 2.594 | .04 | .53 | .98 | 1.981 | .14 | .75 | .** | 1.699 | .24 | .84 | .** |
| 30 | 2.580 | .05 | .65 | .** | 1.974 | .16 | .84 | .** | 1.694 | .27 | .91 | .** |
| 35 | 2.570 | .06 | .75 | .** | 1.969 | .19 | .90 | .** | 1.690 | .30 | .95 | .** |
| 40 | 2.562 | .07 | .83 | .** | 1.965 | .21 | .94 | .** | 1.668 | .33 | .97 | .** |
| 45 | 2.556 | .08 | .89 | .** | 1.962 | .24 | .97 | .** | 1.686 | .36 | .98 | .** |
| 50 | 2.552 | .10 | .93 | .** | 1.959 | .27 | .98 | .** | 1.684 | .39 | .99 | .** |
| 100 | 2.531 | .30 | .** | .** | 1.949 | .54 | .** | .** | 1.677 | .66 | .** | .** |

These tables were created by a computer program written by David J. Pittenger. For more complete power tables, consult Cohen (1988). Discrepancies between these tables and Cohen's are due to differences in rounding.

**Table** N

**Critical Values for the Binomial Test**

## The Use of Table N

This table was prepared to expedite decision making when dealing with binomial populations in which $P \neq Q$. *Example:* A researcher has conducted 12 independent repetitions of the same study, using $\alpha = 0.01$. Four of these studies achieved statistical significance. Is this result (4 out of 12 statistically significant outcomes) itself statistically significant, or is it within chance expectations? Looking in the column headed .01 opposite $N = 12$, we find that two or more differences significant at $\alpha = 0.01$ is in itself significant at $\alpha = 0.01$. Thus, the researcher may conclude that the overall results of his or her investigations justify rejecting $H_0$.

A given value of $x$ is significant at a given $\alpha$-level if it equals or exceeds the critical value shown in the table. All values shown are one-tailed. Since the binomial is not symmetrical when $P \neq Q \neq .50$, there is no straightforward way to obtain two-tailed values.

## Table N (continued)

| N | P / Q | .01 / .99 | .02 / .98 | .03 / .97 | .04 / .96 | .05 / .95 | .06 / .94 | .07 / .93 | .08 / .92 | .09 / .91 | .10 / .90 | .11 / .89 | .12 / .88 | .13 / .87 | .14 / .86 | .15 / .85 | .16 / .84 | .17 / .83 | .18 / .82 | .19 / .81 | .20 / .80 | .21 / .79 | .22 / .78 | .23 / .77 | .24 / .76 | .25 / .75 |
|---|---|---|---|---|---|---|---|---|---|---|---|---|---|---|---|---|---|---|---|---|---|---|---|---|---|---|
| 2 | | 1 | 1 | 2 | 2 | 2 | 2 | 2 | 2 | 2 | 2 | 2 | 2 | 2 | 2 | 2 | 2 | 2 | 2 | 2 | 2 | 2 | 2 | — | — | — |
|   | | 1 | 2 | 2 | 2 | 2 | 2 | 2 | 2 | 2 | 2 | — | — | — | — | — | — | — | — | — | — | — | — | — | — | — |
| 3 | | 1 | 2 | 2 | 2 | 2 | 2 | 2 | 2 | 2 | 2 | 2 | 2 | 2 | 3 | 3 | 3 | 3 | 3 | 3 | 3 | 3 | 3 | 3 | 3 | 3 |
|   | | 2 | 2 | 2 | 2 | 2 | 3 | 3 | 3 | 3 | 3 | 3 | 3 | 3 | 3 | 3 | 3 | 3 | 3 | 3 | 3 | 3 | — | — | — | — |
| 4 | | 1 | 2 | 2 | 2 | 2 | 2 | 2 | 2 | 2 | 3 | 3 | 3 | 3 | 3 | 3 | 3 | 3 | 3 | 3 | 3 | 3 | 3 | 3 | 3 | 4 |
|   | | 2 | 2 | 2 | 2 | 3 | 3 | 3 | 3 | 3 | 3 | 3 | 3 | 3 | 3 | 4 | 4 | 4 | 4 | 4 | 4 | 4 | 4 | 4 | 4 | 4 |
| 5 | | 1 | 2 | 2 | 2 | 2 | 2 | 2 | 3 | 3 | 3 | 3 | 3 | 3 | 3 | 3 | 3 | 3 | 3 | 4 | 4 | 4 | 4 | 4 | 4 | 4 |
|   | | 2 | 2 | 2 | 3 | 3 | 3 | 3 | 3 | 3 | 3 | 4 | 4 | 4 | 4 | 4 | 4 | 4 | 4 | 4 | 4 | 4 | 4 | 5 | 5 | 5 |
| 6 | | 2 | 2 | 2 | 2 | 2 | 2 | 3 | 3 | 3 | 3 | 3 | 3 | 3 | 3 | 3 | 4 | 4 | 4 | 4 | 4 | 4 | 4 | 4 | 5 | 5 |
|   | | 2 | 2 | 3 | 3 | 3 | 3 | 3 | 3 | 4 | 4 | 4 | 4 | 4 | 4 | 4 | 4 | 4 | 5 | 5 | 5 | 5 | 5 | 5 | 5 | 5 |
| 7 | | 2 | 2 | 2 | 2 | 2 | 3 | 3 | 3 | 3 | 3 | 3 | 3 | 4 | 4 | 4 | 4 | 4 | 4 | 4 | 4 | 4 | 4 | 5 | 5 | 5 |
|   | | 2 | 2 | 3 | 3 | 3 | 3 | 3 | 4 | 4 | 4 | 4 | 4 | 4 | 4 | 5 | 5 | 5 | 5 | 5 | 5 | 6 | 6 | 6 | 6 | 6 |
| 8 | | 2 | 2 | 2 | 2 | 3 | 3 | 3 | 3 | 3 | 3 | 3 | 4 | 4 | 4 | 4 | 4 | 4 | 4 | 5 | 5 | 5 | 5 | 5 | 5 | 5 |
|   | | 2 | 3 | 3 | 3 | 3 | 3 | 4 | 4 | 4 | 4 | 4 | 4 | 5 | 5 | 5 | 5 | 5 | 5 | 5 | 6 | 6 | 6 | 6 | 6 | 6 |
| 9 | | 2 | 2 | 2 | 2 | 3 | 3 | 3 | 3 | 3 | 3 | 4 | 4 | 4 | 4 | 4 | 4 | 4 | 5 | 5 | 5 | 5 | 5 | 5 | 5 | 5 |
|   | | 2 | 3 | 3 | 3 | 3 | 4 | 4 | 4 | 4 | 4 | 5 | 5 | 5 | 5 | 5 | 5 | 5 | 6 | 6 | 6 | 6 | 6 | 6 | 6 | 6 |
| 10 | | 2 | 2 | 2 | 3 | 3 | 3 | 3 | 4 | 4 | 4 | 4 | 4 | 4 | 4 | 4 | 5 | 5 | 5 | 5 | 5 | 5 | 6 | 6 | 6 | 6 |
|    | | 2 | 3 | 3 | 3 | 4 | 4 | 4 | 4 | 4 | 5 | 5 | 5 | 5 | 5 | 5 | 6 | 6 | 6 | 6 | 6 | 6 | 7 | 7 | 7 | 7 |
| 11 | | 2 | 2 | 2 | 3 | 3 | 3 | 3 | 4 | 4 | 4 | 4 | 4 | 5 | 5 | 5 | 5 | 5 | 5 | 6 | 6 | 6 | 6 | 6 | 6 | 6 |
|    | | 2 | 3 | 3 | 3 | 4 | 4 | 4 | 4 | 5 | 5 | 5 | 5 | 5 | 6 | 6 | 6 | 6 | 6 | 7 | 7 | 7 | 7 | 7 | 7 | 7 |
| 12 | | 2 | 2 | 2 | 3 | 3 | 3 | 4 | 4 | 4 | 4 | 4 | 5 | 5 | 5 | 5 | 5 | 5 | 6 | 6 | 6 | 6 | 6 | 6 | 6 | 7 |
|    | | 2 | 3 | 3 | 4 | 4 | 4 | 4 | 5 | 5 | 5 | 5 | 6 | 6 | 6 | 6 | 6 | 7 | 7 | 7 | 7 | 7 | 7 | 7 | 8 | 8 |
| 13 | | 2 | 2 | 3 | 3 | 3 | 4 | 4 | 4 | 4 | 4 | 5 | 5 | 5 | 5 | 5 | 6 | 6 | 6 | 6 | 6 | 6 | 7 | 7 | 7 | 7 |
|    | | 2 | 3 | 3 | 4 | 4 | 4 | 5 | 5 | 5 | 5 | 6 | 6 | 6 | 6 | 6 | 7 | 7 | 7 | 7 | 7 | 7 | 8 | 8 | 8 | 8 |
| 14 | | 2 | 2 | 3 | 3 | 3 | 4 | 4 | 4 | 4 | 4 | 5 | 5 | 5 | 5 | 5 | 6 | 6 | 6 | 6 | 6 | 7 | 7 | 7 | 7 | 8 |
|    | | 2 | 3 | 3 | 4 | 4 | 5 | 5 | 5 | 5 | 6 | 6 | 6 | 6 | 7 | 7 | 7 | 7 | 7 | 8 | 8 | 8 | 8 | 8 | 9 | 9 |
| 15 | | 2 | 2 | 3 | 3 | 3 | 4 | 4 | 4 | 5 | 5 | 5 | 5 | 6 | 6 | 6 | 6 | 6 | 7 | 7 | 7 | 7 | 8 | 8 | 8 | 8 |
|    | | 2 | 3 | 3 | 4 | 4 | 5 | 5 | 5 | 5 | 6 | 6 | 6 | 6 | 7 | 7 | 7 | 7 | 8 | 8 | 8 | 8 | 9 | 9 | 9 | 9 |
| 16 | | 2 | 2 | 3 | 3 | 3 | 4 | 4 | 4 | 4 | 5 | 5 | 5 | 5 | 6 | 6 | 6 | 6 | 7 | 7 | 7 | 7 | 7 | 8 | 8 | 8 |
|    | | 3 | 3 | 4 | 4 | 4 | 5 | 5 | 5 | 6 | 6 | 6 | 6 | 7 | 7 | 7 | 7 | 8 | 8 | 8 | 8 | 8 | 9 | 9 | 9 | 9 |
| 17 | | 2 | 2 | 3 | 3 | 4 | 4 | 4 | 4 | 5 | 5 | 5 | 5 | 6 | 6 | 6 | 6 | 7 | 7 | 7 | 7 | 7 | 8 | 8 | 8 | 8 |
|    | | 3 | 3 | 4 | 4 | 4 | 5 | 5 | 5 | 6 | 6 | 6 | 7 | 7 | 7 | 7 | 8 | 8 | 8 | 9 | 9 | 9 | 9 | 9 | 9 | 10 |
| 18 | | 2 | 2 | 3 | 3 | 4 | 4 | 4 | 5 | 5 | 5 | 5 | 6 | 6 | 6 | 6 | 7 | 7 | 7 | 7 | 8 | 8 | 8 | 8 | 8 | 9 |
|    | | 3 | 3 | 4 | 4 | 5 | 5 | 5 | 6 | 6 | 6 | 7 | 7 | 7 | 7 | 8 | 8 | 8 | 9 | 9 | 9 | 9 | 9 | 10 | 10 | 10 |
| 19 | | 2 | 3 | 3 | 3 | 4 | 4 | 4 | 5 | 5 | 5 | 6 | 6 | 6 | 6 | 7 | 7 | 7 | 7 | 8 | 8 | 8 | 9 | 9 | 9 | 9 |
|    | | 3 | 4 | 4 | 5 | 5 | 5 | 6 | 6 | 6 | 7 | 7 | 7 | 8 | 8 | 8 | 8 | 9 | 9 | 9 | 9 | 9 | 10 | 10 | 10 | 10 |
| 20 | | 2 | 3 | 3 | 3 | 4 | 4 | 4 | 5 | 5 | 5 | 6 | 6 | 6 | 7 | 7 | 7 | 7 | 8 | 8 | 8 | 8 | 9 | 9 | 9 | 9 |
|    | | 3 | 3 | 4 | 4 | 5 | 5 | 6 | 6 | 6 | 7 | 7 | 7 | 8 | 8 | 8 | 9 | 9 | 9 | 9 | 10 | 10 | 10 | 10 | 10 | 11 |
| 21 | | 2 | 3 | 3 | 3 | 4 | 4 | 5 | 5 | 5 | 6 | 6 | 6 | 6 | 7 | 7 | 7 | 8 | 8 | 8 | 8 | 9 | 9 | 9 | 9 | 10 |
|    | | 3 | 3 | 4 | 4 | 5 | 5 | 6 | 6 | 6 | 7 | 7 | 7 | 8 | 8 | 8 | 9 | 9 | 9 | 10 | 10 | 10 | 10 | 11 | 11 | 11 |
| 22 | | 2 | 3 | 3 | 4 | 4 | 4 | 5 | 5 | 5 | 6 | 6 | 6 | 7 | 7 | 7 | 8 | 8 | 8 | 9 | 9 | 9 | 9 | 10 | 10 | 10 |
|    | | 3 | 3 | 4 | 5 | 5 | 5 | 6 | 6 | 7 | 7 | 7 | 8 | 8 | 9 | 9 | 9 | 10 | 10 | 10 | 10 | 11 | 11 | 11 | 11 | 11 |
| 23 | | 2 | 3 | 3 | 4 | 4 | 4 | 5 | 5 | 6 | 6 | 6 | 6 | 7 | 7 | 7 | 8 | 8 | 8 | 9 | 9 | 9 | 10 | 10 | 10 | 10 |
|    | | 3 | 4 | 4 | 5 | 5 | 6 | 6 | 6 | 7 | 7 | 7 | 8 | 8 | 9 | 9 | 9 | 9 | 10 | 10 | 10 | 11 | 11 | 11 | 12 | 12 |
| 24 | | 2 | 3 | 3 | 4 | 4 | 5 | 5 | 5 | 6 | 6 | 6 | 7 | 7 | 7 | 8 | 8 | 8 | 9 | 9 | 9 | 9 | 10 | 10 | 10 | 11 |
|    | | 3 | 4 | 4 | 5 | 5 | 6 | 6 | 7 | 7 | 7 | 8 | 8 | 8 | 9 | 9 | 9 | 10 | 10 | 10 | 11 | 11 | 11 | 12 | 12 | 12 |

## Table N (continued)

| N | P | .26 | .27 | .28 | .29 | .30 | .31 | .32 | .33 | .34 | .35 | .36 | .37 | .38 | .39 | .40 | .41 | .42 | .43 | .44 | .45 | .46 | .47 | .48 | .49 | .50 |
|---|---|-----|-----|-----|-----|-----|-----|-----|-----|-----|-----|-----|-----|-----|-----|-----|-----|-----|-----|-----|-----|-----|-----|-----|-----|-----|
|   | Q | .74 | .73 | .72 | .71 | .70 | .69 | .68 | .67 | .66 | .65 | .64 | .63 | .62 | .61 | .60 | .59 | .58 | .57 | .56 | .55 | .54 | .53 | .52 | .51 | .50 |
| 2 |   | — | — | — | — | — | — | — | — | — | — | — | — | — | — | — | — | — | — | — | — | — | — | — | — | — |
|   |   | — | — | — | — | — | — | — | — | — | — | — | — | — | — | — | — | — | — | — | — | — | — | — | — | — |
| 3 |   | 3 | 3 | 3 | 3 | 3 | 3 | 3 | 3 | 3 | 3 | 3 | — | — | — | — | — | — | — | — | — | — | — | — | — | — |
|   |   | — | — | — | — | — | — | — | — | — | — | — | — | — | — | — | — | — | — | — | — | — | — | — | — | — |
| 4 |   | 4 | 4 | 4 | 4 | 4 | 4 | 4 | 4 | 4 | 4 | 4 | 4 | 4 | 4 | 4 | 4 | 4 | 4 | 4 | 4 | 4 | — | — | — | — |
|   |   | 4 | 4 | 4 | 4 | 4 | 4 | — | — | — | — | — | — | — | — | — | — | — | — | — | — | — | — | — | — | — |
| 5 |   | 4 | 4 | 4 | 4 | 4 | 4 | 4 | 4 | 4 | 5 | 5 | 5 | 5 | 5 | 5 | 5 | 5 | 5 | 5 | 5 | 5 | 5 | 5 | 5 | 5 |
|   |   | 5 | 5 | 5 | 5 | 5 | 5 | 5 | 5 | 5 | 5 | 5 | 5 | 5 | 5 | 5 | — | — | — | — | — | — | — | — | — | — |
| 6 |   | 5 | 5 | 5 | 5 | 5 | 5 | 5 | 5 | 5 | 5 | 5 | 5 | 5 | 5 | 5 | 6 | 6 | 6 | 6 | 6 | 6 | 6 | 6 | 6 | 6 |
|   |   | 5 | 5 | 5 | 5 | 6 | 6 | 6 | 6 | 6 | 6 | 6 | 6 | 6 | 6 | 6 | 6 | 6 | 6 | 6 | 6 | 6 | — | — | — | — |
| 7 |   | 5 | 5 | 5 | 5 | 5 | 5 | 5 | 5 | 5 | 6 | 6 | 6 | 6 | 6 | 6 | 6 | 6 | 6 | 6 | 6 | 6 | 6 | 7 | 7 | 7 |
|   |   | 6 | 6 | 6 | 6 | 6 | 6 | 6 | 6 | 6 | 6 | 7 | 7 | 7 | 7 | 7 | 7 | 7 | 7 | 7 | 7 | 7 | 7 | 7 | 7 | 7 |
| 8 |   | 5 | 5 | 5 | 6 | 6 | 6 | 6 | 6 | 6 | 6 | 6 | 6 | 6 | 6 | 6 | 7 | 7 | 7 | 7 | 7 | 7 | 7 | 7 | 7 | 7 |
|   |   | 6 | 6 | 6 | 6 | 7 | 7 | 7 | 7 | 7 | 7 | 7 | 7 | 7 | 7 | 7 | 7 | 8 | 8 | 8 | 8 | 8 | 8 | 8 | 8 | 8 |
| 9 |   | 6 | 6 | 6 | 6 | 6 | 6 | 6 | 6 | 6 | 7 | 7 | 7 | 7 | 7 | 7 | 7 | 7 | 7 | 7 | 8 | 8 | 8 | 8 | 8 | 8 |
|   |   | 7 | 7 | 7 | 7 | 7 | 7 | 7 | 7 | 7 | 8 | 8 | 8 | 8 | 8 | 8 | 8 | 8 | 8 | 8 | 8 | 9 | 9 | 9 | 9 | 9 |
| 10 |   | 6 | 6 | 6 | 6 | 6 | 7 | 7 | 7 | 7 | 7 | 7 | 7 | 7 | 7 | 8 | 8 | 8 | 8 | 8 | 8 | 8 | 8 | 8 | 8 | 9 |
|   |   | 7 | 7 | 7 | 7 | 8 | 8 | 8 | 8 | 8 | 8 | 8 | 8 | 8 | 9 | 9 | 9 | 9 | 9 | 9 | 9 | 9 | 9 | 9 | 9 | 10 |
| 11 |   | 6 | 6 | 7 | 7 | 7 | 7 | 7 | 7 | 7 | 8 | 8 | 8 | 8 | 8 | 8 | 8 | 8 | 9 | 9 | 9 | 9 | 9 | 9 | 9 | 9 |
|   |   | 7 | 8 | 8 | 8 | 8 | 8 | 8 | 9 | 9 | 9 | 9 | 9 | 9 | 9 | 9 | 9 | 10 | 10 | 10 | 10 | 10 | 10 | 10 | 10 | 10 |
| 12 |   | 7 | 7 | 7 | 7 | 7 | 7 | 8 | 8 | 8 | 8 | 8 | 8 | 8 | 9 | 9 | 9 | 9 | 9 | 9 | 9 | 9 | 9 | 10 | 10 | 10 |
|   |   | 8 | 8 | 8 | 8 | 8 | 9 | 9 | 9 | 9 | 9 | 9 | 9 | 10 | 10 | 10 | 10 | 10 | 10 | 10 | 10 | 10 | 11 | 11 | 11 | 11 |
| 13 |   | 7 | 7 | 7 | 8 | 8 | 8 | 8 | 8 | 8 | 8 | 9 | 9 | 9 | 9 | 9 | 9 | 9 | 10 | 10 | 10 | 10 | 10 | 10 | 10 | 10 |
|   |   | 8 | 8 | 9 | 9 | 9 | 9 | 9 | 9 | 10 | 10 | 10 | 10 | 10 | 10 | 10 | 10 | 11 | 11 | 11 | 11 | 11 | 11 | 11 | 11 | 12 |
| 14 |   | 7 | 8 | 8 | 8 | 8 | 8 | 8 | 9 | 9 | 9 | 9 | 9 | 9 | 9 | 10 | 10 | 10 | 10 | 10 | 10 | 11 | 11 | 11 | 11 | 11 |
|   |   | 9 | 9 | 9 | 9 | 9 | 10 | 10 | 10 | 10 | 10 | 10 | 10 | 11 | 11 | 11 | 11 | 11 | 11 | 11 | 12 | 12 | 12 | 12 | 12 | 12 |
| 15 |   | 8 | 8 | 8 | 8 | 9 | 9 | 9 | 9 | 9 | 9 | 10 | 10 | 10 | 10 | 10 | 10 | 10 | 11 | 11 | 11 | 11 | 11 | 11 | 12 | 12 |
|   |   | 9 | 9 | 9 | 10 | 10 | 10 | 10 | 10 | 10 | 11 | 11 | 11 | 11 | 11 | 11 | 12 | 12 | 12 | 12 | 12 | 12 | 12 | 13 | 13 | 13 |
| 16 |   | 8 | 8 | 9 | 9 | 9 | 9 | 9 | 9 | 10 | 10 | 10 | 10 | 10 | 10 | 11 | 11 | 11 | 11 | 11 | 11 | 12 | 12 | 12 | 13 | 13 |
|   |   | 9 | 10 | 10 | 10 | 10 | 10 | 11 | 11 | 11 | 11 | 11 | 11 | 12 | 12 | 12 | 12 | 12 | 12 | 13 | 13 | 13 | 14 | 14 | 14 | 14 |
| 17 |   | 8 | 9 | 9 | 9 | 9 | 9 | 10 | 10 | 10 | 10 | 11 | 11 | 11 | 11 | 11 | 11 | 12 | 12 | 12 | 12 | 12 | 13 | 13 | 13 | 13 |
|   |   | 10 | 10 | 10 | 10 | 11 | 11 | 11 | 11 | 11 | 12 | 12 | 12 | 12 | 13 | 13 | 13 | 13 | 13 | 13 | 14 | 14 | 14 | 14 | 14 | 14 |
| 18 |   | 9 | 9 | 9 | 9 | 10 | 10 | 10 | 10 | 10 | 11 | 11 | 11 | 11 | 12 | 12 | 12 | 12 | 12 | 12 | 13 | 13 | 13 | 13 | 13 | 13 |
|   |   | 10 | 10 | 11 | 11 | 11 | 11 | 12 | 12 | 12 | 12 | 12 | 13 | 13 | 13 | 13 | 13 | 13 | 14 | 14 | 14 | 14 | 14 | 14 | 15 | 15 |
| 19 |   | 9 | 9 | 10 | 10 | 10 | 10 | 10 | 11 | 11 | 11 | 11 | 12 | 12 | 12 | 12 | 13 | 13 | 13 | 13 | 13 | 13 | 14 | 14 | 14 | 14 |
|   |   | 11 | 11 | 11 | 11 | 12 | 12 | 12 | 12 | 12 | 13 | 13 | 13 | 13 | 13 | 14 | 14 | 14 | 14 | 15 | 15 | 15 | 15 | 15 | 15 | 15 |
| 20 |   | 10 | 10 | 10 | 10 | 10 | 11 | 11 | 11 | 11 | 12 | 12 | 12 | 12 | 12 | 13 | 13 | 13 | 13 | 14 | 14 | 14 | 14 | 14 | 14 | 15 |
|   |   | 11 | 11 | 11 | 12 | 12 | 12 | 12 | 13 | 13 | 13 | 13 | 14 | 14 | 14 | 14 | 14 | 15 | 15 | 15 | 15 | 15 | 16 | 16 | 16 | 16 |
| 21 |   | 10 | 10 | 10 | 11 | 11 | 11 | 11 | 12 | 12 | 12 | 12 | 12 | 13 | 13 | 13 | 13 | 14 | 14 | 14 | 14 | 14 | 15 | 15 | 15 | 15 |
|   |   | 11 | 12 | 12 | 12 | 12 | 13 | 13 | 13 | 13 | 14 | 14 | 14 | 14 | 15 | 15 | 15 | 15 | 16 | 16 | 16 | 16 | 16 | 16 | 17 | 17 |
| 22 |   | 10 | 10 | 11 | 11 | 11 | 11 | 12 | 12 | 12 | 12 | 13 | 13 | 13 | 13 | 14 | 14 | 14 | 14 | 15 | 15 | 15 | 15 | 15 | 16 | 16 |
|   |   | 12 | 12 | 12 | 13 | 13 | 13 | 13 | 14 | 14 | 14 | 14 | 15 | 15 | 15 | 15 | 15 | 16 | 16 | 16 | 16 | 17 | 17 | 17 | 17 | 17 |
| 23 |   | 11 | 11 | 11 | 11 | 12 | 12 | 12 | 12 | 13 | 13 | 13 | 13 | 14 | 14 | 14 | 14 | 15 | 15 | 15 | 15 | 16 | 16 | 16 | 16 | 16 |
|   |   | 12 | 12 | 13 | 13 | 13 | 13 | 14 | 14 | 14 | 15 | 15 | 15 | 15 | 15 | 16 | 16 | 16 | 16 | 17 | 17 | 17 | 17 | 18 | 18 | 18 |
| 24 |   | 11 | 11 | 11 | 12 | 12 | 12 | 13 | 13 | 13 | 13 | 14 | 14 | 14 | 14 | 15 | 15 | 15 | 15 | 16 | 16 | 16 | 16 | 17 | 17 | 17 |
|   |   | 13 | 13 | 13 | 13 | 14 | 14 | 14 | 14 | 15 | 15 | 15 | 15 | 16 | 16 | 16 | 16 | 17 | 17 | 17 | 17 | 18 | 18 | 18 | 18 | 19 |

**Table  N** (*continued*)

| N | P<br>Q | .01<br>.99 | .02<br>.98 | .03<br>.97 | .04<br>.96 | .05<br>.95 | .06<br>.94 | .07<br>.93 | .08<br>.92 | .09<br>.91 | .10<br>.90 | .11<br>.89 | .12<br>.88 | .13<br>.87 | .14<br>.86 | .15<br>.85 | .16<br>.84 | .17<br>.83 | .18<br>.82 | .19<br>.81 | .20<br>.80 | .21<br>.79 | .22<br>.78 | .23<br>.77 | .24<br>.76 | .25<br>.75 |
|---|---|---|---|---|---|---|---|---|---|---|---|---|---|---|---|---|---|---|---|---|---|---|---|---|---|---|
| 25 | P | 2 | 3 | 3 | 4 | 4 | 5 | 5 | 5 | 6 | 6 | 6 | 7 | 7 | 8 | 8 | 8 | 8 | 9 | 9 | 9 | 10 | 10 | 10 | 11 | 11 |
|  | Q | 3 | 4 | 4 | 5 | 5 | 6 | 6 | 7 | 7 | 7 | 8 | 8 | 9 | 9 | 9 | 10 | 10 | 10 | 11 | 11 | 11 | 12 | 12 | 12 | 13 |
| 26 | P | 2 | 3 | 3 | 4 | 4 | 5 | 5 | 6 | 6 | 6 | 7 | 7 | 7 | 8 | 8 | 8 | 9 | 9 | 9 | 10 | 10 | 10 | 11 | 11 | 11 |
|  | Q | 3 | 4 | 4 | 5 | 5 | 6 | 6 | 7 | 7 | 8 | 8 | 8 | 9 | 9 | 10 | 10 | 10 | 11 | 11 | 11 | 12 | 12 | 12 | 13 | 13 |
| 27 | P | 2 | 3 | 3 | 4 | 4 | 5 | 5 | 6 | 6 | 6 | 7 | 7 | 8 | 8 | 8 | 9 | 9 | 9 | 10 | 10 | 10 | 11 | 11 | 11 | 12 |
|  | Q | 3 | 4 | 4 | 5 | 6 | 6 | 6 | 7 | 7 | 8 | 8 | 9 | 9 | 9 | 10 | 10 | 11 | 11 | 11 | 12 | 12 | 12 | 13 | 13 | 13 |
| 28 | P | 2 | 3 | 4 | 4 | 4 | 5 | 5 | 6 | 6 | 7 | 7 | 7 | 8 | 8 | 8 | 9 | 9 | 10 | 10 | 10 | 11 | 11 | 11 | 12 | 12 |
|  | Q | 3 | 4 | 4 | 5 | 6 | 6 | 7 | 7 | 8 | 8 | 8 | 9 | 9 | 10 | 10 | 10 | 11 | 11 | 12 | 12 | 12 | 13 | 13 | 13 | 14 |
| 29 | P | 2 | 3 | 4 | 4 | 5 | 5 | 5 | 6 | 6 | 7 | 7 | 8 | 8 | 8 | 9 | 9 | 9 | 10 | 10 | 10 | 11 | 11 | 12 | 12 | 12 |
|  | Q | 3 | 4 | 5 | 5 | 6 | 6 | 7 | 7 | 8 | 8 | 9 | 9 | 9 | 10 | 10 | 11 | 11 | 11 | 12 | 12 | 13 | 13 | 13 | 14 | 14 |
| 30 | P | 2 | 3 | 4 | 4 | 5 | 5 | 6 | 6 | 6 | 7 | 7 | 8 | 8 | 8 | 9 | 9 | 10 | 10 | 10 | 11 | 11 | 11 | 12 | 12 | 13 |
|  | Q | 3 | 4 | 5 | 5 | 6 | 6 | 7 | 7 | 8 | 8 | 9 | 9 | 10 | 10 | 10 | 11 | 11 | 12 | 12 | 12 | 13 | 13 | 14 | 14 | 14 |
| 31 | P | 2 | 3 | 4 | 4 | 5 | 5 | 6 | 6 | 7 | 7 | 7 | 8 | 8 | 9 | 9 | 9 | 10 | 10 | 11 | 11 | 11 | 12 | 12 | 12 | 13 |
|  | Q | 3 | 4 | 5 | 5 | 6 | 6 | 7 | 7 | 8 | 8 | 9 | 9 | 10 | 10 | 11 | 11 | 12 | 12 | 12 | 13 | 13 | 14 | 14 | 14 | 15 |
| 32 | P | 2 | 3 | 4 | 4 | 5 | 5 | 6 | 6 | 7 | 7 | 8 | 8 | 8 | 9 | 9 | 10 | 10 | 10 | 11 | 11 | 12 | 12 | 12 | 13 | 13 |
|  | Q | 3 | 4 | 5 | 5 | 6 | 7 | 7 | 8 | 8 | 9 | 9 | 10 | 10 | 10 | 11 | 11 | 12 | 12 | 13 | 13 | 13 | 14 | 14 | 15 | 15 |
| 33 | P | 2 | 3 | 4 | 4 | 5 | 5 | 6 | 6 | 7 | 7 | 8 | 8 | 9 | 9 | 9 | 10 | 10 | 11 | 11 | 12 | 12 | 12 | 13 | 13 | 13 |
|  | Q | 3 | 4 | 5 | 5 | 6 | 7 | 7 | 8 | 8 | 9 | 9 | 10 | 10 | 11 | 11 | 12 | 12 | 13 | 13 | 14 | 14 | 15 | 15 | 15 |  |
| 34 | P | 2 | 3 | 4 | 4 | 5 | 6 | 6 | 7 | 7 | 7 | 8 | 8 | 9 | 9 | 10 | 10 | 11 | 11 | 11 | 12 | 12 | 13 | 13 | 13 | 14 |
|  | Q | 3 | 4 | 5 | 6 | 6 | 7 | 7 | 8 | 8 | 9 | 9 | 10 | 10 | 11 | 11 | 12 | 12 | 13 | 13 | 14 | 14 | 14 | 15 | 15 | 16 |
| 35 | P | 2 | 3 | 4 | 5 | 6 | 6 | 6 | 7 | 7 | 8 | 8 | 9 | 9 | 9 | 10 | 10 | 11 | 11 | 12 | 12 | 12 | 13 | 13 | 14 | 14 |
|  | Q | 3 | 4 | 5 | 6 | 6 | 7 | 7 | 8 | 9 | 9 | 10 | 10 | 11 | 11 | 12 | 12 | 13 | 13 | 13 | 14 | 14 | 15 | 15 | 16 | 16 |
| 36 | P | 3 | 3 | 4 | 5 | 5 | 6 | 6 | 7 | 7 | 8 | 8 | 9 | 9 | 10 | 10 | 11 | 11 | 11 | 12 | 12 | 13 | 13 | 14 | 14 | 14 |
|  | Q | 3 | 4 | 5 | 6 | 6 | 7 | 8 | 8 | 9 | 9 | 10 | 10 | 11 | 11 | 12 | 12 | 13 | 13 | 14 | 14 | 15 | 15 | 15 | 16 | 16 |
| 37 | P | 3 | 3 | 4 | 5 | 5 | 6 | 6 | 7 | 7 | 8 | 8 | 9 | 9 | 10 | 10 | 11 | 11 | 12 | 12 | 13 | 13 | 13 | 14 | 14 | 15 |
|  | Q | 3 | 4 | 5 | 6 | 6 | 7 | 8 | 8 | 9 | 9 | 10 | 11 | 11 | 12 | 12 | 13 | 13 | 13 | 14 | 14 | 15 | 15 | 16 | 16 | 17 |
| 38 | P | 3 | 3 | 4 | 5 | 5 | 6 | 6 | 7 | 8 | 8 | 9 | 9 | 10 | 10 | 10 | 11 | 11 | 12 | 12 | 13 | 13 | 14 | 14 | 15 | 15 |
|  | Q | 3 | 4 | 5 | 6 | 7 | 7 | 8 | 8 | 9 | 10 | 10 | 11 | 11 | 12 | 12 | 13 | 13 | 14 | 14 | 15 | 15 | 16 | 16 | 17 | 17 |
| 39 | P | 3 | 3 | 4 | 5 | 5 | 6 | 6 | 7 | 8 | 8 | 9 | 9 | 10 | 10 | 11 | 11 | 12 | 12 | 13 | 13 | 14 | 14 | 14 | 15 | 15 |
|  | Q | 3 | 4 | 5 | 6 | 7 | 7 | 8 | 9 | 9 | 10 | 10 | 11 | 11 | 12 | 12 | 13 | 13 | 14 | 14 | 15 | 15 | 16 | 16 | 17 | 17 |
| 40 | P | 3 | 3 | 4 | 5 | 5 | 6 | 7 | 7 | 8 | 8 | 9 | 9 | 10 | 10 | 11 | 11 | 12 | 12 | 13 | 13 | 14 | 14 | 15 | 15 | 16 |
|  | Q | 3 | 4 | 5 | 6 | 7 | 7 | 8 | 9 | 9 | 10 | 10 | 11 | 12 | 12 | 13 | 13 | 14 | 14 | 15 | 15 | 16 | 16 | 17 | 17 | 18 |
| 41 | P | 3 | 3 | 4 | 5 | 6 | 6 | 7 | 7 | 8 | 8 | 9 | 10 | 10 | 11 | 11 | 12 | 12 | 13 | 13 | 14 | 14 | 15 | 15 | 15 | 16 |
|  | Q | 3 | 4 | 5 | 6 | 7 | 8 | 8 | 9 | 9 | 10 | 11 | 11 | 12 | 12 | 13 | 13 | 14 | 14 | 15 | 16 | 16 | 17 | 17 | 18 | 18 |
| 42 | P | 3 | 4 | 4 | 5 | 6 | 6 | 7 | 7 | 8 | 9 | 9 | 10 | 10 | 11 | 11 | 12 | 12 | 13 | 13 | 14 | 14 | 15 | 15 | 16 | 16 |
|  | Q | 3 | 4 | 5 | 6 | 7 | 8 | 8 | 9 | 10 | 10 | 11 | 11 | 12 | 12 | 13 | 14 | 14 | 15 | 15 | 16 | 16 | 17 | 17 | 18 | 18 |
| 43 | P | 3 | 4 | 4 | 5 | 6 | 6 | 7 | 8 | 8 | 9 | 9 | 10 | 10 | 11 | 11 | 12 | 13 | 13 | 14 | 14 | 15 | 15 | 16 | 16 | 17 |
|  | Q | 3 | 5 | 5 | 6 | 7 | 8 | 8 | 9 | 10 | 10 | 11 | 12 | 12 | 13 | 13 | 14 | 14 | 15 | 16 | 16 | 17 | 17 | 18 | 18 | 19 |
| 44 | P | 3 | 4 | 4 | 5 | 6 | 6 | 7 | 8 | 8 | 9 | 9 | 10 | 11 | 11 | 12 | 12 | 13 | 13 | 14 | 14 | 15 | 15 | 16 | 16 | 17 |
|  | Q | 3 | 5 | 5 | 6 | 7 | 8 | 9 | 9 | 10 | 11 | 11 | 12 | 12 | 13 | 14 | 14 | 15 | 15 | 16 | 16 | 17 | 17 | 18 | 18 | 19 |
| 45 | P | 3 | 4 | 4 | 5 | 6 | 7 | 7 | 8 | 8 | 9 | 10 | 10 | 11 | 11 | 12 | 12 | 13 | 13 | 14 | 15 | 15 | 16 | 16 | 17 | 17 |
|  | Q | 4 | 5 | 6 | 6 | 7 | 8 | 9 | 9 | 10 | 11 | 11 | 12 | 13 | 13 | 14 | 14 | 15 | 15 | 16 | 17 | 17 | 18 | 18 | 19 | 19 |
| 46 | P | 3 | 4 | 4 | 5 | 6 | 7 | 7 | 8 | 9 | 9 | 10 | 10 | 11 | 11 | 12 | 13 | 13 | 14 | 14 | 15 | 15 | 16 | 16 | 17 | 17 |
|  | Q | 4 | 5 | 6 | 6 | 7 | 8 | 9 | 9 | 10 | 11 | 11 | 12 | 13 | 13 | 14 | 15 | 15 | 16 | 16 | 17 | 17 | 18 | 19 | 19 | 20 |
| 47 | P | 3 | 4 | 5 | 5 | 6 | 7 | 7 | 8 | 9 | 9 | 10 | 10 | 11 | 12 | 12 | 13 | 13 | 14 | 15 | 15 | 16 | 16 | 17 | 17 | 18 |
|  | Q | 4 | 5 | 6 | 7 | 7 | 8 | 9 | 10 | 10 | 11 | 12 | 12 | 13 | 14 | 14 | 15 | 15 | 16 | 17 | 17 | 18 | 18 | 19 | 19 | 20 |
| 48 | P | 3 | 4 | 5 | 5 | 6 | 7 | 7 | 8 | 9 | 9 | 10 | 11 | 11 | 12 | 12 | 13 | 14 | 14 | 15 | 15 | 16 | 16 | 17 | 18 | 18 |
|  | Q | 4 | 5 | 6 | 7 | 7 | 8 | 9 | 10 | 10 | 11 | 12 | 12 | 13 | 14 | 14 | 15 | 16 | 16 | 17 | 17 | 18 | 19 | 19 | 20 | 20 |
| 49 | P | 3 | 4 | 5 | 5 | 6 | 7 | 8 | 8 | 9 | 10 | 10 | 11 | 11 | 12 | 13 | 13 | 14 | 14 | 15 | 16 | 16 | 17 | 17 | 18 | 18 |
|  | Q | 4 | 5 | 6 | 7 | 8 | 8 | 9 | 10 | 11 | 11 | 12 | 13 | 13 | 14 | 15 | 15 | 16 | 16 | 17 | 18 | 18 | 19 | 19 | 20 | 21 |

**Table N** (*continued*)

| N | P .26 | .27 | .28 | .29 | .30 | .31 | .32 | .33 | .34 | .35 | .36 | .37 | .38 | .39 | .40 | .41 | .42 | .43 | .44 | .45 | .46 | .47 | .48 | .49 | .50 |
|---|---|---|---|---|---|---|---|---|---|---|---|---|---|---|---|---|---|---|---|---|---|---|---|---|---|
| | Q .74 | .73 | .72 | .71 | .70 | .69 | .68 | .67 | .66 | .65 | .64 | .63 | .62 | .61 | .60 | .59 | .58 | .57 | .56 | .55 | .54 | .53 | .52 | .51 | .50 |
| 25 | 11 | 12 | 12 | 12 | 12 | 13 | 13 | 13 | 13 | 14 | 14 | 14 | 15 | 15 | 15 | 15 | 16 | 16 | 16 | 16 | 17 | 17 | 17 | 17 | 18 |
| | 13 | 13 | 13 | 14 | 14 | 14 | 15 | 15 | 15 | 15 | 16 | 16 | 16 | 17 | 17 | 17 | 17 | 18 | 18 | 18 | 18 | 19 | 19 | 19 | 19 |
| 26 | 12 | 12 | 12 | 12 | 13 | 13 | 13 | 14 | 14 | 14 | 14 | 15 | 15 | 15 | 16 | 16 | 16 | 16 | 17 | 17 | 17 | 17 | 18 | 18 | 18 |
| | 13 | 14 | 14 | 14 | 14 | 15 | 15 | 15 | 16 | 16 | 16 | 16 | 17 | 17 | 17 | 18 | 18 | 18 | 18 | 19 | 19 | 19 | 19 | 20 | 20 |
| 27 | 12 | 12 | 12 | 13 | 13 | 13 | 14 | 14 | 14 | 15 | 15 | 15 | 15 | 16 | 16 | 16 | 17 | 17 | 17 | 17 | 18 | 18 | 18 | 18 | 19 |
| | 14 | 14 | 14 | 15 | 15 | 15 | 15 | 16 | 16 | 16 | 17 | 17 | 17 | 18 | 18 | 18 | 18 | 19 | 19 | 19 | 19 | 20 | 20 | 20 | 20 |
| 28 | 12 | 13 | 13 | 13 | 13 | 14 | 14 | 14 | 15 | 15 | 15 | 16 | 16 | 16 | 16 | 17 | 17 | 17 | 18 | 18 | 18 | 18 | 19 | 19 | 19 |
| | 14 | 14 | 15 | 15 | 15 | 16 | 16 | 16 | 17 | 17 | 17 | 17 | 18 | 18 | 18 | 19 | 19 | 19 | 19 | 20 | 20 | 20 | 21 | 21 | 21 |
| 29 | 13 | 13 | 13 | 14 | 14 | 14 | 14 | 15 | 15 | 15 | 16 | 16 | 16 | 17 | 17 | 17 | 18 | 18 | 18 | 18 | 19 | 19 | 19 | 20 | 20 |
| | 14 | 15 | 15 | 15 | 16 | 16 | 16 | 17 | 17 | 17 | 18 | 18 | 18 | 19 | 19 | 19 | 19 | 20 | 20 | 20 | 21 | 21 | 21 | 21 | 22 |
| 30 | 13 | 13 | 14 | 14 | 14 | 15 | 15 | 15 | 16 | 16 | 16 | 17 | 17 | 17 | 17 | 18 | 18 | 18 | 19 | 19 | 19 | 20 | 20 | 20 | 20 |
| | 15 | 15 | 15 | 16 | 16 | 16 | 17 | 17 | 17 | 18 | 18 | 18 | 19 | 19 | 19 | 20 | 20 | 20 | 21 | 21 | 21 | 21 | 22 | 22 | 22 |
| 31 | 13 | 14 | 14 | 14 | 15 | 15 | 15 | 16 | 16 | 16 | 17 | 17 | 17 | 18 | 18 | 18 | 19 | 19 | 19 | 20 | 20 | 20 | 20 | 21 | 21 |
| | 15 | 15 | 16 | 16 | 16 | 17 | 17 | 17 | 18 | 18 | 19 | 19 | 19 | 19 | 20 | 20 | 20 | 21 | 21 | 21 | 22 | 22 | 22 | 23 | 23 |
| 32 | 14 | 14 | 14 | 15 | 15 | 15 | 16 | 16 | 16 | 17 | 17 | 17 | 18 | 18 | 18 | 19 | 19 | 19 | 20 | 20 | 20 | 21 | 21 | 21 | 22 |
| | 15 | 16 | 16 | 16 | 17 | 17 | 18 | 18 | 18 | 19 | 19 | 19 | 20 | 20 | 20 | 21 | 21 | 21 | 22 | 22 | 22 | 22 | 23 | 23 | 24 |
| 33 | 14 | 14 | 15 | 15 | 15 | 16 | 16 | 16 | 17 | 17 | 17 | 18 | 18 | 19 | 19 | 19 | 20 | 20 | 20 | 21 | 21 | 21 | 22 | 22 | 22 |
| | 16 | 16 | 16 | 17 | 17 | 18 | 18 | 18 | 19 | 19 | 19 | 20 | 20 | 20 | 21 | 21 | 21 | 22 | 22 | 22 | 23 | 23 | 23 | 24 | 24 |
| 34 | 14 | 15 | 15 | 15 | 16 | 16 | 16 | 17 | 17 | 18 | 18 | 18 | 19 | 19 | 19 | 20 | 20 | 20 | 21 | 21 | 21 | 22 | 22 | 22 | 23 |
| | 16 | 16 | 17 | 17 | 17 | 18 | 18 | 19 | 19 | 20 | 20 | 20 | 21 | 21 | 21 | 22 | 22 | 22 | 23 | 23 | 23 | 24 | 24 | 24 | 25 |
| 35 | 14 | 15 | 15 | 16 | 16 | 16 | 17 | 17 | 18 | 18 | 18 | 19 | 19 | 19 | 20 | 20 | 21 | 21 | 21 | 22 | 22 | 22 | 23 | 23 | 23 |
| | 16 | 17 | 17 | 18 | 18 | 18 | 19 | 19 | 20 | 20 | 20 | 21 | 21 | 21 | 22 | 22 | 23 | 23 | 23 | 24 | 24 | 24 | 25 | 25 | 25 |
| 36 | 15 | 15 | 16 | 16 | 16 | 17 | 17 | 18 | 18 | 18 | 19 | 19 | 20 | 20 | 20 | 21 | 21 | 21 | 22 | 22 | 22 | 23 | 23 | 24 | 24 |
| | 17 | 17 | 18 | 18 | 18 | 19 | 19 | 20 | 20 | 20 | 21 | 21 | 22 | 22 | 22 | 23 | 23 | 23 | 24 | 24 | 25 | 25 | 25 | 26 | 26 |
| 37 | 15 | 16 | 16 | 16 | 17 | 17 | 18 | 18 | 18 | 19 | 19 | 20 | 20 | 20 | 21 | 21 | 22 | 22 | 22 | 23 | 23 | 23 | 24 | 24 | 24 |
| | 17 | 18 | 18 | 18 | 19 | 19 | 20 | 20 | 20 | 21 | 21 | 22 | 22 | 22 | 23 | 23 | 24 | 24 | 24 | 25 | 25 | 25 | 26 | 26 | 27 |
| 38 | 15 | 16 | 16 | 17 | 17 | 18 | 18 | 18 | 19 | 19 | 20 | 20 | 20 | 21 | 21 | 22 | 22 | 22 | 23 | 23 | 24 | 24 | 24 | 25 | 25 |
| | 17 | 18 | 18 | 19 | 19 | 20 | 20 | 20 | 21 | 21 | 22 | 22 | 23 | 23 | 23 | 24 | 24 | 24 | 25 | 25 | 26 | 26 | 26 | 27 | 27 |
| 39 | 16 | 16 | 17 | 17 | 17 | 18 | 18 | 19 | 19 | 20 | 20 | 20 | 21 | 21 | 22 | 22 | 22 | 23 | 23 | 24 | 24 | 24 | 25 | 25 | 26 |
| | 18 | 18 | 19 | 19 | 20 | 20 | 20 | 21 | 21 | 22 | 22 | 23 | 23 | 23 | 24 | 24 | 25 | 25 | 25 | 26 | 26 | 27 | 27 | 27 | 28 |
| 40 | 16 | 17 | 17 | 17 | 18 | 18 | 19 | 19 | 20 | 20 | 20 | 21 | 21 | 22 | 22 | 23 | 23 | 23 | 24 | 24 | 25 | 25 | 25 | 26 | 26 |
| | 18 | 19 | 19 | 20 | 20 | 20 | 21 | 21 | 22 | 22 | 23 | 23 | 23 | 24 | 24 | 25 | 25 | 26 | 26 | 26 | 27 | 27 | 28 | 28 | 28 |
| 41 | 16 | 17 | 17 | 18 | 18 | 19 | 19 | 20 | 20 | 20 | 21 | 21 | 22 | 22 | 23 | 23 | 23 | 24 | 24 | 25 | 25 | 26 | 26 | 26 | 27 |
| | 18 | 19 | 19 | 20 | 20 | 21 | 21 | 22 | 22 | 23 | 23 | 23 | 24 | 24 | 25 | 25 | 26 | 26 | 26 | 27 | 27 | 28 | 28 | 28 | 29 |
| 42 | 17 | 17 | 18 | 18 | 19 | 19 | 19 | 20 | 20 | 21 | 21 | 22 | 22 | 23 | 23 | 23 | 24 | 24 | 25 | 25 | 26 | 26 | 26 | 27 | 27 |
| | 19 | 19 | 20 | 20 | 21 | 21 | 22 | 22 | 23 | 23 | 23 | 24 | 24 | 25 | 25 | 26 | 26 | 27 | 27 | 27 | 28 | 28 | 29 | 29 | 29 |
| 43 | 17 | 18 | 18 | 18 | 19 | 19 | 20 | 20 | 21 | 21 | 22 | 22 | 23 | 23 | 24 | 24 | 24 | 25 | 25 | 26 | 26 | 27 | 27 | 27 | 28 |
| | 19 | 20 | 20 | 21 | 21 | 22 | 22 | 23 | 23 | 23 | 24 | 24 | 25 | 25 | 26 | 26 | 27 | 27 | 28 | 28 | 28 | 29 | 29 | 30 | 30 |
| 44 | 17 | 18 | 18 | 19 | 19 | 20 | 20 | 21 | 21 | 22 | 22 | 23 | 23 | 24 | 24 | 24 | 25 | 25 | 26 | 26 | 27 | 27 | 28 | 28 | 28 |
| | 19 | 20 | 21 | 21 | 21 | 22 | 22 | 23 | 23 | 24 | 24 | 25 | 25 | 26 | 26 | 27 | 27 | 28 | 28 | 28 | 29 | 29 | 30 | 30 | 31 |
| 45 | 18 | 18 | 19 | 19 | 20 | 20 | 21 | 21 | 22 | 22 | 23 | 23 | 24 | 24 | 24 | 25 | 25 | 26 | 26 | 27 | 27 | 28 | 28 | 29 | 29 |
| | 20 | 20 | 21 | 21 | 22 | 22 | 23 | 23 | 24 | 24 | 25 | 25 | 26 | 26 | 27 | 27 | 28 | 28 | 29 | 29 | 29 | 30 | 30 | 31 | 31 |
| 46 | 18 | 18 | 19 | 20 | 20 | 21 | 21 | 22 | 22 | 22 | 23 | 23 | 24 | 24 | 25 | 25 | 26 | 26 | 27 | 27 | 28 | 28 | 29 | 29 | 30 |
| | 20 | 21 | 21 | 22 | 22 | 23 | 23 | 24 | 24 | 25 | 25 | 26 | 26 | 27 | 27 | 28 | 28 | 29 | 29 | 30 | 30 | 30 | 31 | 31 | 32 |
| 47 | 18 | 19 | 19 | 20 | 20 | 21 | 21 | 22 | 22 | 23 | 23 | 24 | 24 | 25 | 25 | 26 | 26 | 27 | 27 | 28 | 28 | 29 | 29 | 30 | 30 |
| | 21 | 21 | 22 | 22 | 23 | 23 | 24 | 24 | 25 | 25 | 26 | 26 | 27 | 27 | 28 | 28 | 29 | 29 | 30 | 30 | 31 | 31 | 31 | 32 | 32 |
| 48 | 19 | 19 | 20 | 20 | 21 | 21 | 22 | 22 | 23 | 23 | 24 | 24 | 25 | 25 | 26 | 26 | 27 | 27 | 28 | 28 | 29 | 29 | 30 | 30 | 31 |
| | 21 | 21 | 22 | 22 | 23 | 24 | 24 | 25 | 25 | 26 | 26 | 27 | 27 | 28 | 28 | 29 | 29 | 30 | 30 | 31 | 31 | 32 | 32 | 33 | 33 |
| 49 | 19 | 19 | 20 | 21 | 21 | 22 | 22 | 23 | 23 | 24 | 24 | 25 | 25 | 26 | 26 | 27 | 27 | 28 | 28 | 29 | 29 | 30 | 30 | 31 | 31 |
| | 21 | 22 | 22 | 23 | 23 | 24 | 24 | 25 | 26 | 26 | 27 | 27 | 28 | 28 | 29 | 29 | 30 | 30 | 31 | 31 | 32 | 32 | 33 | 33 | 34 |

**Table** $\boxed{N_1}$

**Critical Values of Sign Test**

$x$ is the frequency in the $P$ catagory, and $N - x$ is the frequency in the $Q$ category. The obtained $x$ or $N - x$ must be equal to or greater than the value shown for significance at the chosen level. Dashes indicate that no decision is possible for $N$ at the given $\alpha$-level

| | ONE-TAILED TEST | | TWO-TAILED TEST | |
|---|---|---|---|---|
| $N$ | 0.05 | 0.01 | 0.05 | 0.01 |
| 5 | 5 | — | — | — |
| 6 | 6 | — | 6 | — |
| 7 | 7 | 7 | 7 | — |
| 8 | 7 | 8 | 8 | — |
| 9 | 8 | 9 | 8 | 9 |
| 10 | 9 | 10 | 9 | 10 |
| 11 | 9 | 10 | 10 | 11 |
| 12 | 10 | 11 | 10 | 11 |
| 13 | 10 | 12 | 11 | 12 |
| 14 | 11 | 12 | 12 | 13 |
| 15 | 12 | 13 | 12 | 13 |
| 16 | 12 | 14 | 13 | 14 |
| 17 | 13 | 14 | 13 | 15 |
| 18 | 13 | 15 | 14 | 15 |
| 19 | 14 | 15 | 15 | 16 |
| 20 | 15 | 17 | 16 | 17 |
| 21 | 15 | 17 | 16 | 17 |
| 22 | 16 | 17 | 17 | 18 |
| 23 | 16 | 18 | 17 | 19 |
| 24 | 17 | 19 | 18 | 19 |
| 25 | 18 | 19 | 18 | 20 |
| 26 | 18 | 20 | 19 | 20 |
| 27 | 19 | 20 | 20 | 21 |
| 28 | 19 | 21 | 20 | 22 |
| 29 | 20 | 22 | 21 | 22 |
| 30 | 20 | 22 | 21 | 23 |
| 31 | 21 | 23 | 22 | 24 |
| 32 | 22 | 24 | 23 | 24 |
| 33 | 22 | 24 | 23 | 25 |
| 34 | 23 | 25 | 24 | 25 |
| 35 | 23 | 25 | 24 | 26 |
| 36 | 24 | 26 | 25 | 27 |
| 37 | 24 | 27 | 25 | 27 |
| 38 | 25 | 27 | 26 | 28 |
| 39 | 26 | 28 | 27 | 28 |
| 40 | 26 | 28 | 27 | 28 |
| 41 | 27 | 29 | 28 | 30 |
| 42 | 27 | 29 | 28 | 30 |
| 43 | 28 | 30 | 29 | 31 |
| 44 | 28 | 31 | 29 | 31 |
| 45 | 29 | 31 | 30 | 32 |
| 46 | 30 | 32 | 31 | 33 |
| 47 | 30 | 32 | 31 | 33 |
| 48 | 31 | 33 | 32 | 34 |
| 49 | 31 | 34 | 32 | 35 |
| 50 | 32 | 34 | 33 | 35 |

## Table O

**Factorials of Numbers 1 to 20**

| N | N! |
|---|---|
| 0 | 1 |
| 1 | 1 |
| 2 | 2 |
| 3 | 6 |
| 4 | 24 |
| 5 | 120 |
| 6 | 720 |
| 7 | 5040 |
| 8 | 40320 |
| 9 | 362880 |
| 10 | 3628800 |
| 11 | 39916800 |
| 12 | 479001600 |
| 13 | 6227020800 |
| 14 | 87178291200 |
| 15 | 1307674368000 |
| 16 | 20922789888000 |
| 17 | 355687428096000 |
| 18 | 6402373705728000 |
| 19 | 121645100408832000 |
| 20 | 2432902008176640000 |

## Table Q

**Critical Values for $\chi^2$**

**Level of Significance**
**Two-tailed or Nondirectional Test**

| Degrees of freedom df | .10 | .05 | .02 | .01 |
|---|---|---|---|---|
| 1 | 2.706 | 3.841 | 5.412 | 6.635 |
| 2 | 4.605 | 5.991 | 7.824 | 9.210 |
| 3 | 6.251 | 7.815 | 9.837 | 11.341 |
| 4 | 7.779 | 9.488 | 11.668 | 13.277 |
| 5 | 9.236 | 11.070 | 13.388 | 15.086 |
| 6 | 10.645 | 12.592 | 15.033 | 16.812 |
| 7 | 12.017 | 14.067 | 16.622 | 18.475 |
| 8 | 13.362 | 15.507 | 18.168 | 20.090 |
| 9 | 14.684 | 16.919 | 19.679 | 21.666 |
| 10 | 15.987 | 18.307 | 21.161 | 23.209 |
| 11 | 17.275 | 19.675 | 22.618 | 24.725 |
| 12 | 18.549 | 21.026 | 24.054 | 26.217 |
| 13 | 19.812 | 22.362 | 25.472 | 27.688 |
| 14 | 21.064 | 23.685 | 26.873 | 29.141 |
| 15 | 22.307 | 24.996 | 28.259 | 30.578 |
| 16 | 23.542 | 26.296 | 29.633 | 32.000 |
| 17 | 24.769 | 27.587 | 30.995 | 33.409 |
| 18 | 25.989 | 28.869 | 32.346 | 34.805 |
| 19 | 27.204 | 30.144 | 33.687 | 36.191 |
| 20 | 28.412 | 31.410 | 35.020 | 37.566 |
| 21 | 29.615 | 32.671 | 36.343 | 38.932 |
| 22 | 30.813 | 33.924 | 37.659 | 40.289 |
| 23 | 32.007 | 35.172 | 38.968 | 41.638 |
| 24 | 33.196 | 36.415 | 40.270 | 42.980 |
| 25 | 34.382 | 37.652 | 41.566 | 44.314 |
| 26 | 35.563 | 38.885 | 42.856 | 45.642 |
| 27 | 36.741 | 40.113 | 44.140 | 46.963 |
| 28 | 37.916 | 41.337 | 45.419 | 48.278 |
| 29 | 39.087 | 42.557 | 46.693 | 49.588 |
| 30 | 40.256 | 43.773 | 47.962 | 50.892 |

## Table P

**Binomial Coefficients**

| N | $\binom{N}{0}$ | $\binom{N}{1}$ | $\binom{N}{2}$ | $\binom{N}{3}$ | $\binom{N}{4}$ | $\binom{N}{5}$ | $\binom{N}{6}$ | $\binom{N}{7}$ | $\binom{N}{8}$ | $\binom{N}{9}$ | $\binom{N}{10}$ | Sum of Coefficients |
|---|---|---|---|---|---|---|---|---|---|---|---|---|
| 1 | 1 | 1 | | | | | | | | | | 2 |
| 2 | 1 | 2 | 1 | | | | | | | | | 4 |
| 3 | 1 | 3 | 3 | 1 | | | | | | | | 8 |
| 4 | 1 | 4 | 6 | 4 | 1 | | | | | | | 16 |
| 5 | 1 | 5 | 10 | 10 | 5 | 1 | | | | | | 32 |
| 6 | 1 | 6 | 15 | 20 | 15 | 6 | 1 | | | | | 64 |
| 7 | 1 | 7 | 21 | 35 | 35 | 21 | 7 | 1 | | | | 128 |
| 8 | 1 | 8 | 28 | 56 | 70 | 56 | 28 | 8 | 1 | | | 256 |
| 9 | 1 | 9 | 36 | 84 | 126 | 126 | 84 | 36 | 9 | 1 | | 612 |
| 10 | 1 | 10 | 45 | 120 | 210 | 252 | 210 | 120 | 45 | 10 | 1 | 1,024 |
| 11 | 1 | 11 | 55 | 165 | 330 | 462 | 462 | 330 | 165 | 55 | 11 | 2,048* |
| 12 | 1 | 12 | 66 | 220 | 495 | 792 | 924 | 792 | 495 | 220 | 66 | 4,096 |
| 13 | 1 | 13 | 78 | 286 | 715 | 1287 | 1716 | 1716 | 1287 | 715 | 286 | 8,192 |
| 14 | 1 | 14 | 91 | 364 | 1001 | 2002 | 3003 | 3432 | 3003 | 2002 | 1001 | 16,384 |
| 15 | 1 | 15 | 105 | 455 | 1365 | 3003 | 5005 | 6435 | 6435 | 5005 | 3003 | 32,768 |
| 16 | 1 | 16 | 120 | 560 | 1820 | 4368 | 8008 | 11440 | 12870 | 11440 | 8008 | 65,536 |
| 17 | 1 | 17 | 136 | 680 | 2380 | 6188 | 12376 | 19448 | 24310 | 24310 | 19448 | 131,072 |
| 18 | 1 | 18 | 153 | 816 | 3060 | 8568 | 18564 | 31824 | 43758 | 48620 | 43758 | 262,144 |
| 19 | 1 | 19 | 171 | 969 | 3876 | 11628 | 27132 | 50388 | 75582 | 92378 | 92378 | 524,288 |
| 20 | 1 | 20 | 190 | 1140 | 4845 | 15504 | 38760 | 77520 | 125970 | 167960 | 184756 | 1,048,576 |

* From this point and below, not all the coefficients are shown in the table. However, the column "Sum of Coefficients" includes all values up to $N = 20$.

**Table** R

### Critical Values of $U$ and $U'$ for a One-Tailed Test at $\alpha = .005$ or a Two-Tailed Test at $\alpha = .01$

To be significant for any given $N_1$ and $N_2$, obtained $U$ must be equal to or *less than* the value shown in the table. Obtained $U'$ must be equal to or *greater than* the value shown in the table. *Example:* If $\alpha = 0.01$, two-tailed test, $N_1 = 13$, $N_2 = 15$, and obtained $U = 150$, we cannot reject $H_0$ since obtained $U$ is within the upper (153) and lower (42) critical values.

| $N_2$ \ $N_1$ | 1 | 2 | 3 | 4 | 5 | 6 | 7 | 8 | 9 | 10 | 11 | 12 | 13 | 14 | 15 | 16 | 17 | 18 | 19 | 20 |
|---|---|---|---|---|---|---|---|---|---|---|---|---|---|---|---|---|---|---|---|---|
| 1 | -- | -- | -- | -- | -- | -- | -- | -- | -- | -- | -- | -- | -- | -- | -- | -- | -- | -- | -- | -- |
| 2 | -- | -- | -- | -- | -- | -- | -- | -- | -- | -- | -- | -- | -- | -- | -- | -- | -- | -- | 0/38 | 0/40 |
| 3 | -- | -- | -- | -- | -- | -- | -- | -- | 0/27 | 0/30 | 0/33 | 1/35 | 1/38 | 1/41 | 2/43 | 2/46 | 2/49 | 2/52 | 3/54 | 3/57 |
| 4 | -- | -- | -- | -- | -- | 0/24 | 0/28 | 1/31 | 1/35 | 2/38 | 2/42 | 3/45 | 3/49 | 4/52 | 5/55 | 5/59 | 6/62 | 6/66 | 7/69 | 8/72 |
| 5 | -- | -- | -- | 0/25 | 1/29 | 1/34 | 2/38 | 3/42 | 4/46 | 5/50 | 6/54 | 7/58 | 7/63 | 8/67 | 9/71 | 10/75 | 11/79 | 12/83 | 13/87 | |
| 6 | -- | -- | -- | 0/24 | 1/29 | 2/34 | 3/39 | 4/44 | 5/49 | 6/54 | 7/59 | 9/63 | 10/68 | 11/73 | 12/78 | 13/83 | 15/87 | 16/92 | 17/97 | 18/102 |
| 7 | -- | -- | -- | 0/28 | 1/34 | 3/39 | 4/45 | 6/50 | 7/56 | 9/61 | 10/67 | 12/72 | 13/78 | 15/83 | 16/89 | 18/94 | 19/100 | 21/105 | 22/111 | 24/116 |
| 8 | -- | -- | -- | 1/31 | 2/38 | 4/44 | 6/50 | 7/57 | 9/63 | 11/69 | 13/75 | 15/81 | 17/87 | 18/94 | 20/100 | 22/106 | 24/112 | 26/118 | 28/124 | 30/130 |
| 9 | -- | -- | 0/27 | 1/35 | 3/42 | 5/49 | 7/56 | 9/63 | 11/70 | 13/77 | 16/83 | 18/90 | 20/97 | 22/104 | 24/111 | 27/117 | 29/124 | 31/131 | 33/138 | 36/144 |
| 10 | -- | -- | 0/30 | 2/38 | 4/46 | 6/54 | 9/61 | 11/69 | 13/77 | 16/84 | 18/92 | 21/99 | 24/106 | 26/114 | 29/121 | 31/129 | 34/136 | 37/143 | 39/151 | 42/158 |
| 11 | -- | -- | 0/33 | 2/42 | 5/50 | 7/59 | 10/67 | 13/75 | 16/83 | 18/92 | 21/100 | 24/108 | 27/116 | 30/124 | 33/132 | 36/140 | 39/148 | 42/156 | 45/164 | 48/172 |
| 12 | -- | -- | 1/35 | 3/45 | 6/54 | 9/63 | 12/72 | 15/81 | 18/90 | 21/99 | 24/108 | 27/117 | 31/125 | 34/134 | 37/143 | 41/151 | 44/160 | 47/169 | 51/177 | 54/186 |
| 13 | -- | -- | 1/38 | 3/49 | 7/58 | 10/68 | 13/78 | 17/87 | 20/97 | 24/106 | 27/116 | 31/125 | 34/144 | 38/153 | 42/163 | 45/172 | 49/181 | 53/191 | 56/200 | 60/200 |
| 14 | -- | -- | 1/41 | 4/52 | 7/63 | 11/73 | 15/83 | 18/94 | 22/104 | 26/114 | 30/124 | 34/134 | 38/144 | 42/154 | 46/164 | 50/174 | 54/184 | 58/194 | 63/203 | 67/213 |
| 15 | -- | -- | 2/43 | 5/55 | 8/67 | 12/78 | 16/89 | 20/100 | 24/111 | 29/121 | 33/132 | 37/143 | 42/153 | 46/164 | 51/174 | 55/185 | 60/195 | 64/206 | 69/216 | 73/227 |
| 16 | -- | -- | 2/46 | 5/59 | 9/71 | 13/83 | 18/94 | 22/106 | 27/117 | 31/129 | 36/140 | 41/151 | 45/163 | 50/174 | 55/185 | 60/196 | 65/207 | 70/218 | 74/230 | 79/241 |
| 17 | -- | -- | 2/49 | 6/62 | 10/75 | 15/87 | 19/100 | 24/112 | 29/124 | 34/148 | 39/148 | 44/160 | 49/172 | 54/184 | 60/195 | 65/207 | 70/219 | 75/231 | 81/242 | 86/254 |
| 18 | -- | -- | 2/52 | 6/66 | 11/79 | 16/92 | 21/105 | 26/118 | 31/131 | 37/143 | 42/156 | 47/169 | 53/181 | 58/194 | 64/206 | 70/218 | 75/231 | 81/243 | 87/255 | 92/268 |
| 19 | -- | 0/38 | 3/54 | 7/69 | 12/83 | 17/97 | 22/111 | 28/124 | 33/138 | 39/151 | 45/164 | 51/177 | 56/191 | 63/203 | 69/216 | 74/230 | 81/242 | 87/255 | 93/268 | 99/281 |
| 20 | -- | 0/40 | 3/57 | 8/72 | 13/87 | 18/102 | 24/116 | 30/130 | 36/144 | 42/158 | 48/172 | 54/186 | 60/200 | 67/213 | 73/227 | 79/241 | 86/254 | 92/268 | 99/281 | 105/295 |

(Dashes in the body of the table indicate that no decision is possible at the stated level of significance.)

**Table** R *(continued)*

### Critical Values of U and U' for a One-Tailed Test at α = .01 or a Two-Tailed Test at α = .02

To be significant for any given $N_1$ and $N_2$, obtained $U$ must be equal to or *less than* the value shown in the table. Obtained $U'$ must be equal to or *greater than* the value shown in the table.

| $N_2$ \ $N_1$ | 1 | 2 | 3 | 4 | 5 | 6 | 7 | 8 | 9 | 10 | 11 | 12 | 13 | 14 | 15 | 16 | 17 | 18 | 19 | 20 |
|---|---|---|---|---|---|---|---|---|---|---|---|---|---|---|---|---|---|---|---|---|
| 1 | -- | -- | -- | -- | -- | -- | -- | -- | -- | -- | -- | -- | -- | -- | -- | -- | -- | -- | -- | -- |
| 2 | -- | -- | -- | -- | -- | -- | -- | -- | -- | -- | -- | -- | 0<br>26 | 0<br>28 | 0<br>30 | 0<br>32 | 0<br>34 | 0<br>36 | 1<br>37 | 1<br>39 |
| 3 | -- | -- | -- | -- | -- | -- | 0<br>21 | 0<br>24 | 1<br>26 | 1<br>29 | 1<br>32 | 2<br>34 | 2<br>37 | 2<br>40 | 3<br>42 | 3<br>45 | 4<br>47 | 4<br>50 | 4<br>52 | 5<br>55 |
| 4 | -- | -- | -- | -- | 0<br>20 | 1<br>23 | 1<br>27 | 2<br>30 | 3<br>33 | 3<br>37 | 4<br>40 | 5<br>43 | 5<br>47 | 6<br>50 | 7<br>53 | 7<br>57 | 8<br>60 | 9<br>63 | 9<br>67 | 10<br>70 |
| 5 | -- | -- | -- | 0<br>20 | 1<br>24 | 2<br>28 | 3<br>32 | 4<br>36 | 5<br>40 | 6<br>44 | 7<br>48 | 8<br>52 | 9<br>56 | 10<br>60 | 11<br>64 | 12<br>68 | 13<br>72 | 14<br>76 | 15<br>80 | 16<br>84 |
| 6 | -- | -- | -- | 1<br>23 | 2<br>28 | 3<br>33 | 4<br>38 | 6<br>42 | 7<br>47 | 8<br>52 | 9<br>57 | 11<br>61 | 12<br>66 | 13<br>71 | 15<br>75 | 16<br>80 | 18<br>84 | 19<br>89 | 20<br>94 | 22<br>98 |
| 7 | -- | -- | 0<br>21 | 1<br>27 | 3<br>32 | 4<br>38 | 6<br>43 | 7<br>49 | 9<br>54 | 11<br>59 | 12<br>65 | 14<br>70 | 16<br>75 | 17<br>81 | 19<br>86 | 21<br>91 | 23<br>96 | 24<br>102 | 26<br>107 | 28<br>112 |
| 8 | -- | -- | 0<br>24 | 2<br>30 | 4<br>36 | 6<br>42 | 7<br>49 | 9<br>55 | 11<br>61 | 13<br>67 | 15<br>73 | 17<br>79 | 20<br>84 | 22<br>90 | 24<br>96 | 26<br>102 | 28<br>108 | 30<br>114 | 32<br>120 | 34<br>126 |
| 9 | -- | -- | 1<br>26 | 3<br>33 | 5<br>40 | 7<br>47 | 9<br>54 | 11<br>61 | 14<br>67 | 16<br>74 | 18<br>81 | 21<br>87 | 23<br>94 | 26<br>100 | 28<br>107 | 31<br>113 | 33<br>120 | 36<br>126 | 38<br>133 | 40<br>140 |
| 10 | -- | -- | 1<br>29 | 3<br>37 | 6<br>44 | 8<br>52 | 11<br>59 | 13<br>67 | 16<br>74 | 19<br>81 | 22<br>88 | 24<br>96 | 27<br>103 | 30<br>110 | 33<br>117 | 36<br>124 | 38<br>132 | 41<br>139 | 44<br>146 | 47<br>153 |
| 11 | -- | -- | 1<br>32 | 4<br>40 | 7<br>48 | 9<br>57 | 12<br>65 | 15<br>73 | 18<br>81 | 22<br>88 | 25<br>96 | 28<br>104 | 31<br>112 | 34<br>120 | 37<br>128 | 41<br>135 | 44<br>143 | 47<br>151 | 50<br>159 | 53<br>167 |
| 12 | -- | -- | 2<br>34 | 5<br>43 | 8<br>52 | 11<br>61 | 14<br>70 | 17<br>79 | 21<br>87 | 24<br>96 | 28<br>104 | 31<br>113 | 35<br>121 | 38<br>130 | 42<br>138 | 46<br>146 | 49<br>155 | 53<br>163 | 56<br>172 | 60<br>180 |
| 13 | -- | 0<br>26 | 2<br>37 | 5<br>47 | 9<br>56 | 12<br>66 | 16<br>75 | 20<br>84 | 23<br>94 | 27<br>103 | 31<br>112 | 35<br>121 | 39<br>130 | 43<br>139 | 47<br>148 | 51<br>157 | 55<br>166 | 59<br>175 | 63<br>184 | 67<br>193 |
| 14 | -- | 0<br>28 | 2<br>40 | 6<br>50 | 10<br>60 | 13<br>71 | 17<br>81 | 22<br>90 | 26<br>100 | 30<br>110 | 34<br>120 | 38<br>130 | 43<br>139 | 47<br>149 | 51<br>159 | 56<br>168 | 60<br>178 | 65<br>187 | 69<br>197 | 73<br>207 |
| 15 | -- | 0<br>30 | 3<br>42 | 7<br>53 | 11<br>64 | 15<br>75 | 19<br>86 | 24<br>96 | 28<br>107 | 33<br>117 | 37<br>128 | 42<br>138 | 47<br>148 | 51<br>159 | 56<br>169 | 61<br>179 | 66<br>189 | 70<br>200 | 75<br>210 | 80<br>220 |
| 16 | -- | 0<br>32 | 3<br>45 | 7<br>57 | 12<br>68 | 16<br>80 | 21<br>91 | 26<br>102 | 31<br>113 | 36<br>124 | 41<br>135 | 46<br>146 | 51<br>157 | 56<br>168 | 61<br>179 | 66<br>190 | 71<br>201 | 76<br>212 | 82<br>222 | 87<br>233 |
| 17 | -- | 0<br>34 | 4<br>47 | 8<br>60 | 13<br>72 | 18<br>84 | 23<br>96 | 28<br>108 | 33<br>120 | 38<br>132 | 44<br>143 | 49<br>155 | 55<br>166 | 60<br>178 | 66<br>189 | 71<br>201 | 77<br>212 | 82<br>224 | 88<br>234 | 93<br>247 |
| 18 | -- | 0<br>36 | 4<br>50 | 9<br>63 | 14<br>76 | 19<br>89 | 24<br>102 | 30<br>114 | 36<br>126 | 41<br>139 | 47<br>151 | 53<br>163 | 59<br>175 | 65<br>187 | 70<br>200 | 76<br>212 | 82<br>224 | 88<br>236 | 94<br>248 | 100<br>260 |
| 19 | -- | 1<br>37 | 4<br>53 | 9<br>67 | 15<br>80 | 20<br>94 | 26<br>107 | 32<br>120 | 38<br>133 | 44<br>146 | 50<br>159 | 56<br>172 | 63<br>184 | 69<br>197 | 75<br>210 | 82<br>222 | 88<br>235 | 94<br>248 | 101<br>260 | 107<br>273 |
| 20 | -- | 1<br>39 | 5<br>55 | 10<br>70 | 16<br>84 | 22<br>98 | 28<br>112 | 34<br>126 | 40<br>140 | 47<br>153 | 53<br>167 | 60<br>180 | 67<br>193 | 73<br>207 | 80<br>220 | 87<br>233 | 93<br>247 | 100<br>260 | 107<br>273 | 114<br>286 |

(Dashes in the body of the table indicate that no decision is possible at the stated level of significance.)

**Table** R *(continued)*

### Critical Values of $U$ and $U'$ for a One-Tailed Test at $\alpha = .025$ or a Two-Tailed Test at $\alpha = .05$

To be significant for any given $N_1$ and $N_2$, obtained $U$ must be equal to or *less than* the value shown in the table. Obtained $U'$ must be equal to or *greater than* the value shown in the table.

| $N_2$\$N_1$ | 1 | 2 | 3 | 4 | 5 | 6 | 7 | 8 | 9 | 10 | 11 | 12 | 13 | 14 | 15 | 16 | 17 | 18 | 19 | 20 |
|---|---|---|---|---|---|---|---|---|---|---|---|---|---|---|---|---|---|---|---|---|
| 1 | -- | -- | -- | -- | -- | -- | -- | -- | -- | -- | -- | -- | -- | -- | -- | -- | -- | -- | -- | -- |
| 2 | -- | -- | -- | -- | -- | -- | -- | 0 | 0 | 0 | 0 | 1 | 1 | 1 | 1 | 1 | 2 | 2 | 2 | 2 |
|   |    |    |    |    |    |    |    | 16 | 18 | 20 | 22 | 23 | 25 | 27 | 29 | 31 | 32 | 34 | 36 | 38 |
| 3 | -- | -- | -- | -- | 0 | 1 | 1 | 2 | 2 | 3 | 3 | 4 | 4 | 5 | 5 | 6 | 6 | 7 | 7 | 8 |
|   |    |    |    |    | 15 | 17 | 20 | 22 | 25 | 27 | 30 | 32 | 35 | 37 | 40 | 42 | 45 | 47 | 50 | 52 |
| 4 | -- | -- | -- | 0 | 1 | 2 | 3 | 4 | 4 | 5 | 6 | 7 | 8 | 9 | 10 | 11 | 11 | 12 | 13 | 13 |
|   |    |    |    | 16 | 19 | 22 | 25 | 28 | 32 | 35 | 38 | 41 | 44 | 47 | 50 | 53 | 57 | 60 | 63 | 67 |
| 5 | -- | -- | 0 | 1 | 2 | 3 | 5 | 6 | 7 | 8 | 9 | 11 | 12 | 13 | 14 | 15 | 17 | 18 | 19 | 20 |
|   |    |    | 15 | 19 | 23 | 27 | 30 | 34 | 38 | 42 | 46 | 49 | 53 | 57 | 61 | 65 | 68 | 72 | 76 | 80 |
| 6 | -- | -- | 1 | 2 | 3 | 5 | 6 | 8 | 10 | 11 | 13 | 14 | 16 | 17 | 19 | 21 | 22 | 24 | 25 | 27 |
|   |    |    | 17 | 22 | 27 | 31 | 36 | 40 | 44 | 49 | 53 | 58 | 62 | 67 | 71 | 75 | 80 | 84 | 89 | 93 |
| 7 | -- | -- | 1 | 3 | 5 | 6 | 8 | 10 | 12 | 14 | 16 | 18 | 20 | 22 | 24 | 26 | 28 | 30 | 32 | 34 |
|   |    |    | 20 | 25 | 30 | 36 | 41 | 46 | 51 | 56 | 61 | 66 | 71 | 76 | 81 | 86 | 91 | 96 | 101 | 106 |
| 8 | -- | 0 | 2 | 4 | 6 | 8 | 10 | 13 | 15 | 17 | 19 | 22 | 24 | 26 | 29 | 31 | 34 | 36 | 38 | 41 |
|   |    | 16 | 22 | 28 | 34 | 40 | 46 | 51 | 57 | 63 | 69 | 74 | 80 | 86 | 91 | 97 | 102 | 108 | 111 | 119 |
| 9 | -- | 0 | 2 | 4 | 7 | 10 | 12 | 15 | 17 | 20 | 23 | 26 | 28 | 31 | 34 | 37 | 39 | 42 | 45 | 48 |
|   |    | 18 | 25 | 32 | 38 | 44 | 51 | 57 | 64 | 70 | 76 | 82 | 89 | 95 | 101 | 107 | 114 | 120 | 126 | 132 |
| 10 | -- | 0 | 3 | 5 | 8 | 11 | 14 | 17 | 20 | 23 | 26 | 29 | 33 | 36 | 39 | 42 | 45 | 48 | 52 | 55 |
|   |    | 20 | 27 | 35 | 42 | 49 | 56 | 63 | 70 | 77 | 84 | 91 | 97 | 104 | 111 | 118 | 125 | 132 | 138 | 145 |
| 11 | -- | 0 | 3 | 6 | 9 | 13 | 16 | 19 | 23 | 26 | 30 | 33 | 37 | 40 | 44 | 47 | 51 | 55 | 58 | 62 |
|   |    | 22 | 30 | 38 | 46 | 53 | 61 | 69 | 76 | 84 | 91 | 99 | 106 | 114 | 121 | 129 | 136 | 143 | 151 | 158 |
| 12 | -- | 1 | 4 | 7 | 11 | 14 | 18 | 22 | 26 | 29 | 33 | 37 | 41 | 45 | 49 | 53 | 57 | 61 | 65 | 69 |
|   |    | 23 | 32 | 41 | 49 | 58 | 66 | 74 | 82 | 91 | 99 | 107 | 115 | 123 | 131 | 139 | 147 | 155 | 163 | 171 |
| 13 | -- | 1 | 4 | 8 | 12 | 16 | 20 | 24 | 28 | 33 | 37 | 41 | 45 | 50 | 54 | 59 | 63 | 67 | 72 | 76 |
|   |    | 25 | 35 | 44 | 53 | 62 | 71 | 80 | 89 | 97 | 106 | 115 | 124 | 132 | 141 | 149 | 158 | 167 | 175 | 184 |
| 14 | -- | 1 | 5 | 9 | 13 | 17 | 22 | 26 | 31 | 36 | 40 | 45 | 50 | 55 | 59 | 64 | 67 | 74 | 78 | 83 |
|   |    | 27 | 37 | 47 | 51 | 67 | 76 | 86 | 95 | 104 | 114 | 123 | 132 | 141 | 151 | 160 | 171 | 178 | 188 | 197 |
| 15 | -- | 1 | 5 | 10 | 14 | 19 | 24 | 29 | 34 | 39 | 44 | 49 | 54 | 59 | 64 | 70 | 75 | 80 | 85 | 90 |
|   |    | 29 | 40 | 50 | 61 | 71 | 81 | 91 | 101 | 111 | 121 | 131 | 141 | 151 | 161 | 170 | 180 | 190 | 200 | 210 |
| 16 | -- | 1 | 6 | 11 | 15 | 21 | 26 | 31 | 37 | 42 | 47 | 53 | 59 | 64 | 70 | 75 | 81 | 86 | 92 | 98 |
|   |    | 31 | 42 | 53 | 65 | 75 | 86 | 97 | 107 | 118 | 129 | 139 | 149 | 160 | 170 | 181 | 191 | 202 | 212 | 222 |
| 17 | -- | 2 | 6 | 11 | 17 | 22 | 28 | 34 | 39 | 45 | 51 | 57 | 63 | 67 | 75 | 81 | 87 | 93 | 99 | 105 |
|   |    | 32 | 45 | 57 | 68 | 80 | 91 | 102 | 114 | 125 | 136 | 147 | 158 | 171 | 180 | 191 | 202 | 213 | 224 | 235 |
| 18 | -- | 2 | 7 | 12 | 18 | 24 | 30 | 36 | 42 | 48 | 55 | 61 | 67 | 74 | 80 | 86 | 93 | 99 | 106 | 112 |
|   |    | 34 | 47 | 60 | 72 | 84 | 96 | 108 | 120 | 132 | 143 | 155 | 167 | 178 | 190 | 202 | 213 | 225 | 236 | 248 |
| 19 | -- | 2 | 7 | 13 | 19 | 25 | 32 | 38 | 45 | 52 | 58 | 65 | 72 | 78 | 85 | 92 | 99 | 106 | 113 | 119 |
|   |    | 36 | 50 | 63 | 76 | 89 | 101 | 114 | 126 | 138 | 151 | 163 | 175 | 188 | 200 | 212 | 224 | 236 | 248 | 261 |
| 20 | -- | 2 | 8 | 13 | 20 | 27 | 34 | 41 | 48 | 55 | 62 | 69 | 76 | 83 | 90 | 98 | 105 | 112 | 119 | 127 |
|   |    | 38 | 52 | 67 | 80 | 93 | 106 | 119 | 132 | 145 | 158 | 171 | 184 | 197 | 210 | 222 | 235 | 248 | 261 | 273 |

(Dashes in the body of the table indicate that no decision is possible at the stated level of significance.)

**Table** R *(continued)*

### Critical Values of *U* and *U'* for a One-Tailed Test at α = .05 or a Two-Tailed Test at α = .10

To be significant for any given $N_1$ and $N_2$, obtained *U* must be equal to or *less than* the value shown in the table. Obtained *U'* must be equal to or *greater than* the value shown in the table.

| $N_2$＼$N_1$ | 1 | 2 | 3 | 4 | 5 | 6 | 7 | 8 | 9 | 10 | 11 | 12 | 13 | 14 | 15 | 16 | 17 | 18 | 19 | 20 |
|---|---|---|---|---|---|---|---|---|---|---|---|---|---|---|---|---|---|---|---|---|
| 1 | -- | -- | -- | -- | -- | -- | -- | -- | -- | -- | -- | -- | -- | -- | -- | -- | -- | -- | 0<br>19 | 0<br>20 |
| 2 | -- | -- | -- | -- | 0<br>10 | 0<br>12 | 0<br>14 | 1<br>15 | 1<br>17 | 1<br>19 | 1<br>21 | 2<br>22 | 2<br>24 | 2<br>26 | 3<br>27 | 3<br>29 | 3<br>31 | 4<br>32 | 4<br>34 | 4<br>36 |
| 3 | -- | -- | 0<br>9 | 0<br>12 | 1<br>14 | 2<br>16 | 2<br>19 | 3<br>21 | 3<br>24 | 4<br>26 | 5<br>28 | 5<br>31 | 6<br>33 | 7<br>35 | 7<br>38 | 8<br>40 | 9<br>42 | 9<br>45 | 10<br>47 | 11<br>49 |
| 4 | -- | -- | 0<br>12 | 1<br>15 | 2<br>18 | 3<br>21 | 4<br>24 | 5<br>27 | 6<br>30 | 7<br>33 | 8<br>36 | 9<br>39 | 10<br>42 | 11<br>45 | 12<br>48 | 14<br>50 | 15<br>53 | 16<br>56 | 17<br>59 | 18<br>62 |
| 5 | -- | 0<br>10 | 1<br>14 | 2<br>18 | 4<br>21 | 5<br>25 | 6<br>29 | 8<br>32 | 9<br>36 | 11<br>39 | 12<br>43 | 13<br>47 | 15<br>50 | 16<br>54 | 18<br>57 | 19<br>61 | 20<br>65 | 22<br>68 | 23<br>72 | 25<br>75 |
| 6 | -- | 0<br>12 | 2<br>16 | 3<br>21 | 5<br>25 | 7<br>29 | 8<br>34 | 10<br>38 | 12<br>42 | 14<br>46 | 16<br>50 | 17<br>55 | 19<br>59 | 21<br>63 | 23<br>67 | 25<br>71 | 26<br>76 | 28<br>80 | 30<br>84 | 32<br>88 |
| 7 | -- | 0<br>14 | 2<br>19 | 4<br>24 | 6<br>29 | 8<br>34 | 11<br>38 | 13<br>43 | 15<br>48 | 17<br>53 | 19<br>58 | 21<br>63 | 24<br>67 | 26<br>72 | 28<br>77 | 30<br>82 | 33<br>86 | 35<br>91 | 37<br>96 | 39<br>101 |
| 8 | -- | 1<br>15 | 3<br>21 | 5<br>27 | 8<br>32 | 10<br>38 | 13<br>43 | 15<br>49 | 18<br>54 | 20<br>60 | 23<br>65 | 26<br>70 | 28<br>76 | 31<br>81 | 33<br>87 | 36<br>92 | 39<br>97 | 41<br>103 | 44<br>108 | 47<br>113 |
| 9 | -- | 1<br>17 | 3<br>24 | 6<br>30 | 9<br>36 | 12<br>42 | 15<br>48 | 18<br>54 | 21<br>60 | 24<br>66 | 27<br>72 | 30<br>78 | 33<br>84 | 36<br>90 | 39<br>96 | 42<br>102 | 45<br>108 | 48<br>114 | 51<br>120 | 54<br>126 |
| 10 | -- | 1<br>19 | 4<br>26 | 7<br>33 | 11<br>39 | 14<br>46 | 17<br>53 | 20<br>60 | 24<br>66 | 27<br>73 | 31<br>79 | 34<br>86 | 37<br>93 | 41<br>99 | 44<br>106 | 48<br>112 | 51<br>119 | 55<br>125 | 58<br>132 | 62<br>138 |
| 11 | -- | 1<br>21 | 5<br>28 | 8<br>36 | 12<br>43 | 16<br>50 | 19<br>58 | 23<br>65 | 27<br>72 | 31<br>79 | 34<br>87 | 38<br>94 | 42<br>101 | 46<br>108 | 50<br>115 | 54<br>122 | 57<br>130 | 61<br>137 | 65<br>144 | 69<br>151 |
| 12 | -- | 2<br>22 | 5<br>31 | 9<br>39 | 13<br>47 | 17<br>55 | 21<br>63 | 26<br>70 | 30<br>78 | 34<br>86 | 38<br>94 | 42<br>102 | 47<br>109 | 51<br>117 | 55<br>125 | 60<br>132 | 64<br>140 | 68<br>148 | 72<br>156 | 77<br>163 |
| 13 | -- | 2<br>24 | 6<br>33 | 10<br>42 | 15<br>50 | 19<br>59 | 24<br>67 | 28<br>76 | 33<br>84 | 37<br>93 | 42<br>101 | 47<br>109 | 51<br>118 | 56<br>126 | 61<br>134 | 65<br>143 | 70<br>151 | 75<br>159 | 80<br>167 | 84<br>176 |
| 14 | -- | 2<br>26 | 7<br>35 | 11<br>45 | 16<br>54 | 21<br>63 | 26<br>72 | 31<br>81 | 36<br>90 | 41<br>99 | 46<br>108 | 51<br>117 | 56<br>126 | 61<br>135 | 66<br>144 | 71<br>153 | 77<br>161 | 82<br>170 | 87<br>179 | 92<br>188 |
| 15 | -- | 3<br>27 | 7<br>38 | 12<br>48 | 18<br>57 | 23<br>67 | 28<br>77 | 33<br>87 | 39<br>96 | 44<br>106 | 50<br>115 | 55<br>125 | 61<br>134 | 66<br>144 | 72<br>153 | 77<br>163 | 83<br>172 | 88<br>182 | 94<br>191 | 100<br>200 |
| 16 | -- | 3<br>29 | 8<br>40 | 14<br>50 | 19<br>61 | 25<br>71 | 30<br>82 | 36<br>92 | 42<br>102 | 48<br>112 | 54<br>122 | 60<br>132 | 65<br>143 | 71<br>153 | 77<br>163 | 83<br>173 | 89<br>183 | 95<br>193 | 101<br>203 | 107<br>213 |
| 17 | -- | 3<br>31 | 9<br>42 | 15<br>53 | 20<br>65 | 26<br>76 | 33<br>86 | 39<br>97 | 45<br>108 | 51<br>119 | 57<br>130 | 64<br>140 | 70<br>151 | 77<br>161 | 83<br>172 | 89<br>183 | 96<br>193 | 102<br>204 | 109<br>214 | 115<br>225 |
| 18 | -- | 4<br>32 | 9<br>45 | 16<br>56 | 22<br>68 | 28<br>80 | 35<br>91 | 41<br>103 | 48<br>114 | 55<br>123 | 61<br>137 | 68<br>148 | 75<br>159 | 82<br>170 | 88<br>182 | 95<br>193 | 102<br>204 | 109<br>215 | 116<br>226 | 123<br>237 |
| 19 | 0<br>19 | 4<br>34 | 10<br>47 | 17<br>59 | 23<br>72 | 30<br>84 | 37<br>96 | 44<br>108 | 51<br>120 | 58<br>132 | 65<br>144 | 72<br>156 | 80<br>167 | 87<br>179 | 94<br>191 | 101<br>203 | 109<br>214 | 116<br>226 | 123<br>238 | 130<br>250 |
| 20 | 0<br>20 | 4<br>36 | 11<br>49 | 18<br>62 | 25<br>75 | 32<br>88 | 39<br>101 | 47<br>113 | 54<br>126 | 62<br>138 | 69<br>151 | 77<br>163 | 84<br>176 | 92<br>188 | 100<br>200 | 107<br>213 | 115<br>225 | 123<br>237 | 130<br>250 | 138<br>262 |

(Dashes in the body of the table indicate that no decision is possible at the stated level of significance.)

## Table S

### Critical Values for Wilcoxon Matched-Pairs Signed-Rank Test

The symbol $T$ denotes the smaller sum of ranks associated with differences that are all of the same sign. For any given $N$ (number of ranked differences), the obtained $T$ is significant at a given level if it is equal to or *less than* the value shown in the table. All entries are for the *absolute* value of $T$.

| | Level of significance for one-tailed test | | | | | Level of significance for one-tailed test | | | |
|---|---|---|---|---|---|---|---|---|---|
| | .05 | .025 | .01 | .005 | | .05 | .025 | .01 | .005 |
| | Level of significance for two-tailed test | | | | | Level of significance for two-tailed test | | | |
| $N$ | .10 | .05 | .02 | .01 | $N$ | .10 | .05 | .02 | .01 |
| 5 | 0 | -- | -- | -- | 28 | 130 | 116 | 101 | 91 |
| 6 | 2 | 0 | -- | -- | 29 | 140 | 126 | 110 | 100 |
| 7 | 3 | 2 | 0 | -- | 30 | 151 | 137 | 120 | 109 |
| 8 | 5 | 3 | 1 | 0 | 31 | 163 | 147 | 130 | 118 |
| 9 | 8 | 5 | 3 | 1 | 32 | 175 | 159 | 140 | 128 |
| 10 | 10 | 8 | 5 | 3 | 33 | 187 | 170 | 151 | 138 |
| 11 | 13 | 10 | 7 | 5 | 34 | 200 | 182 | 162 | 148 |
| 12 | 17 | 13 | 9 | 7 | 35 | 213 | 195 | 173 | 159 |
| 13 | 21 | 17 | 12 | 9 | 36 | 227 | 208 | 185 | 171 |
| 14 | 25 | 21 | 15 | 12 | 37 | 241 | 221 | 198 | 182 |
| 15 | 30 | 25 | 19 | 15 | 38 | 256 | 235 | 211 | 194 |
| 16 | 35 | 29 | 23 | 19 | 39 | 271 | 249 | 224 | 207 |
| 17 | 41 | 34 | 27 | 23 | 40 | 286 | 264 | 238 | 220 |
| 18 | 47 | 40 | 32 | 27 | 41 | 302 | 279 | 252 | 233 |
| 19 | 53 | 46 | 37 | 32 | 42 | 319 | 294 | 266 | 247 |
| 20 | 60 | 52 | 43 | 37 | 43 | 336 | 310 | 281 | 261 |
| 21 | 67 | 58 | 49 | 42 | 44 | 353 | 327 | 296 | 276 |
| 22 | 75 | 65 | 55 | 48 | 45 | 371 | 343 | 312 | 291 |
| 23 | 83 | 73 | 62 | 54 | 46 | 389 | 361 | 328 | 307 |
| 24 | 91 | 81 | 69 | 61 | 47 | 407 | 378 | 345 | 322 |
| 25 | 100 | 89 | 76 | 68 | 48 | 426 | 396 | 362 | 339 |
| 26 | 110 | 98 | 84 | 75 | 49 | 446 | 415 | 379 | 355 |
| 27 | 119 | 107 | 92 | 83 | 50 | 466 | 434 | 397 | 373 |

Slight discrepancies will be found between the critical values appearing in the table above and those in Table 2 of the 1964 revision of F. Wilcoxon and R. A. Wilcox, *Some Rapid Approximate Statistical Procedures*, New York: Lederle Laboratories. The disparity reflects the latter's policy of selecting the critical value nearest a given significance level, occasionally overstepping that level. For example, for $N = 8$,

$$\text{the probability of a } T \text{ of } 3 = .0390 \text{ (two-tail)}$$

and

$$\text{the probability of a } T \text{ of } 4 = .0546 \text{ (two-tail)}$$

Wilcoxon and Wilcox selects a $T$ of 4 as the critical value at the 0.05 level of significance (two-tail), whereas Table J reflects a more conservative policy by setting a $T$ of 3 as the critical value at this level.

# Credits

**Table B**

Rand Corporation, *A Million Random Digits*. Glencoe, Ill. Free Press of Glencoe, 1955. Reprinted with Permission.

**Table C**

Table III of R. A. Fisher and F. Yates, *Statistical Tables for Biological, Agricultural, and Medical Research*, 6th edition. London: Longman Group, Ltd., 1974. (Previously published by Oliver and Boyd, Ltd., Edinburgh.) Reprinted with Permission.

**Table G**

E. G. Olds (1949), "The 5 Percent Significance Levels of Sums of Squares of Rank Differences and a Correction," *Ann. Math. Statist.*, 20, 117–118. Reprinted with Permission.

E. G. Olds (1938), "Distribution of Sums of Squares of Rank Difference for Small Number of Individuals," *Ann. Math. Statist.*, 9, 133–148. Reprinted with Permission.

**Table H**

Q. McNemar, Table B of *Psychological Statistics*. New York: John Wiley, 1962. Reprinted with permission of Mrs. Olga W. McNemar.

**Table J**

G. W. Snedecor and William G. Cochran, *Statistical Methods*, 7th edition. Ames, Iowa: Iowa State University Press, copyright © 1980. Reprinted with Permission.

**Table L**

E. S. Pearson and H. O. Hartley, *Biometrika Tables for Statisticians*, vol. 1, 2d ed. New York: Cambridge, 1958. Reprinted with Permission.

**Table N**

R. P. Runyon, Table B of *Nonparametric Statistics*. Reading, MA: Addison-Wesley, 1977. Reprinted with Permission.

**Table N1**

R. P. Runyon, Table A of *Nonparametric Statistics*. Reading, MA: Addison-Wesley, 1977. Reprinted with Permission.

***Table P***

S. Siegel. *Nonparametric Statistics.* New York: McGraw-Hill, 1956. Reprinted with Permission.

***Table Q***

R. A. Fisher, *Statistical Methods for Research Workers,* 14th edition. Reprinted with permission of Macmillan Publishing Company, Inc., © 1970, University of Adelaide.

***Table R***

H. B. Mann and D. R. Whitney (1947), "On a Test of Whether One of Two Random Variables Is Stochastically Larger Than the Other," *Ann. Math Statist.,* 18, 52–54.

D. Auble (1953), "Extended Tables for the Mann-Whitney Statistic," *Bulletin of the Institute of Education Research,* 1, No. 2. Reprinted with Permission.

***Table S***

F. Wilcoxon, S. Katti, and R. A. Wilcox, *Critical Values and Probability Levels for the Wilcoxon Rank Sum Test and the Wilcoxon Signed Rank Test.* New York: American Cyanamid Co., 1963. Reprinted with Permission.

F. Wilcoxon and R. A. Wilcox, *Some Rapid Approximate Statistical Procedures.* New York: Lederle Laboratories, 1964. Reprinted with Permission.

Answers to
Selected
Exercises

## CHAPTER 1

**1. a.** a statistic     **b.** an inference     **c.** data
    **d.** data     **e.** an inference

**3. a.** constant     **b.** variable     **c.** variable
    **d.** variable     **e.** constant     **f.** variable
    **g.** variable

**5.** The numbers themselves represent data. These data are used to calculate statistics.

**7.** In this study, risk-taking behavior measured by the test constitutes a variable. Each student will have a different risk-taking score.

**9.** The average test score of the undergraduates in this sample constitutes a statistic. The average organizes, summarizes, and allows us to make inferences about risk-taking behavior.

**11.** The average score obtained by all undergraduates at the school would constitute a parameter if we treated all the students as a population.

**13. a.** manipulated variable     **b.** not a variable
    **c.** not a variable     **d.** subject variable
    **e.** subject variable     **f.** manipulated variable
    **g.** manipulated variable     **h.** manipulated variable
    **i.** subject variable     **j.** subject variable

**15.** Confounding occurs when there is a variable that is correlated with the independent variable. The presence of a confounding variable prohibits us from making assumptions of cause and effect. For example, we could examine the effectiveness of two teaching methods: An early morning class gets one type of instruction whereas an evening class gets another. Because time of day is correlated with instruction method, we do not know if any differences are due to the teaching method or factors related to the time of day.

**17. a.** correlational     **b.** intact groups comparison
    **c.** true experiment     **d.** descriptive

## CHAPTER 2

**1.** Apply the rules of priority to the following:
**a.** $(6 + 4)^2 + (3 + 4)^2 = (10)^2 + (7)^2 = 100 + 49 = 149$

**b.** $(-3 + 7)^2 = (4)^2 = 16$

**c.** $3(5^2 + 2^2) = 3(25 + 4) = 3(29) = 87$

**d.** $-8(5 + 2)^2 = -8(7)^2 = -8(49) = -392$

**3.** $N = 4$

$20 + N = Y + 2$

$20 + 4 = Y + 2$

$24 = Y + 2$

$22 = Y$

**5.** $90 = \dfrac{360}{N}$     $\dfrac{360}{90} = N$     $N = 4$

**7.** $20 = s^2$     $s^2 = \dfrac{240}{12}$

**9. a.** $\sum_{i=1}^{4} X_i = 25$  **b.** $\sum_{i=1}^{7} X_i = 60$  **c.** $\sum_{i=3}^{6} X_i = 37$

**d.** $\sum_{i=2}^{5} X_i = 31$  **e.** $\sum_{i=1}^{N} X_i = 60$  **f.** $\sum_{i=4}^{N} X_i = 44$

**11. a.** $\Sigma X = 14$    **e.** $\Sigma XY = 78$
**b.** $\Sigma Y = 22$    **f.** $(\Sigma X)(\Sigma Y) = 308$
**c.** $\Sigma X^2 = 62$  **g.** $(\Sigma X)^2 = 196$
**d.** $\Sigma Y^2 = 146$  **h.** $(\Sigma Y)^2 = 484$

**13.** $3600 \neq 588$

**15. a.** ratio    **b.** ratio
**c.** nominal  **d.** ordinal

**17. a.** continuous    **b.** discontinuous
**c.** continuous    **d.** discontinuous
**e.** discontinuous

**19. a.** $4.5 - 5.5$    **b.** $4.95 - 5.05$    **c.** $4.995 - 5.005$
**d.** $0.05 - 0.15$    **e.** $-10.5 - -9.5$    **f.** $0.75 - 0.85$

**21. a.** 0.98    **b.** 1.00    **c.** 9.96    **d.** 0.00
**e.** 7.46    **f.** 1.25    **g.** $-9.14$    **h.** 10.00

**23.**

| Academic Area | Male | Female | Total |
|---|---|---|---|
| Business administration | 400 | 300 | 700 |
| Education | 50 | 150 | 200 |
| Humanities | 150 | 200 | 350 |
| Science | 250 | 300 | 550 |
| Social science | 200 | 200 | 400 |
| Total | 1050 | 1150 | 2200 |

**a.** $52.3\% = (1150/2200) \times 100$
**b.** $38.1\% = (400/1050) \times 100$
    $4.8\% = (50/1050) \times 100$
    $14.3\% = (150/1050) \times 100$
    $23.8\% = (250/1050) \times 100$
    $19.0\% = (200/1050) \times 100$
**c.** $26.1\% = (300/1150) \times 100$
    $13.0\% = (150/1150) \times 100$
    $17.4\% = (200/1150) \times 100$
    $26.1\% = (300/1150) \times 100$
    $17.4\% = (200/1150) \times 100$
**d.**

| Men | Women |
|---|---|
| $18.2\% = (400/2200) \times 100$ | $13.6\% = (300/2200) \times 100$ |
| $2.3\% = (50/2200) \times 100$ | $6.8\% = (150/2200) \times 100$ |
| $6.8\% = (150/2200) \times 100$ | $9.1\% = (200/2200) \times 100$ |
| $11.4\% = (250/2200) \times 100$ | $13.6\% = (300/2200) \times 100$ |
| $9.1\% = (200/2200) \times 100$ | $9.1\% = (200/2200) \times 100$ |

**e.** $42.9\% = (300/700) \times 100$
**f.** $45.5\% = (250/550) \times 100$

**25.**

| | CHARACTERISTICS OF TARGET | | |
|---|---|---|---|
| | **Attractive** | **Unattractive** | **Total** |
| Helped | 17 | 13 | 30 |
| Did not help | 24 | 27 | 51 |
| Total | 41 | 40 | 81 |

**a.** 37.0% = (30/81) × 100
**b.** 41.5% = (17/41) × 100—58.5% = (24/41) × 100
**c.** 32.5% = (13/40) × 100—67.5% = (27/40) × 100

# CHAPTER 3

**1. a.**

| | | |
|---|---|---|
| 4 | 06 | 2 |
| 5 | 2 | 1 |
| 6 | 013678 | 6 |
| 7 | 000456677778899 | 15 |
| 8 | 111122346778 | 12 |
| 9 | 2248 | 4 |

**b.** Highest score = 98
Lowest score = 40
**c.** As = 4   Bs = 12   Cs = 15   Ds = 6   Fs = 3
**d.** B to A = 0   C to B = 2   D to C = 0   F to D = 0
**e.** $Q_1$: 10.25 = (40 + 1) × .25
$Q_1$ = 70
$Q_2$: 20.50 = (40 + 1) × .50
$Q_2$ = 77.5
$Q_3$: 30.75 = (40 + 1) × .75
$Q_3$ = 82.5
**f.** Yes, the data appear to be negatively skewed. The "tail" of the distribution stretches toward the lower end of the scale.

**3. a. and b.**

| X | f | Cum. f | Cum. % | X | f | Cum. f | Cum. % |
|---|---|---|---|---|---|---|---|
| 90 | 1 | 90 | 100.0% | 38 | 2 | 47 | 52.2% |
| 75 | 1 | 89 | 98.9% | 37 | 4 | 45 | 50.0% |
| 67 | 1 | 88 | 97.8% | 36 | 3 | 41 | 45.6% |
| 66 | 1 | 87 | 96.7% | 35 | 1 | 38 | 42.2% |
| 65 | 1 | 86 | 95.6% | 34 | 3 | 37 | 41.1% |
| 64 | 1 | 85 | 94.4% | 33 | 2 | 34 | 37.8% |
| 63 | 1 | 84 | 93.3% | 32 | 2 | 32 | 35.6% |
| 61 | 2 | 83 | 92.2% | 31 | 2 | 30 | 33.3% |
| 59 | 2 | 81 | 90.0% | 29 | 1 | 28 | 31.1% |
| 57 | 2 | 79 | 87.8% | 28 | 1 | 27 | 30.0% |
| 56 | 2 | 77 | 85.6% | 27 | 2 | 26 | 28.9% |
| 55 | 1 | 75 | 83.3% | 26 | 2 | 24 | 26.7% |
| 54 | 2 | 74 | 82.2% | 25 | 2 | 22 | 24.4% |
| 53 | 2 | 72 | 80.0% | 24 | 1 | 20 | 22.2% |
| 52 | 1 | 70 | 77.8% | 23 | 3 | 19 | 21.1% |
| 49 | 2 | 69 | 76.7% | 20 | 1 | 16 | 17.8% |
| 47 | 1 | 67 | 74.4% | 19 | 2 | 15 | 16.7% |
| 46 | 2 | 66 | 73.3% | 17 | 2 | 13 | 14.4% |
| 45 | 6 | 64 | 71.1% | 16 | 2 | 11 | 12.2% |

*(continued)*

**3. a. and b.** *(continued)*

| | | | | | | | |
|---|---|---|---|---|---|---|---|
| 44 | 4 | 58 | 64.4% | 15 | 3 | 9 | 10.0% |
| 43 | 3 | 54 | 60.0% | 14 | 3 | 6 | 6.7% |
| 42 | 1 | 51 | 56.7% | 13 | 1 | 3 | 3.3% |
| 41 | 2 | 50 | 55.6% | 5 | 2 | 2 | 2.2% |
| 40 | 1 | 48 | 53.3% | | | | |

**c.** $Q_1 = 25.5$     $Q_2 = 37.5$     $Q_3 = 48.0$

**d.** 17.8%          **e.** 22.2%

**5. a.**

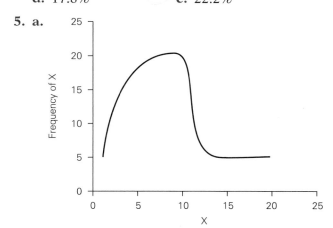

**b.**

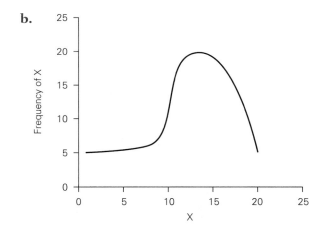

**c.**

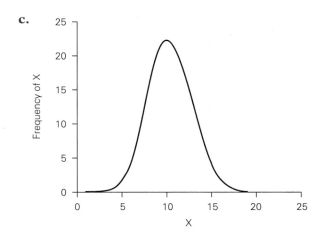

**d.**

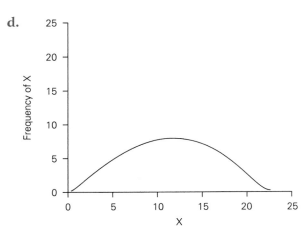

**e.**

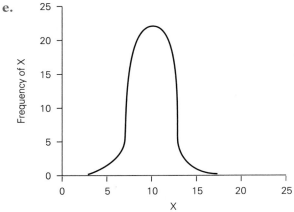

7. **a.** Annual incomes are positively skewed.
   **b.** Heights of women are normally distributed.
   **c.** Heights of men are normally distributed.
   **d.** Heights of men and women are bimodal.
   **e.** If there is a minimum IQ required for entrance into the school and no upper limit, the distribution will be positively skewed.

9. **a.**

| Year | Population | Crimes | Crime/Population × 100 |
|------|-----------|--------|------------------------|
| 1989 | 23,450 | 294 | 1.2537% |
| 1990 | 25,632 | 323 | 1.2601% |
| 1991 | 25,700 | 282 | 1.0973% |
| 1992 | 26,591 | 372 | 1.3990% |
| 1993 | 29,781 | 387 | 1.2995% |
| 1994 | 33,354 | 401 | 1.2023% |
| 1995 | 37,022 | 410 | 1.1074% |
| 1996 | 42,575 | 425 | 0.9982% |
| 1997 | 48,961 | 490 | 1.0008% |
| 1998 | 57,773 | 566 | 0.9797% |

   **b.** The headlines are not appropriate. Although the absolute number of crimes has increased, the rate of crime, as a proportion of the population has decreased. Statistically speaking, citizens are safer in 1998 than they were in 1989.
   **c.** Using the crime rate statistic is more accurate as it accounts for the number of people living in the city.

**11. a., b.**

| Total | f |
|:---:|:---:|
| 0 | 1 |
| 1 | 2 |
| 2 | 3 |
| 3 | 4 |
| 4 | 5 |
| 5 | 6 |
| 6 | 7 |
| 7 | 6 |
| 8 | 5 |
| 9 | 4 |
| 10 | 3 |
| 11 | 2 |
| 12 | 1 |

**c.** 6

# CHAPTER 4

**1.**

| $N$ | $\Sigma X$ | $\overline{X}$ | Median | Mode |
|:---:|:---:|:---:|:---:|:---:|
| 10 | 50 | 5 | 5.5 | 8 |
| 9 | 45 | 5 | 5 | 5 |
| 8 | 140 | 17.5 | 4 | 4 |

**3.** For this answer, we selected two numbers for each data set.

| | $X$ | $(X-5)^2$ | $(X-8)^2$ | $X$ | $(X-5)^2$ | $(X-8)^2$ | $X$ | $(X-17.5)^2$ | $(X-8)^2$ |
|:---:|:---:|:---:|:---:|:---:|:---:|:---:|:---:|:---:|:---:|
| | 10 | 25 | 4 | 1 | 16 | 49 | 119 | 10302.25 | 12321 |
| | 8 | 9 | 0 | 3 | 4 | 25 | 5 | 156.25 | 9 |
| | 6 | 1 | 4 | 3 | 4 | 25 | 4 | 182.25 | 16 |
| | 0 | 25 | 64 | 5 | 0 | 9 | 4 | 182.25 | 16 |
| | 8 | 9 | 0 | 5 | 0 | 9 | 4 | 182.25 | 16 |
| | 3 | 4 | 25 | 5 | 0 | 9 | 3 | 210.25 | 25 |
| | 2 | 9 | 36 | 7 | 4 | 1 | 1 | 272.25 | 49 |
| | 5 | 0 | 9 | 7 | 4 | 1 | 0 | 306.25 | 64 |
| | 8 | 9 | 0 | 9 | 16 | 1 | | | |
| | 0 | 25 | 64 | | | | | | |
| $\Sigma$ | 50 | 116 | 206 | 45 | 48 | 129 | 140 | 11794 | 12516 |

**5.** Because she divided each score by 16, a constant, the measures of central tendency will equal their original value divided by 16.

**7.**

| $X$ |
|:---:|
| 19.0 |
| 5.0 |
| 4.0 |
| 4.0 |
| 4.0 |
| 3.0 |
| 1.0 |
| 0.0 |

| | |
|---|---|
| $\Sigma X$ | 40.0 |
| $\overline{X}$ | 5.0 |
| Median | 4.0 |
| Mode | 4.0 |

**8. & 9.**
   **a.** $\overline{X} = 56$,  Median $= 62$  $\overline{X} <$ Median  therefore negative skew
   **b.** $\overline{X} = 68$,  Median $= 62$  $\overline{X} >$ Median  therefore positive skew
   **c.** $\overline{X} = 62$,  Median $= 62$  $\overline{X} =$ Median  therefore no skew, single mode
   **d.** $\overline{X} = 62$,  Median $= 62$  $\overline{X} =$ Median  therefore no skew, bimodal

**11.** There are several errors with Sam's reasoning. First, the data represent grades at Williams College collected in a specified range of years. These data may not generalize to Sam's college for the years that he will be a student. Second, the average is a measure of central tendency that describes the typical score of all students knowing nothing else about them. Is it possible that Sam is not a good student and will do poorly regardless of major?

**13.** We can assume that the distribution of scores is symmetrical.

**15.** The mean is most affected by the skew of the data. The greater the skew, the more the mean will move toward the tail end of the skew. The skew does not affect the location of the median or the mode.

**17.** **a.** price of new homes in a community: Median—controls for extremely expensive or inexpensive houses.
   **b.** yearly income: Median—controls for extremely high or low incomes.
   **c.** intelligence test scores: Mean—most psychological measures are symmetrically distributed.
   **d.** scores on an exam in an introductory course: Mean—most psychological measures are symmetrically distributed unless the course has two or more large populations (e.g., freshmen and seniors).

**19.**

| Store | $N$ | $\Sigma X$ | $\overline{X}$ | Median | Mode |
|---|---|---|---|---|---|
| Store A | 6 | 180 | 30 | 30 | 30 |
| Store B | 6 | 180 | 30 | 30 | 25, 30, 35 |
| Store C | 6 | 156 | 26 | 27.5 | 25, 30 |

**21.**

| | TYPE A MALE CONDITION | | | TYPE B MALE CONDITION | | |
|---|---|---|---|---|---|---|
| | **A** | **B** | **C** | **A** | **B** | **C** |
| $\Sigma$ | 484 | 458 | 429 | 378 | 396 | 406 |
| $N$ | 20 | 20 | 20 | 20 | 20 | 20 |
| $\overline{X}$ | 24.2 | 22.9 | 21.4 | 18.9 | 19.8 | 20.3 |

## CHAPTER 5

1.

|  | $X$ | $X + 2$ | $X - 2$ | $X \pm 2$ | $X \times 2$ | $X / 2$ |
|---|---|---|---|---|---|---|
|  | 3 | 5 | 1 | 5 | 6 | 1.5 |
|  | 4 | 6 | 2 | 2 | 8 | 2 |
|  | 5 | 7 | 3 | 7 | 10 | 2.5 |
|  | 5 | 7 | 3 | 3 | 10 | 2.5 |
|  | 6 | 8 | 4 | 8 | 12 | 3 |
|  | 7 | 9 | 5 | 5 | 14 | 3.5 |
| $\Sigma X$ | 30.0 | 42.0 | 18.0 | 30.0 | 60.0 | 15.0 |
| $\Sigma X^2$ | 160.0 | 304.0 | 64.0 | 176.0 | 640.0 | 40.0 |
| $\overline{X}$ | 5.0 | 7.0 | 3.0 | 5.0 | 10.0 | 2.5 |
| $s^2$ | 1.67 | 1.67 | 1.67 | 4.33 | 6.67 | 0.42 |
| $s$ | 1.29 | 1.29 | 1.29 | 2.08 | 2.58 | 0.65 |

Adding and subtracting a constant to all numbers has no effect on the variance and standard deviation because the relative difference among the numbers remains the same. By contrast, adding and subtracting 2 to the alternate numbers does increase the variability among the numbers and the variance and standard deviation. Multiplying each number by 2 increased the standard deviation as $2.58 = 1.29 \times 2$. Dividing each number by 2 decreased the standard deviation as $0.65 = 1.29 / 2$.

3. Adding 10 points to each score will increase the mean but not the standard deviation.

5. All the numbers in the distribution are the same value.

7. The standard deviation is large because of the one extraordinary score, 20. It is several times larger than the rest of the numbers. Therefore, its relative distance from the mean is great. The effect is that the standard deviation is large. Extremely deviant scores, scores that are much larger or smaller than the typical score, cause $s$ to be large.

9. a. Comparing students' individual grades to the mean. Calculating variability allows you to know if your score is slightly or much different from the mean.
   b. Determining the accuracy of a measurement. If the same thing is measured many times, the variance of the results should be small.
   c. Comparing two groups. Knowing which group is more variable can allow us to make useful predictions about the future.

11. $\Sigma X = 1262$
    $\Sigma X^2 = 80876$

    a. $\overline{X} = 63.1 = 1262/20$
    b. Range $= 35 = 79 - 44$
       SIR $= 4 = (67.5 - 59.5)/2$
    c. $s^2 = 62.19$, $s = 7.89$

13. a. If we compare the average rainfall among the months then the differences among each month's mean is the between-subject variance and the rainfall within each month is the within-subject variability. By contrast, if we compare the variability among the four communities, the variance among the four means is the between-subject variability, the 12 values for each community is the within-subject variability.

| Stations | Jan | Feb | Mar | Apr | May | June | July | Aug | Sept | Oct | Nov | Dec | $\overline{X}$ | $s^2$ | $s$ |
|---|---|---|---|---|---|---|---|---|---|---|---|---|---|---|---|
| Barrow | 0.2 | 0.2 | 0.1 | 0.1 | 0.1 | 0.4 | 0.8 | 0.9 | 0.6 | 0.5 | 0.2 | 0.2 | 0.36 | 0.07 | 0.27 |
| Burlington | 2.0 | 1.8 | 2.1 | 2.6 | 3.0 | 3.5 | 3.9 | 3.4 | 3.3 | 3.0 | 2.6 | 2.1 | 2.78 | 0.42 | 0.65 |
| Honolulu | 3.8 | 3.3 | 2.9 | 1.3 | 1.0 | 0.3 | 0.4 | 0.9 | 1.0 | 1.8 | 2.2 | 3 | 1.83 | 1.30 | 1.14 |
| Seattle | 5.7 | 4.2 | 3.8 | 2.4 | 1.7 | 1.6 | 0.8 | 1.0 | 2.1 | 4.0 | 5.4 | 6.3 | 3.25 | 3.33 | 1.82 |
| $\overline{X}$ | 2.92 | 2.38 | 2.22 | 1.60 | 1.45 | 1.45 | 1.48 | 1.55 | 1.75 | 2.32 | 2.60 | 2.90 | 2.05 | 1.28 | 0.97 |
| $s^2$ | 4.19 | 2.31 | 1.87 | 1.00 | 1.12 | 1.66 | 1.99 | 1.14 | 1.10 | 1.72 | 3.44 | 4.88 | 1.63 | | |
| $s$ | 2.05 | 1.52 | 1.37 | 1.00 | 1.06 | 1.29 | 1.41 | 1.07 | 1.05 | 1.31 | 1.85 | 2.21 | 1.28 | | |

   **d.** The average between-subject variability among communities is 1.28. The average between-subject variability among months is 1.63. Therefore, the variance among months is greater.
   **e.** Barrow has the most consistent rainfall. Seattle has the greatest variability.

## CHAPTER 6

**1. a.** $0.94 = \dfrac{55 - 45.2}{10.4}$   **b.** $-0.40 = \dfrac{41 - 45.2}{10.4}$   **c.** $0.00 = \dfrac{45.2 - 45.2}{10.4}$

   **d.** $-1.32 = \dfrac{31.5 - 45.2}{10.4}$   **e.** $2.23 = \dfrac{68.4 - 45.2}{10.4}$   **f.** $-2.53 = \dfrac{18.9 - 45.2}{10.4}$

**3. a. and b.**

| $X$ | $z$-score | Proportion and $N$ between Mean and $z$ | Proportion and $N$ above $z$ |
|---|---|---|---|
| 60 | $1.00 = \dfrac{60 - 50}{10}$ | .3413; 341 | .1587; 159 |
| 70 | $2.00 = \dfrac{70 - 50}{10}$ | .4772; 477 | .0228; 23 |
| 45 | $-0.50 = \dfrac{45 - 50}{10}$ | .1915; 192 | .6915; 692 |
| 25 | $-2.50 = \dfrac{25 - 50}{10}$ | .4938; 494 | .9938; 994 |
| 50 | $0.0 = \dfrac{50 - 50}{10}$ | .0000; 0 | .5000; 500 |

   **c.** 60 and 70
   $.4772 - .3413 = .1359$; $N = 136$
   25 and 60
   $.4938 + .3413 = .8351$; $N = 835$
   45 and 70
   $.1915 + .4772 = .6687$; $N = .669$
   25 and 45
   $.4938 - .1915 = .3023$; $N = 302$

**5.** Women:  $\mu = 60$   $\sigma = 10$
   Men:      $\mu = 64$   $\sigma = 8$

   **a.**      $z$-score          Percentile

   $0.20 = \dfrac{62 - 60}{10}$      57.93

   $-0.25 = \dfrac{62 - 64}{8}$      40.13

   **b.** A percentile of 73 is equivalent to a $z$-score of 0.61 for females and a raw score of 66.1. That score compared to male norms is at the 60th percentile (60.26).

$$0.26 = \frac{66.1 - 64}{8}, \text{ which is equivalent to a percentile of } 60.26.$$

**7. a.** $-0.67 = \dfrac{63.96 - 72}{12}$

    **b.** $0.67 = \dfrac{80.04 - 72}{12}$

    **c.** $1.28 = \dfrac{87.36 - 72}{12}$

    **d.** $0.67 = \dfrac{80 - 72}{12}$, 25.14%, score above

    **e.** $-0.50 = \dfrac{66 - 72}{12}$, 30.85%, score below

    **f.** $63.96 - 80.04$

    **g.** $z = \pm 1.64$, below 53.32, above 91.68

    **h.** $z = \pm 2.58$

**9.**

|  | Test I | Test II |
|---|---|---|
| $\mu$ | 500 | 24 |
| $\sigma$ | 40 | 1.4 |
| Larry's scores | 550 | 26 |
| $z$-scores | $1.25 = \dfrac{550 - 500}{40}$ | $1.43 = \dfrac{26 - 24}{1.40}$ |
| Jessica's scores | 600 | 25 |
| $z$-scores | $2.50 = \dfrac{600 - 500}{40}$ | $0.71 = \dfrac{25 - 24}{1.40}$ |

**11.** There is only one normal distribution. Although the means and standard deviations may vary, each normal distribution will have the same shape.

**13. a.** $230 = 500 + 100(-2.70)$
    **b.** $500 = 500 + 100(0.00)$
    **c.** $780 = 500 + 100(2.80)$
    **d.** $640 = 500 + 100(1.40)$
    **e.** $460 = 500 + 100(-0.40)$

**15.** The standard deviation is a measure of the typical deviation between the mean and the observed scores. The smaller the standard deviation, the closer the typical deviation score between the mean and the observed scores. Therefore, if we measure the same thing on many occasions, we would expect a highly precise measurement technique to yield similar scores and a small standard deviation.

## CHAPTER 7

**1. a.**

```
1 |
2 |
3 |
4 | 06
5 | 2
6 | 0167
7 | 00045667778899
8 | 111122346778
9 | 228
```

**b.**

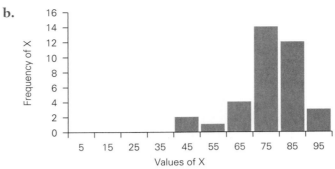

**c.**

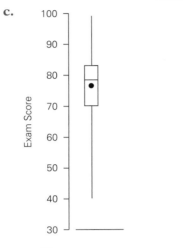

**3. a.**

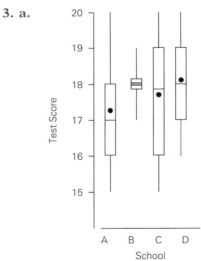

**b.** In general, students in School D did better than the other schools. School B has an extremely restricted range of scores, whereas the other schools have a broader range of scores. School C has an extremely negatively skewed distribution of performance on the test.

**5.**

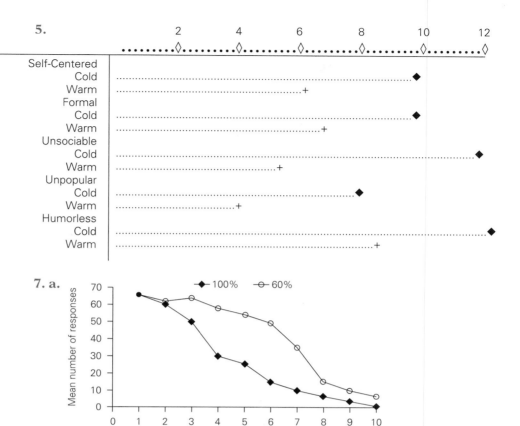

**7. a.**

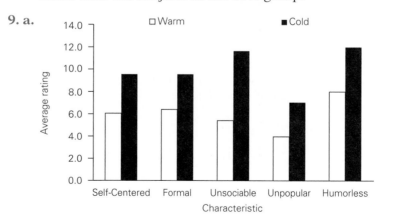

**b.** Although subjects in both groups pressed the bar less frequently as the sessions continued, the subjects in the 100% group decreased faster than the subjects in the 60% group.

**9. a.**

**b.**

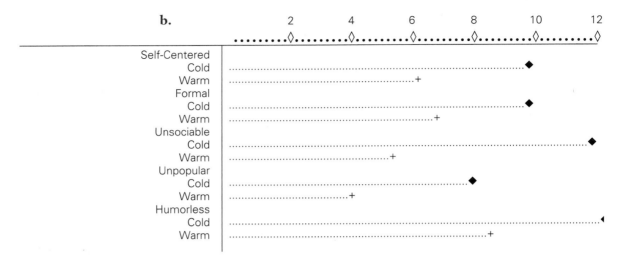

**d.** Overall, the person labeled as cold received a less flattering rating for each characteristic.

**13. a.**

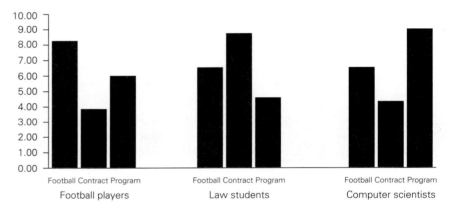

**b.** The data appear to confirm the hypothesis. That is, people with some expertise did appear to remember the material better if it was in their area of expertise.

## CHAPTER 8

1.

| Student | X | X² | Y | Y² | XY |
|---------|-----|-------|-----|-------|-------|
| A | 52 | 2704 | 49 | 2401 | 2548 |
| B | 28 | 784 | 34 | 1156 | 952 |
| C | 70 | 4900 | 45 | 2025 | 3150 |
| D | 51 | 2601 | 49 | 2401 | 2499 |
| E | 49 | 2401 | 40 | 1600 | 1960 |
| F | 65 | 4225 | 50 | 2500 | 3250 |
| G | 49 | 2401 | 37 | 1369 | 1813 |
| H | 49 | 2401 | 49 | 2401 | 2401 |
| I | 63 | 3969 | 52 | 2704 | 3276 |
| J | 32 | 1024 | 32 | 1024 | 1024 |
| K | 64 | 4096 | 53 | 2809 | 3392 |
| L | 43 | 1849 | 41 | 1681 | 1763 |
| M | 35 | 1225 | 28 | 784 | 980 |
| N | 66 | 4356 | 50 | 2500 | 3300 |
| O | 26 | 676 | 17 | 289 | 442 |
| P | 44 | 1936 | 41 | 1681 | 1804 |
| Q | 49 | 2401 | 29 | 841 | 1421 |
| R | 28 | 784 | 17 | 289 | 476 |
| S | 30 | 900 | 15 | 225 | 450 |
| T | 60 | 3600 | 55 | 3025 | 3300 |
| Σ | 953 | 49233 | 783 | 33705 | 40201 |

a.

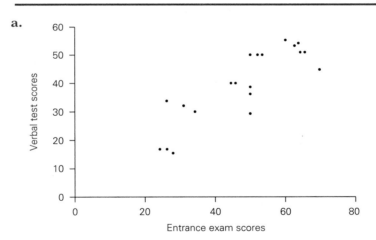

b. $r = \dfrac{\Sigma XY - \dfrac{(\Sigma X)(\Sigma Y)}{N}}{\sqrt{\left[\Sigma X^2 - \dfrac{(\Sigma X)^2}{N}\right]\left[\Sigma Y^2 - \dfrac{(\Sigma Y)^2}{N}\right]}}$

$$r = \frac{40201 - \frac{(953)(783)}{20}}{\sqrt{\left[49233 - \frac{(953)^2}{20}\right]\left[33705 - \frac{(783)^2}{20}\right]}} \qquad r = \frac{2891.05}{\sqrt{(3822.55)(3050.55)}}$$

$$r = \frac{2891.05}{\sqrt{11660879.9}} \qquad r = \frac{2891.05}{3414.8031}$$

$r = .8466$

c. $r^2 = .7168$. Variable $X$ accounts for approximately 72% of the variance in $Y$.

d. Yes, the large correlation indicates that one can make fair predictions from X to Y.

3.

| | GPA | $X^2$ | Salary ($) | $Y^2$ | XY |
|---|---|---|---|---|---|
| | 2.0 | 4.0 | 18 | 324 | 36 |
| | 2.1 | 4.4 | 22 | 484 | 46.2 |
| | 2.1 | 4.4 | 25 | 625 | 52.5 |
| | 2.1 | 4.4 | 26 | 676 | 54.6 |
| | 2.7 | 7.3 | 27 | 729 | 72.9 |
| | 2.0 | 4.0 | 28 | 784 | 56 |
| | 2.0 | 4.0 | 28 | 784 | 56 |
| | 2.9 | 8.4 | 30 | 900 | 87 |
| | 2.3 | 5.3 | 31 | 961 | 71.3 |
| | 2.6 | 6.8 | 31 | 961 | 80.6 |
| | 2.1 | 4.4 | 32 | 1,024 | 67.2 |
| | 2.2 | 4.8 | 35 | 1,225 | 77 |
| | 3.4 | 11.6 | 38 | 1,444 | 129.2 |
| | 3.1 | 9.6 | 36 | 1,296 | 111.6 |
| | 3.2 | 10.2 | 38 | 1,444 | 121.6 |
| | 3.4 | 11.6 | 39 | 1,521 | 132.6 |
| | 3.8 | 14.4 | 42 | 1,764 | 159.6 |
| | 3.2 | 10.2 | 45 | 2,025 | 144 |
| | 3.0 | 9.0 | 49 | 2,401 | 147 |
| $\Sigma$ | 50.2 | 138.8 | 620.0 | 21372.0 | 1702.9 |

a.

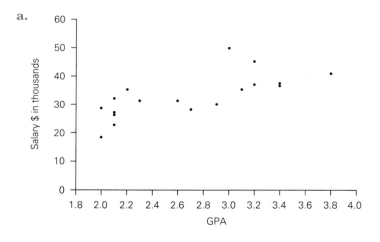

**b.**
$$r = \frac{1702.9 - \frac{(50.2)(620)}{19}}{\sqrt{\left[138.8 - \frac{(50.2)^2}{19}\right]\left[21372 - \frac{(620)^2}{19}\right]}}$$

$$r = \frac{64.7947}{\sqrt{(6.1663)(1140.4211)}} \quad r = \frac{64.7947}{\sqrt{7032.1786}}$$

$$r = \frac{64.7947}{83.8581}$$

$$r = .7727$$

**c.** $r^2 = .5971$. Variable $X$ accounts for almost 60% of the variance in $Y$.

**d.** Yes, the strong correlation indicates that one can make fair predictions from $X$ to $Y$.

**5. a.** Data may be curvilinear.

  **b.** Using honor students may restrict the range of scores for grades and test scores.

  **c.** The scores may be restricted in range because of the population sampled.

  **d.** There are two problems here. First, men and women earn different incomes. Therefore, mixing the populations will confuse the data analysis. Second, the range of age is relatively narrow and may reduce the correlation.

**7. a.** Test 3, $r = -.410$; $r^2 = .1681$

  **b.** $.1682 \times 2 = .3362$; $r = .5798$

  **c.** They ask the same types of questions.

**9. a.**

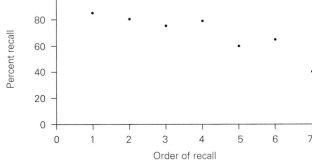

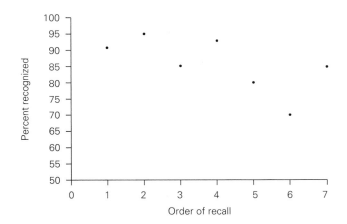

**b.**

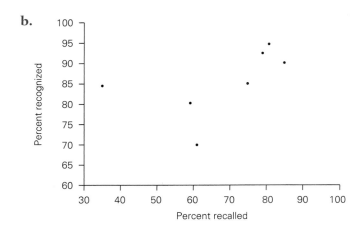

9. **c.**

| Dwarf | Order of Recall X | Rank % Recalled Y | D | D² |
|---|---|---|---|---|
| Sleepy | 1 | 7 | −6 | 36 |
| Dopey | 2 | 6 | −4 | 16 |
| Grumpy | 3 | 4 | −1 | 1 |
| Sneezy | 4 | 5 | −1 | 1 |
| Doc | 5 | 2 | 3 | 9 |
| Happy | 6 | 3 | 3 | 9 |
| Bashful | 7 | 1 | 6 | 36 |
| Σ | 28 | 28 | 0 | 108 |

$$r_S = 1 - \frac{6(108)}{7(7^2 - 1)}$$

$$r_S = 1 - \frac{648}{336}$$

$$r_S = -.9286$$

| Dwarf | X | Y | D | D² |
|---|---|---|---|---|
| Sleepy | 1 | 5 | −4 | 16 |
| Dopey | 2 | 7 | −5 | 25 |
| Grumpy | 3 | 4 | −1 | 1 |
| Sneezy | 4 | 6 | −2 | 4 |
| Doc | 5 | 2 | 3 | 9 |
| Happy | 6 | 1 | 5 | 25 |
| Bashful | 7 | 3 | 4 | 16 |
| Σ | 28 | 28 | 0 | 96 |

$$r_S = 1 - \frac{6(96)}{7(7^2 - 1)}$$

$$r_S = 1 - \frac{576}{336}$$

$$r_S = -.7143$$

| Dwarf | % Recalled | X² | % Recognized | Y² | XY |
|---|---|---|---|---|---|
| Sleepy | 86 | 7396 | 91 | 8281 | 7826 |
| Dopey | 81 | 6561 | 95 | 9025 | 7695 |
| Grumpy | 75 | 5625 | 86 | 7396 | 6450 |
| Sneezy | 78 | 6084 | 93 | 8649 | 7254 |
| Doc | 58 | 3364 | 80 | 6400 | 4640 |
| Happy | 62 | 3844 | 70 | 4900 | 4340 |
| Bashful | 38 | 1444 | 84 | 7056 | 3192 |
| Σ | 478 | 34318 | 599 | 51707 | 41397 |

$$r = \frac{41397 - \frac{(478)(599)}{7}}{\sqrt{\left[34318 - \frac{(478)^2}{7}\right]\left[51707 - \frac{(599)^2}{7}\right]}}$$

$$r = \frac{493.8571}{\sqrt{(1677.4286)(449.7143)}}$$

$$r = \frac{493.8571}{868.5411}$$

$$r = .5686$$

**d.** There is a strong relation between order of recall and the other measures of recall. In general, Sleepy is the most remembered dwarf by all measures. By contrast, Bashful is the least likely to be remembered.

**11. a.**

| Feeling | Hairdressers | Bartenders | D | D² |
|---|---|---|---|---|
| Gratified | 1 | 4 | −3 | 9 |
| Sympathetic | 2 | 3 | −1 | 1 |
| Encouraging | 3 | 1 | 2 | 4 |
| Supportive | 4 | 2 | 2 | 4 |
| Puzzled | 5 | 7 | −2 | 4 |
| Helpless | 6 | 5.5 | 0.5 | 0.25 |
| Uncomfortable | 7 | 9 | −2 | 4 |
| Bored | 8 | 8 | 0 | 0 |
| Trapped | 9.5 | 5.5 | 4 | 16 |
| Depressed | 9.5 | 10 | −0.5 | 0.25 |
| Angry | 11 | 11 | 0 | 0 |
| Σ | 66 | 66 | 0 | 42.5 |

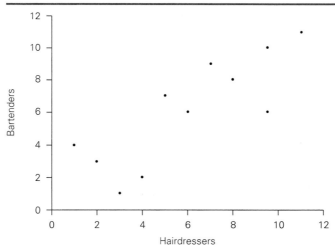

**b.** Whereas there was a low correlation represented between problems discussed, there is a stronger correlation represented between reactions.

**c., d.** $r_S = 1 - \frac{6(42.5)}{11(11^2 - 1)}$, $r_S = .8068$: The hairdressers and bartenders tend to have similar reactions.

**e.** Although people may talk about different things with hairdressers and bartenders, both occupations have similar reactions to having people share their problems.

**13.** Stuart needs to recognize that we don't know which factor came first, the anxiety or the health problems. Because the data were probably recorded at the same time, we cannot be sure whether the anxiety caused the health problems or if the health problems caused the anxiety.

**15.** $r = 41.3/50 = .826$

## CHAPTER 9

**1.**

| | Age | $X^2$ | Responses | $Y^2$ | XY |
|---|---|---|---|---|---|
| | 2 | 4 | 11 | 121 | 22 |
| | 4 | 16 | 10 | 100 | 40 |
| | 5 | 25 | 11 | 121 | 55 |
| | 6 | 36 | 10 | 100 | 60 |
| | 7 | 49 | 12 | 144 | 84 |
| | 9 | 81 | 7 | 49 | 63 |
| | 11 | 121 | 6 | 36 | 66 |
| | 12 | 144 | 5 | 25 | 60 |
| | 3 | 9 | 12 | 144 | 36 |
| | 4 | 16 | 14 | 196 | 56 |
| | 5 | 25 | 9 | 81 | 45 |
| | 7 | 49 | 7 | 49 | 49 |
| | 9 | 81 | 8 | 64 | 72 |
| | 10 | 100 | 3 | 9 | 30 |
| | 11 | 121 | 5 | 25 | 55 |
| | 12 | 144 | 3 | 9 | 36 |
| Σ | 117 | 1021 | 133 | 1273 | 829 |

**a.**

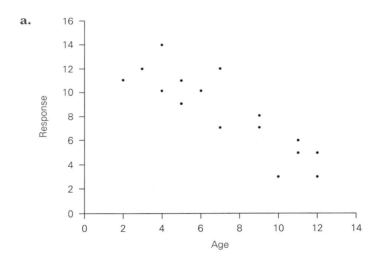

**b.** There appears to be a strong negative correlation. As age increases, the number of irrelevant responses decreases.

**c.** Yes, these data appear to fit the researcher's expectation.

**d.** $r = \dfrac{829 - \dfrac{(117)(133)}{16}}{\sqrt{\left[1021 - \dfrac{(117)^2}{16}\right]\left[1273 - \dfrac{(133)^2}{16}\right]}}$

$r = -.8626$

e. $r^2 = .7441$. Approximately 74% of the variance in responses can be predicted by age.

f. $b_Y = r_{XY}\left(\dfrac{s_Y}{s_X}\right)$ $\qquad b_Y = -.8626\left(\dfrac{3.2349}{3.2156}\right)$

$b_Y = -0.8678$

$a_Y = \overline{Y} - b_Y\overline{X}$ $\qquad a_Y = 8.3125 - -08678(7.3125)$

$a_Y = 14.6583$

g. $Y' = 14.6583 + -0.8678(X)$ $Y' = 14.6583 + -0.8678(8)$

$Y' = 7.7159$

$Y' = 7.7$ rounded to 8 as this is a discrete variable.

3. $\overline{X} = 49.0$ $\qquad\qquad\qquad \overline{Y} = 2.85$

$s_X = 12.0$ $\qquad\qquad\qquad s_Y = 0.50$

$\qquad\qquad r = .36$

$\qquad\qquad N = 60$

a. $b_Y = r_{XY}\left(\dfrac{s_Y}{s_X}\right)$ $\qquad b_Y = .36\left(\dfrac{0.50}{12}\right)$

$b_Y = 0.0150$

$a_Y = \overline{Y} - b_Y\overline{X}$ $\qquad a_Y = 2.85 - 0.0150(49.0)$

$a_Y = 2.115$

b.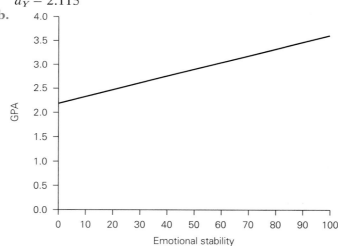

c. $Y' = 2.115 + .015(X)$ $\qquad Y' = 2.115 + .015(65)$

$Y' = 3.09$

d. $s_{\text{est } Y} = s_Y\sqrt{\dfrac{N(1 - r^2)}{N-2}}$ $\qquad s_{\text{est } Y} = .50\sqrt{\dfrac{60(1 - .36^2)}{60 - 2}}$

$s_{\text{est } Y} = 0.4745$

e. $r^2 = .1296$. The $X$-variable accounts for approximately 13% of the variance in the $Y$-variable.

5. For each of the following data sets, what is the slope of the regression line?

|  | a. $r = .30$ | b. $r = -.60$ | c. $r = .25$ | d. $r = -.80$ |
|---|---|---|---|---|
|  | $s_X = 3.5$ | $s_X = 8.4$ | $s_X = 2.0$ | $s_X = 12.0$ |
|  | $s_Y = 3.4$ | $s_Y = 9.1$ | $s_Y = 6.0$ | $s_Y = 3.0$ |

$b_Y = .30\left(\dfrac{3.4}{3.5}\right)$ $\quad b_Y = -.60\left(\dfrac{9.1}{8.4}\right)$ $\quad b_Y = .25\left(\dfrac{6.0}{2.0}\right)$ $\quad b_Y = -.80\left(\dfrac{3.0}{12.0}\right)$

$b_Y = .2914$ $\qquad b_Y = -0.6500$ $\qquad b_Y = 0.7500$ $\qquad b_Y = -0.2000$

e. First, the sign of the slope reflects the sign of the correlation; when the correlation is negative, the slope is negative. Second, the magnitude of the slope is the function of the ratio of the size of the standard deviation of $Y$ to the standard deviation of $X$ and the correlation coefficient.

f. Only the correlation reflects the magnitude of the relation between the two variables. Because the slope reflects the combined effects of the correlation and the standard deviation, the slope alone does not represent the relation between the two variables.

7. **i. a.** $r = .00$      $0 + .00(1.5) = 0.00$
    **b.** $r = .40$      $0 + .40(1.5) = 0.60$
    **c.** $r = .80$      $0 + .80(1.5) = 1.20$
    **d.** $r = .97$      $0 + .97(1.5) = 1.46$
    **e.** $r = .60$      $0 + .60(1.5) = 0.90$

**ii.** Correlation $a$, $r = 0$.

**iii.** The smaller the correlation, the greater the regression to the mean.

9. $b_Y = 0.40\left(\dfrac{0.40}{25.0}\right)$    $b_Y = 0.0064$    $a_Y = 2.95 - 0.0064(500)$    $a_Y = -0.25$

$Y' = -0.25 + 0.0064(X)$

$s_{\text{est } Y} = 0.40\sqrt{\dfrac{2500(1 - .40^2)}{2500 - 2}}$    $s_{\text{est } Y} = 0.3668$

**a.** 3.014

**b.** $1.324 = \dfrac{3.5 - 3.014}{0.3668}$, $p = .0934$. There is a 9.34% chance that the GPA will be 3.5 or greater.

**c.** $2.000 = -0.25 + 0.0064(351.5625)$ Test score should be 352.

**d.** $1.67 = -0.25 + 0.0064(300.0)$

   $0.8997 = \dfrac{2.0 - 1.67}{0.3668}$, $p = .1841$. There is a 18.41% chance that the GPA will be 2.00 or greater.

**e.** $3.27 = -0.25 + 0.0064(550.0)$

   $-3.46 = \dfrac{2.0 - 3.27}{0.3668}$, $p = .0002$. There is a 0.02% chance that the GPA will be less than 2.00.

**f.** $3.40 = -0.25 + 0.0064(570.31)$ Test score should be 570.

11. This is a good example of a post hoc fallacy. We know that the two variables are related, but we cannot use the data to infer that the moon causes lunacy. There may be other explanations. For example, the research could have been done during the summer when, coincidentally, the temperature rose as the moon became full. If true, we cannot be sure whether it was the heat or the moon that caused the calls to the 911 line.

13. This is an example of post hoc fallacy. There may be other variables besides education that account for these data. Perhaps students who stay in school longer are more likely to live in a social and economic environment that allows a person to achieve financial success without resorting to crime. In other words, it is not the education that "causes" the person's chances of becoming a criminal, but the environment in which he or she was raised.

15. When the correlation is .20, there is little relation between the two measures. Therefore, there is a good chance that if he took the test again he could obtain a better score. On the other hand, if the correlation is high then there is little regression to the mean. Under such circumstances, there is less chance that his score will increase.

# CHAPTER 10

1. Mr. Smyth is not correct to assume that the next child will be a girl. The sex of each child is independent of the others. Therefore, the next child is equally likely to be a boy or girl. Mr. Smyth shows us an example of the gambler's fallacy when he assumes that the next child has to be a girl.

3. This is an example of the "man-who" statistic. Denise is using a single example to attempt to counter a statistical generalization. Her biology professor used statistics to describe population statistics. The generalization holds true when considering the general trends in the population.

5. **a.** The following table presents the original data. The percentage column represents the probability of selecting a student from each of the four schools.

| School | Frequency | Percent |
|---|---|---|
| College of Arts and Sciences | 12,546 | 36.94% |
| College of Business | 8,534 | 25.13% |
| College of Education | 2,543 | 7.49% |
| College of Engineering | 10,343 | 30.45% |
| Total | 33,966 | 100.00% |

   **b.** A simple random sampling procedure would allow each student to have an equal probability of being selected. The registrar could use a random number table to generate numbers corresponding with the students' position in an alphabetical list. The simple random sample procedure will not guarantee that each college will be equally represented.
   **c.** This procedure is called sequential selection. The procedure is easy to conduct and is generally considered to produce a random selection. Although easy to use, the procedure does not guarantee a random sample nor does it guarantee that each college will be equally represented.
   **d.** To use a stratified procedure, the registrar would select students in proportion to the size of the college. For example, the registrar would select 37% of the sample from the College of Arts of Sciences.

7. **a.** $p(W) = .3333$.   $p(W \text{ and } W) = .3333 \times .3333$   $p(W \text{ and } W) = .1111$
   **b.** $p(R) = .3333$.   $p(R \text{ and } R) = .3333 \times .3333$   $p(R \text{ and } R) = .1111$
   $p(W) = .3333$.   $p(W \text{ and } W) = .3333 \times .3333$   $p(W \text{ and } W) = .1111$
   $p(B) = .3333$.   $p(B \text{ and } B) = .3333 \times .3333$   $p(B \text{ and } B) = .1111$
   $p(W \text{ and } W, \text{ or } R \text{ and } R, \text{ or } B \text{ and } B) = .1111 + .1111 + .1111$
   The probability of two of the same color is .3333.
   **c.** $p(R \text{ and } W) = .3333 \times .3333$   $p(R \text{ and } W) = .1111$

9.

|  | Normal | Unattractive | Total |
|---|---|---|---|
| Helped | 19 | 13 | 32 |
| Did not help | 22 | 27 | 49 |
| Total | 41 | 40 | 81 |

### JOINT PROBABILITIES

|  | Normal | Unattractive |  |
|---|---|---|---|
| Helped | .2346 | .1605 | .3951 |
| Did not help | .2716 | .3333 | .6049 |
|  | .5062 | .4938 | 1.0000 |

### CONDITIONAL PROBABILITIES: B|A

|  | Normal | Unattractive |  |
|---|---|---|---|
| Helped | .4634 | .3250 |  |
| Did not help | .5366 | .6750 |  |
|  | 1.0000 | 1.0000 |  |

### CONDITIONAL PROBABILITIES: A|B

|  | Normal | Unattractive |  |
|---|---|---|---|
| Helped | .5938 | .4063 | 1.0000 |
| Did not help | .4490 | .5510 | 1.0000 |

**11.**

|  | Sexual Abuse | No Sexual Abuse | Total |
|---|---|---|---|
| Physical abuse | 12 | 36 | 48 |
| No physical abuse | 23 | 27 | 50 |
| Total | 35 | 63 | 98 |

### JOINT PROBABILITIES

|  | Sexual Abuse | No Sexual Abuse |  |
|---|---|---|---|
| Physical abuse | .1224 | .3673 | .4898 |
| No physical abuse | .2347 | .2755 | .5102 |
|  | .3571 | .6429 | 1.0000 |

### CONDITIONAL PROBABILITIES: B|A

|  | Sexual Abuse | No Sexual Abuse |  |
|---|---|---|---|
| Physical abuse | .3429 | .5714 |  |
| No physical abuse | .6571 | .4286 |  |
|  | 1.0000 | 1.0000 |  |

### CONDITIONAL PROBABILITIES: A|B

|  | Sexual Abuse | No Sexual Abuse |  |
|---|---|---|---|
| Physical abuse | .2500 | .7500 | 1.0000 |
| No physical abuse | .4600 | .5400 | 1.0000 |

**13. a.** There is a 20% probability that a person will have Type A blood.
   **b.** $p(A \text{ and } A) = .2 \times .2 = .04$
   **c.** $p(\text{not } A) = 1 - .20 = .80$
   **d.** $p(\text{not } A \text{ and not } A) = .8 \times .8 = .64$

**15. a.** .1960, .516, .114, .086, .042, .036, .006, .004
   **b. i.** .804
       **ii.** .196
       **iii.** .630
   **c.** 1.41
   **d.** The data have a positive skew.

**17.**

| Number of Changes | Frequency | Proportion of Total |
|---|---|---|
| 0 | 1 | 0.0080 |
| 1 | 5 | 0.0400 |
| 2 | 35 | 0.2800 |
| 3 | 45 | 0.3600 |
| 4 | 23 | 0.1840 |
| 5 | 12 | 0.0960 |
| 6 | 3 | 0.0240 |
| 7 | 1 | 0.0080 |
| | 125 | 1.0000 |

   **b.** $p(X \geq 3) = .3600 + .1840 + .0960 + .0240 + .0080$
       $p(X \geq 3) = .672$
   **c.** $p(X \leq 2) = .0080 + .0040 + .2800$
       $p(X \leq 2) = .2920$
   **d.** $p(2 \geq X < 4) = .2800 + .3600 + .1840$
       $p(2 \geq X < 4) = .824$
   **e.** $387/125 = 3.096$
   **f.** The data have a slight positive skew.

**18. a.** .3413       **b.** .4505       **c.** .0495
     **d.** .8413       **e.** .0250       **f.** .9750
     **g.** .6826       **h.** .9010       **i.** .9500

**20. a.** −1.960       **b.** −0.675       **c.** 0.84
     **d.** 1.65        **e.** −0.675—0.675       **f.** −1.96—1.96

**22. a.** .9987        **b.** .0228       **c.** .975
     **d.** .1587       **e.** .5000       **f.** .025

**24. a.** .0838        **b.** 126.4       **c.** .4714
     **d.** .0070, .2222, .0395       **e.** 120.48

**26. a.** .0228        **b.** 48.66       **c.** 50.00
     **d.** 52.56       **e.** 53.28       **f.** .9544
     **g.** $.0228^2 = .00052$       **h.** $.9544^2 = .91088$
     **i.** $1.04 = \dfrac{X - 50}{2.0}$, $X = 52.08$

# CHAPTER 11

**1.** First, we use the descriptive statistics to infer the value of the parameters of the population. We assume that the sample is representative of the population and therefore the statistical summaries will represent the parameters. Second, we can use sample statistics to determine if specific characteristics are different from the population parameters. In these situations, we know or can estimate the population parameters, and want to know if the difference between the parameters and the samples are greater than expected by chance. Finally, we use sample statistics to determine if the difference between two samples is greater than we would expect by chance. In all cases, we say that the inferences are conditional because we use random sampling from the population to create the samples. Therefore, each time we create a sample, we will obtain slightly different statistics.

3. For a point estimate, we use a sample statistic to infer the value of a population parameter. For an interval estimate, we use the sample statistic to estimate a range of potential values that could occur if one were to continue to sample from the population.

5. **a.** $p(5) = .246$    **b.** $p(3) = .117$
   **c.** $p(\leq 3) = .172$    **d.** $p(0) = .001$
   **e.** $p(\geq 7) = .172$    **f.** $p(10) = .001$

*p.268*

7. The sampling distribution of means is normally distributed. The mean of the sampling distribution will equal the mean of the population. The standard deviation of the sampling distribution will equal the standard deviation of the population divided by the square root of the sample size.

9. **a.** The standard deviation of the sampling distribution will decrease by the square root of $N$.
   **b.** The distribution will "fill-in" as a normal distribution.

11. **a.** .6836    **b.** .9544
    **c.** .0228    **d.** .0668

13. One cannot "prove" the null hypothesis or the lack of a difference between two groups, especially on the basis of one set of samples. All that we can infer is there is insufficient evidence to reject the hypothesis that there is no difference.

15. Yes, the two hypotheses differ. For the one-tailed test we use the algebraic expressions "<" or ">". When determining whether to reject the null hypothesis, the magnitude of the test and its sign must conform to the expected difference. For the two-tailed test, we use the algebraic expression "$\neq$". To reject the null hypothesis in favor of the alternative, only the magnitude of the statistic must be considered.

17. $H_0: \mu_1 = \mu_2$    $H_1: \mu_1 \neq \mu_2$

19. $H_0: \rho = 0$    $H_1: \rho \neq 0$

21. .05

23. Correct Decision

25. Correct Decision

27. The purpose of research is to collect data. We sample data from the population. Our goal is to collect data that show that the null hypothesis is not correct. If we reject the null hypothesis, we can be confident in its alternative statement.

# CHAPTER 12

1. The relation between $\sigma^2$ and $s^2$ is $\sigma^2 \cong \dfrac{N}{N-1} s^2$. When the sample size is small, $s^2$ will underestimate $\sigma^2$. If we divide the sum of squares by $N - 1$, we will have an unbiased estimate of the population variance.

**3.** The term $\hat{s}$ is the unbiased estimate of the population parameter, $\sigma$. The term $s_{\bar{X}}$ is an estimate of $\sigma_{\bar{X}}$. We calculate $s_{\bar{X}}$ as $s_{\bar{X}} = \dfrac{\hat{s}}{\sqrt{n}}$. The term $s$ represents the sample version of the standard deviation. We use $N$ in the denominator to calculate $s$ and $n - 1$ to determine $\hat{s}$.

**5. a.** The term $s^2$ is a biased estimate of $\sigma^2$.

   **b.** The term $s^2$ is an unbiased estimate of $\sigma^2$.

**7.** We use the $z$-score when we know the value of $\sigma$. We use the $t$-ratio when we must estimate $\sigma$ using $\hat{s}$.

**9.** $H_0$: $\mu_{\bar{X}} = \mu_0$

   $H_1$: $\mu_{\bar{X}} \neq \mu_0$

**11.**

| $df$ | $t_{\text{critical}}$ |
|------|-----------------------|
| 10   | 2.228                 |
| 15   | 2.131                 |
| 20   | 2.086                 |
| 25   | 2.060                 |

**13. a.** $t_{\text{critical}} = 2.131$ : $t_{\text{observed}} < t_{\text{critical}}$ therefore do not reject $H_0$.
   **b.** $t_{\text{critical}} = 2.131$ : $t_{\text{observed}} > t_{\text{critical}}$ therefore reject $H_0$.
   **c.** $t_{\text{critical}} = 1.753$ : $t_{\text{observed}} > t_{\text{critical}}$ therefore reject $H_0$.
   **d.** $t_{\text{critical}} = 2.602$ : $t_{\text{observed}} > t_{\text{critical}}$ therefore reject $H_0$.

**15.** $t = \dfrac{82 - 78}{\dfrac{7}{\sqrt{22 - 1}}}$ $\quad t = \dfrac{4}{\dfrac{7}{4.5826}}$ $\quad t = \dfrac{4}{1.5275}$ $\quad t = 2.619, df = 21$

   $t_{\text{critical}} = 2.831$
   $t_{\text{observed}} < t_{\text{critical}}$ therefore do not reject $H_0$.

**17.** $z = \dfrac{3.1 - 2.1}{\dfrac{0.50}{\sqrt{27}}}$ $\quad z = \dfrac{1.0}{\dfrac{0.50}{5.1962}}$ $\quad z = \dfrac{1.0}{.0962}$ $\quad z = 10.39$

   $z_{\text{critical}} = 2.32$
   $z_{\text{observed}} > z_{\text{critical}}$ therefore reject $H_0$.

**19.** $t = \dfrac{29.61 - 32.11}{\dfrac{6.00}{\sqrt{25}}}$ $\quad t = \dfrac{-2.50}{\dfrac{6.00}{5.0}}$ $\quad t = \dfrac{-2.5}{1.2}$ $\quad t = -2.08, df = 25$

   $t_{\text{critical}} = 2.485$
   $t_{\text{observed}} < t_{\text{critical}}$ therefore do not reject $H_0$.

**21.** $r_{\text{critical}} = .6319$. Because $.31 < r_{\text{critical}}$ do not reject $H_0$.

**23.** As the sample size increases, the criterion needed to reject $H_0$: $\rho = 0$ decreases.

**25. a.** $z = \dfrac{z_r - Z_r}{\sqrt{\dfrac{1}{(N - 3)}}}$ $\quad z = \dfrac{.604 - .460}{\sqrt{\dfrac{1}{(52 - 3)}}}$ $\quad z = \dfrac{.144}{\sqrt{0.0204}}$

   $z = \dfrac{.144}{.1428}$
   $z = 1.01$
   $z_{\text{critical}} = 1.96$
   Do not reject $H_0$.

**b.** $z = \dfrac{z_r - Z_r}{\sqrt{\dfrac{1}{(N - 3)}}}$ $\qquad z = \dfrac{.709 - .460}{\sqrt{\dfrac{1}{(67 - 3)}}}$ $\qquad z = \dfrac{.249}{\sqrt{0.0156}}$

$z = \dfrac{.249}{.1249}$

$z = 1.99$

$z_{\text{critical}} = 1.96$

Reject $H_0$.

**27.** $r_{S \text{ critical}} = .400 = (.409 + .392)/2$; do not reject $H_0$.

**29.** CI $= 45 \pm 2.131 \times 2.2$, CI $= 45 \pm 4.688$, CI $= 40.312$ to $49.688$

**31.** The issue has to do with sample size. As a generality, the larger the sample, the lower the critical value for rejecting the null hypothesis. In this example the sample size was too small to allow $r = .337$ to reject the null hypothesis. The published correlations, which were statistically significant, had large sample sizes.

**33–39.**

| Problem: | 33 | 35 | 37 | 39 |
|---|---|---|---|---|
| $\Sigma X$ | 60 | 105 | 200 | 180 |
| $n$ | 6 | 7 | 8 | 9 |
| $\overline{X}$ | 10.00 | 15.00 | 25.00 | 20.00 |
| $\hat{s}$ | 2.00 | 3.00 | 2.00 | 3.00 |
| $\mu_0$ | 12.00 | 20.00 | 23.00 | 17.00 |
| $t_{\text{observed}}$ | −2.45 | −4.41 | 2.83 | 3.00 |
| $t_{\text{critical}}$ | 2.015 | 2.45 | 2.36 | 1.83 |
| Reject $H_0$ | Yes | Yes | Yes | No |

| Problem: | 41 | 43 | 45 | 47 |
|---|---|---|---|---|
| $1 - \beta$ | .08 | .82 | .22 | .34 |

# CHAPTER 13

**1.**

| | | $t_{\text{critical}}$ | decision |
|---|---|---|---|
| **a.** | $t = 1.78$, $df = 15$, $\alpha = .05$, two-tailed | **2.131** | **Fail to reject $H_0$** |
| **b.** | $t = 2.18$, $df = 15$, $\alpha = .05$, two-tailed | **2.131** | **Reject $H_0$** |
| **c.** | $t = 1.90$, $df = 15$, $\alpha = .05$, one-tailed | **1.753** | **Reject $H_0$** |
| **d.** | $t = 1.90$, $df = 15$, $\alpha = .01$, one-tailed | **2.602** | **Fail to reject $H_0$** |

**3.** $t = \dfrac{82.0 - 77.0}{\sqrt{\dfrac{384.16 + 1536.64}{25(25 - 1)}}}$ $\qquad t = \dfrac{5.0}{\sqrt{\dfrac{1920.80}{600}}}$ $\qquad t = \dfrac{5.0}{1.7892}$ $\qquad t_{\text{observed}} = 2.795$

$df = 25 + 25 - 2 \qquad df = 48$

$t_{\text{critical}} = 2.68$ (determined by interpolation)

$t_{\text{observed}} > t_{\text{critical}}$ therefore reject $H_0$.

**5.**

| | Large Target | Small Target |
|---|---|---|
| $\Sigma X$ | 40 | 37 |
| $\Sigma X^2$ | 326 | 279 |

$$t = \frac{8.0 - 7.4}{\sqrt{\dfrac{326 - \dfrac{40^2}{5} + 279 - \dfrac{37^2}{5}}{5(5-1)}}} \qquad t = \frac{0.60}{\sqrt{\dfrac{6 + 5.2}{20}}} \qquad t = \frac{0.60}{\sqrt{0.560}} \qquad t = \frac{0.60}{0.7483}$$

$t_{\text{observed}} = 0.802$

$df = 5 + 5 - 2 \; df = 8$

$t_{\text{critical}} = 2.306$

$t_{\text{observed}} < t_{\text{critical}}$ therefore fail to reject $H_0$.

**7.** $t = \dfrac{17.8196 - 19.5903}{\sqrt{\dfrac{198503 - \dfrac{10371^2}{582} + 427764 - \dfrac{20609^2}{1052}}{582 + 1052 - 2}\left(\dfrac{1}{582} + \dfrac{1}{1052}\right)}}$

$t = \dfrac{-1.7707}{\sqrt{\dfrac{13696.0567 + 24027.4211}{1632}(.0017 + .00095)}}$

$$t = \frac{-1.7707}{\sqrt{23.1149(.00265)}} \qquad t = \frac{-1.7707}{\sqrt{0.06125}} \qquad t = \frac{-1.7707}{0.2475}$$

$t_{\text{observed}} = -7.1543 \qquad df = 1632$

$t_{\text{critical}} = 1.960$

$t_{\text{observed}} > t_{\text{critical}}$ therefore reject $H_0$.

**9.** $t = \dfrac{1.759 - 1.6103}{\sqrt{\dfrac{2712 - \dfrac{1024^2}{582} + 4318 - \dfrac{1694^2}{1052}}{582 + 1052 - 2}\left(\dfrac{1}{582} + \dfrac{1}{1052}\right)}}$

$t = \dfrac{0.1487}{\sqrt{\dfrac{910.3230 + 1590.2091}{1632}(.0017 + .00095)}}$

$$t = \frac{0.1487}{\sqrt{1.532(.00265)}} \qquad t = \frac{0.1487}{\sqrt{0.00406}} \qquad t = \frac{0.1487}{.0637}$$

$t_{\text{observed}} = 2.33 \qquad df = 1632$

$t_{\text{critical}} = 1.960$

$t_{\text{observed}} > t_{\text{critical}}$ therefore reject $H_0$.

**11.** $\sigma_{\bar{X}_1 - \bar{X}_2} = \sqrt{\left(\dfrac{6}{\sqrt{36}}\right)^2 + \left(\dfrac{6}{\sqrt{36}}\right)^2} \qquad \sigma_{\bar{X}_1 - \bar{X}_2} = \sqrt{1^2 + 1^2} \qquad \sigma_{\bar{X}_1 - \bar{X}_2} = \sqrt{2}$

$\sigma_{\bar{X}_1 - \bar{X}_2} = 1.4142$

**a.** $z = \dfrac{(5) - (80 - 77)}{1.4142} \qquad z = \dfrac{2}{1.4142} \qquad z = 1.41 \qquad p = .0793$

**b.** $z = \dfrac{(0) - (80 - 77)}{1.4142} \qquad z = \dfrac{-3}{1.4142} \qquad z = -2.12 \qquad p = .9830$

**c.** $z = \dfrac{(0) - (80 - 77)}{1.4142} \qquad z = \dfrac{-3}{1.4142} \qquad z = -2.12 \qquad p = .0170$

**d.** $z = \dfrac{(-5) - (80 - 77)}{1.4142} \qquad z = \dfrac{-8}{1.4142} \qquad z = -5.66 \qquad p < .00003$

**13.** As sample size increases the probability of the $z$-score decreases, all else being equal.

15. $d_2 = \dfrac{3.6}{6} = .6$

| $n$ | $1 - \beta$ |
|-----|-------------|
| 10 | .37 |
| 20 | .60 |
| 30 | .75 |

Increases in sample size increase power.

17.

|  | | $k$ | $df$ | $F_{\text{critical}}$ | |
|---|---|-----|------|-----------------------|---|
| a. | $F_{\text{max}} = 5.02,$ | 2 | 12 | 3.28 | Reject $H_0$ |
| b. | $F_{\text{max}} = 2.11,$ | 2 | 10 | 3.72 | Fail to reject $H_0$ |
| c. | $F_{\text{max}} = 2.33,$ | 2 | 9 | 4.03 | Fail to reject $H_0$ |
| d. | $F_{\text{max}} = 5.09,$ | 2 | 9 | 4.03 | Reject $H_0$ |

19. $t = \dfrac{6.3 - 3.3}{\sqrt{\dfrac{20.1 + 12.1}{10(10 - 1)}}}$      $t = \dfrac{3.0}{\sqrt{0.3578}}$      $t = 5.0153$

$t_{\text{observed}} = 5.02$
$df = 10 + 10 - 2 = 18$
$t_{\text{critical}} = 2.101$
$t_{\text{observed}} > t_{\text{critical}}$ therefore reject $H_0$.

21. $t = \dfrac{19.8 - 24.7}{\sqrt{\dfrac{25.6 + 20.1}{10(10 - 1)}}}$      $t = \dfrac{-4.9}{\sqrt{0.50777}}$   $t = -6.8764$

$t_{\text{observed}} = -6.88$
$df = 10 + 10 - 2 = 18$
$t_{\text{critical}} = 2.101$
$t_{\text{observed}} > t_{\text{critical}}$ therefore reject $H_0$.

23.

| Employee | A | B | D | $D^2$ |
|----------|---|---|---|-------|
| 1 | 5 | 2 | −3 | 9 |
| 2 | 6 | 3 | −3 | 9 |
| 3 | 7 | 4 | −3 | 9 |
| 4 | 4 | 3 | −1 | 1 |
| 5 | 8 | 4 | −4 | 16 |
| 6 | 9 | 4 | −5 | 25 |
| 7 | 6 | 3 | −3 | 9 |
| 8 | 5 | 1 | −4 | 16 |
| 9 | 7 | 5 | −2 | 4 |
| 10 | 6 | 4 | −2 | 4 |
|  | 63 | 33 | −30 | 102 |

$t = \dfrac{-3.0}{\sqrt{\dfrac{102 - \dfrac{(-30)^2}{10}}{10(10 - 1)}}}$      $t = \dfrac{-3.0}{\sqrt{\dfrac{12}{10(10 - 1)}}}$   $t = \dfrac{-3.0}{0.3651}$   $t = -8.2169$

$t_{\text{observed}} = -8.22$
$df = 10 - 1 = 9$
$t_{\text{critical}} = 2.262$
$t_{\text{observed}} < t_{\text{critical}}$ therefore, do not reject $H_0$.

## CHAPTER 14

**1.**

|  | $F_{observed}$ | $\alpha = .05$ $F_{critical}$ | Reject $H_0$ | $\alpha = .01$ $F_{critical}$ | Reject $H_0$ |
|---|---|---|---|---|---|
| a. | $F(3, 23) = 3.56$ | 3.03 | Yes | 4.76 | No |
| b. | $F(5, 40) = 4.12$ | 2.45 | Yes | 3.51 | Yes |
| c. | $F(2, 4) = 5.23$ | 6.94 | No | 18.00 | No |
| d. | $F(3, 12) = 4.16$ | 3.49 | Yes | 5.95 | No |

**3.**

| Source | SS | df | MS | F |
|---|---|---|---|---|
| Between-groups | 39.636 | 3 | 13.212 | 6.25 |
| Within-groups | 33.824 | 16 | 2.114 | |
| Total | 73.460 | 19 | | |

a. four levels
b. $20/4 = 5$ subjects per group
c. $df_N = 3$, $df_D = 16$
d. $F_{critical} = 3.24$
e. yes, because $F_{observed} > F_{critical}$
f. $\underline{F(3,16)} = 6.25$, $\underline{MSE} = 2.114$, $\underline{p} < .05$

g. $\omega^2 = \dfrac{df_N(F - 1)}{df_N(F - 1) + N}$     $\omega^2 = \dfrac{3(6.25 - 1)}{3(6.25 - 1) + 20}$     $\omega^2 = .4406$

The independent variable can explain or predict approximately 44% of the variance among subjects.

h. $\eta^2 = \dfrac{SS_{between}}{SS_{total}}$     $f = \sqrt{\dfrac{\eta^2}{1 - \eta^2}}$

$\eta^2 = \dfrac{39.636}{73.460}$     $f = \sqrt{\dfrac{.5396}{1 - .5396}}$

$\eta^2 = .5396$     $f = 1.08.$

The effect size of this experiment is extremely large.

**5.**

| Source | SS | df | MS | F |
|---|---|---|---|---|
| Between-groups | 42.596 | 4 | 10.649 | 2.950 |
| Within-groups | 162.450 | 45 | 3.610 | |
| Total | 205.046 | 49 | | |

a. five levels
b. There are 10 subjects in each group.
c. $df_N = 4$, $df_D = 45$
d. $F_{critical} = 2.575$
e. Yes, because $F_{observed} > F_{critical}.$
f. $\underline{F(4,45)} = 2.95$, $\underline{MSE} = 3.610$, $\underline{p} < .05$

g. $\omega^2 = \dfrac{df_N(F - 1)}{df_N(F - 1) + N}$     $\omega^2 = \dfrac{4(2.95 - 1)}{4(2.95 - 1) + 50}$     $\omega^2 = .1349$

The independent variable can explain or predict approximately 13% of the variance among subjects.

**h.** $\eta^2 = \dfrac{SS_{between}}{SS_{total}}$    $\mathbf{f} = \sqrt{\dfrac{\eta^2}{1 - \eta^2}}$

$\eta^2 = \dfrac{42.596}{205.046}$    $\mathbf{f} = \sqrt{\dfrac{.2077}{1 - .2077}}$

$\eta^2 = .2077$    $\mathbf{f} = .5120$

The effect size of this experiment is large.

**i.** 56%

**j.** Between 15 and 20 subjects per group or a total of 75 to 100 subjects.

**7. a.**

| $50 | Extra Credit | No Reward |
|---|---|---|
| 00 | | |
| | 11 | |
| | | 33 |
| 44 | 4 | |
| 7 | 77 | 77 |
| 1 | 1 | 1 0 |

The groups do not look different from each other. There is considerable overlap of the three groups.

**b.**

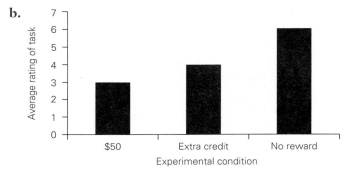

**c.** $H_0$: $\mu_1 = \mu_2 = \mu_3$
$H_1$: Not $H_0$

**d.**

| | GROUP | | | |
|---|---|---|---|---|
| | **1** | **2** | **3** | |
| $X_{\bullet j}$ | 15 | 20 | 30 | $\Sigma X_{ij} = 65$ |
| $X_{\bullet j}^2$ | 81 | 116 | 216 | $\Sigma X_{ij}^2 = 413$ |

Between-Groups Variance

$SS_{between} = \Sigma \dfrac{(X_{\bullet j})^2}{n_j} - \dfrac{(\Sigma X_{ij})^2}{N}$    $df_{between} = k - 1$

$SS_{between} = \dfrac{15^2}{5} + \dfrac{20^2}{5} + \dfrac{30^2}{5} - \dfrac{(65)^2}{15}$    $df_{between} = 3 - 1$

$SS_{between} = 305 - 281.667$    $df_{between} = 2$

$SS_{between} = 23.333$

**e.** Within-Groups Variance

$$SS_{\text{within}} = \Sigma X_{ij}^2 - \Sigma \frac{(X_{\bullet j})^2}{n_j} \qquad df_{\text{within}} = \Sigma(n_j - 1)$$

$$SS_{\text{within}} = 413 - 305.0 \qquad df_{\text{within}} = (5-1) + (5-1) + (5-1)$$

$$SS_{\text{within}} = 108.0 \qquad df_{\text{within}} = 12$$

Total Variance

$$SS_{\text{total}} = \Sigma X_{ij}^2 - \frac{(\Sigma X_{ij})^2}{N} \qquad df_{\text{total}} = N - 1$$

$$SS_{\text{total}} = 413 - 281.667 \qquad df_{\text{total}} = 15 - 1$$

$$SS_{\text{total}} = 131.333 \qquad df_{\text{total}} = 14$$

| Source | SS | df | MS | F |
|---|---|---|---|---|
| Between-groups | 23.333 | 2 | 11.667 | 1.296 |
| Within-groups | 108.000 | 12 | 9.000 | |
| Total | 131.333 | 14 | | |

The researcher cannot reject the null hypothesis. The data do not allow the researcher to claim that there is a statistically significant relation between the two variables.

**f.** $\omega^2 = \dfrac{df_{\text{between}}(F - 1)}{df_{\text{between}}(F - 1) + N}$

$\omega^2 = .038 = \dfrac{2(1.296 - 1)}{2(1.296 - 1) + 15}$

According to the data, $\omega^2 = .038$. The independent variable accounts for approximately 4% of the differences among subjects rating of the task. Although $\omega^2$ is usually not calculated when $F$ is not significant, the calculations are provided for illustrative purposes.

**g.** $\eta^2 = \dfrac{SS_{\text{between}}}{SS_{\text{total}}} \qquad f = \sqrt{\dfrac{\eta^2}{1 - \eta^2}}$

$\eta^2 = \dfrac{23.333}{131.333} \qquad f = \sqrt{\dfrac{.1777}{1 - .1777}}$

$\eta^2 = .1777 \qquad f = .464$

The effect size of this experiment is large.

**h.** Using Tukey's HSD is inappropriate as the $F$-ratio is not statistically significant.

**9. a.**

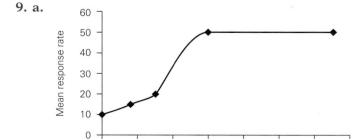

**b.** $H_0: \mu_1 = \mu_2 = \mu_3 = \mu_4 = \mu_5$
$H_1:$ Not $H_0$

**c.**

| | GROUP | | | | | | |
|---|---|---|---|---|---|---|---|
| | **1** | **2** | **3** | **4** | **5** | | |
| $X_{\bullet j}$ | 60 | 80 | 110 | 250 | 300 | $\Sigma X_{ij} =$ | 800 |
| $X_{\bullet j}^2$ | 680 | 1344 | 2514 | 12564 | 15080 | $\Sigma X_{ij}^2 =$ | 32182 |
| | 6 | 5 | 5 | 5 | 6 | $N =$ | 27 |

Between-Groups Variance

$$SS_{between} = \Sigma \frac{(X_{\bullet j})^2}{n_j} - \frac{(\Sigma X_{ij})^2}{N}$$

$$df_{between} = k - 1$$

$$SS_{between} = \frac{60^2}{6} + \frac{80^2}{5} + \frac{110^2}{5} + \frac{250^2}{5} + \frac{300^2}{6} - \frac{(800)^2}{27}$$

$$df_{between} = 5 - 1$$

$SS_{between} = 31800 - 23703.7037$  $df_{between} = 4$
$SS_{between} = 8096.2963$

Within-Groups Variance

$$SS_{within} = \Sigma X_{ij}^2 - \Sigma \frac{(X_{\bullet j})^2}{n_j}$$ 
$$df_{within} = \Sigma(n_j - 1)$$

$SS_{within} = 32182.0 - 31800.0$  $df_{within} = (6-1) + (5-1) +$
$(5-1) + (5-1) + (6-1)$

$SS_{within} = 382.0$  $df_{within} = 22$

Total Variance

$$SS_{total} = \Sigma X_{ij}^2 - \frac{(\Sigma X_{ij})^2}{N}$$
$$df_{total} = N - 1$$

$SS_{total} = 32182.0 - 23703.7037$  $df_{total} = 27 - 1$
$SS_{total} = 8478.2963$  $df_{total} = 26$

| Source | SS | df | MS | F |
|---|---|---|---|---|
| Between-groups | 8096.30 | 4 | 2024.08 | 116.59 |
| Within-groups | 382.00 | 22 | 17.36 | |
| Total | 8478.30 | 26 | | |

**d.** The researcher can reject the null hypothesis. The data allow the researcher to conclude that the experimental conditions affected performance.

**e.** $\omega^2 = \dfrac{df_{between}(F - 1)}{df_{between}(F - 1) + N}$   $\omega^2 = .9448 = \dfrac{4(116.59 - 1)}{4(116.59 - 1) + 27}$

According to the data, $\omega^2 = .94$. The independent variable accounts for approximately 94% of the differences among subjects' rating of the task.

**f.** $\text{HSD} = q_{\text{critical}} \sqrt{\dfrac{MS_{\text{within}}}{n}}$  $n' = 5.357 = \dfrac{5}{\dfrac{1}{6} + \dfrac{1}{5} + \dfrac{1}{5} + \dfrac{1}{5} + \dfrac{1}{6}}$

$\text{HSD} = 4.20 \sqrt{\dfrac{17.36}{5.357}}$  $\text{HSD} = 7.56$

| | GROUPS | | | | |
|---|---|---|---|---|---|
| | **1** | **2** | **3** | **4** | **5** |
| | 10.0 | 16.0 | 22.0 | 50.0 | 50.0 |
| 10.0 | — | 6.0 | 12.0* | 40.0* | 40.0* |
| 16.0 | — | — | 6.0 | 34.0* | 34.0* |
| 22.0 | — | — | — | 28.0* | 28.0* |
| 50.0 | — | — | — | 10.0* | 10.0* |
| 50.0 | — | — | — | — | 0.0 |

*Reject $H_0$

It would appear, therefore, that the concentration of sweetener does affect performance.

**11. a.** three levels

**b.** 22 subjects

**c.** $\omega^2 = \dfrac{2(3.75 - 1)}{2(3.75 - 1) + 22}$, $\omega^2 = .20$

The independent variable accounts for approximately 20% of the differences among subjects.

**d.** $\eta^2 = \dfrac{2(3.75)}{2(3.75) + 19}$  $f = \sqrt{\dfrac{.28}{1 - .28}} = 0.62$

$\eta^2 = .28$

According to Cohen, this is a large treatment effect.

**e.** No. The value of $\alpha$ determines the probability of committing a Type I error if the Null Hypothesis is a true statement. Similarly, $p$ represents the probability of obtaining the $F$-ratio at least as small as the observed value.

**f.** The researcher will need between 20 and 25 subjects in each of the three treatment groups.

**13.** $F(1, 13) = 6.791$

$t(13) = 2.606$

$F = t^2$

## CHAPTER 15

**1.**

| Source | SS | df | MS | F |
|--------|------|----|--------|-------|
| A | 160.0 | 1 | 160.00 | 4.72 |
| B | 372.1 | 1 | 372.10 | 10.97 |
| AB | 3.6 | 1 | 3.60 | 0.11 |
| Within | 1221.1 | 36 | 33.92 | |
| Total | 1756.8 | 39 | | |

**a.** two levels of Factor A
**b.** two levels of Factor B
**c.** 10

| Source | Degrees of Freedom | $F_{critical}$ | Statistical Decision |
|--------|--------------------|----------------|----------------------|
| Factor A | $df_N = 1, df_D = 36$ | 4.11 | Reject $H_0$ |
| Factor B | $df_N = 1, df_D = 36$ | 4.11 | Reject $H_0$ |
| AB | $df_N = 1, df_D = 36$ | 4.11 | Do not reject $H_0$ |

**3.**

| Source | SS | df | MS | F |
|--------|---------|----|-------|------|
| A | 162.60 | 3 | 54.20 | 2.15 |
| B | 251.09 | 4 | 62.77 | 2.49 |
| AB | 704.87 | 12 | 58.74 | 2.33 |
| Within | 2016.80 | 80 | 25.21 | |
| Total | 3135.36 | 99 | | |

**a.** four levels of Factor A
**b.** five levels of Factor B
**c.** 5

| Source | Degrees of Freedom | $F_{critical}$ | Statistical Decision |
|--------|--------------------|----------------|----------------------|
| Factor A | $df_N = 3, df_D = 80$ | 2.72 | Reject $H_0$ |
| Factor B | $df_N = 4, df_D = 80$ | 2.48 | Reject $H_0$ |
| AB | $df_N = 12, df_D = 80$ | 1.88 | Reject $H_0$ |

**5. a.** $A_1 = 10$   $A_2 = 15$   $A_3 = 20$
**b.** $B_1 = 10$   $B_2 = 15$   $B_3 = 20$
**c.** The lines are parallel, therefore there is no interaction.

**7.**

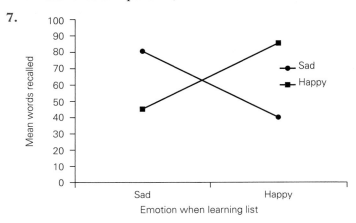

## EMOTION EXPERIENCED
## DURING RECALL OF LIST

|  | Sad ($a_1$) | Happy ($a_2$) |  |
|---|---|---|---|
| **Sad ($b_1$)** | $X_{\bullet11} = 381.0$ | $X_{\bullet21} = 229.0$ | $X_{\bullet\bullet1} = 610.0$ |
|  | $n_{11} = 5$ | $n_{21} = 5$ | $n_{\bullet1} = 10$ |
| **Happy ($b_2$)** | $X_{\bullet12} = 193.0$ | $X_{\bullet22} = 430.0$ | $X_{\bullet\bullet2} = 623.0$ |
|  | $n_{12} = 5$ | $n_{22} = 5$ | $n_{\bullet2} = 10$ |
|  | $X_{\bullet1\bullet} = 574.0$ | $X_{\bullet2\bullet} = 659.0$ | $X_{\bullet\bullet\bullet} = 1233.0$ |
|  | $n_{1\bullet} = 10$ | $n_{2\bullet} = 10$ | $N = 20$ |
|  |  |  | $\Sigma X_{ijk}^2 = 84073.0$ |

Factor A Variance

$$SS_A = \Sigma \frac{(X_{\bullet j\bullet})^2}{n_{j\bullet}} - \frac{(\Sigma X_{ijk})^2}{N} \qquad df_A = j - 1$$

$$SS_A = \frac{574^2}{10} + \frac{659^2}{10} - \frac{1233^2}{20} \qquad df_A = 2 - 1$$

$$SS_A = 76375.7 - 76014.45 \qquad df_A = 1$$

$$SS_A = 361.25$$

Factor B Variance

$$SS_B = \Sigma \frac{(X_{\bullet\bullet k})^2}{n_{\bullet k}} - \frac{(\Sigma X_{ijk})^2}{N} \qquad df_B = k - 1$$

$$SS_B = \frac{610.0^2}{10} + \frac{623.0^2}{10} - \frac{1233^2}{20} \qquad df_B = 2 - 1$$

$$SS_B = 76022.9 - 76014.45 \qquad df_B = 1$$

$$SS_B = 8.25$$

Interaction Variance

$$SS_{AB} = \Sigma \frac{(X_{\bullet jk})^2}{n_{jk}} - \frac{(\Sigma X_{ijk})^2}{N} - (SS_A + SS_B) \qquad df_{AB} = (j-1)(k-1)$$

$$SS_{AB} = \frac{381^2}{5} + \frac{229^2}{5} + \frac{193^2}{5} + \frac{430^2}{5} - 76014.45 - (8.450 + 361.250)$$

$$df_{AB} = (2-1)(2-1)$$

$$SS_{AB} = 83950.20 - 76014.45 - (8.450 + 361.250)$$

$$SS_{AB} = 7566.05 \qquad df_{AB} = 1$$

Within-Groups Variance

$$SS_{\text{within}} = \Sigma X_{ijk}^2 - \Sigma \frac{(X_{\bullet jk})^2}{n_{jk}} \qquad df_{\text{within}} = \Sigma(n_{jk} - 1)$$

$$SS_{\text{within}} = 84073 - 83950.20 \qquad df_{\text{within}} \; (5-1) + (5-1) +$$
$$(5-1) + (5-1)$$

$$SS_{\text{within}} = 122.805 \qquad df_{\text{within}} = 16$$

Total Variance

$$SS_{\text{total}} = \Sigma X_{ijk}^2 - \frac{(\Sigma X_{ijk})^2}{N} \qquad df_{\text{total}} = N - 1$$

$$SS_{\text{total}} = 84073 - 76014.45 \qquad df_{\text{total}} = 20 - 1$$

$$SS_{\text{total}} = 8058.55 \qquad df_{\text{total}} = 19$$

| Source | SS | df | MS | F |
|--------|------|------|----------|---------|
| A | 361.250 | 1 | 461.250 | 47.067 |
| B | 8.450 | 1 | 8.450 | 1.101 |
| AB | 7566.050 | 1 | 7566.050 | 985.767 |
| Within | 122.805 | 16 | 7.675 | |
| Total | 8058.550 | 19 | | |

Omega Squared:

$$\omega^2 = \frac{df_{\text{effect}}(F_{\text{effect}} - 1)}{df_{\text{effect}}(F_{\text{effect}} - 1) + N}$$

A

$$\omega^2 = .697 = \frac{1(47.067 - 1)}{1(47.067 - 1) + 20}$$

B

$$\omega^2 = .005 = \frac{1(1.101 - 1)}{1(1.101 - 1) + 20}$$

AB

$$\omega^2 = .980 = \frac{1(985.767 - 1)}{1(985.767 - 1) + 20}$$

**9.**

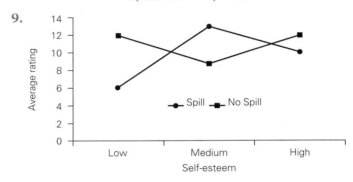

**EXPECTANCY**

| Blunder | Low (a₁) | Medium (a₂) | High (a₃) | |
|---------|----------|-------------|-----------|---|
| Spill (b₁) | $X_{\bullet 11} = 25.0$ | $X_{\bullet 21} = 53.0$ | $X_{\bullet 31} = 41.0$ | $X_{\bullet \bullet 1} = 119.0$ |
| | $n_{11} = 4$ | $n_{21} = 4$ | $n_{31} = 4$ | $n_1 = 12$ |
| No spill (b₂) | $X_{\bullet 12} = 49.0$ | $X_{\bullet 22} = 35.0$ | $X_{\bullet 32} = 53.0$ | $X_{\bullet \bullet 2} = 137.0$ |
| | $n_{12} = 4$ | $n_{22} = 4$ | $n_{32} = 4$ | $n_2 = 12$ |
| | $X_{\bullet 1 \bullet} = 74.0$ | $X_{\bullet 2 \bullet} = 88.0$ | $X_{\bullet 3 \bullet} = 94.0$ | $X_{\bullet \bullet \bullet} = 256.0$ |
| | $n_1 = 8$ | $n_2 = 8$ | $n_3 = 8$ | $N = 24$ |
| | | | | $\Sigma X_{ijk}^2 = 2940.0$ |

Factor A Variance

$$SS_A = \Sigma \frac{(X_{\bullet j \bullet})^2}{n_{j \bullet}} - \frac{(\Sigma X_{ijk})^2}{N} \qquad df_A = j - 1$$

$$SS_A = \frac{74^2}{8} + \frac{88^2}{8} + \frac{94^2}{8} - \frac{256^2}{24} \qquad df_A = 3 - 1$$

$$SS_A = 2757.0 - 2730.6667 \qquad df_A = 2$$

$$SS_A = 26.333$$

Factor B Variance

$$SS_B = \Sigma \frac{(X_{\bullet\bullet k})^2}{n_{\bullet k}} - \frac{(\Sigma X_{ijk})^2}{N} \qquad\qquad df_B = k - 1$$

$$SS_B = \frac{119.0^2}{12} + \frac{137^2}{12} - \frac{256^2}{24} \qquad\qquad df_B = 2 - 1$$

$$SS_B = 2744.1667 - 2730.6667 \qquad\qquad df_B = 1$$

$$SS_B = 13.4997$$

Interaction Variance

$$SS_{AB} = \Sigma \frac{(X_{\bullet jk})^2}{n_{jk}} - \frac{(\Sigma X_{ijk})^2}{N} - (SS_A + SS_B) \qquad df_{AB} = (j - 1)(k - 1)$$

$$SS_{AB} = \frac{25^2}{4} + \frac{53^2}{4} \cdots \frac{35^2}{4} + \frac{53^2}{4} - 2730.6667 - (26.333 + 13.4997)$$

$$df_{AB} = (3 - 1)(2 - 1)$$

$$SS_{AB} = 2887.5 - 2730.6667 - (26.333 + 13.4997)$$

$$SS_{AB} = 117.0 \qquad\qquad df_{AB} = 2$$

Within-Groups Variance

$$SS_{\text{within}} = \Sigma X_{ijk}^2 - \Sigma \frac{(X_{\bullet jk})^2}{n_{jk}} \qquad\qquad df_{\text{within}} = \Sigma(n_{jk} - 1)$$

$$SS_{\text{within}} = 2940.0 - 2887.5 \qquad\qquad df_{\text{within}} (4 - 1) + (4 - 1) + \cdots + (4 - 1)$$

$$SS_{\text{within}} = 52.50 \qquad\qquad df_{\text{within}} = 18$$

Total Variance

$$SS_{\text{total}} = \Sigma X_{ijk}^2 - \frac{(\Sigma X_{ijk})^2}{N} \qquad\qquad df_{\text{total}} = N - 1$$

$$SS_{\text{total}} = 2940.0 - 2730.6667 \qquad\qquad df_{\text{total}} = 24 - 1$$

$$SS_{\text{total}} = 209.333 \qquad\qquad df_{\text{total}} = 23$$

| Source | SS | df | MS | F |
|--------|-----|-----|--------|--------|
| A | 26.333 | 2 | 13.167 | 4.514 |
| B | 13.500 | 1 | 13.500 | 4.629 |
| AB | 117.000 | 2 | 58.500 | 20.057 |
| Within | 52.500 | 18 | 2.9167 | |
| Total | 209.333 | 23 | | |

Omega Squared:

$$\omega^2 = \frac{df_{\text{effect}}(F_{\text{effect}} - 1)}{df_{\text{effect}}(F_{\text{effect}} - 1) + N}$$

A

$$\omega^2 = .227 = \frac{2(4.514 - 1)}{2(4.514 - 1) + 24}$$

B

$$\omega^2 = .131 = \frac{1(4.629.0 - 1)}{1(4.629 - 1) + 24}$$

AB

$$\omega^2 = .614 = \frac{2(20.057 - 1)}{2(20.057 - 1) + 24}$$

# CHAPTER 16

**1. a.** The sequence of the videos and questions may influence the subject's answers.
   **b.** She should attempt to randomly order the presentation of the film clips such that an equal number of subjects see each possible sequence of videos.
   **c.** Using a correlated groups design will allow her to have greater power because the effects of individual differences will be removed by partitioning the effect out of the within-subjects term.

**3.** If the same subjects are observed under different treatment conditions or observed on several occasions, then the research has used a within-subjects factor. If the researcher assigns the subjects to groups using a matching variable, then the researcher is using a within-subjects factor.

**5. a.**

| 2\| | 2\| | 2\| | 2\| | 2\|68 | 2\|79 |
|---|---|---|---|---|---|
| 3\| | 3\| | 3\|278 | 3\|25679 | 3\|003 | 3\|115 |
| 4\|79 | 4\|35556 | 4\|01 | 4\| | 4\| | 4\| |
| 5\|012 | 5\| | 5\| | 5\| | 5\| | 5\| |

**b.** $H_0$:  $\mu_1 = \mu_2 = \mu_3 = \mu_4 = \mu_5 = \mu_6$
$H_1$: Not $H_0$.

| Subject | 1 | 2 | 3 | 4 | 5 | 6 | $X_{i\bullet}$ |
|---|---|---|---|---|---|---|---|
| 1 | 47 | 45 | 32 | 32 | 26 | 27 | 209 |
| 2 | 51 | 45 | 37 | 35 | 30 | 31 | 229 |
| 3 | 52 | 46 | 40 | 36 | 33 | 29 | 236 |
| 4 | 50 | 45 | 41 | 37 | 30 | 35 | 238 |
| 5 | 49 | 43 | 38 | 39 | 28 | 31 | 228 |
| $X_{\bullet j}$ | 249 | 224 | 188 | 179 | 147 | 153 | $X_{\bullet\bullet} = 1140$ |
|  |  |  |  |  |  |  | $\Sigma X_{ij}^2 = 45074$ |

Total Variance

$$SS_{total} = \Sigma X_{ij}^2 - \frac{(\Sigma X_{ij})^2}{N} \qquad\qquad df_{total} = N - 1$$

$$SS_{total} = 45074 - \frac{(1140)^2}{30} = 45074.0 - 43320.0 \qquad df_{total} = 30 - 1$$

$$SS_{total} = 1754.0 \qquad\qquad df_{total} = 29$$

Between-Groups Variance

$$SS_{between} = \frac{\Sigma X_{\bullet j}^2}{n_j} - \frac{(\Sigma X_{ij})^2}{N} \qquad\qquad df_{between} = j - 1$$

$$SS_{between} = \frac{249^2 + 224^2 + 188^2 + 179^2 + 147^2 + 153^2}{5} - \frac{(1140)^2}{30}$$

$$SS_{between} = \frac{224580}{5} - \frac{1299600}{30}$$

$$SS_{between} = 44916 - 43320 \qquad\qquad df_{between} = 6 - 1$$

$$SS_{between} = 1596.0 \qquad\qquad df_{between} = 5$$

Subjects Variance

$$SS_{subjects} = \frac{\Sigma X_{i\bullet}^2}{j} - \frac{(\Sigma X_{ij})^2}{N} \qquad\qquad df_{subjects} = n - 1$$

$$SS_{subjects} = \frac{209^2 + 229^2 + 236^2 + 238^2 + 228^2}{6} - \frac{(1140)^2}{30}$$

$$SS_{subjects} = \frac{260446}{6} - 43320$$

$$SS_{subjects} = 43407.6667 - 43320 \qquad\qquad df_{subjects} = 5 - 1$$

$$SS_{subjects} = 87.667 \qquad\qquad df_{subjects} = 4$$

Within-Groups Variance

$$SS_{within} = \Sigma X_{ij}^2 - \frac{\Sigma X_{i\bullet}^2}{j} - \frac{\Sigma X_{\bullet j}^2}{n} + \frac{(\Sigma X_{ij})^2}{N} \qquad df_{within} = (j-1)(n-1)$$

$$SS_{within} = 45074 - 43407.6667 - 44916 + 43320$$

$$df_{within} = (5)(4)$$

$$SS_{within} = 70.3333 \qquad\qquad df_{within} = 20$$

| Source | SS | df | MS | F |
|---|---|---|---|---|
| Between-groups | 1596.00 | 5 | 319.20 | 90.68 |
| Subjects | 87.67 | 4 | 21.92 | |
| Within-groups | 70.33 | 20 | 3.52 | |
| Total | 1754.00 | 29 | | |

$F_{critical} = 2.71$: Reject $H_0$

e. $\omega^2 = \dfrac{df_{between}(F_{between} - 1)}{df_{between}(F_{between} - 1) + F_{subjects}(n) + j(n)}$

$\omega^2 = .88 = \dfrac{5(90.68 - 1)}{5(90.68 - 1) + 6.23(5) + 6(5)}$

f. $HSD = 3.73 = 4.45\sqrt{\dfrac{3.52}{5}}$

**7. a.**

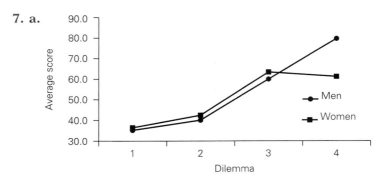

The data suggest that men and women responded in the same way to three of the dilemmas. There is, however, an apparent difference for Dilemma 4. Also, there are differences among each of the four dilemmas.

|       | Subject | 1 | 2 | 3 | 4 | $X_{\bullet ij}$ | |
|-------|---------|-----|-----|-----|-----|-----------------|------|
| Men   | 1       | 26  | 34  | 60  | 70  |                 | 190  |
|       | 2       | 47  | 51  | 71  | 98  |                 | 267  |
|       | 3       | 24  | 36  | 57  | 59  |                 | 176  |
|       | 4       | 39  | 49  | 66  | 89  |                 | 243  |
|       | 5       | 44  | 54  | 67  | 73  |                 | 238  |
|       | $X_{\bullet 1k}$ | 180 | 224 | 321 | 389 | $X_{\bullet 1 \bullet} =$ | 1114 |
|       | 6       | 32  | 49  | 86  | 65  |                 | 232  |
|       | 7       | 37  | 49  | 73  | 69  |                 | 228  |
| Women | 8       | 47  | 47  | 70  | 51  |                 | 215  |
|       | 9       | 37  | 45  | 53  | 82  |                 | 217  |
|       | 10      | 33  | 43  | 53  | 57  |                 | 186  |
|       | $X_{\bullet 2k}$ | 186 | 233 | 335 | 324 | $X_{\bullet 2 \bullet} =$ | 1078 |
|       | $X_{\bullet \bullet k}$ | 366 | 457 | 656 | 713 | $X_{\bullet \bullet \bullet} =$ | 2192 |
|       |         |     |     |     |     | $\Sigma X_{ijk}^2 =$ | 132006 |

Between-Subjects Variable Variance: Factor A

$$SS_A = \frac{\Sigma (X_{\bullet j \bullet})^2}{nk} - \frac{(\Sigma X_{ijk})^2}{N} \qquad df_A = j - 1$$

$$SS_A = \frac{1114^2 + 1078^2}{5(4)} - \frac{(2192)^2}{40} \qquad df_A = 2 - 1$$

$$SS_A = \frac{2403080}{20} - \frac{4804864}{40}$$

$$SS_A = 120154 - 120121.6$$

$$SS_A = 32.40 \qquad\qquad df_A = 1$$

Variance Due to Subjects Across Factor A

$$SS_{subjects} = \frac{\Sigma (X_{i \bullet \bullet})^2}{k} - \frac{\Sigma (X_{\bullet j \bullet})^2}{nk} \qquad df_{subjects} = j(n - 1)$$

$$SS_{subjects} = \frac{190^2 + 267^2 + \cdots 217^2 + 186^2}{4} - \frac{1114^2 + 1078^2}{5(4)}$$

$$df_{subjects} = 2(5 - 1)$$

$$SS_{subjects} = \frac{487776}{4} - \frac{2403080}{20} \qquad df_{subjects} = 2(4)$$

$SS_{\text{subjects}} = 121944 - 120154$

$SS_{\text{subjects}} = 1790.0$ $\hspace{2cm}$ $df_{\text{subjects}} = 8$

## Within-Subjects Variable Variance: Factor B

$$SS_B = \frac{\Sigma(X_{\bullet\bullet k})^2}{nj} - \frac{(\Sigma X_{ijk})^2}{N} \hspace{2cm} df_B = k - 1$$

$$SS_B = \frac{366^2 + 457^2 + 656^2 + 713^3}{5(2)} - \frac{(2192)^2}{40} \hspace{0.5cm} df_B = 4 - 1$$

$$SS_B = \frac{1281510}{10} - \frac{4804864}{40}$$

$SS_B = 128151 - 120121.6$

$SS_B = 8029.4$ $\hspace{3cm}$ $df_B = 3$

## Interaction Variance

$$SS_{AB} = \frac{\Sigma(X_{\bullet ij})}{n} - \frac{(\Sigma X_{ijk})^2}{N} - SS_A - SS_B \hspace{1cm} df_{AB} = (j - 1)(k - 1)$$

$$SS_{AB} = \frac{180^2 + 224^2 + \cdots 335^2 + 324^2}{5} - \frac{(2192)^2}{40} - 32.40 - 8029.40$$

$$df_{AB} = (2 - 1)(4 - 1)$$

$SS_{AB} = 128604.8 - 120121.6 - 32.40 - 8029.40$

$$df_{AB} = (1)(3)$$

$SS_{AB} = 421.4$ $\hspace{3cm}$ $df_{AB} = 3$

## Factor B × Subjects Variance

$$SS_{B \times \text{subjects}} = \Sigma X_{ijk}^2 - \frac{\Sigma(X_{\bullet ij})}{n} - \frac{\Sigma(X_{i\bullet\bullet})^2}{k} + \frac{\Sigma(X_{\bullet j\bullet})^2}{nk}$$

$$df_{B \times \text{subjects}} = j(n - 1)(k - 1)$$

$SS_{B \times \text{subjects}} = 132006 - 128604.8 - 121944 + 120154$

$$df_{B \times \text{subjects}} = 2(5 - 1)(4 - 1)$$

$SS_{B \times \text{subjects}} = 1611.20$ $\hspace{1.5cm}$ $df_{B \times \text{subjects}} = 24$

$$SS_{\text{total}} = \Sigma X_{ijk}^2 - \frac{(\Sigma X_{ijk})^2}{N} \hspace{2cm} df_{\text{total}} = N - 1$$

$SS_{\text{total}} = 132006 - 120121.6$

$SS_{\text{total}} = 11884.4$ $\hspace{3cm}$ $df_{\text{total}} = 39$

| Source | SS | df | MS | F |
|---|---|---|---|---|
| A | 32.40 | 1 | 32.40 | 0.15 |
| Subjects | 1790.00 | 8 | 223.75 | 3.33 |
| B | 8029.40 | 3 | 2676.47 | 39.87 |
| AB | 421.40 | 3 | 140.47 | 2.09 |
| B×subjects | 1611.20 | 24 | 67.13 | |
| Total | 11884.40 | 39 | | |

A $\hspace{0.5cm}$ Fail to Reject

B $\hspace{0.5cm}$ Reject

AB $\hspace{0.3cm}$ Fail to Reject

**d.** Common denominator for omega squared.
$$215.67 = .15(1) + 3.38(8) + 39.87(3) + 2.09((1)(3)) + (9)(7)$$

The numerators for the three $\omega^2$s are:

| | | |
|---|---|---|
| $A = (F_A - 1)(j - 1)$ | $= (0.15 - 1)(2 - 1)$ | $= -0.85$ |
| $B = (F_B - 1)(k - 1)$ | $= (39.87 - 1)(4 - 1)$ | $= 116.61$ |
| $AB = (F_{AB} - 1)(j - 1)(k - 1)$ | $= (2.09 - 1)(2 - 1)(4 - 1)$ | $= 3.27$ |

A   $\omega_A^2 = \dfrac{-.85}{215.67} = -.004$

B   $\omega_B^2 = \dfrac{116.61}{215.67} = .54$

AB   $\omega_{AB}^2 = \dfrac{3.26}{215.67} = 0.02$

# CHAPTER 17

**1. a.** $\chi^2 = 4.12$   $df = 1$   $\chi_{critical}^2 = 6.635$   Do not reject $H_0$.
   **b.** $\chi^2 = 3.94$   $df = 2$   $\chi_{critical}^2 = 9.210$   Do not reject $H_0$.
   **c.** $\chi^2 = 7.99$   $df = 3$   $\chi_{critical}^2 = 11.341$   Do not reject $H_0$.
   **d.** $\chi^2 = 7.99$   $df = 1$   $\chi_{critical}^2 = 6.635$   Reject $H_0$.

**3.** The data are not nominal. The student has recorded the total number of responses made by each subject. Therefore, the student should examine the differences among reinforcement rates using an ANOVA.

**5.**

| Games | $O$ | $E$ | $\dfrac{(O_i - E_i)^2}{E_i}$ |
|---|---|---|---|
| 4 | 11 | 17 | 2.1176 |
| 5 | 15 | 17 | 0.2353 |
| 6 | 13 | 17 | 0.9412 |
| 7 | 29 | 17 | 8.4706 |
| | 68 | 68 | 11.7647 |

$\chi^2(N = 68, 3) = 11.7647, p < .05$

**7.**

| Program | $O$ | $E$ | $\dfrac{(O_i - E_i)^2}{E_i}$ |
|---|---|---|---|
| 1 | 12 | 12.5714 | 0.0260 |
| 2 | 23 | 12.5714 | 8.6510 |
| 3 | 8 | 12.5714 | 1.6623 |
| 4 | 7 | 12.5714 | 2.4691 |
| 5 | 15 | 12.5714 | 0.4692 |
| 6 | 5 | 12.5714 | 4.5600 |
| 7 | 18 | 12.5714 | 2.3442 |
| | 88 | 88.0000 | 20.1818 |

$\chi^2(N = 88, 6) = 20.182, p < .05$
Erin can conclude that there are differences among the programs.

**9.** $\chi^2(N = 300, 3) = 6.00$, not significant. Fail to reject $H_0$.

The data indicate that the accounts are not equally popular among the two weave levels. Accounts A and C appear to be except initially different from one another.

**11.** $O_{11} = 12$    $E_{11} = 2.2535 = (24 \times 20)/213$

$O_{22} = 25$    $E_{22} = 9.6620 = (49 \times 42)/213$

$O_{33} = 45$    $E_{33} = 20.0845 = (62 \times 69)/213$

$O_{44} = 23$    $E_{44} = 11.2300 = (46 \times 52)/213$

$O_{55} = 12$    $E_{44} = 4.5070 = (32 \times 30)/213$

Total 117        47.7370

$$\kappa = \frac{117 - 47.737}{213 - 47.737} \qquad \sigma_\kappa = \sqrt{\frac{117(213 - 117)}{213(213 - 47.737)^2}}$$

$\kappa = .419$,

$\sigma_\kappa = .044$. The level of agreement is moderate for the two friends.

**13. a.** $N = 20$, 10 reported 30+ hours, Critical value = 13: Do not reject $H_0$.
    **b.** $N = 20$, 14 reported 30+ hours, Critical value = 13: Reject $H_0$.
    **c.** $N = 24$, 14 reported 30+ hours, Critical value = 15: Do not reject $H_0$.
    **d.** $N = 24$, 18 reported 30+ hours, Critical value = 15: Reject $H_0$.

**15.** $N = 46$, 28, Critical value = 31: Do not reject $H_0$.

Remember to use Table $N$, when $P = Q = 5$.

**17. a.** $N = 20$, 10, Critical value = 17: Do not reject $H_0$.
    **b.** $N = 20$, 14, Critical value = 17: Do not reject $H_0$.
    **c.** $N = 24$, 20, Critical value = 19: Reject $H_0$.
    **d.** $N = 24$, 22, Critical value = 19: Reject $H_0$.

## CHAPTER 18

**1.**

### NUMBER OF STOLEN BASES

| Team Standing | League 1 $X_1$ | Rank | League 2 $X_2$ | Rank | Difference $X_{i1} - X_{i2}$ | $R_1 - R_2$ |
|---|---|---|---|---|---|---|
| 1 | 91 | 15 | 81 | 12.5 | 10 | 3 |
| 2 | 46 | 4.5 | 51 | 6.5 | −5 | −1 |
| 3 | 108 | 18 | 63 | 9 | 45 | 4 |
| 4 | 99 | 16 | 51 | 6.5 | 48 | 5 |
| 5 | 110 | 19 | 46 | 4.5 | 64 | 9 |
| 6 | 105 | 17 | 45 | 3 | 60 | 8 |
| 7 | 191 | 20 | 66 | 11 | 125 | 10 |
| 8 | 57 | 8 | 64 | 10 | −7 | −2 |
| 9 | 34 | 2 | 90 | 14 | −56 | −7 |
| 10 | 81 | 12.5 | 28 | 1 | 53 | 6 |
| Totals | 922 | 132 | 585 | 78 | −10 | 45 |

$T_W = 10$

a. Sign Test
   Positive Differences = 7
   Negative Differences = 3
   Critical value for $N = 10$, $\alpha = .05$: 10, Fail to Reject $H_0$.

b. Wilcoxon Matched-Pairs Signed-Rank Test
   $T_W = 10$
   Critical value for $N = 10$, $\alpha = .05$: 8, Fail to Reject $H_0$.

c. Mann-Whitney $U$-Test

$$23 = 10(10) + \frac{10(10 + 1)}{2} - 132 \quad 77 = 10(10) + \frac{10(10 + 1)}{2} - 78$$

   Critical range for $U$-test, $\alpha = .05$, two tailed: $23 - 77$, Reject $H_0$.

d. For the question posed, the Wilcoxon Matched-Pairs test is the best test because the test maintains information concerning the number of stolen bases, an important variable that affects winning a baseball game.

3.

| PERSONAL-SOCIAL TRAINING | | CONTROL GROUP | |
|---|---|---|---|
| **X** | **Rank** | **X** | **Rank** |
| 18 | 20 | 12 | 14 |
| 15 | 18 | 13 | 15.5 |
| 9 | 10.5 | 9 | 10.5 |
| 10 | 12 | 8 | 9 |
| 14 | 17 | 1 | 1 |
| 16 | 19 | 2 | 2.5 |
| 11 | 13 | 7 | 8 |
| 13 | 15.5 | 5 | 6 |
| 19 | 21 | 3 | 4 |
| 20 | 22 | 2 | 2.5 |
| 6 | 7 | 4 | 5 |
| Totals | 175.0 | | 78.0 |

a. $H_0$: $U = U'$  $H_1$: $U \neq U'$

b.

| **Training** | | **Control** |
|---|---|---|
| 96 | 0 | 122345789 |
| 98654310 | 1 | 23 |
| 0 | 2 | |

c. Mann-Whitney $U$-test.

d. $12 = 11(11) + \dfrac{11(11 + 1)}{2} - 175 \quad 109 = 11(11) + \dfrac{11(11 + 1)}{2} - 78$

e. Critical range for $U$-test, $\alpha = .01$, two-tailed: $21 - 100$, Reject $H_0$.

**5.**

| Husband $X_1$ | Wife $X_2$ | Difference $X_2 - X_1$ | Rank − | + |
|---|---|---|---|---|
| 37 | 33 | −4 | −4.0 | |
| 46 | 44 | −2 | −1.0 | |
| 59 | 48 | −11 | −11.0 | |
| 17 | 30 | 13 | | 12.0 |
| 41 | 56 | 15 | | 13.0 |
| 36 | 30 | −6 | −6.5 | |
| 29 | 35 | 6 | | 6.5 |
| 38 | 38 | 0 | | |
| 32 | 46 | 14 | | 14.0 |
| 35 | 32 | −3 | −2.5 | |
| 39 | 29 | −10 | −10.0 | |
| 37 | 45 | 8 | | 9.0 |
| 36 | 29 | −7 | −8.0 | |
| 45 | 48 | 3 | | 2.5 |
| 40 | 35 | −5 | −5.0 | |
| | | | −48.0 | 57.0 |

$$T_W = 48$$

a. $H_0$: The sum of positive and negative rank differences are equal.
   $H_1$: The sum of positive and negative rank differences are not equal.

b.

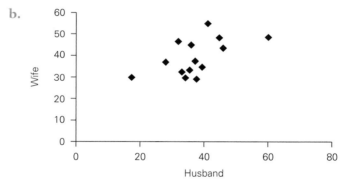

c. Wilcoxon Matched-Pairs Test
d. $T_W = 48$
e. Critical value for $N = 14$, $\alpha = .05$: 21, Fail to Reject $H_0$.
   Critical value for $N = 14$, $\alpha = .01$: 12, Fail to Reject $H_0$.

7.

| A<br>$X_1$ | B<br>$X_2$ | Difference<br>$X_2 - X_1$ | Rank<br>− | + |
|---|---|---|---|---|
| 10.2 | 9.9 | −0.3 | −4.5 | |
| 11.1 | 10.3 | −0.8 | −7.0 | |
| 10.5 | 11.0 | 0.5 | | 6.0 |
| 10.0 | 10.1 | 0.1 | | 2.0 |
| 9.7 | 9.8 | 0.1 | | 2.0 |
| 12.0 | 9.5 | −2.5 | −10.0 | |
| 10.7 | 10.8 | 0.1 | | 2.0 |
| 10.9 | 10.6 | −0.3 | −4.5 | |
| 11.5 | 9.6 | −1.9 | −9.0 | |
| 10.4 | 9.4 | −1.0 | −8.0 | |
| | | Totals | −43.0 | 12.0 |

$T_W = 12$

Critical value for $N = 10$, $\alpha = .05$: 8, Fail to Reject $H_0$.

Critical value for $N = 10$, $\alpha = .01$: 3, Fail to Reject $H_0$.

# References

## Chapter 1

Runyon, R. P., Haber, A., & Coleman, K. A. (1994). *Behavioral Statistics: The Core*. New York: McGraw-Hill, Inc.

## Chapter 2

"Erosion and dental enamel among competitive swimmers–Virginia" (1983), *Morbidity and Mortality Weekly Report, 32*(28).

Sinrod, B. & Grey, M. (1998). *Just Married*. Kansas City, MO: Andrews McMeel Publishers.

## Chapter 3

Bolles, R. C. (1988). Why you should avoid statistics. *Biological Psychiatry 23*, 79–85.

Stapp, J., Tucker, A. M., & Vandenbox, G. R. (1985). Census of Psychological Personnel: 1983. *American Psychologist, 40*, 1317–1351.

Tukey, J. W. (1977). *Exploratory data analysis*. Reading, MA: Addison-Wesley.

## Chapter 4

Manstead et al., (1983) *Motivation and Emotion, 7*, 279–289.

National Climatic Center, NOAA, US Department of Commerce.

Sabor, R. & Wakeman, L. (1991) *Journal of Economic Perspectives, 5*, 1, 159–170.

Based on survey conducted by Survey USA, copyright by Hypotenuse Inc. To reach them, call 1-800-685-8500.

## Chapter 7

Cleveland, W. S. (1984). *The elements of graphing data*. Monterey, CA: Wadsworth.

Cleveland, W. S. (1984). Graphs in scientific publication. *American Statistician, 38*, 261–269.

Cleveland, W. S. (1984). Graphical methods for data presentation: Full scale breaks, dot charts, and multibased logging. *American Statistician, 38*, 270–280.

Fiske, D. W. & Fogg, L. (1990). But the reviewers are making different criticisms of my paper!: Diversity and uniqueness in reviewers comments. *American Psychologist, 45*, 591–598.

Hare, R. D. (1965). Acquisition and generalization of a conditioned-fear response in psychopathic and nonpsychopathic criminals. *Journal of Psychology, 59*, 367–370.

Huff, D. (1954). *How to lie with statistics,* New York: Norton.

Stapp, Tucker, & VandenBos (1985). *American Psychologist, 40*, 1317–1351.

## Chapter 8

Casey, V. A., Dwyer, J. T., Coleman, K. A., & Valadian, I. (1992). Body massindex from childhood to middle age: A 50-year follow up. *American Journal of Clinical Nutrition, 56*, 14–18.

Meyer, G. E., & Hildebrand, K. (1984). Does it pay to be 'bashful'?: The seven dwarfs and long-term memory. *American Journal Psychology, 97*, 47–55.

Snyder, M. & Simpson, J. A. (1984). Self-monitoring and dating relationships. *Journal of Personality and Social Psychology, 74*, 1281–1291.

## Chapter 10

Nisbett, R. E., & Ross, L. (1980). *Human inference: Strategies and shortcomings of social judgment*. Englewood Cliffs, NJ: Prentice-Hall.

Rand Corporation (1955). *A million random digits with 100,000 normal deviates*. Glenco, IL: Free Press.

Snyder, M. (1984). When belief creates reality. In L. Berkowitz (Ed.), *Advances in experimental social psychology.* (Vol. 18, pp. 248–306). New York: Academic Press.

Tversky, A., & Kahneman, D. (1974). Judgment under uncertainty: Heuristics and biases. *Science, 185,* 1124–1131.

Tversky, A., & Kahneman, D. (1982). Evidential impact of base rates. In D. Kahneman, P. Slovic, & A. Tversky (Eds.), *Judgment under uncertainty: Heuristics and biases.* Cambridge: Cambridge University Press.

Tversky, A., & Kahneman, D. (1983). Extensional versus intuitive reasoning: The conjunction fallacy in probability judgment. *Psychological Review, 90,* 93–315.

## Chapter 14

Abelson, R. P. (1985). A variance explanation paradox: When a little is a lot. *Psychological Bulletin, 97,* 129–133.

Charter, R. A. (1982). Practical formulas for strength of association measures. *Educational and Psychological Measurement, 42,* 969–974.

Jaccard, J., Becker, M. A., & Wood, G. (1984). Pairwise multiple comparison procedures: A review. *Psychological Bulletin, 96,* 589–596.

Kirk, R. E. (1982). *Experimental design: Procedures for the behavioral sciences* (2nd ed.). Monterey, CA: Brooks-Cole.

Maxwell, S. E., Camp, C. J., & Arvey, R. D. (1981). Measures of strength of association: A comparative examination. *Journal of Applied Psychology, 66,* 525–534.

Miller, R. G. (1981). *Simultaneous statistical inference.* New York: Springer-Verlag.

Milligan, G. W., Wong, D. S., & Thompson, P. A. (1987). Robustness properties of nonorthogonal analysis of variance. *Psychological Bulletin, 101,* 464–470.

Pittenger, D. J., & Pavlik, W. B. (1989). Resistance to extinction in humans: Analysis of the generalized partial reinforcement effect. *Learning and Motivation, 20,* 60–72.

Toothaker, L. E. (1991). *Multiple comparisons for researchers.* Newbury Park, CA: Sage.

Tukey, J. W. (1953). *The problem of multiple comparisons.* Princeton University, Mimeographed monograph.

## Chapter 15

Cohen, J. (1960). A coefficient of agreement for nominal scales. *Educational and Psychological Measurement, 20,* 37–46.

Hayes, L. V. (1981). *Statistics.* New York: Holt, Rinehart, and Winston.

Kirk, R. E. (1982). *Experimental design* (2nd ed.). Monterey, CA: Brooks/Cole.

Sandelands, L. E., Brocker, J., & Glynn, M. A. (1988). If at first you don't succeed, try, try again: Effects on persistence-performance contingencies, ego involvement, and self-esteem on task performance. *Journal of Applied Psychology, 73,* 208–216.

Winer, B. J., Brown, D. R., & Michels, K. M. (1991). *Statistical principles in experimental design* (3rd ed.). New York: McGraw-Hill.

## Chapter 16

Dodd, D. H., & Schultz, R. F. (1973). Computational procedures for estimating magnitude of effect for some analysis of variance designs. *Psychological Bulletin, 79,* 391–394.

## Chapter 17

Cohen, J. (1988). *Statistical power analysis for the behavioral sciences* (2nd ed.). Hillsdale, NJ: Lawrence Erlbaum Associates.

Delucchi, K. L. (1993). On the use and misuse of the chi-square. In G. Keren, & C. Lewis (Eds.) *A handbook for data analysis in the behavioral sciences: Statistical issues.* Hillsdale, NJ: LEA.

Good, I. J., Grover, T. N., & Mitchell, G. J. (1977). Exact distributions for chi-squared and for the likelihood-ratio statistic for the equiprobable multinomial distribution. *Journal of the American Statistical Association, 65,* 267–283.

Haberman, S. J. (1973). The analysis of residuals in cross-classified tables. *Biometrics, 29,* 205–220.

Siegel, S., & Castellan, N. J. (1988). *Nonparametric statistics for the behavioral sciences* (2nd ed.). New York: McGraw-Hill.

# Index

## ONE-WAY ANOVA

| | Sum of squares | Degrees of freedom | Mean square | F-ratio |
|---|---|---|---|---|

$$SS_{between} = \Sigma \frac{(X_{\bullet j})^2}{n_j} - \frac{(\Sigma X_{ij})^2}{N} \qquad j - 1 \qquad MS_{between} = \frac{SS_{between}}{df_{between}} \qquad F = \frac{MS_{between}}{MS_{within}}$$

$$SS_{within} = \Sigma X_{ij}^2 - \Sigma \frac{(X_{\bullet j})^2}{n_j} \qquad \Sigma(n_j - 1) \qquad MS_{within} = \frac{SS_{within}}{df_{within}}$$

$$SS_{total} = \Sigma X_{ij}^2 - \frac{(\Sigma X_{ij})^2}{N} \qquad N - 1$$

### Omega Squared

$$\omega^2 = \frac{df_{between}(F - 1)}{df_{between}(F - 1) + N}$$

### Effect Size

$$\mathbf{f} = \sqrt{\frac{\eta^2}{1 - \eta^2}} \quad \text{where} \quad \eta^2 = \frac{df_{between}(F)}{df_{between}(F) + df_{within}} \quad \text{or} \quad \eta^2 = \frac{SS_{between}}{SS_{total}}$$

## TWO-WAY ANOVA

| Sum of Squares | Degrees of Freedom | Mean Square | F-ratio |
|---|---|---|---|

$$SS_A = \Sigma \frac{(X_{\bullet j \bullet})^2}{n_{j\bullet}} - \frac{(\Sigma X_{ijk})^2}{N} \qquad df_A = j - 1 \qquad MS_A = \frac{SS_A}{df_A} \qquad F_A = \frac{MS_A}{MS_{within}}$$

$$SS_B = \Sigma \frac{(X_{\bullet\bullet k})^2}{n_{\bullet k}} - \frac{(\Sigma X_{ijk})^2}{N} \qquad df_B = k - 1 \qquad MS_B = \frac{SS_B}{df_B} \qquad F_B = \frac{MS_B}{MS_{within}}$$

$$SS_{AB} = \Sigma \frac{(X_{\bullet jk})^2}{n_{jk}} - \frac{(\Sigma X_{ijk})^2}{N} - (SS_A + SS_B) \quad df_{AB} = (j - 1)(k - 1) \quad MS_{AB} = \frac{SS_{AB}}{df_{AB}} \quad F_{AB} = \frac{MS_{AB}}{MS_{within}}$$

$$SS_{within} = \Sigma X_{ijk}^2 - \Sigma \frac{(X_{\bullet jk})^2}{n_{jk}} \qquad df_{within} = \Sigma(n_{ik} - 1) \qquad MS_{within} = \frac{SS_{within}}{df_{within}}$$

$$SS_{total} = \Sigma X_{ijk}^2 - \frac{(\Sigma X_{ijk})^2}{N} \qquad df_{total} = N - 1$$

### Omega squared

$$\omega^2 = \frac{df_{effect}(F_{effect} - 1)}{df_{effect}(F_{effect} - 1) + N}$$

### Effect Size

$$f = \sqrt{\frac{\eta_{effect}^2}{1.0 - \eta_{effect}^2}} \quad \text{where} \quad \eta^2 = \frac{df_{effect}F_{effect}}{df_{effect}F_{effect} + df_{within}} \quad \text{or} \quad \eta^2 = \frac{SS_{effect}}{SS_{total}}$$

## ONE-WAY ANOVA WITH CORRELATED GROUPS

| Sum of squares | Degrees of freedom | Mean square | F-ratio |
|---|---|---|---|

$$SS_{between} = \frac{\Sigma X_{\bullet j}^2}{n_j} - \frac{(\Sigma X_{ij})^2}{N} \qquad df_{between} = j - 1 \qquad MS_{between} = \frac{SS_{between}}{df_{between}}$$

$$F_{between} = \frac{MS_{between}}{MS_{within}}$$